Lecture Notes in Computer Science 13901

Founding Editors

Gerhard Goos
Juris Hartmanis

The series Lecture Notes in Computer Science (LNCS), including its subseries Lecture Notes in Artificial Intelligence (LNAI) and Lecture Notes in Bioinformatics (LNBI), has established itself as a medium for the publication of new developments in computer science and information technology research, teaching, and education.

LNCS enjoys close cooperation with the computer science R & D community, the series counts many renowned academics among its volume editors and paper authors, and collaborates with prestigious societies. Its mission is to serve this international community by providing an invaluable service, mainly focused on the publication of conference and workshop proceedings and postproceedings. LNCS commenced publication in 1973.

Marta Indulska · Iris Reinhartz-Berger ·
Carlos Cetina · Oscar Pastor
Editors

Advanced Information Systems Engineering

35th International Conference, CAiSE 2023
Zaragoza, Spain, June 12–16, 2023
Proceedings

 Springer

Editors
Marta Indulska 🆔
The University of Queensland
Brisbane, QLD, Australia

Iris Reinhartz-Berger 🆔
University of Haifa
Haifa, Israel

Carlos Cetina 🆔
Universidad San Jorge
Zaragoza, Spain

Oscar Pastor 🆔
Universitat Politècnica de València
Valencia, Spain

ISSN 0302-9743   ISSN 1611-3349 (electronic)
Lecture Notes in Computer Science
ISBN 978-3-031-34559-3   ISBN 978-3-031-34560-9 (eBook)
https://doi.org/10.1007/978-3-031-34560-9

This Springer imprint is published by the registered company Springer Nature Switzerland AG
The registered company address is: Gewerbestrasse 11, 6330 Cham, Switzerland

Preface

The 35th edition of the International Conference on Advanced Information Systems Engineering (CAiSE 2023) was held in Zaragoza, Spain, during June 12–16, 2023. It took place at the Palacio de Congresos and was hosted by the SVIT Research Group at San Jorge University.

CAiSE 2023 continued the CAiSE conference tradition as the premiere venue for innovative and rigorous research across the whole spectrum of information systems (IS) engineering. The program had a special focus on "Cyber-Human Systems". Our choice of this theme was based on the increasingly coupled relationships between humans and computing, giving rise to cyber-human systems that aim to advance human abilities to work in complex environments. The theme refers to various aspects of the interface between humans and technology, with the intention to advance models, methods and theories relating to such systems. The call for papers solicited research papers in the categories of Technical, Empirical, and Exploratory papers, in all areas of IS engineering, including novel approaches to IS engineering; models, methods, and techniques in IS engineering; architectures and platforms for IS engineering; and domain-specific and multi-aspect IS engineering. We received a total of 169 full paper submissions and followed a five-phase selection process. First, we desk-rejected 8 papers that were clearly out of scope or deviated substantially from the required paper layout and length limitations. We then assigned two Program Committee (PC) members to each of the remaining 161 papers. As an outcome of this phase, we rejected 59 papers as they had two negative and constructive reviews. The remaining papers were assigned a member of the Program Board (PB) as a third reviewer. Out of this process, we further rejected 27 papers on which there was a consensus on rejection between the assigned program members. We then facilitated an online discussion for the remaining 75 papers, and, as a result, we accepted 14 papers and rejected 5 papers. The remaining 56 papers were further discussed in the Program Board meeting, held in Valencia, Spain. This resulted in overall accepting 36 papers (17 of which were first conditionally accepted, and then accepted after gatekeepers reviewed revisions). An additional outcome of the PB meeting was to invite 16 papers to submit shorter versions for presentation at the CAiSE Forum, due to their focus on innovative research, tools and prototypes while being at a relatively early stage. Overall, the review process resulted in the selection of 36 papers, which amounted to an acceptance rate of 21%.

Through the Journal First initiative, the CAiSE 2023 program also included six additional papers for presentation and discussion. Overall, the 42 papers cover core and emerging fields of research relating to topics of cyber-human systems, requirements engineering, IoT, environmental applications, process mining, event-driven process mining, ontology knowledge representation, model-driven approaches, process monitoring, conformance compliance, data centric approaches, privacy security, explainable AI and service-related approaches. Each of the main days of the conference started with a keynote, presented by Giancarlo Guizzardi (University of Twente), Bran Selic (Malina Software Corp) and Pnina Soffer (University of Haifa).

In addition, the program included presentations of papers accepted to the different tracks, including the Forum, workshops, co-located working conferences EMMSAD and BPMDS, and Doctoral Consortium. The program also featured three keynote talks, three tutorials, a panel, and a new Research Projects Exhibition, which provided a forum for discussing research projects that are currently under development.

We are grateful to the whole team that worked collaboratively for the success of CAiSE 2023 and its related events. We sincerely thank the General Chairs, Carlos Cetina and Oscar Pastor, the Local Organization Chair, Raul Lapeña; and the Proceedings Chair, Pierluigi Plebani, for facilitating our work as Program Chairs. We are also thankful to Giancarlo Guizzardi, Bran Selic and Pnina Soffer for their inspirational keynote presentations. We further wish to thank: the Forum Chairs, Cristina Cabanillas and Francisca Pérez; the Workshop Chairs, Pnina Soffer and Marcela Ruiz; the Tutorial Chairs, Fabiano Dalpiaz and Jelena Zdravkovic; the Panel Chairs, Hajo A. Reijers and Stefanie Rinderle-Ma; the Doctoral Consortium Chairs, Daniel Méndez and Raimundas Matulevicius; the Journal-first Track Chairs, Jan Mendling and Lola Burgueño; the Publicity Chairs, Jolita Ralyté, Guilherme H. Travassos, Anna Segooa and Anna Kalenkova; the Web and Social Media Chairs, Jorge Echeverria and Africa Domingo; the Sustainability Chairs, Sergio España and Monica Vitali; the Sponsor Chairs, Pedro Valderas and Antonio Ruiz; the Student Chairs, Selmin Nurcan and Estefania Serral; the PhD Award Chairs, John Krogstie and Camille Salinesi; and the Research Project Exhibition Chairs, Giovanni Giachetti, Jaime Font, Lorena Arcega and José Fabián Reyes.

It was also our great pleasure to collaborate with the chairs of the two working conferences traditionally co-located with CAiSE: Dominik Bork and Henderik Proper, who co-chaired EMMSAD 2023, and Han van der Aa and Rainer Schmidt, who co-chaired BPMDS 2023. We would also like to thank all Program Committee and Program Board members, who played a fundamental role in the review and selection process. We appreciate the time, knowledge, insights and effort they contributed during the five-phase selection process. The conference would not be a success without their hard work.

We would like to extend our sincerest gratitude to all those who served at the event itself as workshop organizers, session chairs, hosts, volunteer helpers, technical staff, and the many others who went above and beyond to ensure that CAiSE continues to provide an engaging and high value forum for scientific exchange and networking within the information systems engineering community, leading conversations on how information systems engineering leveraging emerging technologies. Finally, we would like to thank our sponsors, CSIC Aragon, Zaragoza Congresos and Expo Zaragoza Empresarial, VRAIN (Valencian Research Institute of Artificial Intelligence, UPV, Valencia, Spain), as well as Springer for their generous support for the best paper and PhD-thesis awards.

June 2023   Iris Reinhartz-Berger
                                                                                                                    Marta Indulska

Organization

General Chairs

Carlos Cetina   San Jorge University, Spain
Oscar Pastor   Universitat Politècnica de València, Spain

Program Committee Chairs

Iris Reinhartz-Berger   University of Haifa, Israel
Marta Indulska   University of Queensland, Australia

Organization Chair

Raul Lapeña   San Jorge University, Spain

Workshops Chairs

Pnina Soffer   University of Haifa, Israel
Marcela Ruiz   Zurich University of Applied, Switzerland

Forum Chairs

Cristina Cabanillas   University of Sevilla, Spain
Francisca Pérez   San Jorge University, Spain

Journal First Track Chairs

Jan Mendling   Wirtschaftsuniversität Wien, Austria
Lola Burgueño   Universitat Oberta de Catalunya, Spain

Tutorial Chairs

Fabiano Dalpiaz   Utrecht University, The Netherlands
Jelena Zdravkovic   Stockholm University, Sweden

Panel Chairs

Hajo A. Reijers   Utrecht University, The Netherlands
Stefanie Rinderle-Ma   Technical University of Munich, Germany

Sustainability Chairs

Sergio España   Universitat Politècnica de València, Spain
Monica Vitali   Politecnico di Milano, Italy

Publicity Chairs

Jolita Ralyté   University of Geneva, Switzerland
Guilherme H. Travassos   Universidade Federal de Rio de Janeiro, Brazil
Anna Segooa   Tshwane University of Technology, South Africa
Anna Kalenkova   University of Adelaide, Australia

Sponsor Chairs

Pedro Valderas   Universitat Politècnica de València, Spain
Antonio Ruiz   University of Sevilla, Spain

Student Chairs

Selmin Nurcan   Université Paris 1 Panthéon-Sorbonne, France
Estefania Serral   KU Leuven, Belgium

Web and Social Media Chairs

Jorge Echeverria   San Jorge University, Spain
Africa Domingo   San Jorge University, Spain

Proceedings Chair

Pierluigi Plebani   Politecnico di Milano, Italy

Ph.D. Award Chairs

John Krogstie   Norwegian University of Science and Technology
                           (NTNU), Norway
Camille Salinesi   Université Paris 1, Panthéon-Sorbonne, France

Doctoral Consortium Chairs

Daniel Méndez   Blekinge Institute of Technology, Sweden
Raimundas Matulevicius   University of Tartu, Estonia

Research Projects Exhibition Chairs

Giovanni Giachetti   Universitat Politècnica de València, Spain
Jaime Font   San Jorge University, Spain
Lorena Arcega   San Jorge University, Spain
José Fabián Reyes   Universitat Politècnica de València, Spain

Program Board

Sjaak Brinkkemper   Utrecht University, The Netherlands
Johann Eder   Alpen Adria Universität Klagenfurt, Austria
Xavier Franch   Universitat Politècnica de Catalunya, Spain
Giancarlo Guizzardi   Federal University of Espirito Santo, Brazil
John Krogstie   Norwegian University of Science and Technology,
                           Norway
Jan Mendling   Humboldt-Universität zu Berlin, Germany
Selmin Nurcan   Université Paris 1 Panthéon – Sorbonne, France

Program Committee

Ulrich Frank	Universität Duisburg-Essen, Germany
Lidia Fuentes	University of Malaga, Spain
Chiara Ghidini	Fondazione Bruno Kessler (FBK), Italy
Paolo Giorgini	University of Trento, Italy
Maria-Teresa Gomez Lopez	University of Seville, Spain
Jaap Gordijn	Vrije Universiteit Amsterdam, The Netherlands
Renata Guizzardi	Universidade Federal do Espirito Santo, Brazil
Mirjana Ivanovic	University of Novi Sad, Serbia
Matthias Jarke	RWTH Aachen University, Germany
Paul Johannesson	Royal Institute of Technology, Sweden
Mārīte Kirikova	Riga Technical University, Latvia
Julio Cesar Leite	PUC-Rio, Brazil
Henrik Leopold	Kühne Logistics University, Germany
Sebastian Link	University of Auckland, New Zealand
Lin Liu	Tsinghua University, China
Wolfgang Maass	Deutsches Forschungszentrum für Künstliche Intelligenz (DFKI), Germany
Felix Mannhardt	Eindhoven University of Technology, The Netherlands
Andrea Marrella	Sapienza University of Rome, Italy
Raimundas Matulevicius	University of Tartu, Estonia
Massimo Mecella	Sapienza University of Rome, Italy
Marco Montali	KRDB Research Centre, Free University of Bozen-Bolzano, Italy
Haralambos Mouratidis	University of Essex, UK
Jeffrey Parsons	Memorial University of Newfoundland, Canada
Günther Pernul	Universität Regensburg, Germany
Pierluigi Plebani	Politecnico di Milano, Italy
Artem Polyvyanyy	University of Melbourne, Australia
Luise Pufahl	TU Berlin, Germany
Gil Regev	Ecole Polytechnique Fédérale de Lausanne, Switzerland
Stefanie Rinderle-Ma	Technical University of Munich, Germany
Marcela Ruiz	Zurich University of Applied Sciences, Switzerland
Camille Salinesi	CRI, Université de Paris 1, Panthéon-Sorbonne, France
Michael Sheng	Macquarie University, Australia
Veda Storey	Georgia State University, USA
Arnon Sturm	Ben-Gurion University, Israel
Sagar Sunkle	Tata Consultancy Services, India
Yutian Tang	ShanghaiTech University, China

Earnest Teniente	UPC, Spain
Han van der Aa	University of Mannheim, Germany
Seppe Vanden Broucke	Katholieke Universiteit Leuven, Belgium
Tony Wasserman	Carnegie Mellon University Silicon Valley, USA
Matthias Weidlich	Humboldt-Universität zu Berlin, Germany
Hans Weigand	Tilburg University, The Netherlands
Carson Woo	University of British Columbia, Canada
Moe Wynn	Queensland University of Technology, Australia
Jian Yang	Macquarie University, Australia
Eric Yu	University of Toronto, Canada

Additional Reviewers

Affia, Abasi-Amefon
Agostinelli, Simone
Alfonso, Iván
Ali, Syed Juned
Alkhammash, Hanan
Amaral de Sousa, Victor
Andrews, Robert
Ayala, Inmaculada
Bagozi, Ada
Bakhtina, Mariia
Beerepoot, Iris
Benzin, Janik-Vasily
Buchmann, Robert Andrei
Buliga, Andrei
Cai, Taotao
Cappiello, Cinzia
Christ, Sven
Dasht Bozorgi, Zahra
Dell'Anna, Davide
Durán Toro, Amador
Empl, Philip
Fernandez, Pablo
Friedl, Sabrina
Furutanpey, Alireza
García, José María
Garda, Massimiliano
Glas, Magdalena
Goel, Kanika
Grill, Johannes
Grundspenkis, Janis

Hellmanzik, Ben
Iqbal, Mubashar
Kaczmarek-Heß, Monika
Khayatbashi, Shahrzad
Klessascheck, Finn
Lu, Xixi
López-Gil, Juan-Miguel
Mahmood, Adnan
Maicher, Lutz
Maier, Pierre
Mangat, Amolkirat Singh
Marquez-Chamorro, Alfonso
Mattei, Luca
Morais, Gabriel
Morales, Sergio
Morichetta, Andrea
Pettinari, Sara
Pfeiffer, Peter
Pusztai, Thomas
Rebmann, Adrian
Reittinger, Tobias
Reiz, Achim
Riss, Uwe
Rivkin, Andrey
Rizzi, Williams
Ronzani, Massimiliano
Rossi, Lorenzo
Sadeghianasl, Sareh
Sarkar, Sandip Kumar
Scheibel, Beate

Seeba, Mari
Smuts, Hanlie
Stevens, Alexander
Su, Xin
Su, Xing

Su, Zihang
Tour, Andrei
Van der Merwe, Alta
Winter, Karolin
Zaib, Munazza

Contents

Model-Driven Approaches

Process Monitoring

Conformance, Compliance and Workarounds

Service-Related Approaches

Tutorial Papers

Cyber-Human and Cyber Physical Systems

Comparing User Perspectives in a Virtual Reality Cultural Heritage Environment

Luana Bulla[1,3], Stefano De Giorgis[2], Aldo Gangemi[1,2],
Chiara Lucifora[1,2(✉)], and Misael Mongiovì[1]

[1] ISTC - National Research Council, Rome and Catania, Italy
{luana.bulla,aldo.gangemi,chiara.lucifora,misael.mongiovi}@istc.cnr.it
[2] University of Bologna, Bologna, Italy
{stefano.degiorgis,aldo.gangemi,chiara.lucifora}@unibo.it
[3] University of Catania, Catania, Italy

Abstract. Virtual reality enables the creation of personalized user experience that brings together people of different cultures and ethnicity. We consider a novel concept of virtual reality innovation in museums, which is cognitively grounded and supported by data and their semantics, to enable users sharing their experiences, as well as to take the perspective of other users, with the ultimate goal of increasing social cohesion. The implementation of this scenario requires an autonomous artificial system that detects emotions and values from a dialogue involving museum visitors who express their personal point of view, listen to those from other visitors, and possibly take the perspective of others.

An important feature of this system is the ability of detecting similarity and dissimilarity between user perspectives expressed in speech, when exposed to artworks. This ability helps defining an effective strategy for sharing diverse user perspectives for increasing social cohesion. Moreover, it enables an unbiased quantification of the success of the interaction in terms of change in the user perspective. Based on results from previous work, we employ the Ekman's emotion model and Haidt's moral value model to extract emotional and moral value profiles from user descriptions of artworks. We propose a novel method for measuring the similarity between user perspectives by comparing emotional and moral value profiles. Our results show that the employment of unsupervised text classification models is a promising research direction for this task.

Keywords: Text similarity · Emotion detection · Moral value detection · Virtual reality

1 Introduction

Virtual Reality (VR) is an innovative technology that, by isolating the perceptive channels of users, makes them feel immersed in a virtual environment, through the sensations of virtual embodiment [39]. Its effectiveness is mainly due to its imaginative power, which allows users to experience situations as they were real

© The Author(s), under exclusive license to Springer Nature Switzerland AG 2023
M. Indulska et al. (Eds.): CAiSE 2023, LNCS 13901, pp. 3–15, 2023.
https://doi.org/10.1007/978-3-031-34560-9_1

[26]. This sensation of reality is given by the system's ability to process the information received, and to offer visual and sound feedback in real time [40]. Today VR is applied in many domains related to cognitive sciences, including social technology, which facilitates interactions by promoting the psychological well-being of people in social contexts. As a countermeasure, as a part of a wider project[1], which aims to ensure social cohesion, participation and inclusion through cultural engagement, we use virtual reality technology to build an innovative system, in which users are subjected to the Interpretation-Reflection Loop (IRL) [8] in an immersive environment that makes them share their personal interpretations with others, listen to others' interpretations given by different people, and take another point of view through virtual embodiment. We are implementing a system that supports continuous communication between its constituent parts, i.e., a VR interface jointly with an external server that detects emotions and moral values from user speech, and the user itself. The system selects a specific avatar for each user, based on their personal characteristics such as age, gender and nationality; subsequently, following the user's first interpretation, the external server detects emotions and moral values to select an appropriate avatar that will interact with the user. All users' interpretations are recorded and associated with specific avatars. These data are saved in an external dataset that the server can access for further reuse (Fig. 1).

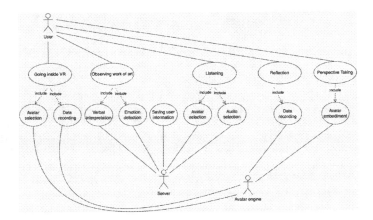

Fig. 1. A use case diagram of the mixed VR-AI system for emotion-value-based perspective taking.

An essential feature of the system is the ability to quantify similarity between user perspectives. For instance, presenting perspectives that are different from those of users can make them reflect about their standpoint, and encourage them to adopt a wider perspective, ultimately increasing social cohesion. The

---

[1] SPICE: Social Cohesion, Participation and Inclusion through Cultural Engagement – EC Grant Agreement number 870811.

experiments conducted until now focus on the emotional and axiological (moral) meaning of those perspectives, which will be eventually combined with other semantic features in future work. The task can also be useful for comparing perspectives of a user at two different points in time, e.g. before and after an interaction, to quantify the propensity of people to change their point of view under certain circumstances (e.g., when impersonating an avatar holding a different standpoint). Considering the large volume of data to process, and the necessity of performing the task on-line and autonomously, it is essential that the system is able to reason with user perspectives and quantify their similarity.

We adopt a novel method to quantify the similarity between user perspectives through emotional and moral values lenses [25]. We leverage text classifiers to extract emotional profiles and moral value profiles from text obtained after speech-to-text conversion. We then compare profiles from different speeches by means of cosine similarity. To evaluate our method, we collected data from our VR prototype, obtaining a total of 396 interpretations on 6 works of art associated to 6 avatars. We compared some state-of-the-art supervised or unsupervised classifiers based on Transformers [1] and adopt the top-performing one for computing the similarity between perspectives.

The remainder of the paper is structured as follows. Next, we present some background on social and technological aspects of our work (Sect. 2). In Sect. 3 we present our VR scenario used for data collection. Section 4 introduces our method for evaluating and comparing user perspectives. We report our results in Sect. 5, and then conclude in Sect. 6.

2 Background

We provide some background on social (Sect. 2.1) and technological (Sect. 2.2) aspects related to this work. First, we briefly overview recent work on social cohesion, which motivates the importance of implementing suitable strategies and developing effective tools for favouring it. Second, we discuss the reference models we employ and evaluate for automatically detecting emotions and moral values evoked by people's speech. We also describe state-of-the-art metrics for computing the semantic similarity between natural language sentences, which we employ as a starting point for out method.

2.1 Improving Social Cohesion

In the field of cognitive science, social cohesion represent an important topic that needs to be investigated since, as shown in recent studies [21,22,34,35], the lack of social cohesion, which increases social isolation, can have a strong impact on people's health, impacting life expectancy and increasing the risk of death, as well as the risk of developing dementia. In general, social exclusion is mainly characterized by rejection (i.e. being denied) and ostracism (i.e. being ignored) [41], that lead to what social psychologists call social pain that has a strong impact on people's emotions and behaviours [34]. Previous studies have shown that virtual embodiment enables empathetic sharing of personal experiences that boosts social inclusion [6,39] as well as a reduction of prejudices towards different people [43]. For instance, Slater et al. [38] have shown that adopting another point of view allows the user to be more sensitive to violent behavior, leading to a reduction in racial aggression [23] and a decrease in child maltreatment [19]. In this line, in our previous work (Lucifora et al., under revision), we used an ecological paradigm in virtual reality to promote social cohesion through the virtual embodiment. Our results show that the percentages of people who change their interpretation (totally or partially) when they embody the avatar are equal to or greater than the ones who do not change their interpretation at all (Chi square between subjects p-level 0.018; Chi-square within subjects group n.1 p-level 0.007; Chi-square within subjects group n.2 p-level 0.016). This result allows us to state that the use of virtual embodiment can improve social cohesion and reduce ostracism and prejudice.

2.2 Reference Models

The following paragraphs describe the two theoretical frameworks adopted to extract users' emotion and value profile, in turn used to measure social cohesion.

Basic Emotions Theory. Originally developed by Paul Ekman [12], the Basic Emotions (BE) theory adopted in this work is a 2018 revised version [13], available online[2]. In this version of the theory, complex emotions are traced back to 6 main emotions, used here for classification tasks: Anger, Fear, Sadness, Disgust, Enjoyment, and Surprise. The Basic Emotions theory is adopted in this context because, among models that consider emotions as discrete categories, it is a widely used framework in well-known datasets used for tasks of automatic extraction of emotional content from natural language text [3,24,37], and thus lends itself to meeting the intentions of the work.

Moral Foundations Theory. The theoretical framework adopted to map moral values is the Moral Foundations Theory (MFT) [15], by Graham and Haidt. This framework organizes values in six "foundations", namely dyads of positive pole (value) vs negative pole (violation). The six dyads are:

- *Care/Harm:* caring versus harming behavior, it is grounded in mammals attachment system and cognitive appraisal mechanism of dislike of pain. It grounds virtues of kindness, gentleness and nurturance.
- *Fairness/Cheating:* it is based on social cooperation and typical nonzero-sum game theoretical situations based on reciprocal altruism. It underlies ideas of justice, rights and autonomy.
- *Loyalty/Betrayal:* it is based on tribalism tradition and the positive outcome coming from cohesive coalition, as well as the ostracism towards traitors.

---

[2] The Atlas of Emotions developed from a revised version of Ekman's Basic Emotions theory is available here: https://atlasofemotions.org/.

- *Authority/Subversion:* social interactions in terms of societal hierarchies, it underlies ideas of leadership and deference to authority, as well as respect for tradition.
- *Purity/Degradation:* derived from psychology of disgust, it implies the idea of a more elevated spiritual life; it is expressed via metaphors like "the body as a temple", and includes the more spiritual side of religious beliefs.
- *Liberty/Oppression:* it expresses the desire of freedom and the feeling of oppression when it is negated.

MFT is adopted in this work since it is described as "nativist, cultural-developmentalist, intuitionist, and pluralist approach to the study of morality" [15]. It is "Nativist", due to its neurophysiological grounding; "cultural-developmentalist" because it consider environmental variables in the morality-building process [16]; "intuitionist" in asserting that there is no unique moral or non-moral trigger, but rather many co-occurring patterns resulting in a rationalized judgment [17]; "pluralist" in considering that more than one narrative could fit the moral explanation process [18]. This final aspect of perspective pluralism is particularly relevant according to the this work's aim of fostering social cohesion.

Previous work on moral values and emotions detection focuses mainly on machine learning techniques and quantitative or semantic text document analysis [1,28,29,32].

For the purposes of our study, we selected three different methods based on natural language models to classify the emotional and moral perspective of users based on their natural language descriptions of artworks[3]. The first is based on Asprino et al. [5], which employs a zero-shot classification in an unsupervised way, drawing inspiration from Yin et al. [44]. This approach is based on the use of a model trained for a natural language inference (NLI) task, where a *premise* is determined whether or not it entails a *hypothesis*. Starting from the input text document as a premise, the system recognizes if one or more taxonomic labels, provided as hypotheses, are semantically coherent with the input. The advantage of this method is that it does not require training on an annotated dataset and hence it is directly applicable in our scenario, where we cannot rely on a large annotated dataset. We evaluate two additional supervised BERT-based machine learning models trained on available datasets. Both systems take textual data as input to perform a multi-class classification task based on Ekman's emotion taxonomy. [20,30]. The former is trained on a set of tweets, while the latter has a greater heterogeneity, as it is fine-tuned on a large number of different sources such as Twitter, Reddit, student self-assessments and television dialogue expressions. Both these methods suffer from the data shift problem, i.e. their performances degrade when applied to data with different characteristics than the training set [42].

To measure the change of user perspective and compare perspectives of different users, we consider as a baseline a state-of-the-art technique for semantic

---

[3] All methods take as input text documents, which can be generated by a speech-to-text tool.

similarity among text documents, consisting on computing a vector representation of each text document and compare them by means of cosine similarity. We employ Sentence-BERT [33] for computing the text representation. Sentence-BERT is a variant of the pre-trained BERT model [11] that generates semantically significant sentence embeddings using siamese and triplet network structures. The limit of this method in our scenario is that it considers the overall semantic similarity and cannot focus on a specific lens (emotional or value) to compare perspectives.

3   Data Collection

We applied an ecological paradigm in VR, made up by a helmet of virtual reality (Oculus Quest 2), equipped with a headphone that provides 3D audio effects, and an immersive and realistic virtual museum based on Blue Dot Studios- Art Gallery, developed with Unity Engine 3D 2020.3.33 as software. Inside the virtual museum, we included some artworks of the Modern Art Gallery in Turin (Italy) and avatars, which we built using Ready-player.me and Mixamo.com for the animations. To have a representative sample of the world population we used three main variables, that are i) age (children, adults, elderly), ii) gender (male, female, no gender), iii) nationality (European, African, Asian). In total we built 27 avatars, multiplying 3 variables to 9 categories (Fig. 2).

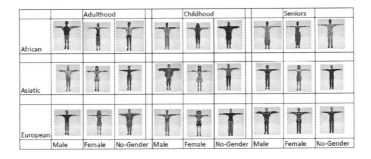

Fig. 2. Avatar generation based on age, gender and nationality.

We carried out an experimental study between subjects, on a total sample of 44 subjects, divided into two experimental groups (N = 22) in order to balance our stimuli in relation to the main characteristics of the avatars and art movements. So far, we recording 396 verbal interpretations (in Italian language) on 6 works of art, related to 6 avatars. We have prepared an interview based on four questions based on widely used theories for emotions [12] and moral values [15]. Two questions are related to the user's feeling (Q1 "How does this work of art make you feel?"; Q2 "What moral value does this work of art inspire you?"), while two questions are related to the specific categorization of emotions and values (Q3 "Among these emotions (Ekman's model) which do you think the work of art arouses?"; Q4 "Of these values (Haidt's model) which one do you think the work of art arouses?"). Our procedure is based on a 4-step timeline: At time 0 the user provides its personal interpretation of the work, based on an interview given by the researcher. At time 1 the user is invited to listen to the (verbally expressed) interpretation provided by the avatar who shares the scene with him. At time 2, users give their personal reflection, discussing their interpretations against those of the avatar. No specific questions are asked here. At the last time (time 3), the user is invited to respond again to the structured interview, given by the researcher, but this time users take the role of the avatar through virtual embodiment. Time 2 and time 3 were reversed in the two experimental groups in order to understand how much virtual embodiment can influence the interpretation-reflection loop. We have recorded 3 verbal interpretations (time 0, time 2, time 3) for each participant.

4   Comparing Perspectives by Emotion and Moral Value Classification

In order to detect the emotions and moral values from human-avatar dialogues, we analyzed the answers to Q1 and Q2 at time 0 and time 3, plus the free reflection at time 2, using the supervised and unsupervised AI systems for natural language understanding discussed in Sect. 2.2. Following Asprino et all. [5], we apply a pre-trained Natural Language Inference system as ready-made zero-shot sequence classifier (namely NLI-based). We use the framework to categorize emotions and moral values, developing two different system configurations based respectively on the taxonomies of Ekman and Haidt. We compared the results with two distinct BERT-based supervised models for emotion detection: E-BERTweet [30] and E-DistilRoBERTa [20] trained on annotated benchmark data [4,9,10,27,31,36].

We propose a novel method to determine how emotionally and morally comparable the text documents are. Specifically, we compare the answers to Q1 and Q2 at time 0 and time 3 to understand whether the users changed their perspective after the virtual embodiment (time 3) with respect to their first interpretation of the artwork (time 0). Since to the best of our knowledge there is no approach available to measure the similarity of perspective through an emotional and/or value lens, we consider as a baseline the cosine similarity between Sentence-BERT text representations (Sect. 2.2).

Our approach considers the output function of the (emotion or moral value) classifier, typically a probability distribution over the set of classes computed by a softmax normalization function, of each text document and compute their cosine similarity. Specifically:

$$emotional\_similarity(t_1, t_2) = \frac{\boldsymbol{f}_e(t_1) \cdot \boldsymbol{f}_e(t_2)}{||\boldsymbol{f}_e(t_1)|| \, ||\boldsymbol{f}_e(t_2)||} \tag{1}$$

$$value\_similarity(t_1, t_2) = \frac{\boldsymbol{f}_v(t_1) \cdot \boldsymbol{f}_v(t_2)}{||\boldsymbol{f}_v(t_1)|| \, ||\boldsymbol{f}_v(t_2)||} \tag{2}$$

where $f_e(t)$ and $f_v(t)$ are the output vectors of the emotional and value classifiers on text t, respectively; $\cdot$ is the dot product between vectors and $||x||$ is the 2-norm of vector x.

The result is a value between 0 and 1, where 0 represent completely different perspectives, while 1 represent perfectly coincident perspectives. For example, let's assume that the emotional profile of a user is equal to "joy" at time 0 and "sadness" at time 3. The emotional similarity score will therefore be equal to a 0.13 point in percentage, which indicates a sharp change in his emotional state. The method can be applied even when the output does not represent a probability distribution, provided that it is given as a vector of N non-negative values, where N is the number of classes. In our experiments (Sect. 5) we consider the output of the zero-shot NLI-based emotion and moral value classifiers normalized by softmax.

5   Results and Evaluation

We consider two basic experimental frameworks dealing with emotional and value-based detection and similarity in text, respectively. Next we describe the setup and results of detection, then we discuss the results concerning similarity.

Emotion and Moral Detection. For the moral and emotion classification we considered the answers to questions Q1 and Q2 at time 0 (t0), time 2 (t2) and time 3 (t3) for both experimental groups (see Sect. 3) and divided our sample in three categories, that are: (i) *irrelevant* answers, which do not contain any emotions or moral values; (ii) *incoherent* answers, which contain emotions incompatible with their annotations; (iii) *relevant* (and coherent) answers, which express and annotate clear emotions or moral values. The splitting process was done manually, with the support of human experts. We consider the user's annotations of emotions and moral values (answers to questions Q3 and Q4, respectively) as the ground truth and compare the system's predictions with them to measure performances. For the emotion classification task we compare the unsupervised NLI-based model [5], and the supervised E-BERTeet [30] and E-DistilRoBERTa [20] models, introduced in Sect. 2.2. We adopt the unsupervised NLI-based [5] method for detecting moral values.

We report the results in terms of weighted F1-score. We compute the outcomes considering six basic emotions and six value dimensions, respectively. The results show that the models are able to detect the emotions and values from relevant (and coherent) answers with significant accuracy, for any step (Table 1 and Table 2). As expected, the performances degrade for irrelevant and incoherent answers, since in that case user annotations are not representative of the emotions and moral values expressed in the free answer.

With the exception of time t0 of the second trial, the NLI-based model [5] performs noticeably better in both the first and second group for the emotion detection task. In this scenario, the F1-score ranges from 0.56 to 0.72. For the task of identifying moral values the F1 score fluctuates between 32% and 49% on relevant answers. Considering the difficulty of the task, because of subjectivity and ambiguity of moral values expressed in natural language statements, we consider this result promising.

Table 1. Emotion detection results for the unsupervised zero-shot model (NLI-based) and supervised BERT-based models (E-BERTweet and E-DistilRoBERTa) in terms of weighted F1-score. In relevant (and coherent) answers, NLI-based outperforms supervised methods (which have been trained on third-part datasets). As expected, the F1-score is low for irrelevant and incoherent answers since the users' annotations do not represent the real emotions expressed in the free answers.

Category	Model	Group n. 1			Group n. 2		
		t0	t2	t3	t0	t2	t3
Relevant	NLI-based	**.72**	**.62**	**.70**	.56	**.56**	**.47**
	E-BERTweet	.56	.34	.47	.36	.36	.22
	E-DistilRoBERTa	.67	.48	.61	**.66**	.55	**.47**
Irrelevant	NLI-based	.26	.05	.26	.11	.20	.09
	E-BERTweet	.11	.01	.01	.42	.10	.04
	E-DistilRoBERTa	.44	.01	.06	.36	.01	.04
Incoherent	NLI-based	.19	.18	.13	.06	.25	.20
	E-BERTweet	.00	.00	.00	.00	.00	.00
	E-DistilRoBERTa	.00	.23	.22	.08	.00	.00

Table 2. Moral value detection results for the unsupervised NLI-based zero-shot model in terms of weighted F1-score. As for the emotion detection case, the F1-score is low for irrelevant and incoherent answers since the users' annotations do not represent the real moral values expressed in the free answers.

Category	Group n. 1			Group n. 2		
	t0	t2	t3	t0	t2	t3
Relevant	.48	.49	.35	.38	.32	.29
Irrelevant	.09	.30	.42	.18	.30	.33
Incoherent	.27	.30	.33	.18	.32	.19

Emotional and Moral Similarity. To evaluate the emotional and moral similarity scores, we consider the portion of cases of our sample that are consistent and relevant with user annotations. Two annotators evaluated the statements given at time 0 and time 3 to determine whether there is a change in the user's emotional and moral perspective. Annotators specifically highlighted sentences that expressed distinctions with a "yes" (corresponding to non similar perspectives) and coherent text with a "no" (corresponding to similar perspectives). We compare the scores with the conforming annotations to see how well our emotional and moral similarity score can predict a change in perspective by applying a threshold and predicting a change when the similarity is below the threshold.

We use the Area Under the Curve (AUC) measure to evaluate the performances of our change-in-perspective classifier. AUC provides an aggregate measure of performances against all possible similarity thresholds. AUC is also recommended in an unbalanced dataset framework when comparing continuous and binary variables. Results are reported in Table 3. The outcomes show that our tool consistently produces AUC comparable or higher than the reference BERT-based semantic similarity system Sentence-BERT [33] discussed in Sect. 2.2. We obtained an AUC score of 81% and 70% for emotional and moral semantic similarity, respectively.

Table 3. AUC of the similarity metrics for predicting a change in perspective. We evaluate emotional, moral, and semantic similarity for coherent statements between answers at time 0 and time 3.

Task	Emotional Similarity	Moral Similarity	SBert	Support
Emotional validation	**0,81**		**0,81**	25
Moral validation		**0,70**	0,66	19

In summary, NLI-based emotion and moral detection systems show do not match the annotation), significant performances when the user annotation is coherent with the free description. Furthermore, the NLI model outcomes for the emotion detection task are superior to those of supervised systems trained on third-part datasets. This confirms the versatility of unsupervised architectures in out-of-domain tasks. The results obtained from the emotional and moral similarity system show an overall positive trend in capturing the emotional and value nuances of sentences.

6 Conclusion

In order to improve social cohesion, we implement an integration of VR and AI to deploy perspective taking into museums, and automatically update VR environment objects, works of art, and user metadata. To this end, we have recorded a total of 396 verbal interpretations from 44 subjects, using an experimental procedure based on a 4-step workflow, employed on an immersive VR system enriched with automated extraction of emotions and moral values. Our results lead to two important considerations. The first one is related to the utility of VR interfaces to promote social cohesion. In this sense, in line with recent literature [2], our results show that virtual embodiment is able to increase prosocial behavior and arouse empathy among users. These results motivate us to investigate perspective taking in immersive environments for different contexts e.g., including political or religious conflicts.

Our data relating to the higher number of empathic people compared to non-empathic people during virtual embodiment confirms previous studies that show that the first perspective in an immersive virtual reality leads to a strong feeling of embodiment towards an artificial body [7], which on its turn allows users to be more empathetic in relation to the feeling of other people [14]. The second result of our research is related to the use of natural language processing models. Our results show that zero-shot learning with transformers is able to detect emotions and moral values that are evoked by the personal interpretation of artworks. Furthermore, we proposed a method for determining the degree of emotional and moral coherence between two statements, and show that it is useful to infer the change of user's perspectives.

In conclusion, our results point to the feasibility of building an innovative VR system based on data semantics, as a valid tool to sensitize people to other interpretations, improving social cohesion through virtual embodiment.

Acknowledgements. This work is supported by the H2020 projects TAILOR: Foundations of Trustworthy AI - Integrating Reasoning, Learning and Optimization – EC Grant Agreement number 952215 – and SPICE: Social Cohesion, Participation and Inclusion through Cultural Engagement – EC Grant Agreement number 870811, as well as by the Italian PNRR MUR project PE0000013-FAIR.

References

1. Acheampong, F.A., Nunoo-Mensah, H., Chen, W.: Transformer models for text-based emotion detection: a review of BERT-based approaches. Artif. Intell. Rev. **54**(8), 5789–5829 (2021)
2. Ahn, S.J., Le, A.M.T., Bailenson, J.: The effect of embodied experiences on self-other merging, attitude, and helping behavior. Media Psychol. **16**(1), 7–38 (2013)
3. Alm, E.C.O.: Affect in* text and speech. University of Illinois at Urbana-Champaign (2008)
4. del Arco, F.M.P., Strapparava, C., Lopez, L.A.U., Martín-Valdivia, M.T.: Emo-event: a multilingual emotion corpus based on different events. In: Proceedings of the 12th Language Resources and Evaluation Conference, pp. 1492–1498 (2020)
5. Asprino, L., Bulla, L., De Giorgis, S., Gangemi, A., Marinucci, L., Mongiovì, M.: Uncovering values: detecting latent moral content from natural language with explainable and non-trained methods. In: Proceedings of Deep Learning Inside Out (DeeLIO 2022): The 3rd Workshop on Knowledge Extraction and Integration for Deep Learning Architectures, pp. 33–41 (2022)
6. Blascovich, J., Loomis, J., Beall, A.C., Swinth, K.R., Hoyt, C.L., Bailenson, J.N.: Immersive virtual environment technology as a methodological tool for social psychology. Psychol. Inq. **13**(2), 103–124 (2002)
7. Casula, E.P., et al.: Feeling of ownership over an embodied avatar's hand brings about fast changes of fronto-parietal cortical dynamics. J. Neurosci. **42**(4), 692–701 (2022)
8. Daga, E., et al.: Integrating citizen experiences in cultural heritage archives: requirements, state of the art, and challenges. ACM J. Comput. Cult. Herit. (JOCCH) **15**(1), 1–35 (2022)

9. Dan-Glauser, E.S., Scherer, K.R.: The difficulties in emotion regulation scale (DERS). Swiss J. Psychol. (2012)
10. Demszky, D., Movshovitz-Attias, D., Ko, J., Cowen, A., Nemade, G., Ravi, S.: Goemotions: a dataset of fine-grained emotions. arXiv preprint arXiv:2005.00547 (2020)
11. Devlin, J., Chang, M.W., Lee, K., Toutanova, K.: Bert: pre-training of deep bidirectional transformers for language understanding. arXiv preprint arXiv:1810.04805 (2018)
12. Ekman, P.: Basic emotions. In: Handbook of Cognition and Emotion, vol. 98, no. 45–60, p. 16 (1999)
13. Ekman, P.: Atlas of emotion (2018)
14. Fusaro, M., Tieri, G., Aglioti, S.M.: Seeing pain and pleasure on self and others: behavioral and psychophysiological reactivity in immersive virtual reality. J. Neurophysiol. **116**(6), 2656–2662 (2016)
15. Graham, J., et al.: Moral foundations theory: the pragmatic validity of moral pluralism. In: Advances in Experimental Social Psychology, vol. 47, pp. 55–130. Elsevier (2013)
16. Graham, J., Nosek, B.A., Haidt, J.: The moral stereotypes of liberals and conservatives: exaggeration of differences across the political spectrum. PLoS ONE **7**(12), e50092 (2012)
17. Haidt, J.: The emotional dog and its rational tail: a social intuitionist approach to moral judgment. Psychol. Rev. **108**(4), 814 (2001)
18. Haidt, J.: The righteous mind: why good people are divided by politics and religion. Vintage (2012)
19. Hamilton-Giachritsis, C., Banakou, D., Garcia Quiroga, M., Giachritsis, C., Slater, M.: Reducing risk and improving maternal perspective-taking and empathy using virtual embodiment. Sci. Rep. **8**(1), 1–10 (2018)
20. Hartmann, J.: Emotion english distilroberta-base (2022). https://huggingface.co/j-hartmann/emotion-english-distilroberta-base/
21. Holt-Lunstad, J., Smith, T.B., Baker, M., Harris, T., Stephenson, D.: Loneliness and social isolation as risk factors for mortality: a meta-analytic review. Perspect. Psychol. Sci. **10**(2), 227–237 (2015)
22. Holt-Lunstad, J., Smith, T.B., Layton, J.B.: Social relationships and mortality risk: a meta-analytic review. PLoS Med. **7**(7), e1000316 (2010)
23. Kishore, S., Spanlang, B., Iruretagoyena, G., Halan, S., Szostak, D., Slater, M.: A virtual reality embodiment technique to enhance helping behavior of police toward a victim of police racial aggression. PRESENCE: Virtual Augmented Reality **28**, 5–27 (2022)
24. Li, Y., Su, H., Shen, X., Li, W., Cao, Z., Niu, S.: Dailydialog: a manually labelled multi-turn dialogue dataset. arXiv preprint arXiv:1710.03957 (2017)
25. Lieto, A., Pozzato, G.L., Striani, M., Zoia, S., Damiano, R.: Degari 2.0: a diversity-seeking, explainable, and affective art recommender for social inclusion. Cogn. Syst. Res. **77**, 1–17 (2023)
26. Lucifora, C., et al.: Cyber-therapy: the use of artificial intelligence in psychological practice. In: Russo, D., Ahram, T., Karwowski, W., Di Bucchianico, G., Taiar, R. (eds.) IHSI 2021. AISC, vol. 1322, pp. 127–132. Springer, Cham (2021). https://doi.org/10.1007/978-3-030-68017-6_19
27. Mohammad, S., Bravo-Marquez, F., Salameh, M., Kiritchenko, S.: Semeval-2018 task 1: affect in tweets. In: Proceedings of the 12th International Workshop on Semantic Evaluation, pp. 1–17 (2018)

28. Nandwani, P., Verma, R.: A review on sentiment analysis and emotion detection from text. Soc. Netw. Anal. Min. **11**(1), 1–19 (2021)
29. Pacheco, M.L., Goldwasser, D.: Modeling content and context with deep relational learning. Trans. Assoc. Comput. Linguist. **9**, 100–119 (2021)
30. Pérez, J.M., Giudici, J.C., Luque, F.: pysentimiento: a python toolkit for sentiment analysis and socialnlp tasks. arXiv preprint arXiv:2106.09462 (2021)
31. Poria, S., Hazarika, D., Majumder, N., Naik, G., Cambria, E., Mihalcea, R.: Meld: a multimodal multi-party dataset for emotion recognition in conversations. arXiv preprint arXiv:1810.02508 (2018)
32. Priniski, J.H., et al.: Mapping moral valence of tweets following the killing of George Floyd. arXiv preprint arXiv:2104.09578 (2021)
33. Reimers, N., Gurevych, I.: Sentence-BERT: sentence embeddings using Siamese BERT-networks. In: Proceedings of the 2019 Conference on Empirical Methods in Natural Language Processing. Association for Computational Linguistics (2019). https://arxiv.org/abs/1908.10084
34. Riva, P., Eck, J.: The many faces of social exclusion. In: Social Exclusion: Psychological Approaches to Understanding and Reducing Its Impact, pp. ix–xv (2016)
35. Riva, P., Wirth, J.H., Williams, K.D.: The consequences of pain: the social and physical pain overlap on psychological responses. Eur. J. Soc. Psychol. **41**(6), 681–687 (2011)
36. Saravia, E., Liu, H.C.T., Huang, Y.H., Wu, J., Chen, Y.S.: Carer: contextualized affect representations for emotion recognition. In: Proceedings of the 2018 Conference on Empirical Methods in Natural Language Processing, pp. 3687–3697 (2018)
37. Scherer, K.R., Wallbott, H.G.: Evidence for universality and cultural variation of differential emotion response patterning. J. Pers. Soc. Psychol. **66**(2), 310 (1994)
38. Slater, M., et al.: Bystander responses to a violent incident in an immersive virtual environment. PLoS ONE **8**(1), e52766 (2013)
39. Slater, M., Spanlang, B., Sanchez-Vives, M.V., Blanke, O.: First person experience of body transfer in virtual reality. PLoS ONE **5**(5), e10564 (2010)
40. Steuer, J.: Defining virtual reality: dimensions determining telepresence. J. Commun. **42**(4), 73–93 (1992)
41. Wesselmann, E.D., Grzybowski, M.R., Steakley-Freeman, D.M., DeSouza, E.R., Nezlek, J.B., Williams, K.D.: Social exclusion in everyday life. In: Social Exclusion: Psychological Approaches to Understanding and Reducing Its Impact, pp. 3–23 (2016)
42. Wright, D., Augenstein, I.: Transformer based multi-source domain adaptation. arXiv preprint arXiv:2009.07806 (2020)
43. Yee, N., Bailenson, J.N.: Walk a mile in digital shoes: the impact of embodied perspective-taking on the reduction of negative stereotyping in immersive virtual environments. Proc. PRESENCE **24**, 26 (2006)
44. Yin, W., Hay, J., Roth, D.: Benchmarking zero-shot text classification: datasets, evaluation and entailment approach (2019)

Can Information System Engineering Make Cyber-Human Systems Smarter?

Steven Alter[✉] [iD]

University of San Francisco, 2130 Fulton Street, San Francisco 94117, USA
alter@usfca.edu

Abstract. The term smart is often used carelessly in relation to systems, devices, and other entities such as cities that capture or otherwise process or use information. This exploratory paper takes the idea of smartness seriously as a way to reveal basic issues related to IS engineering and its possibilities and limitations. This paper defines work system, cyber-human system, digital agent, smartness of systems and devices, and IS engineering. It links those ideas to IS engineering challenges related to cyber-human systems. Those challenges call for applying ideas that are not applied often in IS engineering, such as facets of work, roles and responsibilities of digital agents, patterns of interaction between people and digital agents, knowledge objects, and a range of criteria for evaluating cyber-human systems and digital agents. In combination, those ideas point to new possibilities for expanding IS engineering to reflect emerging challenges related to making cyber-human systems smarter.

Keywords: Cyber-Human System · Work System · Information System Engineering · Smartness of Systems and Devices · Facets of Work

1 Steps Toward IS Engineering for Cyber-Human Systems

One might wonder how cyber-human systems are fundamentally different from the vast number of IT-enabled work systems that operate in the world of commerce. That seemingly innocent question leads to many important issues related to describing, analyzing, designing, and evaluating cyber-human systems (and other IT-enabled work systems). The important question is not about fundamental differences between cyber-human systems and other systems. Rather, it is about describing and analyzing cyber-human systems while attending to roles of digital agents within those systems and interactions between digital agents and their human participants.

This paper treats *cyber-human system* (CHS) as a type of work system in which human participants and digital agents interact in nontrivial ways that involve conscious attention by human participants. This paper summarizes work system theory (WST) as a theoretical core and then switches to focusing on CHSs and digital agents, both of which are special cases with some properties not shared by work systems in general. Examples of CHSs and related digital agents include health monitoring CHSs that use

M. Indulska et al. (Eds.): CAiSE 2023, LNCS 13901, pp. 16–32, 2023.
https://doi.org/10.1007/978-3-031-34560-9_2

wearable devices, hospital CHSs that use digital agents for suggestions and alarms, factory production CHSs that people control with the help of dashboards, and design CHSs in which engineers use digital agents to specify and evaluate artifacts. Excluded from this discussion are implanted devices such as pacemakers that are not used consciously and imperceptible digital agents that are embedded in devices such as network controllers or dishwashers.

Goal. This paper's central premise is that thinking broadly about CHSs leads to IS engineering ideas that are not at the core of current IS engineering approaches. Those ideas are related to topics such as dimensions of smartness, facets of work, roles and responsibilities of digital agents, patterns of interaction between humans and digital agents, different types of knowledge objects that may be created and/or used, and a broad range of evaluation criteria. This paper shows how those and other ideas can be integrated into IS engineering for CHSs.

Organization. The next section identifies and defines basic concepts including work, work system, work system theory, CHS, digital agent, and IS engineering. A table uses the nine elements of the work system framework to identify CHS-related challenges that might lead to incorporating new ideas into IS engineering. The remainder of the paper focuses on ideas that could help in addressing some of those challenges. Those ideas include dimensions of smartness for systems and devices, facets of work, roles and responsibilities of digital agents, patterns of interaction between people and devices, different types of knowledge objects, and criteria for evaluating CHSs. In combination, those ideas and others point to important issues that IS engineering for CHSs ideally should address in attempts to make CHSs smarter.

2 Basic Definitions

2.1 Work

In relation to purposeful systems, work is defined as the use of resources to produce product/services for human or nonhuman customers or for oneself. Those resources include human, informational, physical, financial, and other types of resources. Work involves activities that try to be productive and that may occur in any business, societal, or home setting. This definition of work is not directly related to careers, jobs, or business organizations.

2.2 Work Systems

This term appeared in the first edition of *MIS Quarterly* [1] and is a natural unit of analysis for thinking about systems in organizations. Work systems (WSs) are described by the three elements of work system theory (WST – [2]). WST (Fig. 1) include the definition of WS, the work system framework, and the work system life cycle model. The first *and/or* in the definition of WS addresses trends toward automation of work by saying that WSs may be sociotechnical systems (with human participants doing some of the work) or totally automated systems. Many of the same WS properties apply equally to sociotechnical WSs and totally automated WSs regardless of the extent to which machines in those systems are viewed as smart. The work in WSs may be structured to varying degrees, e.g., unstructured (designing a unique advertisement), semi-structured (diagnosing an ambiguous medical condition), workflows (processing invoice payments), or highly structured (manufacturing semiconductors).

Definition of work system. A system in which human participants *and/or* machines perform work (processes and activities) using information, technology, and other resources to produce specific product/services for internal and/or external customers and/or for themselves.

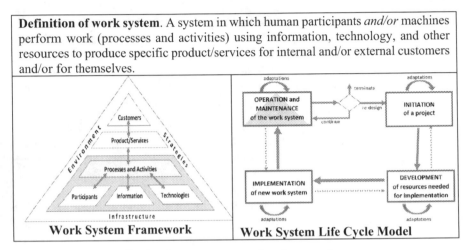

Work System Framework

Work System Life Cycle Model

Fig. 1. Three components of work system theory

Work System Framework. This framework in Fig. 1 identifies nine elements of a basic understanding of a WS's form, function, and environment during a period when it retains its identity even as incremental changes may occur. *Processes and activities, participants, information*, and *technologies* are completely within the WS. *Customers* and *product/services* may be partially inside and partially outside because customers often participate in activities within a WS. (Thus, customers are not viewed as part of a WS's environment.) *Environment, infrastructure*, and *strategies* are external to the WS even though they have direct impacts on its operation.

Core components of the work system framework have appeared in the BPM literature at least since 2005, when a BPR framework in a paper on best practices in business process redesign [3] cited a "work centered analysis framework" from a 1999 IS textbook and included *customers, products, information, technology, business process*, and organization (consisting of structure and "population"). In 2021, [4] extended that BPR framework by proposing a redesign space for exploring process redesign alternatives. Five of six layers of that redesign space are core elements of the work system framework in Fig. 1, (*customer, product/service, business process, information, technology*); the other layer replaces *participants* with organization.

Information Systems and Other Special Cases. An IS is a WS most of whose activities are devoted to capturing, transmitting, storing, retrieving, deleting, manipulating, and/or displaying information. This definition differs from 20 previous definitions in [5] and was one of 34 definitions of IS noted in [6]. An example is a sociotechnical accounting IS in which accountants decide how specific transactions and assets will be handled for tax purposes and then produce monthly or yearend financial statements. This is an IS because its activities are devoted to processing information. It is also supported by a totally automated IS that performs calculations and generates reports. In both cases, an IS that is an integral part of another WS cannot be analyzed, designed, or improved thoughtfully without considering how changes in the IS affect that WS. Projects, service systems, self-service systems, and some supply chains (interorganizational WSs) are other special cases. E.g., software development projects and projects that create or customize a machine are WSs that produce specific product/services and then go out of existence.

2.3 Human Agency and Workarounds

Human WS participants in sociotechnical WSs may not perform work exactly as designated by designers or managers. The deviations may stem from mistakes, from lack of training, or from intentional workarounds [7–10] in which WS participants deviate from expected practices when they encounter obstacles that prevent them from achieving organizational or personal goals. A related issue is intentional nonconformance with process specifications or expectations [11, 12]. Workarounds and nonconformance generate significant challenges for process mining [13, 14]. Ideally, IS engineering should try to anticipate mistakes, workarounds, and other types of nonconformance that might be possible to predict.

2.4 Digital Agents

The concept of digital agent is useful for understanding cyber-human systems. An agent is an entity that performs task(s) delegated by another entity. An algorithmic agent is a physical or digital agent that operates by executing algorithms, i.e., specifications for achieving specified goals within stated or unstated constraints by applying specific resources such as data inputs. Algorithmic agents are WSs because they perform work using information, technologies, and other resources to produce product/services for their direct customers, which may be people or non-human entities. A digital agent is a totally automated IS that is an algorithmic agent serving a specific purpose. A gigantic ERP system would not be viewed as a digital agent because it is better described as IT infrastructure that serves needs of many different WSs with many different customers.

2.5 Cyber-Human Systems

Cyber-human systems (CHSs) can be viewed as sociotechnical WSs in which human participants and digital agents interact in nontrivial ways that involve complex attention by human participants. For example, using a digital twin to try to solve a difficult problem is a nontrivial interaction, quite different from simply selecting a document from a list. Much of this paper uses the abbreviation CHS to emphasize its focus on CHSs rather than other sociotechnical WSs that may not involve nontrivial interactions between people and software-driven devices.

Alternative Configurations of Cyber-Human Systems. CHSs occur along a continuum involving different forms of initiation of interactions between people and machines. Alternatives along that spectrum of arrangements can be described as machine-in-the-loop, mixed initiative interactions, and human-in-the-loop.

With machine-in the-loop (e.g., [15]), CHS participants guide the operation of the CHS and interact with digital agents to request status or performance information or to obtain suggestions concerning decisions. With mixed initiative interactions, either CHS participants or digital agents may take the initiative. For example, a digital agent monitoring a process might issue a warning and might request a response from a CHS participant about whether corrective action is needed. From the other side, a CHS participant might initiate an interaction to request a nonstandard action or status report from the digital agent. With human-in-the-loop interactions (e.g., [16, 17], the digital agent performs activities autonomously, but requests confirmation or instructions from CHS participants when it encounters situations requiring human judgment.

2.6 IS Engineering

IS engineering is a CHS involving the development, evaluation, and improvement of specifications of systems devoted to processing information, thereby supporting, controlling, or executing activities that stakeholders recognize and care about. Interactions between WS participants and digital agents in IS engineering may lie anywhere along the spectrum of CHS arrangements that goes from machine-in-the-loop to mixed initiative interactions to human-in-the-loop.

3 Cyber-Human System Challenges Related to Elements of the Work System Framework

Table 1 uses the elements of the work system framework (Fig. 1) to identify some of the IS engineering challenges related to making CHSs smarter. Subsequent sections of this paper present ideas that help in addressing some these challenges.

Table 1. IS engineering challenges related to making cyber human systems smarter

Work system element	Challenges related to making cyber-human systems smarter
Technologies	• Providing technologies whose use increases the smartness of a CHS regardless of the extent to which the technologies themselves are smart • Integrating smarter and less smart technologies within a CHS
Information	• Extending the idea of information in CHSs to include explicit knowledge that smarter cyber-human systems can use
Participants	• Anticipating and adjusting for predictable mistakes, workarounds, or other reasons why people may or may not perform work in exactly the way that designers or managers imagined it would be performed • Anticipating and adjusting for human sensitivity issues in CHSs, e.g., people may dislike performing work in which machines play a major role, especially when the machines monitor human work closely or tell people what to do
Processes and activities	• Finding effective ways to integrate CHSs into activities in processes that may range from unstructured to semi-structured to highly structured • Finding effective ways to support different facets of work in CHSs, such as making decisions, communicating, coordinating, and many other facets of work that may present other challenges • Making effective use of different possibilities for interaction patterns between WS participants and digital agents within CHSs
Product/services	• Making product/services smarter so that they provide greater benefit for customers while fitting within work practices and contexts of customers
Customers	• Recognizing that customers often are involved in activities in CHSs and may not be trained about capabilities and quirks of digital agents or other parts of the CHS
Environment	• Recognizing that the surrounding competitive, political, legal, organizational, and technological environments may present challenges that seem far removed from the operation of specific CHSs and digital agents
Infrastructure	• Recognizing that human, informational, and technical infrastructures may not be adequate for CHSs that use smarter digital agents
Strategies	• Recognizing that strategies related to advanced technology uses may be little more than slogans

4 Dimensions of Smartness for Systems and Devices

Supporting the development of smarter CHSs is a possible aspiration for IS engineering. An approach to smartness of devices and systems is explained in [18], which says that the smartness of purposefully designed entity X is a design variable related to the extent to which X uses physical, informational, technical, and/or intellectual resources for processing information, interpreting information, and/or learning from information that may not be specified by its designers. That definition leads to four broad categories of smartness that are each related to 5 to 7 capabilities that might be built into devices or systems:

- **Information processing**. Capture information, transmit information, store information, retrieve information, delete information, manipulate information, display information.
- **Action in the world**. Sensing, actuation, coordination, communication, control, physical action.
- **Internal regulation**. Self-detection, self-monitoring, self-diagnosis, self-correction, self-organization.
- **Knowledge acquisition**. Sensing or discovering, classifying, compiling, inferring or extrapolating from examples, inferring or extrapolating from abstractions, testing and evaluating.

The smartness built into a device or system for any of the above capabilities can be characterized along the following dimension [18]:

- **Not smart at all**. Does not perform activities that exhibit the capability.
- **Scripted execution**. Performs activities related to a specific capability according to prespecified instructions.
- **Formulaic adaptation**. Adaptation of capability-related activities based on prespecified inputs or conditions.
- **Creative adaptation**. Adaptation of capability-related activities based on unscripted or partially scripted analysis of relevant information or conditions.
- **Unscripted or partially scripted invention**. Invention of capability-related activities using unscripted or partially scripted execution of a workaround or new method.

The four categories of smartness, the various capabilities within each category, and the related dimensions for describing smartness reveal that most "smart" entities in current use are not very smart after all because they perform only scripted execution for a limited number of capabilities. For example, many current uses of machine learning are built on transforming a dataset into an algorithm for making choices or predictions, but have no ability to process other kinds of data and very limited ability to take action in the world, self-regulate, or acquire new knowledge autonomously. Similarly, many nominally smart devices can capture data and use it in a scripted way, but cannot perform other kinds of activities at a level that seems "smart," especially when compared with the smartness of sentient robots in science fiction.

5 Facets of Work

One possible approach for trying to make a CHS smarter is to increase the smartness of individual facets of work within that CHS. Facets of work are aspects of work that can be observed or analyzed, such as making decisions, communicating, processing information, and coordinating. The idea of facets of work is an extension of WST that is useful for describing and analyzing the use of a digital agent by a CHS. That idea grew out of research for bringing richer and more evocative concepts to systems analysis and design to facilitate interactions between analysts and stakeholders, as is explained in [19]. The notion of "facet" is an analogy to how a cut diamond consists of a single thing with many facets that can be observed or analyzed. Psychology, library science, information science, and computer science have used the idea of facets, but with quite different meanings and connotations.

All 18 of the facets of work in Table 2 apply to all CHSs, are associated with specific concepts, bring evaluation criteria and design trade-offs, have sub-facets, and bring open-ended questions for analysis and design [19]. Some facets overlap in many situations (e.g., making decisions and communication). The iterative design process that led to selection of the 18 facets might have led to a different set of facets, perhaps 14 or 27. Determination of whether or not to include a type of activity as one of the 18 facets of work in [19] was based on the extent to which that type of activity was associated with a nontrivial set of concepts, evaluation criteria, design trade-offs, sub-facets, and open-ended questions that could be useful in analysis and design. In relation to digital agents, facets of work provide a way to be specific about requirements for many types of capabilities that might be overlooked otherwise.

Table 2. 18 facets of work [19].

Making decisions	Communicating	Providing information
Representing reality	Learning	Coordinating
Performing physical work	Providing service	Applying knowledge
Planning	Improvising	Performing support work
Creating value	Thinking	Controlling execution
Processing information	Interacting socially	Maintaining security

There is no assumption that the facets of work should be independent. To the contrary, the facet *making decisions* often involves other facets such as *communicating, learning,* and *processing information*. The main point is that each facet can be viewed as part of lens for thinking about where and how CHSs might use digital agents.

6   Roles and Responsibilities of Digital Agents

Another possible direction for finding ways to make CHS smarter is to focus on roles and responsibilities of digital agents within CHSs. Roles that digital agents might play in supporting or performing work in a CHS can be identified along a spectrum from the lowest to the highest degree of direct involvement of the digital agent in the execution of the CHS's activities. Shneiderman's human-centered AI (HCAI) framework [20, 21] was a starting point for developing a spectrum of such roles. That framework has two dimensions: low vs. high computer automation and low vs. high human control. Deficiency or excess along either dimension may lead to worse results for organizations, for

CHS participants, and/or for customers. For current purposes, however, the low vs. high distinctions in those dimensions provide too little detail to inspire vivid visualization and discussion of how or why a digital agent might be applied in a CHS's operation or might affect its stakeholders.

An iterative attempt to expand on Shneiderman's HCAI framework to make it more useful for detailed description and analysis of WSs focused initially on the low vs. high automation dimension. The three roles were identified initially: support, control, and perform. Trial and error consideration of many familiar examples led to six types of roles that a digital agent might play for a WS (and hence a CHS). Specific instances of each type might support HCAI values and aspirations or might oppose those values and aspirations (e.g., micromanagement or surveillance capitalism). The following comments about the six roles include examples that promote human-centric values and other examples that seem contrary to those values:

Monitor a Work System. A digital agent might monitor and measure aspects of work to assure that a CHS's processes and activities are appropriate for CHS participants. In some cases the digital agent might generate alarms when digital traces of work start going out of accepted bounds regarding health, safety, and cognitive load. On the other hand, the digital agent might monitor work so closely that people would feel micromanaged or disrespected.

Provide Information. A digital agent might provide information that helps people achieve their work goals safely and comfortably without infringing on privacy and other rights of people whose information is used. On the other hand, the digital agent might provide real time comparisons that lead to toxic levels of competition between workers.

Provide Capabilities. A digital agent might provide analytical, visualization, and computational capabilities that help CHS participants achieve their work objectives safely and with appropriate effort. On the other hand, new digital agent capabilities might erode or eliminate the importance of skills that CHS participants had developed over many years (e.g., de-skilling of insurance underwriters by partial automation).

Control Activities. A digital agent might control CHS activities directly to prevent specific activities from going out of bounds related to worker safety, time on the job, stress, and other variables that can be measured and used to control a CHS. On the other hand, a digital agent's frequent feedback about performance gaps (e.g., rate of call completions in support centers) might increase anxiety about whether goals can be met.

Coproduce Activities. A digital agent might be deployed in a division of responsibility in which the digital agent and human CHS participants have complementary responsibilities for performing their parts of the work. In some instances the initiative for the next step might shift back and forth between the digital agent and the CHS participants depending on the status of the work. On the other hand, giving the digital agent a leading role might leave some CHS participants feeling that they are working for a machine.

Execute Activities. A digital agent might execute activities that should not or cannot be delegated to people. For example, a digital agent might perform activities that are difficult, dangerous, or impossible for people to perform as the CHS produces product/services. On the other hand, a digital agent might automate activities that people could perform more effectively due to their ability to understand and evaluate exceptions and unexpected situations.

6.1 Agent-Responsibility Framework

The agent-responsibility (AR) framework in Fig. 2 [22, 23] combines the facets of work in Table 2 with the six digital agent roles introduced above. It assumes that digital agent usage occurs when a digital agent performs one or more roles (the horizontal dimension) related to one or more facets of work (the vertical dimension). For the sake of easy visualization, the abbreviated version of the AR framework in Fig. 2 uses only 6 of the 18 facets in Table 2.

Combining the AR framework's two dimensions leads to pinpointing design issues concerning the extent to which a digital agent should have responsibilities involving roles related to facets of work, e.g., monitoring decisions, providing capabilities used in coordinating, or performing security-related activities automatically. The AR framework can be used in many ways. For example, [22] and [23] show how different roles might apply to many different facets of work in CHSs such as a hiring system, use of an electronic medical records system, an ecommerce system, and in other work systems such as an automated auction and the IS that partly controls a self-driving car.

Facet of work >>>		Monitoring the CHS	Providing information	Providing capabilities	Controlling activities	Coproducing activities	Executing activities
	Making decisions						
	Communicating						
	Processing information						
	Coordinating						
	Creating value						
	Maintaining security						
		<<<<<<<		Spectrum of roles		>>>>>>>	

Fig. 2. (Abbreviated) Agent responsibility framework with six roles and six facets of work

7 Patterns of Interaction Between CHS Participants and Digital Agents

Yet another approach for increasing the smartness of an CHS is to improve interactions between CHS participants and digital agents. Those interactions may include unidirectional, mutual, or reciprocal actions, effects, relationships, and influences. IS engineering can look at those interactions by adapting system interaction patterns from preliminary research [24] that used four categories to organize 19 patterns of interaction between work systems. The idea of system interaction pattern was inspired by an analogy to software design patterns (solutions to recurring software problems), an idea that was inspired by design patterns for architecture [25]. Features of software design patterns include name, intent, problem, solution, entities involved in the pattern, consequences, and implementation, i.e., a concrete manifestation of a pattern [26].

Table 3 uses four categories to organize 16 or the 19 *system interaction patterns* that [24] explains. (The other three are not relevant for interactions between CHS participants and digital agents.). In specific situations, instances of most of the 16 interaction patterns can be described in detail in terms of roles and responsibilities of the CHS participant and digital agent, cause or trigger of the interaction, desired outcome, typical process during the interaction, and alternative versions of that process. Occasionally relevant aspects of those interactions include constraints, risks and risk factors, byproducts, and verification of interaction (important in some cases, but not all). The interaction patterns in Table 3 do not need the rigor or specificity of software design patterns because they serve more as a map for identifying different types of interaction situations and related issues that need to be addressed.

Table 3. Sixteen Patterns of Interaction between CHS Participants and Digital Agents

One-way patterns (unidirectional)	Co-production patterns (bilateral)
• Inform	• Converse
• Command	• Negotiate
• Request	• Mediate
• Commit	• Share resource
• Refuse	• Supply resource
Access and visibility patterns	**Unintentional impact patterns**
• Monitor	• Spillover
• Hide	• Indirect interaction
• Protect	• Accidental interaction

One-way patterns are unidirectional interactions that have been studied in relation to the language action perspective (LAP). These patterns include *inform, command, request, commit,* and *refuse,* all of which appeared in a study of email [27]. Examples show how all five might occur: the digital agent might *inform* the CHS participant about a condition that requires action; the digital agent might *command* the CHS participant to take a particular action that is necessary to avoid a breakdown or for other reasons; the digital agent might *request* that the CHS participant to take a particular action that seems appropriate; the digital agent might *commit* to taking a particular action that depends on a nonobvious aspect of its internal state; the digital agent might *refuse* to take a particular action, perhaps because that action is infeasible due to its internal state.

Coproduction patterns are bilateral patterns whose jointly produced interactions involve multiple unidirectional interactions, some of which may be described as speech acts. Coproduction patterns include *converse, negotiate, mediate, share resource,* and *supply resource.* The first three are fundamentally about bilateral speech situations. The other two are fundamentally about coordination as described by coordination theory [28, 29]. For example, the digital agent and CHS participant might *converse* or *negotiate* about how to proceed toward achieving a goal; the digital agent might *mediate* in activities involving several CHS participants; the digital agent and CHS participant might *share* a physical resource; the digital agent might *supply* the CHS participant with a resource by providing convenient access to a tool.

Access and visibility patterns are unidirectional interaction patterns through which one entity achieves or blocks access to resources that may include information about the state of either entity. These patterns include *monitor, hide,* and *protect*. For example, the CHS participant might *monitor* the state of the digital agent to make sure that it is fully operable. The CHS participant might *hide* information that might otherwise cause the digital agent to malfunction, e.g., a workaround that might be necessary when an exception condition dictates that typically expected interactions are not appropriate. A CHS participant might *protect* a digital agent by intentionally modifying data that that otherwise might cause it to malfunction due to limits in its algorithms.

Unintentional impact patterns may occur in *spillover, indirect,* and *accidental* interactions. These are the least articulated patterns because of the great uncertainty about the sources and effects of many unintentional impacts. A *spillover* interaction could occur when a CHS participant's inability to complete a task requires the digital agent to operate in a nonstandard or unplanned manner. An *indirect* interaction occurs when a mistake by a CHS participant creates a situation that requires corrective action by the digital agent. An *accidental* interaction occurs when a CHS participant's behavior accidentally causes the digital agent to stop operating. Unintentional impacts often are difficult to anticipate, but ignoring the possibility that they will occur certainly is not beneficial for either CHS design or CHS operation.

An attempt to make a CHS smarter might involve changing elements of typical interaction patterns in any of the first three categories. Those elements include actor roles (e.g., requestor/respondent, initiator/recipient, partner, or intermediary), actor type (e.g., CHS participant or digital agent), actor rights for each role, actor responsibilities for each role, cause or trigger of the interaction, desired outcome, expected process for the interaction, possible states of an interaction, and alternative enactments. Other elements of interaction patterns that sometimes might point to paths for improvement include constraints, risks and risk factors, relevant concepts, verification of completion, and evaluation of the interaction.

8 Knowledge Objects

Information processing and knowledge acquisition are two of the categories of smartness identified earlier. The taxonomy of knowledge objects (KOs) in Fig. 3 points to ways to make CHSs and digital agents smarter even though it is an extension of ideas developed for a different purpose. That purpose was describing science as the creation, evaluation, accumulation, dissemination, synthesis, and prioritization of KOs, including the reevaluation, improvement, or replacement of existing KOs by other KOs that are more effective for understanding aspects of the relevant domain.

In relation to current concerns, human CHS participants and digital agents have quite different capabilities in regard to the KOs in the taxonomy in Fig. 3. People can make

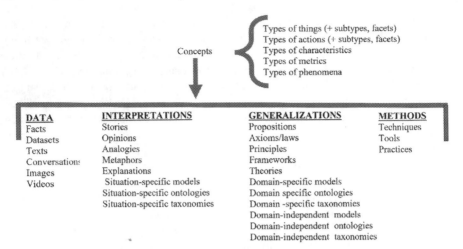

Fig. 3. Taxonomy of knowledge objects (revision of a figure in [30])

explicit use of abstract KOs that Fig. 3 categorizes as types of generalizations or methods. For example, when confronted with issues or obstacles they can think about which concepts, principles, or theories might be helpful. In contrast, most current digital agents and computerized components of other parts of CHSs can only process data (the non-abstract category in Fig. 3). Without engaging in debates about the strengths and limits of current machine learning algorithms and generative AI capabilities (e.g., producing texts and images starting from user prompts), it seems fair to say that greater ability to process and apply abstractions that express generalizations or methods might make CHSs smarter. [31] suggests that activities in the human parts of CHSs might become smarter if the human CHS participants had greater access to codified knowledge, possibly through knowledge graphs. In contrast, it might be possible to make digital agents smarter by embedding capabilities for processing and applying abstractions. Both aspirations might lead to beneficial results, but the path toward those capabilities is quite unclear.

9   Evaluating Cyber-Human Systems and Digital Agents

Both CHSs and digital agents should be evaluated based on multiple criteria that address different types of issues. Big picture criteria such as efficiency, effectiveness, equity, engagement, empathy, explainability, exceptions, and externalities (the 8 E's) [32] apply to most nontrivial CHSs and to many digital agents that they use. The first two evaluation criteria are fundamentally about how well a CHS or digital agent achieves its operational goals. The other six are not as directly linked to operational goals but often affect CHS performance and/or perceptions of product/services that a CHS produces. Beyond the 8 E's, a full picture of the performance of a CHS or digital agent requires metrics related to individual elements of the work system framework (e.g., accuracy and timeliness of the information in the CHS). Different metrics for the various work system elements have been discussed elsewhere, but only the 8 E's will be discussed here.

Efficiency. Both a CHS and a digital agent that supports it should be efficient and should support the efficiency of related work systems, i.e., the minimally wasteful production of the product/services of those work systems.

Effectiveness. Both a CHS and a digital agent that supports it should meet or exceed expectations regarding effectiveness in satisfying needs and expectations of their customers, which are often other work systems.

Equity. Both a CHS and a digital agent that supports it should operate in ways that are fair to stakeholders including CHS participants, CHS customers, and others affected directly and indirectly. Equity often presents challenges because designers, managers, and others may be unaware of their own biases and biases built into the CHS and/or the digital agent.

Engagement. CHSs and digital agents should engage CHS participants wherever that might maximize benefits from their insights or might make their work environments healthier, more satisfying, and more productive.

Empathy. CHSs and digital agents should reflect realistic consideration of the goals, capabilities, health, and comfort of CHS participants and customers that use the CHS's product/services. Lack of such empathy could have negative impacts on CHS participants, on the CHS's operational performance, on product/services that it produces, or on customers who receive and use its product/services.

Explainability. Both a CHS and a digital agent that supports it should be understandable by people who are affected by it and/or by product/services that it produces. This issue has been discussed widely in regard to AI applications whose outputs cannot be linked in an understandable way to inputs related to individuals, groups, or situations. Inadequate explainability results in confusions, errors, misuse of product/services, and possible harm to people who are affected directly or indirectly.

Exceptions. Frequent exceptions challenge many real world processes. Those challenges are amplified in CHSs because exceptions may come from the environment or from mistakes by participants or digital agents in the CHS.

Externalities. Current attention to sustainability is a strong reminder that the evaluation of both CHSs and digital agents should also consider identifiable externalities that may affect people or property not directly involved with the WS.

10   Conclusion: Toward Smarter Cyber-Human Systems

This paper defined cyber-human system, identified a series of challenges related to making CHSs smarter (Table 1), and explained how smartness of systems and devices can be described in relation to capabilities for information processing, action in the world, internal regulation, and knowledge acquisition. This paper presented ideas related to some of the challenges in Table 1 but could only cite references related to others, such as anticipating workarounds, noncompliance, and other impacts of human agency. The ideas covered here suggest the following directions that IS engineering might pursue when attempting to increase the smartness of CHSs:

Use More Powerful Digital Agents. A central purpose of many IS engineering efforts is to create or extend digital agents whose information processing activities enable the CHS to be smarter in terms of action in the world, internal regulation, and/or knowledge acquisition. This path toward smarter CHSs does not require impressively smart digital agents. It only requires scripted execution of programs that capture, transmit, store, retrieve, delete, manipulate, and/or display information that increases CHS capabilities related to any of the multiple dimensions of smartness.

Extend Roles and Responsibilities of Digital Agents. The discussion of facets of work, roles of digital agents, and responsibilities of digital agents in relation to facets of work identifies possible directions for making a CHS smarter by increasing its capabilities related to any of the digital agent roles (the horizontal axis of the AR framework) and any of the 18 facets of work in Table 3 (the vertical axis of the AR framework). IS engineering also could pursue those possibilities through more focused attention to the AR framework, e.g., how could digital agents with specific roles improve results for specific facets of work. It is easy to imagine interactive tools that might display the roles, facets of work, or combinations that would help in identifying roles and responsibilities that could be executed more successfully, and possibly in a smarter manner.

Improve Interactions Between Digital Agents and Other Parts of CHSs. The big picture choices of machine-in-the-loop, mixed initiative interaction, and human-in-the-loop plus the 16 interaction patterns in Table 3 point to many possibilities that IS engineering might pursue for making CHSs smarter. In all cases, the question is not whether machine-in-the-loop, mixed initiative, or human-in-the-loop is better in general. The key question is whether changes in the form and details of interactions between CHS participants and digital agents will result in better CHS capabilities, especially greater flexibility that might lead to greater smartness.

Introduce and Use New Knowledge Objects. The different types of knowledge objects in Fig. 3 raise the possibility that IS engineering might make CHSs and/or digital agents smarter by enabling their direct use of abstract knowledge objects such as principles, theories, models, and methods. Efforts directed toward explicit use of abstract knowledge objects would try to open new possibilities because current IS engineering methods focus primarily on pre-defined processing of pre-defined data.

Use the Eight Evaluation Criteria. IS engineering uses the criteria of efficiency and effectiveness routinely in evaluating CHSs and digital agents. Greater attention to the other six criteria might provide an impetus toward smarter CHSs and/or digital agents. Greater attention to equity, engagement, empathy, and explainability could lead to enhancing CHS smartness through fuller use of human rather than machine intelligence. Greater attention to exceptions and externalities might help in seeing the limits of efficiency and effectiveness as overriding criteria for action in the world.

References

1. Bostrom, R.P., Heinen, J.S.: MIS problems and failures: a socio-technical perspective, part II: the application of socio-technical theory. MIS Q. **1**(1), 11–28 (1977)
2. Alter, S.: Work system theory: overview of core concepts, extensions, and challenges for the future. J. Assoc. Inf. Syst. **14**(2), 72–121 (2013)
3. Reijers, H.A., Mansar, S.L.: Best practices in business process redesign: an overview and qualitative evaluation of successful redesign heuristics. Omega **33**(4), 283–306 (2005)
4. Gross, S., et al.: The business process design space for exploring process redesign alternatives. Bus. Process. Manag. J. **27**(8), 25–56 (2021)
5. Alter, S.: Defining information systems as work systems: implications for the IS field. Eur. J. Inf. Syst. **17**(5), 448–469 (2008)
6. Boell, S.K., Cecez-Kecmanovic, D.: What is an information system? In: Proceedings of HICSS (2015)
7. Alter, S.: Theory of workarounds. Commun. Assoc. Inf. Syst. **34**(55), 1041–1066 (2014)
8. Röder, N., Wiesche, M., Schermann, M., Krcmar, H.: Why managers tolerate workarounds– the role of information systems. In: Proceedings of AMCIS (2104)
9. Alter, S.: A workaround design system for anticipating, designing, and/or preventing workarounds. In: Gaaloul, K., Schmidt, R., Nurcan, S., Guerreiro, S., Ma, Q. (eds.) CAISE 2015. LNBIP, vol. 214, pp. 489–498. Springer, Cham (2015). https://doi.org/10.1007/978-3-319-19237-6_31
10. Beerepoot, I., Van De Weerd, I.: Prevent, redesign, adopt or ignore: improving healthcare using knowledge of workarounds. In: Proceedings of ECIS (2018)
11. Alter, S.: Beneficial noncompliance and detrimental compliance: expected paths to unintended consequences. In: Proceedings of AMCIS (2015)
12. Mertens, W., Recker, J., Kohlborn, T., Kummer, T.: A framework for the study of positive deviance in organizations. Deviant Behav. **37**(11), 1288–1307 (2016)
13. Outmazgin, N., Soffer, P.: Business process workarounds: what can and cannot be detected by process mining. In: Nurcan, S., et al. (eds.) BPMDS/EMMSAD -2013. LNBIP, vol. 147, pp. 48–62. Springer, Heidelberg (2013). https://doi.org/10.1007/978-3-642-38484-4_5
14. Wijnhoven, F., Hoffmann, P., Bemthuis, R., Boksebeld, J.: Using process mining for workarounds analysis in context: Learning from a small and medium-sized company case. Int. J. Inf. Manag. Data Insights **3**(1), 1–15 (2023)
15. Clark, E., et al.: Creative writing with a machine in the loop: case studies on slogans and stories. In: Proceedings of 23rd International Conference on Intelligent User Interfaces, pp. 329–340 (2018)
16. Munir, S., et al.: Cyber physical system challenges for human-in-the-loop control. In: 8th International Workshop on Feedback Computing (2013)
17. Smith, A., et al.: Closing the loop: user-centered design and evaluation of a human-in-the-loop topic modeling system. In: 23rd International Conference on Intelligent User Interfaces, pp. 293–304 (2018)
18. Alter, S.: Making sense of smartness in the context of smart devices and smart systems. Inf. Syst. Front. **22**(2), 381–393 (2019). https://doi.org/10.1007/s10796-019-09919-9
19. Alter, S.: Facets of work: enriching the description, analysis, design, and evaluation of systems in organizations. Commun. Assoc. Inf. Syst. **49**(13), 321–354 (2021)
20. Shneiderman, B.: Human-centered artificial intelligence: reliable, safe & trustworthy. Int. J. Hum.-Comput. Interact. **36**(6), 495–504 (2020)
21. Shneiderman, B.: Human-centered artificial intelligence: three fresh ideas. AIS Trans. Hum.-Comput. Interact. **12**(3), 109–124 (2020)

22. Alter, S.: Agent Responsibility Framework for Digital Agents: Roles and Responsibilities Related to Facets of Work. In: Augusto, A., Gill, A., Bork, D., Nurcan, S., Reinhartz-Berger, I., Schmidt, R. (eds.) Enterprise, Business-Process and Information Systems Modeling, pp. 237–252. Springer, Cham (2022). https://doi.org/10.1007/978-3-031-07475-2_16

23. Alter, S.: Responsibility Modeling for Operational Contributions of Algorithmic Agents. AMCIS (2022)

24. Alter, S.: System interaction patterns. In: Proceedings of the Conference on Business Informatics (2016)

25. Alexander, C.: A Pattern Language: Towns, Buildings, Construction. Oxford University Press, Oxford (1977)

26. Shalloway, A., Trott, J.R.: Design Patterns Explained: A New Perspective on Object-Oriented Design. Pearson Education (2004)

27. Cohen, W.V., Carvalho, V.R., Mitchell, T.M.: Learning to classify email into "speech acts". In: EMNLP, pp. 309–316 (2004)

28. Malone, T.W., Crowston, K.: The interdisciplinary study of coordination. ACM Comput. Surv. **26**(1), 87–119 (1994)

29. Crowston, K., Rubleske, J., Howison, J.: Coordination theory: a ten-year retrospective. In: Zhang, P., Galletta, D. (eds.) Human-Computer Interaction in Management Information Systems, Vol. I. M. E. Sharpe (2006)

30. Alter, S.: Taking different types of knowledge objects seriously: a step toward generating greater value from is research. ACM SIGMIS Database Adv. Inf. Syst. **51**(4), 123–138 (2020)

31. Alter, S.: Extending a Work System Metamodel Using a Knowledge Graph to Support IS Visualization and Development. ER Forum (2022)

32. Alter, S.: How can you verify that i am using AI? Complementary frameworks for describing and evaluating AI-based digital agents in their usage contexts. In: HICSS (2023)

Perceptual Risk-Aware Adaptive Responsibility Sensitive Safety for Autonomous Driving

Xiwei Li[1], Xi Wu[2], Yongxin Zhao[1(✉)], and Yongjian Li[3]

[1] Shanghai Key Laboratory of Trustworthy Computing, Shanghai, China
yxzhao@sei.ecnu.edu.cn
[2] The University of Sydney, NSW, Australia
[3] State Key Laboratory of Computer Science, Institute of Software,
Chinese Academy of Sciences, Beijing, China

Abstract. The Responsibility-Sensitive Safety (RSS) model is a state-of-the-art parametrizable approach to facilitating safety planning and control, which has been widely used in autonomous driving systems. However, the current RSS model neither considers perceptual risks, nor can adaptively adjust its parameter settings according to different scenarios. These limitations may lead to unsafe or inefficient behavior of the autonomous vehicles. Therefore, this paper proposes a novel perceptual risk-aware adaptive RSS approach, which trains the interpretable perceptual risk assessment model to evaluate the risk level of different scenarios and provides interpretable reasons for reference, then adaptively selects the corresponding parameters in the RSS model for safety monitoring according to the obtained perceptual risk level. This new risk-aware adaptive approach significantly reduces safety margins and increases traffic density, while maintaining risk limits. Our experiments illustrate that our approach can well balance the safety and practicality of autonomous driving systems for complex scenarios.

Keywords: RSS Model · Risk Assessment · Autonomous Driving

1 Introduction

Recently, with the rapid development of the field of information systems engineering and the increasingly coupled relationships between humans and computing, technologies related to autonomous driving have received substantial attention from both academia and industry. A lot of companies, such as Google, Toyota and Ford [13], are developing their own autonomous driving vehicles. There are several key factors in the field of autonomous driving, among which how to ensure safe driving is the top priority [10].

The safety warning system is a system that enables autonomous vehicles to detect potential dangers in advance and warn of possible traffic accidents to ensure safe driving [20]. It has become an important part of autonomous driving systems, and is considered to be a prerequisite for safe driving. In 2017,

M. Indulska et al. (Eds.): CAiSE 2023, LNCS 13901, pp. 33–49, 2023.
https://doi.org/10.1007/978-3-031-34560-9_3

Intel/Mobileye proposed the Responsibility-Sensitive Safety (RSS) approach [17], which is a white-box, interpretable, parametrizable, mathematical model with safety assurances. This approach is the latest specification to facilitate safety planning and control of autonomous driving. However, two key limitations [16] with the current RSS model are that it neither considers the perceptual risks that exist in the environment nor can adjust its parameter settings according to different scenarios adaptively. The uncertainty in the perception of autonomous driving systems may lead to cognitive errors of the surrounding environment of the systems, resulting in unsafe behaviors of the autonomous vehicles. Safety margins for autonomous vehicles in the RSS are determined based on a parametric mathematical model, and vary depending on the parameter selection. Since the model purely relies on its current state without considering past experience, it cannot provide an efficient safety assurance for different scenarios.

The research on the perceptual risk assessment of RSS has been receiving increasing interests. Salay et al. [16] sketched a formal RSS perception module to mitigate the impact of misperception by using perceptual uncertainty. However, it does not consider the scenario factors that make perception uncertain, resulting in no guarantee of the scalability for different scenarios. Some of the existing risk assessment methods [7] captured the effect of speed and distance on the risk of different driving situations in their mathematical models. However, these risk assessment methods do not take into account factors such as perception, road conditions and past risk experience.

In this paper, we propose a perceptual risk-aware adaptive RSS approach for real-time safety monitoring of autonomous vehicles. We mainly focus on answering the research question: whether it is possible to synthetically obtain sets of images with different scenario features and to extract rules that are used to decide the perceptual risk in the perceptual module, in order to detect scenes perceptual risk in autonomous driving and to explain their root causes. Firstly, we generate an initial scene dataset of different traffic flows and road types through sampling and simulation. It consists of two parts including a scene feature set and an image information set. The scene feature set captures the environment features and vehicle features generated by Scenic samplying [8], and the image information set is made of synthetic images generated by the scene feature simulation and the nearest horizontal and nearest vertical vehicle bounding box positions corresponding to the images. Secondly, based on the perception module, we evaluate the image information set to obtain risk level labels, which are used to train the perceptual risk assessment model. An interpretable perceptual risk assessment model is then obtained by bringing the training dataset with scene features and corresponding risk level labels into the Anchor method [15]. Finally, we set the parameters of the RSS model according to the perceptual risk level to provide interpretable runtime safety monitoring for autonomous vehicles, achieving a balance between the safety and efficiency of autonomous driving.

The main contributions of this paper are listed as follows:

- **Interpretable Perceptual Risk Assessment Model**. We propose an interpretable perceptual risk assessment model for evaluating the perceptual risk of complex scenarios during autonomous driving. Compared with traditional risk assessment, it not only considers perceptual risk information but also provides interpretable auxiliary help, thereby improving the accuracy and interpretability of the risk assessment model.

- **Adaptive Adjustment of RSS Parameters**. We have implemented a new information engineering software that considers the scenario perceptual risk for the safe driving of autonomous vehicles and obtain the perceptual risk level of the current scenario based on the new interpretable perceptual risk assessment model. If the autonomous vehicle is at a high-risk level, interpretable risk information will be displayed and safe braking action will be taken or the control of the vehicle will be transferred into a trusted mode. We select the corresponding parameters for the RSS model adaptively according to the perceptual risk level for real-time safety monitoring.

The remainder of this paper is organized as follows. An introduction to the recent safety assistance technologies, RSS model and failure prediction approach is provided in Sect. 2. Section 3 describes the framework of perceptual risk-aware adaptive RSS and Sect. 4 describes the details of the underlying technologies integrated into our model. In Sect. 5, we discuss the implementation of interpretable perceptual risk assessment models via experiments and explain the selection of parameters for RSS models according to different perceptual risk levels. Section 6 concludes the paper and points out the future direction.

2 Preliminaries

2.1 Vehicle Safety Assist Technology

Over the past few decades, more and more safety assistance technologies have been proposed to improve safe driving. Technologies [4,9,14,18], such as blind spot checking, lane keeping, adaptive cruise control, and forward collision avoidance, alert drivers to potential risks while driving. However, safe driving in autonomous driving is still facing a lot of challenges [1], including identifying unavoidable collisions, liability determination, validation costs for reasonable scenario coverage, and extra costs for re-validating the update of the autonomous driving system. There are many safety standards for autonomous driving, such as UL 4600 [11], ISO PAS 21448 SOTIF (Safety of Intended Function) [3] and simulation-based testing. Recently, programming methods Scenic [8] and Paracosm [12] have been proposed to specify and generate scenarios for autonomous driving tests, which are verified by the simulation to guarantee the safety of autonomous driving. However, these methods can only pre-validate the model and lack strong safety guarantees while driving. Our work instead uses Scenic for sampling to generate a dataset of scene features for training a real-time perceptual risk assessment model.

2.2 Responsibility Sensitive Safety

In 2017, Intel/Mobileye proposed Responsibility Sensitive Safety (RSS), which translates the concepts of safe driving and accident liability classification into mathematical models and reference parameters for decision control. It includes the following five key rules [17].

1) Do not hit someone from behind.
2) Do not cut-in recklessly.
3) Right-of-way is given, not taken.
4) Be careful of areas with limited visibility.
5) If you can avoid an accident without causing another one, you must do it.

These rules are described by parametric mathematical equations and logical rules that can be used to determine whether an autonomous vehicle is in a safe state or not. If the current state is unsafe, the RSS will bring the autonomous vehicle back to a safe state by limiting the actuator to execute unreasonable commands. Therefore, RSS can be used as an independent safety layer within the technology stack of autonomous driving. Due to the limitation of space, we will give an intuitive explanation about the first rule of RSS by using the following example in Fig. 1. A more detailed explanation of the second rule on lateral safety distances is given in Sect. 4.4.

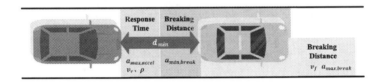

Fig. 1. Longitudinal safety distance

It indicates that a safe longitudinal distance $d_{rss-safe}$ (i.e., $d_{rss-safe} \geq d_{min}$) should be maintained between vehicles so that the autonomous vehicle (i.e., blue vehicle in Fig. 1) is able to react to any sudden emergency braking of the vehicle in front. The minimal safe longitudinal distance is calculated in the Eq. 1.

$$d_{min} = [v_r\rho + \frac{1}{2}a_{max,accel}\rho^2 + \frac{(v_r + \rho a_{max,accel})^2}{2a_{min,break}} - \frac{v_f^2}{2a_{max,break}}]_+ \quad (1)$$

In this equation, ρ represents the reaction time of the vehicle behind (i.e., the blue one in Fig. 1), $a_{max,accel}$ is the maximum acceleration of the vehicle behind during the reaction time, $a_{min,break}$ is the minimum braking acceleration that must be applied by the vehicle behind after the reaction time, and v_r is the current speed of the vehicle behind. Similarly, v_f is the speed of the vehicle in front (i.e., the yellow one in Fig. 1), and $a_{max,break}$ is the maximum braking acceleration of the vehicle in front. Finally, $[x]_+$ is defined as $max[0, x]$. If the blue autonomous vehicle enters into a dangerous situation, i.c., the distance between the above two vehicles is less than d_{min}, RSS will ask the blue vehicle behind to slow down at least $a_{min,break}$ to avoid an accident.

Since the RSS model is parametrised, according to different scenarios, a safe distance can be set up by using conservative parameters to make driving more cautious or by using loose parameters to make driving more confident. Therefore, an adaptive parameter selection is very important for achieving safe driving. Our work considers perceptual risk without imposing excessive safety margins.

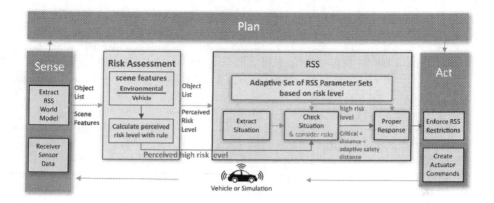

Fig. 2. Example of integrating RSS as a separate safety layer into the planning component of autonomous driving

2.3   Failure Prediction

Recently, more and more work takes the uncertainty of autonomous driving into account. Salay et al. [16] proposed a new perceptual module in combination with a formal RSS model to mitigate the effects of misperception by using information about perceptual uncertainty. Cornelius Buerkle et al. [5] proposed a new solution that used a monitoring-recovery approach based on a dynamic occupancy grid to detect common faults in a perceptual system and to successfully recover from these errors. Fremont et al. [8] implemented a SCENIC simulation-based test of the perception module, but they neither captured the semantic features of the scenario to build a perceptual risk assessment model, nor extended it to real-time monitoring of autonomous driving. Our work will implement a new interpretable perceptual risk assessment model, with which the RSS model is extended to obtain a perceptual risk-aware adaptive RSS model. In addition to creating warnings that contain the root cause of risks, the perceptual assessment algorithms that we are going to use can achieve an effective balance between safety and efficiency by adaptively selecting the parameters of the RSS model according to different scenarios.

3   Framework of Perceptual Risk-Aware Adaptive RSS

In this section, a perceptual risk-aware adaptive RSS model is proposed to guarantee that autonomous vehicles can drive safely and efficiently in real time under different scenarios. The model is shown in Fig. 2. Compared to the standard RSS model[1], we highlight in orange all extensions required to make RSS decisions with perceptual risk assessment and adaptive parameter selection. The details of each extension are described as follows.

Extract Scene Features. Our approach mainly focuses on the scene perception part of autonomous driving. According to the basic elements of scene perception and the components of a simulator scene library [6], we define scene features into two categories, including environment features and vehicle features. The environment features consist of nine indicators: time, cloudiness, precipitation, road water accumulation, wind, fog density, fog distance, wetting intensity, and road type (i.e., straight road represented as I, circle road represented as R, T-intersection represented as T, and cross intersection represented as X). The vehicle features include seven indicators: vehicle HSV value, vehicle type, vehicle distance, pitch angle, heading angle, cross-roll angle, and traffic flow. According to the rules of the RSS model, the vehicles at risk are mainly the nearest frontal vehicles and lateral vehicles. Therefore, in our approach, we mainly consider the vehicle features of these vehicles when calculating the perceptual risk. Vehicle features can be obtained through the self-sensing module.

Assess Perceptual Risk. Sensor detection of nearby scene objects is always subject to uncertainty, which depends on scene features such as environment, vehicle features and location factors. Therefore, a set of rules (i.e., a perception assessment model) is needed to determine the perceptual risk level of the current scene. The perceptual risk level can be classified as Safety, Low Risk, Medium Risk, and High Risk. If the perceptual risk assessment level is Safety, it is considered that the scene is perceptual safe for autonomous vehicles at this time, whereas if the perceptual risk assessment level is High Risk, a warning is issued to alert the decision-making system of the autonomous vehicle to take appropriate emergency measures to ensure the safety of the occupants.

Adjust RSS Parameters. After we get the perceptual risk level of the current scenario, the parameters in the RSS formula can then be selected adaptively according to the risk level (e.g., autonomous vehicles at the high-risk level need to emergency brake or to continue driving with a stricter safety distance). The Extraction Situation module listed in Fig. 2 will extract the required important information from the surrounding vehicles and bring it together with the RSS parameters into the Check Situation module to check and determine whether vehicles are in a safe state or not according to the RSS rules. Finally, the Proper Response module calculates the limits when unsafe situations happen.

4   Data-Driven Approach to Perceptual Risk Assessment

In this section, we describe the workflow of the technologies integrated in our model, as shown in Fig. 3. Specifically, an initial scene data set is generated

---

[1] The remaining grey parts are the Sense, Plan and Act modules for autonomous driving [1].

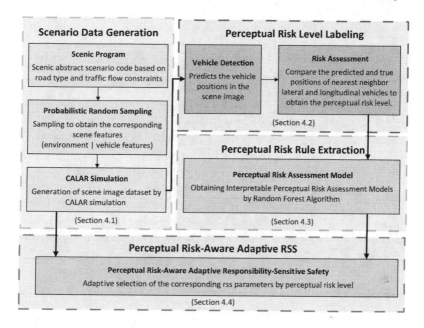

Fig. 3. Perceptual risk-aware adaptive responsibility sensitive safety process

through sampling and simulation, and the perceptual risk level is assessed and labelled on the generated data set according to the perception module. Combining the scene features and perceptual risk levels that we obtained above, an interpretable perceptual risk assessment model is trained, and by setting the RSS parameters based on perceptual risk levels, it finally provides interpretable runtime safety monitoring for autonomous vehicles.

The key idea of our approach is to capture the rules of the subspace of the feature space defined in the given SCENIC program corresponding to the different perceptual risk levels, and to interpret the sufficient conditions for accurate detection of the perceptual module based on these features. Since these features describe the important features that should be present in the scene and they are much fewer than the original low-level pixels, we can obtain fewer, compact interpretable rules [15], with significant improvements in efficiency and interpretability. We apply it to autonomous driving, providing interpretable warnings of perceptual risks and the run-time safety.

4.1 Scenario Data Generation

Considering the fact that 1) collecting real-world data can be slow and expensive, since it must be preprocessed (i.e., scene feature vector acquisition) and correctly labelled (i.e., vehicle bounding box labelling) before use; and 2) being difficult or impossible to collect data of rare or even dangerous corner cases which are indeed necessary for training to obtain a model with a wider situation coverage, we therefore propose a new method for generating road scenario datasets based on SCENIC.

The raw scenario dataset for perceptual discrimination is generated by the following steps. We first write the SCENIC program, which has high-level semantic feature constraints relevant to a specific application domain, and derive a scene feature space $D_1 \times D_2 \times \cdots \times D_n$ based on its defined feature dependencies and soft and hard constraints, where road type and traffic flow are the constrained features to be set and the rest are sample features that can be assigned. Then, SCENIC as a probabilistic programming language can generate a set of high-coverage scene feature vectors $[f_1, f_2, \cdots, f_n] \in D_1 \times D_2 \times \cdots \times D_n$ by sampling from a specified distribution, containing the environmental and vehicle features mentioned in the previous section. Finally, the simulator can simulate the scene feature vector with a mapping function m. A scenario specific pixel matrix $M_{x \times y}$ is generated from ego's camera sensor and the position $[(x_{1,low}, y_{1,low}, x_{1,high}, y_{1,high}), (x_{2,low}, y_{2,low}, x_{2,high}, y_{2,high})]$ of the nearest lateral and longitudinal vehicle bounding box on the pixel matrix can be calculated based on the transformation from world to pixel coordinates.

4.2   Perceptual Risk Level Labeling

The perceptual risk assessment of the scenario is achieved based on the perceptual performance of the nearest lateral and longitudinal vehicles by the perception module (i.e., target detection algorithm [2]). The synthetic scenario pixel matrix with the vehicle location information is provided to the target detection recognition model O. Based on the perceptual performance P of the target detection model on the images, each image is assigned a perceptual risk level label $L(P(O(m([f_1, f_2, \cdots, f_n]))))$, such as Safety, Low, Medium and High Risk.

The perceptual risk level label L of the acquired image will be calculated by using the perceptual performance P for classification. High risk is the presence of ground truth box that are not detected correctly, i.e., the nearest neighboring lateral or longitudinal vehicle is not detected correctly. If all detections are successful, the perceptual score of each image is then calculated based on the set of predicted candidate boxes and the set of real marked boxes obtained from the simulation by Eq. 2,

$$Score_{perception} = \frac{PBox_h \cap TBox_h}{PBox_h \cup TBox_h} \times C_h + \frac{PBox_l \cap TBox_l}{PBox_l \cup TBox_l} \times C_l \qquad (2)$$

where $PBox_h$ is the lateral prediction candidate box position, $TBox_h$ is the lateral true marker box position, and C_h is the target detector lateral prediction confidence. Similarly, $PBox_l$, $TBox_l$ and C_l represent the corresponding longitudinal variables. Two thresholds θ_1 and θ_2 (i.e., $\theta_1 < \theta_2$) have been set so that different scenarios can be classified into corresponding perceptual risk levels. Specifically, scenarios with perception scores less than θ_1 are at medium risk, scenarios with perception scores between θ_1 and θ_2 are at low risk, and scenarios with perception scores greater than θ_2 are safe. The labels obtained for each image are mapped back to the scene feature vectors that previously resulted in the generation of the corresponding image. The final result is a dataset of scene features labelled with perceptual risk levels, which maps each high-level feature vector to its respective label.

4.3 Perceptual Risk Rule Extraction

We train the scene feature dataset with perceptual risk level labels to obtain the perceptual risk assessment model. Specifically, we use the anchoring method [15] to capture the rules of a subspace of the scene feature space defined in a given SCENIC program.

$$\max_{R}(R([f_1, f_2, \cdots, f_n]) - L(P(O(m([f_1, f_2, \cdots, f_n]))))) \tag{3}$$

As shown in Eq. 3, we extract rules from the dataset using anchoring methods. The result is a set of rules that encode conditions on high-level features of the scenario that may lead to different perceptual risk levels. The obtained rules can be used to monitor the perceptual risk level of the real-time autonomous vehicle operating environment and provide explanations for perceptual errors in safe driving.

4.4 Perceptual Risk-Aware Adaptive RSS

In order to adaptively generate the RSS model, it is necessary to obtain the customised parameters in the lateral safety distance and the longitudinal safety distance.

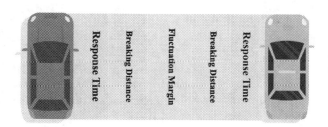

Fig. 4. Lateral safety distance

As shown in Fig. 4, the lateral safety distance in the RSS model is calculated by both the distance of braking in the reaction time of the left and right vehicles and the lateral holding distance. The specific calculation is shown in Eq. 4,

$$d_{min} = \mu + [\frac{v_1 + v_{1,\rho}}{2}\rho + \frac{1}{2}a^{lat}_{min,break}v^2_{1,\rho} -$$
$$(\frac{v_2 + v_{2,\rho}}{2}\rho) - \frac{1}{2}a^{lat}_{min,break}v^2_{2,\rho}] +$$
$$v_{1,\rho} = v_1 + \rho a^{lat}_{max,accel}$$
$$v_{2,\rho} = v_2 - \rho a^{lat}_{max,accel}$$
$$\tag{4}$$

where, ρ represents the reaction time of the left vehicle, $v_{1,\rho}$ and $v_{2,\rho}$ are the speed of the left and right vehicles after the reaction time, $a^{lat}_{min,break}$ is the minimum braking acceleration that must be implemented by both vehicles after the reaction time, v_1 and v_2 are the current speed of the left vehicle and the right vehicle respectively, and μ is the lateral safe braking distance. Finally, $[x]_+$ is defined as $max[0, x]$.

Considering both Eqs. 1 and 4, we can obtain the following customized parameters in RSS: reaction time ρ, longitudinal maximum acceleration $a_{max,accel}$, longitudinal minimum braking acceleration $a_{min,break}$, longitudinal maximum braking acceleration $a_{max,break}$, lateral maximum acceleration $a^{lat}_{max,accel}$, lateral minimum braking acceleration $a^{lat}_{min,break}$, and lateral safety braking distance μ. All these parameters will then be set according to the perceptual risk level. An example about the parameter setting could be found in Table 5 in Sect. 5.

5   Experimental Evaluation

In this section, to evaluate the effectiveness and performance of the proposed perceptual risk-aware adaptive RSS approach, we conduct extensive experiments in the simulated environments with different levels of complexity and road conditions.

5.1   Scenarios

We experiment our approach in four abstract SCENIC scenarios with different road types and traffic flow constraints. The scene features for each scene are divided into two categories, namely environmental features and vehicle features as mentioned in Sect. 3. The high-coverage scene feature vectors can be obtained by probabilistic random sampling of the corresponding scene feature space for four different abstract scenarios. Although each abstract scenario can be sampled to obtain multiple scene feature vectors, only one feature vector is shown here for each abstract scenario due to space limitations, the rest of the data can be viewed on github[2]. The corresponding scene features are shown in Table 1.

Table 1. The features corresponding to the scenario.

Scenario	Environment Feature					Vehicle Feature			
	Time	Cloudiness	Fogden	...	Roadtype[a]	Distance	Type	...	Traffic
a	18	65	6	...	I	4 - 13	nissan.micra - jeep.rubicon	...	4
b	19	42	11	...	R	28 - 6	toyota.prius - nissan.micra	...	5
c	6	14	85	...	T	19 - Nan	volkswagen.t2 - Nan	...	5
d	11	5	3	...	X	4 - 10	chevrolet.impala seat.leon	...	6

[a] I: straight road, R: circle road, T: T-intersection, X: cross intersection.

[2] https://github.com/DeltaViv/Perceptual-Risk-Aware-Adaptive-Responsibility-Sensitive-Safety-for-Autonomous-Driving.

The sampled scene feature vector is passed to the simulator CARLA for simulation, and the images from the camera sensor of the ego vehicle are acquired to obtain the scene features and their corresponding synthetic images. Images generated from these scenarios are shown in Fig. 5. Scenario 5(a) describes the operation of an autonomous vehicle on a straight road with a traffic flow of 4 on a rainy day with a lot of water on the ground. Scenario 5(b) describes the operation of an autonomous vehicle on a circular road with a traffic flow of 5 on a rainy day with low visibility. Scenario 5(c) describes the operation of an autonomous vehicle on a T-intersection with a traffic flow of 5 on a foggy day. Scenario 5(d) describes the operation of an autonomous vehicle at an intersection with a traffic flow of 6 on a sunny day at noon.

(a) Straight road

(b) Circle intersection

(c) T-intersection

(d) Cross intersection

Fig. 5. Set of image scenes generated by image feature simulation

Due to the scene features contain both discrete and continuous variables, we use the Eq. 5 to evaluate the situation coverage of the synthetic data to guarantee that the data we have obtained to be able to cover the distribution of the real scene data as much as possible.

$$
\begin{aligned}
score = &\frac{1}{N_\mathbf{F}} \sum_{f \in \mathbf{F}} \{1 - [\max(\frac{min(s_f) - min(r_f)}{max(s_f) - min(r_f)}, 0) + \\
&\max(\frac{max(r_f) - max(s_f)}{max(s_f) - min(r_f)}, 0)]\} + \frac{1}{N_\mathbf{C}} \sum_{i \in \mathbf{C}} \frac{s_c}{r_c}
\end{aligned}
\tag{5}
$$

where $\mathbf{F}$ and $\mathbf{C}$ represent the set of continuous and discrete features in the synthetic scene, respectively. $N_\mathbf{F}$ and $N_\mathbf{C}$ represent the number of features in the corresponding set. After the evaluation, the situation coverage rate of our synthetic data is 90.5%, which proves that the synthetic data covers the distribution of the real scene data quite well.

5.2 Perceptual Risk Assessment

We use the object detection code in Tensorflow Garden [2] to identify the vehicles in the synthetic images that are closest to the autonomous vehicle in both longitudinal and lateral directions. We then calculate the perceptual safety score of the scenarios in synthesized images based on the Eq. 2 and map the score to the scene features corresponding to the synthesized images. It is worth noting that our model is portable and scalable. Once we have a realistic dataset that fits the required format as we mentioned, it can be easily added to or substituted for the raw dataset to perform the current process and subsequent processes.

(a) Object detection   (b) Score calculation

Fig. 6. Perceptual safety score

As shown in Fig. 6(b), the green boxes represent the vehicle locations predicted by the object detection algorithm, while the remaining boxes (i.e., red boxes and yellow boxes) represent the nearest lateral and longitudinal vehicle actual locations. Specifically, red boxes represent undetected vehicles among the nearest vehicles, whereas yellow boxes represent detected vehicles among the nearest vehicles. The perceptual safety score of Fig. 6(b) is calculated as 0.288. However, it is still set as High Risk due to the presence of the nearest lateral or longitudinal vehicles undetected. In addition, we set thresholds $\theta_1 = 0.25$ and $\theta_2 = 0.5$ to classify risk levels for non-high-risk scenarios.

As shown in Table 2, in order to obtain a larger dataset to train the perceptual risk assessment model, for each abstract scenario, we generate 2000 scene features while calculating its perceptual risk level as the training and test set (i.e., 8,000 scene features with perceptual risk level labels for training and testing). The details of the dataset are shown in the above github on page 10.

Table 2. The perceptual risk assessment model dataset

Id	Features									Score	Level
1	8	38	42	49	32	99	...	I	3	0.414	Low Risk
2	18	74	16	5	94	30	...	I	3	——	High Risk
...				...				...		...	...
7998	20	38	57	46	83	42	...	T	2	0.855	Safety
7999	18	5	26	53	43	37	...	T	2	0.3	Low Risk
8000	16	27	28	24	41	9	...	T	2	0.483	?Low Risk?

Table 3. The confusion matrix, recall, precision and F1-score of the interpretable perceptual risk assessment model

True Labels	Predicted Labels				Sum
	Safety	Low Risk	Medium Risk	High Risk	
Safety	179	4	10	0	193
Low Risk	19	152	5	13	189
Medium Risk	7	1	169	15	192
High Risk	0	3	1	190	194
Recall	92.75%	80.42%	88.02%	97.94%	89.84%
Precision	87.32%	95.00%	91.35%	87.16%	90.18%
F1-score	89.95%	87.10%	89.65%	91.35%	89.75%

Finally, the generated training set is brought into the random forest classifier for training and the Anchor algorithm for parsing to obtain an interpretable perceptual risk assessment model. As shown in Table 3, the confusion matrix, recall, precision and F1-score of the interpretable perceptual risk assessment model on the test dataset show that it has an excellent recall (>90%) and a good precision (>85%) in both safety and high risk scenarios, and an excellent precision (>90%) and a good recall (>80%) in both low and medium risk scenarios. Overall, our model has an excellent performance on perceptual risk assessment.

Table 4. Perceptual risk assessment results

Scenario	Perceptual Risk Level	Interpretable Rule
a	Low Risk	cloudiness <= 75.00 AND time <= 19.00 AND cardistance < 5.00 AND wind <= 76.00 AND roadtype = I
b	High Risk	cardistance > 25.0 AND cloudiness > 24.0 AND fogden > 50.0 AND roadtype = R AND yaw > 100 AND time >= 18.0
c	Medium Risk	cardistance <= 21.00 AND cloudiness <= 50.00 AND fogdis <= 6.00 AND fogden > 69.00
d	High Risk	roadtype = X AND carnumber > 5.00 AND cardistance <= 4.00

As shown in Table 4[3], the generated scene features are brought into the assessment model to obtain their perceptual risk level and the reasons for that level. For scenario c, we can observe that even though the fog visibility is low and the fog source is too close, it is still assessed as medium risk due to the moderate distance between vehicles and the good lightness of the sky. In summary, the model can predict the perceptual risk level of the current scenario with relative accuracy and distinguish which features of the current scenario are likely to cause faults in the perception module.

5.3   Adaptive RSS Model

Parameters corresponding to different perceived risk situations were developed based on the perceived risk classification thresholds of the dataset θ_1, θ_2 and the range of data from the real driving study $[l_1, l_2]$ [19]. The Table 5 shows the parameters corresponding to the different perceived risk scenarios. The strictest parameter l_2 is chosen for the high risk level, the stricter parameter $(1 - \theta_1)l_2 + \theta_1 l_1$ is chosen for the medium risk level, the looser parameter $(1 - \theta_2)l_2 + \theta_2 l_1$ is chosen for the low risk level and the loosest parameter l_1 is chosen for the perceived safety situation to achieve a balance between safety and efficiency.

We take the scenario shown in Table 5 that contains other vehicles in the longitudinal direction as an example, assuming that the current speed of the vehicle ahead is half of the maximum urban speed of 25 km/h (i.e., no danger to the ego vehicle when the speed of the vehicle ahead is too high). Figure 7 illustrates the safety distance that the ego vehicle should keep under different risk levels and the corresponding throughput, through which the results clearly demonstrate that the higher the perceived risk, the greater the minimum safe distance between vehicles and the safer the vehicles, but the smaller the accompanying throughput and the lower the efficiency. Our model achieves a dynamic balance between safety and efficiency by adaptively adjusting the RSS parameters through the perceptual risk level.

Table 5. The RSS parameters corresponding to different perceptual risk levels

Parameter	Safety	Low Risk	Medium Risk	High Risk
$\rho(s)$	0.1	0.3	0.4	0.5
$a_{max,accel}(m/s^2)$	1	2	2.5	3
$a_{max,break}(m/s^2)$	5	6.5	7.25	8
$a_{min,break}(m/s^2)$	4	2.5	1.75	1
$a_{max,accel}^{lat}(m/s^2)$	0.2	0.3	0.35	0.4
$a_{min,break}^{lat}(m/s^2)$	0.3	0.2	0.15	0.1
$\mu(m)$	0.55	0.73	0.82	0.92

---

[3] The perceptual rules corresponding to the completed test data set can be found on the GitHub repository mentioned on page 10.

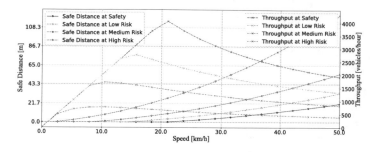

Fig. 7. Longitudinal safety distance and throughput at different perceptual risk levels

The results show that our approach is effective in scenario-aware assessment, interpretable rule generation and adaptive adjustment of RSS parameters, enabling interpretable safety warnings for autonomous vehicles and achieving a balance between safety and efficiency. However, due to the effectiveness of our method in practical scenarios depends on both the distribution and the size of the data set, the accuracy of the method therefore can be further improved by increasing the size of the data set and by selecting data set with different scenarios. Moreover, various optimisation techniques could be used to further reduce the response time of the model in order to improve the efficiency of the method and better apply the method to different scenarios in the real world. Finally, since our approach is a proven general method, for any specific vehicle perception module, it can easily generate scenarios based on our model and obtain perception rules based on real data sets to dynamically adapt the RSS model for safe and efficient autonomous vehicle operation.

6   Conclusion and Future Work

In this paper, we proposed a new perceptual risk assessment model for evaluating the perceptual risk of the environment in autonomous driving, while providing interpretable assessment rules that can be used for driving vehicle safety warnings and subsequent perceptual module improvements. Compared with the traditional risk assessment model, our approach considered perceptual risk factors and provided interpretable safety alerts, thus improving the accuracy and interpretability of the risk assessment model. Our approach also allowed to select RSS parameters adaptively for safety monitoring according to the perceptual risk level, achieving a balance between safety and efficiency of autonomous driving.

In future work, we will use a variety of optimisation techniques to further improve the response time of our models and extend the perceptual risk assessment to a road risk assessment that takes into account the motion risk of other vehicles to achieve a safer and more efficient framework for autonomous driving assurance.

Acknowledgement. This work is supported by National Key Research and Development Program (2020AAA0107800), National Natural Science Foundation of China

(62272165), the "Digital Silk Road" Shanghai International Joint Lab of Trustworthy Intelligent Software (Grant No.22510750100), and Shanghai Trusted Industry Internet Software Collaborative Innovation Center.

References

1. Anderson, J., Kalra, N., Stanley, K., Sorensen, P., Samaras, C., Oluwatola, T.: Autonomous Vehicle Technology: A Guide for Policymakers (2014)
2. Banna, V., et al.: An experience report on machine learning reproducibility: guidance for practitioners and tensorflow model garden contributors. arXiv abs/2107.00821 (2021)
3. Birch, J., et al.: A structured argument for assuring safety of the intended functionality (SOTIF). In: Casimiro, A., Ortmeier, F., Schoitsch, E., Bitsch, F., Ferreira, P. (eds.) SAFECOMP 2020. LNCS, vol. 12235, pp. 408–414. Springer, Cham (2020). https://doi.org/10.1007/978-3-030-55583-2_31
4. Carvalho, A., Lefevre, S., Schildbach, G., Kong, J., Borrelli, F.: Automated driving: the role of forecasts and uncertainty - a control perspective. Eur. J. Control **24**, 14–32 (2015). https://doi.org/10.1016/j.ejcon.2015.04.007
5. Cho, H., Seo, Y.W., Kumar, B., Rajkumar, R.: A multi-sensor fusion system for moving object detection and tracking in urban driving environments (2014). https://doi.org/10.1109/ICRA.2014.6907100
6. Dosovitskiy, A., Ros, G., Codevilla, F., López, A.M., Koltun, V.: CARLA: an open urban driving simulator. CoRR abs/1711.03938 (2017). https://arxiv.org/abs/1711.03938
7. Eggert, J., Mueller, F.: A foresighted driver model derived from integral expected risk, pp. 1223–1230 (2019). https://doi.org/10.1109/ITSC.2019.8916978
8. Fremont, D., et al.: Scenic: a language for scenario specification and data generation. Mach. Learn. 1–45 (2022). https://doi.org/10.1007/s10994-021-06120-5
9. Jain, A., Koppula, H., Raghavan, B., Soh, S., Saxena, A.: Car that knows before you do: anticipating maneuvers via learning temporal driving models, pp. 3182–3190 (2015). https://doi.org/10.1109/ICCV.2015.364
10. Kohli, P., Chadha, A.: Enabling pedestrian safety using computer vision techniques: a case study of the 2018 Uber Inc. Self-driving car crash. In: Arai, K., Bhatia, R. (eds.) FICC 2019. LNNS, vol. 69, pp. 261–279. Springer, Cham (2020). https://doi.org/10.1007/978-3-030-12388-8_19
11. Koopman, P., Ferrell, U., Fratrik, F., Wagner, M.: A safety standard approach for fully autonomous vehicles. In: Romanovsky, A., Troubitsyna, E., Gashi, I., Schoitsch, E., Bitsch, F. (eds.) SAFECOMP 2019. LNCS, vol. 11699, pp. 326–332. Springer, Cham (2019). https://doi.org/10.1007/978-3-030-26250-1_26
12. Majumdar, R., Mathur, A., Pirron, M., Stegner, L., Zufferey, D.: Paracosm: a language and tool for testing autonomous driving systems (2019)
13. Pandey, G., McBride, J., Eustice, R.: Ford campus vision and lidar data set. I. J. Robot. Res. **30**, 1543–1552 (2011). https://doi.org/10.1177/0278364911400640
14. Rezaei, M., Klette, R.: Look at the driver, look at the road: no distraction! no accident! (2014). https://doi.org/10.1109/CVPR.2014.24
15. Ribeiro, M., Singh, S., Guestrin, C.: Anchors: high-precision model-agnostic explanations. In: Proceedings of the AAAI Conference on Artificial Intelligence, vol. 32 (2018). https://doi.org/10.1609/aaai.v32i1.11491

16. Salay, R., Czarnecki, K., Elli, M.S., Alvarez, I.J., Sedwards, S., Weast, J.: PURSS: towards perceptual uncertainty aware responsibility sensitive safety with ML. In: Espinoza, H., et al. (eds.) Proceedings of the Workshop on Artificial Intelligence Safety, co-located with 34th AAAI Conference on Artificial Intelligence, SafeAI@AAAI 2020, New York City, NY, USA, 7 February 2020. CEUR Workshop Proceedings, vol. 2560, pp. 91–95. CEUR-WS.org (2020). https://ceur-ws.org/Vol-2560/paper34.pdf
17. Shalev-Shwartz, S., Shammah, S., Shashua, A.: On a formal model of safe and scalable self-driving cars (2017)
18. Shia, V., et al.: Semiautonomous vehicular control using driver modeling. IEEE Trans. Intell. Transp. Syst. **15**, 2696–2709 (2014). https://doi.org/10.1109/TITS.2014.2325776
19. Xu, X., Wang, X., Wu, X., Hassanin, O., Chai, C.: Calibration and evaluation of the responsibility-sensitive safety model of autonomous car-following maneuvers using naturalistic driving study data. Transp. Res. Part C Emerg. Technol. **123**, 102988 (2021). https://doi.org/10.1016/j.trc.2021.102988
20. Zhao, S., Qu, X., Li, Y.: Curve driving safety warning system for vehicle with driver-vehicle-environment synergy, vol. 42, pp. 112–118 (2016). https://doi.org/10.11936/bjutxb2015020042

Requirements Engineering

Configuration Optimization with Limited Functional Impact

Edouard Guégain[1]([✉]) [ID], Amir Taherkordi[2] [ID], and Clément Quinton[1] [ID]

[1] Univ. Lille, CNRS, Inria, Centrale Lille, UMR 9189 CRIStAL, 59000 Lille, France
{edouard.guegain,clement.quinton}@univ-lille.fr
[2] University of Oslo, Oslo, Norway
amirhost@ifi.uio.no

Abstract. Dealing with a large configuration space is a complex task for developers, especially when configurations must comply with both functional constraints and non-functional goals. In this paper, we introduce an approach to optimize any set of performance indicators for an existing configuration, while meeting functional requirements. The efficiency of this approach is assessed by exhaustively optimizing a configurable system, and by analyzing how the algorithm navigates through the configuration space. This approach proves especially efficient at optimizing configurations through a minimal number of changes, thus limiting the impact on their functional behavior.

Keywords: Software · Variability · Optimization · Performance

1 Introduction

Modern software-intensive systems are highly configurable. Software engineers thus have to develop, test and maintain a significant number of options, or *features*, that are then combined together to produce a specific software configuration. As the number of features grows, the number of configurations (*i.e.*, the *configuration space*) consequently grows exponentially and modern systems face the ever-increasing complexity of their configurations [20]. Dealing with large configuration spaces is challenging, especially when configurations must comply with both functional constraints and non-functional performance goals. To avoid facing this complexity, developers may stick to default configurations or sub-optimal ones [12].

Based on this observation and inspired by our previous work on measuring the energy consumption of configurable systems [2], we propose in this paper an approach that optimizes a configuration regarding multiple performance objectives. Contrarily to prior work that samples or predicts performance models seeking for the best configuration of the whole configuration space [4,7,9,10,22], our approach optimizes existing configurations by maximizing performance gains while minimizing changes to such configurations. The objective is to provide the developer with the best-performing configuration by altering as little as possible

M. Indulska et al. (Eds.): CAiSE 2023, LNCS 13901, pp. 53–68, 2023.
https://doi.org/10.1007/978-3-031-34560-9_4

the initial one, in order to remain as close as possible to the developer's functional requirements. Our contribution is threefold. First, we propose ICO, a novel optimization approach for configurable systems that addresses the aforementioned objective. Second, we release an up-and-running Java-based implementation of the approach. Third, we provide an in-depth analysis of the behavior of our approach and assess its efficiency on a real-world system.

In the remainder of this paper, Sect. 2 explains fundamentals and a running example. Sect. 3 explains our optimization approach. Section 4 and Sect. 5 present the design and results of our experiments, respectively. Section 6 provides a critical discussion. Section 7 discusses related work and Sect. 8 concludes the paper.

2 Motivation and Running Example

Feature models are commonly used to define the configuration space of highly-variable software systems. A feature model is a tree or a directed acyclic graph of features [8], organized hierarchically in parent/sub-feature(s) relationships. Features can be mandatory, optional, or alternative and the selection of a feature may require or exclude the selection of other features. While most of these relationships can be encoded in a feature tree, *require* and *exclude* relationships are usually defined using cross-tree constraints. Therefore, the feature model describes the configuration space of a software system encoded both as a feature tree and a set of cross-tree constraints. It thus defines, in an implicit yet compact way, the set of possible configurations for that software.

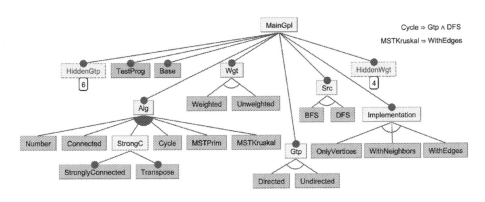

Fig. 1. Excerpt of the feature model of GPL-FH-Java.

Figure 1 presents an excerpt of the GPL-FH feature model (some features, like HiddenWgt, are collapsed and only two constraints are shown). GPL-FH is a testbed, used in particular to evaluate different implementations and algorithms that can be executed on a graph. The graph under test is generated at runtime through the TestProg feature. GPL-FH exhibits 156 configurations for

37 features and 14 constraints. These features represent different characteristics of the generated graph, such as `Weighted` or `Unweighted`, and cross-tree constraints define what algorithm can be run depending on the implementation of the graph, *e.g.*, `MSTKruskal` can only be run with a `WithEdges` implementation.

When running a configuration, a few questions arise regarding its performance, such as: *Are there better (*e.g., *faster regarding* GPL-FH*) configurations? If yes, is there one that is close enough so it still complies with the user's requirements? What would be the gain of running this configuration? How to make sure changing feature(s) will not result in a worst configuration?* These questions arise for several reasons. In particular, the large number of configurations makes picking the *best* configuration on the first try almost impossible, unless having the proper background knowledge of the configuration space. Developers usually do not have this background knowledge and only consider less than 20% of the available configurations [20]. Another reason is the use of the default configuration or a legacy one, *e.g.*, to make sure functional requirements are met. Running such a configuration does not guarantee running the optimal one; On the contrary, it may result in running worst or incorrect configurations [10,12].

In both cases, it is necessary to explore the configuration space to seek configurations providing better performance. Yet, the size of the configuration space increases exponentially with the number of functionalities, making this exploration impractical manually. There is thus a need for an approach that optimizes the performance of an existing configuration while minimizing the impact on functional requirements for such a configuration.

3 ICO: Iterative Configuration Optimization Approach

To address these challenges, we propose the Iterative Configuration Optimization (ICO) approach. The core idea is as follows: From an initial configuration, ICO explores the remaining configuration space in search of configurations that *(i)* are neighbors of the initial configuration, *(ii)* comply with the user's functional requirements (*i.e.*, features that have to be selected or excluded) and *(iii)* optimize given performance indicators. It then provides optimization suggestions to the developer. ICO is inspired by the energy consumption optimization approach presented in [2], but the approach in this paper differs from the one in [2] in several aspects. In particular, the approach proposed in this paper addresses the limitations listed in [2]. That is, we propose an approach that is feature model agnostic and supports multi-objective optimization, in contrast to an optimization method that was tightly coupled to the feature model under test and dedicated to only one performance indicator, the energy consumption. In addition, ICO supports cross-tree constraints in its optimization process, while the approach presented in [2] only focused on switching selected features based on the feature tree structure.

3.1 Optimizing Configurations

To perform the optimization process, ICO relies on the performance of each feature regarding all the considered metrics. That is, as shown by Eq. 1, the overall performance P of a feature f with respect to n metrics is the sum, for each metric, of p_{if} the normalized performance of the feature regarding this metric, multiplied by w_i the weight associated to this metric and by d_i the objective optimization for this metric, $i.e.$, 1 or -1, respectively to maximize or minimize.

$$P_f = \sum_{i=1}^{n} d_i w_i p_{if} \qquad (1)$$

As interactions between features impact performance [15], ICO is able to optimize configurations $w.r.t$ tuples of features of any size, in which case f defines a tuple of features instead of a single one. The performance of a configuration is then computed as the average performance of features - or tuples of features in interaction-wise optimization - contained in this configuration.

The ICO approach is realized by Algorithm 1, which takes the set of features, the list of constraints and the initial configuration as input to compute a set of improvement suggestions. The algorithm starts by creating a set of

---

Algorithm 1: ICO optimization algorithm

    Input: features, constraints, $conf_{init}$;
    Output: suggestions
1   $candidates \leftarrow \emptyset$
2   $suggestions \leftarrow \emptyset$
3   $addable \leftarrow (features \backslash conf_{init}) \backslash constraints_{exclude}$
4   $removable \leftarrow conf_{init} \backslash constraints_{include}$
5   **for** $rem \in removable$ **do**
6 | $candidates \leftarrow candidates \cup \texttt{newConfig}(conf_{init} \backslash rem)$
7   **end**
8   **for** $add \in addable$ **do**
9 | $candidates \leftarrow candidates \cup \texttt{newConfig}(add \cup conf_{init})$
10   **end**
11   **for** $add \in addable, rem \in removable$ **do**
12 | $candidates \leftarrow candidates \cup \texttt{newConfig}(addable \cup conf_{init} \backslash removable)$
13   **end**
14   $candidates \leftarrow \texttt{sortByPerfGain}(candidates)$
15   **for** $c \in candidates$ **do**
16 | **if** $isValid(c, constraints) \wedge perf(c) > perf(conf_{init})$ **then**
17 | | $suggestions \leftarrow suggestions \cup \texttt{diff}(c, conf_{init})$
18 | **end**
19   **end**
20   **return** suggestions

---

candidate configurations for the configuration to optimize (lines 5–13). Candidate configurations are the set of configurations that are one change away from the initial configuration, *i.e.*, *neighbor* configurations, since they differ by the selection/deselection of one feature. For instance, a GPL-FH configuration for a Weighted graph is a neighbor of the same configuration where Unweighted graph is selected since both features are mutually exclusive. In a general way, each unselected feature leads to a candidate configuration where this feature is selected (lines 5–7), each selected feature leads to a candidate configuration where this feature is unselected (lines 8–10), and each exclusive relationship of both a selected and unselected features leads to a candidate configuration where the selected feature is deselected and the unselected one is selected (lines 11–13). Candidate configurations are then ordered by performance gain (line 14), and finally filtered regarding their validity and performance (line 16), to ensure that the returned suggestions *(i)* cannot turn a valid configuration into an invalid one and *(ii)* can only improve the performance of the configuration, according to the performance model[1].

For each candidate configuration, the algorithm then computes the difference between this candidate configuration and the initial one (line 17). This difference takes the form of a feature to add or a feature to remove – or both, and its estimated performance gain. As a result, the algorithm provides a set of improvement suggestions, ordered by potential performance gains. For instance, a possible suggestion for a GPL-FH configuration is to replace the Undirected feature by the Directed feature which offers better performances, while other features remain unchanged.

The approach can thus be entirely automated by applying, while new suggestions are provided, the one providing the highest performance gain. ICO also offers an interactive mode, where developers select the suggestion to apply according to their functional requirements and domain knowledge.

3.2 Implementation

ICO has been implemented as a series of tools, namely the ICO tool suite. This tool suite has been built with the objectives of *(i)* providing developers with feedback about the performances of a given configuration and *(ii)* providing suggestions to optimize its performance by adding or removing a feature. ICO is composed of three software components: (1) ICOLIB, a Java implementation of the proposed approach; (2) ICOCLI, a command-line interface; and (3) ICOPLUGIN, an Eclipse plugin. The ICO tool suite takes as input a configuration, a feature model and performance files, and then returns optimized configurations based on the suggestions provided by Algorithm 1. Figure 2 provides an overview of the architecture of ICO: through either ICOCLI or ICOPLUGIN, user instructions are sent to ICOLIB which then performs various operations based on input files.

---

[1] The computation of the performance model is out of the scope of this paper. Yet, we discuss this particular point in Sect. 6.

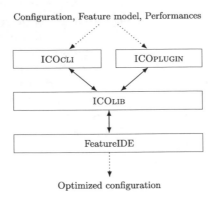

Fig. 2. The architecture of the ICO tool suite.

The tool suite is centered on ICOLIB, a Java library that exposes the API managing all operations that can be performed with ICO: loading a project, displaying current performances, managing constraints (*i.e.*, the lists of features required or excluded by the developer), listing or applying improvement suggestions and saving the new configurations. In particular, ICOLIB delegates to the FeatureIDE [19] library the responsibility to load, update, validate and save the configurations. Taken as a standalone component, ICOLIB can be integrated as a Java dependency into any tool requiring an implementation of Algorithm 1. ICOPLUGIN is an Eclipse Plugin developed to interact with ICOLIB and implemented as an Eclipse view. It thus provides a GUI that assists developers when seeking optimized configurations, in particular by proposing visual feedback on suggested optimizations. ICOCLI is a command-line interface to interact with ICOLIB, enabling an in-depth exploration of the variability of the software and its performances. It can be used directly by the developer or integrated into automated processes such as CI/CD. The source code of ICO is publicly available[2], and [3] covers the specifics of its implementation.

4 Experimental Methodology

Our goal is to assess the validity and effectiveness of our approach. In particular, we aim to answer the following research questions:

RQ 1: Can any configuration be optimized? Considering a configuration space, we investigate whether or not any configuration from that space can be optimized using our approach.

RQ 2: How effective is the ICO optimization approach? When the ICO approach provides a better configuration, we measure the performance discrepancy between that configuration and the initial one.

---

[2] https://gitlab.inria.fr/ico.

RQ 3: How many iterations does it take to optimize a configuration? We evaluate the number of iterations of ICO required to converge from an initial configuration to its respective optimal one.

We evaluate our approach on the real-world configurable system GPL-FH presented in Sect. 2. This system was selected for several reasons. First, both its source code and feature model are publicly available, and they seamlessly integrate as GPL-FH can be run from the command line. Second, its feature model (presented in Fig. 1) exhibits 156 configurations, thus providing a large-enough configuration space for the optimization process to be significant.

The experiments consist in optimizing all 156 configurations regarding a pair of performance indicators, namely the execution time (`time`) and the number of lines of code (`LoC`). This exhaustive optimization highlights how the approach navigates through the configuration space. To not interfere with the `time` measurements, the logging functionality that comes as a default option of the GPL-FH system was disabled, as it might misrepresent the actual execution time. The GPL-FH default number of vertices was changed from 10 to 3500 to yield a larger graph and be able to properly measure the `time`, thus getting meaningful readings. The building time of the graph itself is excluded from the `time` measurement, since constant across configurations. In order to consolidate the measure of the `time` of each configuration, the experiment was repeated 20 times. Beyond that point, the average execution time converges.

The performance of each feature $w.r.t$ `LoC` and `time` is computed according to the method proposed in [2], $i.e.$, the performance of a feature $w.r.t$ a metric is the average performance in this metric of configurations containing this feature. The global performance of each feature ($i.e.$, the performance taking all metrics into consideration) is then calculated using Formula 1. Both metrics were given the same weight, while the optimization goal was set to a minimization of both performance indicators. The optimization algorithm has then been applied on each of the 156 configurations of GPL-FH: for each initial configuration, it seeks for a better neighbor configuration that minimizes `LoC` and `time`. All measurements were performed on a machine with an Intel Core i5 CPU at 2.9 GHz and 8 GB of RAM.

5   Results

The configuration space of GPL-FH has been exhaustively measured, providing insight into the performance of each of the 156 configurations $w.r.t$ `LoC` and `time`. Figure 3 presents such performances. The best and worst `time` are respectively 0.09 and 23.4 s, while `LoC` ranges from 282 to 632. The optimization of a configuration should thus provide higher variations in `time` than in `LoC`, as the ratio between the worst and best readings for `time` (260) is orders of magnitude higher than the one for `LoC` (2.2).

Investigating RQ1: Can any Configuration be Optimized? Applying the best suggestion (if any) provided by Algorithm 1 to a given configuration results in either

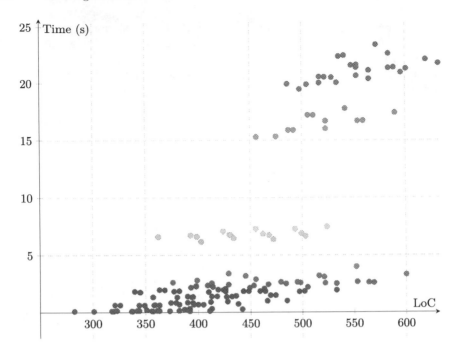

Fig. 3. Performance of each GPL-FH configuration *w.r.t* LoC and time (lower left corner is better).

one of the following situations: (S_1) the configuration improved regarding both performance indicators; (S_2) the configuration improved regarding one performance indicator and worsened regarding the other; (S_3) the configuration did not improve nor worsen, *i.e.*, ICO returned no suggestion; (S_4) the configuration worsened on both indicators[3].

Table 1 summarizes the performance gains resulting from applying Algorithm 1 on the GPL-FH configuration space regarding the four situations discussed above. Out of the 156 configurations, 138 were modified while 18 remained unchanged. Among the 138 modified configurations, 110 were improved regarding both performance indicators, and 16 regarding only one. As a matter of fact, all these 16 single-indicator optimizations relate to an improvement of LoC at the expense of time. The remaining 12 configurations worsened on both performance indicators.

> **RQ 1:** These results show the efficiency of ICO: only 8% of the configuration space could not be improved by our approach. 12% remained unchanged as there was no way to further optimize them, and 80% were successfully optimized.

---

[3] Due to inaccuracies in the performance model. See Sect. 6 for further analysis.

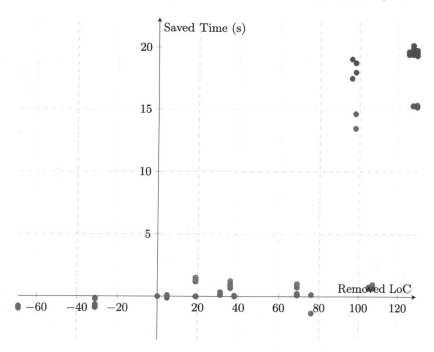

Fig. 4. Performance gains for each GPL-FH configuration *w.r.t* LoC and time (top right corner is better).

Investigating RQ2: How effective is the ICO *optimization approach?* Figure 4 shows the performance gains when running ICO on the GPL-FH configuration space. As anticipated above, variations in time were more significant than the Loc-related ones, *i.e.*, ranging from +96,6% to −133,6% regarding time and from +26,5% to −17,7% regarding Loc. The 12 configurations discussed in Table 1 worsen both performance indicators (situation S_4) thus represent a negative gain and as depicted below the horizontal axis and the left side of the vertical axis. The figure highlights that the performance loss on such features is very limited when compared to the performance gains in other situations.

Table 1. The effect of ICO on the GPL-FH configuration space.

Performance change	Configurations		Removed LoC			Saved Time (s)		
w.r.t indicators (*Situation*)	Count	%	worst	med.	best	worst	med	best
Optimized - both indicators (S_1)	110	70	5	69	129	∼0	0,78	20,21
Optimized - one indicator (S_2)	10	10	5	5	76	−1,35	−0,01	∼0
Unchanged (S_3)	18	12	-	-	-	-	-	-
Worsened - both indicators (S_4)	12	8	−69	−31	−31	−0,99	−0,74	−0,15

RQ 2: ICO provides efficient optimizations, especially for poorly performing configurations, but can sometimes worsen configurations' performance. Nevertheless, although worsened, these configurations remain in the top-tier performance ranking.

Investigating RQ3: How Many Iterations Does it Take to Optimize a Configuration? Since an initial configuration cannot be turned into an invalid one by Algorithm 1 (see line 16), running the algorithm on each configuration of the configuration space thus results in a set of optimized configurations which are a subset of the initial configurations. These optimized configurations cannot be further optimized, as they have no neighbor configuration with better performances. Based on this inclusion, it is then possible to build a directed graph representing all successive iterations of the algorithm.

Figure 5 depicts such a graph for the GPL-FH case study, where each node represents a configuration. For the sake of readability, nodes are placed on a relative logarithmic scale representing their related configuration's time and LoC, respectively on the vertical axis and on the horizontal axis. Each edge represents the application of the first suggestion returned by Algorithm 1: the initial configuration is the source node for that edge, while the optimized configuration resulting from applying this first suggestion is the target node. Thus, an edge represents the removal of a feature, the addition of a feature, or the substitution of a feature by another one. This graph is composed of 18 disconnected sub-graphs. Each sub-graph converges towards one of the 18 configurations that could not be optimized and remained unchanged (see Table 1, situation S_3). These 18 configurations are thus local optima, and one of them is the global optimum.

Table 2. Applying ICO on the GPL-FH configuration space.

Nb Iterations	0	1	2	3	4	5
Nb Configurations	18	61	48	22	6	1
Nb Configurations, cumulative	18	79	127	149	155	156
% remaining configurations		11.5	44.2	62.3	75.8	85.7	100
% total configurations		11.5	39.1	30.7	14.1	3.8	0.6
% total configurations, cumulative	11.5	51	81	95	99	100

Table 2 shows the number of iterations of Algorithm 1 required by all configurations to converge towards their related optimized configuration. As explained before, 18 configurations remain unchanged and therefore do not need any iteration of the ICO algorithm to reach their convergence point. Regarding the 138 other configurations, a single iteration drives 61 of them (44.2%) toward their convergence point. That is, after one iteration, 79 configurations (more than half

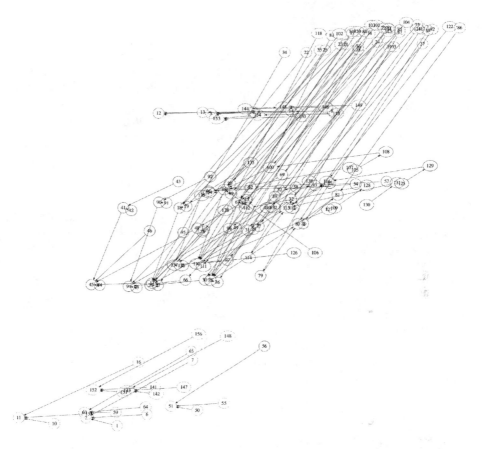

Fig. 5. ICO transition graph between configurations of GPL-FH. Configurations on a relative logarithmic scale for readability, `time` on the vertical axis, `LoC` on the horizontal axis, lower left is better.

the configuration space) have already converged. After a second iteration, 81% of configurations have reached their convergence point. Up to five iterations are required to optimize the whole set of configurations, but the last two iterations only apply to 3.8% of the configurations.

> **RQ 3**: The number of iterations required by ICO to optimize a configuration is very limited, as *(i)* half of configurations are optimized after a single iteration and *(ii)* the number of configurations yet to be optimized decreases dramatically after each iteration. In this experiment, only 1 configuration required the maximum number of five iterations to be optimized.

6   Discussion

A thorough analysis of the GPL-FH optimization graph depicted in Fig. 5 provides additional findings regarding the ICO approach. The graph is composed of four clusters of nodes: (C_1) the green nodes at the bottom left; (C_2) the black nodes in the center; (C_3) the "horizontal" cluster of blue nodes in the upper part above cluster (C_2); and (C_4) the red nodes in the upper right corner. In particular, we observe that all the configurations located in C_4 move to C_2 once optimized. Such configurations thus share the same optimization. In particular, they are optimized by removing the MSTPrim feature, which is characterized by both the worst LoC and time performance.

Feature Model Design. One can also notice that no optimization edge enters or leaves clusters C_1 and C_3. These two clusters are characterized by the presence of features that are mutually dependent such as Directed, WithEdges and DirectedWithEdges (a sub-feature of the collapsed HiddenGtp feature), which are tightly-coupled by the Directed $\wedge$ WithEdge $\leftrightarrow$ DirectedWithEdge cross-tree constraint. In addition, C_3 contains configurations whose couple of features StronglyConnected and Transpose are selected, complying with the StronglyConnected $\leftrightarrow$ Transpose cross-tree constraint, thus preventing the removal or addition of these features. The best-performing configuration from C_3 is actually similar to a configuration from C_1, with the addition of Transpose and StronglyConnected features that, as explained before, must be removed together. It is thus impossible to enter or leave these clusters without changing two or three features at once, or without turning the configuration into an invalid transitional state, which is not supported by the ICO approach. Configurations from these clusters can only be optimized by changing other features, and configurations from C_2 and C_4 cannot be optimized towards C_1 or C_3. Feature relationships and cross-tree constraints also explain why the optimization process converges towards 18 different configurations: these configurations only contain mutually-dependent features and cannot be further improved while remaining valid. The shape of the feature model and related cross-tree constraints can thus hinder the capacity of ICO to optimize the entire configuration space.

Performance Model. To perform its optimization process, ICO relies on a performance model. This model provides an estimated performance for each feature, measured based on the method proposed in [2]. As the performance model is estimated, it may contain measurement inaccuracies which in turn may impact the efficiency of the approach. For instance, we observed that, while optimizing GPL-FH, the performance of twelve configurations worsened after an iteration. When analyzing the initial and "optimized" configurations, we found out that the twelve performance regressions were caused by the addition of either the feature Number or Cycle. Both of these features happen to be present in all the configurations from C_1, the cluster of best-performing configurations. However, such good performances are actually not related to Number or Cycle alone, but to the presence of other features in combination. The performance model seems thus biased toward Number and Cycle, which causes inaccuracies during the execution of ICO.

Validity Threats. To assess our approach, we ran our experiments on a specific configurable system (GPL-FH) and optimized it based on specific metrics, *i.e.*, minimizing the execution time and the number of lines of code of configurations from this system. Results such as the performance gains or the number of iterations are thus only related to this single system, and cannot be generalized. Nonetheless, our contribution can be easily applied to any configurable system as long as a feature model is provided. The optimization gains resulting from applying our approach to other configurable systems will depend on the initial performance of each configuration for such systems. We leave the evaluation of our approach across a larger set of domains to a future study.

We ran the ICO optimization algorithm on the whole configuration space of GPL-FH. While relying on an exhaustive performance model was convenient, we acknowledge that this may not be practical for any case study, in particular regarding performance models of software systems exhibiting larger configuration spaces. Yet, it is still possible to use our approach by sampling or predicting performance models for such larger spaces, using approaches such as [1,2,10].

7 Related Work

The management of highly configurable systems has been widely studied in the last decade. Research has mainly addressed one of the following three areas: *(i)* performance prediction, intending to estimate the performance of a configuration without actually measuring it, *(ii)* performance optimization, to generate optimal configurations of a system, and *(iii)* recommender systems, to assist developers during the feature selection process.

Performance Prediction. Performance prediction approaches have been proposed by many researchers [4,7,14]. The aim of such approaches is to build an estimated performance model of the system's features. These approaches rely on machine learning techniques to infer performance data from a sample of configurations. One of their main objectives is to detect feature interactions – as they can have significant impact on performances, and provide more accurate prediction than approaches that do not consider such interactions. Relying on such performance models, Siegmund *et al.* [15,17] predict the performance of configurations as the sum of the impact of each feature on performances. Such approaches are complementary to the current performance model of ICO, which originates from [2], and can extend its current implementation.

Performance Optimization. Many approaches have been proposed to address performance optimization for configurable systems. Such approaches strive to locate optimal or near-optimal configurations *w.r.t* some performance indicators. Several studies provide deterministic approaches [10,11,22] to tackle this challenge. Other authors like Hierons *et al.* rely on genetic algorithms to minimize the number of measurements needed to optimize configurations [5], or leverage the performance predictions methods discussed above [16]. Such approaches do not take an initial configuration into consideration. For instance, Nair *et al.* [10] start their optimization process from a random configuration. In contrast to such approaches, the approach proposed in this paper aims at optimizing a set of performance indicators while remaining as close as possible to the initial user-defined configuration. This optimization goal is shared with the approach of Soltani *et al.*, which takes user's preferences into consideration to optimize a configuration, but yet does not support the optimization of pre-existing configurations [18].

Recommender Systems. In recent years, we observed an increased interest in studies applying tools and approaches to assist users during the configuration of their systems. Such systems provide recommendations to the users based on their functional needs. For instance, Pereira *et al.* propose a visual recommender system [13] based on proximity and similarity between features. Similarly, Zhang *et al.* [21] use dynamic profiling and analyze the stack trace of the system to locate features that can be changed without altering the functional behavior of the system. Other approaches, such as [9] or [6], aim at updating the configuration of the system while it is running, in order to adapt it to the evolution of its environment. To the best of our knowledge, no recommender system provides suggestions based on both functional and performance considerations.

8   Conclusion

This paper introduced ICO, an iterative approach to optimize configurations regarding defined performance indicators. Considering an initial configuration to optimize, ICO estimates the performance of neighbor configurations, *i.e.*, configurations that distinguish from the initial one by a single feature (de)selection change. ICO provides performance improvement suggestions to drive the optimization process, which can be run either in fully automated mode or based on the developer's inputs. We evaluated our approach on a real-world example by running ICO on its entire configuration space, and our experiments showed that ICO significantly improved 80% of the configurations.

As future work, we plan to improve the accuracy of performance suggestions provided by ICO by relying on more accurate performance models and performance prediction techniques. We also plan to extend the capabilities of ICO supporting multiple feature changes at once, *e.g.*, in highly heterogeneous systems such as Edge and Fog computing systems. In such systems, the wide range of possibilities (*e.g.*, component-level resource allocation and computation models) results in a huge configuration space that is not manually manageable.

Acknowledgement. The research leading to these results received funding from French Research Agency through the ANR-19-CE25-0003 KOALA project and from the Norwegian Research Council through the DILUTE project (Grant No. 262854/F20).

References

1. Acher, M., et al.: Feature subset selection for learning huge configuration spaces: the case of Linux kernel size. In: Proceedings of the 26th ACM International Systems and Software Product Line Conference - Volume A, SPLC 2022, pp. 85–96. Association for Computing Machinery, New York (2022)
2. Guégain, E., Quinton, C., Rouvoy, R.: On reducing the energy consumption of software product lines. In: Proceedings of the 25th ACM International Systems and Software Product Line Conference - Volume A, SPLC 2021, pp. 89–99 (2021)
3. Guégain, E., Taherkordi, A., Quinton, C.: The ICO Tool Suite: Optimizing Highly Configurable Systems (2022). Preprint. https://hal.archives-ouvertes.fr/hal-03874051
4. Guo, J., Czarnecki, K., Apel, S., Siegmund, N., Wasowski, A.: Variability-aware performance prediction: a statistical learning approach, pp. 301–311 (2013)
5. Hierons, R.M., Li, M., Liu, X., Segura, S., Zheng, W.: SIP: optimal product selection from feature models using many-objective evolutionary optimization. ACM Trans. Softw. Eng. Methodol. $25(2)$, 1–39 (2016)
6. Horcas, J.M., Pinto, M., Fuentes, L.: Context-aware energy-efficient applications for cyber-physical systems. Ad Hoc Netw. 82, 15–30 (2019)
7. Kaltenecker, C., Grebhahn, A., Siegmund, N., Apel, S.: The interplay of sampling and machine learning for software performance prediction. IEEE Softw. 37, 58–66 (2020)
8. Metzger, A., Pohl, K.: Software product line engineering and variability management: achievements and challenges. In: Future of Software Engineering, FOSE 2014, Hyderabad, India, 31 May–7 June 2014, pp. 70–84 (2014)
9. Metzger, A., Quinton, C., Mann, Z.Á., Baresi, L., Pohl, K.: Realizing self-adaptive systems via online reinforcement learning and feature-model-guided exploration. Computing 1–22 (2022). https://doi.org/10.1007/s00607-022-01052-x
10. Nair, V., Yu, Z., Menzies, T., Siegmund, N., Apel, S.: Finding faster configurations using flash. IEEE Trans. Software Eng. $46(7)$, 794–811 (2020)
11. Olaechea, R., Stewart, S., Czarnecki, K., Rayside, D.: Modelling and multi-objective optimization of quality attributes in variability-rich software. In: Proceedings of the Fourth International Workshop on Nonfunctional System Properties in Domain Specific Modeling Languages. NFPinDSML 2012 (2012)
12. Pereira, J.A., Acher, M., Martin, H., Jézéquel, J.M., Botterweck, G., Ventresque, A.: Learning software configuration spaces: a systematic literature review. J. Syst. Softw. 182, 111044 (2021)
13. Pereira, J.A., Matuszyk, P., Krieter, S., Spiliopoulou, M., Saake, G.: A feature-based personalized recommender system for product-line configuration. In: Proceedings of the 2016 ACM SIGPLAN International Conference on Generative Programming: Concepts and Experiences, pp. 120–131 (2016)
14. Siegmund, N., Grebhahn, A., Apel, S., Kästner, C.: Performance-influence models for highly configurable systems. In: Proceedings of the 2015 10th Joint Meeting on Foundations of Software Engineering, ESEC/FSE 2015, pp. 284–294 (2015)
15. Siegmund, N., et al.: Predicting performance via automated feature-interaction detection, pp. 167–177 (2012)
16. Siegmund, N., Rosenmüller, M., Kuhlemann, M., Kästner, C., Apel, S., Saake, G.: SPL conqueror: toward optimization of non-functional properties in software product lines. Software Qual. J. 20, 487–517 (2012)

17. Siegmund, N., Rosenmüller, M., Kästner, C., Giarrusso, P.G., Apel, S., Kolesnikov, S.S.: Scalable prediction of non-functional properties in software product lines: footprint and memory consumption. Inf. Softw. Technol. **55**, 491–507 (2013)
18. Soltani, S., Asadi, M., Gašević, D., Hatala, M., Bagheri, E.: Automated planning for feature model configuration based on functional and non-functional requirements. In: Proceedings of the 16th International Software Product Line Conference, SPLC 2012, vol. 1, pp. 56–65 (2012)
19. Thüm, T., Kästner, C., Benduhn, F., Meinicke, J., Saake, G., Leich, T.: Featureide: an extensible framework for feature-oriented software development. Sci. Comput. Program. **79**, 70–85 (2014)
20. Xu, T., Jin, L., Fan, X., Zhou, Y., Pasupathy, S., Talwadker, R.: Hey, you have given me too many knobs!: understanding and dealing with over-designed configuration in system software. In: Proceedings of the 2015 10th Joint Meeting on Foundations of Software Engineering, ESEC/FSE 2015, pp. 307–319. Association for Computing Machinery, New York (2015)
21. Zhang, S., Ernst, M.D.: Which configuration option should i change? In: Proceedings of the 36th International Conference on Software Engineering, ICSE 2014, pp. 152–163. Association for Computing Machinery, New York (2014)
22. Švogor, I., Crnković, I., Vrček, N.: An extensible framework for software configuration optimization on heterogeneous computing systems: time and energy case study. Inf. Softw. Technol. **105**, 30–42 (2019)

IoT

Modeling Context-Aware Events and Responses in an IoT Environment

Marc Vila[1,2](✉) [iD], Maria-Ribera Sancho[1,3] [iD], and Ernest Teniente[1] [iD]

[1] inLab FIB, Universitat Politècnica de Catalunya, Barcelona, Spain
{marc.vila.gomez,maria.ribera.sancho,ernest.teniente}@upc.edu
[2] Worldsensing, Barcelona, Spain
[3] Barcelona Supercomputing Center, Barcelona, Spain

Abstract. The Internet of Things (IoT) involves the use of devices that exchange information about the state of things in the real world. In IoT, monitoring is regarded to be the most fully researched use case. However, research on the use and manipulation of control and maintenance applications has not yet been fully addressed. An important step forward in this direction may be provided by executing automatic context-aware actuations. These may be achieved by delivering responses based on the context gathered with components endowed in some device. In this paper, we propose a solution that uses ontological knowledge for this purpose, thus improving the interoperability of IoT devices. We focus on real-time data collection to fully automate monitoring, context gathering, and appropriate responses. Our proposal is illustrated via the lens of a railroad use case, where maintaining track safety is critical to avoid accidents.

Keywords: Internet of Things · Interoperability · Context-Awareness · Semantics · Cyber-Physical Systems

1 Introduction

The Internet of Things (IoT) comprises a large number of *smart* devices: physical objects aimed at connecting and exchanging information with other devices, entities, or systems via the Internet. IoT sensors generate data that can be used for various purposes, such as monitoring, data analysis, or decision-making. IoT actuating devices are typically used to convert a signal input into a physical action or movement or to modify the logical state of an entity.

Physical infrastructures must be effectively monitored to ensure their reliability, security, and performance, and to detect and resolve any possible difficulties or problems. There are situations where entities, whether real or virtual, need to be watched over and, if necessary, reacted to. When an informational condition has to be taken into account, a responsive capacity is required; if it is urgent, it has to be handled accordingly. This situational context is mostly gained by employing IoT devices with sensors and logical entities, such as data transmission information, depending on whether the state can be inferred from the outside world or from any value associated to software. This knowledge or ability, namely "context-aware", involves considering the data that the IoT devices gather and allowing the system to understand its context. The system can then react since it is aware of the situation where it is. Context awareness is a key aspect of the IoT domain that enables systems to provide a more precise understanding of the environment [24]. As a result, they can provide accurate responses to events. For example, context-aware situations can be used in a factory to monitor machinery performance and optimize production by considering factors such as temperature, humidity, and energy consumption.

In IoT, communication is straightforward when the systems are in the same working environment. However, with entities from other companies or platforms, communication becomes more complicated. This complexity is due to the fact that two different environments must agree to establish communication. This has implications for information properties, data structures, and communication technologies. The *Interoperability of Things* aims to homogenize data communication between IoT devices so that software systems can provide generic solutions to enable interoperability across applications, contexts, and domains [9].

In this paper, we contribute to the Interoperability of Things as follows:

- We propose an ontology for automatic monitoring using IoT devices. We focus on the definition of context-aware entities that enable to specify the responsive behavior to be taken when a certain situation is met. We allow for defining the entities to be observed, receiving the measurement data from the sensors, and also specifying the actions or response procedures to be taken when a given event occurs.
- Our ontology is domain-independent, and it is based on existing ontologies such as SSN/SOSA, GeoSPARQL, OWL-Time, and IoTMA. All software systems dealing with its components are able to handle different IoT installations with almost no changes in the code. A small number of components might be needed to update, for instance, how the various devices feed information to the ontology or extend actuation procedures.
- We provide an implementation based on a rail-track safety monitoring scenario, to show the feasibility of our approach.

Section 2 reviews related work. Section 3 highlights the key elements of the ontology and compares them with previous work. Section 4 depicts our use case and matches the proposed ontology with it. Section 5 shows the experimentation carried out. The paper ends with our conclusions and further work.

2   Related Work

The term *IoT* was originally coined in 1999 for supply chain management by Ashton [5] and was later used to encompass the devices aimed at exchanging information with other elements on the Internet [11]. One of the most notorious characteristics of IoT is the heterogeneity of the ecosystem, i.e. the *Interoperability of Things*, one of the challenges to be solved. There is heterogeneity in the devices, not only from differences in capacity and features but also for application requirements and information transmission [26]. This can also be seen in the technologies used to communicate and in the information data structure.

According to Noura et al. [19], interoperability in IoT can be classified into different levels. The *device* level is related to output capacity and communication protocols; the *syntactic* one to the data format, schemas, and interfaces; *networking* to the network protocols; *platform* to the operating system, and programming language; and *semantic* to the data and information models. Our work aims at improving the interoperability of IoT devices at the semantic level in the context-awareness domain. This allows for the abstraction of the particular syntax and data formats, providing common semantics to all the managed data.

Context-awareness is known as the ability of software applications to discover and react to changes in the environment in which they are situated. In the IoT setting, this concept enables the contextualization of the information linked to sensor data so that interpretations can be easily and meaningfully performed, as stated Schilit et al. [27] in 1994. Some years later, Abowd et al. [1] provided a more precise definition: "A system is context-aware if it uses context to provide relevant information and/or services to the user, where relevancy depends on the user's task". In 2004, contextual information began to be combined with ontologies [13,28,31], in which human, machine, physical, and abstract things are combined, using ontologies, modeling, and semantic reasoning.

In the general scope of context-awareness in the IoT, Perera et al. [23] proposed an IoT context-aware architecture with the purpose of automatically selecting sensor data from some user-based inputs. However, they focus on the ability to select the most significant sensor for a particular task and do not provide a middleware solution for managing its context. Kim et al. [17] developed a system to support an autonomous context-aware environment where they proposed low complexity rules to execute *if-else* kind of rules. These rules are useful in certain restricted contexts but they are not general enough since they do not allow combining sensors for instance. Dobrescu et al. [7] proposed a middleware architecture for IoT context-aware field monitoring using environmental and real-time sensors. However, it is not clear how they support the use of different sensors beyond the ones they already considered. Jiang et al. [16] stated that context-awareness with semantics is a recent research area, and sketched an ontology for the integration of several data sources to extract contextual information. Gaur et al. [10] proposed a context-aware proof-of-concept framework, but it is not clear how context actions can be incorporated and handled. In Zhang et al. [33], authors propose an approach to capture events from sensor streams. However, it is not clear how the data is structured in the sense of heterogeneity of things. Dörndorfer et al. [8], developed a modeling tool that includes data aggregation and definition for sensors, context, and decision outputs. It is not clear how multiple context-aware rules can be defined, as it seems to remain in the *if-else* theory.

Improving interoperability has also been achieved through ontology definition. Therefore, the Semantic Sensor Network Incubator Group developed the

SSN [12] ontology in 2011 to specify sensors and sensor network resources. In 2017, the W3C Consortium proposed the SOSA [15] ontology, an extension of SSN, to be used when the Semantic Web and linked data technologies are needed. Xue et al. [32] proposed a semantic sensor network but the proposal is not complete as far as managing the network. Maarala et al. [18], examine the different types of semantic reasoning and different data models for context-aware IoT applications. They also propose an ontology for information contextualization. However, they do not provide means to understand the sensing part of the process. Alirezaie et al. [3] and Choi et al. [6] propose a context-aware system for smart homes and cities. CAMeOnto [2] proposes a meta-ontology for modeling context-awareness systems, including *user, activity, time, device, services,* and *location.* Yet, they do not take into account the sensorization part, and the relationship between what is being observed and what is being controlled or acted upon is not clear. MSSN-Onto [4] proposes an ontology that models sensors, events, and their corresponding types. They use SOSA/SSN as a base ontology, but do not go beyond its observation perspective.

In conclusion, context awareness with semantics and ontologies is a hot topic that only recently began to receive significant attention. Previous work mostly uses only a subset of features, among all those encompassed by the IoT. Moreover, finding proposals like ours that successfully combine context awareness systems, ontologies for the IoT, and the modeling of sensors and actuators is still a challenging issue.

3   Our Context-Aware Responsive Ontology

The ontology we present in this paper is aimed at enabling the monitoring of real-world entities using IoT devices in computing continuum applications. The context-aware responsive behavior of our ontology is based on two different concepts: *Actuation* and *ContextAwareRule.* Context-aware rules specify the general policies that will be applied when a certain situation is satisfied, such as when a sensor detects a value that is higher than a certain threshold and takes some action. These are the *Actuations,* which specify the specific corrections or actions made after an event. In our approach, the designer can precisely specify the events to be monitored, under which conditions, and the actions to be taken when a condition is satisfied.

Our ontology, Context-Aware Responsive ontology (ConAwarIoT) extends the IoTMA ontology [29] by incorporating the specification of context-aware events and responses to these events, which were not considered. Our proposal includes two key concepts from IoTMA: *Sensor,* the element capable of making measurements of a given feature; and *Actuator,* the executors of actions that modify the state of a given feature. We extend these concepts here with the new key concept *ContextAwareRule,* which allows users to specify the events to monitor, conditions to apply and response procedures to execute.

Our ontology is defined in Fig. 1 by means of a UML class diagram, showing the *classnames* and the relations between *classes*:

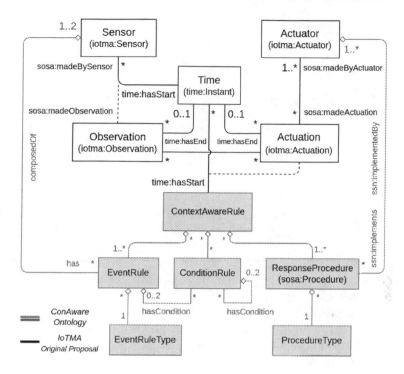

Fig. 1. Overview of our Context-Aware Responsive ontology

We share with IoTMA the concepts *Sensor*, *Actuator*, *Observation*, *Actuation*, and *Time*. This is because we want to stress that the definition and treatment of responsive behavior require this information to be effective. In the previous figure, ConAwarIoT is the default namespace when none is provided.

3.1   Resource URIs

In our work, *Classnames* are expressed in the Uniform Resource Identifier (URI) format, a unique sequence of characters that identifies a resource, to increase the simplicity and manageability of systems. In Table 1 we show the URI additions defined in our ontology. The first column represents the *classname* of the entity. The second is the URI, the format that follows the pattern defined below. BASE_URI refers to the URL entry point located in a test domain. CLASS_NAME indicates the name of the entity. CLASS_ID the identifier for each instance of an entity. In addition to CLASS_PROPERTY_N, which holds N properties of the entity: {BASE_URI}:{CLASS_NAME}/{CLASS_ID}?{CLASS_PROPERTY_1}&{CLASS_PROPERTY_N}

3.2   Description of the Concepts for Our ConAwarIoT

ContextAwareRule. It states the rules or conditions that define how the system reacts when some condition is met. If so, an *ResponseProcedure* is executed

Table 1. Main URIs added in our Context-Aware Responsive Ontology

Class	URI Patterns

ContextAwareRule	`ConAwarIoT:ContextAwareRule/{ContextAwareRuleName}?`
	`{EventRulesName}&{ConditionRulesName}&`
	`{ResponseProceduresName}&{Executing}`

EventRule	`ConAwarIoT:EventRule/{EventRuleName}?{ContextAwareRule-`
	`Name}&{EventRuleTypeName}&{Sensor1Name}&{Sensor2Name}&`
	`{ValueBoolean|ValueString|ValueInteger|ValueFloat}`

ConditionRule	`ConAwarIoT:ConditionRule/{ConditionRuleName}?{Context-`
	`AwareRuleName}&{EventRule1Name}&{EventRule2Name}&`
	`{ConditionRule1Name}&{ConditionRule2Name}&`
	`{ConditionComparationType}`

ResponseProcedure	`ConAwarIoT:ResponseProcedure/{ResponseProcedureName}?` `{ContextAwareRuleName}&{ProcedureTypeName}&{ActuatorName}`

via an *Actuator*'s *Actuation*. Context-aware rules hold metadata information about sensor-actuator mechanisms and are made up of events (*EventRule*), conditions (*ConditionRule*), and responses (*ResponseProcedure*). It is also possible to state which sensors should be taken into account, for what reason, and what to do when *that* occurs. In addition, these rules can be toggled, enabled, or disabled, to enable all event detection and responses using the *executing* attribute.

A simple example could be, when a certain EventRule is true, it executes a certain ResponseProcedure action as a response, as can be seen in Fig. 2.

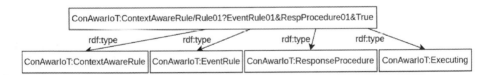

Fig. 2. Example of a ContextAwareRule description

EventRule. It is used to check whether a sensor measurement complies with a predefined criterion. Starting from a *Sensor* or a set of sensors, it allows defining in *EventRuleType* which comparison types should be made, either one sensor compared to a constant (*Value*) or with another sensor (*Sensor*). In *EventRuleType*, we assume the following comparison operators (*EventRuleComparationType*) available to compare among *Sensors* or against constant values:

- `EQUALS` or `NOT_EQUALS`: Numeric values such as `INTEGER` or `FLOAT`, also `STRING` and `BOOLEAN`.
- `LESS_THAN` or `MORE_THAN`: Numeric values such as `INTEGER` or `FLOAT`.
- Mathematical operators such as the *arithmetic mean*, *median*, *harmonic mean* or the *standard deviation*.

As an example, Fig. 3 represents an *EventRule*, named `EventRule01` that compares a sensor `Sensor01` against a constant `ValueInt1`. The comparison is about two `integers`, and it is desired to know if the contents are `equal` or not. And it could be similar to the comparison between a temperature sensor that is being compared over being equal to a value, for example, 20 °C.

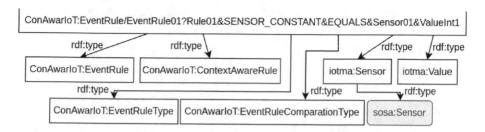

Fig. 3. Example of an EventRule description, comparing one sensor - one constant

ConditionRule. *EventRules* can be combined using *ConditionRules*. This is required when two or more entities in the real world have to be checked together. The operators we are able to deal with are `AND`, `OR`, `NAND`, `NOR`, and `XOR`. Moreover, *ConditionRules* can be linked, as components of the condition itself, to take advantage of the possibility of specifying different conditions that handle *EventRules*. Two side operators are available: one operator to be *EventRule* and one *ConditionRule*, as well as a couple of *EventRule* or a couple *ConditionRule*. If more complex *Rule* are needed, they can be nested using this concept.

ResponseProcedure. Handles the definition of actions to be executed when defined criteria are met. It contains the *Procedure* to follow and the predefined steps to improve in the target scenario. It also allows the user to state which type of actuation is needed, for instance, the *HTTP + GET* method in Fig. 4, which means that when the *Actuation* is executed, an HTTP GET request will be executed. The *ProcedureType* allows the designer to define other methods as answers. Thus, the user is able to handle a diverse number of these types, for instance, defining URLs for sending notifications via some local URL or a cloud-based URL, depending on the urgency of the action; sending an email, etc.

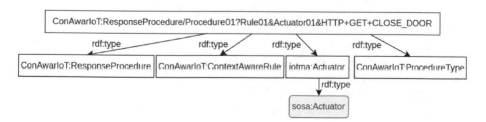

Fig. 4. Example of a ResponseProcedure description

3.3   Relationship with Related Ontologies

ConAwarIoT is based on several existing ontologies, making it compliant with current standards and existing solutions. Most of the concepts are drawn from *SSN/SOSA*, which in turn extends primarily from the *IoTMA* ontology. We also use concepts from *OWL-Time* and *GeoSPARQL* in our ontology.

IoTMA - IoT Monitoring and Actuation ontology [29]. IoTMA, which is a previous work of us, is aimed at understanding sensor-actuation contexts, thus incorporating concepts of general monitoring and actuation terms. It incorporates basic semantics for reacting to predefined conditions, in the case of critical events, although, it does not allow defining in a detailed way the conditions for which events to apply and how the system should handle its responses.

Our main contribution in this paper is that of improving the expressiveness of context-awareness rules in IoTMA. This is achieved through the *ContextAware-Rule* concept, which now allows the definition and treatment of more complex and responsive behaviors as required by current IoT applications.

Semantic Sensor Network and Sensor-Observation-Sample-Actuator - SSN/SOSA [15]. Provides a lightweight core for defining classes and properties of data managed in the IoT scenario. It supports sensing and actuation device capabilities, for modeling interoperability. Here, we make use of the *sosa:Procedure* for providing the steps for changing the state of the world via an *Actuator*.

GeoSPARQL [21]. It is used to describe the location properties of entities. We use *geo:Location* to describe the location of physical entities in the ontology.

OWL-Time [30]. It states temporal concepts and properties. *Time* is used to define when there is an *Observation* and an *Actuation* (*time:hasStart*).

3.4   Research Methodology

We have followed the *Design-Science Research* methodology (Hevner et al. [14]): "In this research methodology, a designer answers questions relevant to human problems via the creation of innovative artifacts [...]. The designed artifacts are useful and fundamental to understanding that problems."

At some points of the ontology development, we also follow Noy et al. [20] recommendation: the *Knowledge-Engineering Methodology*. They suggest there is no single way to develop semantics, as domain modeling depends on several factors, including the purpose of the system it supports. The modeling of an ontology is an iterative process: Determine the domain and scope; sketch a list of competency questions that should be answered; consider reusing existing ontologies; enumerate important terms in the ontology; develop the ontology (classes, hierarchy, properties, ...); and, lastly, validate the list of competency questions. In case the outcomes are not as predicted, then return to the first stage.

4   Use Case Description

We focus on a railway use case as an illustration of a cyber-physical system which is very relevant in the IoT scenario. However, it is worth mentioning that the semantics endowed in our ontology are defined at an abstract level and can be applied to different domains, other than railways.

There are several aspects of railway systems that can be improved. One of the duties that must be automated using IoT devices is safety, which involves maintaining the entire railway system. Rail tracks are one of the components in the rail industry that need to be checked on a regular basis. Corrective maintenance is currently carried out based on sparse data and no short-term vision. With this use case, we pave the way for real-time data-based maintenance services, the point at which predictive maintenance begins.

In tracks, certain important elements need to be monitored as they require active maintenance. The geometry of the tracks is an extremely relevant area for ensuring the safe operation of the railway infrastructure. Two of the most important parameters to monitor are the *cant* and *twist* factors of these tracks.

Currently, ADIF[1], the Spanish railway infrastructure manager, uses an auscultation train to check various parameters of the track, including *cant* and *twist* factors. The use of a train to monitor elements on the track has some drawbacks. First, when this train is in use, the normal use of the track is affected, which makes it necessary to take into account in case there is another train with the need to circulate there, and it is usually run in the early hours of the morning. The second is that these checks are run every few months, as due to the great extension of the railway network, this train passes 1 to 2 times a year through each section of the Spanish railway. This implies that if something happens between the checks, no one will be warned about a possible failure.

Our method enables the provision of a viable solution to the aforementioned issues, such as continuous monitoring of trains without service interruptions. We consider using IoT devices to perform checks more frequently, and our method is complementary to the train approach. When an anomaly is found, the area becomes of interest, and when work is to be done in a nearby section or underneath the train track, our approach can be employed as a preventive measure.

The first characteristic to be checked, the *cant* factor (Fig. 5a), is the height difference between the two parallel tracks. Using one sensor (tiltmeter[2]), placed in the sleeper, we can provide the difference in angle from one track to the other. The sensor provides information in microvolts for the angle and then, through some calculations, converts it to degrees, and from there, knowing the distance between tracks and basic trigonometry, we can establish the height of the deviation in *millimeters*, as indicated in the ADIF guidelines.

Twist, i.e. the measurement of the rotation of the railway track, (Fig. 5b) is the second feature to monitor. It describes the variation in cross-level measured

---

[1] https://www.adif.es.

[2] Tiltmeter: A sensitive inclinometer designed to measure very small changes from the horizontal plane, either on the ground or in structures.

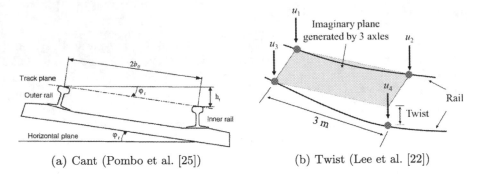

(a) Cant (Pombo et al. [25])   (b) Twist (Lee et al. [22])

Fig. 5. Usecase Ilustrations

across five sleepers along the track. This permits comparing the height between each of the four points, resulting in a plane. It can be seen as two *cant* factors at once. In this case, the use of at least two sensors (tiltmeters) is mandatory.

One of the causes of the *cant* factor is the temperature variation in tracks. Tracks expand and contract according to temperature. To correlate this, a sensor near the tracks is also added. Thus, two different sensors need to be monitored at the same time. This is a derived factor from the other already existing one, also contemplated in our use case.

There are several *cant* and *twist* values to compare in the *ADIF* guidelines; based on the measured value, a low-severity warning can be sent, while others can result in high-severity alerts requiring quick action. These elements are monitored in this use case to actuate when certain circumstances are reached.

4.1   Using Our Context-Aware Responsive Ontology

Our solution enables the definition of rules to keep track of the measurements reported by the sensors. Rules can be understood as something simple, like monitoring the events for one sensor, or something more sophisticated, as a combination of different *EventRules* or chained *ConditionRules*. We refer to the former as *simple* and the latter as *complex* to distinguish between them.

Supporting Single Events

In our system, measurements can be compared with other sensor measurements or constants using *ContextAwareRules*. A case of a simple rule is that of the *cant* factor. It is a feature that can be monitored using a single tiltmeter sensor. This feature consists of using the last measurement to determine the state, and each measurement provides one degree of inclination per axis. For this purpose, Fig. 6 shows the visual representation of a sensor named TILTMETER_1 that is compared to COMPARATOR_MORE_THAN against a constant CONSTANT_1.

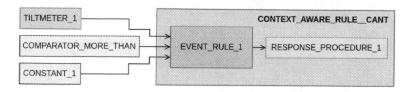

Fig. 6. Representation of a ContextAwareRule with a simple use case - Cant

This evaluation is done in the EVENT_RULE_1 component, and if it is evaluated as true, it will trigger the RESPONSE_PROCEDURE_1.

Supporting Multiple Events or Conditions

More complex rules are useful to model when an element to be monitored depends on two or more variables, such as the *twist* factor, which must be monitored with at least two sensors. One way to measure this factor is to use a pair of tiltmeters and compare the measured values to determine whether each one has a different rotation.

In our system, sensors report measurements from entities to be monitored. If these values are compared with other sensor measurements, constants, or chain conditions, they are called *complex* rules. Figure 7 shows the visual representation of a sensor named TILTMETER_1 compared to COMPARATOR_MORE_THAN against a constant CONSTANT_1, evaluated in the EVENT_RULE_1 component. Additionally, a sensor named TILTMETER_2 that is compared with COMPARATOR_MORE_THAN against a constant CONSTANT_1, evaluated in the EVENT_RULE_2 component.

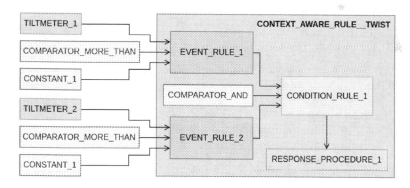

Fig. 7. Representation of a ContextAwareRule with a complex use case - Twist

Furthermore, the two *EventRule* are compared using a COMPARATOR_AND, so if both are evaluated as true, it will trigger the RESPONSE_PROCEDURE_1.

Another complex example for our use case is to check the correlation between the *cant* or *twist* factor and the temperature. For this, sensor values are compared with other measurements or constants, using the combination of *EventRules* and *ConditionRules*. Figure 8 shows the visual representation of a sensor named TILTMETER_1 compared to COMPARATOR_MORE_THAN against a constant CONSTANT_1, evaluated in EVENT_RULE_1. Furthermore, a sensor named TILTMETER_2 compared to COMPARATOR_MORE_THAN against a constant CONSTANT_1, evaluated in EVENT_RULE_2. Additionally, a sensor named TEMPERATURE_1 that is compared with COMPARATOR_LESS_THAN against a constant CONSTANT_2, evaluated in the EVENT_RULE_3. Then, EVENT_RULE_1 and EVENT_RULE_2 are evaluated in CONDITION_RULE_1 using a COMPARATOR_OR, and this condition is analyzed together with EVENT_RULE_3 in CONDITION_RULE_2. If both are evaluated as true (COMPARATOR_AND), the RESPONSE_PROCEDURE_1 will be triggered.

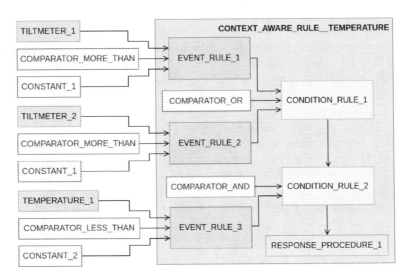

Fig. 8. Represent. of a ContextAwareRule with a complex use case - Temperature

5   Experimentation

We have performed some experiments to demonstrate the validity of our ontology for incorporating context-aware entities to increase semantic interoperability in the IoT. With this purpose in mind, we have established the foundation for our studies on the interoperability of IoT devices in railways. Using the entities provided in our ontology, we handle data interoperability for IoT devices, from monitoring to actuating situations. Although our ontology is sufficiently generic to be used in different domains, the experiment is focused on a specific use case.

Our experimentation is shown in Fig. 9 and aims to demonstrate the *cant* use case. In this way, IoT sensors read information about railway tracks, monitor it, and trigger emails as *ResponseProcedure* if *ContextAwareRules* are triggered. With this, we enable another way to monitor safety on railways.

Our setup consists of two Raspberry Pi 4B devices to monitor the railway tracks. Each Raspberry reads one track tilt using a tilt sensor as a critical sensor. On top of both Raspberry, there is a GrovePi Shield[3], used to wire sensors to the device. Both devices are capable of reaching the Internet using WiFi mechanisms and submitting measurements to the *Cloud* server, using an HTTP API as the communication method.

In the experiment, each Raspberry is taking measures (Observations) of the track tilt and sending them to the server. We have defined entities to monitor in the *Cloud* server for this purpose. At least two *Things*, one per Raspberry, with two *Sensors*, one per tilt sensor. Also, the *Actuator*, with its module to send emails, has been specified. In addition, the *ContextAwareRules* with its corresponding *EventRules* and *ResponseProcedures* have also been set. The defined *Procedure* is to communicate with an *Actuator* to send an email as a warning.

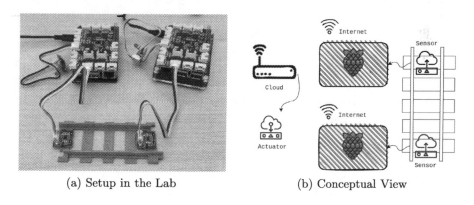

(a) Setup in the Lab   (b) Conceptual View

Fig. 9. Experimentation setup for showcasing the twist scenario

We have developed a context-aware engine in addition to the code that supports the ontology. This engine periodically queries the state of the system in terms of *ContextAwareRules*. If there are some that have the *executing* flag active, the engine checks the *EventRules* it has, and together with the *ConditionRules*, it identifies whether any *ResponseProcedure* has to be performed. If this is the case, it sends it to execution.

In Fig. 10 we see the *Observations* received from a *Sensor* named *TiltSensor*. The tilt sensor of the Raspberry is located on the train track, and the spikes that are seen in the graph represent movements in height of the track, which could be understood as the cant factor value in millimeters when the train runs.

---

[3] GrovePi Shield for Raspberry Pi: https://www.seeedstudio.com/GrovePi.html.

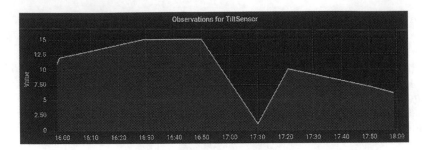

Fig. 10. Our Grafana frontend showing the Observations of the *TiltSensor*

For the graph, we have used Grafana, an open-source data visualization tool. In Grafana we performed an SQL query to the database, where all the experimental information is stored. The *observation* table is where all the metadata information about the *Observations* is stored, and *obs_integer* to store *Observations* that are *integers*.

```
SELECT observation.time_start as"time",
    obs_integer.value as "value"
FROM observation
INNER JOIN obs_integer ON obs_integer.ID=observation.ID
WHERE observation.sensor_name = 'TiltSensor'
```

In this work, we include a functional code of the ontology, available in https://github.com/worldsensing/conawariot-modelling-context-aware. This code is composed of a backend made in Python Flask and PostgreSQL together with Grafana for visualization. In addition, there is also a first implementation of the context-aware client for the rules, which this ontology supports. As well as the code that supports sensing the *Observations* from the Raspberry Pi.

Our Cloud setup consists of a GCP E2-small instance that has 1 vCore and 2 GB of RAM under Debian 11 Linux. In this instance, we have deployed our own server code. The setup handles the incoming measurements and the context-aware rules. It also maintains the state of the entities using our ontology.

Lessons Learnt: The experiments we have performed in this paper have allowed us to learn some lessons from the approach we have proposed in this paper. They are the following:

– We have been able to show the feasibility of our approach in the sense that we have declaratively and semantically handled the responses to the critical events related to the real-time measurement of the cant and twist factors.
– With our ontology, we have been able to abstract from the technological aspects of IoT devices, thus being able to concentrate on the specification of the responses to the context-aware events.
– The software solution we have implemented in our experiments is able to provide the response to our particular scenario, but it could be easily applied,

without having to change any single line of code, to other railway system characterizations, provided that their IoT infrastructure is specified in terms of our *ConAwarIoT* ontology.

6 Conclusions and Future Work

With a large number of IoT devices being used, the need to homogenize the information that is being manipulated is acknowledged. This work contributes to this homogenization by proposing an ontology for context awareness in the sensing and actuation domains, using IoT devices. The proposed ontology builds upon concepts of well-known ontologies and specifies the knowledge required by context-aware rules for defining the possible reactions to some events if they occur thus enabling the users to define in detail the events needed to be monitored and the actions that modify real-world elements when the conditions are met.

With the proposed railway use case, we enable the possibility of manipulating data in real time in settings where sensors and their potential reactions must be monitored. This use case has been demonstrated using an experiment to showcase the functionality enabled by the proposed ontology. With that, a ready-to-use system is provided, including the backend orchestrated components. In addition, a client code is provided that handles the observations, as well as the context-aware engine code the status and actuations to be executed by *Actuators*.

In future work, we plan to develop a framework that combines the work presented in this article with actual *Worldsensing* IoT devices that use LoRaWAN or related technologies like NB-IoT. Also, other than sending emails when an actuation is desired, introducing more options such as MQTT, emails, and so forth. Further work can go down the Machine Learning path to perform predictive maintenance using the real-time data that is being sent.

Acknowledgments. This work is partially funded by Industrial Doctorates from Generalitat de Catalunya (2019 DI 001), the SUDOQU project, PID2021-126436OB-C21 from MCIN/AEI, 10.13039/ 501100011033, FEDER, UE, and the Grup de Recerca Consolidat IMP, 2021-SGR-01252. We thank Ignasi Garcia-Milà for his help in the definition of the use case and to the anonymous reviewers for their valuable comments.

References

1. Abowd, G.D., Dey, A.K., Brown, P.J., Davies, N., Smith, M., Steggles, P.: Towards a better understanding of context and context-awareness. In: Gellersen, H.-W. (ed.) HUC 1999. LNCS, vol. 1707, pp. 304–307. Springer, Heidelberg (1999). https://doi.org/10.1007/3-540-48157-5_29
2. Aguilar, J., Jerez, M., Rodríguez, T.: Cameonto: context awareness meta ontology modeling. Appl. Comput. Inform. **14**(2), 202–213 (2018)
3. Alirezaie, M., Renoux, J., et al.: An ontology-based context-aware system for smart homes: E-care@home. Sensors **17**(7), 1586 (2017)
4. Angsuchotmetee, C., Chbeir, R., Cardinale, Y.: MSSN-Onto: an ontology-based approach for flexible event processing in multimedia sensor networks. Futur. Gener. Comput. Syst. **108**, 1140–1158 (2020)

5. Ashton, K.: That internet of things thing. RFID J. **22**(7), 97–114 (2009)
6. Choi, C., Esposito, C., et al.: Intelligent power equipment management based on distributed context-aware inference in smart cities. IEEE Commun. Mag. **56**(7), 212–217 (2018)
7. Dobrescu, R., Merezeanu, D., Mocanu, S.: Context-aware control and monitoring system with IoT and cloud support. Comput. Electron. Agric. **160**, 91–99 (2019)
8. Dörndorfer, J., Hopfensperger, F., Seel, C.: The SenSoMod-modeler - a model-driven architecture approach for mobile context-aware business applications. In: Cappiello, C., Ruiz, M. (eds.) CAiSE 2019, pp. 75–86. Springer, Cham (2019). https://doi.org/10.1007/978-3-030-21297-1_7
9. Elkhodr, M., Shahrestani, S., Cheung, H.: The internet of things: new interoperability, management and security challenges. Int. J. Netw. Secur. Appl. **8**(2), 85–102 (2016)
10. Gaur, S., Almeida, L., et al.: CAP: context-aware programming for cyber physical systems. In: 24th IEEE International Conference on Emerging Technologies and Factory Automation, pp. 1009–1016. ETFA (2019)
11. Gubbi, J., Buyya, R., et al.: Internet of things (IoT): a vision architectural elements and future directions. Future Gener. Comput. Syst. **29**(7), 1645–1660 (2013)
12. Haller, A., et al.: The modular SSN ontology: a joint W3C and OGC standard specifying the semantics of sensors, sampling, and actuation. Semant. Web (2018)
13. Henricksen, K., Indulska, J.: Modelling and using imperfect context information. In: IEEE Annual Conference on Pervasive Computing and Communications Workshops, pp. 33–37. PerCom (2004)
14. Hevner, A., Chatterjee, S.: Design Research in Information Systems: Theory and Practice. Springer, New York (2010). https://doi.org/10.1007/978-1-4419-5653-8
15. Janowicz, K., Haller, A., et al.: SOSA: a lightweight ontology for sensors, observations, samples, and actuators. J. Web Semant. **56**, 1–10 (2019)
16. Jiang, S., Angarita, R., Chiky, R., Cormier, S., Rousseaux, F.: Towards the integration of agricultural data from heterogeneous sources: perspectives for the French agricultural context using semantic technologies. In: Dupuy-Chessa, S., Proper, H.A. (eds.) CAiSE 2020. LNBIP, vol. 382, pp. 89–94. Springer, Cham (2020). https://doi.org/10.1007/978-3-030-49165-9_8
17. Kim, G., Kang, S., et al.: An MQTT-based context-aware autonomous system in oneM2M architecture. IEEE Internet Things J. **6**(5), 8519–8528 (2019)
18. Maarala, A.I., Su, X., Riekki, J.: Semantic reasoning for context-aware internet of things applications. IEEE Internet Things J. **4**(2), 461–473 (2017)
19. Noura, M., Atiquzzaman, M., et al.: Interoperability in internet of things: taxonomies and open challenges. Mob. Netw. Appl. **24**, 796–809 (2019)
20. Noy, N.F., McGuiness, D.L.: Ontology development 101: a guide to creating your first ontology. Technical report, Knowledge Systems - Stanford University (2001)
21. OGC - GeoSPARQL: A Geographic Query Language for RDF Data (2012). https://www.ogc.org/standards/geosparql. Accessed 02 Nov 2022
22. Park, J.W., Lee, K.C., et al.: Traffic safety evaluation for railway bridges using expanded multisensor data fusion. Comput.-Aided Civil Infrastruct. Eng. **31**(10), 749–760 (2016)
23. Perera, C., Zaslavsky, A., et al.: CA4IOT: context awareness for internet of things. In: IEEE International Conference on Green Computing and Communications, pp. 775–782. GreenCom (2012)
24. Perera, C., Zaslavsky, A., et al.: Context aware computing for the internet of things: a survey. IEEE Commun. Surv. Tutor. **16**(1), 414–454 (2014)

25. Pombo, J., Ambrósio, J.: General spatial curve joint for rail guided vehicles: kinematics and dynamics. Multibody Syst. Dyn. **9**, 237–264 (2003)
26. Razzaque, M.A., Milojevic-Jevric, M., et al.: Middleware for internet of things: a survey. IEEE Internet Things J. **3**(1), 70–95 (2016)
27. Schilit, B., Theimer, M.: Disseminating active map information to mobile hosts. IEEE Network **8**(5), 22–32 (1994)
28. Sheng, Q., Benatallah, B.: ContextUML: a UML-based modeling language for model-driven development of context-aware web services. In: International Conference on Mobile Business, pp. 206–212. ICMB (2005)
29. Vila, M., Casamayor, V., Dustdar, S., Teniente, E.: Edge-to-cloud sensing and actuation semantics in the industrial internet of things. Pervasive Mob. Comput. **87**, 101699 (2022)
30. W3C - OWL-Time: Time Ontology in OWL (2020). https://www.w3.org/TR/owl-time/. Accessed 02 July 2022
31. Wang, X., Zhang, D., et al.: Ontology based context modeling and reasoning using OWL. In: IEEE Annual Conference on Pervasive Computing and Communications Workshops, pp. 18–22. PerCom (2004)
32. Xue, L., Liu, Y., et al.: An ontology based scheme for sensor description in context awareness system. In: IEEE International Conference on Information and Automation, pp. 817–820. ICIA (2015)
33. Zhang, Z., Liu, C., Li, X., Han, Y.: A service-based declarative approach for capturing events from multiple sensor streams. In: Pahl, C., Vukovic, M., Yin, J., Yu, Q. (eds.) ICSOC 2018. LNCS, vol. 11236, pp. 255–263. Springer, Cham (2018). https://doi.org/10.1007/978-3-030-03596-9_17

Modular Quality-of-Service Analysis of Software Design Models for Cyber-Physical Systems

Riccardo Pinciroli[1]([✉]) [iD], Raffaela Mirandola[2] [iD], and Catia Trubiani[1] [iD]

[1] Gran Sasso Science Institute, L'Aquila, Italy
{riccardo.pinciroli,catia.trubiani}@gssi.it
[2] Politecnico di Milano, Milan, Italy
raffaela.mirandola@polimi.it

Abstract. Emerging applications such as collaborative and autonomous cyber-physical systems (CPS) seek for innovative techniques that support Quality-of-Service (QoS) analysis as key concern to be considered. The objective of this paper is to complement the software design models with an approach that provides a set of *modules* that are (i) representative of multiple QoS-based properties, and (ii) equipped with strategies aimed to establish rules of interaction among them in a feedback loop fashion. We propose a novel methodology that builds upon the specification of QoS-based modules and enables the generation of design alternatives as outcome of an internal intertwining of different QoS analysis results for CPS. The approach is applied to a collaborative and autonomous network of sensors, and experimental results show that software designers are supported in the selection of design alternatives by quantitative information. A comparison with an integrated model is performed to show the advantages of our novel modular QoS-based analysis.

Keywords: Software Design Models · Quality-of-Service Analysis · Modularity · Cyber-Physical Systems

1 Introduction

Cyber-physical systems (CPS) are complex systems where both hardware and software components interact together in a tight way to offer the required services. This complexity exacerbates when considering CPS that are *collaborative* [18] (i.e., components collaborate and establish new services for mutual benefit) and *autonomous* [20] (i.e., components take the initiative of interacting with other components for mutual advantage). These characteristics of CPS may reveal a major impact when evaluating the quality of applications, since quality-of-service (QoS) attributes (e.g., energy consumption and performance) are affected by collaborative and autonomous behaviours of system components.

In the literature, early validation of QoS-based requirements and their continuous monitorability has been assessed as fundamental in the software development process [23], and several methodologies have been defined to analyze

© The Author(s), under exclusive license to Springer Nature Switzerland AG 2023
M. Indulska et al. (Eds.): CAiSE 2023, LNCS 13901, pp. 88–104, 2023.
https://doi.org/10.1007/978-3-031-34560-9_6

services enriched with annotations about their QoS attributes [29]. However, the problem to combine the behaviour of system components (and their quality) in an appropriate way is still challenging [26], even more so if we consider that each QoS attribute may bring its own specification. Hence, it becomes necessary to integrate multiple formalisms and supporting their heterogeneity.

In this paper, we investigate the problem of bridging multiple and heterogeneous QoS attributes to support their collaborative and autonomous analysis, thus reflecting the characteristics of CPS, with the underlying goal of achieving a mutual profit among the attributes. Consider as an example, camera devices that operate in different modes on the basis of their battery levels. Dependencies arise between QoS attributes, e.g., battery charge impacts the quality of the pictures, and consequently the system performance. State-of-the-art approaches *separately* derive the QoS attributes and combine them afterward by analyzing the Pareto front, adopting ad-hoc weighted sums, or studying their trade-off [7,16,25]. Instead, we pursue an approach that aims to establish rules of *interaction* among components and their QoS analysis results. This means to decide, in a feedback loop fashion, when a QoS-based model (due to its analysis results) is supposed to trigger design changes required by another QoS-based specification.

To evaluate the quality of collaborative and autonomous CPS we need a change of perspective w.r.t. more traditional systems. We claim the need for a modular multi-view approach, namely MODULO (MODular qUaLity-of-service mOdels), that adopts different connected models to help the software designer in selecting alternatives for collaborative and autonomous CPS. The main advantages of this approach are as follows: (i) it puts together different aspects of the system still maintaining a separation of concerns; (ii) it avoids the complexity of defining a unique flat model including all the system aspects; (iii) the adoption of QoS-based *modules* (i.e., models of a specific QoS characteristics of the systems) allows the plug-and-play of different models that focus on the attribute of interest, or that reflect the different knowledge about the system itself.

Our approach allows the continuous interaction of collaborative and autonomous QoS-based modules, where the results of a module can feed a different one in a feedback loop fashion to empower the system quality evaluation. Similarly to all model-based analysis approaches, numerical values of input parameters can be customized by software designers (reflecting end-users expectation) to grasp different operational profiles and/or varying software and hardware characteristics. The main advantage of the proposed approach is to provide quantitative information to software designers that are supported in the selection of design alternatives. This is achieved through a novel modular analysis technique that considers the intertwining of different QoS-based modules interacting on the basis of model-based analysis results.

The rest of the paper is organized as follows. Section 2 motivates our investigation through an illustrative scenario. Section 3 describes our approach, and Sect. 4 reports the experimental results of a case study[1]. Section 5 discusses the main limitations of the approach. Section 6 presents related work, and Sect. 7 concludes the paper by outlining future research directions.

---

[1] Replication package: https://doi.org/10.5281/zenodo.7773975.

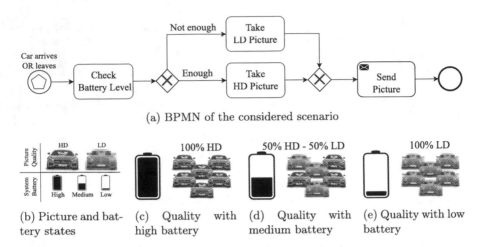

(a) BPMN of the considered scenario

(b) Picture and bat-
tery states

(c) Quality with
high battery

(d) Quality with
medium battery

(e) Quality with low
battery

Fig. 1. The analyzed application: a collaborative and autonomous smart parking system where the camera resolution depends on the battery charge.

2   Motivating Example

Inspired by [4], we consider the case of a collaborative and autonomous smart parking as a motivating scenario. We assume that, in the analyzed system, there are battery-powered cameras that observe cars entering/leaving a parking lot. Figure 1(a) depicts the BPMN of the picture collection process.

When a car enters or leaves the parking lot, the system checks the camera battery level. Cameras take HD or LD pictures of the car depending on their battery level. Collected pictures are forwarded to a cloud application where they are analyzed, e.g., to charge car owners based on the length of their staying in the parking lot. Figure 1(b) depicts camera working modes, i.e., low and high definition modes (LD and HD, respectively). In the former case, cameras capture LD pictures, while high-quality pictures (i.e., with more details) are taken in the latter one. For example, when the cloud application analyzes LD pictures, it may be able to extract only a few information, such as car color and body style (e.g., hatchback, sedan, wagon). The cloud application may get more data from HD pictures, e.g., the registration plate and the car manufacturer.

When a new picture is captured, some energy is consumed and the battery state-of-charge (SoC) decreases; taking a LD picture uses less energy than collecting a HD one. The system battery is characterized by different states defined by its available charge. For the sake of the presentation, in this section, we consider only three battery states (i.e., high, medium, and low charge); more states are considered when MODULO is evaluated in Sect. 4. Cameras autonomously adapt their working mode to the battery SoC to make the battery live longer, i.e., delay the discharge process. For example, when the battery is in the *high charge* state, all cameras work in HD mode, see Fig. 1(c). When the battery SoC decreases and less energy is available, some cameras work in HD mode while others operate in LD mode as in Fig. 1(d). If the battery is almost discharged, see Fig. 1(e), all cameras capture LD pictures to reduce the required energy.

The smart parking goal is to maximize a score, i.e., low- and high-quality pictures provide a reward ρ_{ld} and ρ_{hd}, with $\rho_{ld} < \rho_{hd}$, depending on the information contained in each picture. If cameras work only in HD mode, they generate highly rewarding pictures for a short time (i.e., the battery drains fast). If they work in LD mode, the battery lasts longer, but collected pictures provide a small reward. Reasons that make this application well-suited for our analysis are discussed in the following: (i) the system is characterized by three main QoS attributes (i.e., battery depletion, system performance, and reward computation) that need to be modeled with their interactions; (ii) the battery depletion and the system performance affect each other in a complex feedback loop fashion; (iii) naive (i.e., static) configurations of the considered system can be modeled by standard approaches, hence allowing comparing MODULO to other modeling frameworks.

The smart parking system also emphasizes the strengths of using modular approaches like MODULO instead of an integrated one. Specifically, MODULO allows modeling systems whose components interact in a complex way, e.g., in the smart parking, we analyze the system reward obtained by continuously adapting the performance of the system to the battery SoC. Moreover, MODULO gives software designers the freedom to model each QoS-based module using the preferred solution, e.g., processes of the smart parking system are analyzed using state-of-the-art models and algorithms.

3   Our Approach

The MODULO approach aims to empower the software designer with the ability to assess the quality of the system in the early design stage. To this end, quality assurance (QA) experts are involved to define modules and interactions based on the system requirements.

CPS are composed of highly intertwined software and hardware components that interact with the environment to offer their service and achieve their goal. To guarantee the quality objectives of CPS, it is crucial to evaluate how different QoS attributes influence each other. This calls for an interactive modular approach that considers the intertwining of all QoS attributes. To this end, the MODULO approach (see Fig. 2) devises the following main operational steps.

Step ① - System Modeling. The first step consists in modeling the software system: services are specified, and key quality attributes A_i (i = 0, ..., N, where the value of N depends on the specific software system) are identified. For example, these attributes may be A_1: performance and A_2: energy consumption for a battery powered system, or A_1: reliability (to model possible component malfunctions), A_2: performance, and A_3: security for a health-care system, or A_1: availability (to model the probability of invoking services conditioned by environmental changes) and A_2: performance for a wind-generator system.

Step ② - QoS-based Modules Modeling. A module M_i is associated with each attribute A_i and will include the appropriate model(s) for the evaluation of A_i,

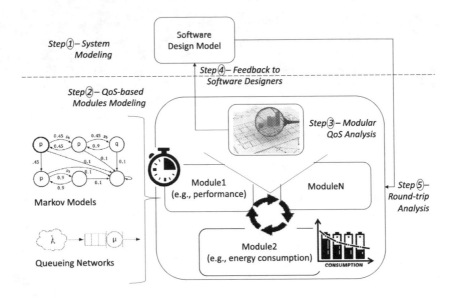

Fig. 2. High-level vision of our MODULO approach.

defined according to the present level of knowledge. For example, if A_i denotes the system performance and we have only a very high level description of the system, a simple Queueing network (QN) model [14] can be defined and evaluated. A deeper knowledge of the system allows the definition of a more detailed and precise QN, Discrete/Continuous-time Markov models [5] (as illustrated in Fig. 2), or any other software performance engineering formalism.

Step ③ - Modular QoS Analysis. Each module M_i is evaluated and results are fed to other modules M_j. Due to the modular nature of the approach, QA experts can adopt different formalisms and analysis techniques for each module. The rules of interaction among modules are meant to define how different aspects of a system affect each other when the behavior depends on the state of the environment or of the system itself [19]. MODULO offers trade-off and parametric sensitivity analysis to identify the system configuration that allows optimizing the satisfaction of quality objectives. This way, software designers are supported with quantitative information on service quality analysis and trade-offs.

Step ④ - Feedback to Software Designers. The software designer is informed about the trade-off and sensitivity analysis of parameters that support their design choices in the early stages of software development. After analysing the received feedback, the QA expert can suggest updates to the software model that represent design alternatives most likely not leading to QoS-based shortcomings. This process enables the early detection and diagnosis of issues, and avoids increased costs to fix errors later in the project life-cycle [12].

Step ⑤ - *Round-trip Analysis.* The QoS evaluation can be repeated when the knowledge about the whole system or part of it increases. This leads to the definition of more precise models for the corresponding module(s) with subsequent new analysis and evaluation steps. Rules of interaction among modules are not supposed to change at this stage. Instead, results of the model-based analysis may vary and trigger different QoS attributes changes.

4   Evaluation

In the following, we use the MODULO approach (see Sect. 3) to analyse the smart parking scenario presented in Sect. 2. We focus on steps ②–④ which constitute the key novelty of the MODULO. For step ① we plan to adopt state-of-the art methods [6], whereas step ⑤ is left for future work.

4.1   Step ② – QoS-Based Modules Modeling

Here, we discuss all modules used to model the three identified QoS attributes (i.e., battery depletion, system performance, and reward computation) of the smart parking. Specifically, each QoS attribute is deployed with different models or analysis techniques. This way, we aim to emphasize the plug-and-play capability of MODULO, as well as its other benefits (i.e., adoption of different formalisms for each module, independent model-based analysis techniques, and interaction among analysis results of different modules). It is worth remarking that the selection of QoS attributes (i.e., battery, performance, and reward) is one of the possible interpretations of the smart parking scenario. The MODULO approach allows implementing other modules and defining further interactions that may differently describe the system and its requirements.

Figure 3 depicts the overview of MODULO modules developed for analyzing the smart parking. The three modules are drawn as boxes, their interactions are shown using arrows. Interactions are labeled with metrics exchanged between the modules. Specifically, the Battery Depletion module passes the number of low- and high-quality requests, i.e., $\vec{N} =$

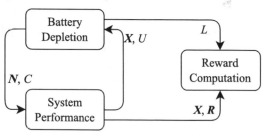

Fig. 3. Modules and their interactions developed using MODULO to study the smart parking system.

(N_{ld}, N_{hd}), and the number of active cameras C to the System Performance module. This module computes the system throughput and response time for the two types of request, i.e., $\vec{X} = (X_{ld}, X_{hd})$ and $\vec{R} = (R_{ld}, R_{hd})$, respectively, as well as the overall sensor utilization, i.e., U. The system throughput and sensor utilization are forwarded to the Battery Depletion module that uses these metrics to determine the battery longevity (i.e., L) before reaching the new SoC.

This loop is repeated until the battery is fully discharged. $\vec{X}$, $\vec{R}$, and L are continuously communicated to the `Reward Computation` module that uses these values to compute the system reward.

Battery Models. We deploy the `Battery Depletion` module using two different models, i.e., the *Linear Model* and the *Kinetic Battery Model* (KiBaM) [17]. These models analytically evaluate the longevity (i.e., L) before moving to the new battery state when the system undergoes a given electrical current load (i.e., I). The battery longevity can be studied using different models, e.g., those discussed in [10]. Our choice of implementing the linear model and the KiBaM aims to show that different existing models and their analysis affect the QoS. Software designers can decide to adopt one of these alternatives based on system requirements. The Linear Model is a naive implementation of the discharge process of a battery, it does not account for two essential battery characteristics (i.e., rate capacity and recovery). For a constant load I, it is defined as:

$$L = \frac{SoC_{init} - SoC_{end}}{I}, \tag{1}$$

where SoC_{init} and SoC_{end} are two battery states, with $SoC_{end} \leq SoC_{init}$. In the case of LD and HD requests, I is computed as:

$$I = \frac{X_{ld} \cdot E_{ld} + X_{hd} \cdot E_{hd} + P_{idle} \cdot (1 - U) \cdot C}{V}, \tag{2}$$

where the energy to capture low- and high-quality pictures is E_{ld} and E_{hd}, respectively, P_{idle} is the power required by cameras to stay on without taking any picture, C is the number of active cameras, and V is the battery voltage.

The KiBaM is a simple, non-linear, and effective battery model that represents the battery discharge process using two connected tanks, see Fig. 4. The energy required to serve an external load, i.e., $I(t)$, is taken from the *Available Charge* tank whose capacity at time t is $Q_A(t)$. The *Bound Charge* tank represents energy that is not

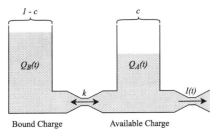

Fig. 4. The Kinetic Battery Model (KiBaM) [17].

directly available, but that can flow in the *Available Charge* tank (with rate k) to recover the battery SoC. The capacity of the *Bound Charge* at time t is $Q_B(t)$. The initial available charge ratio is $c = Q_A(0)/[Q_A(0) + Q_B(0)]$. The battery is considered fully discharged when the *Available Charge* tank is empty, however the SoC can recover if some energy is in the *Bound Charge* tank, i.e., $Q_B > 0$. Numerical values used with both battery models are reported in Table 1.

Performance Model and Two Analysis Techniques. The smart parking is modeled as a QN to be deployed in the System Performance module. Fixed parameters of this module are the think time, $\vec{Z} = (Z_{ld}, Z_{hd})$, the camera service time, $\vec{S^{cam}} = (S_{ld}^{cam}, S_{hd}^{cam})$, and the cloud service times, $\vec{S^{cloud}} = (S_{ld}^{cloud}, S_{hd}^{cloud})$, whose numerical values are given in Table 1.

Table 1. Numerical values of models used for the three modules in Fig. 3. Energy consumption of low- and high-quality requests, as well as their service time at cameras are derived from [15] assuming 1 MP and 8 MP resolutions for low- and high-quality pictures, respectively.

Module	Parameter	Value	Parameter	Value
Battery Depletion	$Q_A(0)$	23220 W-sec	E_{ld}	0.0299 W-sec
	$Q_B(0)$ (only KiBaM)	23220 W-sec	E_{hd}	0.1286 W-sec
	c (only KiBaM)	0.5	P_{idle}	0.2254 W Watt
	k (only KiBaM)	2.5 A	V	3.8 V
System Performance	Z_{ld}	0.1 sec	Z_{hd}	0.1 sec
	S_{ld}^{cam}	0.085 sec	S_{hd}^{cam}	0.4 sec
	S_{ld}^{cloud}	1.0 sec	S_{hd}^{cloud}	2.5 sec
	N	100	–	–
Reward Computation	ρ_{ld}	1	ρ_{hd}	5
	SLA (only penalty)	2 sec	–	–

Table 2 reports the numerical value of input parameters that depends on the battery SoC, i.e., the number of requests, $\vec{N} = (N_{ld}, N_{hd})$, and the number of active cameras C. The performance analysis makes use of two widely adopted techniques, i.e., Mean Value Analysis (MVA) and its approximate solution [14]. MVA is an iterative algorithm based on the *Arrival theorem* [2]. It allows retrieving accurate performance metrics (e.g., system response time and throughput) of closed QN with a contained computational cost. Its time and space complexity depend on the number of service centers and the number of customers. A faster and still accurate solution for closed QN is provided by the approximate MVA technique (AMVA) whose complexity depends only on the number of service centers. Note that we model the system performance with QN and solve it using the (approximate) MVA since this is a standard technique in performance engineering [28]. Other formalisms (e.g., Petri nets or Markov chains) can be adopted to analyze different systems. Moreover, if the scenario is too complex to be solved with MVA (e.g., the workload is dynamic [1]), other solution techniques (e.g., simulation) can be used to analyze the system performance at the cost of a longer computation time.

Reward Models. Two reward models (i.e., with and without penalties) are envisioned for the Reward Computation module. The model without penalties (namely W/O) always assigns the whole reward to the system, independently of the time spent to capture and analyze a picture. This reward model may be used when timeliness is not a crucial system aspect and is computed as:

$$\rho = (X_{ld} \cdot \rho_{ld} + X_{hd} \cdot \rho_{hd}) \cdot L, \tag{3}$$

where X_{ld} and X_{hd} are the average throughput of low- and high-quality requests (i.e., req/sec, from the System Performance module), ρ_{ld} and ρ_{hd} are the reward for every low- and high-quality request that is processed, and L is the battery longevity (in seconds, from the Battery Depletion module). The reward model with penalties (namely $W/$) allows penalizing slow systems. To this end, a Service Level Agreement (i.e., SLA) is provided and the reward is computed as:

Table 2. System configurations with low- and high-quality requests (N_{ld}, N_{hd}), and the number of active cameras C depends on the battery SoC. Cameras are turned on/off so that $96\% \leq U \leq 98\%$.

$$\rho = (X_{ld} \cdot \rho_{ld} + X_{hd} \cdot \rho_{hd}) \cdot L \cdot$$
$$\left(1 - \frac{\max(\bar{R} - SLA, 0)}{SLA}\right), \tag{4}$$

where $\bar{R}$ is the average system response time of low- and high-quality requests. Similar to the Battery and Performance models, also in this case, other models that better represent system requirements can be implemented and used. Our choice of modeling the reward as in Eqs. (3) and (4) intends to stress the plug-and-play features of the MODULO approach.

Conf.	N_{ld}	N_{hd}	C	SoC_{init}	SoC_{end}
c_1	0	100	14	100%	90%
c_2	10	90	13	90%	80%
c_3	20	80	12	80%	70%
c_4	30	70	12	70%	60%
c_5	40	60	11	60%	55%
c_6	50	50	10	55%	50%
c_7	60	40	9	50%	40%
c_8	70	30	9	40%	30%
c_9	80	20	8	30%	20%
c_{10}	90	10	8	20%	10%
c_{11}	100	0	7	10%	0%

Numerical values of reward model parameters are reported in Table 1.

4.2   Steps ③ and ④ – Modular QoS Analysis and Feedback to Software Designers

Results obtained by analyzing the smart parking using MODULO are shown in Fig. 5. On the x-axis the system configuration identifier is reported, see first column of Table 2. Note that the *Mix* configuration means varying the numerical values of parameters (N_{ld}, N_{hd}, and C) during the analysis based on the battery SoC. All other configurations ($c_1, \ldots, c_{11}$) are fixed ones (i.e., N_{ld}, N_{hd}, and C are set at the beginning of the analysis and do not change). Every row of Fig. 5 depicts a different metric: (i) battery depletion time, (ii) reward percentage increment over the configuration with the minimum reward, and (iii) time required by MODULO to complete the analysis. Columns account for the effect of different models and analysis techniques, e.g., the first column shows results obtained using the Linear model for the Battery Depletion module, the MVA algorithm for the System Performance module, and the reward without penalties for the Reward Computation module.

The battery longevity is depicted in Figs. 5(a)–(d). The largest variation is observed when the Battery Depletion module uses the Linear model, Fig. 5(a), or the KiBaM, Figs. 5(b)–(d). With the Linear model, the battery depletion time is 4 to 15 min shorter than the one observed with the KiBaM due to the recovery process modeled only by the latter approach. Models used to deploy the System Performance and Reward Computation modules do not affect significantly the battery life, i.e., the observed variation is less than 2 min.

Figures 5(e)–(h) show the reward increment obtained by each configuration over the minimum reward, i.e., *Reward Gain [%]* $= [(\rho - \rho_{min})/\rho_{min}] \cdot 100$, where ρ is the reward of the considered configuration and ρ_{min} is the minimum reward.

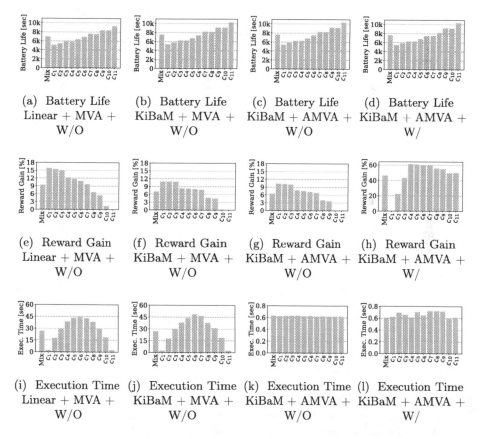

(a) Battery Life Linear + MVA + W/O

(b) Battery Life KiBaM + MVA + W/O

(c) Battery Life KiBaM + AMVA + W/O

(d) Battery Life KiBaM + AMVA + W/

(e) Reward Gain Linear + MVA + W/O

(f) Reward Gain KiBaM + MVA + W/O

(g) Reward Gain KiBaM + AMVA + W/O

(h) Reward Gain KiBaM + AMVA + W/

(i) Execution Time Linear + MVA + W/O

(j) Execution Time KiBaM + MVA + W/O

(k) Execution Time KiBaM + AMVA + W/O

(l) Execution Time KiBaM + AMVA + W/

Fig. 5. System behavior (i.e., battery life, reward gain), and scalability (i.e., execution time) using MODULO with different models and analysis techniques.

The configuration whose *Reward Gain* is 0% scored $\rho = \rho_{min}$. This is the metric that depends the most on the deployed modules since some variations are observed every time a model is changed. When penalties are not included in the reward, i.e., Figs. 5(e)–(g), serving a large number of high-quality requests (i.e., c_1, c_2, c_3) allows maximizing the reward. The smaller gain observed when modeling the battery with KiBaM is due to the longer battery life of configurations with small N_{hd} (i.e., those with small rewards). Since the battery takes longer to run out of energy, there is more time to process requests and increase the minimum reward. The model used for the System Performance module slightly affects the system reward, smaller rewards observed with the Approximate MVA are due to the reduced accuracy w.r.t. the exact MVA. When the reward accounts also for penalties, see Fig. 5(h) whose y-axis goes from 0% to 60%, there are new configurations with the maximum gain (i.e., c_4, c_5, c_6, c_7). This is due to the long response time of configurations serving mainly high-quality requests.

Figures 5(i)–(l) depict the time MODULO takes to analyze the smart parking with considered configurations. The scalability of MODULO is highly affected by the technique used to analyze the System Performance (i.e., MVA or Approximate MVA). This is due to the different time complexity of the two algorithms, see Sect. 4.1. Despite system results (i.e., battery life and reward gain) obtained with the exact and approximate MVA are very similar, see Figs. 5(b)–(c) and 5(f)–(g), the approximate solution allows MODULO to complete its analysis in less than a second, note the different y-axis scale.

4.3   Validation of MODULO

To evaluate the accuracy of MODULO, we analyze the smart parking using an *integrated* (i.e., non-modular) model. Specifically, we use a Queueing Petri Nets (QPN) [13] due to its capability of modeling performance and reliability aspects. The choice of using QPN as a benchmark method to compare MODULO is motivated by our interest in highlighting the modular analysis as a key contribution, and QPN nicely fits with the need of showing differences w.r.t. an integrated model. Other related works (see Sect. 6) are excluded from comparison, since they separately evaluate quality attributes and eventually combine them using techniques such as Pareto analysis.

Figure 6 depicts the QPN model used in this section for comparison, where white (gray) transitions are driven by Exponential (Deterministic) processes, and solid (dashed) arrows describe the performance (battery) workflow. Note that QPN does not support the online adaptation of system configuration to the observed battery SoC, only fixed configurations are analyzed. Moreover, for the sake of simplicity, the developed QPN assumes a linear battery consumption. *These are two advantages of using MODULO , i.e., it allows analyzing collaborative and autonomous systems, and enables an ease adoption of different models.*

For a fair comparison,
MODULO is deployed with
the Linear battery model
and the MVA algorithm.
The performance aspect is
modeled as follows: $\vec{N}$ =
(N_{ld}, N_{hd}) requests are in
the Trigger place that,
after an exponentially distributed Delay (with aver-

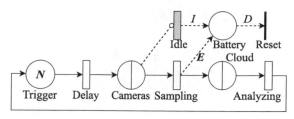

Fig. 6. QPN model of the smart parking.

age Z_{ld} and Z_{hd}, see Table 1), move to the Cameras place. Here, requests are
processed, low- and high-quality pictures are taken (i.e., Sampling transition)
and sent to the Cloud application to be analyzed (i.e., Analyzing transition),
before returning to the initial place. The system throughput is measured observing the throughput of low- and high-quality requests at the Analyzing transition.
To model the battery consumption aspect in the proposed QPN, every time a
picture is captured, $\vec{E} = (E_{ld}, E_{hd})$ tokens are inserted into the Battery place
depending on the quality of the taken picture. Energy is consumed also when
cameras are idle (i.e., Cameras is empty), in this case I tokens are generated into
the Battery place every $S_{Idle} = 1$ second. When D tokens are collected into the
Battery place, the immediate transition Reset fires. In this case, the average
battery longevity is $L = 1/\phi_{Reset}$, where ϕ_{Reset} is the firing frequency of the
Reset transition.

Comparison of the two approaches, i.e., MODULO and Integrated (in this case
a QPN) is shown in Fig. 7, where we consider prediction (i.e., battery life,
low-, and high-quality throughput) and scalability perspectives. Battery life,
low-, and high-quality throughput are the metrics of choice since they are used
(together with the response time that is derived from the response time law
[14] through N, X, and Z) to compute the system reward, Eqs. (3) or (4).
Since MODULO uses analytical formulas to model the smart parking system, exact
values are obtained by solving equations presented in Sect. 4.1. The QPN is
simulated on a commodity machine (Intel Core i7-10750H CPU @ 2.60 GHz
and 16 GB memory) using the discrete-event simulator of the Java Modelling
Tools [3], a widely used tool for performance analysis. Average values are collected with 99% confidence interval. Figure 7(a) depicts the battery life estimated by the two approaches for different configurations. The observed error, i.e.,
$Error \ [\%] = (|M_{Integrated} - M_{MODULO}|/M_{Integrated}) \cdot 100$, is always smaller
than 5%, and MODULO underestimates the battery depletion time. The throughput of low- and high-quality requests estimated by the two approaches are very
similar and errors are negligible, see Figs. 7(b) and 7(c), respectively. Figure 7(d)
shows that the scalability of the two approaches largely differs. MODULO takes less
than a minute to generate results (and it is even shorter when the approximate
MVA is used for the System Performance module, see Fig. 5).

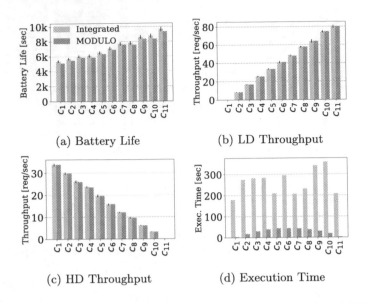

(a) Battery Life (b) LD Throughput

(c) HD Throughput (d) Execution Time

Fig. 7. MODULO vs. QPN integrated approach – *prediction* and *scalability*.

4.4 Threats to Validity

Internal Validity. Threats are caused by bias in establishing cause-effect relationships in our experiments. To limit these threats, we extensively experiment with the considered system. We vary input parameters, look at different output metrics, and compare MODULO to a widely used mathematical modeling language (i.e., QPN). We also make code of MODULO and replication data publicly available.

External Validity. Threats arise due to modeling assumptions. To mitigate these threats and assess the appropriateness of claims in Sect. 4, we use models and data inspired by established case studies in the literature [4,15]. We are aware that the generalization of results is not guaranteed, the application of MODULO to additional scenarios and other domains is left for future work.

Construct Validity. Threats related to the design of experiments. We state the purpose of our experimentation, i.e., (i) assessment of MODULO efficacy in modeling collaborative and autonomous CPS and (ii) validation of MODULO results. We analyze different system configurations and show that MODULO can model collaborative and autonomous CPS (e.g., the smart parking with the *Mix* configuration). We compare MODULO to QPN on performance and energy metrics.

Conclusion Validity. Threats are due to incorrect relationships between input parameters and model outputs. Results obtained through MODULO are derived from state-of-the-art equations and algorithms whose accuracy is assessed in the literature [14,17]. Results simulated using the QPN are provided with 99% confidence intervals and a maximum relative error of 3%.

5   Discussion

The choice of models for each module is an open issue in the QoS domain [11], and there is no silver bullet for this scope. Modules can be implemented differently, e.g., the system performance can be evaluated using Markov models or QN. Such choices depend on the application domain and are delegated to QA experts. This is a limitation of MODULO since the required expertise might not be available in the development team. In the future, we want to explore the effect of different models on the accuracy of our approach as well as on module interactions.

MODULO is applied to a case study concerned with battery depletion, system performance, and reward computation. Other scenarios may call for different QoS attributes (e.g., reliability and availability) and models. For instance, the system reliability (i.e., malfunction of components) can be captured by Fault-Tree Analysis [21], whereas environmental changes affecting the system (e.g., the speed of the wind may activate different turbines, or the illumination may trigger more/less powerful sensors) is modeled with Bayesian Networks in [24]. As future work, we foresee an orchestrator component that is in charge of capturing the system run-time changes by (i) sensing the environment, (ii) adding the proper modules, and (iii) triggering QA experts for defining the corresponding models and the interactions with other modules already specified.

When considering many QoS attributes, MODULO complexity inevitably increases due to the large number of modules and the difficulty of defining their interactions. If non-analytic solutions are needed to study one or more modules, the execution time to solve the overall model may increase as well. In Figs. 5(i)–(l), we investigate the impact of different solution techniques on MODULO execution time, relatively to the considered case study. In the future, we plan to investigate the effect of increasing the number of modules and their interactions on the scalability of our approach.

6   Related Work

The work presented in this paper relates to all the approaches concerned with QoS-based analysis of software design models, e.g., [9,29]. Seminal work on non-functional requirements and their correlation through softgoal interdependency graphs is presented in [8]. MODULO extends [8] by enabling the definition of interactions among different modules and their parameters. Here, we discuss recent techniques that are closely related to MODULO, and we group them into those more concerned with: (i) the relationships between quality attributes and design choices, and (ii) the trade-off analysis between multiple QoS properties.

Relationships Between Quality Attributes and Design Choices. Lytra et al. [16] confirm that quality attributes are the major driver of the design process to achieve high quality systems, and they investigate the relationships between quality attributes and design decisions. They observe that performance is the most frequently analyzed attribute, and the cost is also well perceived as a rewarding factor. Differently from [16] we contribute to improve performance as effort from the analysis of other QoS-based system properties. Verginadis et al. [26] consider applications with alternative architecture variants that can be optimized only considering all their services. They extend two modeling frameworks (i.e., CAMEL and MDS) to improve the analysis of such applications in a multi-cloud environment. Despite sharing similar goals, MODULO profoundly differs from the approach discussed in [26]. Specifically, the approach proposed by Verginadis et al. applies to a single domain (i.e., cloud applications) and allows software developers to use the provided language to study concepts already implemented in the modeling framework. MODULO allows using any modeling language to define different services, study their interactions, and analyze the effect of design decisions on QoS attributes. Schneider et al. [22] consider informal knowledge to improve design decisions in software architectures by annotating design models for qualitative-quantitative reasoning. Differently from [22], MODULO does not explore the whole design space. It gets alternative decisions by analyzing results obtained from the interaction of different QoS-based modules.

Trade-Off Analysis Between Multiple QoS Properties. Vitali [27] presents the Sustainable Application Design Process (SADP) to support software developers in designing sustainable microservice applications. The proposed methodology allows developers to specify different working modalities that account for the trade-off between power consumption and other QoS attributes (e.g., system performance). While the purpose of the SADP methodology is to draw the developers' attention to the sustainability of their applications, MODULO allows analyzing any set of QoS attributes and their interactions. Vale et al. [25] present an empirical study on quality trade-offs involving patterns when designing microservices, and performance emerges as a key concern in industry practice, in conjunction with scalability that is also perceived as a major challenge in software development. Our work inherits from [25] the goal of supporting software designers when evaluating different QoS analysis results. Cámara et al. [7] explicitly link design decisions to satisfaction of quality requirements, while facilitating the comprehension of trade-offs. Our work differs from [7] since we do not use machine learning techniques to explore the design space, we generate specific design alternatives out of QoS analysis results.

Summarizing, to the best of our knowledge, approaches in the literature consider quality trade-offs design decisions that are supported by an integrated analysis of system models. The MODULO novelty is in the underlying reasoning engine that builds upon a modular analysis of different QoS-based properties. The interaction of those properties driven by model-based results allows identifying the most appropriate design alternative.

7   Conclusion and Future Work

In this paper we present MODULO, a modular approach that enables the interaction among different quality-of-service (QoS) properties. Its novelty relies on the interplay of results from the model-based analysis of different modules. Our approach is viable when studying intertwined QoS-based properties, each one with its own model and showing interacting features. Experiments assess the benefits of adopting MODULO to analyse the quality of cyber-physical systems. As future work, we plan to (i) investigate the last step of MODULO (i.e., Round-trip Analysis) and its integration with other steps; (ii) extend the modeling of other interacting QoS properties since we are interested to consider a larger number of relationships; (iii) apply the approach to industrial applications from different domains, to further investigate its usability and scalability.

Acknowledgements. We thank the anonymous reviewers for their valuable feedback. This work has been partially funded by MUR PRIN project 2017TWRCNB SEDUCE, and the PNRR MUR project VITALITY (ECS00000041) Spoke 2 ASTRA - Advanced Space Technologies and Research Alliance.

References

1. Ali, A., et al.: It's not a sprint, it's a marathon: stretching multi-resource burstable performance in public clouds. In: International Middleware Conference, pp. 36–42 (2019)
2. Asmussen, S.: Applied Probability and Queues, vol. 51, 2nd edn. Springer, New York (2003). https://doi.org/10.1007/b97236
3. Bertoli, M., et al.: JMT: performance engineering tools for system modeling. Perf. Eval. Rev. **36**(4), 10–15 (2009)
4. Bock, F., et al.: Smart parking: using a crowd of taxis to sense on-street parking space availability. IEEE Trans. Intell. Transp. Syst. **21**(2), 496–508 (2019)
5. Bolch, G., et al.: Queueing Networks and Markov Chains - Modeling and Performance Evaluation with Computer Science Applications. Wiley, Hoboken (2006)
6. Budgen, D.: Software Design. Pearson Education, London (2003)
7. Cámara, J., Silva, M., Garlan, D., Schmerl, B.: Explaining architectural design tradeoff spaces: a machine learning approach. In: Biffl, S., Navarro, E., Löwe, W., Sirjani, M., Mirandola, R., Weyns, D. (eds.) ECSA 2021. LNCS, vol. 12857, pp. 49–65. Springer, Cham (2021). https://doi.org/10.1007/978-3-030-86044-8_4
8. Chung, L., et al.: Non-functional Requirements in Software Engineering, vol. 5. Springer, New York (2012)
9. Fadda, E., Plebani, P., Vitali, M.: Optimizing monitorability of multi-cloud applications. In: Nurcan, S., Soffer, P., Bajec, M., Eder, J. (eds.) CAiSE 2016. LNCS, vol. 9694, pp. 411–426. Springer, Cham (2016). https://doi.org/10.1007/978-3-319-39696-5_25
10. Gazafrudi, S., Nikdel, M.: Various battery models for various simulation studies and applications. Renew. Sustain. Energy Rev. **32**, 477–485 (2014)
11. Gerasimou, S., Calinescu, R., Tamburrelli, G.: Synthesis of probabilistic models for quality-of-service software engineering. Autom. Softw. Eng. **25**(4), 785–831 (2018). https://doi.org/10.1007/s10515-018-0235-8
12. Haskins, B., et al.: Error cost escalation through the project life cycle. In: INCOSE Annual International Symposium, pp. 1723–1737 (2004)
13. Kounev, S., et al.: Introduction to queueing petri nets: modeling formalism, tool support and case studies. In: International Conference on Performance Engineering, pp. 9–18 (2012)
14. Lazowska, E.D., et al.: Quantitative System Performance - Computer System Analysis Using Queueing Network Models. Prentice Hall, Hoboken (1984)

15. LiKamWa, R., et al.: Energy characterization and optimization of image sensing toward continuous mobile vision. In: International Conference on Mobile Systems, Applications, and Services, pp. 69–82 (2013)
16. Lytra, I., et al.: Quality attributes use in architecture design decision methods: research and practice. Computing **102**(2), 551–572 (2020)
17. Manwell, J.F., McGowan, J.G.: Lead acid battery storage model for hybrid energy systems. Sol. Energy **50**(5), 399–405 (1993)
18. Nazarenko, A.A., Camarinha-Matos, L.M.: Collaborative cyber-physical systems design approach: smart home use case. In: Camarinha-Matos, L.M., Ferreira, P., Brito, G. (eds.) DoCEIS 2021. IAICT, vol. 626, pp. 92–101. Springer, Cham (2021). https://doi.org/10.1007/978-3-030-78288-7_9
19. Pinciroli, R., Trubiani, C.: Performance analysis of fault-tolerant multi-agent coordination mechanisms. IEEE Trans. Ind. Inform. (2023, Early Access)
20. Platzer, A.: The logical path to autonomous cyber-physical systems. In: Parker, D., Wolf, V. (eds.) QEST 2019. LNCS, vol. 11785, pp. 25–33. Springer, Cham (2019). https://doi.org/10.1007/978-3-030-30281-8_2
21. Rao, K.D., et al.: Dynamic fault tree analysis using Monte Carlo simulation in probabilistic safety assessment. Reliab. Eng. Syst. Saf. **94**(4), 872–883 (2009)
22. Schneider, Y., Busch, A., Koziolek, A.: Using informal knowledge for improving software quality trade-off decisions. In: Cuesta, C.E., Garlan, D., Pérez, J. (eds.) ECSA 2018. LNCS, vol. 11048, pp. 265–283. Springer, Cham (2018). https://doi.org/10.1007/978-3-030-00761-4_18
23. Shi, H., et al.: How big service and internet of services drive business innovation and transformation. In: Franch, X., Poels, G., Gailly, F., Snoeck, M. (eds.) CAiSE 2022. LNCS, vol. 13295, pp. 517–532. Springer, Cham (2022). https://doi.org/10.1007/978-3-031-07472-1_30
24. Trubiani, C., Mirandola, R.: Continuous rearchitecting of QoS models: collaborative analysis for uncertainty reduction. In: Lopes, A., de Lemos, R. (eds.) ECSA 2017. LNCS, vol. 10475, pp. 40–48. Springer, Cham (2017). https://doi.org/10.1007/978-3-319-65831-5_3
25. Vale, G., et al.: Designing microservice systems using patterns: an empirical study on quality trade-offs. In: International Conference on Software Architecture, pp. 69–79 (2022)
26. Verginadis, Y., Kritikos, K., Patiniotakis, I.: Data and cloud polymorphic application modelling in multi-clouds and fog environments. In: La Rosa, M., Sadiq, S., Teniente, E. (eds.) CAiSE 2021. LNCS, vol. 12751, pp. 449–464. Springer, Cham (2021). https://doi.org/10.1007/978-3-030-79382-1_27
27. Vitali, M.: Towards greener applications: enabling sustainable-aware cloud native applications design. In: International Conference of Advanced Information Systems Engineering, pp. 93–108 (2022)
28. Woodside, C.M., et al.: The future of software performance engineering. In: Workshop on the Future of Software Engineering (FOSE), pp. 171–187 (2007)
29. Woodside, C.M., et al.: Transformation challenges: from software models to performance models. Softw. Syst. Model. **13**(4), 1529–1552 (2014)

Environmental Applications

Simulating and Analyzing Crowdsourcing Impacts in Flood Management: A Geo-spatial Agent-Based Approach

Aurélien Richa[ID], Chihab Hanachi[(✉)][ID], and Patricia Stolf[ID]

IRIT Laboratory, University of Toulouse, Toulouse, France
{hanachi,stolf}@irit.fr

Abstract. Crowdsourcing is becoming essential to facilitate disaster management. It can help to gather or check information and delegate collective physical tasks (alerting, rescuing, sheltering, food distribution...) to volunteers. In this context, the management of volunteers, with possible uncertain behavior, cannot be improvised, for both security and efficiency reasons. Therefore, it is necessary to provide officials with tools to anticipate and prepare coordination with volunteers. For that purpose, this paper proposes a geospatial agent-based simulator to visualize, measure and analyze the influence of crowdsourcing in natural disasters management. More precisely, this tool allows the authorities to visualize a crisis situation (actors, environment) and its evolution throughout time and space, improve their situation awareness and explore several what-if scenarios so as to ease coordination with official responders. Moreover, task assignment is implemented according to the contract net protocol to select the volunteers according to their variable characteristics: availabilities, positions, skills... This paper describes the design and implementation of this simulator, which is based on a conceptual model representing the environment, agents' behaviors and their interactions. We also demonstrate its use through a real-world case study based on a flood that took place in 2018 in Trèbes, a French town. We demonstrate with quantitative indicators the positive impacts of crowdsourcing on this crisis management. This simulator could be easily reused for other natural disaster situations.

Keywords: Agent based Modelling and Simulation · Crowdsourcing · disaster management

1 Introduction

Context. Nowadays, the number of natural disasters (floods, fires, earthquakes, tsunamis...) as well as their impacts are increasing worldwide, notably due to climate change. In Europe for example, in 2021 summer floods affected Germany, Belgium and Turkey and caused the death of hundreds of people and more than 10 billion euros of property damage. Nowadays, during the response phase of such crisis, the authorities cannot handle these events alone anymore. Citizen volunteers (i.e. contributors) are commonly included in crisis management activities such as rescuing, hosting, alerting people, providing materials and food, or gathering and checking information on the field [1, 5].

In this context, the management of volunteers, with possible uncertain behavior (availability, motivation, movement...), cannot be improvised, both for security and efficiency reasons. Indeed, coordination is necessary for limiting redundant actions, avoiding collisions, or synchronizing them. Besides, it is important that contributors follow explicit and well-defined protocols (to be engaged and also during tasks allocation) to avoid misinterpretation of orders and therefore reduce risks. Since preparation drills in the field are costly and time-consuming, it becomes necessary to provide officials with simulation tools to anticipate, test and prepare volunteers coordination policies, calibrate the number of volunteers (number, distribution...) and measure the overall impact of their actions on the quality of the disaster management process (reduce the number of victims and damage, improve reaction time, increase citizens and responders awareness...). Moreover, the acceptability of digital solutions by officials requires coordination policies to be experimented, visualized, discussed, and adapted in *a shared and user-friendly information space* that shows the geospatial context in which the crisis occurs, and the scope of damage.

Given these observations, *the goal of this work* is to design and implement a simulation framework to simulate, visualize and analyze the impact of crowdsourcing in natural crisis management. It should make it possible to test and elaborate in an interactive way, coordination policies while taking into account the following requirements: the variable behavior of the contributors, their interactions with the officials, and the geospatial representation and evolution of the disaster phenomena in its environment.

Existing work about crowdsourcing applied to disaster management (see [1, 2, 5] for a review) features several limitations. They mainly focus on optimization aspects (task allocation, information accuracy improvements) without measuring the global impacts of crowdsourcing on crisis management and the possible risks and vulnerability attached to it. In addition, as noticed by [8], most of them rely on idealized models that do not consider uncertainty due to the variability of human behavior. [12] specifies an interesting approach to formalize and integrate motivation in an agent-based simulation devoted to model the spontaneous volunteers' convergence phenomena but it provides neither a comprehensive approach nor a geo-spatial setting for its execution, as discussed in Sect. 2.

To the best of our knowledge, no work provides an interactive framework simulating contributors' behaviors and visualizing the geo-spatial environment, its evolution and the global effect of crowdsourcing on the crisis resolution.

Contributions. To overcome these limitations and thanks to interviews with officials involved in crisis management, we developed a geospatial simulator for visualizing, measuring and analyzing the impact of crowdsourcing for disaster management. Our work follows an agent-based modeling and simulation (ABMS) approach [4] allowing to capture the complexity of the crisis universe: the different actors (contributors, citizens and officials) with their variable and parallel behaviors, their interactions protocols and the representation of the evolving environment. It also allows officials to conduct what-if scenarios (exploratory, predictive or normative) interactively.

Our simulator is designed to be used by the authorities in charge of the crisis response to prepare coordination plans, or to react to an imminent flood in their locality. In such situations, hydrologic and meteorological data to predict the dynamic of the flood represented in the simulation. Based on output indicators and the dynamic visualization of the map, representing the flood's impacts on the population and the infrastructures, authorities are then able to evaluate different scenarios and determine the most adequate contributors' configuration.

More precisely, *the contributions of our work* are as follows:

- A *conceptual model* representing the agents (citizens, contributors, official responders), their interactions and the dynamic environment (river, flooded areas...) in which they evolve. Task allocation is represented by the contract net communication protocol [11].
- A *simulator implementing the previous model* with the Gama multi-agent platform [4] that allows spatial visualizations of the simulations based on GIS real-world data. Our user interface also allows to try different what-if scenarios, and visualize different output metrics.
- A *set of experiments* applied to a real case study validates and demonstrates the interest of our approach. It is about a flood that took place in the Southern French City of Trèbes in October 2018. In our experiments, contributors have three possible tasks: informing citizens to increase their awareness of the event, helping them to shelter and closing roads to help traffic regulation.

The remainder of the paper is organized as follows. Related works, about crowdsourcing and ABMS applied to disaster management are discussed in Sect. 2. Our conceptual model is described in Sect. 3. The simulator interface and its context of use are presented in Sect. 4. The experiments and validation are presented in Sect. 5. A discussion about our work concludes the paper in Sect. 6.

2 Related Work

The concept of Crowdsourcing is gaining widespread popularity to complete cooperatively complex activities. Besides research interests, crowdsourcing also has a practical relevance notably in information technology, business, education, health and more recently disaster management [1].

In the context of *disaster management*, numerous crowdsourcing tools and platforms (Ushahidi, Tweet4Act, CrowdTasker, RE-ACTA, Staying Alive, GDACSmobile...) have been developed and several of them have been used during one or several steps of the crisis life-cycle (mitigation, preparedness, response or recovery) see [1, 2, 6] for a review. [2] presents lessons learned from an exercise using a combination of two tools (Crowdrasker and GDACSmobile). Tools are either *information-oriented*, by providing means to gather, aggregate or check information, or *task-oriented* by delegating to volunteers collective physical tasks in the field (alerting, rescuing, sheltering, food distribution...). Our simulator is task-oriented and could be used at different steps of the life-cycle: to prepare coordination plans, organize an imminent reaction with what-if scenarios, or replay past events to better understand what happened. Its objective is to improve the coordination of volunteers in a geo-spatial context: physical distribution and task allocation (informing the population in their houses or in the streets, helping them to shelter).

While geo-spatial crowdsourcing [7] has been addressed in the literature, existing works mainly concentrate on optimization aspects (task allocation, information accuracy improvements) without considering the disaster context and linking the solutions to their possible consequences in terms of risks and vulnerability. In addition, as noticed by [8], most of optimization methods rely on idealized models that do not consider uncertainty accurately due to the *variability of human behavior*: actions and movements based on interactions and the dynamic environment state, availability, position... At the opposite, Agent-based modelling brings two interesting features, used in our simulator, that better reflect reality: goal-oriented behavior (e.g., saving population, sheltering...) and high-level interactions between agents with protocols (e.g., matchmaking, contracting protocol). In addition, *the interactivity* provided by our simulator is a key and original feature to associate decision-makers (authorities) to the incremental building of the crowdsourcing configuration. Indeed, we believe that the acceptability of the solution could be improved by providing a visual information space to decision makers and by enabling them to launch what-if scenarios based on their knowledge of the domain and the specific situation.

Regarding the ABMS approach, [13] defines 25 attributes that feature and influence the behavior and coordination of agents representing spontaneous unaffiliated volunteers. It also classifies these attributes into three groups: individual, social and environmental attributes. Even if we didn't take into account all these attributes (e.g. motivation, group affiliation), our agents are able to perceive their environment, coordinate and interact with others, and decide by themselves the actions to perform (e.g. decide to shelter or not, and where). Adding attributes to our model will not change the overall agents architecture and reasoning (see Sect. 3). [12] aims at understanding through simulations the spontaneous volunteers' convergence phenomena according to their motivation and information sharing. The motivation is formalized using the Theory of Planned Behavior (TPB) while our agents have a simple probability-based decision process for accepting or refusing to perform a service. However in [12], authors do not measure the real impacts of their work on the rescue of individuals and their awareness of the situation. They do not formalize either the interaction protocols between stakeholders as we do with the contract net protocol, to coordinate volunteers. Moreover, we provide a more comprehensive approach, taking into account agents, their interaction protocols, their organizations and the environment. Our simulator is also more realistic thanks to a spatialized agent-based model and an interactive interface, more useful for decision makers.

Regarding *ABMS and GIS coupling*, several simulators have already been proposed for floodings [2], bushfires [10], tsunamis [9] but they do not address crowdsourcing (impacts) which remains a key requirement from an official crisis responders' point of view.

3   Agent-Based Model for Crowdsourcing Management

We will present hereafter our agent-based conceptual model for crowdsourcing management in the context of flooding. This model represents the concepts involved and their relationships: agents, the environment, interactions between agents and the environment.

Here, only the environment is specific to flooding while the other concepts are invariant and crisis independent.

We first present the structure of the different entities involved in our model and their relationships, and then the behaviors of the active entities, namely agents, and their interaction protocol. Agents exhibit an autonomous and intelligent behavior that captures uncertainty and improve realism: i) they perceive their surrounding environment, and so can be aware of the situation ii) they decide of their actions (move, shelter, help…) and iii) they communicate with one another through protocols. Part of the model has been elaborated thanks to interviews, we conducted with crisis managers.

Structure of the Entities

The model in Fig. 1 represents, with a UML class diagram, the following aspects:

i) the environment (Building, RescueCenter, RoadSegment, River) and its dynamic state (FloodSituation);
ii) the agents (Citizens, responders Actors: Contributors and Officials) that are able to move, to perceive their environment and act;
iii) the services (tasks) that Actors can provide (skills) and possibly realize.

More precisely, let us detail each class:

- **Building**: A building may be affected by a flood, and may host one or several people when its type is residential.
- **RescueCenter**: represents a safe public building that will not be affected by the flood, where people can shelter.
- **RoadSegment**: corresponds to a portion of a road. It can be used by citizens to move from and to different locations, and may be submerged by a flood.
- **FloodSituation**: defines a flooded area at a specific moment. It starts at a predefined time and affects the infrastructures of a predefined area.
- **River**: describes a watercourse as a line from where the flood starts and is mainly used for visualization purposes on the map. This entity does not have any activity nor interactions with other agents.
- **Agent**: defined by the common attributes and behaviors of the human agents of the model. They notably have a location, a perception radius and they can move according to a speed value.
- **Citizen**: regular inhabitant (not involved in crowdsourcing activities), living in the case study area, who may decide to shelter during the flood according to his/her awareness state about the flood. A citizen inherits the attributes and behaviors from agent.
- **Actor**: abstract class describing the common attributes and methods of contributors and officials involved in the crisis response. Like a citizen, an actor inherits the attributes and behaviors from agent. An actor can offer several services: close a road, help citizens by sheltering and informing them (at home or in the street).
- **Contributor**: an agent contributing to crowdsourcing crisis response activities according to his/her skills and current state.
- **Official**: an official person representing the authorities (e.g. professional rescuer, police officer) and taking part in crisis response operations. As for contributors, an official is a subclass of the actor class.

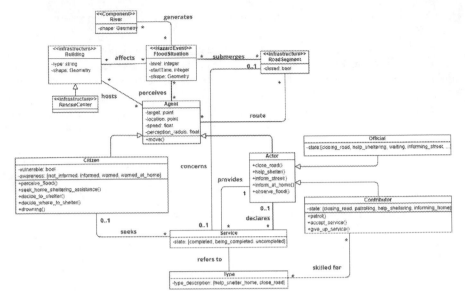

Fig. 1. UML class diagram of the model

- **Service:** describes an assistance task sought by a citizen or a general community (e.g. close a road). A service requires a specific skill, depending on its type, for the completion of the task. Its state could be: "completed", "uncompleted", "under completion"
- **Type:** describes the type of a service.

Agents' Behavior

We will present hereafter the behavior of the active agents: citizen, contributor and official.

Citizen States and Behavior. Figure 2 represents the evolution of a citizen's state according to his/her flood awareness. Initially, a citizen is not informed about the flood. Citizens get the strongest level of awareness when they are warned at home by contributors (who physically visit them at home), and get the lowest level (*informed*) when they perceive the flood by themselves. They become *warned* when they are informed of the flood by phone (at home by officials), or in the street by officials or contributors. According to their level of awareness of the flood, citizens decide to shelter with different probabilities represented by the following parameters:

- Shelter$_{informed}$: is the probability of an *informed* citizen to shelter
- Shelter$_{warned}$: represents the probability of a *warned* citizen to shelter
- Shelter$_{warned\ at\ home}$: is the probability of a *warned_at_home* citizen to shelter

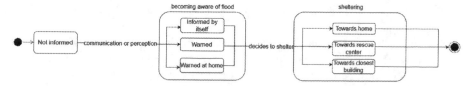

Fig. 2. Citizen state diagram

Once a citizen has decided to shelter, he/she chooses the nearest sheltering location (home, rescue center or other safe buildings).

Contributor States and Behavior. The states are summarized in Fig. 3. Initially, a contributor is patrolling in the area using random successive destinations. This state consists in the following on-field activities: observing the flood, creating a *close_road* service if a road is submerged, and informing citizens in the street about the flood. Once the predefined time for informing citizens at home has been reached, a predefined proportion of contributors starts a walking tour to inform the citizens directly at home. When contributors have finished their home informing tour (they have visited all the buildings to inform in the flood-prone area) they recover their initial *Patrolling* state. While they are informing citizens at home or patrolling, contributors can interrupt their activity to accept a service: *closing road* or *help sheltering*. When the service is completed or if the completion failed, contributors recover the original state they were in before accepting the service.

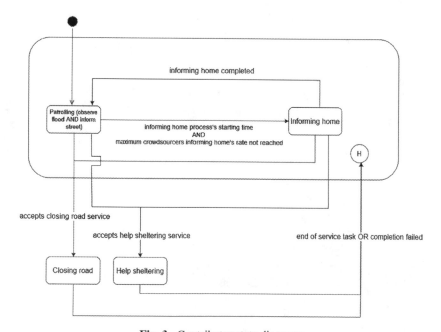

Fig. 3. Contributor state diagrams

Official States and Behavior (See Fig. 4). The initial state for officials is to be waiting for interventions. When the predefined time for informing citizens at home has been reached, officials who have this role start to phone to citizens at home to inform them of the flood. This informing citizens at home process is quicker than the volunteers' informing home process. However, officials are less likely to reach citizens on the phone and thus inform them. Similarly, to the informing home process, when the predefined time for informing citizens in the street has been reached, officials having the corresponding role start informing citizens in the street. They remain in this state until the end of the simulation.

When officials are waiting, they can be allocated task services to complete. Unlike contributors, officials have no choice to accept or refuse a task service and must accept it. When the task is performed, officials recover their waiting state.

At any time (in any state), officials keep observing the flood. Unlike volunteers, officials' flood observations are not performed on the field. One observation comes up randomly among flooded roads every 15 min and results in the creation of a *close_road* service for the observed flooded road. This process aims at reproducing the way authorities are being informed of field situation by the population in real situations.

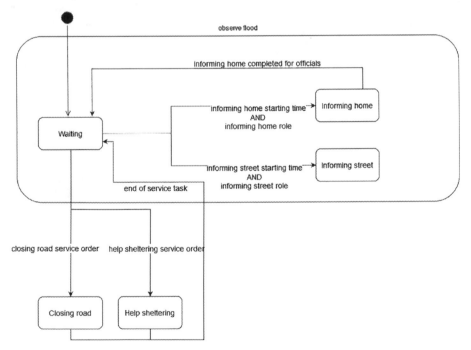

Fig. 4. Officials state diagram

Task Allocation Protocol

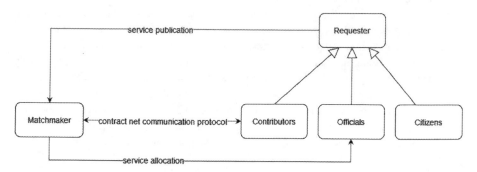

Fig. 5. Service publication diagram

As described in Fig. 5, services are created and published to the matchmaker by contributors, officials and citizens, who are represented by the requester class, The requester class is not implemented in the model and is represented on the diagram only to facilitate its reading. When a service is published, the matchmaker tries to allocate it either to officials (in priority), i.e. through an order, or to contributors through the contract net interaction protocol (see Fig. 6). The matchmaker class corresponds to the manager agent of the Gama model, which is basically the main program of the model orchestrating simulations.

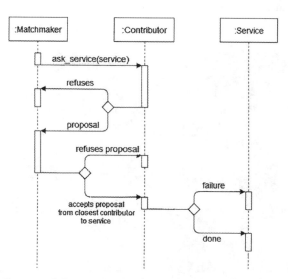

Fig. 6. Sequence diagram of the contract net interaction protocol used to allocate services to contributors (adapted from [3]).

The services allocation process uses the contract net interaction protocol (defined by [11]) and depicted in Fig. 6 (UML model adapted from [3]). The principle is that the manager (here matchmaker) sends the specification of a task (service) to several agents (here contributors), waits for proposals from some of them and then chooses one of them to whom the task is subcontracted. In our context, at each time step of the simulation, the matchmaker sends requests to contributors. The service specification contains the type of service and its location. Each Contributor may accept to perform a service depending on his/her availability, on whether or not the location is safely accessible (without having to cross flooded areas) and on a service acceptance probability. When the matchmaker receives the responses from contributors for a given service, he/she allocates the service's task completion to the contributor who is the closest to the service's location. The elected contributor then performs the service which results in its completion or failure.

4   The Simulator Engine and Interface

4.1   The Simulator Engine

The main program initiates the simulation with the creation of all the agents of all the different classes of our model (see Fig. 1). When the simulation is launched, at each timestep, all the agents automatically compute the methods representing their behaviors (e.g. the "drowning" or "perceive_flood" methods for citizens) known as reflex methods in the Gama terminology. The execution of the reflex methods is sequential and follows the creation order of the agents performed at the initialization.

4.2   The Simulator Interface

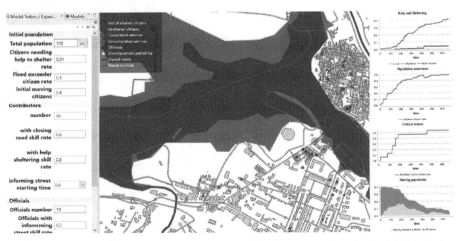

Fig. 7. Interface of the crowdsourcing-based flood management model under the GAMA platform with input parameters (left hand side), real-time chart indicators (right), and dynamic map of the case study area with simulated agents (contributors, citizens, officials) in the middle.

The interface allows to visualize the environment of the studied area (road network, buildings, rivers), the spread of the flood, the location and state of citizens (e.g. level of awareness about the flood, sheltered or not), the location and state of contributors and officials (movements and activities they are involved in) and of services (completed, being completed or uncompleted) (Fig. 7).

Input Simulation Parameters. The main input parameters, specified at the initialization of the simulation and used to define the initial population are for each type of actor, as follows:

- *Population (citizens):* total population, percentage of citizens needing help to shelter, percentage of citizens initially moving.
- *Contributors:* total number, percentages of them offering the following services: "closing road", "sheltering", "informing citizens at home"; maximum rate of contributors informing citizens at home; starting time for informing citizens at home.
- *Officials:* total number, percentages of officials involved in the following services: "informing citizens in the street", "Informing citizens at home"; starting time for informing citizens in the street; "starting time for informing citizens at home".

Output Indicators. The indicators used to evaluate the different crowdsourcing scenarios are the following:

- *Dead and sheltered citizens graph:* represents the evolution of the percentage of sheltered and dead citizens
- *Population awareness graph:* represents the evolution of the percentage of citizens aware of the flood, whether they are *informed*, *warned* or *warned at home*.
- *Percentage of identified critical stakes graph:* this indicator is used to give an insight about authorities' situation awareness. In our experiments critical stakes are defined by 12 vulnerable citizens that need help to shelter and 3 strategically chosen roads (crossing or near the rivers) that need to be closed. A critical stake is considered as identified/discovered when an associated service is created either to close the corresponding road or to help the corresponding vulnerable citizen to shelter.

5 Validation and Experiments

5.1 The Trèbes Case Study

As mentioned before, our model is evaluated using real world data from a flood that took place in the Southern French town of Trèbes in October 2018 where 6 deaths and consequent material damages were recorded. The flood that occurred in Trèbes was caused by a rainfall event. The water level started to rise on the 14th of October at approximately 11:00 pm and reached its maximum level at 5:25 am on the 15th of October.

The data of the simulation scenario are based on feedback report of the Trèbes event. As we focus on the study of the response phase of the crisis management and in order to reduce computational time of simulations, we consider a relatively small time frame (3 h and 45 min), starting at the beginning of the flood (when the flood threshold is reached), and terminating 30 min after the maximum water level has been reached. In addition, we launched our experiments with a reduced but representative population, 1000 citizens, instead of the approximate number of 5500 inhabitants living in the area.

For the other inputs, real data of the Trèbes event are used:

- The IGN (National Institute of Geographical Information) BD TOPO® database provides GIS data representing different aspects of the study area (buildings, roads, and rivers);
- the feedback report provides the dynamics of the flood, i.e. the evolution over time of the areas covered by the flood (provided through shapefiles);
- Approximation based on data from the national statistics bureau of France INSEE (National Institute of Statistics and Economic Studies) provides us demographic and sociological values for parameters such as the number of vulnerable people (provided through input simulation parameters).

5.2 Experiments and Results

Scenarios. To demonstrate the advantage of using crowdsourcing for flood crisis management, two scenarios, defined by the absence or presence of contributors, are studied. The first scenario, abbreviated as *"without CS"* (without crowdsourcing) only involves professional rescuers, called *officials,* in the response effort while the second one, referred to as *"with CS"* involves both contributors and professional rescuers. All the actors are randomly geographically distributed.

The two scenarios are evaluated with the same population characteristics, synthetized as follows:

- Number of citizens: 1000
- Rate of citizens needing help to shelter (rate): 1%
- Rate of Citizens not reacting to the flood: 10%
- Rate of initially moving citizens: 40%
- Number of vulnerable citizens: 12

The scenario without crowdsourcing consists in 50 officials involved in the response effort. 10 of them have an informing-home role and 10 others have an informing-street role. Both groups start their activities, informing home and informing street, at the beginning of the simulation.

The scenario with crowdsourcing consists in the same officials' configuration as the latter one and involves 100 contributors. 80% of the contributors have the capacity (skill) to close a road and to help citizens to shelter at home. A maximum of 20% of them can be allocated the informing activity of citizens at their home. As for officials, this activity starts at the beginning of the simulation.

For each scenario, we launch five simulations and aggregate the results to obtain the average values of each indicator. We then compare the two scenarios by superposing the obtained average graphs for each indicator.

Scenarios Analysis
Influence of Crowdsourcing in the Percentage of Sheltered and Dead Citizens. From

Fig. 8a, we can draw the following observations. The presence of contributors allows to shelter more citizens and more rapidly. After 47 min, 50% of the population is sheltered with crowdsourcing, while 1 h and 6 min are needed (19 more minutes) to reach the same proportion without crowdsourcing. The final rate of sheltered citizens also tends to be relatively higher with crowdsourcing with 66.5% (665 persons) of the population sheltered, compared to 63.1% (631 persons) without crowdsourcing: this represents 34 additional persons sheltered thanks to crowdsourcing. This difference could be higher if contributors started their service before the arrival of the officials, which is sometimes the reality since contributors are most often citizens of the impacted area.

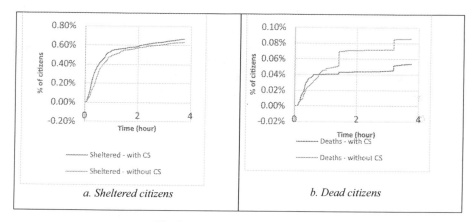

Fig. 8. Sheltered and dead citizens

The total number of deaths (cf. Fig. 8b) represents 5.4% of the population with crowdsourcing and 8.6% without. In other words, the presence of contributors allows to save 32 persons in comparison with the scenario involving only professional rescuers.

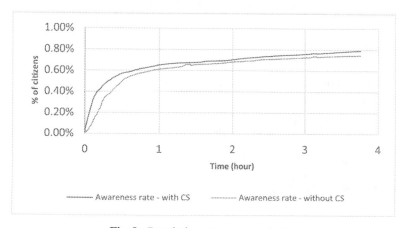

Fig. 9. Population awareness evolution

Influence of Crowdsourcing in Population Awareness. The analysis of Fig. 9 reveals that the presence of contributors enhances the diffusion of flood-awareness: more citizens are aware of the flood more rapidly. 50% of the population is aware of the flood after 19 min with crowdsourcing, while 30 min are needed to reach the same rate without crowdsourcing. The final number of aware citizens is also slightly higher in the crowdsourcing scenario, with 42 more citizens being aware.

In both scenarios, the final number of citizens aware is higher than the final number of sheltered citizens: for the crowdsourcing scenario 790 (79.0%) citizens are aware while 665 (66.5%) are sheltered; for the officials-only scenario 748 (74.8%) citizens are aware whereas 631 (63.1%) are sheltered. This corresponds to 125 (12.5%) and 117 (11.7%) citizens who are aware but not sheltered at the end of the simulation respectively in the crowdsourcing and the officials-only scenario. This difference highlights two elements. Firstly, the sheltering of citizens process is not immediate (some citizens can be aware and engaged in a sheltering process, but not yet sheltered). Secondly, although citizens are aware, they might not decide to shelter according to their sheltering decision probability (see description of *Fig. 2. Citizen state diagram*).

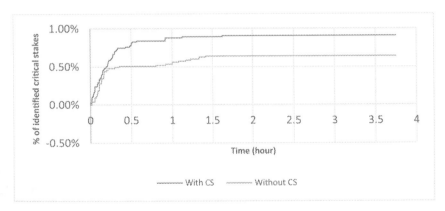

Fig. 10. Critical stakes identification

Influence of Crowdsourcing on the Identification of Critical Stakes. Figure 10 enlightens the positive impact of crowdsourcing on the authorities' situational awareness. Indeed, on-ground information (critical stakes in this case) is gathered quicker and in a higher volume. 50% of the critical stakes are discovered after 12 min with crowdsourcing, whereas the same proportion is reached after 21 min without their contribution. In average 90.7% of the critical stakes is discovered with the help of contributors, while only 64.0% without their help.

6 Conclusion and Discussion

In this paper, we have proposed a new approach aiming at developing a generic agent-based model to simulate and measure the impacts of crowdsourcing in flood crisis management. The main interest of our simulator is to provide a visual and shared information space on top of which decision makers can simulate and visualize floods interactively and incrementally elaborate a coordination policy thanks to what-if scenarios.

We used a real-world case study to evaluate our model and launched *several* experiments that underlined the interest of using crowdsourcing in flood crisis management through output quantitative indicators. The results have showed that the presence of contributors allows to increase the level of the populations' flood-awareness and the number of sheltered citizens. Moreover, sheltering activities were speeded up. In addition, a reduction in the number of dead citizens was observed and the authorities' situational awareness was improved both in terms of the number of stakes discovered and the discovering speed.

In future work, we would like to represent additional realistic characteristics and psychological factors in the population, such as: family links, motivation, emotion, etc. Additional interaction protocols (vote, negotiation…) could also be included to allow the authorities to select the most appropriate one according to the situation.

Acknowledgments. This work was carried out as part of the CRIZ'INNOV project.

References

1. Poblet, M., García-Cuesta, E., Casanovas, P.: Crowdsourcing roles, methods and tools for data-intensive disaster management. Inf. Syst. Front. **20**(6), 1363–1379 (2017). https://doi.org/10.1007/s10796-017-9734-6
2. Middelhoff, M., et al.: Crowdsourcing and crowdtasking in crisis management: lessons learned from a field experiment simulating a flooding in the city of the Hague. In: 3rd International Conference on Information and Communication Technologies for Disaster Management (ICT-DM) Proceedings. IEEE (2016)
3. FIPA: FIPA Contract Net Interaction Protocol Specification. Foundation for Intelligent Physical Agents (2002). http://www.fipa.org/specs/fipa00029/
4. Taillandier, P., et al.: Building, composing and experimenting complex spatial models with the GAMA platform. GeoInformatica **23**(2), 299–322 (2018). https://doi.org/10.1007/s10707-018-00339-6
5. Schimak, G., Havlik, D., Pielorz, J.: Crowdsourcing in crisis and disaster management – challenges and considerations. In: Denzer, R., Argent, R.M., Schimak, G., Hřebíček, J. (eds.) ISESS 2015, vol. 448, pp. 56–70. Springer, Cham (2015). https://doi.org/10.1007/978-3-319-15994-2_5
6. Batard, R., et al.: Integrating citizen initiatives in a technological platform for collaborative crisis management. In: ISCRAM 2019 Conference Proceedings, pp 1346–1356 (2019)
7. Tong, Y., Zhou, Z., Zeng, Y., Chen, L., Shahabi, C.: Spatial crowdsourcing: a survey. VLDB J. **29**(1), 217–250 (2019). https://doi.org/10.1007/s00778-019-00568-7
8. Roy, S.B., et al.: Crowds, not drones: modeling human factors in interactive crowdsourcing. In: DBCrowd 2013 Workshop, pp. 39–42. CEUR-WS (2013)
9. Le, N.-T.-T., Nguyen, P.-A.-H.-C., Hanachi, C.: Agent-based modeling and simulation of citizens sheltering during a Tsunami: application to Da Nang City in Vietnam. In: Wojtkiewicz, K., Treur, J., Pimenidis, E., Maleszka, M. (eds.) ICCCI 2021. CCIS, vol. 1463, pp. 199–211. Springer, Cham (2021). https://doi.org/10.1007/978-3-030-88113-9_16
10. Mancheva, L., Adam, C., Dugdale, J.: Multi-agent geospatial simulation of human interactions and behaviour in bushfires. In: ISCRAM Conference Proceedings, pp. 352–366 (2019)

11. Smith, R.G.: The contract net protocol: high-level communication and control in a distributed problem solver. IEEE Trans. Comput. **29**(12), 1104–1113 (1980)
12. Feinberg, C., Malur, A.: Modeling spontaneous volunteer convergence using agent-based simulation. In: IISE Annual Conference Proceedings (2020)
13. Lindner, S., Betke, H., Sackmann, S.: Attributes for simulating spontaneous on-site volunteers. In: ISCRAM Conference Proceedings (2017)

A Data-Centric Approach for Reducing Carbon Emissions in Deep Learning

Martín Anselmo and Monica Vitali$^{(\boxtimes)}$ ⓘ

Dipartimento di Elettronica, Informazione e Bioingegneria, Politecnico di Milano, Milan, Italy
martinfelix.anselmo@mail.polimi.it, monica.vitali@polimi.it

Abstract. The growing popularity of Deep Learning (DL) in recent years has had a large environmental impact. Training models require a lot of processing and computation and therefore require a lot of energy. The size of these models and the amount of data required for training them have grown exponentially, not comparable to the performance improvements. Recently, some model-centric approaches have been proposed to limit the environmental impact of AI. This paper complements them by proposing a data-centric "Green AI" approach, focusing on the data preparation phase of the DL pipeline. A general methodology, valid for any DL task, is proposed. This methodology is based on analyzing data characteristics, mainly the data quality and volume dimensions, and observing how these affect carbon emissions and performance on different models. With this information, a human-in-the-loop (HITL) approach is provided to support researchers in obtaining a modified and reduced version of a dataset that can decrease the environmental impact of training while achieving a specified performance goal. To demonstrate its validity, the proposed methodology is applied to the time series classification task and a prototype has been developed which demonstrates the possibility of reducing the carbon emissions of DL training by up to 50%.

Keywords: Data-centric AI · Green AI · Data Preparation · Data Quality · Deep Learning · Big Data

1 Introduction

In recent years, Deep Learning (DL) has become very popular for extracting knowledge from non-structured data, such as images or time series. The increase in computing power made possible with the development of new computing hardware and new deep neural network architectures has allowed for unprecedented results in previously complex tasks. From 2012 to 2019, the computing power required by state-of-the-art results has increased by 300,000× [17]. More recently, there has been an even bigger increase with models such as GPT-3, which has 175 billion parameters and was trained on a dataset of nearly a trillion words.

This rise of DL results in a huge environmental impact since the hardware required is very power-hungry. Recently, a distinction between "Red AI" and

© The Author(s), under exclusive license to Springer Nature Switzerland AG 2023
M. Indulska et al. (Eds.): CAiSE 2023, LNCS 13901, pp. 123–138, 2023.
https://doi.org/10.1007/978-3-031-34560-9_8

"Green AI" has been introduced in [17]: the former refers to Artificial Intelligence (AI) research focusing on performance aspects only, the latter refers to environmentally-aware research on AI. Most of the research on "Green AI" has been addressed to developing better and more efficient algorithms and architectures. However, DL training is always preceded by a data preparation phase, in charge of preparing the dataset for the training task. Information Systems Engineering (ISE) expertise can be beneficial in the design of the data preparation phase and can impact the overall energy consumption of the DL task.

This work aims at complementing the existing model-centric approaches with a data-centric approach. We propose a methodology that improves data preparation by transforming the original training set such that: (i) the performance constraints of the resulting model are satisfied; (ii) the environmental impact of the training phase is reduced. These goals are reached by taking into account the characteristics of the dataset, such as data volume and Data Quality (DQ).

The proposed methodology is validated on time series classification using Deep Neural Networks (DNNs). The prototype of a tool that researchers interested in reducing their carbon emissions in this task can use is also provided.

The paper is organized as follows. Section 2 describes existing work. Section 3 motivates the approach and set the goals of the methodology. Section 4 and Sect. 5 introduce an architecture for Data-centric Green AI and describe an implementation in the context of time series classification. Section 6 validates the methodology, while Sect. 7 summarizes the approach and outlines future developments.

2   State of the Art

AI has become pervasive in all fields, and its strong interdependency with climate change has been demonstrated [16]. Several applications of AI can play a role in the reduction of the effects of climate change. At the same time, AI is also the application affecting the environmental impact of IT the most. In 10 years, the computing power required by AI has increased 300'000 times [10]. DL is a subset of AI which uses DNNs as predictive models. The learning process requires several iterations and can take many hours or days, on very power-hungry hardware. Models such as Convolutional Neural Networks (CNNs), Fully Convolutional Networks (FCNs), and Residual Networks (ResNet) have proved to be very effective in terms of performance at the expense of a relevant environmental impact [7,8]. The most power-hungry phase in DL is the hyperparameter (HP) search, since it considers the training of many models with different configurations to find the one with the best performance [20].

The issue of the environmental impact of AI has been discussed in [17], introducing and comparing the two opposite concepts of "Red AI" and "Green AI". The former refers to a performance-focused approach, where all the efforts are put into accuracy, disregarding costs and efficiency. The second envisions a more sustainable approach to AI, encouraging a reduction in resources spent. The main aspects to consider for reducing the environmental impact of AI are analyzed, focusing mainly on architectural and algorithm-related aspects.

This can also be seen in [25] and [15], where the environmental impact of DL is considered focusing on the infrastructural, architectural, and location aspects. They partially consider the data perspective through transfer learning and active learning approaches. In [6], authors focus instead on the environmental impact of the model selection and the hyperparameter search. As shown in [4], modelling the DL task is only one step, preceded by a data preparation phase, which might affect as well the environmental impact of the overall task.

Data preparation is essential in many contexts for the analysis of large volumes of data [13,14]. Data preparation is the preliminary phase of every DL task, which can improve the resulting model performance [11,19] or affect the dataset balance [22]. Data preparation can also affect the environmental impact of DL tasks. The main factor to consider is data volume [12], affecting the training time and the number of resources needed, with sometimes marginal effects in terms of performance [21]. A preliminary data-centric empirical study on Green AI [23] has shown that modifications on the volume of datasets can drastically reduce energy consumption, with a limited decline in accuracy. Data selection should be DQ-driven. The data preparation step in the AI lifecycle is necessary to prevent incorrect results and biases due to poor quality data [2]. A study on the effect of DQ issues on several ML models have been performed in [3], where completeness, accuracy, consistency, completeness, and class balance have been considered, suggesting a limited relevance of class balancing on the model performance as far as the balance is higher than or equal to the original dataset.

This paper takes a data-centric perspective to Green AI to complement existing model-centric approaches with improved training data management.

3   Motivation and Goals for Data-Centric Green AI

AI is a first-class citizen in modern data centers, and the amount of computational and storage resources employed for supporting AI has been increasing and keeps growing. AI applications have become a utility, as demonstrated by the wide and continuously increasing adoption in different fields and for diverse purposes. Current approaches to AI focus on performance optimization and consider sustainability mainly from a model-centric perspective. The availability of huge datasets has enabled the training of complex models and boosted their performance. However, the data size used for training significantly affects the time and the resources needed for the training, impacting the environmental sustainability of AI applications [20]. Not all data have the same relevance for building the model: good quality datasets are necessary for creating high-quality models able to perform accurate predictions [9]. This problem is amplified by big data [5]. This paper adopts a sustainability-driven perspective on DL, with a data-centric focus: the environmental impact of DL applications is reduced by selecting a proper subset of the data for training the model while ensuring a required performance level. This paper identifies three incremental goals:

– **Goal 1:** Explore which data-centric characteristics of DL pipelines contribute the most to energy usage, and find out which can be tweaked so the overall environmental impact is reduced.

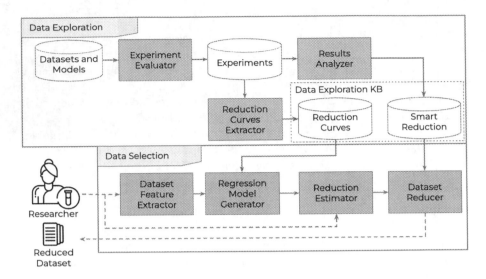

Fig. 1. Architecture for Data-Centric Green DL

- **Goal 2:** Model the relation between the discovered data-centric characteristics and the resulting model's performance.
- **Goal 3:** Reduce the DL impact on carbon emissions by making more efficient use of data while being constrained by performance requirements.

To reach them, a general and data-centric methodology valid for any DL task is proposed, including two phases: a **Data Exploration Phase** in charge of reaching the first two goals through the generation of a knowledge base, and a **Data Selection Phase** focused on the third goal. The proposed approach can be integrated with existing model-centred techniques to improve AI sustainability.

4   An Architecture for Data-Centric Green DL

In this section, we present a detailed architecture for supporting Data-Centric Green DL in Fig. 1. The architecture is split into two parts, corresponding to each one of the phases. Since each DL task has different characteristics (i.e., models, algorithms, datasets and performance metrics), the actual implementation of the architecture depends on the specific DL task to support. To validate our approach, an implementation for time series classification is presented in Sect. 5.

4.1   Data Exploration

The **Data Exploration** part of the architecture focuses on the components required for addressing Goal 1 and Goal 2. The output is a *Data Exploration KB* containing information about how an experiment (defined here as a dataset-model pair) is affected by the manipulation of a data-centric characteristic.

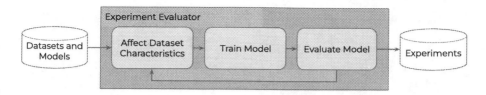

Fig. 2. Overview of the Experiment Evaluator component behaviour

The performance of the resulting model and the carbon emissions generated during training will be considered. This part consists of three components.

The *Experiments Evaluator* executes a set of experiments to collect useful data and learn the trade-offs between data volume vs performance, data volume vs emissions, and DQ vs performance. More specifically, the *Experiments Evaluator* runs a set of experiments, defined as:

$$exp = <mod, ds>$$ (1)

where *mod* is a specific DL model and *ds* is a dataset for training the model. For each experiment, the *Experiments Evaluator* runs a set of sub-experiments, changing its configurations. A sub-experiment is defined as:

$$sub\_exp = <exp, [conf]>$$ (2)

where [*conf*] is the set of configurations to test (data volume or DQ), each one identifying a specific aspect and a specific value for that aspect (e.g., $volume = 50\%$). In order to isolate side effects, only one configuration is tested at each time and for each aspect, several values are tested. For each sub-experiment, the resulting modified dataset is used to train the model and a set of performance metrics is evaluated and stored. The overall process is shown in Fig. 2. The component uses as input a set of models and relative datasets stored in the *Datasets and Models* DB. The output of the component is stored in the *Experiments* DB as a table containing the following information for each sub-experiment:

$$exp\_res = <ds, mod, [conf], [perf]>$$ (3)

where [*perf*] is the set of performance metrics evaluated with their assessed values. The set of metrics to evaluate depends on the task (e.g., recall, precision, accuracy, F1-score for classification tasks).

The data stored in the *Experiments* DB have a dual use. The *Results Analyzer* component analyzes the impact of data volume and DQ on the model performance. It accesses the experiments with different configurations involving DQ aspects and provides a ranking of which DQ metric degradation mostly affects the model performance. It also validates the carbon emission reduction capabilities for each configuration to detect which data aspects mostly affect CO_2 emissions. This information is stored in the *Smart Reduction* DB.

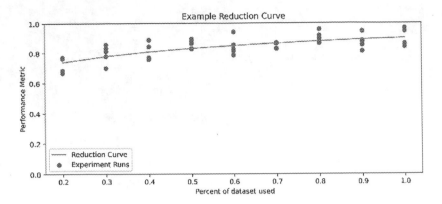

Fig. 3. Sample reduction curve for an experiment

The *Reduction Curves Extractor* component focuses on the data volume vs performance trade-off and aggregates the information collected by the *Experiment Evaluator* to build a reduction curve for each experiment. An example can be seen in Fig. 3, in which actual data are collected only for nine configurations of the data volume, while the generated curve enables us to estimate which will be the performance metric also for intermediate configurations.

All the activities in this phase are executed only once and aim at collecting information to enable the **Data Selection Phase**.

4.2   Data Selection

The **Data Selection** part of the architecture exploits the results collected in the previous phase to support a researcher willing to execute a new training task in reducing its environmental impact.

The most relevant component of this part of the architecture is the *Regression Model Generator*. At first, this component uses the data stored in the *Reduction Curves* DB to train a predictive regression model that will be able to build a new reduction curve for an unseen experiment starting from the reduction curves examples contained in the DB. Once the regression model is built, it can be used to perform a prediction every time a researcher submits a new experiment.

The *Regression Model Generator* is the only component of this part of the architecture running partially in batch mode. All other components run interactively, providing a human-in-the-loop (HITL) approach. The researcher is, in fact, in charge of providing some preliminary information to the system. The information provided by the researcher belongs to four different categories:

- **Dataset Information**: $\mathcal{DI} = <ds, d\_type>$. The researcher provides the dataset ds for training the model and specifies the data type d_type from a list of supported types (e.g., image, sensor data, etc.).
- **Model Information**: $\mathcal{MI} = <arch\_type, \#par>$. The researcher provides the features of the model to be trained, consisting in the type of architecture

$arch\_type$, selected from a list of available architectures, and in the number of parameters of the model $\#par$;

- **Baseline Execution Information**: $\mathcal{BI} = <ds_p, perf_{val}>$. The researcher provides the results of a preliminary execution of the experiment using a randomly reduced dataset. More specifically, the researcher provides the tested dataset size ds_p and the obtained performance value with that size $perf_{val}$;
- **Performance Goal**: $\mathcal{G} = <perf_{metric}, perf_{val}>$ the researcher sets the minimum acceptable value $perf_{val}$ for a specific performance metric $perf_{metric}$.

The inputs provided by the researcher are used by the different components of the architecture. The dataset ds is first processed by the *Dataset Features Extractor* component, which performs profiling activities to extract metadata and compute DQ metrics about the dataset. The enriched dataset information $\mathcal{DI}'$ and the model information $\mathcal{MI}$ are used by the *Regressor Model Generator* that matches them with the parameters and configurations of its internal model and predicts a regression curve for the new experiment. With this curve and $\mathcal{G}$, the *Reduction Estimator* suggests the volume of data $\hat{p}$ that ensures $\mathcal{G}$ while reducing energy consumption. The *Dataset Reducer* extracts a subset $ds_{\hat{p}} \subset ds$ of size $\hat{p}$ exploiting the information provided in the *Smart Reduction DB* about the DQ metric ranking. As an output, the researcher gets the *Reduced Dataset* $ds_{\hat{p}}$, with higher DQ and lower data volume, that can be used to perform a new training with a limited environmental impact.

5   Implementation of the Architecture

The actual implementation of the architecture presented in Sect. 4 depends on the specific DL task to be addressed. To demonstrate it, we describe its implementation for the time series classification task. In this context, we can define a *dataset ds* as a collection of *data points DP*, where each data point dp is a time series consisting of L *values* collected over a time period.

A collection of datasets and models have been used to implement the **Data Exploration Phase** and stored in the *Dataset and Models* DB:

- the datasets are selected from the UCR/UEA repository[1], consisting of over 100 datasets with different characteristics over a variety of fields;
- three different architectures - MLP, FCN, and ResNet [24] were used.

For the sake of simplicity, we limited our evaluation to a single performance metric, and we selected the F1-Score, which represents both the correctly classified series (precision) and the incorrect ones (recall).

The experiments were run on Google Colab[2], on Intel(R) Xeon(R) CPU and a Nvidia Tesla T4 GPU instances. Carbon emissions were measured in $KgCO_2e$ with CodeCarbon[3], manually setting the execution in Italy to reduce variability. All the code is freely available on GitHub[4].

---

[1] https://www.timeseriesclassification.com/dataset.php.

[2] https://colab.research.google.com.

[3] https://codecarbon.io/.

[4] https://github.com/mfanselmo/Time-Series-Classification-GreenAI.

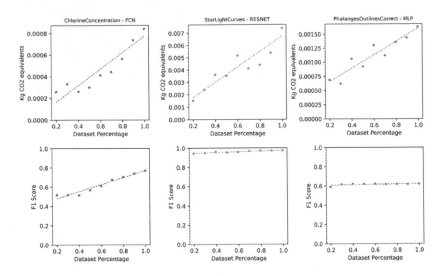

Fig. 4. Volume and carbon emissions (top) or F1-Score (bottom) trade-off

5.1   Data Exploration Implementation

As described in Sect. 4.1 and depicted in Fig. 2, several experiments are executed combining the datasets and models contained in the *Dataset and Models* DB and storing the results in the *Experiments* DB. In each sub-experiment a different dataset configuration was tested, considering two aspects:

- **Data Volume:** from 100% all the way down to 20%, in steps of 10%. At this stage, data points are selected randomly from the dataset;
- **DQ:** injecting errors on accuracy, consistency, and completeness, from 1 to 0.2 in steps of 0.1. To obtain the dirty dataset, we apply *data pollution* as described in [3]: for each DQ metric and for each step, the set of data points to pollute is randomly extracted, and the data points are properly modified:
    - Accuracy: it is computed as the percentage of data points with a correct target value associated. For each of the selected data points, the target value is substituted with a different one;
    - Completeness: it is computed as the complement of the percentage of missing values in the time series composing the dataset. For each of the selected data points, values of the time series are randomly removed;
    - Consistency: it is computed as the percentage of data points that follow the consistency rule: two series with the same values must be associated with the same target value. Each of the selected data points is duplicated and a different target value is assigned to the copy.

For each configuration, five experiments are executed to reduce noise for a total of 1'215 experiments.

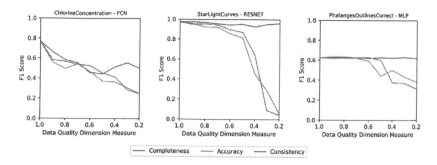

Fig. 5. Impact of different DQ dimensions on model performance

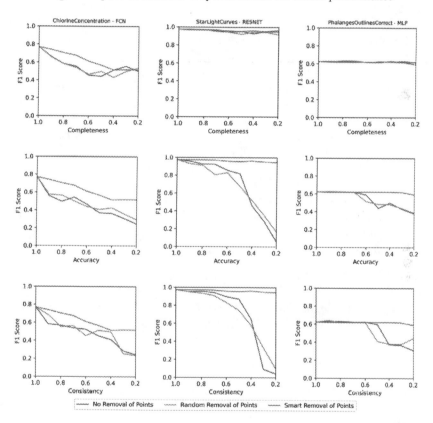

Fig. 6. Comparison of the impact on the performance of different data reduction strategies: smart removal, random removal, no removal

The *Results Analyzer* uses part of these data to (i) evaluate the volume vs performance and the volume vs emissions trade-off, and (ii) to rank the DQ dimensions according to their impact on the model performance. As an example, the results of these two analyses performed by the *Results Analyzer* for three datasets and three models are shown and discussed here. In Fig. 4, the impact of data volume on CO_2 emissions (top row) can be compared to its impact on the model performance (bottom row). While the degradation in performance due to a reduced training set grows slowly, the CO_2 emissions have a steeper trend, suggesting that the gain in terms of environmental sustainability beats the loss in terms of performance. It can be seen that volume reduction has a limited effect on the second and third experiments. This can be due to the dataset characteristics (a better class separability, which makes it easier to build a high-performance model with fewer data) and its intertwining with the selected DL model and HP configuration. Figure 5 shows the impact of DQ degradation on the resulting model performance, considering three different DQ metrics: completeness, consistency, and accuracy. It can be observed that not all the metrics have the same impact, with completeness being the less relevant aspect. A ranking of the most relevant DQ dimensions is extracted from these experiments and stored in the *Smart Reduction* DB. The intuition is that removing poor-quality data improves the overall model performance. To validate this intuition, we executed some experiments showing the results of the model performance under three different conditions: given a dataset with a percentage p of poor quality data (i) no data are removed; (ii) all the poor quality data are removed (Smart Removal); (iii) the same percentage p of data is removed but with a random selection. The experiments tested different percentages of affected data points for different DQ metrics. Results are shown in Fig. 6. As can be observed, smart removal performs similarly or better than the other two options.

The *Reduction Curves Extractor* uses the experiments DB to build a set of reduction curves modeling the trade-off between performance and volume. To build the *Reduction Curves* DB, 42 datasets and three models were used. The reduction curves were modeled as shown in Eq. 4:

$$F1\_Score = C_1 + C_2 \times \log(ds_p) \tag{4}$$

where ds_p is the percentage of the original dataset to be considered, C_1 and C_2 are the regression parameters, and $F1\_Score$ is the resulting model performance.

5.2   Data Selection Implementation

The content of the *Reduction Curves* DB is used by the *Regression Model Generator* to build a Regression Model. In our implementation, we tested several algorithms and selected the Random Forest Regression [18]. All the details about the inputs and output of this model can be seen in Table 1.

As described in Sect. 4, our methodology considers a HITL approach. For this, it is expected for a researcher to provide all the necessary information ($\mathcal{DI}$, $\mathcal{MI}$, $\mathcal{G}$) and to perform a preliminary HP search process with a reduced dataset ($\mathcal{BI}$). In our tests, we set the dataset size $ds_p = 50\%$ since this value resulted in a good trade-off between performance and emissions in the analysed scenario. The *Dataset Feature Extractor* extract from the dataset the missing characteristics for the selected data type and model (as described in Table 1) and assesses DQ.

Table 1. Inputs of the regression model

Input Type	Attribute Name	Description
Model Metadata	Dataset Type	What is the source of the data (chosen from categories)
	Number of Classes	How many classes has the dataset
	Number of Training Samples	How many training samples are available in the full dataset
	Length of Sequence	How long is each time series
	Dimensions	How many dimensions are in each time series
Dataset Metadata	Architecture Type	Which is the general architecture type of the model (chosen from categories)
	Number of Parameters	How many parameters does the model have

Using this information, the Regression Model can be exploited to obtain the C_2 coefficient for the new regression curve. The C_1 coefficient is computed using the baseline $F1 - Score$ result from $\mathcal{BI}$, using Eq. 5. With this reduction curve and the performance goal $\mathcal{G}$, the required dataset percentage is computed by the *Reduction Estimator* using Eq. 6. Finally, the dataset is reduced by the *Dataset Reducer* component by removing low-quality data first according to the DQ dimensions ranking until the required percentage is met: (i) for completeness, data points containing null values are removed; (ii) for consistency, data points with the same values but different target values are removed. Since data points associated with a wrong label cannot be automatically detected, no action is taken to improve accuracy unless additional information is provided. The Data Selection phase additionally allows the researcher to express preferences on the class balance of the resulting dataset: the user can decide if to keep the same distribution or reduce as much as possible the imbalance between classes.

$$\hat{C}_1 = ReportedF1Score - \hat{C}_2 \times \log(ds_p) \tag{5}$$

$$RequiredPercentage = e^{\frac{GoalMetric - \hat{C}_1}{\hat{C}_2}} \tag{6}$$

To ease the interaction with the researcher, we provided a prototype including a web interface (Fig. 7a). To tool increases the sustainability awareness of the researcher by estimating the emissions reduction of the approach (Fig. 7b).

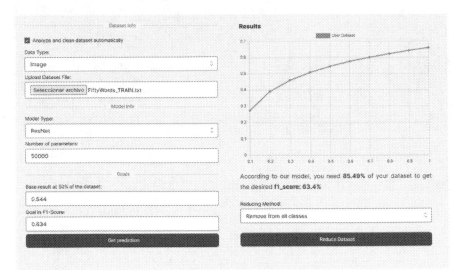

(a) User Interface of the tool

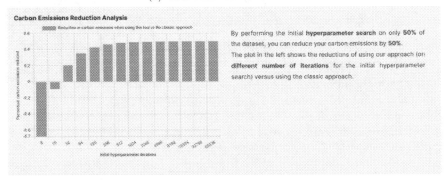

(b) Prediction of the reduction in CO_2 emissions

Fig. 7. The Data-Centric Green DL tool GUI

6   Validation

The validation of the proposed methodology needs to focus on two aspects: (i) using the approach, the environmental impact of DL model training is reduced; (ii) the performance goals set by the researchers are met.

The majority of carbon emissions produced in a DL pipeline come from the HP search. Using a classic method for this process, N training iterations are usually performed on the full dataset changing the HP values, and the resulting best model is chosen. This paper proposes to perform this search in two steps: (i) N training iterations are performed on a reduced dataset $ds_p = 50\%$ to generate the required input for the methodology; (ii) a final HP search is refined on the resulting reduced dataset $ds_{\hat{p}}$ with n final iterations. If $N > n$ by a significant

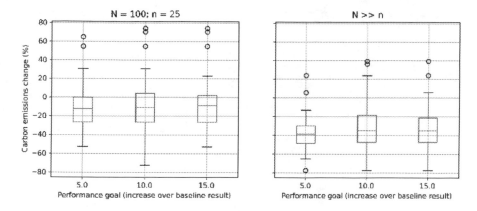

Fig. 8. Carbon emissions change due to the proposed approach

amount, the carbon emissions of the new method will be less than the ones in the classic method, up to half in the limit case where $N \gg n$. The values for N and n used for the experiments were defined part experimentally and part from the literature [1].

In order to extensively and systematically validate the approach, the same experimental data obtained in Sect. 5 were used. The data contained in the *Experiments* DB were split into a training set (70% of the experiments) for training the regression model and a testing set (30% of the experiments) to simulate new experiments requested by researchers. The baseline result $\mathcal{BI}$ was obtained from one of the sub-experiments performed from the validation set, and the performance goal $\mathcal{G}$ was set as the performance of the selected sub-experiment plus 5%, 10%, and 15%. Taking an extreme case, where $N \gg n$, the emissions were reduced by around 40%, on the three performance goal cases. When using more reasonable values of iterations for the HP search ($N = 100; n = 25$), the reduction in emissions was closer to 15% (Fig. 8). Figure 9 shows instead the average error of the approach of predicting the model performance for a specific dataset volume, which resulted to be near 1.5%.

Finally, an extra end-to-end experiment was performed, to test how the researcher can reduce carbon emissions on a new and unseen DL model. This was done using the Swedish Leaf dataset[5], modified to have *consistency* = 0.85 and with a performance goal set as $\mathcal{G} : F1 - Score = 0.95$. After the first HP search with $N = 100$, a baseline result of $F1 - Score = 0.91$ was achieved. With the proposed approach, the original dataset was reduced using 68% of the original data, with a resulting consistency of 1. The new dataset was used to perform a second HP search with $n = 1$, with a resulting performance of $F1 - Score = 0.961$. Table 2 shows a comparison between the proposed method and the results of the

---

[5] http://www.timeseriesclassification.com/description.php?Dataset=SwedishLeaf.

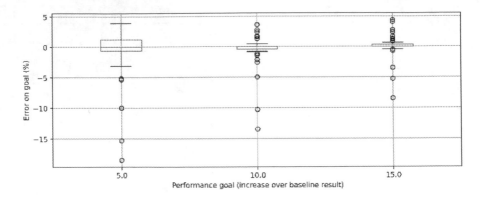

Fig. 9. Error in the satisfaction of the performance goal set by researcher

Table 2. Performance and emissions results of the Green DL compared with classic DL training on the Swedish Leaf dataset

Approach	Data Volume	Consistency	Emissions	F1-Score
Proposed	50%	1	$0.0424\,kg\,CO_2e$	0.961
	68%	1		
Classic	100%	0.85	$0.07451\,kg\,CO_2e$	0.91
Classic	85%	1	$0.05654\,kg\,CO_2e$	0.944

classic method in two different cases: one where the full dataset was used (with the inconsistent series present), and one with all the inconsistent data removed (85% of the dataset). The proposed method generated fewer emissions when compared to both cases while reaching the performance goal set.

All the experiments executed in this paper generated $6.7\,kg\,CO_2e$. Using the tool on datasets with a size similar to the ones used for development, with $N = 100; n = 25$, we can estimate that the generated emissions would be offset with 274 uses of the tool. This number is reduced to only 12 uses with $N = 1000$.

The preliminary results obtained in testing the approach have proven the relevance of data preparation for Green DL. However, the approach can be enriched by i) integrating it with the existing model-centric approaches, providing a holistic view to Green DL; ii) exploiting additional data features affecting either model performance or energy consumption (e.g., data augmentation and class balancing). Namely, the approach can also be applied to other DL tasks, however, additional experiments will be needed to check its efficiency and to provide a way to automatize the parameters optimization in different scenarios.

7   Conclusion

Motivated by the increasing environmental impact that DL is having, this paper proposes a data-centric approach for reducing carbon emissions in DL training pipelines as part of what is called "Green AI". This research is data-centric since all the considerations to reduce energy usage are addressed to more efficient use of the training data, rather than focusing on more efficient hardware or algorithms. For this, characteristics like data volume and DQ were taken into account. A general methodology, valid for any DL task, was proposed, consisting of two phases. First, a Data Exploration Phase inspected the characteristics of the data and generated a knowledge base for efficient data reduction. Second, a Reduction Building System Phase is defined to support researchers in reducing their carbon emissions by operating on the training dataset. This process follows a HITL approach, where the researcher needs to interact with it, providing all the necessary information.

An implementation of the approach focusing on the time series classification task using DNNs is provided. The result of the implementation is a prototype that can be used by the researchers. Experimental results showed that the approach can reduce carbon emissions by up to 50%. With time, more data from experiments of new model architectures and datasets can be included, further increasing the accuracy of the predictions provided by the proposed system.

Future work will focus on testing a more extensive set of data-centric characteristics, to reduce more or in a better way the dataset. Also, the proposed system could be integrated with a location-aware deployment service, which can train models in locations with a more favourable energy mix.

Acknowledgements. This research was supported by the EU Horizon Framework grant agreement 101070186 (TEADAL) and by the Spoke 1 "FutureHPC & BigData" of the Italian Research Center on High-Performance Computing, Big Data and Quantum Computing (ICSC) funded by MUR Missione 4 - Next Generation EU (NGEU).

References

1. Bergstra, J., Bengio, Y.: Random search for hyper-parameter optimization. J. Mach. Learn. Res. **13**(2), 281–305 (2012)
2. Berti-Equille, L.: Learn2Clean: optimizing the sequence of tasks for web data preparation. In: The World Wide Web Conference, pp. 2580–2586 (2019)
3. Budach, L., et al.: The effects of data quality on machine learning performance. preprint arXiv:2207.14529 (2022)
4. Castanyer, R.C., Martínez-Fernández, S., Franch, X.: Which design decisions in AI-enabled mobile applications contribute to greener AI? preprint arXiv:2109.15284 (2021)
5. Dong, X.L., Srivastava, D.: Big data integration. In: 2013 IEEE 29th International Conference on Data Engineering (ICDE), pp. 1245–1248. IEEE (2013)
6. Frey, N.C., et al.: Energy-aware neural architecture selection and hyperparameter optimization. In: 2022 IEEE International Parallel and Distributed Processing Symposium Workshops (IPDPSW), pp. 732–741. IEEE (2022)
7. He, K., et al.: Deep residual learning for image recognition. In: Proceedings of the IEEE Conference on Computer Vision and Pattern Recognition, pp. 770–778 (2016)
8. Hsiao, T.Y., et al.: Filter-based deep-compression with global average pooling for convolutional networks. J. Syst. Archit. **95**, 9–18 (2019)

9. Jain, A., et al.: Overview and importance of data quality for machine learning tasks. In: Proceedings of the 26th ACM SIGKDD International Conference on Knowledge Discovery & Data Mining, pp. 3561–3562 (2020)

10. Knight, W.: AI can do great things - if it doesn't burn the planet. Wired Magazine (2020)

11. Konstantinou, N., Paton, N.W.: Feedback driven improvement of data preparation pipelines. Inf. Syst. **92**, 101480 (2020)

12. Lucivero, F.: Big data, big waste? A reflection on the environmental sustainability of big data initiatives. Sci. Eng. Ethics **26**(2), 1009–1030 (2020). https://doi.org/10.1007/s11948-019-00171-7

13. Maccioni, A., Torlone, R.: KAYAK: a framework for just-in-time data preparation in a data lake. In: Krogstie, J., Reijers, H.A. (eds.) CAiSE 2018. LNCS, vol. 10816, pp. 474–489. Springer, Cham (2018). https://doi.org/10.1007/978-3-319-91563-0_29

14. Miao, Z., et al.: A data preparation framework for cleaning electronic health records and assessing cleaning outcomes for secondary analysis. Inf. Syst. **111**, 102130 (2023)

15. Patterson, D., et al.: Carbon emissions and large neural network training. preprint arXiv:2104.10350 (2021)

16. Rolnick, D., et al.: Tackling climate change with machine learning. ACM Comput. Surv. (CSUR) **55**(2), 1–96 (2022)

17. Schwartz, R., et al.: Green AI. Commun. ACM **63**(12), 54–63 (2020)

18. Segal, M.R.: Machine learning benchmarks and random forest regression. UCSF: Center for Bioinformatics and Molecular Biostatistics (2004)

19. Shin, Y., et al.: Practical methods of image data preprocessing for enhancing the performance of deep learning based road crack detection. ICIC Express Lett. Part B Appl. **11**(4), 373–379 (2020)

20. Strubell, E., Ganesh, A., McCallum, A.: Energy and policy considerations for deep learning in NLP. preprint arXiv:1906.02243, June 2019

21. Sun, C., et al.: Revisiting unreasonable effectiveness of data in deep learning era. In: Proceedings of the IEEE International Conference on Computer Vision, pp. 843–852 (2017)

22. Werner de Vargas, V., et al.: Imbalanced data preprocessing techniques for machine learning: a systematic mapping study. Knowl. Inf. Syst. **65**(1), 31–57 (2023). https://doi.org/10.1007/s10115-022-01772-8

23. Verdecchia, R., et al.: Data-centric green AI: an exploratory empirical study. preprint arXiv:2204.02766 (2022)

24. Wang, Z., Yan, W., Oates, T.: Time series classification from scratch with deep neural networks: a strong baseline. In: 2017 International Joint Conference on Neural Networks (IJCNN), pp. 1578–1585. IEEE (2017)

25. Xu, J., et al.: A survey on green deep learning. preprint arXiv:2111.05193 (2021)

Process Mining

Unsupervised Task Recognition from User Interaction Streams

Adrian Rebmann$^{(\boxtimes)}$ and Han van der Aa

Data and Web Science Group, University of Mannheim, Mannheim, Germany
{rebmann,han.van.der.aa}@uni-mannheim.de

Abstract. User interaction events can give an accurate picture of tasks executed in a process, since they capture work performed across applications in a detailed manner. However, such data is too low level to be used for process analysis directly, since the underlying tasks are typically not apparent from individual events. Therefore, several task-recognition techniques were recently proposed that are able to abstract user interaction data to a higher level. However, these techniques work in an offline manner, requiring user interaction data to be stored in event logs. Such storage is often infeasible, though, due to the data's sheer volume and its privacy-sensitive nature. While this can be avoided by analyzing user interaction data in a streaming manner, existing task-recognition techniques cannot be applied to such settings, since they require multiple, post-hoc passes over the entire data collection. To overcome this, we propose the first approach for unsupervised task recognition from user interaction streams. For a given stream, our approach continuously identifies task instances, groups them according to their type, and emits task-level events to an output stream. Our evaluation demonstrates our approach's efficacy and shows that it outperforms two baseline approaches.

Keywords: Streaming process mining · User interaction data · Task recognition

1 Introduction

Process mining comprises methods for the analysis of event data recorded by information systems in order to gain insights into the true behavior of organizational processes [1]. To be able to apply these methods, events that correspond to the execution of tasks have to be recorded by the systems supporting a process. However, any tasks performed outside of those systems, e.g., involving email, spreadsheets, or web applications, will not be included in such data, and, therefore, will not be taken into account when applying process mining methods.

By contrast, user interaction data [3, 19] has the potential to give an accurate picture of such tasks, since it records all actions performed by a user across applications, at a detailed level and with no need to extract or integrate data from heterogeneous systems. Yet, the fine-granular nature of this data is both a blessing and a curse: raw interaction events are too low-level to be used for process analysis directly, since the purpose of the individual events from a process perspective is typically not apparent. For instance,

© The Author(s), under exclusive license to Springer Nature Switzerland AG 2023
M. Indulska et al. (Eds.): CAiSE 2023, LNCS 13901, pp. 141–157, 2023.
https://doi.org/10.1007/978-3-031-34560-9_9

what was the role of *Click button* and *Edit field* events in a purchase-to-pay setting? Therefore, so-called *task recognition* is required to infer which higher-level tasks are described in low-level user interaction data. Though a challenging problem in an unsupervised setting, some initial approaches to address it [18,23] were recently proposed.

However, these existing approaches are designed for offline analysis of stored user interaction logs, whereas we argue that there are two key benefits to performing task recognition in an online manner, i.e., by analyzing streams of user interaction events. First, offline analysis requires large amounts of low-level data to be stored, including data on events that are not relevant from the perspective of process analysis (e.g., a user logging into an SAP system) or that contain personal information (e.g., records of visits to news websites or private communication). By contrast, performing task recognition in an online manner means that only high-level, process-relevant event data is emitted for further analysis or storage. Second, offline task recognition means that downstream process analysis can only give post-hoc insights into a process, whereas performing it an online manner enables the subsequent application of streaming process mining techniques [9], which can provide a timely understanding of current process behavior and enable process predictions on-the-fly.

Because of these benefits of online task recognition and because existing approaches cannot be applied in online settings, since they perform multiple passes over an entire data collection, we use this paper to propose a novel approach for unsupervised task recognition based on user interaction streams. Our approach continuously identifies task instances and categorizes them according to their type, while adhering to the constraints of the streaming setting it operates in. In this manner, we turn a stream of user interaction events into a stream of task-related events, ready for downstream analysis.

In the following, Sect. 2 illustrates the challenges of unsupervised task recognition over streams and Sect. 3 presents key definitions. Section 4 presents our approach itself, which is evaluated in Sect. 5. Finally Sect. 6 summarizes related work and Sect. 7 discusses limitations and concludes.

2   Problem Illustration

Our work deals with task recognition in situations where user interaction events arrive in a stream and there is no information available about the relation between user interactions and high-level tasks. This section illustrates the problem of such unsupervised task recognition from events in general, before introducing the additional challenges of doing this in a streaming setting.

Unsupervised Task Recognition. To illustrate the goal of (unsupervised) task recognition, consider the excerpt of an event stream in Table 1, where the events record how a user handles requests related to orders. Although the user interaction events show what a user does at a low level (e.g., which buttons are clicked), it fails to give a clear impression about the actual process that is executed. For example, it is hard to recognize that events $u1$–$u8$ correspond to the execution of a specific task, i.e., creating a new order, and events $u9$–$u16$ to a different one, i.e., updating an existing order after a change request was made. Task recognition aims to extract such insights from user interaction data, which involves two parts:

Table 1. An excerpt of a user interaction stream recording the execution of two tasks.

ID	Action	Application	Timestamp	Element	Label	Value
...	...	...	...	...	...	...
u1	click	Mail	15:41:32	list	Order	-
u2	input	Chrome	15:42:10	field	Login	-
u3	input	Chrome	15:42:26	field	Password	-
u4	click	Chrome	15:42:31	button	ok	-
u5	click	Chrome	15:43:01	button	Create order	-
u6	input	Chrome	15:43:29	field	Search	Pete Miller
u7	input	Chrome	15:43:43	field	Customer	C0075
u8	click	Chrome	15:43:58	button	Save	O007501
u9	click	Mail	15:44:32	list	Change request	-
u10	input	Chrome	15:44:41	field	Search	C0081
u11	click	Chrome	15:45:39	button	Edit	O008102
u12	input	Chrome	15:45:48	field	Quantity	4
u13	click	Chrome	15:46:05	button	Save	O008102
u14	click	Chrome	15:46:39	button	Edit	O008102
u15	input	Chrome	15:46:48	field	Quantity	5
u16	click	Chrome	15:46:55	button	Save	O008102
...	...	...	...	...	...	...

1. *Task identification.* The first step in task recognition is to identify sequences of user interaction events that together form individual tasks, also referred to as *segmentation* [18]. Working under the assumption that a user performs one task before moving to the next, this involves the identification of points in the data where one task completes and the next one starts. In the given example, this is the case after events *u8* and *u16*, which denote the completion of two higher-level tasks. The difficulty here is that such end points are not explicitly indicated in the data. For instance, although *u8* ends the first task by the press of a *Save* button, event *u13* involves such a button as well, even though it occurs only halfway through the execution of the second task. As such, task identification must infer when execution has moved to the next task, based on clues from the context and attributes of events.
2. *Task categorization.* Having identified individual tasks, task categorization strives to recognize which tasks correspond to the same type of task (such as *creating an order* or *updating a quantity*), and which to different ones. Due to variability, such categorization is difficult, though, since the same process-level task may be executed by performing different sequences of user interaction events. For instance, the *create order* task (*u1–u8*) could also be executed without first logging in (*u2–u4*) or by having to search multiple times (*u6*) until the right customer is found.

Challenges of the Streaming Setting. Performing task recognition over a user interaction stream is more complex than doing it in an offline manner using an event log, due to the general constraints of streaming settings [8]. Specifically, we have to identify tasks and categorize them as they are observed, using just a limited buffer to temporarily store a small number of events. This leads to two main difficulties:

1. *Single-pass processing.* Offline task-recognition approaches can do multiple passes over an entire collection of events, allowing them to use global information such as co-occurrence counts and similarity scores [23]. In a streaming setting, decisions have to be made as events are recorded, which means that they can only consider local information. For example, we have to decide if events $u1$ to $u16$ form one or more tasks in the moment, without being able to revise this decision later.
2. *Adapting to changes over time.* An associated issue is that when dealing with streams, decisions have to be made without knowing what kind of events will arrive in the future. For example, while offline task-recognition approaches can be certain that all types of tasks they need to identify and categorize are already available, this is not the case in a streaming setting. At any point in time, events corresponding to new kinds of applications, actions, or task types may be observed. For instance, for the running example, events $u9$–$u16$ must be properly analyzed, even if no such *update order* task has been seen before, which requires on-the-fly updating of the task-identification and categorization mechanisms.

3   Preliminaries

User Interactions and User Interaction Events. A *user interaction* is a manual activity performed on a user interface, e.g., clicking a button or entering a value into a text field [2]. In line with the definitions of Leno et al. [18], a *user interaction event* (simply *event* in the remainder) $ue = (id, ts, P, V)$ is a tuple that records a user interaction, with $\mathcal{E}$ the universe of all events. Each event has a unique identifier $ue.id$, a timestamp $ue.ts$, a set of context attribute values $ue.P$, capturing the interaction type and information about the affected user interface element, and a set of data attribute values $ue.V$, capturing data associated with an interaction, e.g., what the user typed into a field. For instance, $u6=(u6, 15{:}43{:}29, \{input, Chrome, field, Search\}, \{Pete\ Miller\})$.

Event Class. Given an event, we let its context attributes values, i.e., $ue.P$, define its event class. For instance, the event class of $u6$ is given as $\{input, Chrome, field, Search\}$.

User Interaction Stream. A user interaction stream S_E is a potentially infinite sequence of events recorded during task execution, i.e., $S_E \in \mathcal{E}^* \forall_{1 \leq i < j \leq |S_E|} S_E(i) \neq S_E(j)$.

Tasks and Task-level Events. A task is a single unit of work that is part of an organizational process. A *task-level event* $te = (id, type, ts, D)$ is a tuple that corresponds to the execution of a task, with $\mathcal{T}$ the universe of all task-level events. Each task-level event has a unique identifier $te.id$, relates to a task type $te.type$, has a timestamp $te.ts$, and has optional information captured in its set of attribute-value pairs $te.D$, such as life cycle information that, e.g., indicates whether the event corresponds to the start or completion of a task. For instance, the start of the task that corresponds to $u9$–$u16$, is given by $te_1 =(1, Change\ order, 15{:}44{:}32, \{(\texttt{lifecycle}, start)\})$.

Task-level Event Stream. A task-level event stream S_T is a potentially infinite sequence of task-level events, i.e., $S_T \in \mathcal{T}^* \forall_{1 \leq i < j \leq |S_T|} S_T(i) \neq S_T(j)$.

4   Approach

Figure 1 provides a high-level overview of our approach, which we complement with a formalization in Algorithm 1. As depicted, our approach collects user interaction events from a stream S_E into a buffer B. In this work, we assume that the buffer's size is large enough to store the events corresponding to a single task instance. Given the events collected in the buffer, task recognition consists of two components: the *task-identification component* identifies sequences of events that correspond to individual tasks, whereas the *task-categorization component* subsequently assigns a type to them. Finally, for each task recognized in this manner, our approach emits a start and a completion event to a task-level event stream S_T.

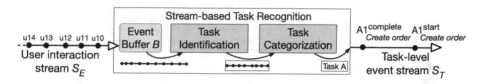

Fig. 1. Overview of our task-recognition approach.

Algorithm 1. Stream-based task recognition

Input S_E: User interaction stream, b: Maximum buffer size
Output S_T: Task-level event stream

 ▷ Initialize buffer B, clustering model M, and chunk list C
1: $B \leftarrow$ new FIFOQueue(b), $M \leftarrow$ new OnlineClusteringModel(), $C \leftarrow []$
2: **loop forever**
3:   $e \leftarrow S_E$.observeEvent()   ▷A new event is consumed from the stream
4:   B.insert(e)   ▷Add the new event to the buffer
  ▷ **Task identification**
5:   **if** completesChunk(e) **then**
6:    C.add(B.getEventsSinceLastChunk(C)) ▷Create and store new chunk

7:   **if** $|C| \geq 3$ **then**   ▷Check if enough chunks available
8:    $c_i, c_{i+1} \leftarrow C[-3], C[-2]$ ▷Get chunks to be checked
9:    **if** endsTask(B, C, c_i, c_{i+1}) **then** ▷Check if c_i completes a task
10:     $task \leftarrow$ new Task(B.dequeueUpThrough(c_i)) ▷De-queue events to
  create task
11:     $C \leftarrow C$.removeRange($C[0], c_i$) ▷Remove chunks that are part of new
  task
  ▷ **Task categorization**
12:     $v \leftarrow$ vectorize($task$) ▷Create a feature vector of the task
13:     M.update(v)   ▷Update the clustering model
14:     $task.type \leftarrow M$.categorizeTask(v) ▷Assign a type to the task
  ▷ **Emit task-level events**
15:     emit($S_T, task$.startEvent(), $task$.completionEvent())

4.1 Task Identification

The task-identification component identifies sequences of events from the stream that correspond to individual tasks. It consists of two main operations, as visualized in Fig. 2. Here, *chunking* identifies sequences of observed events that represent sub-tasks, such as filling in a form or sending an e-mail, whereas *segmenting* determines if consecutive sub-tasks corresponds to the same process-level task, or rather to different ones. Once such a transition from one task to the next has been detected, we forward the segment that corresponds to the completed task to our task-categorization component.

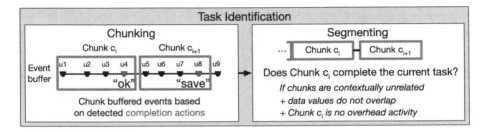

Fig. 2. Task-identification component.

Chunking. We recognize sub-tasks by looking for common keywords in user interaction data that indicate the conclusion of an interaction sequence, achieved through the completesChunk function in Algorithm 1 (line 5). To operationalize this function, we established a set of completion actions K_A, which consists of 20 keywords stemming from design guidelines for user interfaces by IBM [17], covering typical terms that indicate the conclusion of a smaller part in a process, such as *ok* (to go to the next step in a user interface), *submit* (for a form), *send* (e-mail), or *save* (changes).[1]

For an event e, completesChunk(e) returns true if e's event class contains a mention of an action in K_A. Based on the events stored in B, a sub-task is formed by the events that occurred since the last completed chunk in C (line 6). For instance, for the running example, *u4, u8, u13*, and *u16* complete chunks (due to their *ok* and *save* labels), which results in *u1–u4, u5–u8, u9–u13*, and *u14–u16* as chunks.

Segmenting. The segmenting operation aims to decide whether a chunk c_i corresponds to the end of a task or if it continues with the next chunk, c_{i+1} (function endsTask in line 9). Specifically, as shown in Fig. 2, endsTask identifies c_i as finalizing a task if: (1) the chunks are contextually unrelated to each other, (2) the chunks have no overlap in data values, and (3) c_i does not represent an overhead activity. Otherwise, c_i and c_{i+1} are considered to belong to the same task.

(1) Assessing Contextual Relatedness. Our approach first checks if c_i and c_{i+1} are contextually related. We do this by lifting the notion of contextual relatedness proposed by Urabe et al. [23], which targets offline segmentation, to our setting. The idea is to check

---

[1] We refer to our repository for the full list of keywords, though K_A can naturally be extended with, e.g., self-defined keywords or other languages.

if the event classes contained in c_i and c_{i+1} commonly co-occurred so far (indicating a shared context) or not (suggesting that the chunks are part of different tasks).

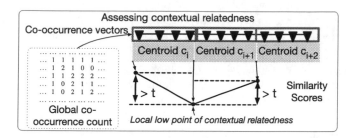

Fig. 3. Adapted contextual-relatedness approach by Urabe et al. [23]

As illustrated in Fig. 3, contextual relatedness is quantified on the basis of a global co-occurrence matrix, which tracks how often pairs of event classes have been observed to be part of the same chunk. Based on the global counts, we obtain the co-occurrence vectors of the event classes per chunk (i.e., rows in the co-occurrence matrix) and compute their centroid. Then, we compute the similarity score $\text{sim}(c_i, c_{i+1})$ as the cosine similarity between the centroids of c_i and c_{i+1}.

Finally, we place $\text{sim}(c_i, c_{i+1})$ into the context of other scores to determine if the chunks are contextually related or not. Specifically, we check if $\text{sim}(c_i, c_{i+1})$ represents a local minimum by comparing it to the highest similarity score observed since the last identified task ($prev_{max}$) and to the next similarity score ($\text{sim}(c_{i+1}, c_{i+2})$). Given a similarity threshold t,[2] if $prev_{max} - \text{sim}(c_i, c_{i+1}) > t$ and $\text{sim}(c_{i+1}, c_{i+2}) - \text{sim}(c_i, c_{i+1}) > t$, chunks c_i and c_{i+1} are considered contextually unrelated, since their contextual-relatedness score negatively stands out.

In this manner, given the four chunks identified in the previous operation, we would determine that the transitions from $u1$–$u4$ (logging in) to $u5$–$u8$ (creating an order), and from $u5$–$u8$ (creating an order) to $u9$–$u13$ (updating a quantity) are both clear changes in context. By contrast, the transition from $u9$–$u13$ to $u14$–$u16$ occurs within the same context (updating and fixing an order quantity), due to its strongly related event classes.

(2) Checking for Data Value Overlap. Next, we recognize that sub-tasks may be part of the same tasks, even when they relate to different contexts, such as opening a request sent by a customer per e-mail and subsequently updating one of their orders in a system. Therefore, we check if events belonging to chunks c_i and c_{i+1} share particular attribute values, such as a customer name or an order ID. Specifically, we check the last two events of c_i and the first two of c_{i+1} for exact matches in their attribute sets V, and if these are present, determine that there should be no segmentation between c_i and c_{i+1}.

In this manner, we would, for instance, recognize that chunks $u9$–$u13$ and $u14$–$u16$ also relate to each other in terms of their data attributes, because events $u13$ and $u14$ both refer to order number $O008102$, thus avoiding segmentation here.

---

[2] t is configurable, yet, we set it to 0.1 as done by the authors of the offline approach [23].

(3) Checking for Overhead Sub-tasks. Finally, we check if c_i actually corresponds to a sub-task performed for a particular process instance or that it, rather, corresponds to overhead being performed. Common examples of this include logging into a system, launching an application, or visiting non-work related websites. If c_i represents such an overhead sub-task, we do not want to treat this chunk as a distinct task on a process level, which is why we would not segment after c_i (even though contextual relatedness or shared data values between c_i and c_{i+1} are unlikely).

To operationalize this final check, we established a set K_O of overhead keywords based on the guidelines [17] we also use for chunking, including *log in*, *sign up*, *reload*, and *open*. Using this set, we check if a member of the last two event classes of c_i is contained in K_O and, if so, avoid segmentation. In this manner, we, e.g., recognize that the first sub-task in our running example (*u1–u4*), which corresponds to the user logging into a web app, belongs to the same task as the next chunk *u5–u8*, where the same system is used to create an order.

Post Processing. When our approach has detected that c_i represents the final chunk of a task (line 9), this means that all events currently in the buffer, up to and including the final event of c_i, together form a task. This completed task is then forwarded to the categorization component, whereas its individual events are removed from buffer B and chunk list C (lines 10–11), so that the first event in B is the first event of the next task.

4.2   Task Categorization

The task-categorization component assigns a type to tasks identified by the previous component. Given that we cannot store identified tasks in a streaming setting, we categorize them directly after identification. This is complex, though, because it means we may not yet have observed all possible task types.

To deal with this challenge, we perform task categorization on the basis of an online clustering model M, which is incrementally updated as new task instances arrive. As shown in Fig. 4, this involves the transformation of a task into a feature vector, updating the model M, then using it to assign a cluster and a corresponding cluster explanation. The latter part is necessary, because the clustering only indicates that certain tasks belong to the same type (e.g., *Task A*), but not what this type entails [22].

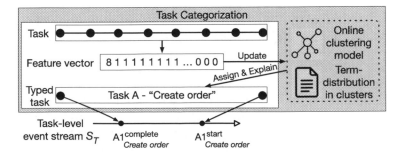

Fig. 4. Task-categorization component.

Establishing Feature Vectors of Tasks. Given an identified task, we first transform its contents into a feature vector that can be used for clustering (line 12). We use a vector encoding that accounts for variability in the executions of tasks of the same type, such as tasks that consist of slightly different sets of events or that are performed in a different order. Therefore, we capture the number of unique event classes (as an indicator of a task's complexity) and the frequency of each event class (to capture its contents) as features. For instance, the task $u1$–$u8$ in our running example consists of eight event classes, all performed once, resulting in a vector $\langle 8, 1, 1, 1, 1, 1, 1, 1, 1, \ldots, 0, 0, 0 \rangle$. Here, the zeros at the end are used to ensure that vectors remain of the same size s_v throughout the stream[3], accounting for a number of event classes not seen so far.

Clustering Tasks. We use an online clustering model M to recognize that tasks are of the same type, based on their vector representation. Specifically, we use *Den-Stream* [10], a density-based online clustering technique building on the DBSCAN algorithm [15]. It dynamically creates, updates, and deletes so-called micro-clusters in the online feature space it maintains. This technique has two key benefits. First, the technique is highly memory efficient, since it only stores summaries of vector sets (the micro-clusters), rather than the vectors themselves. Second, unlike many other clustering techniques, it does not depend on a user-defined number of desired clusters.

As shown in Fig. 4 and Algorithm 1, we update the clustering model M with the vector v that corresponds to an identified task (line 13), before using it to assign the task to a cluster (line 14). For instance, due to the distinct features of the two tasks in our running example, these are assigned to different clusters (e.g., types *A* and *B*).

Providing Type Explanations. After using clustering to recognize tasks that belong to the same or to different types, we aim to provide useful indicators of what these types (like *A* or *B*) actually mean. For this, we detect parts of event classes that are distinctive for the detected clusters, e.g., that tasks of type *A* uniquely involve interactions with a *Create order* button or that type *B* involves the editing of a *Quantity* field.

To this end, we use the well-known *term frequency-inverse document frequency* (tf-idf) score. For this, we use a term dictionary to keep track of the frequency of terms used in the event classes within tasks of a specific type, where a *term* is an attribute value part of P, such as *click*, *Chrome*, *button*, or *Create order*. Using $M.types$ to refer to the types (i.e., clusters) currently recognized by the clustering model M, we write $\mathtt{tf\text{-}idf}(x, type)$ as the score for a term x and a type $type \in M.types$.

Then, we set the *explanation* of *type* as the term x with the highest $\mathtt{tf\text{-}idf}(x, type)$, e.g., *Create order* for type *A*. If multiple types are assigned the same explanation (e.g., if *Quantity* is the most distinctive term for types *B* and *C*), we add the term with the next highest $\mathtt{tf\text{-}idf}$ score to each explanation, until they are all unique. For example, *B* may get *Quantity, update*, while *C* gets *Quantity, Confirm*.

4.3 Output

The output of our approach is a stream of task-related events based on the identified and categorized tasks. For each task, we emit a start event with the timestamp of its first

---

[3] Given that the final number of event classes is unknown, s_v should be set sufficiently large. We set 1,000 as the default for s_v, which already covers more than 6 times the total number of event classes in our evaluation data.

user interaction event and a completion event with the last timestamp (line 15). Both task-level events are assigned a unique identifier, as well as the type and explanation assigned by the categorization component. For instance, for $u1$–$u8$, we emit:

$$te_1 = \{1, A, 15\!:\!41\!:\!32, \{(\texttt{lifecycle}, start), (\texttt{explain}, Create\ order)\}\}$$
$$te_2 = \{2, A, 15\!:\!43\!:\!58, \{(\texttt{lifecycle}, complete), (\texttt{explain}, Create\ order)\}\}$$

For $u9$–$u16$ we emit:

$$te_3 = \{3, B, 15\!:\!44\!:\!32, \{(\texttt{lifecycle}, start), (\texttt{explain}, Edit,\ Quantity)\}\}$$
$$te_4 = \{4, B, 15\!:\!46\!:\!55, \{(\texttt{lifecycle}, complete), (\texttt{explain}, \{Edit,\ Quantity\})\}\}$$

Compared to the fine-grained input events in our running example, our approach thus only emits events that are important for process analysis, whereas potentially sensitive or irrelevant user behavior and information is omitted from consideration.

5 Experimental Evaluation

We describe the data collection used in our experiments in Sect. 5.1 and the setup in Sect. 5.2. In Sect. 5.3 we present the evaluation results showing our approach's capability to recognize tasks in a stream of events and compare it against two baselines. The implementation, data collection, evaluation pipeline, and raw results are all available in our repository.[4]

5.1 Data Collection

There are no publicly available event logs (let alone streams) that contain interaction data related to different task types, associated with a necessary gold standard. Therefore, we follow the idea of Urabe et al. [23] and take available task logs, each recording various instances of the same task type, and combine these into three evaluation logs, which thus cover multiple different task types, in various orders. Finally, we use these event logs as a basis to simulate event streams.

Task logs. As depicted in Table 2, we have eight task logs available, stemming from three sources. The tasks can be divided into two groups, with types 1–4 involving *copying data* from spreadsheets to web forms, filing *reimbursement* requests, entering *student records* into a web-based app, and filling out *travel requests*, whereas types 5–8 all relate to the creation of informational objects in an SAP system. Six out of these eight task logs contain overhead tasks such as logging into a system, starting an application, or opening a file. As shown in the table, the logs also differ considerably in their variation and task lengths.

User Interaction Streams. We established three evaluation logs (available on our repository) by combining and shuffling the tasks contained in individual task logs, which we use to simulate three streams (S_{E1}–S_{E3}):

---

[4] https://gitlab.uni-mannheim.de/processanalytics/task-recognition-from-event-stream.

- S_{E1} consists of 200 tasks, covering types 1–3, with a total of 6,114 events. This stream includes the same task types as used in the evaluation of Urabe et al. [23].
- S_{E2} consists of 240 tasks, covering types 1–4, with a total of 9,054 events. It is an extension of $L1$, based on the recently released task log of type 4.
- S_{E3} consists of 120 tasks, covering types 5–8, with a total of 1,386 events. We use the task types included here in isolation from the others, since their event attributes differ considerably from those in the other task logs, which would bias the results.

We unified the data structure across the task logs as much as possible before merging them, such that attribute names are the same for all task types.

Table 2. Characteristics of the task logs used in our experiments

Type	Source	Description	#Tasks	Avg. length	#Variants	#Events	#Classes
1	[18]	Copy data	100	14.5	7	1,462	15
2	[18]	Request reimbursement	50	2.3	2	3,113	32
3	[18]	Enter student records	50	30.8	1	1,539	23
4	[4]	Fill in travel request	40	73.5	2	2,940	48
5	[3]	Create group	30	10.9	30	331	9
6	[3]	Create keyword	30	10.1	30	425	12
7	[3]	Create version	30	14.2	30	304	8
8	[3]	Create document	30	11.0	30	326	9

5.2 Setup

Environment. We implemented our approach in Python and ran our experiments single-threaded on a laptop with a 2 GHz Intel Core i5 processor and 16GB of memory.

Configurations. Our approach requires a buffer size b that can store all events belonging to a single task. We report on the results using a buffer size of 250 events (also for the baselines), which covers 3× the number events of the longest task in our data. Furthermore, we consider that two parts of our approach need to be initialized at the beginning of a stream and populated over time: the global co-occurrence matrix used during task identification and the online clustering model used for task categorization. Given that the accuracy of these two parts may improve as more events are observed, we test the value of a *warm-up phase*, where our approach populates the matrix and clustering model using the first 0, 100, 250, 500, or 1,000 events, before starting to perform identification and categorization on them.

Baselines. Because there are currently no techniques capable of recognizing tasks based on a stream of user interactions, we established two baselines by adapting existing works. The task-identification component of each baseline consists of an existing, offline identification technique, lifted to an online setting (as described below). Their task-categorization components, by contrast, are operationalized with the same clustering technique used in our proposed approach, which is necessary because offline categorization techniques cannot be lifted to an online setting.

- *BL1: Back-edge-based identification.* Leno et al. [18] proposed a log segmentation technique based on back-edges identified from a directly-follows graph (DFG). We adapted the technique to build the DFG incrementally using the same event classes as available to our approach and apply the authors' back-edge detection method periodically, after every b events (i.e., each time the buffer is full).
- *BL2: Co-occurrence-based identification.* The approach by Urabe et al. [23], which also inspired parts of our work, leverages co-occurring event classes in fixed windows to segment a log. We adapted it to count co-occurrence incrementally and compute similarities on a buffer of events. We use the same parameter configurations as reported in the original paper.

Measures. We use the following measures for quality and efficiency in our experiments.

Identification quality. We assess identification quality by comparing the identified task segments to those of the corresponding gold standard, for which we use two measures:

- *# of tasks.* To assess if an approach makes the right amount of segmentation decisions, we compare the numbers of identified and gold-standard tasks.
- *Normalized edit distance (nor.ED).* To quantify how similar the identified tasks are in comparison to the gold standard, we calculate the average normalized edit distance between identified tasks and their closest task in the gold standard.

Categorization Quality. We assess categorization quality through measures for cluster quality, by comparing the tasks that are assigned to the same category to the gold-standard categorization (i.e., task types):

- *Rand index (R).* We compute the Rand index, which considers the fraction of pairs (tasks at macro level, events at micro level) that are correctly assigned to the same or to different categories, i.e., $(TP+TN)/(TP+TN+FP+FN)$, where a true positive (TP) indicates that two tasks/events are correctly assigned to the same category.
- *Jaccard index (J).* We also compute the weighted average Jaccard index to quantify the similarity between identified clusters and the gold-standard clusters, which is given as $A \cap B / A \cup B$ per cluster, with A a cluster's identified contents and B its gold-standard contents (i.e., tasks at the macro level, events at the micro level).

Efficiency. Finally, we assess the memory and response time efficiency of our approach:

- *Memory consumption.* We measure the maximum memory required by our approach, which is the sum of the largest buffer size during runtime, the final size of the global co-occurrence matrix, and the final size of the clustering model.
- *Response time.* We measure how long it takes our approach to perform task identification after an event arrives, i.e., determining if a task has been completed, as well as how long it takes to categorize an identified task.

5.3 Results

We first present the overall results of our approach compared to the baselines, before discussing the impact of the warm-up phase, memory consumption, and response time.

Table 3. Results of our approach and the baselines (warm-up of 250 events). ↑ and ↓ indicate the desired direction per measure.

Stream	Approach	Identification		Categorization			
		# tasks	nor.ED ↓	R(mi) ↑	R(ma) ↑	J(mi) ↑	J(ma) ↑
S_{E1}	*Our approach*	**198**	**0.04**	**0.94**	**0.95**	**0.92**	**0.92**
	BL1	202	0.83	0.58	0.82	0.38	0.89
	BL2	159	0.33	0.74	0.80	0.64	0.71
	Perfect ident.	200	0.00	1.00	1.00	1.00	1.00
S_{E2}	*Our approach*	**231**	**0.06**	**0.89**	**0.95**	**0.82**	**0.89**
	BL1	99	0.32	0.42	0.80	0.24	0.56
	BL2	198	0.33	0.69	0.71	0.50	0.51
	Perfect ident.	240	0.00	0.97	0.97	0.95	0.95
S_{E3}	*Our approach*	**138**	**0.23**	**0.87**	**0.88**	**0.76**	**0.76**
	BL1	29	0.58	0.34	0.49	0.16	0.35
	BL2	58	0.37	0.45	0.57	0.31	0.46
	Perfect ident.	120	0.00	1.00	1.00	1.00	1.00

Overall Results. Table 3 shows the results obtained using our approach (with a warm-up of 250 events), the two baselines, and a perfect identification strategy (to show the quality of our categorization step independently of identification quality).

Identification Results. Our approach achieves highly accurate identification results for S_{E1} and S_{E2}, identifying approximately the same numbers of tasks as in the gold standard (198 vs 200 and 231 vs 240), to which they are very close in terms of contents, yielding edit distances of just 0.04 and 0.06. Stream S_{E3} is more challenging, though. Our approach overestimates the total number of tasks (138 versus 120), and achieves an edit distance of 0.23. Taking an in-depth look at the results, we find that our approach occasionally fails to recognize that certain sub-tasks belong to the same gold-standard task, since they lack contextual relatedness and overlapping data values.

Compared to the baselines, our approach consistently obtains better results in terms of edit distances. This indicates that the tasks they identify differ more from their gold-standard counterparts than the ones identified by our approach. Both baselines often miss segmentation points, resulting in much lower numbers of identified tasks than contained in the gold standard. *BL1*, specifically, only finds 99 tasks for S_{E2} (out of 240) and 29 for S_{E3} (out of 120). Although *BL2* generally performs better than *BL1*, we find that its results are heavily dependent on the selection of two parameter values, with the edit distances differing by up to 0.5 across configurations.[5]

Overall, these results indicate that our approach, which takes the semantic and data perspectives into account, on top of the control-flow perspective also considered by the baselines, leads to more accurate task identification, whereas our approach also does not depend on user-defined parameters (unlike *BL2*).

---

[5] See our repository for detailed experiments regarding *BL2*'s parameter configurations.

Categorization Results. Our approach achieves high macro Rand scores of 0.95 for S_{E1} and S_{E2} and 0.87 for S_{E3}, which shows that it accurately assigns pairs of tasks to the same category as their gold-standard counterparts. The comparable micro-level scores show that this categorization quality generally also holds for pairs of events, which thus accounts for tasks of different lengths. The Jaccard index, which provides insights into the quality per cluster, rather than per task (or event) pair, confirms the accurate categorization quality, achieving macro scores of 0.92 for S_{E1}, 0.89 for S_{E2} and 0.76 for S_{E3} and the comparable scores on the micro level (0.92, 0.82, and 0.76).

The lower scores for S_{E3} can largely be attributed to the more challenging nature of this stream when it comes to task identification, as evidenced by the results obtained when using our categorization component on perfectly identified tasks (gray row in Table 3). The results reveal that categorization itself is highly accurate, achieving perfect scores for S_{E1} and S_{E3}, and near-perfect ones (≥ 0.95) for S_{E2}. As also confirmed by the results of the baselines, which use the same categorization technique as our approach, it is thus clear that lower identification quality leads to lesser categorization results.

Table 4. Results of our approach with warm-up phases of 0, 250, 500, and 1,000 events. ↑ and ↓ indicate the desired direction per measure.

Stream	Warm-up	Identification		Categorization			
		# tasks	nor.ED ↓	R(mi) ↑	R(ma) ↑	J(mi) ↑	J(ma) ↑
S_{E1}	0 events	198	0.04	0.89	0.84	0.84	0.79
	250 events	198	0.04	0.94	0.95	0.92	0.92
	500 events	198	0.04	**0.96**	**0.96**	**0.94**	**0.94**
	1,000 events	198	0.04	0.96	0.96	0.94	0.94
S_{E2}	0 events	231	0.06	0.89	0.95	0.82	0.89
	250 events	231	0.06	0.89	0.95	0.82	0.89
	500 events	231	0.06	0.89	0.95	0.82	0.89
	1,000 events	**236**	**0.05**	**0.95**	**0.96**	**0.92**	**0.94**
S_{E3}	0 events	138	0.23	0.76	0.79	0.57	0.57
	250 events	138	0.23	0.87	0.88	0.76	0.76
	500 events	138	0.23	**0.90**	0.91	**0.83**	0.82
	1,000 events	138	0.23	0.90	**0.94**	0.83	**0.88**

Impact of Warm-up Phase. Table 4 shows the results of our approach for warm-up phases of 0, 250, 500, and 1,000 events. We find that there is little to no impact on identification quality, since only for S_{E2} the number of identified tasks and edit distance improve slightly (by 5 resp. 0.01), when setting the warm-up to 1,000 events compared to no warm-up at all. For categorization quality, the benefit of a warm-up phase becomes clear, though. While for 0 warm-up events, we achieve a macro Rand score of 0.84 and Jaccard score of 0.79 for S_{E1}, setting the warm-up phase to 500 events increases the scores by 0.12 resp. 0.15. A further increase to 1,000 has no substantial impact, though, only leading to improvements for S_{E2}. Overall, these results show that a warm-up phase is not necessary for task identification, but that it is beneficial for task categorization, if an application context allows for it. However, its length can be relatively short (e.g., just one to two times the buffer size).

Efficiency. We find that our approach requires less than 1% of the memory that would be needed to store all events from the streams, thus clearly demonstrating its memory efficiency. When it comes to response time, we find that our approach requires between 2 and 4 ms for task identification and between 40 to 150 ms for task categorization. Given that the average time between user interactions is over 2.5 s in the available data, this means that our approach can easily keep up in terms of responses.

6   Related Work

Our work primarily relates to task recognition from user interaction logs and other low-level event data as well as pre-processing techniques for stream-based process mining.

Urabe et al. [23] segment logs in a post-hoc manner based on contextual relatedness, which we lift to an online setting as part of our identification component and use as a baseline in our evaluation. Other offline approaches [12,18] segment logs by focusing on frequent execution patterns in the logs assuming that task execution is deterministic. Therefore, these approaches cannot handle cases with multiple execution variants well. Agostinelli et al. [4,5] take a supervised approach based on the computation of alignments between user interaction logs and task models that they require as input. Finally, Linn et al. [20] combine transactional data recorded by information systems with user interaction logs, to integrate interaction data with traditional process mining. Beyond user interaction events, related approaches recognize process-related tasks from ambient or wearable sensors [11,21] or network traffic data [14]. However, due to the low-level, highly abstract nature of the data used by these approaches, they depend on supervised recognition strategies, as opposed to our unsupervised approach.

Research on stream pre-processing in process mining mostly focuses on cleaning noisy event streams. Van Zelst et al. [24] filter a stream based on estimates of how likely new events belong to real process behavior, whereas Hassani et al. [16] filter noise by extracting frequent sequential patterns from an event stream before applying streaming process discovery. Finally, Awad et al. [6] propose an approach to resolve situations in which events arrive in an incorrect order on a stream. However, these techniques assume arriving events to be on the task level, even though, in practice, streaming data is commonly at a lower-level of abstraction, such as taken into account by our approach.

7   Conclusion

In this paper, we proposed an approach to recognize tasks from a stream of user interaction events in a fully unsupervised manner. To this end, our approach continuously segments the stream to identify task instances and categorizes these according to their type. The output is a stream of task-related events, to which subsequent streaming analysis techniques can subscribe. We demonstrated our approach's efficacy in an experimental evaluation on real data and showed that it outperforms two baseline approaches.

In its current form, our work has limitations that we aim to address in the future. With respect to our evaluation, we acknowledge that, although the considered data includes a variety of task types, it does not capture a user's real sequence of process-related and overhead tasks conducted during a workday. Therefore, we plan to conduct further experiments as soon as more suitable data becomes available. As for our approach, we recognize that it currently does not consider event timestamps. It has been shown that these can help make correct segmentation decisions when there are large time differences between events, though [7]. Therefore, we aim to incorporate a strategy based on time differences into our identification component. Furthermore, our approach is currently limited to task recognition, so it does not identify information about the process instance or business objects to which a task relates. In the future, we aim to tackle this by building on existing work on case correlation [13] and leveraging data values associated with events (such as identifiers of orders and customers). Finally, our approach (and other unsupervised task-recognition approaches) so far assumes that tasks are executed sequentially, i.e., one task must be completed before another one is started. In the future, we aim to loosen this assumption, by also dealing with interleaving task executions, which again largely depends on the detection of data values that allow us to infer inter-relations between non-consecutive events.

References

1. van der Aalst, W.M.P.: Process Mining: Data Science in Action. Springer, Berlin (2016). https://doi.org/10.1007/978-3-662-49851-4
2. Abb, L., Bormann, C., van der Aa, H., Rehse, J.R.: Trace clustering for user behavior mining. In: ECIS 2022 Research Papers, vol. 34 (2022)
3. Abb, L., Rehse, J.R.: A reference data model for process-related user interaction logs. In: Di Ciccio, C., Dijkman, R., del Río Ortega, A., Rinderle-Ma, S. (eds.) Business Process Management. BPM 2022. LNCS, vol. 13420, pp. 57–74. Springer, Cham (2022). https://doi.org/10.1007/978-3-031-16103-2_7
4. Agostinelli, S.: Automated segmentation of user interface logs using trace alignment techniques. In: ICPM Doctoral Consortium/Tools, pp. 13–14 (2020)
5. Agostinelli, S., Marrella, A., Mecella, M.: Automated segmentation of user interface logs. In: Robotic Process Automation, pp. 201–222. De Gruyter Oldenbourg (2021)
6. Awad, A., Weidlich, M., Sakr, S.: Process mining over unordered event streams. In: ICPM, pp. 81–88. IEEE (2020)
7. Bernard, G., Senderovich, A., Andritsos, P.: Cut to the trace! process-aware partitioning of long-running cases in customer journey logs. In: La Rosa, M., Sadiq, S., Teniente, E. (eds.) CAiSE 2021. LNCS, vol. 12751, pp. 519–535. Springer, Cham (2021). https://doi.org/10.1007/978-3-030-79382-1_31
8. Bifet, A., Gavalda, R., Holmes, G., Pfahringer, B.: Machine learning for data streams: with practical examples in MOA. MIT Press (2018)
9. Burattin, A.: Streaming process mining. In: van der Aalst, W.M.P., Carmona, J. (eds.) Process Mining Handbook. LNBIP, vol. 448, pp. 349–372. Springer, Cham (2022). https://doi.org/10.1007/978-3-031-08848-3_11
10. Cao, F., Ester, M., Qian, W., Zhou, A.: Density-based clustering over an evolving data stream with noise. In: International Conference on Data Mining, pp. 328–339. SIAM (2006)
11. Chen, L., Hoey, J., Nugent, C.D., Cook, D.J., Yu, Z.: Sensor-based activity recognition. IEEE Trans. Syst. Man Cybern. **42**(6), 790–808 (2012)

12. Dev, H., Liu, Z.: Identifying frequent user tasks from application logs. In: Proceedings of the 22nd International Conference on Intelligent User Interfaces, pp. 263–273 (2017)
13. Diba, K., Batoulis, K., Weidlich, M., Weske, M.: Extraction, correlation, and abstraction of event data for process mining. WIRES **10**(3), 1–31 (2020)
14. Engelberg, G., Hadad, M., Soffer, P.: from network traffic data to business activities: a process mining driven conceptualization. In: Augusto, A., et al. (eds.) BPMDS/EMMSAD - 2021. LNBIP, vol. 421, pp. 3–18. Springer, Cham (2021). https://doi.org/10.1007/978-3-030-79186-5_1
15. Ester, M., Kriegel, H.P., Sander, J., Xu, X.: A density-based algorithm for discovering clusters in large spatial databases with noise. In: KDD. p. 226–231. AAAI Press (1996)
16. Hassani, M., Siccha, S., Richter, F., Seidl, T.: Efficient process discovery from event streams using sequential pattern mining. In: SSCI, pp. 1366–1373. IEEE (2015)
17. IBM: Carbon Design System - Action Labels (2022). https://carbondesignsystem.com/guidelines/content/action-labels/
18. Leno, V., Augusto, A., Dumas, M., La Rosa, M., Maggi, F.M., Polyvyanyy, A.: Identifying candidate routines for robotic process automation from unsegmented UI logs. In: ICPM, pp. 153–160. IEEE (2020)
19. Leno, V., Polyvyanyy, A., Dumas, M., La Rosa, M., Maggi, F.M.: Robotic process mining: vision and challenges. Bus. Inf. Syst. Eng. **63**(3), 301–314 (2021)
20. Linn, C., Zimmermann, P., Werth, D.: Desktop activity mining-a new level of detail in mining business processes. In: Workshops der INFORMATIK 2018-Architekturen, Prozesse, Sicherheit und Nachhaltigkeit. Köllen Druck+ Verlag GmbH (2018)
21. Rebmann, A., Emrich, A., Fettke, P.: Enabling the discovery of manual processes using a multi-modal activity recognition approach. In: Di Francescomarino, C., Dijkman, R., Zdun, U. (eds.) BPM 2019. LNBIP, vol. 362, pp. 130–141. Springer, Cham (2019). https://doi.org/10.1007/978-3-030-37453-2_12
22. Rebmann, A., Pfeiffer, P., Fettke, P., van der Aa, H.: Multi-perspective identification of event groups for event abstraction. In: Montali, M., Senderovich, A., Weidlich, M. (eds.) Process Mining Workshops. ICPM 2022. LNBIP, vol. 468, pp. 31–43. Springer, Cham (2022). https://doi.org/10.1007/978-3-031-27815-0_3
23. Urabe, Y., Yagi, S., Tsuchikawa, K., Oishi, H.: Task clustering method using user interaction logs to plan RPA introduction. In: Polyvyanyy, A., Wynn, M.T., Van Looy, A., Reichert, M. (eds.) BPM 2021. LNCS, vol. 12875, pp. 273–288. Springer, Cham (2021). https://doi.org/10.1007/978-3-030-85469-0_18
24. van Zelst, S.J., Fani Sani, M., Ostovar, A., Conforti, R., La Rosa, M.: Filtering spurious events from event streams of business processes. In: Krogstie, J., Reijers, H.A. (eds.) CAiSE 2018. LNCS, vol. 10816, pp. 35–52. Springer, Cham (2018). https://doi.org/10.1007/978-3-319-91563-0_3

Revealing the Importance of Setting Parameters in Declarative Discovery Algorithms: An Evolutionary-Based Methodology

Vanessa Pradas Fernández⬤, Ángel Jesús Varela-Vaca⬤,
and María Teresa Gómez-López(✉)⬤

University of Seville, IDEA Research Group, Seville, Spain
{vpradas,ajvarela,maytegomez}@us.es
https://www.idea.us.es

Abstract. Through constraints, declarative process models represent the permitted behaviour associated with a business process, by limiting the potential correct traces. These models can be discovered by analysing an event log. However, various declarative business models can be extracted from a single event log, depending on the desirable level of metrics, such as fitness and generalisation. Existing discovery algorithms enable the type of discovered declarative process model to be customised through a set of configuration parameters. Depending on the values of these parameters, the discovered process can be of high or low quality. Unfortunately, the high number of combinatorial parameters and the high time consumption of process discovery make it impractical to conduct an exhaustive analysis of the configuration parameters to determine the most suitable declarative process model discovered. As a solution, we propose a methodology supported by an implemented framework that uses evolutionary algorithms to reduce computational complexity and to select the highest quality declarative business processes. An experiment is included to show the feasibility of our proposal.

Keywords: Process mining · Declarative process model discovery · Evolutionary algorithms

1 Introduction

Process mining [1] is a discipline aimed at creating a union between *data mining* and *business process management*. By combining model-based process analysis and data-driven analysis techniques to better understand business performance. Although this discipline encompasses three subareas (discovery, enhancement, and conformance checking), in this paper, we focus on *process discovery*. Process discovery aims to produce process models from a given event log. An event log represents the execution traces for a business process, including the timestamp of when the activities are executed. Process discovery algorithms can be orientated

© The Author(s), under exclusive license to Springer Nature Switzerland AG 2023
M. Indulska et al. (Eds.): CAiSE 2023, LNCS 13901, pp. 158–173, 2023.
https://doi.org/10.1007/978-3-031-34560-9_10

to obtain *imperative* or *declarative* models. An imperative process model explicitly describes the acceptable behaviour of the process with regard to control-flow patterns, whereas a declarative process model is used in environments of a more flexible nature where constraints limit undesirable traces. The use of declarative models takes place when the precise order of the activities remains unknown, although there are certain constraints between the different activities. Since any behaviour that is not explicitly prohibited by such constraints is assumed to be allowed, the number of possible discovered models can be vast.

Existing declarative discovery algorithms [25] take an event log and a set of configuration parameters to discover a process model. The nature of these configuration parameters varies depending on the characteristics of the algorithm employed, such as the maximum branching level for discovered constraints and the minimum confidence level threshold required to consider a discovered constraint as significant; in this respect, different settings of these parameters can discover a variety of process models that differ from each other in terms of multiple aspects (metrics), although a number thereof can optimise major quality metrics according to user requirements [5]. However, to obtain these optimal models, it is necessary to explore the entire domain space to set the configuration parameters [3]; furthermore, it is impossible to previously ascertain the characteristics of the process models generated by these parameters. Moreover, this search for the setting that produces the most suitable process models could require excessive computational resources and time.

Given this situation, we propose tackling three main research questions.

- *RQ1: How can we handle the computational complexity of exploring the entire domain space of configuration parameters for discovery algorithms?* Configuration parameters can take hundreds of thousands of possible values. It is even more difficult since the domain of the parameters can be real-valued, which would make it necessary to discretise the possible values evaluated or divide them into segments.
- *RQ2: What is/are 'the best' process model(s) discovered?* According to the configuration parameters, one or a subset thereof can be chosen as the most suitable. One process model can be better than another, for example, when one optimises the fitting or another optimises the simplicity. This means that several models can be 'the best', since multiple objectives can be taken into account.
- *RQ3: How can we face (dis)similarity in process models to select the most representative in a set?* Many of the discovered processes can be very similar, as there are numerous parameter configurations that generate small changes. It is impossible to present all of them as a solution, although they can be optimal yet slightly different.

To face these challenges, we propose the Selevminer methodology which is supported by an implemented framework that includes the following:

- Related to *RQ1*, we propose combining the discovery of the declarative process with *evolutionary algorithms* to reduce the evaluation of the setting of every configuration parameter.

- Related to *RQ2*, we include a multi-objective optimisation algorithm in order to obtain a Pareto front with the process models that optimise a set of quality metrics.
- Related to *RQ3*, we propose including clustering techniques to select the canonical representative solutions by obtaining a set of non-similar process models.

The rest of this paper is organised as follows: Sect. 2 presents the fundamentals for understanding the paper. Section 3 describes the details of the approach. Section 4 contains the experiments carried out and the analysis of the results. Section 5 analyses related work in the area. Finally, Sect. 6 summarises several conclusions and presents various lines of research.

2   Preliminaries

Declarative processes describe permissible and prohibited actions in a business process. Declarative models enable the specification of *what* is to be performed in a business process, instead of *how* it must be performed [17]. These are described by a set of activities and constraints between them, for example, "Activity B cannot be executed before activity A", and "if A is executed, B must be executed later". This example supports various traces where A and/or B can or cannot be executed. An example of a declarative process model is given in Fig. 1. There are multiple examples of constraints in the figure, e.g., the precedence between *order* and *accepted* activities, or the cardinality '0..1' on *accepted* that indicates that it can execute at most once. Derived from the flexibility of declarative models, various models can represent the same trace of events.

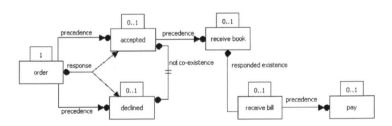

Fig. 1. A book-purchase process modelled in Declare [18].

From a process modelling perspective, imperative models should be completely known and specified at design time, since they explicitly represent the allowed sequences of activities. However, declarative models describe which orders of activities are permitted in an open-world assumption (everything that is not explicitly specified is permitted). For example, if activity A is executed, activity B has to be executed afterwards, and, as long as this rule is satisfied, any behaviour is allowed. Several languages are proposed in the literature to describe declarative processes, such as the Compliance Rule Graph [10], EM-BrA2CE [8], Declare [19].

In an equivalent way to which Process Mining techniques are defined for imperative models, they can be used for declarative models [1]. Stated earlier, our focus is on process discovery, a paradigm that aims to create a process model through the analysis of event logs, but that has to date focused mainly on imperative process models [1].

Declarative process discovery [13, 25] has also been consolidated as a mature discipline in the Process Mining arena. In this respect, there exist a plethora of techniques, approaches, and tools in the literature, such as Declare Miner [12], MINERful [4], HeuristicMiner [15], ILP Miner [9], AGNEsMiner [7], DisCoveR [2], and DeciClareMiner [16].

Depending on the algorithm used and the parameters settings, a variety of process models can be discovered, which can be measured using quality metrics. Typical measurements related to control flow include those of simplicity, fitness, precision, and generalisation, although several metrics can also be extracted, such as density, cyclic number, coefficient of connectivity, and control flow complexity [20] by conducting the possible process discovery algorithms.

3 Selevminer: An Evolutionary-Based Methodology to Discover Optimal Declarative Process Models

We present Selevminer as a methodology for discovering optimal declarative processes that evaluate the possible configuration parameters used in the discovering algorithms. Optimisation is based on a multi-objective function that integrates a set of quality metrics of the discovered processes. The Selevminer workflow (shown in Fig. 2) is aligned with the three research queries presented: discover various declarative processes to configure the input parameters; extract the optimal solution based on a multi-objective solution; and apply clustering techniques to ascertain the representative solutions from among all the potential solutions. This methodology combines a multi-objective optimisation algorithm (in particular, evolutionary algorithms), a declarative process discovery algorithm, a clustering algorithm, and a selection algorithm. Furthermore, to support this methodology, we provide a framework developed for the community at https:// doi.org/10.5281/zenodo.7730789.

In the following, each research query is related to Selevminer's task devoted to it's solution.

1. **Discover and Measure models:** Given an event log and the set of configuration parameters that are used as input in the discovery algorithms, this task performs a discovery algorithm to obtain a declarative process model based on the configuration parameters. The discovered model must be measured in terms of a set of quality metrics defined by a user in order to ascertain where a discovered process is better or worse than another. This task is crucial for the handling of *RQ1 and RQ2* concerning the models discovered and for the assessment of their quality.

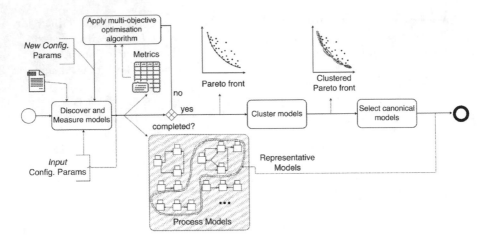

Fig. 2. Selevminer workflow overview.

2. **Apply multi-objective optimisation algorithm:** This task aims to solve *RQ1*, by considerably minimising the computational complexity of the search for the configuration parameter. In order to obviate the need for the analysis of every possible configuration parameter, we propose the use of an algorithm based on a local search instead of on an exhaustive search. In this case, an evolutionary algorithm is employed that infers another setting for the configuration parameters to optimise the quality metrics during the search. This is performed as many times as the number of generations established for the evolutionary algorithm. This task answers *RQ2* by generating a Pareto front of "optimal" models based on the set of quality metrics.

3. **Cluster models:** This task applies a clustering technique to the process models that belong to Pareto front solutions, to reduce the number of similar solutions obtained in response to *RQ3*. In this way, similar redundant results are avoided and a set of models that can be assumed by a user is obtained.

4. **Select canonical models:** Since the ultimate goal of Selevminer is to obtain a set of models, a canonical model from each cluster is selected and returned as a result. This task strives to respond to *RQ3*.

3.1   Discovering and Measuring Declarative Process Models

A fundamental aspect of any discovery approach is the event log used. An event log can be seen as a collection of cases, where a case is a sequence of events. Any event can contain multiple attributes, such as the identifier of the activity that produces it and the timestamp when the event occurred. Different processes can be discovered even when utilising the same event log and the same discovery algorithm, depending on the configuration parameters employed. In general, a set of configuration parameters $\{p_0, p_1, \ldots, p_n\}$ is used as input to a discovery algorithm to customise the features of the obtained business process.

These parameters are usually Float, Integer (that can be bounded), and Boolean values.

There are various algorithms for discovering declarative business processes, such as Declare Miner [14] and UnconstrainedMiner [30]. In Selevminer, we incorporate MINERful [4] because, based on the analysis performed in [4], its performance scales better than other proposals with respect to the number of traces, the length of traces, and the number of activities of the process. In addition, MINERful includes various configuration parameters. We may consider the maximum branching level for discovered constraints, the minimum confidence level threshold required to consider a discovered constraint significant, the hiding of redundant or inconsistent constraints, and the minimum interest factor threshold required for a discovered constraint to be considered significant.

Once the discovery process is complete and the process models are obtained, a set of quality metrics is measured, that is, $\{q_1, \ldots, q_m\}$. A wide range of metrics can be found in the literature [21], such as the number of states, transitions, and constraints. Slightly more advanced metrics include the coefficient of connectivity, the ratio of states to transitions, and the cyclomatic complexity. More robust in nature are the dimensions of process mining, that is, precision, fitness, simplicity, and generalisation. It should be borne in mind to note that the desired value of each metric can be maximised or minimised, depending on the case.

3.2 Apply Multi-objective Optimisation Algorithms

The use of several metrics to evaluate the discovered declarative process calls for the definition of a multi-objective function for the optimisation. From our point of view, no metric is more important than another, and hence no special weights have been associated with each partial objective. However, as explained above, the metrics could be maximised or minimised. In a multi-objective optimisation where not all objectives can be optimised at the same time, the Pareto optimal solutions are usually employed. The well-known Pareto front describes a set of solutions as the best according to a multi-objective function if no solution improves in any of the objectives without degrading at least one of the others.

Whenever there are n functions the so-called **Pareto front**, f_i, must be found, which is a set containing all the solutions to the optimisation problems given by any function. In our approach, the discovery algorithm is performed iteratively until the best possible result is obtained for the quality metrics, by changing the setting of the configuration parameter values in each execution. When the latter has been achieved, the Pareto front is generated from the values they provide.

In order to obviate the need to study every possible combination of the configuration parameters, which can imply an untractable problem, we propose the use of a local search algorithm. There is a wide range of local search algorithms, such as Simulated Annealing, Local Beam Search, Genetic, and Hill-climbing Search [26]. In our solution, genetic algorithms are applied because this is a mature area used in several scenarios. Furthermore, the similarity between the set of metrics to be improved and the chromosomes used has made it easier to develop. In particular, we have used the evolutionary algorithm of NSGA-II [6], which is an extended algorithm utilised to solve multi-objective optimisation problems by finding multiple Pareto solutions. Selevminer works on populations of numerical chromosomes of size n, where n is the number of configuration parameters used as input in the MINERful discovery algorithm. These chromosomes use this discovery algorithm when calculating fitness, which is the m different quality metrics predefined by the user before execution. With respect to these metrics, it is important to note that they depend on the output used (finite-state machines, in the case of MINERful).

Therefore, given quality metrics $\{q_1, \ldots, q_m\}$, the *fitness* of a chromosome c would be calculated as the tuple $(c, \{q_1, q_2, \ldots, q_m\})$. All these quality metrics, some of which may be opposed to each other, are those that the algorithm strives to optimise over the generations specified as input variables. For the current implementation, declarative process models have been analysed in the form of declarative finite state machines where activities, constraints and cardinalities are mapped to states, transitions and guards[1] respectively. Then, the quality metrics are related to the number of states, the ratio of states to transitions, the cyclomatic complexity, and the number of transition guards (i.e., choice conditions to split or join paths between states). The objective is to minimise all of these metrics.

The output of this multi-objective optimisation algorithm is an approximation of the Pareto front for the given metrics with as many points as the number of elements in the population. Normally, this final number of elements should be and is too large to deal with manually, since evolutionary algorithms require a large population to converge quickly. Our approach proposes solving it by using clustering techniques, as explained in the following section.

3.3   Cluster Models

Different configuration parameters can discover very similar declarative process models, where some parameters optimise certain metrics but not others. The number of solutions obtained as a Pareto front is often too large for a human to analyse. Additionally, the process models obtained can be very similar and can hinder the subsequent analysis carried out by the expert. For this reason, we propose the creation of clusters with the found solutions, where each cluster gathers similar declarative models. We propose the selection of one model of each cluster as a representative thereof. Cluster analysis measures the similarity between elements, by creating clusters with those that have similar characteristics. To this end, a clustering algorithm has been proposed to reduce the number of optimal discovered models returned.

All clustering techniques require a distance metric between the elements that make up the clusters; our approach proposes using a metric based on *Manhattan Distance* between the quality metrics of the models. Other distance metrics could be used if necessary, but this is the most efficient and the easiest to interpret.

---

[1] Conditions allow transitions to occur only under specific circumstances.

The algorithm that has been employed to apply clustering in Selevminer is *Single-Linkage Agglomerative Clustering*: a hierarchical clustering technique of extended use. This is a computationally efficient algorithm that can be applied to large datasets. It starts with one cluster for each of the elements and gradually merges the clusters using a distance metric between them. Thus, it only needs the calculation of the distance between the two closest objects or clusters at each step, which can be very efficient. The two clusters closest to each other are unified in each iteration until the desired number of clusters is found. This raises the question of which particular algorithm has been employed to define the distance between clusters in process models, since there are several alternatives. In that case, the selected algorithm is the average distance between all the elements of the first cluster (cl_1) and all the elements of the second cluster (cl_2).

$$\text{clusterdist}(cl_1, cl_2) = \frac{1}{|cl_1| \cdot |cl_2|} \cdot \sum_{a \in cl_1} \sum_{b \in cl_2} dist(a, b) \tag{1}$$

3.4   Selection of Canonical Models

The obtained clusters can include a high number of declarative models, which can be very similar. To tackle this issue, a selection algorithm is proposed that consists of selecting one element from each cluster to return, under the assumption that this element subsumes all the others in the cluster. Therefore, this element can be understood as representative canonical process model.

In our approach, assumptions cannot be made regarding the structure of the data, since these could be incorrect; therefore, the approach currently implemented in Selevminer would be *random selection*. Based on the heuristic that the clustering algorithm uses, this is responsible for grouping the most similar models according to their metrics.

4   Experimentation

In this section, we intend to demonstrate the feasibility of our implementation of the Selevminer methodology. To this end, an exhaustive analysis of the configuration parameters was conducted to compare our solution, by using various event logs from the literature.

4.1   Experimental Settings

Since there is more than one metric to optimise in the discovered processes, various processes can be chosen as the most feasible. For this reason, we propose the Pareto front as a reference to manage optimisation with multiple objectives. More similar to the exhaustive solutions are those found with Selevminer, better than our solution. To obtain every best solution: (1) every possible process model has been discovered for all combinations for the five configuration parameters by using MINERful; and (2) the optimal front (with non-dominated solutions) has been chosen, which are the set of the discovered models with the optimised metric.

Note that the optimal front obtained exhaustively does not necessarily correspond to the Pareto front of the possible models, since the granularity of the partitions in which Float parameters are discretised, the timeout, and the computational power of the systems used may cause certain models not to be discovered. However, it should be noted that the non-dominated solutions would correspond to the current Pareto front, in the case where all possible models in the event log are discovered. This cannot be assured in any simple way, and hence partitions are as small as possible, without excessively compromising performance.

Once this front is obtained, several Selevminer executions are performed with different numbers of configurations as population, to compare their discovered models with the optimal solutions obtained by the exhaustive solution. This answers the question of whether this new approach is capable of generating satisfactory results in a significantly shorter time.

The following MINERful parameters have been set in the implementation of the exhaustive discovery: (MBL) the maximum branching level for discovered constraints; (MCL) the minimum confidence level threshold required for a discovered constraint to be considered as meaningful; (HRIC) the hiding of redundant or inconsistent constraints; (MIF) the minimum interest factor threshold required for a discovered constraint to be considered as meaningful; and (MST) the minimum support threshold required for a discovered constraint to be considered as meaningful. For each of these parameters, a partition has been made according to their nature and the range of values that they allow, in the order in which they appear in Table 1a. Given these, the total possible combinations to set the parameters are calculated from the resulting fragments as $3 \cdot 21 \cdot 2 \cdot 21 \cdot 21$, resulting in $55,566$ possible discovered processes.

Both the exhaustive discovery and the Selevminer have been evaluated on a system with an Intel Xeon at 2.6GHz (4 cores), 8GB of RAM, and a 256GB SSD disk. By running both tests on the same server, we ensure that time and computation capacity bias are eliminated. Furthermore, the event logs used to run the tests, which are provided by the Business Process Intelligence Challenges, are listed in Table 1b. In this table, it can be observed that datasets of different sizes are employed to assess how discovery time is affected.

Once the exhaustive Pareto fronts and the different Selevminer solutions have been extracted, the Averaged Hausdorff Distance (AHD) [24] is employed to check how close are the two solutions are in terms of the Manhattan distance. The result of this metric determines the effectiveness of Selevminer in converging to the optimal front provided by the exhaustive algorithm. Furthermore, the *Minimum Pairwise Distance* (MPD) is utilised to measure the dissimilarity between the models returned after clustering. The higher the value of this metric, the more separated the models are.

Table 1. Discovery algorithm resources.

Parameter	Type	Domain	Partitions
MBL	Integer	[1 − 3]	2
MCL	Float	[0 − 1]	20
HRIC	Boolean	{true,false}	1
MIF	Float	[0 − 1]	20
MST	Float	[0 − 1]	20

(a) Configuration Parameters.

Name	Year	Traces	Cases	Size
Financial[1]	2012	13,087	262,200	70.6MB
Incidents[2]	2013	7,554	65,533	37.7MB
Open[3]	2013	819	2,871	1.37MB
Closed[4]	2013	1,487	6,660	4.1MB

(b) Event Logs.

[1] doi:10.4121/uuid:3926db30-f712-4394-aebc-75976070e91f
[2] doi:10.4121/500573e6-accc-4b0c-9576-aa5468b10cee
[3] doi:10.4121/3537c19d-6c64-4b1d-815d-915ab0e479da
[4] doi:10.4121/c2c3b154-ab26-4b31-a0e8-8f2350ddac11

4.2 Results of the Experimentation

The exhaustive algorithm has been executed with all event logs described in Table 1b to obtain the optimal reference fronts. The detailed results of each of these executions are given in Table 2. Both the elapsed time and the number of models returned by each execution are shown here. It can be observed that as the size of the dataset (number of traces and cases) increases, so does the execution time. To perform the discovery with both algorithms (exhaustive and Selevminer), the discovery process timeout has been set to 20 s, since this is high enough to perform the model search but low enough not to exceed it when searching with the full parametric configuration. Furthermore, the number of generations has been set to 10 in Selevminer as the standard value and the population to three executions with sizes 100, 200, and the number of non-dominated models returned by the exhaustive algorithm. The "Opt. models" column represents the number of models returned by Selevminer that coincide with one of the models returned by the exhaustive execution. Finally, note that the number of models requested for Selevminer to provide is the same as the number of models in its corresponding exhaustive Pareto front.

Regarding the three executions for each event log in Selevminer, Table 2 shows the number of optimal models discovered and the time taken. In relation to the exhaustive solution, it can be observed by contrasting the time that, as the size of the data increases, so does the time. Most important is the difference between the time taken by the exhaustive solution to find the optimal front and the time taken by Selevminer for each of the four datasets.

Once all these executions have been carried out, it is necessary to compare the Pareto fronts obtained by Selevminer with the optimal fronts of the exhaustive solution. In all the analysed event logs, it can be observed that many models obtained by Selevminer seem to correspond to optimal models in the front generated by the exhaustive algorithm. Since Selevminer does not execute an exhaustive solution, it is expected that the models obtained in the Pareto Front are less than those obtained in an exhaustive way. Depending on the case, the obtained models can differ. The best examples are 'Incident' and 'Open', where

Table 2. Comparison of performance measures between Selevminer and an exhaustive algorithm.

Event Log	Exhaustive		Selevminer			
	Models in P. Front	Time	Population	Models in P. Front	Opt. models	Time
Financial	35	375 h 30 m	35	9	8	3 h 26 m
			100	22	13	7 h 10 m
			200	20	9	8 h 48 m
Incidents	12	35 h 49 m	12	6	3	5 m
			100	11	7	49 m
			200	9	4	1 h 39 m
Open	14	4 h 59 m	14	6	5	40 s
			100	8	6	4 m
			200	9	7	9 m
Closed	10	8 h 22 m	10	4	0	54 s
			100	8	4	8 m
			200	6	3	16 m

58% and 50% of the optimal solutions are found, respectively. In contrast, with 10 elements of the population, no solutions have been found for the 'Closed' example. In the case of 'Financial', since the number of optimal models is high, Selevminer provides only 37% of the optimal solutions. For more details, we provide full information on the results at the following link https://doi.org/10.5281/zenodo.7730789.

For an in-depth comparison of these executions, the results given in Table 3 are provided. In this table, several metrics are computed to analyse our approach quantitatively. First, *Averaged Hausdorff Distance* (AHD) is utilised to obtain the similarity between the exhaustive and evolutionary solutions. Since each of the metrics is *min-max normalised* (in the range $[0, 1]$), it should be borne in mind that the maximum value for this metric is 5. This is also the maximum value for *Manhattan distance*, which is used internally to calculate AHD. This metric is primarily employed to check the effectiveness of the Selevminer optimisation step.

Table 3 presents a summary of the results obtained by executing Selevminer with different population settings and exhaustive models. The columns "O - E", "E - O", "C - E", and "E - C" represent the non-symmetric distance from the different combinations of the exhaustive models (E), optimised models with Selevminer (O), and the clustered models for Selevminer or Exhaustive (C). *Averaged Hausdorff Distance* (AHD) is defined as the maximum value of the two corresponding reciprocals. These and *Minimum Pairwise Distance* (MPD) are measured before and after applying clustering to analyse the evolution of these metrics.

Table 3. Summary of the comparative of the results

Log	Population	Before clustering				After clustering			
		O - E	E - O	AHD	MPD	C - E	E - C	AHD	MPD
Financial	35	0.0023	0.5945	0.5945	0.00017	-	-	-	-
	100	0.0495	0.2135	0.2135	0.00016	0.0679	0.2820	0.2820	0.0298
	200	0.019	0.0565	0.0565	0.00026	0.0190	0.0961	0.0961	0.0163
	Exhaustive	-	-	-	0.00016	-	0.1040	0.1040	0.0237
Incidents	12	0.1295	0.2915	0.2915	0.2469	-	-	-	-
	100	0.077	0.09	0.09	0.0381	0.075	0.1423	0.1423	0.2023
	200	0.069	0.3525	0.35	0.0316	0.0927	0.3757	0.3757	0.0381
	Exhaustive	-	-	-	0.1671	-	0.0917	0.0917	0.1671
Open	14	0.0648	0.4465	0.4465	0.2562	-	-	-	-
	100	0.1155	0.2585	0.2585	0.2562	0.1155	0.3180	0.3180	0.2562
	200	0.1025	0.2425	0.2425	0.2217	0.1027	0.3022	0.3022	0.2217
	Exhaustive	-	-	-	0.0776	-	0.1608	0.1608	0.8270
Closed	10	0.6485	0.7575	0.7575	0.02587	-	-	-	-
	100	0.417	0.1665	0.4117	0.2557	1.6763	0.4138	1.6763	0.2557
	200	0.4565	0.3155	0.4565	0.4067	0.5238	0.5710	0.5710	0.4066
	Exhaustive	-	-	-	0.1252	-	0.0679	0.0679	0.1752

It is important to note that clustering will seek as many models for the 100 and 200 population Selevminer runs and for Exhaustive as optimal models are found in the lower population that Selevminer runs. This step is performed 50 times for each run and the results obtained are averaged. Due to the fact that the selection algorithm applied is random, we cannot determine the result obtained by a single run.

As can be observed, in general, the values for the AHD metric are low[2] with regard to the near-perfect solutions for the Financial log. In contrast, the closed problem log yields worse results due to its low model count. In most cases, when AHD has a high value, it is because Selevminer returned fewer models than the exhaustive algorithm, although these models tend to be highly optimised. This is represented by a low value in the "O - E" or "C - E" columns and a high value in the "E - O" or "E - C" columns. In certain cases, the two values are similar and close to 0, such as in the financial event log for a population size of 200. In general, the results given by Selevminer appear to be close to the optimal results given by the exhaustive algorithm, with a considerably lower order of magnityde regarding time.

This also confirms the data shown in Table 2, where it can be observed that Selevminer almost always returns some models that also appear in the exhaustive Pareto front. This means that the convergence of the Selevminer is good and that many optimal solutions can be feasibly obtained without using exhaustive approaches.

---

[2] The value of AHD lies within the range of 0 to 5, whereby a lower value indicates a better result.

Regarding the clustering and selection, since their main objective is to create dissimilarity in the final result, we use *Minimum Pairwise Distance* (MPD) to quantify the separation of the models in the solutions. As expected, the results for MPD are much higher subsequent to the clustering step. In certain cases, the values for this metric go higher for Selevminer solutions than for their corresponding clustered exhaustive models, probably because the dominated models provide better conditions for the clustering algorithms. In general, it appears that the clustering and selection steps successfully manage to increase the separation of the results without excessively compromising their precision.

Finally, a visualisation of the different fronts is provided by the Financial and Incident logs using *Principal Component Analysis* (PCA) [28] of the model metrics in Fig. 3. These visualisations can be employed to perceive the apparent overlap of the Pareto fronts returned by Selevminer and those returned by the exhaustive algorithm. It should be borne in mind that this reduction in dimension skipped 3 dimensions from our metric space, which has 5 dimensions. Figure 3 shows the relation between the solutions found by Selevminer and that obtained with the exhaustive solution. When the red, green, or orange symbols are above the blue square, it means that the solution is one of those found by the exhaustive solution. When these symbols are not above the blue symbols, then it means that the solutions found by Selevminer do not belong to the optimal declarative models.

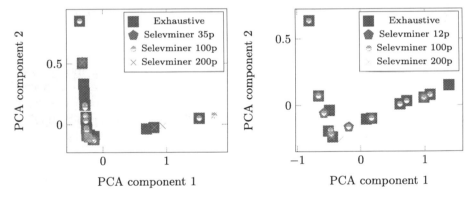

Fig. 3. *PCA* visualisation of Selevminer executions and the exhaustive algorithm for Financial and Incident logs, respectively.

5   Related Work

Most approaches to improving process discovery focus on techniques to recommend or select the best discovery algorithm for particular event data [23, 27] to achieve the highest quality process model in terms of fitness, generalisation, precision, etc. However, these approaches are related to imperative process discovery techniques. Furthermore, setting parameters for discovery algorithms is a challenging problem [5]. Ribero et al. [23] state that "the selection of parameters for discovery algorithms is considered one of the most challenging issues . . ."

Several approaches exist that analyse the impact of setting parameters on discovery algorithms [3,11,22,29]. In [3], the authors demonstrate that it is unfeasible to tackle the domains of real values of the parameters and propose utilising the discretisation of parameters to reduce the domain space. In [11], the authors present an evaluation framework that includes mechanisms to optimise the setting of parameters in the discovery algorithms, whereas the optimisation of the setting parameters is based on k-fold cross-validation. In [22], the authors use sensitive analysis techniques to assess the impact of parameters on discovery algorithms. In [29], an optimisation framework is proposed for the evaluation of the process discovery algorithms in their best parameter settings. However, all of these approaches have been developed for imperative-oriented process discovery algorithms.

To the best of our knowledge, no work can be found in the literature that addresses the problem of assessing the impact of configuration parameters in declarative discovery algorithms.

6   Conclusion

This paper proposes a framework to determine the configuration parameters to discover the most suitable Declarative Process Models based on a set of quality metrics. To achieve this objective, we propose three actions: (i) the use of an evolutionary algorithm to reduce the complexity of the problem; (ii) the application of a multi-objective algorithm to integrate the optimisation of the various metrics; and (iii) the application of clustering techniques to withdraw equivalent declarative models as a solution. To evaluate the suitability of our proposal, we have compared it with the exhaustive solution, and have included a multi-objective function using AHD to measure the feasibility, and MPD to measure the diversity of the clusters. From this analysis, we can conclude that our solution drastically reduces computational time, and obtains solutions close to the optimal results.

As future lines of research, we plan to extend the design of a more general framework that enables the type of algorithm to be composed for the selection the configuration parameter, the multi-objective algorithm, and the clustering techniques. Moreover, this paper can be extended by including more logs in the experiments.

Acknowledgement. This work has been funded by the following projects: AETHER-US (PID2020-112540RB-C44), ALBA-US (TED2021-130355B-C32) AEI/10.13039/501100011033/Unión Europea NextGenerationEU/PRTR, METAMORFOSIS (US-1381375), and COPERNICA (P20-01224).

References

1. van der Aalst, W.M.P.: Foundations of process discovery. In: van der Aalst, W.M.P., Carmona, J. (eds.) Process Mining Handbook, LNBIP, vol. 448, pp. 37–75. Springer, Cham (2022). https://doi.org/10.1007/978-3-031-08848-3_2
2. Back, C.O., Slaats, T., Hildebrandt, T.T., Marquard, M.: Discover: accurate and efficient discovery of declarative process models. Int. J. Softw. Tools Technol. Transf. **24**(4), 563–587 (2022)
3. Burattin, A., Sperduti, A.: Automatic determination of parameters' values for heuristics miner++. In: IEEE Congress on Evolutionary Computation, pp. 1–8. IEEE (2010)
4. Ciccio, C.D., Mecella, M.: On the discovery of declarative control flows for artful processes. ACM Trans. Manage. Inf. Syst. **5**(4) (2015)
5. De Weerdt, J., De Backer, M., Vanthienen, J., Baesens, B.: A multi-dimensional quality assessment of state-of-the-art process discovery algorithms using real-life event logs. Inf. Syst. **37**(7), 654–676 (2012)
6. Durillo, J.J., Nebro, A.J.: Jmetal: a java framework for multi-objective optimization. Adv. Eng. Softw. **42**(10), 760–771 (2011)
7. Goedertier, S., Martens, D., Vanthienen, J., Baesens, B.: Robust process discovery with artificial negative events. J. Mach. Learn. Res. **10**, 1305–1340 (2009)
8. Goedertier, S., Vanthienen, J.: Declarative process modeling with business vocabulary and business rules. In: Meersman, R., Tari, Z., Herrero, P. (eds.) OTM 2007. LNCS, vol. 4805, pp. 603–612. Springer, Heidelberg (2007). https://doi.org/10.1007/978-3-540-76888-3_83
9. Ponce-de León, H., Carmona, J., vanden Broucke, S.K.L.M.: Incorporating negative information in process discovery. In: Motahari-Nezhad, H.R., Recker, J., Weidlich, M. (eds.) Business Process Management, pp. 126–143. Springer International Publishing, Cham (2015)
10. Ly, L.T., Rinderle-Ma, S., Knuplesch, D., Dadam, P.: Monitoring business process compliance using compliance rule graphs. In: Meersman, R., et al. (eds.) OTM 2011. LNCS, vol. 7044, pp. 82–99. Springer, Heidelberg (2011). https://doi.org/10.1007/978-3-642-25109-2_7
11. Ma, L.: How to evaluate the performance of process discovery algorithms. Ph.D. thesis, Master thesis, Eindhoven University of Technology, Netherlands (2012)
12. Maggi, F.M., Bose, R.P.J.C., van der Aalst, W.M.P.: A knowledge-based integrated approach for discovering and repairing declare maps. In: Salinesi, C., Norrie, M.C., Pastor, Ó. (eds.) CAiSE 2013. LNCS, vol. 7908, pp. 433–448. Springer, Heidelberg (2013). https://doi.org/10.1007/978-3-642-38709-8_28
13. Montali, M.: Declarative process mining. In: Specification and Verification of Declarative Open Interaction Models. LNBIP, vol. 56, pp. 343–365. Springer, Heidelberg (2010). https://doi.org/10.1007/978-3-642-14538-4_15
14. Maggi, F.M., Bose, R.P.J.C., van der Aalst, W.M.P.: Efficient discovery of understandable declarative process models from event logs. In: Ralyté, J., Franch, X., Brinkkemper, S., Wrycza, S. (eds.) CAiSE 2012. LNCS, vol. 7328, pp. 270–285. Springer, Heidelberg (2012). https://doi.org/10.1007/978-3-642-31095-9_18
15. Mannhardt, F., de Leoni, M., Reijers, H.A., van der Aalst, W.M.P.: Data-driven process discovery - revealing conditional infrequent behavior from event logs. In: Dubois, E., Pohl, K. (eds.) Advanced Information Systems Engineering, pp. 545–560. Springer International Publishing, Cham (2017). https://doi.org/10.1007/978-3-319-59536-8_34

16. Mertens, S., Gailly, F., Van Sassenbroeck, D., Poels, G.: Integrated declarative process and decision discovery of the emergency care process. Inf. Syst. Front. **24**(1), 305–327 (2022)
17. Parody, L., Gomez-Lopez, M.T., Gasca, R.M.: Hybrid business process modeling for the optimization of outcome data. Inf. Softw. Technol. **70**, 140–154 (2016)
18. Pesic, M., van der Aalst, W.M.P.: A declarative approach for flexible business processes management. In: Eder, J., Dustdar, S. (eds.) Business Process Management Workshops, pp. 169–180. Springer, Heidelberg (2006). https://doi.org/10. 1007/11837862_18
19. Pesic, M., Schonenberg, H., van der Aalst, W.M.P.: Declarative workflow. In: ter Hofstede, A.H.M., van der Aalst, W.M.P., Adams, M., Russell, N. (eds.) Modern Business Process Automation - YAWL and its Support Environment, pp. 175–201. Springer, Heidelberg (2010). https://doi.org/10.1007/978-3-642-03121-2_6
20. Ramos-Gutiérrez, B., Varela-Vaca, Á.J., Galindo, J.A., Gómez-López, M.T., Benavides, D.: Discovering configuration workflows from existing logs using process mining. Empir. Softw. Eng. **26**(1), 1–41 (2021). https://doi.org/10.1007/s10664-020-09911-x
21. Ramos-Gutiérrez, B., Varela-Vaca, Á.J., Ortega, F.J., Gómez-López, M.T., Wynn, M.T.: A NLP-oriented methodology to enhance event log quality. In: Augusto, A., Gill, A., Nurcan, S., Reinhartz-Berger, I., Schmidt, R., Zdravkovic, J. (eds.) BPMDS/EMMSAD -2021. LNBIP, vol. 421, pp. 19–35. Springer, Cham (2021). https://doi.org/10.1007/978-3-030-79186-5_2
22. Ribeiro, J., Carmona, J.: A method for assessing parameter impact on control-flow discovery algorithms. In: Koutny, M., Désel, J., Kleijn, J. (eds.) Transactions on Petri Nets and Other Models of Concurrency XI. LNCS, vol. 9930, pp. 181–202. Springer, Heidelberg (2016). https://doi.org/10.1007/978-3-662-53401-4_9
23. Ribeiro, J., Carmona, J., Mısır, M., Sebag, M.: A recommender system for process discovery. In: Sadiq, S., Soffer, P., Völzer, H. (eds.) Business Process Management, pp. 67–83. Springer International Publishing, Cham (2014). https://doi.org/10. 1007/978-3-319-10172-9_5
24. Schutze, O., Esquivel, X., Lara, A., Coello, C.A.C.: Using the averaged Hausdorff distance as a performance measure in evolutionary multiobjective optimization. IEEE Trans. Evol. Comput. **16**(4), 504–522 (2012)
25. Slaats, T.: Declarative and hybrid process discovery: recent advances and open challenges. J. Data Semant. **9**(1), 3–20 (2020)
26. Stützle, T.: Local search algorithms for combinatorial problems - analysis, improvements, and new applications. Ph.D. thesis, Darmstadt University of Technology, Germany (1999)
27. Tavares, G.M., Junior, S.B., Damiani, E.: Automating process discovery through meta-learning. In: Sellami, M., Ceravolo, P., Reijers, H.A., Gaaloul, W., Panetto, H. (eds.) Cooperative Information Systems, pp. 205–222. Springer International Publishing, Cham (2022). https://doi.org/10.1007/978-3-031-17834-4_12
28. Tipping, M.E., Bishop, C.M.: Mixtures of probabilistic principal component analyzers. Neural Compu. **11**(2), 443–482 (1999)
29. Weijters, A.: An optimization framework for process discovery algorithms. In: Proceedings of the International Conference on Data Mining, Las Vegas, Nevada, USA (2011)
30. Westergaard, M., Stahl, C.: Leveraging super-scalarity and parallelism to provide fast declare mining without restrictions. In: Fauvet, M., van Dongen, B.F. (eds.) Proceedings of the BPM Demo sessions 2013, Beijing, China, 26–30 August 2013. CEUR Workshop Proceedings, vol. 1021. CEUR-WS.org (2013)

Why Am I Waiting? Data-Driven Analysis of Waiting Times in Business Processes

Katsiaryna Lashkevich⬤, Fredrik Milani⬤, David Chapela-Campa⬤,
Ihar Suvorau⬤, and Marlon Dumas(✉)⬤

University of Tartu, Tartu, Estonia
{katsiaryna.lashkevich,fredrik.milani,david.chapela-campa,
ihar.suvorau,marlon.dumas}@ut.ee

Abstract. Waiting times in a business process often arise when a case transitions from one activity to another. Accordingly, analyzing the causes of waiting times of activity transitions can help analysts to identify opportunities for reducing the cycle time of a process. This paper proposes a process mining approach to decompose the waiting time observed in each activity transition into multiple direct causes and to analyze the impact of each identified cause on the cycle time efficiency of the process. An empirical evaluation shows that the proposed approach is able to discover different direct causes of waiting times. The applicability of the proposed approach is demonstrated in a real-life process.

Keywords: Process mining · Waiting time · Cycle time efficiency

1 Introduction

Waiting time is a common source of waste in business processes [6]. Although it is impractical to completely eliminate waiting times in business processes, there are various approaches to reduce them [11]. Waiting times typically arise during transitions between activities, i.e. when the execution of a case moves from one activity to another. There are different reasons why waiting times occur during activity transitions. For instance, when two consecutive activities in a case are executed by different resources (a.k.a. a handoff [22]), the processing of the case is put on hold until the next resource becomes available to execute it. In this scenario, the cause of the waiting time is resource contention, i.e. a resource is not available to execute an activity instance because they are busy executing other activity instances [7]. Waiting times may also be caused by data exchanges [17], coordination issues [18], or synchronization points [18].

Process mining techniques allow us to analyze data generated by business process executions, a.k.a. *event logs*, to unveil performance and conformance issues, and associated improvement opportunities [1]. In particular, process mining techniques support the discovery of sources of waste, including waiting times [1]. However, while existing process mining techniques enable analysts to visualize

Work funded by the European Research Council (PIX Project).

M. Indulska et al. (Eds.): CAiSE 2023, LNCS 13901, pp. 174–190, 2023.
https://doi.org/10.1007/978-3-031-34560-9_11

activity transitions with high waiting time (i.e. bottlenecks), they provide limited support for identifying the causes of waiting times and how to reduce them.

To tackle this gap, this paper addresses the following research questions: (RQ1) *"What causes of waiting times between pairs of activity instances can be identified from event logs?"*, (RQ2) *"How can these causes of waiting time be identified from event logs?"*, and (RQ3) *"How can improvement opportunities, expressed as inefficiencies due to waiting times, be identified from event logs?"*

The contribution of the paper is two-fold. First, we conceptualize the causes of waiting time arising from activity transitions. Second, we propose a process mining approach to (1) discover waiting times associated with activity transitions; (2) identify their causes; and (3) analyze their impact w.r.t. a well-known measure of temporal efficiency called Cycle Time Efficiency (CTE): the ratio of processing time to cycle time in a process [7].

The proposed approach has been implemented as a software tool and empirically evaluated to verify its ability to discover different causes of waiting time using synthetic event logs. In addition, the applicability of the approach has been tested by applying it to a real-life event log.

The rest of the paper is structured as follows. Section 2 introduces background and related work. Section 3 presents the proposed approach. Section 4 describes the empirical evaluation, and Sect. 5 concludes the paper.

2   Background and Related Work

In this section, we introduce relevant conceptual foundations and notations from the fields of business process management and process mining, and position our contribution w.r.t. existing approaches to discover and analyze waiting times.

2.1   Business Processes and Temporal Performance Measures

A business process is a collection of events, activities, and decisions that lead from a customer need to an outcome that is of value to this customer [7]. Each execution of a business process is called a *case*. A common measure of temporal performance of a business process is its *cycle time*: the time between the moment a case of the process starts, and the case ends, aggregated to the level of the set of cases of a process observed during a period of time. The cycle time of a process consists of *processing time* (the time during which a case is being processed) and *waiting time* (the time when a case waits to be processed) [7].

Waiting time may be caused by resource contention, i.e. no suitable resource is available to execute an activity instance [11]. Other causes of waiting time include: synchronization between resources within a process [18] or across multiple processes [7], coordination between resources executing different activities [18], data transfer [7], batching [12], handoffs [18], and external inputs [2].

The temporal efficiency of a process can be measured by its CTE: the ratio of processing time to cycle time. When CTE is close to 1, there is relatively little waiting time. Conversely, if the CTE is close to 0, the waiting times are longer relative to processing times and there are opportunities to improve the CTE by reducing waiting times [7].

2.2   Event Logs and Activity Instance Logs

Modern IT systems record and store process execution data in *event logs*, i.e. sets of timestamped events capturing the execution of the activities in a process [7]. An event log contains information about state changes of each activity instance (e.g. enablement, start, end, or cancellations of activity instances). In this paper, we use the concept of *activity instance log* to represent the execution of a set of cases in a process. An activity instance log is an event log in which each entry contains information about the start time and end time of an activity instance [16]. Below, we introduce several notations used in the paper, leading to a definition of an activity instance log.

We consider a business process that involves a set of *activities* A. We denote each of these activities with α. An *activity instance* $\varepsilon = (\varphi, \alpha, \tau_e, \tau_s, \tau_c, \rho)$ denotes one execution of activity α, where φ identifies the *process case* to which this execution belongs to, τ_e, τ_s, and τ_c denote, respectively, the instants in time in which this activity instance was *enabled*, *started*, and *completed*, and ρ identifies the *resource* that processed the activity. Accordingly, we use $\varphi(\varepsilon_i)$, $\alpha(\varepsilon_i)$, $\tau_e(\varepsilon_i)$, $\tau_s(\varepsilon_i)$, $\tau_c(\varepsilon_i)$ and $\rho(\varepsilon_i)$ to denote, respectively, the process case, the activity, the enablement time, the start time, the completion time, and the resource associated with the activity instance ε_i. We use (τ_i, τ_j) to denote the time interval between τ_i and τ_j. We write $\omega(\varepsilon_i) = (\tau_e(\varepsilon_i), \tau_s(\varepsilon_i))$ to denote the *waiting time* of ε_i, representing the interval since ε_i became available for processing ($\tau_e(\varepsilon_i)$), until its recorded start ($\tau_s(\varepsilon_i)$). The processing time of ε_i is $pt(\varepsilon_i) = (\tau_s(\varepsilon_i), \tau_c(\varepsilon_i))$. We use $(\tau_i, \tau_j) \in (\tau_k, \tau_l)$ to denote that the interval (τ_i, τ_j) is contained in (τ_k, τ_l), i.e. $\tau_i \geq \tau_k$ and $\tau_j \leq \tau_l$. With $(\tau_i, \tau_j) \perp (\tau_k, \tau_l)$ we denote that both intervals (partially or fully) overlap, i.e. $\exists (\tau_m, \tau_n) \in (\tau_i, \tau_j) \mid (\tau_m, \tau_n) \in (\tau_k, \tau_l)$.

Given the above, an *activity instance log* L is a collection of activity instances recording the data of the execution of a set of cases of a business process. Table 1 shows an example of 10 activity instances from an activity instance log, whereas Fig. 1 depicts the corresponding process model.

Table 1. Fragment of an activity instance log composed of 10 activity instances.

Case ID	Activity	Enabled Time	Start Time	End Time	Resource
...					
510	Register invoice	08:30:12	08:30:12	11:30:00	Jack
511	Notify acceptance	09:10:11	09:10:11	10:01:01	Carolyn
511	Post invoice	09:10:11	09:10:11	10:14:15	Sarah
512	Post invoice	10:25:45	10:25:45	10:30:00	Sarah
513	Post invoice	10:34:15	10:34:15	12:00:00	Sarah
514	Post invoice	09:10:11	11:30:00	13:00:00	Jack
515	Register invoice	12:08:10	12:08:10	13:00:00	Sarah
512	Pay invoice	10:30:00	15:55:50	17:00:11	Jack
513	Pay invoice	12:00:00	17:00:11	17:55:40	Jack
511	Pay invoice	10:14:15	17:55:40	18:30:15	Jack
...					

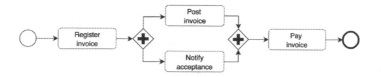

Fig. 1. Process model example corresponding to the event log of Table 1.

2.3   Related Work

Process mining is a family of techniques that support the discovery of process models from data as well as the analysis of business processes with respect to efficiency, quality, and compliance. Some of these techniques address the question of how to discover and analyze waiting times in specific application domains. For instance, Uysal et al. [21] present a case study where process mining is used to identify bottlenecks and reduce the cycle time in a production process. Similarly, Erdogan et al. [8] apply process mining techniques to identify waiting times in a hospital emergency process, while Yampaka & Chongstitvatana [24] describe an application of process mining combined with a queuing system to analyze and improve temporal performance in a healthcare process. Similarly, Antunes et al. [3] combine process mining with discrete event simulation to optimize waiting time in an emergency department. However, none of these domain-specific studies considers the question of how to attribute waiting times to their causes, which is the focus of this paper.

Ferreira & Vasilyev [9] present a technique to identify why some cases in a process take longer time to complete. They identify case characteristics correlating with higher delays, e.g., when a given activity occurs in a case, or when a given resource is involved, the case is likely to have higher waiting time. Likewise, De Leoni & van der Aalst [5] combine some of the existing correlation analysis techniques to identify how different process characteristics correlate with the process performance, e.g. if process deviations cause delays. Similarly, Hompes et al. [10] propose an approach based on time series analysis to detect cause-effect relations between process characteristics and performance indicators, e.g., if the waiting time for the receipt of payment depends on the time of day. Toosinezhad et al. [20] introduce an approach to detect event patterns that frequently precede, i.e. lead to, dynamic bottlenecks. While these studies take a correlation-based approach to analyze waiting times, we classify the causes of waiting times and consider their impact on process performance.

Some process mining techniques support the identification of waiting times caused by queuing effects, i.e. when activity instances wait in a queue until a resource becomes available [19]. Similarly, in [12], the authors present an approach to discover waiting times caused by batch processing. However, these techniques focus on identifying a singular cause of waiting time. In contrast, in the present paper, we seek to decompose the observed waiting time into multiple causes.

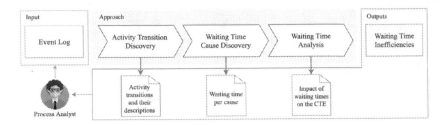

Fig. 2. Overview of the proposed approach.

3 Waiting Time Discovery and Analysis

In this section, we describe our approach to discover and analyze waiting times in a business process. The approach takes an event log as input and, as a result, produces a report comprising the causes of waiting times and their impact on the CTE. Figure 2 depicts an overview of the three main steps of the approach.

In the first step, we discover the transitions between activities and their characteristics – total frequency, case frequency, and total waiting time – from the event log. In the second step, we identify the causes of waiting time of each transition. In the third and final step, we analyze the impact of each cause on the temporal efficiency of the process.

3.1 Activity Transition Discovery

The first step of our approach is to discover transitions between activities and their waiting times. We define an *activity transition instance* as a pair of activity instances $\langle a_1, b_1 \rangle$ in a single case, such that the completion of a_1 enables b_1, i.e. b_1 cannot be executed before a_1 is completed. We call the first element of an activity transition instance the *source activity instance*, while the latter is the *target activity instance*. An *activity transition* is a set of activity transition instances with the same source and target activities, where the *source activity* is the activity executed in all its source activity instances, and the *target activity* is the activity executed in all its target activity instances. For example, the activity transition $\langle a, b \rangle$ is composed of the set of activity transition instances $\{\langle a_1, b_1 \rangle, \langle a_2, b_2 \rangle, \ldots \langle a_n, b_n \rangle\}$. For simplicity, we refer to activity transitions as *transitions* and to activity transition instances as *transition instances*.

As input, we require an activity instance log as defined in Sec. 2.2, where the resources sharing the same role are considered separately, and the enabled time of each activity instance is optional. If this latter element is missing, we estimate it as follows. In a sequential process, each activity instance of a case is enabled by the completion of the preceding activity instance. However, concurrency is common in real-life processes. For example, Fig. 3 shows the execution of a case with concurrency between two activities. The order of the activity instances is "Register invoice", "Post invoice", "Notify acceptance", and "Pay invoice". However, "Post invoice" and "Notify acceptance" are enabled when the activity

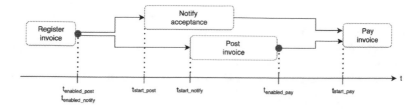

Fig. 3. Waiting time in a case with concurrent activity instances.

instance "Register invoice" completes. In the same way, "Pay invoice" is enabled only when "Post invoice" is completed. Accordingly, there are only three activity transitions in this example, namely $\langle RegisterInvoice, NotifyAcceptance\rangle$, $\langle RegisterInvoice, PostInvoice\rangle$, and $\langle PostInvoice, PayInvoice\rangle$. In this way, we consider each activity instance to be enabled by its closest non-concurrent preceding activity instance. We assume that once an activity instance is enabled, it remains enabled until its processing starts.

To detect concurrent activities (e.g. if activities "Post invoice" and "Notify acceptance" are concurrent), we use the concurrency oracle of the Heuristics Miner [23]. This method computes, for each pair of activities related via a directly-follows relation, a coefficient indicating whether these activities are in a concurrent relation or not. This coefficient is computed based on the percentage of times the two activities directly-follow each other in either order, e.g. "Post invoice" followed by "Notify acceptance" versus "Notify acceptance" followed by "Post invoice". The concurrency oracle then determines which pairs of activities are concurrent based on certain thresholds.

Once the transition instances are discovered, we calculate their *duration*, i.e. the waiting times they induce. The waiting time of a target activity instance in a transition instance is the interval between its enablement and its start time. For example, in Fig. 3, the waiting time in the transition $\langle PostInvoice, PayInvoice\rangle$ corresponds to the interval $(t_{enabled\_pay}, t_{start\_pay})$. In this way, we identify the waiting time of each target activity instance per transition.

Finally, we compute the following characteristics for each identified transition (composed of all its transition instances): *Case frequency* illustrates the proportion of process cases from the total number of cases where this transition is observed. *Total frequency* indicates the number of occurrences of this transition in the process. *Total duration* is the sum of the waiting times of all transition instances. The output of this step is a report depicting all identified transitions and their characteristics, sorted by total duration in descending order. Based on this information, the analysts can see what transitions cause the highest waiting times and how frequently they are executed.

3.2   Waiting Time Cause Discovery

Once the activity transitions and their characteristics are discovered, we analyze the waiting time of each transition instance and identify their causes. In this section, we define the proposed causes of waiting times (RQ1) and describe how they can be identified from an event log (RQ2).

Given the event log information, we consider that an enabled activity instance can wait for *i)* other activity instances to be enabled (so they are processed together) or *ii)* the assigned resource to become available. Below, we analyze each of these situations and we relate them to direct causes of waiting time. *i)* When an activity instance waits for another activity instance to be enabled, we observe a batch processing behavior, and thus, *waiting time due to batching*. *ii)* If an activity instance is not waiting for this reason, it might wait for the assigned resource. The assigned resource might be busy processing other activity instances, enabled before or after the waiting activity instance. Thus, we observe *waiting times due to resource contention* or *due to prioritization*, respectively. If the resource is not busy, they might be unavailable due to working schedules, causing *waiting time due to resource unavailability*. Finally, if there is waiting time that cannot be explained by any of the above causes, we consider the cause to be *due to extraneous factors*, i.e. causes that cannot be identified from the log. Accordingly, we propose to target five causes of waiting time: batching, resource contention, prioritization, resource unavailability, and extraneous factors.

The waiting time within a given transition instance may stem from one or multiple causes –e.g. the resource was busy performing another activity instance during half of this waiting time, while the resource was off-duty (outside their working hours) during the other half. If there are multiple waiting time causes for a given transition instance, we decompose this waiting time into non-overlapping time intervals and attribute each interval to one cause using the decision procedure in Fig. 4. According to this decision procedure, we first identify if any intervals of the transition duration are caused by batching. Then we look for intervals of waiting time caused by resource contention and prioritization, followed by resource unavailability and extraneous factors. This order is determined by the dominance relations between these causes. Batching dominates resource contention, prioritization, and unavailability, because regardless of the availabil-

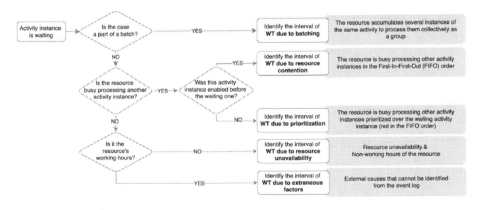

Fig. 4. Overview of the waiting time cause discovery process and their definitions.

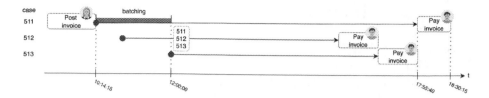

Fig. 5. Waiting time due to batching.

ity status of any given resource, an activity instance that is part of a batch is not ready to be assigned (and started) until the batch is ready. Resource contention and prioritization dominate resource availability, because if a resource has a work queue, they cannot start an activity instance until the latter reaches the front of the queue, or until this activity instance has the highest priority among all activity instances in the queue, regardless of the resource's availability status. Extraneous factors are dominated by all other causes, as they act as a "catch-all" cause for any waiting time that cannot be attributed to other causes.

Note that since each interval of waiting time is attributed to a single cause, this approach ensures the identified waiting time are additive, i.e. the sum of the waiting time causes is equal to the total waiting time of the transition instance.

Below, we define each waiting time cause in turn, and we specify how it is discovered within an activity instance log.

Waiting Time Due to Batching. The first cause that we identify is *waiting time due to batching*. Batch processing occurs when a set of instances of the same activity are accumulated to be processed together (either simultaneously or one after the other) [12]. In this context, a batch is a set of activity instances $\mathcal{E}_b \subseteq L$, such that all $\varepsilon_i \in \mathcal{E}_b$ record the execution of the same activity, performed by the same resource, and processed as a batch (i.e. all of them were enabled before any of them started, and they were processed as a group). We use the technique proposed in [12] to identify batch processing. In batch processing, when an activity instance is enabled and ready to be processed, it can wait for other instances of the same activity until the batch is accumulated, i.e. until all instances that are part of a batch are collected. Accordingly, when the target activity instance of a transition instance is detected as part of a batch, the waiting time interval from its enablement time to the batch accumulation time is classified as *waiting time due to batching*. The waiting time due to batching of an activity instance is then defined as follows:

Definition 1 (Waiting Time Due to Batching). Given an activity instance log L, a batch $\mathcal{E}_b \subseteq L$, and an activity instance $\varepsilon_i \in \mathcal{E}_b$, the waiting time due to batching of ε_i is $\omega_{ba}(\varepsilon_i) = (\tau_e(\varepsilon_i), \tau_{bc}) \mid \tau_{bc} = max(\{\tau_e(\varepsilon_j) \mid \varepsilon_j \in \mathcal{E}_b\})$, i.e. the interval of time between the enablement of ε_i and the last enablement of the activities in the batch.

Consider the transition instance between "Post invoice" and "Pay invoice" of case 511 in the running example (Fig. 5) with a waiting time between 10:14:15

and 17:55:40. The activity "Pay invoice" is a batch-processed activity where the resource accumulates instances and then processes them one by one (sequential batch processing) [16]. The batch is accumulated until the last activity instance of "Pay invoice" is enabled, i.e. case 513 is ready to be processed ($t_{enabled} = 12:00:00$). Therefore, if we analyze the transition instance $\langle PostInvoice, PayInvoice\rangle$ of case 511, its waiting time due to batching corresponds to the interval between 10:14:15 and 12:00:00.

Waiting Time Due to Resource Contention. There are situations where the resources that have to process a certain activity are busy processing other activity instances that were enabled earlier than the waiting one, and thus, it's understood that they start processing them before the current one (following a first-in-first-out order).[1] When this situation occurs, we classify as *waiting time due to resource contention* those intervals in which the resource that performed the activity instance was working in other activity instances enabled before it. Therefore, the waiting time due to resource contention of an activity instance is defined as follows:

Definition 2 (Waiting Time Due to Resource Contention). Given an activity instance log L, and an activity instance $\varepsilon_i \in L$, the waiting time due to resource contention of ε_i is $\Omega_{rc}(\varepsilon_i) = \{(\tau_i, \tau_j) \mid \tau_i = max(\tau_e(\varepsilon_i), \tau_s(\varepsilon_j)) \wedge \tau_j = min(\tau_s(\varepsilon_i), \tau_c(\varepsilon_j)) \wedge \varepsilon_j \in L \wedge \varepsilon_j \neq \varepsilon_i \wedge \rho(\varepsilon_j) = \rho(\varepsilon_i) \wedge \tau_e(\varepsilon_j) \leq \tau_e(\varepsilon_i) \wedge pt(\varepsilon_j) \perp \omega(\varepsilon_i)\}$, i.e. the set of intervals of processing time of all ε_j of L (executed by the same resource as ε_i, and enabled before it) overlapping with the waiting time of ε_i.

Coming back to the running example, during the transition instance between "Post invoice" and "Pay invoice" of case 511, the resource works on case 514 that has an earlier enabled instance of "Post invoice" (see Fig. 6). Therefore, there is waiting time due to resource contention between 12:00:00 and 13:00:00.

Waiting Time Due to Prioritization. However, the resources might not always follow the FIFO policy. In some situations, the resources might give priority to certain activity instances over others. We call this behavior *prioritization*, meaning that an activity instance is processed out of turn w.r.t. a FIFO policy, thus causing other activity instances to wait longer. When this situation occurs, we classify as *waiting time due to prioritization* those intervals in which the resource that performed the activity instance was working in other activity instances enabled after it. Therefore, the waiting time due to prioritization of an activity instance is defined as follows:

Definition 3 (Waiting Time Due to Prioritization). Given an activity instance log L, and an activity instance $\varepsilon_i \in L$, the waiting time due to prioritization of ε_i is $\Omega_{prior}(\varepsilon_i) = \{(\tau_i, \tau_j) \mid \tau_i = \tau_s(\varepsilon_j) \wedge \tau_j = min(\tau_s(\varepsilon_i), \tau_c(\varepsilon_j)) \wedge \varepsilon_j \in$

---

[1] We assume that resources work only on one activity at a time, i.e. there is no multitasking. Thus, we foresee that the proposed estimation technique will not be suitable for event logs with a high proportion of multitask activity instances.

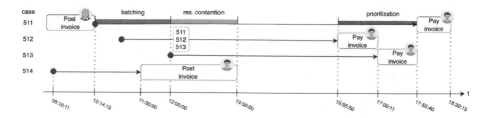

Fig. 6. Waiting time due to resource contention and due to prioritization.

$L \wedge \varepsilon_j \neq \varepsilon_i \wedge \rho(\varepsilon_j) = \rho(\varepsilon_i) \wedge \tau_e(\varepsilon_j) > \tau_e(\varepsilon_i) \wedge pt(\varepsilon_j) \perp \omega(\varepsilon_i)\}$, i.e. the set of intervals of processing time of all ε_j of L (executed by the same resource as ε_i, and enabled after it) overlapping with the waiting time of ε_i.

In Fig. 6, when the resource starts processing the batch of cases 511–513, instead of processing cases in their order of enablement, he prioritizes cases 512 and 513 over 511. Waiting time due to prioritization then corresponds to the interval between 15:55:50 and 17:55:40.

Waiting Time Due to Resource Unavailability. The fourth cause of waiting time that we propose to consider is resource unavailability, which corresponds to the intervals in time in which the resource is not available to work due to their working schedules. To identify this waiting time, we need to first discover the working schedules of the resources. We propose to use the technique presented in [14] to discover calendars over time granules not fully described by the input data. This technique analyzes the instants in time when each resource interacted with the system (i.e. the start and end of each activity instance) to build a weekly working calendar composed of time intervals in which there was enough evidence, based on given support and confidence values, that the resource is working.[2] Given the weekly calendars of each resource, we transform them to absolute time intervals to compare them with the waiting times observed in the log. Then, we classify as *waiting time due to resource unavailability* those intervals where the resource is not available for working. Therefore, the waiting time due to resource unavailability of an activity instance is defined as follows:

Definition 4 (Waiting Time Due to Resource Unavailability). Given an activity instance log L, an activity instance $\varepsilon_i \in L$, and being $cal_{av}(\rho) = \{(\tau_{avs}, \tau_{ave})\}$ a resource availability calendar with the set of time intervals in which the resource is available to work, the waiting time due to resource unavailability of ε_i is $\Omega_{unav}(\varepsilon_i) = \{(\tau_i, \tau_j) \mid (\tau_i, \tau_j) \in \omega(\varepsilon_i) \wedge \nexists(\tau_k, \tau_l) \in cal_{av}(\rho(\varepsilon_i)) \mid (\tau_i, \tau_j) \perp (\tau_k, \tau_l)\}$, i.e. the set of intervals of the waiting time of ε_i that do not overlap with the availability calendar of the resource $\rho(\varepsilon_i)$ that executed c_i.

---

[2] Although we use this resource calendar discovery algorithm, the approach can be applied with other calendar discovery algorithms or with manually defined calendars.

In the running example (Fig. 7), the resource executing "Pay invoice" does not work between 13:00:00 and 15:00:00. Thus, in the transition instance of case 511, the respective waiting time interval is due to resource unavailability.

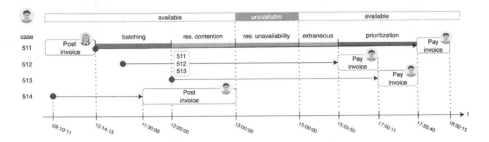

Fig. 7. Waiting time due to resource unavailability and due to extraneous factors.

Waiting Time Due to Extraneous Factors. The last cause of waiting time that we propose to consider is "extraneous factors". We propose to classify as *waiting time due to extraneous factors* the waiting time intervals caused by the external effects that cannot be identified from the event log – e.g. the resource is working on another process, the activity instance cannot start until some unrecorded event has occurred, fatigue effects, or context switch In Fig. 7, the interval between 15:00:00 and 15:55:50 cannot be explained by the data available in the log and is considered due to extraneous factors. Thus, the waiting time of an activity instance due to extraneous factors is defined as follows:

Definition 5 (Waiting Time Due to Extraneous Factors). Given an activity instance log L and an activity instance $\varepsilon_i \in L$, the waiting time due to extraneous factors of ε_i is $\Omega_{extr}(\varepsilon_i) = \{(\tau_i, \tau_j) \mid (\tau_i, \tau_j) \in \omega(\varepsilon_i) \wedge \nexists(\tau_k, \tau_l) \in (\{\omega_{ba}(\varepsilon_i)\} \bigcup \Omega_{rc}(\varepsilon_i) \bigcup \Omega_{prior}(\varepsilon_i) \bigcup \Omega_{unav}(\varepsilon_i)) \mid (\tau_i, \tau_j) \perp (\tau_k, \tau_l)\}$, i.e. the set of intervals within the waiting time of ε_i that does not overlap with waiting times due to batching, resource contention, prioritization, or resource unavailability.

3.3   Waiting Time Analysis

The final step is to analyze how much each waiting time cause contributes to the temporal performance of the process and their impact on the CTE. With that purpose, we propose to compute the percentage of time that each cause induces in the CTE of the process. In this context, we measure the CTE as the processing time divided by the sum of the processing and the waiting time (PT + WT), where PT is the sum of the processing time of all activity instances in the process, and WT is the sum of their waiting time. The impact of waiting times per cause is calculated as the difference between the original process CTE and the CTE if a particular waiting time is eliminated. In this way, we can measure

(1) the impact that each waiting time cause has on the process CTE, (2) the impact that each transition has on the process CTE, and (3) the impact that each waiting time cause has in each transition. These metrics can indicate the potential CTE improvement if a particular cause of waiting time is addressed.

As a result, we can analyze the discovered waiting time causes and their impact on CTE. With this information, process analysts can identify where the inefficiencies due to waiting times are localized, choose which transitions and/or waiting time causes to address, and which redesign alternatives to apply.

4   Evaluation

In this section, we present the evaluation of our approach. We evaluate the approach by addressing two evaluation questions: (EQ1) *To which extent is the technique able to detect the presence or absence of certain waiting time causes?*, (EQ2) *To what extent is the technique able to correctly quantify the amount of waiting time waste per each cause?* In this experimentation, we use synthetic data to validate the ability of the technique to accurately discover transitions, their waiting times and the waiting time causes known to be present in the event logs. Then, we demonstrate the approach's applicability on a real-life event log. The approach implementation, the event logs and experiment results are all available on GitHub.[3]

4.1   Evaluation on Synthetic Data

To answer EQ1, we used a business process simulation model (BPS model) of a loan application process to simulate a set of event logs with different combinations of waiting time causes. To simulate waiting time due to resource contention, we set a low number of available resources in the BPS model, so that in some cases, there were no resources available to process an enabled activity instance. To create waiting time due to resource unavailability, we set resource working calendars so that some resources worked from Monday to Wednesday, and others from Thursday to Friday. To simulate waiting time due to extraneous factors, we added timer events before some of the activities in the BPS model, thus delaying their start. Waiting time due to batching and prioritization cannot be injected by modifying the simulation parameters, as current BPS engines do not support them. Therefore, in batching, we added a set of new cases delaying the start of some activity instances so that they are processed as a batch. To simulate prioritization, we added a set of new cases changing the order of execution of some activity instances, so they are processed following a prioritization order. Combining these modifications, we simulated a set of 32 event logs with all the combinations of causes of waiting time and measured the performance using precision and recall. True positives and false positives stand for the discovery of

---

[3] https://github.com/AutomatedProcessImprovement/waiting-time-analysis/tree/caise2023.

a waiting time cause that, respectively, was and was not injected in the event log. True and false negatives denote an undiscovered waiting time cause that, respectively, was not and was injected.

Table 2. Results for the simulated event logs with all waiting time causes, depicting the true positives with '✓', the false positives with '✗', and the true negatives with an empty cell (there are no false negatives).

	S01	S02	S03	S04	S05	S06	S07	S08	S09	S10	S11	S12	S13	S14	S15	S16
Batching		✓					✓	✓	✓	✓				✗		
Prioritization			✓				✓				✓	✓	✓	✗	✗	
Res. Contention				✓				✓			✓			✓	✓	
Res. Unavailability					✓	✗			✓	✗		✓	✗	✓	✗	✓
Extraneous factors						✓				✓			✓		✓	✓

	S17	S18	S19	S20	S21	S22	S23	S24	S25	S26	S27	S28	S29	S30	S31	S32
Batching	✓	✓	✓	✓	✓	✓	✗			✗	✓	✓	✓	✓	✗	✓
Prioritization	✓	✓	✓		✗		✓	✓	✓	✗	✓	✓	✓	✗	✓	✓
Res. Contention	✓			✓	✓		✓	✓		✓	✓	✓		✓	✓	✓
Res. Unavailability		✓	✗	✓	✗	✓	✓	✗	✓	✓	✓	✗	✓	✓	✓	✓
Extraneous factors		✓		✓	✓		✓	✓	✓		✓	✓	✓	✓	✓	✓

Table 2 depicts the results for the simulated event logs used to evaluate EQ1. Our approach discovered the injected waiting time causes in all the event logs (no false negatives) resulting in a recall of 100%. However, due to the influence that some waiting time causes have between them, the results contain 17 false positives (precision of 83%). False positives in waiting time due to resource unavailability (S06, S10, S13, S15, S19, S21, S24, and S28) are caused by the presence of extraneous waiting time, combined with limited data for the discovery of resources' working calendars. To simulate these logs, we set 24/7 working calendar for all resources (high availability). However, when a resource has low occupation (executes few events), there is not enough data for the calendar discovery to identify a 24/7 calendar and some intervals are interpreted as non-working time. When these non-working intervals overlap with extraneous waiting time, the tool classifies them as waiting time due to resource unavailability. This limitation is inherent to the discovery of the resource calendar, if there is no data showing that a resource was active during a period of time, it cannot be assumed that they were working.

The injection of waiting time due to extraneous factors also induced false positives of prioritization (S15, S21, S26, S30). When an activity instance is enabled but waiting due to extraneous factors, the resource might execute other activities enabled after the waiting one, being detected as waiting time due to prioritization. These false positives are due to the absence of an explicit indicator of the extraneous factors (i.e. extraneous waiting time is only detected when no other causes are identified). False positives due to batching (S14, S23, S26, S31) are caused by the appearance of a batch processing behavior that was not intentionally added. To create waiting time due to resource contention and unavailability, in some scenarios, we assigned working calendars with low resource availability. In such cases, while instances were waiting until the resource became available, they were collected and processed by the same resource. This resulted in an unassigned but correctly discovered batch processing behavior.

EQ2 aimed at assessing if our approach is able to correctly identify waiting time intervals and their causes. We could not use the set of event logs used for EQ1 to answer EQ2, as the logs were created through stochastic business process simulation – we know we have introduced a certain cause of waiting time, but we don't know to what extent. Therefore, we manually created a set of 5 event logs with activity transitions having different waiting time causes. Due to the low number of events per resource, we manually defined the resource working calendars for this experiment. We ran our technique over these logs and obtained accurate waiting time intervals and their causes. The input and results for the EQ2 experiment are available on GitHub.

4.2   Evaluation on a Real-Life Log

To evaluate the applicability of the proposed approach in a real-life scenario, we used an event log of a manufacturing production process [13]. The event log has 225 cases recording the execution of 24 activities in a total of 4,503 activity instances, executed by 46 resources.

First, we discovered the transition instances – 91 transitions with 3,421 transition instances (i.e. executions of each transition) –, and their characteristics – case frequency, total frequency, and total duration (i.e. total waiting time).

Then, we discovered the waiting time causes, producing a report that captures to what extent each cause (per transition) contributes to the total waiting time of the process. The highest waiting times originated from the self-loop transitions, i.e. when the same activity is executed twice in a row. For instance, the self-loop of "Turning & Milling Q.C." induced a total waiting time of 1,101 days, 2 h, and 54 min (see Fig. 8), being the greatest contributor to the total waiting time. The largest portion of the waiting time in this transition (54.74%) was caused by resource unavailability (602 days, 19 h, and 59 min).

Finally, we analyzed to what extent each waiting time cause contributes to the total waiting time of the process, and how they affect the CTE. Resource unavailability was the primary source of waiting time (as it caused 57% of the total waiting time), followed by batching (22%), prioritization (9%), extraneous (8%), and resource contention (4%). Then, we measured the impact of the waiting times by cause on the process CTE (CTE = 6.81%). The highest CTE increase (up to 14.62%) can be achieved if the waiting time due to resource unavailability is eliminated. Regarding individual transitions, addressing the "Turning & Milling Q.C" self-loop is the highest improvement opportunity. If the waiting time in this transition is addressed, the CTE could increase to 7.69%.

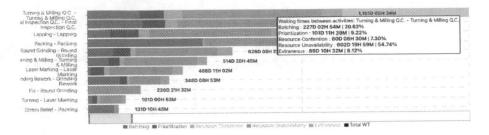

Fig. 8. Waiting time causes in activity transitions of the production process.

5   Conclusion

This paper outlines a process mining-based approach for identifying causes of waiting times and their impact. To address research question RQ1, we propose a method to attribute the waiting time of activity transitions to one of five causes: *batching, resource contention, prioritization, resource unavailability,* and *extraneous factors*. To address RQ2, we outline how these five causes of waiting time can be discovered, for each activity transition, from an event log. Finally, we propose to measure the impact of each waiting time cause on the CTE of a process, to help analysts to prioritize opportunities to reduce these waiting times (RQ3). The empirical evaluation shows that our approach can accurately classify the waiting times in a process into the five causes, in (synthetic) event logs where the causes of waiting time are known. Finally, we illustrated the applicability of our approach using an event log of a production process.

In its current form, the proposed approach only considers waiting times in transitions between activity instances. Yet waiting times may also arise in at least two other settings: (i) between case creation and start of the first activity instance; and (ii) within an activity instance due to interruptions (e.g. the resource interrupts their work and resumes it later). The first of these waiting times could be analyzed by applying methods that estimate the inter-arrival time of each case [4,15]. The second requires new methods for modeling and inferring interruptions, possibly using additional attributes of the log or other additional data. Another limitation of the approach is that it does not consider multitasking. This could be addressed by inferring multitasking patterns from the log, and using this data to estimate at what point in time a resource would normally have started an activity instance, given their past multitasking behavior.

In future work, we plan to develop a method for discovering business process simulation models from event logs, which considers the causes of waiting times considered in this paper. Such simulation models could be used to support analysts in identifying combinations of redesign options to optimize CTE, while also considering other performance dimensions (e.g. cost).

References

1. van der Aalst, W.M.P.: Process Mining: Data Science in Action, 2nd edn. Springer, Heidelberg (2016). https://doi.org/10.1007/978-3-662-49851-4
2. Andrews, R., Wynn, M.: Shelf time analysis in CTP insurance claims processing. In: Kang, U., Lim, E.-P., Yu, J.X., Moon, Y.-S. (eds.) PAKDD 2017. LNCS (LNAI), vol. 10526, pp. 151–162. Springer, Cham (2017). https://doi.org/10.1007/978-3-319-67274-8_14
3. Antunes, B.B.P., Manresa, A., Bastos, L.S.L., Marchesi, J.F., Hamacher, S.: A solution framework based on process mining, optimization, and discrete-event simulation to improve queue performance in an emergency department. In: Di Francescomarino, C., Dijkman, R., Zdun, U. (eds.) BPM 2019. LNBIP, vol. 362, pp. 583–594. Springer, Cham (2019). https://doi.org/10.1007/978-3-030-37453-2_47
4. Berkenstadt, G., Gal, A., Senderovich, A., Shraga, R., Weidlich, M.: Queueing inference for process performance analysis with missing life-cycle data. In: Proceedings of the 2nd International Conference on Process Mining (ICPM 2020), pp. 57–64. IEEE (2020)
5. De Leoni, M., van der Aalst, W.M., Dees, M.: A general process mining framework for correlating, predicting and clustering dynamic behavior based on event logs. Inf. Syst. **56**, 235–257 (2016)
6. Delias, P.: A positive deviance approach to eliminate wastes in business processes: the case of a public organization. Ind. Manag. Data. Syst. **117**, 1323–1339 (2017)
7. Dumas, M., La Rosa, M., Mendling, J., Reijers, H.A., et al.: Fundamentals of Business Process Management, 2nd edn. Springer, Heidelberg. (2018). https://doi.org/10.1007/978-3-662-56509-4
8. Erdogan, T.G., Tarhan, A.K.: Multi-perspective process mining for emergency process. Health Inform. J. **28**(1), 14604582221077196 (2022)
9. Ferreira, D.R., Vasilyev, E.: Using logical decision trees to discover the cause of process delays from event logs. Comput. Ind. **70**, 194–207 (2015)
10. Hompes, B.F., Maaradji, A., La Rosa, M., Dumas, M., Buijs, J.C., van der Aalst, W.M.: Discovering causal factors explaining business process performance variation. In: Dubois, E., Pohl, K. (eds.) Advanced Information Systems Engineering. CAiSE 2017. LNCS, vol. 10253, pp. 177–192. Springer, Cham (2017). https://doi.org/10.1007/978-3-319-59536-8_12
11. Jansen-Vullers, M., Reijers, H.: Business process redesign in healthcare: towards a structured approach. Information **43**(4), 321–339 (2005)
12. Lashkevich, K., Milani, F., Chapela-Campa, D., Dumas, M.: Data-Driven Analysis of Batch Processing Inefficiencies in Business Processes. In: Guizzardi, R., Ralyté, J., Franch, X. (eds.) RCIS, pp. 231–247. Springer, Cham (2022). https://doi.org/10.1007/978-3-031-05760-1_14
13. Levy, D.: Production analysis with process mining technology (2014). https://doi.org/10.4121/uuid:68726926-5ac5-4fab-b873-ee76ea412399
14. López-Pintado, O., Dumas, M.: Business process simulation with differentiated resources: does it make a difference? In: Di Ciccio, C., Dijkman, R., del Río Ortega, A., Rinderle-Ma, S. (eds.) Business Process Management. BPM 2022. LNCS, vol. 13420, pp. 361–378. Springer, Cham (2022). https://doi.org/10.1007/978-3-031-16103-2_24
15. Martin, N., Depaire, B., Caris, A.: Using event logs to model interarrival times in business process simulation. In: Reichert, M., Reijers, H.A. (eds.) BPM 2015. LNBIP, vol. 256, pp. 255–267. Springer, Cham (2016). https://doi.org/10.1007/978-3-319-42887-1_21

16. Martin, N., Pufahl, L., Mannhardt, F.: Detection of batch activities from event logs. Inf. Syst. **95**, 101642 (2021)
17. Ramakrishnan, S., Kumaran, S., Chang, H., Kulkarni, N., Srihari, K.: Defining and categorizing handoff points for the service domain. In: Proceedings of the 29th Annual Conference of ASEM, pp. 12–15 (2008)
18. Rummel, J.L., Walter, Z., Dewan, R., Seidmann, A.: Activity consolidation to improve responsiveness. Eur. J. Oper. Res. **161**(3), 683–703 (2005)
19. Senderovich, A., Weidlich, M., Gal, A., Mandelbaum, A.: Queue mining for delay prediction in multi-class service processes. Inf. Syst. **53**, 278–295 (2015)
20. Toosinezhad, Z., Fahland, D., Köroğlu, Ö., Van Der Aalst, W.M.: Detecting system-level behavior leading to dynamic bottlenecks. In: 2020 2nd ICPM, pp. 17–24. IEEE (2020)
21. Uysal, M.S., et al.: Process mining for production processes in the automotive industry. In: Industry Forum at BPM, vol. 20 (2020)
22. Van Der Aalst, W.M., et al.: Business process mining: an industrial application. Inf. Syst. **32**(5), 713–732 (2007)
23. Weijters, A.J.M.M., Ribeiro, J.T.S.: Flexible heuristics miner (FHM). In: Proceedings of the IEEE Symposium on CIDM. IEEE (2011)
24. Yampaka, T., Chongstitvatana, P.: An application of process mining for queueing system in health service. In: 13th International JCSSE, pp. 1–6. IEEE (2016)

Event-Driven Process Mining

Extracting Event Data from Document-Driven Enterprise Systems

Diego Calvanese[1,2], Mieke Jans[3,4(✉)], Tahir Emre Kalayci[5],
and Marco Montali[1]

[1] Free University of Bozen-Bolzano, 39100 Bolzano, Italy
{calvanese,montali}@inf.unibz.it
[2] Umeå University, 90187 Umeå, Sweden
diego.calvanese@umu.se
[3] Hasselt University, 3500 Hasselt, Belgium
mieke.jans@uhasselt.be
[4] Maastricht University, 6200, MD Maastricht, Netherlands
mj.jans@maastrichtuniversity.nl
[5] Virtual Vehicle Research GmbH, 8010 Graz, Austria
emre.kalayci@v2c2.at

Abstract. The preparation of input event data is one of the most critical
phases in process mining projects. Different frameworks have been developed to offer methodologies and/or supporting toolkits for data preparation. One of these frameworks, called OnProm, relies on sophisticated
semantic technologies to extract event logs from relational databases.
The toolkit consists of a series of general steps, meant to work on arbitrary, legacy databases. However, in many settings, the input database
is not a legacy one but is structured with conceptually understandable
object types and relationships that can be effectively employed to support business users in the extraction process. This is, for example, the
case for document-driven enterprise systems. In this paper, we focus on
this class of systems and propose a guided approach, erprep, to support a
group of business and technical users in setting up OnProm with minimal
effort. We demonstrate the approach in a real-life use case.

Keywords: Data preparation · event log extraction · ERP systems ·
Ontology-based event modeling

1 Introduction

Many business processes are supported by an information system, recording large
amounts of data about the underlying process. Extracting useful knowledge and
insights from this process data is the purpose of the field of process mining.
Process mining has brought forward various algorithms and techniques that are
used to discover, analyze, and improve business processes. A process mining
project requires the availability of event data in a standardized format, the IEEE

M. Indulska et al. (Eds.): CAiSE 2023, LNCS 13901, pp. 193–209, 2023.
https://doi.org/10.1007/978-3-031-34560-9_12

XES standard. Although the standard is a good format to represent process logs, different perspectives on the data can be taken, and it is often hard to understand how to identify and extract events from legacy data sources. Hence, different event logs can be extracted from the same system [8]. Once a perspective has been chosen, the extraction is typically handled via coding, e.g., through ETL-scripts for relational databases. This is error-prone, does not directly reflect the taken perspective, and requires to write new code from scratch whenever one wants to change perspective when analyzing the data (e.g., when changing the case notion).

To mitigate these issues, a novel approach, called OnProm, has recently been put forward to facilitate and semi-automate this log extraction process in the case of relational databases [4,5], leveraging the *ontology-based data access paradigm* [21]. Event data extraction in OnProm consists of three phases: *(1)* creating a domain ontology to conceptually capture the relevant concepts and relations of the domain of interest, *(2)* mapping this domain ontology to the underlying database structure, and *(3)* annotating the domain ontology to indicate where to find cases, events, and their attributes. While these three phases are free of procedural code, they may still be very demanding as they intensively rely on human knowledge and expertise, due to the intrinsic complexity of the extraction process, and the complete generality of the approach, which does not make any assumption on how data is structured in the underlying relational database.

The goal of this work is to study these three phases in the setting where the underlying database is a so-called *document-driven enterprise system*, like an ERP-system. In such systems, the database is organized around conceptually understandable document objects and their mutual relationships, with specific modeling structures to store events. This leads to the following research question: *how can one simplify the definition of an OnProm pipeline in the case of document-driven enterprise systems?*

We answer this question by introducing the erprep guided approach, which supports domain and IT experts in the incremental, semi-automated definition of a suitable domain ontology and the corresponding mappings, and helps them in easily defining case- and event-annotations depending on the perspective of interest. We show through a case study in the manufacturing domain that, by applying erprep, we can indeed smoothly (in terms of procedure) and feasibly (in terms of performance) extract multiple XES event logs that, together, provide a suitable basis to conduct process mining analyses.

2   Related Work

To guide projects aiming to improve process performance or compliance to rules and regulations, the PM^2 methodology has been developed [7]. This methodology defines the stages that a successful process mining project entails and it describes the accompanied activities to these stages. Stages 1, 2, and 3 (Planning – Extraction – Data processing) represent the labor-intensive preparation of the core project (which starts at Stage 4). Although these stages are presented as clear-cut different stages in the PM^2 methodology, it is difficult to disentangle the activities related to these stages. With much less research conducted on these stages, important research problems remain unaddressed, like how to effectively extract and process your data as event log [8].

The availability of a (high-quality) event log in a standardized format is essential for every process mining project, but most information systems are currently not capable of automatically producing the required kind of event logs. Hence it is paramount to identify novel methods for improving the log extraction process. Some work has been done on the topic of extracting event logs in the context of specific environments (like SAP) or domains (like accounting) [10,16].

In general, process mining requires a clear notion of a case. However, many database systems that provide the input for process mining analyses are document-oriented: they associate a chain of documents to one process execution. Selecting one specific document as case identifier is therefore providing only a single perspective on the process. To avoid the problems of *data divergence* and *convergence* that arise when forcing event data from these systems to adopt a single case notion, artifact-centric process mining has been proposed as a more generic solution [6,14,17]. This approach tries to solve the aforementioned problem by discovering the life-cycles of interrelated data objects (i.e., artifacts) and their interactions. The authors of [13] take another approach and present the eXtensible Object-Centric (XOC) event log format, which does not require a case notion, hereby avoiding the flattening of reality into an event log.

Two key frameworks that tackle the manual, labor-intensive aspect of event data extraction are [5,8]. The authors of [8] introduce a meta-model and tool-chain to connect databases with processes through bridging concepts. Data from three source environments (redo logs, SAP-style change tables, and in-table version storage) are transformed into a common representation and missing values are automatically inferred where possible. The authors envision this model to assist in multi-perspective event log building in a more intuitive way and provide a solution for extracting multiple event logs without having to restart from scratch when changing perspective. The other framework is called OnProm [4,5] and is briefly recalled in the next section.

3   The OnProm Approach

The OnProm approach [4,5] aims at the semi-automatic extraction of event logs from various kinds of legacy information systems, reflecting different process-related views on the same data, and consequently supporting analysts in the application of process mining along multiple perspectives. The approach leverages the *ontology-based data access* (OBDA) paradigm [21] and is based on the use of an ontology that captures the semantics of the domain of interest.

Intuitively, an ontology represents the domain of interest in terms of a set of *classes* (which denote sets of objects), *object properties* (which connect pairs of objects), and *data properties* (which connect objects to values), and captures domain knowledge by means of suitable axioms. Ontologies in OnProm are formalized using the lightweight description logic *DL-Lite$_A$* [2], belonging to the

DL-Lite family [3][1]. In OnProm, in order to facilitate the understanding of the ontology and the annotation of ontology elements (see below), we rely on the tight correspondence between the *DL-Lite* family and conceptual data models (see, e.g., [2]), and actually represent $DL\text{-}Lite_\mathcal{A}$ ontologies by means of UML Class Diagrams. Specifically, OnProm considers a fragment of UML Class Diagrams that allows for specifying *(i)* classes and *(ii)* class hierarchies (specified through ISA and generalizations), *(iii)* binary associations (corresponding to object properties) with *(iv)* multiplicity constraints (of the form 0..1, 1, *, and 1..*), and *(v)* class attributes (corresponding to data properties) [4].

In OBDA, the domain ontology is linked to the underlying legacy data through declarative (as opposed to procedural) mappings that specify how the ontology elements (i.e., classes and properties) are to be populated from the data in the sources. In line with the OBDA paradigm, we assume that the legacy data sources are relational databases, typically equipped with integrity constraints, notably keys and foreign keys. To represent database schemas, we resort here to a simple box notation for tables, where we show the name of the table and its columns, and where we indicate referential integrity constraints using ER crow-foot notation (to distinguish one-to-many and one-to-one dependencies).

Considering a $DL\text{-}Lite_\mathcal{A}$ ontology $\mathcal{O}$ (represented as a UML Class Diagram) and a relational schema of data sources, consisting of a set $\mathcal{R} = \{R_1, \ldots, R_n\}$ of relation schemas, an *OBDA Specification* is a triple $\mathcal{S} = \langle \mathcal{O}, \mathcal{M}, \mathcal{R} \rangle$, where $\mathcal{M}$ is a set of *(OBDA) mappings* [2]. To formalize such mappings, we refer to a (countably infinite) set $\mathcal{V}$ of values (i.e., strings, numbers, dates, timestamps, etc.) that may be stored in the data source relations, and to a (countably infinite) set $\mathcal{F}$ of function symbols. These are exploited to construct the identifiers of the ontology objects, by applying a function symbol to data values extracted from the sources through the mappings. Specifically, each such identifier is a term of the form $f(v_1, \ldots, v_k)$, where $f \in \mathcal{F}$ is a function symbol of arity k and $v_1, \ldots, v_k$ are values in $\mathcal{V}$. We call such terms *object terms*. Then, each mapping in $\mathcal{M}$ has the form $Q_{sql}(\vec{x}) \rightsquigarrow \Phi(\vec{y}, \vec{t})$, where *(i)* $Q_{sql}(\vec{x})$ is an arbitrary SQL query over schema $\mathcal{R}$, having the (non-empty) set $\vec{x}$ of answer variables, *(ii)* $\vec{y} \subseteq \vec{x}$, *(iii)* $\vec{t}$ is a set of object terms, each of the form $f(\vec{z})$, where $f \in \mathcal{F}$ and $\vec{z} \subseteq \vec{x}$, and *(iv)* $\Phi(\vec{y}, \vec{t})$ is a set of atoms over the variables $\vec{y}$ and the object terms $\vec{t}$. Each such atom has as predicate symbol a class or a data/object property of the ontology $\mathcal{O}$. Intuitively, each mapping creates a link between the database and the ontology, expressing how instances of the involved classes/properties are obtained from the answers of queries posed over the database. Function symbols from $\mathcal{F}$, applied to the values retrieved from the data sources, are used to construct the object terms that act as identifiers of objects populating the ontology (For the formal semantics, we refer interested readers to [2].)

Example 1. Consider the portion of the domain ontology in Fig. 6 consisting of the class **SalesDoc** and its subclass **Order**. Consider further just the VBAK table

---

[1] The *DL-Lite* family provides the formal counterpart of the lightweight ontology language OWL 2 QL, standardized by the W3C [15].

in the database schema in Fig. 1, storing sales documents identified through the combination of the columns MANDT and VBELN, and where entries with AUART = 'ZOR' denote orders. Taking this into account, we can use the following two mappings to link the VBAK table to **SalesDoc** and **Order**, respectively:

SELECT MANDT, VBELN FROM VBAK   ⤳   **SalesDoc**(sd(MANDT, VBELN))

SELECT MANDT, VBELN FROM VBAK
WHERE AUART='ZOR'   ⤳   **Order**(sd(MANDT, VBELN))

Notice that in both mappings, in the right-hand side we have chosen to use the binary function symbol sd, applied to the answer variables MANDT and VBELN of the SQL query in the left-hand side, to construct object terms denoting sales documents. The mappings specify that these sales documents become instances of the **SalesDoc** and **Order** classes. For example, if the VBAK table contains the two tuples (c25, d362, ZCN) and (c25, d571, ZOR), the mappings generate the two instances sd(c25, d362) and sd(c25, d571) of **SalesDoc**, of which the latter is also an instance of **Order**.   ◁

As mentioned, OnProm relies on the availability of a domain ontology and of the mappings to the underlying data. Producing these two artifacts might be very time-consuming, as they encode human knowledge and expertise about the underlying data sources. However, one can make use of well-established method- ologies for ontology design [9] and of sophisticated tools that facilitate the con- struction of mappings even in complex real-world scenarios[2].

Finally, in OnProm, the domain ontology is graphically annotated to sin- gle out, among all possible alternatives, which classes and properties define the desired notions of case object, events, and their relevant attributes. This method aims to let domain experts focus solely on the high-level process characteristics, while the connection with the underlying data is handled by the OBDA system. Notably, the OnProm approach is particularly effective for multi-perspective pro- cess mining, since changing the notion of case only requires changing the (graph- ical) annotation of the domain ontology, without the need to revise the entire extraction process. Case and event annotations follow the OnProm notation [4], as shown in Fig. 6 for our running example (and discussed in Step 4 in the next section).

4   The erprep Guided Approach

The erprep guided approach provides a series of steps for a group of experts collaborating in a process mining project. The approach is inspired by the pro- cedure in [11] and systematically explores it as an intermediate layer between the group of users and OnProm, providing guidance in taking decisions on the log structure in a conscious manner [12]. Following the PM^2 methodology [7], we assume the group contains people covering three main roles/competencies:

---

[2] See, e.g., the tools developed by Ontopic, https://ontopic.ai/.

(i) domain expertise of the organizational domain and the main questions to be answered through process mining; *(ii) data engineering* to access and query the information systems used by the organization to (implicitly) store events and process-related data; *(iii) analytics/process mining expertise* regarding analysis techniques and tools.

The main purpose of erprep is to drive extracting event data from document-driven enterprise systems in agreement with the questions the group wants to find an answer for, thus relieving the group from manual, ad-hoc data preparation procedures. We therefore need to better clarify what a document-driven enterprise system is. It is a relational database tracking the evolution of documents and related objects, obeying to three assumptions.

– Every document type is represented as a pair of tables, respectively storing information about the main (material) documents of that type, and the parts of those documents. A typical example is that of order and order lines, which typically coexist in the same material document (but may later be altered in different moments, through different activities). The document-part table points to the document table via a foreign key.
– Every document table is linked, directly or indirectly, to the other (document and non-document tables), hence navigational queries can be expressed to retrieve related documents and objects.
– Timestamps are used to denote the evolution of documents and other objects. Given a table C denoting an object or document type, a timestamp can be added in one of the two following ways:
  • *Column timestamp*, added directly as one or more columns of C to mark the transition of its instances from one phase to another; different timestamp columns (or groups of columns) can be used to mark different *phase transitions* of instances of C.
  • *History-table timestamp*, where the timestamp belongs to a separate *history-table* (or bundle of history-tables) listing all the changes applied to instances of C, indicating which column was affected, how, and *when*.[3]

Document-driven enterprise systems abstractly characterize the typical structure of ERP systems, such as SAP.

Example 2. Consider the database schema of Fig. 1, showing a fragment of the order-to-cash tables of SAP, which are used by the international company subject of the real case study reported in Sect. 5. The structure of the schema is a typical structure similarly adopted in other ERP systems, and uses 6 tables and 4 referential integrity constraints to capture the evolution of sales/billing documents and their lines. Specifically, VBAK and VBAP store sales documents and their lines, related via Ref_1; VBRP stores billing document lines; VBFA stores document flows, where each entry relates a sales document line with its next document, which sometimes is indeed a billing document (this depends on the complex join condition attached to Ref_3).

---

[3] History-tables closely relate to the notion of *redo logs* in databases, previously studied within process mining in [8].

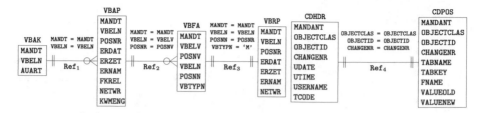

Fig. 1. Excerpt of the SAP order-to-cash database schema, in a Belgian installment. Naming is kept as in the original schema.

Both column and history-table timestamps are present. For example, the creation of a sales order line is traced via the combination of the ERDAT (date) and ERZET (time) columns of the VBAP table (cf. Figure 1), which is in fact the same table used to store order lines. The additional columns ERNAM, NETWR, and KWMENG in the same table respectively indicate the person who created the line, and its initial price and quantity.

The fact that a customer changes the quantity of a line is instead separately traced in the CDHDR and CDPOS history-tables from Fig. 1. Each entry in CDHDR indicates that change number CHANGENR occurred at date UDATE and time UTIME for the concept OBJECTCLAS, and in particular for its entry identified by OBJECTID. A corresponding entry in table CDPOS (where the correspondence is given by table, entry identifier, and change number) indicates the specifics of the change, in particular that the change is about modifying the value for the column FNAME from VALUEOLD to VALUENEW for table TABNAME.   ◁

With this premise at hand, the four steps of the erprep procedure are:

1. *Data Understanding:* definition of the process mining questions/cornerstones and decision of which relevant tables to use for the procedure;
2. *Conceptual Understanding:* identification and documentation of which document/object/relationship types are represented in these tables;
3. *Activity Elicitation:* elicitation of the main activities of interest;
4. *Perspective, Granularity, and Scoping:* identification of a suitable notion of case and of the relevant events pertaining the elicited activities.

These steps are depicted in Fig. 2, together with their relationship to the OnProm approach. The first three steps are used to semi-automatically generate the domain ontology and mappings required by OnProm, whereas the last one guides the user in the semi-automatic generation of annotations used by OnProm to generate the desired XES log. We next detail the four steps of erprep, using a running example that covers an excerpt of the use case reported in Sect. 5.

Step 1: Data Understanding. This step corresponds to the classical initialization step of any process mining project [7]. The domain expert narrates in own words the process steps that are perceived as the cornerstones of the process. These are often a combination of activities and statuses. At the same time, the domain expert needs to explicitly formulate the key questions driving the

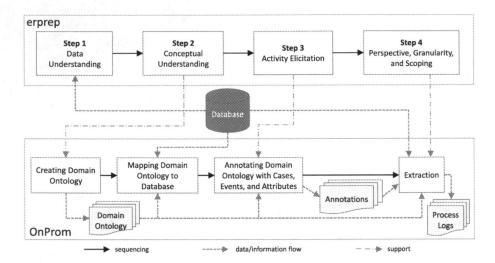

Fig. 2. The four steps of the erprep procedure and their relationship to OnProm.

process mining analysis. The data engineer then assists in identifying the tables that capture the timestamps of the cornerstones. These tables, the foreign keys between them, and the relevant fields are displayed in a relational schema so as to understand the underlying relations. This step provides the anchor for selecting out of thousands of tables of the database the set $\mathcal{R}$ of relevant tables that are part of the OBDA Specification $\langle \mathcal{O}, \mathcal{M}, \mathcal{R} \rangle$ to be provided (together with annotations) as input to OnProm.

Step 2: Conceptual Understanding. This step focuses on the conceptual understanding of the selected documents and related concepts. The purpose is to understand how the following key concepts are stored therein: *(i)* documents and their parts; *(ii)* document flows, mutually linking documents in a logical sequence; *(iii)* other relevant classes and associations. The focus here is on structural aspects (classes, attributes, and associations), while dynamic aspects related to activities executed on these structural elements are handled later.

Before entering in the description of the sub-steps, we describe the two main information sources used to identify classes, associations, and documents/document-parts, in corresponding *tabs*, that is, forms structured as depicted in Fig. 3. These tabs are filled in by the data engineer, on the basis of interaction with the domain expert. A *class tab* describes a relevant class whose instances can be obtained from an underlying table, possibly using a filter on its entries. Identifiers of objects in this class have to be consequently constructed from one or multiple columns from the table, where the default choice is that of selecting the primary key of the table. Also each relevant attribute of the class is obtained by taking the value of one or more columns (in the latter case, the semantics is that of concatenation). Sub-classes of the considered class could also implicitly be identified from the table, by looking into a so-called *discriminator column* whose values indicate to which sub-class the corresponding entry

Class ⟨cla-name⟩

DESCRIPTION	⟨text⟩		
TABLE	⟨tab-name⟩		
FILTER	⟨sql-filter⟩		
OBJECT ID	⟨col-name⟩⁺		
	NAME	DESCR.	COLS
ATTRIBUTES	⟨att-name⟩	⟨text⟩	⟨col-name⟩⁺
	...	...	

	⟨col-name⟩	
SUBCLASSES	SUBCLASS	COL VALUE
	⟨cla-name⟩	⟨text⟩
	...	...

(a) Class tab template

Association ⟨rel-name⟩

DESCRIPTION	⟨text⟩	
	CLASS	MULT.
SOURCE	⟨cla-name⟩	⟨min-max⟩
TARGET	⟨cla-name⟩	⟨min-max⟩
LINK	⟨sql-nav⟩	

(b) Association tab template

Main document ⟨cla-name⟩

CLASS TAB

Document Part ⟨cla-name⟩

CLASS TAB	
LINK	⟨sql-nav⟩

(c) Document tab template

Fig. 3. Templates of documentation tabs for document classes and other classes/associations; the document tab uses twice the class tab (once for the main document, once for its parts). Sections can be omitted if not needed. Symbols inside angles indicate the entry type: ⟨text⟩ free text; ⟨cla-name⟩, ⟨rel-name⟩, and ⟨att-name⟩ class, association, and attribute names (at the conceptual level); ⟨tab-name⟩ and ⟨col-name⟩ table and column names (at the database level); ⟨sql-filter⟩ and ⟨sql-nav⟩ "SQL notes", sketching filters over single tables and join/navigational queries relating multiple tables; ⟨min-max⟩ multiplicity constraints à la UML (0..1, 1, *, 1..*).

belongs to; this tackles the common pattern where a class hierarchy is mapped to a single database table. An example of usage is given in Fig. 4.

An *association tab* describes a relevant association between two classes, previously described using class tabs. Such classes are linked through a so-called *navigation expression* that relates the two corresponding class tables. This is done in two possible ways: either by defining a full-fledged query that relates the two tables via joins and filters, or as a sequence of one or more referential constraints of the database schema. In the former case, the participating multiplicities of the source and target classes to the association have to be defined manually (possibly validating them using the data stored in the database). In the latter case, the multiplicities are instead directly obtained by considering the concatenation of the constraints: if, by moving from the source to the target, all referential constraints indicate mandatory participation, the source multiplicity has 1 as lower bound, 0 otherwise; similarly if, by moving from the source to the target, all referential constraints are functional, the source multiplicity has 1 as upper bound, * otherwise. The same line of reasoning applies from the target to the source, to define the target multiplicity.

In this phase, queries and filters have not to be thought as full SQL queries, but more as SQL "notes" used by the data engineer.

Step 2.1: Identification of documents and their flows. The main entry point for Step 2 is to start from the elicitation of the *document classes* of interest, identifying their document- and document-part- tables. To do so, one compiles a *document tab* that, as shown in Fig. 3(c), consists of three sections: *(i)* a *main document* section, defined using a class tab as described above; *(ii)* a *document*

Main document SalesDoc

DESCRIPTION	Doc. for sales-specific info	
TABLE	VBAK	
OBJECT ID	MANDT, VBELN	
SUBCLASSES	AUART	
	SUBCLASS	COL VALUE
	Order	ZOR
	DebitNote	...
	CreditNote	...

Document part SalesDocLine

DESCRIPTION	Entry for sales of a single item		
TABLE	VBAP		
FILTER	FKREL='a'		
OBJECT ID	MANDT, VBELN, POSNR		
ATTRIBUTES	NAME	DESCR.	COLS
	lineNo	line number	POSNR
LINK	VBAP->Ref$_1$->VBAK		

Fig. 4. Document tab for sales document in our running example.

part section, also defined using a class tab; *(iii)* a *link* section, containing a navigation expression to relate all parts of the same document to their unique, main document. The navigation expression must induce a one-to-many association from the main document to its parts – which can be directly checked if the navigation expression is a sequence of referential constraints.

Example 3. By applying Step 2.1 to the database schema of Fig. 1, we encode the knowledge described in Example 2 into a document tab for sales document, instantiating the template in Fig. 3(c) into Fig. 4. The tab shows that sales documents are identified through the combination of the columns MANDT (identifying the SAP client) and VBELN (identifying a specific sales document within a SAP client), and that the AUART column acts as discriminator column to identify the three types of sales documents existing in the system; for example, VBAK entries with AUART = 'ZOR' denote orders (as we had anticipated in Example 1). The tab further captures the knowledge that only VBAP entries with FKREL = 'a' (sales document lines that are relevant for billing) should be included in the event log. Each sales document line is identified by combining its MANDT and VBELN columns (actually referencing the two corresponding VBAK columns via Ref$_1$) together with POSNR, which denotes the line number. Ref$_1$ also provides the navigation for linking sales document lines to their sales documents.   ◁

Step 2.2: Identification of additional classes and associations. Additional, relevant classes and associations can be defined similarly to documents and their parts, until all the tables isolated in Step 1 are inspected. Notice that not all the tables should be promoted to classes, as some of them are actually used to establish associations. This is for example the case of the VBFA table in Fig. 1, which is used to implicitly link different documents in a flow.

Step 2.3: Generation of core domain ontology and mappings. All the tabs filled in Steps 2.1 and 2.2 are used to automatically generate a domain ontology $\mathcal{O}$ that describes the domain of interest at a pure conceptual level, and constitutes a further component of the OBDA Specification $\langle \mathcal{O}, \mathcal{M}, \mathcal{R} \rangle$ to be used for data

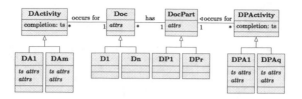

Fig. 5. Domain ontology fragment for document **Doc**, its parts, and related activities.

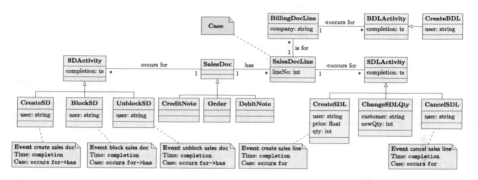

Fig. 6. Annotated domain ontology for the SAP schema fragment of Fig. 1. The green part denotes what is obtained after Step 2, the blue part the addition obtained after Step 3, and the annotations what done in Step 4. (Color figure online)

extraction via OnProm. Such an ontology will be later expanded with additional components. This is done by simply fetching all classes, subclasses, attributes, associations, and multiplicities introduced in the different documentation tabs. The green, central part of Fig. 5 shows the generic contribution that a specific document tab provides to the ontology $\mathcal{O}$ (the presence or absence of subclasses there depends on what indicated in the tab), while the central, green part of Fig. 6 shows the ontology generated for Example 3.

Documentation tabs also provide a basis to semi-automatically derive mappings $\mathcal{M}$ to link the database schema $\mathcal{R}$ isolated in Step 2 to the ontology $\mathcal{O}$. In this respect, each class tab provides the basis for generating one mapping to populate the instances of the class, using the table as a target for the selection of values, and what indicated in the OBJECT ID entry to construct objects from the retrieved database values. The same mechanism, using filters based on the discriminator column, is used to populate the subclasses. Also, every attribute entry leads to a dedicated mapping. In addition to the mapping for its two classes, each document tab leads to a further mapping, used to connect document part instances to their main document instance based on what indicated in the LINK entry. Finally, similar mappings are generated based on the association tabs.

Example 4. The document tab in Fig. 4 leads to the generation of the mappings that we have anticipated in Example 1 (where we have shown only one subclass mapping for brevity), together with the following mapping:

Activities

NAME	TABLE	COMPLETION TIME	TARGET CLASS	FILTER	LINK	OTHER ATTRS		
						NAME	DESCR.	QUERY
⟨text⟩	⟨tab-name⟩	⟨col-name⟩⁺	⟨cla-name⟩	− or ⟨sql-filter⟩	− or ⟨sql-nav⟩	⟨att-name⟩	⟨text⟩	⟨sql-nav⟩
						...	...	...
...	...	...	...	...	...	...		

Fig. 7. Template of the activity tab for defining relevant activities; each entry depends on whether the timestamp is retrieved by column or by history-table.

```
SELECT MANDT, VBELN, POSNR FROM VBAP WHERE FKREL='a'
  ↝ SalesDocLine(sdl(MANDT, VBELN, POSNR)), lineNo(sdl(MANDT, VBELN, POSNR), POSNR),
    has(sd(MANDT, VBELN), sdl(MANDT, VBELN, POSNR))
```

Note how this last mapping populates at the same time the class **SalesDocLine**, its data property **lineNo**, and the object property **has**, which connects instances of **SalesDoc** to their sales document lines.   ◁

Step 3: Activity Elicitation. Step 3 enriches the ontology $\mathcal{O}$ (and the mappings $\mathcal{M}$) obtained at the end of Step 2 with all the relevant activities that are executed on the documents and objects instantiating the classes mentioned therein. This is done by iterating over all document/document-part types and other classes that may be subject to activities. For each such class, the data engineer identifies the relevant timestamp columns in the database schema, considering the two patterns of column and history-table timestamps. For simplicity of exposition, we concentrate here on timestamps marking the completion of activities. Timestamp attributes are used to decide, together with the domain expert, which activities should be modeled.

Step 3.1: Turn timestamps into activities. This step singles out all relevant activities, and populates an overall activity tab following the template in Fig. 7. Each activity is described there by a name, the table containing the timestamp of interest, and a selection of columns providing that timestamp (more columns may be needed if, e.g., the date and time are stored separately, as it happens in our running example). In addition, the target class C containing the instances that are the subject of the activity is provided. Here, the two patterns of column and history-table timestamps have to be considered. In the case of column timestamp, no further details need to be given, as each instance of C will go through that activity whenever a timestamp in the selected column(s) is given. In the case of history-table timestamp, instead, since the table contains different changes for the same or different classes, and may be related to additional history tables, two information units have to be provided: a filter indicating under which circumstances a change actually describes an occurrence of the activity of interest, and a navigation expression to explain how entries in the history table relate to instances of C. In both cases, additional attributes (such as the resource responsible for the activity) can be declared.

Example 5. We continue our running example by eliciting two activities for sales document lines, following the description in Example 2. The creation of a sales order line can be simply tracked by looking into the columns ERDAT and ERZET of the VBAP table - according to the column timestamp pattern. A change of sales order line quantity is instead tracked following the history-table pattern, specifically by filtering the CDHDR table on those entries where TCODE = 'VA02', OBJECTCLAS = 'VERKBELEG', and whose corresponding entry in CDPOS (obtained by navigating Ref_4) is so that FNAME = 'KWMENG', with the new quantity retrieved also from CDPOS by selecting VALUENEW. To link occurrences of this activity to corresponding lines, one can define a complex navigation expression connecting CDHDR to VBAP, using the aforementioned columns.   ◁

Step 3.2: Extension of domain ontology and mappings. The core ontology $\mathcal{O}$ obtained at the end of Step 2 is automatically extended using the activity tab produced in Step 3.1. Specifically, every class **C** that has at least one activity gets associated via a one-to-many association to a corresponding **CActivity** class, denoting a generic activity, and equipped with the completion timestamp as attribute. Every entry in the activity tab filled for **C** in Step 3.1 becomes a dedicated subclass of **CActivity**, possibly carrying additional attributes. The result of this extension for a generic document is shown in the blue part of Fig. 5, whereas the result in the context of our running example is shown in the blue part of Fig. 6 (including the two activities elicited in Example 5).

Additional mappings linking the underlying database to such activity classes are semi-automatically devised, following again the procedure of Step 2.3.

Step 4: Perspective, Granularity, and Scoping. In this final step, the domain and the process mining experts finally concentrate only on the domain ontology $\mathcal{O}$, without considering anymore the specific storage mechanisms provided by the underlying database. The purpose is to define the perspective and scope of the analysis, identifying which notion of case best serves this purpose, and which events should be included (or not). Thanks to the ontology annotation mechanism provided by OnProm to identify cases and events, this final step is performed directly using OnProm in a guided way.

Step 4.1: Perspective and granularity selection. Based on the questions elicited in Step 1, the domain expert indicates which document provides the main angle for the analysis. This is not enough, as one has to consequently indicate the granularity of the analysis, either choosing the main document class, or the class for document-parts, as case notion. Depending on this choice, there may be *convergence* and *divergence* issues that the two experts have to be aware of [1]. Specifically, if the main document class is selected, all events related to its lines will be merged together in a single overall sequence, making it impossible to distinguish which events refer to the same line. On the other hand, if the document part class is selected, all events related to the main document will be replicated in the traces of all its parts. Thanks to the explicit annotation scheme provided by OnProm, and the fact that association multiplicities are explicitly shown in the ontology, these aspects are clearly communicated to the user group.

For example, Fig. 6 indicates that the decision has been to declare the sales document line as case class. This implies that all activities attached to the main sales document are replicated in each line trace, and the activities of multiple billing documents referring to the same line are merged in the same line trace.

Step 4.2: Scoping and definition of events. The very last step consists in selecting which activities are in the scope of the analysis, providing corresponding event annotations for those activities that are kept. As required by OnProm, every event must come with an event label (that is provided manually), an indication of the associated timestamp, and a navigation expression to indicate how the event is related to its reference case(s). The latter two information units are instead directly defined using what produced in previous steps of erprep, in particular by using the completion timestamps available in the abstract activity classes, and by exploiting the associations generated in Steps 3 and 4. The latter requires the intervention of the expert group to manually disambiguate those cases where multiple associations exist between two classes.

Figure 6 shows event annotations reflecting that the domain expert is interested in the creation and cancellation of sales lines, in the creation, blocking and unblocking of their parent sales documents, without considering the billing flow.

At this stage, OnProm has all the necessary information to automatically generate an XES event log from the database, reflecting the decisions taken. Alternative logs for different perspectives and scopes can be easily obtained by re-executing Step 4 with different annotations.

5   Case Study

To select an appropriate evaluation strategy for erprep, we applied the *framework for evaluation in design science* of [20] and selected the 'Human Risk & Effectiveness' evaluation strategy. This led to a case study evaluation of erprep in a formative-naturalistic setting, following [18,19]. Ideally, an evaluation benchmarks the new approach against a baseline setting where the approach has not been followed. However, this is nearly impossible in a naturalistic setting that involves industry, as it would require the case company to build several event logs in the traditional, labor-intensive way first, only to redo the exercise differently.

By applying erprep, we aim to answer the following questions: *(1)* Can the three envisioned phases of the OnProm approach be smoothly applied in a real-life setting? *(2)* Is performance playing a role in the feasibility of erprep?

To test these, we collaborated with an international manufacturing company that uses SAP. One of the authors interacted with the company. This researcher has expertise in process mining and event log building, but no prior experience with OnProm, thus representing a process mining expert that is knowledgeable of erprep, but not of ontology nor mapping design. The lack of knowledge on the OnProm approach by this person is key to this study. This set-up allowed us to evaluate whether erprep is capable of employing domain knowledge on both the process and the event data structure in its traditional form, not manipulated towards the OnProm approach. Orthogonal to the OnProm steps, the same researcher also executed the data extraction on premises of the company. The other authors are experts in the OnProm approach and toolchain.

The case study was conducted following the steps described in Sect. 4. In particular, the running example covers a fragment of what was conducted during the case study. The main difference is that, in the case study, the focus has been on the entire order-to-cash process, which requires to consider additional tables, and in turn a wider repertoire of documents, including documents related to accounting and delivery. Since compliance to financial regulations is of interest to the company, the accounting document was selected as case notion. However, by choosing the accounting document (the invoice) as case, it was not possible to answer some of the identified key questions, since they would require a different view on the process. Hence, a second event log was generated by taking the sales document perspective, which only required to repeat Step 4 of erprep a second time. Building these logs using erprep resulted in a smooth process, with a single workshop to gather the domain knowledge and the key questions.

The result was directly encoded into an ontology and mappings, following erprep without the need of taking further decisions. This led to the direct generation of 21 mappings linking the database to the ontology. Using also the annotations, OnProm automatically transformed them into 251 mappings linking the database to the XES concepts of trace, event, and event attributes. Two logs based on the result of erprep were generated on a computer with an Intel i7-7820HQ CPU and 64 GB of RAM. The input data were stored in a PostgreSQL database on the same machine, setting 48 GB as the maximum heap size for log extraction. We obtained the following indicators, witnessing feasibility; *(i)* using the sales document perspective, 238 806 traces, 1 345 269 events, and 10 489 169 attributes were extracted in 241 s, resulting in a log of 338 MB; *(ii)* using the invoice perspective, 247 051 traces, 1 742 127 events, and 10 497 414 attributes were extracted in 362 s, resulting in a log of 457 MB.

6 Conclusion

We have defined a guided approach, called erprep, to help expert groups in extracting event logs from relational databases of document-driven, enterprise information systems. The approach relies on OnProm as a technical pipeline for data extraction, while simplifying the set up of such pipeline. We have evaluated erprep on a real-world industrial use case, answering relevant research questions that show feasibility in an industrial setting.

The next, natural step is to make erprep able to generate object-centric logs, such as those conforming to the recent OCEL log format. This is directly implementable, considering a recent extension of OnProm to provide object-centric log annotations and the capability of generating OCEL logs [22].

References

1. Aalst, W.M.P.: Object-centric process mining: dealing with divergence and convergence in event data. In: Ölveczky, P.C., Salaün, G. (eds.) SEFM 2019. LNCS, vol. 11724, pp. 3–25. Springer, Cham (2019). https://doi.org/10.1007/978-3-030-30446-1_1

2. Calvanese, D., et al.: Ontologies and databases: the *DL-Lite* approach. In: Tessaris, S., et al. (eds.) Reasoning Web 2009. LNCS, vol. 5689, pp. 255–356. Springer, Heidelberg (2009). https://doi.org/10.1007/978-3-642-03754-2_7

3. Calvanese, D., De Giacomo, G., Lembo, D., Lenzerini, M., Rosati, R.: Tractable reasoning and efficient query answering in description logics: The DL-Lite family. J. of Autom. Reason. **39**(3), 385–429 (2007)

4. Calvanese, D., Kalayci, T.E., Montali, M., Santoso, A.: OBDA for Log extraction in process mining. In: Ianni, G., Lembo, D., Bertossi, L., Faber, W., Glimm, B., Gottlob, G., Staab, S. (eds.) Reasoning Web 2017. LNCS, vol. 10370, pp. 292–345. Springer, Cham (2017). https://doi.org/10.1007/978-3-319-61033-7_9

5. Calvanese, D., Kalayci, T.E., Montali, M., Tinella, S.: Ontology-based data access for extracting event logs from legacy data: the onprom tool and methodology. In: Abramowicz, W. (ed.) BIS 2017. LNBIP, vol. 288, pp. 220–236. Springer, Cham (2017). https://doi.org/10.1007/978-3-319-59336-4_16

6. Cohn, D., Hull, R.: Business artifacts: a data-centric approach to modeling business operations and processes. IEEE Bull. Data Eng. **32**(3) (2009)

7. van Eck, M.L., Lu, X., Leemans, S.J.J., van der Aalst, W.M.P.: PM^2: a process mining project methodology. In: Zdravkovic, J., Kirikova, M., Johannesson, P. (eds.) CAiSE 2015. LNCS, vol. 9097, pp. 297–313. Springer, Cham (2015). https://doi.org/10.1007/978-3-319-19069-3_19

8. González López de Murillas, E., Reijers, H.A., van der Aalst, W.M.P.: Connecting databases with process mining: a meta model and toolset. Softw. Syst. Model. 18(2) (2019)

9. Guarino, N., Welty, C.A.: An overview of OntoClean. In: Staab, S., Studer, R. (eds.) Handbook on Ontologies. International Handbooks on Information Systems, pp. 151–171. Springer, Berlin, Heidelberg (2004). https://doi.org/10.1007/978-3-540-24750-0_8

10. Ingvaldsen, J.E., Gulla, J.A.: Preprocessing support for large scale process mining of SAP transactions. In: ter Hofstede, A., Benatallah, B., Paik, H.-Y. (eds.) BPM 2007. LNCS, vol. 4928, pp. 30–41. Springer, Heidelberg (2008). https://doi.org/10.1007/978-3-540-78238-4_5

11. Jans, M., Soffer, P.: From relational database to event log: decisions with quality impact. In: Teniente, E., Weidlich, M. (eds.) BPM 2017. LNBIP, vol. 308, pp. 588–599. Springer, Cham (2018). https://doi.org/10.1007/978-3-319-74030-0_46

12. Jans, M., Soffer, P., Jouck, T.: Building a valuable event log for process mining: an experimental exploration of a guided process. Enterp. Inf. Syst. **13**(5) (2019)

13. Li, G., de Murillas, E.G.L., de Carvalho, R.M., van der Aalst, W.M.P.: Extracting object-centric event logs to support process mining on databases. In: Mendling, J., Mouratidis, H. (eds.) CAiSE 2018. LNBIP, vol. 317, pp. 182–199. Springer, Cham (2018). https://doi.org/10.1007/978-3-319-92901-9_16

14. Lu, X., Nagelkerke, M., v. d. Wiel, D., Fahland, D.: Discovering interacting artifacts from ERP systems. IEEE Trans. Serv. Comput. 8(6) (2015)

15. Motik, B., Cuenca Grau, B., Horrocks, I., Wu, Z., Fokoue, A., Lutz, C.: OWL 2 Web Ontology Language profiles (second edition). W3C Recommendation, W3C (2012). https://www.w3.org/TR/owl2-profiles/

16. Mueller-Wickop, N., Schultz, M.: ERP event log preprocessing: timestamps vs. accounting logic. In: vom Brocke, J., Hekkala, R., Ram, S., Rossi, M. (eds.) i. LNCS, vol. 7939, pp. 105–119. Springer, Heidelberg (2013). https://doi.org/10.1007/978-3-642-38827-9_8

17. Nooijen, E.H.J., van Dongen, B.F., Fahland, D.: Automatic discovery of data-centric and artifact-centric processes. In: La Rosa, M., Soffer, P. (eds.) BPM 2012. LNBIP, vol. 132, pp. 316–327. Springer, Heidelberg (2013). https://doi.org/10.1007/978-3-642-36285-9_36
18. Runeson, P., Höst, M.: Guidelines for conducting and reporting case study research in software engineering. Emp. Softw. Eng. **14**(2) (2008)
19. Shull, F., et al.: Replicating software engineering experiments: addressing the tacit knowledge problem. In: Proceedings of International Symposium on Empirical Software Engineering (2002)
20. Venable, J., Pries-Heje, J., Baskerville, R.: FEDS: a framework for evaluation in design science research. Eur. J. Inf. Syst. **25**(1) (2016)
21. Xiao, G., et al.: Ontology-based data access: a survey. In: Proceedings of IJCAI (2018)
22. Xiong, J., Xiao, G., Kalayci, T.E., Montali, M., Gu, Z., Calvanese, D.: Extraction of object-centric event logs through virtual knowledge graphs (extended abstract). In: Proceedings of DL. CEUR, vol. 3263. CEUR-WS.org (2022)

Event Data-Driven Feasibility Checking
of Process Schedules

Hannes Häfke[1]([✉])[ID] and Sebastiaan J. van Zelst[1,2][ID]

[1] Fraunhofer Institute for Applied Information Technology, Sankt Augustin,
Germany
{hannes.haefke,sebastiaan.van.zelst}@fit.fraunhofer.de
[2] RWTH Aachen University, Aachen, Germany

Abstract. Numerous processes require dedicated scheduling of their to-
be-executed activities. Various algorithms have been developed to computationally solve many different scheduling problems, allocating the
available resources to predefined time slots of activity execution to (theoretically) maximize resource utilization efficiency. Yet, in industry, creating schedules for future process executions often remains a (primarily)
manual, spreadsheet-based endeavor. Typically, manually created schedules are sub-optimal and potentially infeasible. At the same time, the
event data stored in the information systems supporting the process can
act as valuable input to further improve the general alignment of the
schedule to the actual process execution. Therefore, in this paper, we
propose a novel method that enables schedule feasibility checking based
on historically recorded event data corresponding to the actual execution
of the scheduled process. Our method serves as an input to detect significant issues in the project scheduling problems, which can be used to
further improve the overall quality of the schedules computed. Our initial
results confirm the general applicability of the proposed framework.

Keywords: Business Process Management · Process Mining ·
Data-driven Scheduling · Business Process Organization

1   Introduction

The efficient execution of business processes includes decision-making from various perspectives to achieve the desired business outcomes. One such perspective
is *scheduling* [20], i.e., a sub-field of the broader field of Operations Research
(OR) [23,24], concerned with the assignment of to-be-executed activities to available resources at a predefined designated time-slot. It is generally recognized that
accurate scheduling is vital in many areas, e.g., in production and service industries, to ensure a competitive advantage. Hence, several scheduling algorithms
exist that allow for computationally solving many different scheduling problems,
i.e., either yielding an optimal solution (defined in terms of some desirable outcome of the schedule, e.g., overall lead time) or an approximate solution.

Albeit numerous classes of scheduling problems and their associated solution approaches have been investigated in tremendous depth, creating schedules

M. Indulska et al. (Eds.): CAiSE 2023, LNCS 13901, pp. 210–225, 2023.
https://doi.org/10.1007/978-3-031-34560-9_13

in the industry remains a largely manual, spreadsheet-based endeavor. In [6], two main causes are presented for the lack of adoption: (i) Advanced Planning Systems (APS) are considered a black box, and (ii) financial gains of APS adoption are unclear. However, the advantages of APS adoption are numerous, e.g., reduced manual labor in planning, varying optimization criteria, reduced errors, etc. At the same time, the information systems supporting scheduled processes, e.g., Enterprise Resource Planning (ERP) and Manufacturing Execution Systems (MES), track the historical process execution in great detail. These recorded data, i.e., referred to as *event data*, provide a valuable source of, arguably, objective evidence of the actual execution performance of the company. Said event data can, in turn, be used to detect problems in a schedule (created either manually or by an APS) and recommend alternative resource allocations.

Scheduling and the structured (semi-automated) analysis of event data (i.e., *process mining* [1]) have both been intensively studied. Yet, work focusing on their intersection remains scarce. Some work focuses on resource allocation [2,4] or combining event data with queueing theory [5,22]. However, none of these techniques allow for improving operational schedules based on historical behavior. Yet, at the same time, it is clear that historical event data is a precious resource in increasing the overall quality of the application of scheduling in practice. Therefore, this paper presents a novel approach for assessing scheduling feasibility based on event data. Our approach learns a statistical characterization of the past performance of resources, which it subsequently uses to detect potential infeasibilities in the given schedule. To the best of our knowledge, our work is the first to seek to connect the operational history of a process with an organization's scheduling function.

We present an initial evaluation of our approach using real event data combined with artificially generated corresponding schedules. We assess the parameter sensitivity of two instantiations of our framework and show that our approach is computationally feasible. Furthermore, we investigate typical distributions that tend to fit concerning the training event data.

The remainder of this paper is structured as follows. In Sect. 2, we present related work. In Sect. 3, we present key background concepts. Section 4 presents our newly developed framework. In Sect. 5, we evaluate our approach. Section 6 concludes this work.

2   Related Work

Ample work exists on scheduling, i.e., covering scheduling theory, algorithms, models, systems, etc. [13,20]. Most work in scheduling research is algorithm oriented and focuses on static scheduling problems. A smaller subset focuses on the notion of *dynamic scheduling* [18], i.e., an ongoing reactive scheduling process in which real-time events and information forces schedule reconsideration.

A limited amount of work has considered the intersection of process-generated event data and scheduling. In [16], a revised WfMS implementation is presented that supports both *flow* and *schedule tasks*, which allows integration of employee calendars within the task-scheduling. In [17, Section 11.3], process mining algorithms are used to identify future task scheduling, based on event logs containing (historical) appointment information. In [15], the authors propose event-log-based visualization techniques to visualize changes in the process execution, primarily focusing on the resource and time dimension. Whereas the framework is generic, the proposed instantiation heavily focuses on the resource and temporal dimension, allowing the analysis of the impact of alternative work schedules. In [8], a scheduling approach is proposed for workforce scheduling. The authors do not exploit recorded event data, yet, illustrate how the inputs of the proposed scheduling problem relate to the BPM discipline, e.g., covering the *organizational perspective*, the *control-flow perspective*, etc. In [21], the authors propose to learn static scheduling models from event data. The approach learns a timed Petri net from the event data which is converted into a constraint programming problem. In [12], the authors propose to embed process mining techniques in the context of scheduling. However, the integration of process mining is on the output side, i.e., the solutions of an optimization problem are converted into synthetic event data which are used for the analysis of the proposed solution. Another line of work aims to transform event data into Gantt charts (rather than process models) for further analysis [3].

Some authors have considered using queueing models to explicitly model timing-related aspects of business processes. In [22], Senderovich et al. propose to convert an event log and a schedule of a process into a *Fork/Join Queuing Network*, which are subsequently compared to assess conformance and performance aspects of the schedule. In [5], the authors propose to estimate missing lifecycle data for the purpose of performance analysis based on queueing models.

Several authors have focused on exploiting event data in the context of (human) resource allocation, i.e., in the context of business process executions. For example, in [2], Arias et al. propose a framework that exploits contextual information together with event data to improve human resource allocation. In [4], the authors propose to learn, i.e., based on event data, which resource allocations may lead to execution problems and propose a resource selection mechanism that minimizes the risk of execution problems when executing future tasks. In [11], Ihde et al. focus on a software design for a resource-aware task allocation service that can replace existing task schedulers in BPM systems. Havur et al. [9,10] propose a resource allocation mechanism based on answer set programming that is able to handle resource dependencies and conflicts.

Whereas the works mentioned consider event data and schedules/resource allocation, to the best of our knowledge, our work is the first to seek to connect the operational history of a process with an organization's scheduling function.

3   Preliminaries

In this section, we present the basic background concepts used in this paper. In Sect. 3.1, we briefly present the notation used. In Sect. 3.2, we formally define the notion of schedules. Finally, in Sect. 3.3, we present event data.

3.1 Notation

$\mathbb{Z}$ denotes the set of integers and $\mathbb{N}$ denotes the set of natural numbers including 0. We let $\mathbb{R}$ denote the set of real-valued numbers and we let $\mathbb{R}^+ = \{x \in \mathbb{R} | x \geq 0\}$ denote the non-negative real-valued numbers. A *timestamp* $t \in \mathbb{R}^+$ is a point in time.[1] An *interval* is a set of real-valued numbers containing all numbers that lie between its two boundaries. Let $a, b \in \mathbb{R}$, the *closed interval* between a and b is defined as $[a, b] = \{x \in \mathbb{R} | a \leq x \leq b\}$. Observe that a closed interval can be empty (i.e., if $b > a$) and it can be a singleton set (i.e., if $a = b$), referred to as a *degenerate interval*. Any interval that is non-empty and not degenerate is a *proper interval*.

We assume that the reader is reasonably familiar with *probability theory* [14]. We particularly focus on *continuous probability functions*, with an associated *probability density function* f, e.g., the *normal distribution* [19] has density function $f(x) = \frac{1}{\sigma\sqrt{2\pi}} e^{-\frac{1}{2}\left(\frac{x-\mu}{\sigma}\right)^2}$ for average value μ and standard deviation σ. Various methods exist to *fit* a probability distribution. Generally, given some $X \subset \mathbb{R}$, we let $\hat{f} = \theta(X)$ denote the result of applying a probability distribution fitting algorithm θ applied on X, where $\hat{f}$ represents the fitted distribution. Various different methods exist to assess the *goodness of fit* of $\hat{f}$ w.r.t. X. We generally let ϵ denote the error of $\hat{f}$ with respect to X.

3.2 Schedules

In the context of this paper, we formalize the notion of a schedule. Conceptually, a schedule describes a collection of *tasks* that describe that some *activity* is intended to be executed by a *resource* within a predefined *time-frame*. For example, consider Fig. 1, in which we present visual examples of two schedules of an academic reviewing process. In the schedule in Fig. 1a, *John* is scheduled to "Collect Reviews" in time window $[t_0, t_1]$, and activity "Decide" in time window $[t_6, t_8]$. *Mike* is scheduled to "Invite Reviewers" in time window $[t_3, t_5]$. *Anne* is scheduled to "Collect Reviews" in time window $[t_1, t_3]$. In the example schedule in Fig. 1b, the same activities are scheduled to the same set of resources. However, in the schedule, there is no obsolete idle time in between any tasks, and, the tasks are scheduled as early as possible (e.g., Anne starts inviting reviewers directly at t_0, reviews are directly collected after reviewer invitation is completed, etc.). As such, schedule Fig. 1b is expected to finish earlier. In the context of this paper, we define the notion of a *task* and corresponding as follows.

Definition 1 (Task; Schedule). *Let Σ denote the universe of business activities and let $\mathcal{R}$ denote the universe of resources. A task τ is a tuple $\tau = (a, r, t_1, t_2) \in \Sigma \times \mathcal{R} \times \mathbb{R}^+ \times \mathbb{R}^+$, s.t. $t_2 > t_1$. We let $\mathcal{T}$ denote the universe of tasks. A schedule is a set of tasks, i.e., $S \subseteq \mathcal{T}$. We let $\mathcal{S}$ denote the universe of schedules.*

Observe that, for a given task $\tau = (a, r, t_1, t_2)$, the intended timeframe of execution is the interval $[t_1, t_2]$. Since $t_2 > t_1$, any task

---

[1] We assume the existence of some minimal timestamp $t_0 \in \mathbb{R}^+$ and $t' \in \mathbb{R}^+$ s.t. any timestamp t can be expressed as $t = t_0 + t'$.

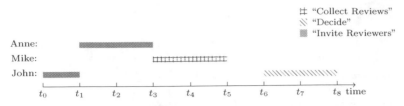

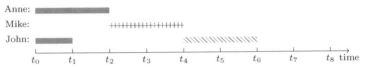

(a) Example of a *non-optimal schedule* of an academic reviewing process. *John* is scheduled to "Invite Reviewers" in time window $[t_0, t_1]$, and activity "Decide" in time window $[t_6, t_8]$. *Mike* is scheduled to "Collect Reviews" in time window $[t_3, t_5]$. *Anne* is scheduled to "Invite Reviewers" in time window $[t_1, t_3]$.

(b) Example of an *optimal schedule* of an academic reviewing process. *John* is scheduled to "Invite Reviewers" in time window $[t_0, t_1]$, and activity "Decide" in time window $[t_4, t_6]$. *Mike* is scheduled to "Collect Reviews" in time window $[t_2, t_4]$. *Anne* is scheduled to "Invite Reviewers" in time window $[t_0, t_2]$.

Fig. 1. Two example schedules. The schedule in Fig. 1a is non-optimal, the schedule in Fig. 1b is optimal and is expected to finish earlier.

is assumed to be scheduled in a *proper interval*. We let $\Delta(\tau) = [t_1, t_2]$ denote said interval. Reconsider Fig. 1a, which can be written as {("InviteReviewers", John, t_0, t_1), ("Decide", John, t_6, t_8), ("CollectReviews", Mike, t_3, t_5), ("InviteReviewers", Anne, t_2, t_6)}.

Various *constraints* can render a schedule (in)feasible. For example, if we only require a resource to work on one task at a time, both schedules in Fig. 1 are feasible. However, suppose we require a minimal setup time of four time-units (idle time in-between two consecutive activities executed by a resource). In that case, the example schedule in Fig. 1b is not feasible (John only has three time-units of setup time between his two activities). Finally, a strict subset of all feasible schedules, i.e., given a set of constraints, is *optimal*. Optimality of a schedule is determined by an *objective function*, i.e., a function that needs to be minimized or maximized. For example, assuming that no setup times are required, if we aim to optimize the *makespan* (minimizing the end time of any task), the schedule in Fig. 1a is not optimal whereas Fig. 1b is (assuming that the schedule needs to adhere to the general control-flow of academic reviewing). A schedule may be optimal under a particular set of constraints yet infeasible for a slightly different set of constraints. In the context of this paper, we primarily assume that a given schedule is *feasible*, yet, it may be sub-optimal.

3.3 Event Data

The information systems supporting business processes, e.g., Enterprise Resource Planning (ERP) systems, track the execution of the different activities executed,

Table 1. Event data required for scheduling

Event ID	Case ID	Task	Start Time	End Time	Resource
⋮	⋮	⋮	⋮	⋮	⋮
1337	331	Invite reviewers	01/15/2009 15:40	01/15/2009 15:59	Mike
1338	331	Get review	02/19/2009 07:30	02/19/2009 15:22	Carol
1339	332	Invite reviewers	05/15/2009 12:10	05/15/2009 13:01	Anne
⋮	⋮	⋮	⋮	⋮	⋮

i.e., referred to as an *event log*. Consider Table 1, in which we present a simplified example of an event log. Each row in the table describes an *activity instance*, i.e., a historical recording of the execution of an activity. The first row represents a recording of the "Invite reviewers" activity. The activity instance has a *unique identifier*, i.e., 1337. Similarly, the activity instance has a unique *case identifier*, i.e., 331, representing the process instance for which the activity was executed. Two *timestamps* are recorded for the activity instance, i.e., a *start* and *end timestamp*. Finally, the activity instance records which *resource* executed the activity. Generally, additional data attributes may be available for activity instances, e.g., a customer ID, product ID, or associated costs. However, for simplicity, we only focus on the data attributes strictly required for our approach.[2] We formalize the notion of event data as follows.

Definition 2 (Activity Instance, Event Log). *Let Σ denote the universe of activity labels and let $\mathcal{R}$ denote the universe of resources. An* activity instance, *i.e., a tuple $v = (i, c, a, r, t_1, t_2) \in \mathbb{N} \times \mathbb{N} \times \Sigma \times \mathcal{R} \times \mathbb{R}^+ \times \mathbb{R}^+$, describes the historical recording of an activity a, executed by resource r during time-frame $[t_1, t_2]$ $(t_1 < t_2)$, in the context of case c. Attribute i represents the activity instance's unique identifier. We let $\mathcal{I}$ denote the universe of activity instances, i.e., for any $v, v' \in \mathcal{I}$ with $v = (i, c, a, r, t_1, t_2)$, $v' = (i', c', a', r', t_1', t_2')$, if $i = i'$ then $v = v'$.*

An event log *L is a collection of activity instances, i.e., $L \subseteq \mathcal{I}$.*

Let $v = (i, c, a, r, t_1, t_2)$ be an activity instance. Similarly to tasks, we let $\Delta(v) = [t_1, t_2]$, yet, $\Delta(v)$ describes the *actual time interval* in which the activity instance was observed (opposed to the scheduled/expected time).

4   Event-Data-Driven Feasibility Checking

In this section, we present our main contribution, i.e., *event-data-driven feasibility checking of schedules*. We present a general overview of our approach in Sect. 4.1. In Sect. 4.2, we present a generic definition and two instantiations of *duration estimators*, i.e., data-driven statistics to estimate the duration of a task executed by a resource. Finally, in Sect. 4.3, we describe the general mechanism to revise a given schedule based on the learned estimators to be subsequently used for feasibility checking.

---

[2] Unlike most process mining works, we do not explicitly require the presence of a case identifier. However, Definition 2 follows the conventional definition.

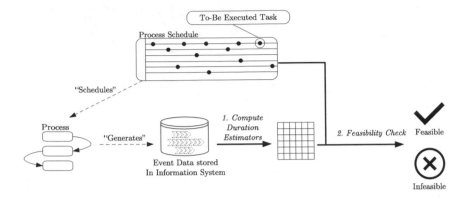

Fig. 2. Schematic overview of the proposed approach. The proposed approach consists of two steps, i.e., *1. learning an activity-resource statistics matrix* and *2. Checking schedule feasibility*

4.1 Overview

In this section, we briefly present an overview of our proposed framework. Consider Fig. 2, in which we present a schematic overview. Our framework consists of two main steps. In the first step, from the input event log, we derive a *duration estimator*. We use the event data to record different statistics (e.g., averages, distributions, etc.) of the historical execution performance of an activity-resource combination. In the second step, we perform a feasibility check of a given theoretically feasible schedule. The core idea of the feasibility check is to find scheduled tasks that, according to the data-based duration estimator, are either *overly optimistic or overly pessimistic*, i.e., in terms of their expected duration. Suppose we detect such a task in the schedule. In that case, we use the activity-resource statistic to compute a more reasonable expected duration, i.e., we use a statistic based on historical $\Delta(v)$ values to revise $\Delta(\tau)$ values (for $v \in \mathcal{I}$ and $\tau \in \mathcal{T}$). We subsequently replace the $\Delta(\tau)$ values in the given schedule with a more realistic data-driven timeframe $[t'_1, t'_2]$ and assess if the schedule remains feasible. We generally assume that the underlying scheduling problem is known, i.e., used to generate the schedule, or, that domain knowledge regarding general schedule feasibility is known. For example, there may be working hours in which tasks must be scheduled, mandatory setup times between two tasks, breaks, etc. We additionally assume that checking the feasibility of a given schedule w.r.t. a set of constraints is (programmatically) handled outside of our approach.

4.2 Deriving Activity-Resource Duration Estimators

In this section, we define the notion of duration estimators. We aim to compute an estimator for the expected duration of an activity $a \in \Sigma$ executed by a resource $r \in \mathcal{R}$. For example, if we assume that event 1337 in Table 1 is representative for the performance of *Mike* for the activity "Invite reviewers", we assign an estimated value of 19 minutes. We first define the general notion of duration estimator, after which we present two corresponding instantiations.

Definition 3 (Duration Estimator). *Let Σ denote the universe of activities and let $\mathcal{R}$ denote the universe of resources. A duration estimator is a function $\hat{\Delta} \colon \Sigma \times \mathcal{R} \to \mathbb{R}^+$ estimating the expected duration of task execution.*

Given a task $\tau = (a, r, t_1, t_2)$ in some schedule S, for simplicity, we let $\hat{\Delta}(\tau) = \hat{\Delta}(a, r)$. Observe that $\tau' = (a, r, t_1, t_1 + \hat{\Delta}(\tau))$ is a derived task, i.e., based on τ, starting at the same timestamp as τ, with the estimated duration for the activity and resource described by τ.

In the remainder, we propose two concrete instantiations for the duration estimator, i.e., an estimator based on the *empirical average* and a *distribution-based* duration estimator.

The empirical-average-based estimator uses the measured average duration of a task executed by a resource. Additionally, the standard deviation is added a number of $k \in \mathbb{N}$ times to the measured average. We formalize the empirical-average-based estimator as follows.

Definition 4 (Empirical Average Estimator). *Let $L \subseteq \mathcal{I}$ be an event log and let $k \in \mathbb{Z}$. The empirical average duration estimator $\hat{\Delta}_{avg,k} \colon \Sigma \times \mathcal{R} \to \mathbb{R}^+$ is a duration estimation function with:*

$$\hat{\Delta}_{avg,k}(a, r) = \overline{x} + k \cdot \sigma_{\overline{x}} \tag{1}$$

where $X = \{\Delta(v) | v \in L \wedge v = (i, c, a, r, t_1, t_2)\}$, $\overline{x} = \frac{\sum_{x \in X} x}{|X|}$, and $\sigma_{\overline{x}} = \sqrt{\frac{\sum_{x \in X} (x - \overline{x})}{|X| - 1}}$

The empirical-average-based estimator ignores the underlying distribution of the duration of the activity executed by the resource. Furthermore, parameter k allows us to tune the degree of under or overestimation of the estimator w.r.t. the data, i.e., a negative value for k yields a low estimated value, a positive value yields a high value.

Additionally, we propose a distribution-based estimator. In the estimator, we fit a number of different probability distributions and select the best fitting value. Subsequently, we use the k-th percentile of the fitted probability distribution as an estimator.

Definition 5 (Distribution Estimator). *Let $L \subseteq \mathcal{I}$ be an event log and let $k \in [0, 1]$. The distribution-based duration estimator $\hat{\Delta}_{dist,\hat{f},k} \colon \Sigma \times \mathcal{R} \to \mathbb{R}^+$ is a duration estimation function with:*

$$\hat{\Delta}_{dist,\hat{f},k}(a, r) = b, \ s.t. \int_{-\infty}^{b} \hat{f}(x)dx = k \tag{2}$$

where $X = \{\Delta(v) | v \in L \wedge v = (i, c, a, r, t_1, t_2)\}$ and $\hat{f} = \theta(X)$ is some fitted continuous probability function.

Observe that, for $k = 0.1$, we obtain the 10-th percentile of the cumulative distribution of $\hat{f}$ as an estimator. In practice, when computing $\hat{f} = \theta(X)$, we fit a number of different distributions based on X, e.g., the log-normal distribution, the Gamma distribution, etc. We pick the fitted distribution that minimizes the corresponding error ϵ, e.g., by using the *residual sum of squares*.

Observe that Definition 3 assumes that every repeated execution of a task by the same resource, i.e., for the same case, has the same duration. In practice, this needs not to be the case, i.e., the 2nd execution of the same activity by the same resource may be generally significantly faster or slower. Clearly, the signature of the domain of the $\hat{\Delta}$-function can be extended to cover more contextual attributes than just activity and resource, e.g., other available attributes. However, notably, it is likely that the most effective context to use depends on both the process under study as well as the corresponding event data.

4.3   Feasibility Checking

As a second step of our proposed framework, we assess the feasibility of the schedule. The feasibility check consists of two major steps, i.e., *task duration replacement* and *constraint-compliance checking*. The latter step depends primarily on either the constraints used to generate the schedule (in case scheduling is applied) or on domain knowledge regarding general scheduling feasibility, e.g., task may only be executed during work hours. However, the former step, i.e., *task duration replacement*, can be performed either in a *conservative* or in a *progressive manner*.

Given some schedule $S \in \mathcal{S}$ and $\tau = (a, r, t_1, t_2)$. In the conservative replacement strategy, we only replace task durations that are overly optimistic in the given schedule, i.e., if $\Delta(\tau) < \hat{\Delta}(a, r)$ we replace τ in S by $\tau' = (a, r, t_1, t_1 + \hat{\Delta}(a, r))$. However, if $\Delta(\tau) > \hat{\Delta}(a, r)$, we keep τ in the schedule, i.e., as it is assumed to take longer than the estimator and thus, is not expected to lead to problems. Reconsider Fig. 1b, and assume that we predict *Anne* to require 4 time units for "Invite Reviewers", *Mike* to require 3 time units for "Collect Reviews", and *John* only 1 time unit for the "Decide" activity. Figure 3a depicts the revised schedule, using the conservative strategy. Observe that the schedule inviting reviewers is expected to overlap with the review collection. Similarly, the decision activity is expected to partially overlap with the review collection.

In the progressive replacement strategy, we replace τ in S by $\tau' = (a, r, t_1, t_1 + \hat{\Delta}(a, r))$ if $\Delta(\tau) \neq \hat{\Delta}(a, r)$. Hence, in the progressive strategy, we allow tasks to be shortened in the expected duration as well. Observe that the consequences of shortening tasks in the schedule are more profound. Reconsider the previous example and consider Fig. 3b, illustrating the corresponding result of applying the progressive strategy. The "Decide" task of *John* is expected to only take one time-unit. However, as the original schedule reserved the time-frame $[t_4, t_6]$, the activity can be positioned to be starting anywhere in the time-frame $[t_4, t_5]$.

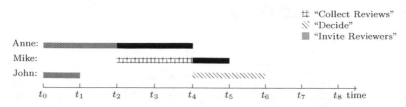

(a) Example of *conservative task duration replacement*. The tasks of *Anne* and *Mike* are expected to take longer (extended time-frame highlighted in black). John is expected to take only one time-unit for the "Decide" activity. However, the conservative strategy does not alter the scheduled "Decide" task for John.

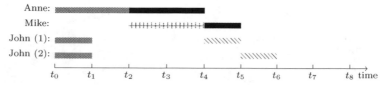

(b) Example of *progressive task duration replacement*. The progressive strategy shortens the scheduled "Decide" task for John. We are able to schedule the start of the "Decide" activity for *John* in-between t_4 and t_5. The earliest and latest scheduling of the decide activity are both visualized (*John (1)* and *John (2)*) respectively.

Fig. 3. Different examples of task duration replacement of the schedule depicted in Fig. 1b, i.e., covering both the *conservative* (Fig. 3a) and *progressive strategy* (Fig. 3b).

5   Evaluation

In this section, we evaluate our proposed event-data-driven schedule feasibility check. We present the experimental setup in Sect. 5.1. Section 5.2 presents the results.

5.1   Experimental Setup

In this section, we present the general experimental setup of our evaluation. We present the research questions considered, discuss the event data used and the general setup of the experiments, including the preprocessing steps conducted to prepare the event data for our experiments.[3]

Research Questions. The primary focus of our evaluation is an assessment of the computational aspects. In the context of our evaluation, we aim to answer the following research questions:

1. Is there a (significant) difference in the parameter sensitivity of the proposed estimators?

---

[3] The source code of our experiments is publicly available at https://github.com/ HannesHf/FeasibilityCheckingofProcessSchedules.

Table 2. Descriptive statistics of the BPIC17 event log, used in the experiments.

Events	1,202,267
Events with Start	128,227
Events with Complete	475,306
Resulting Tasks	44,503
Total Timeframe	Jan. 2016 - Jan. 2017
Training Window	Jan. 2016 - Apr. 2016
Test Data (Schedule Proxies)	May 2016 - Oct. 2016

Fig. 4. Schematic control-flow view of the steps conducted in the experiments.

2. Is there a (significant) difference in the computational complexity of the proposed estimators?
3. Which distributions are most often fitted when using the distribution-based estimator?

Event Data Selection. In our experiments, we use *real event data*. A primary requirement of the event data is the availability of both start and end timestamps as well as resource information. However, most publicly available event data (https://data.4tu.nl/) only records one timestamp per event. In the BPI Challenge 2017 log (BPIC17) [7] (https://data.4tu.nl/articles/dataset/BPI_Challenge_2017/12696884), a subset of the recorded events describe both a start and end timestamp (respectively $128,227$ start and $475,306$ end timestamps, out of a total of $1,202,267$ events). Additionally, the event data is mapping of a task to a specific resource, where the set resource is to some extent constant. The event log pertains to a loan application process of a Dutch financial institute, and as such several tasks performed by human resources differ in duration. We match the events describing a start and complete timestamp to create tasks. Note that only a small subset of the events can be matched because either the started task is aborted, i.e., there exists no corresponding complete timestamp, or the events are atomic events, i.e., there is no corresponding start timestamp. Consider Table 2, in which we present general descriptive statistics of the BPIC17 event log in the context of our experiments.

Setup. Figure 4 depicts the control flow of the experimental setup. In the first step, we retain all activity instances with a non-zero duration. The final number of extracted tasks for our experiments is $44,503$. We use the event data both as a training set, i.e., to compute the task estimator, as well as to present schedules (i.e., *schedule proxies*). To create a training data set we use the tasks occurring in the time period *Jan. 2016 - Apr. 2016*, yielding $13,131$ tasks.

We use the events recorded in the time period *May 2016 - Oct. 2016* as *proxy schedules*. The sizes of the derived schedules are (# tasks): 05/16: 3,383; 06/16: 4,408; 07/16: 4,289; 08/16: 3,648; 09/16: 4115; 10/16: 3,715 We use all activity instances between Jan. 1st, 2016, and Apr. 30th, 2016, as a training window (cf. Table 2). For every experiment, we repeat the subsequent three steps, i.e., *training the estimator*, *selecting the test data*, and finally *checking the schedule feasibility*.

We consider the empirical average estimator $(\hat{\Delta}_{\text{avg},k})$, with $k \in \{-2, -1.5, \ldots, 1.5, 2\}$. For the distribution based estimator $(\hat{\Delta}_{\text{dist}, \hat{f}, k}(a, r))$, we perform distribution fitting on the *normal, exponential, beta* and *gamma* distributions and use $k \in \{0.01, 0.05, 0.1, 0.2, 0.3, \ldots, 0.8, 0.9, 0.95, 0.99\}$ for feasibility checking. As no schedules are available for BPIC17, we select a subset of the event log to represent a schedule, i.e., as test data (which we refer to as a *proxy schedule*). In terms of task replacement, we only apply the conservative replacement strategy.

5.2   Results

In this section, we discuss the results of our experiments. We first consider *parameter sensitivity*, after which we focus on *computational complexity*. Finally, we briefly investigate the *most frequently occurring distribution* for the task-duration estimator.

Parameter Sensitivity. In this section, we compare the parameter sensitivity of the average-based estimator against the distribution-based estimator. In particular, we investigate the sensitivity of both approaches in terms of their conflict-detection ratio for different parameterizations of the algorithm. Generally, we compute a revised schedule, for which we measure the ratio of the number of tasks that overlap with another task to be executed by the same resource.[4] Let z denote the number of tasks that have such an issue; the ratio q we compute is $q = \frac{z}{|S'|}$. Hence, if $q = 0$, no problems have been detected. If $q = 1$, all tasks have a problem.

Consider Fig. 5, in which we depict the results for both estimators. Observe that, in the figures, the previously described q values are listed as percentages, and, similarly, for the distribution-based estimator (Fig. 5b), the k-values are represented as percentages. The empirical-average-based estimator (Fig. 5a) shows a much stronger parameter sensitivity compared to the distribution-based estimator (Fig. 5b). This makes sense as, for example, for a normal distribution, a value of k close to 0 or 1 for the distribution-based approach describes the results at $\overline{x} +/- 2\sigma_{\overline{x}}$ for the empirical-average-based approach. In that regard, even though

---

[4] Observe that, since we use real event data, we are not aware of the actual constraints of the process.

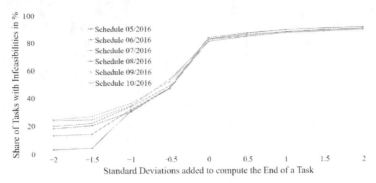

(a) Measurement of schedule compliance/feasibility based on mean values and varied standard deviations

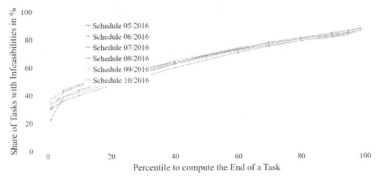

(b) Measurement of schedule compliance/feasibility based on distribution fitting with varying percentiles

Fig. 5. Results for parameters sensitivity of the two proposed estimators, i.e., *empirical average* (Fig. 5a) and *distribution-based* (Fig. 5b)

different underlying distributions are used for activity-resource combinations, using $k \in \{0.2\dots0.8\}$ for the distribution-based estimator broadly covers $\overline{x} + / - \sigma_{\overline{x}}$ for the empirical-average-based. Generally, the distribution-based approach is less sensitive to parameter changes, except for the extremes of parameter k.

Interestingly, in both cases, the highly "optimistic" values of the parameters (i.e., -2 for Fig. 5a and close to 0 for Fig. 5b) still yield a detection value of $q = 0.2$. Upon inspection of the results, we observed that this is because some activity-resource pairs infrequently occur in the training data, even yielding large estimated values for optimistic parameter settings. In other cases, some tasks still overlap, i.e., even though the estimated duration is very low. In such cases, either the tasks were already overlapping in time in the real execution (i.e., used as a proxy), or the low duration is still an overestimate of the actual duration at that point in time.

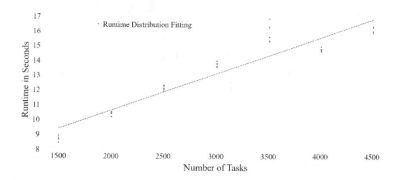

Fig. 6. Runtime of distribution fitting and computation of percentiles per size of event log combined with a linear trend-line ($R^2 = 0.895132$). The experimental results show a linear trend in terms of the number of activity instances present in the training data.

Table 3. Distribution fitting results.

Distribution	Absolute	Relative
Beta	99	54.4%
Gamma	60	33%
Exponential	22	12.1%
Normal	1	0.5%

Computational Complexity. Here, we focus on the computational complexity of the estimators. Clearly, computing the average and standard deviation of a set of numbers is a linear operation in terms of its input. Even for extremely large numbers, such statistic can be computed on commodity hardware, as such, we refrain from presenting run-time measurements. Similarly, schedule revision has a theoretical run-time of $O(|S|)$. Measuring the number of errors has a theoretical run-time of $O(|S|^2)$. As we expect schedules to be of reasonable size, we do not further investigate the runtime of said check.

Distribution fitting may have a wider range of theoretical runtime complexity and is, as such, more interesting to study, i.e., particularly as we perform multiple tests. In Fig. 6, we present the run-time of the training time of the distribution-based estimator. To generate training data of increasing sizes, we randomly sampled relevant activity instances from the BPIC17 data (cf. Table 2). We apply distribution fitting on top of the collection of recorded instances. We observe that the results show a linear trend regarding the number of instances.

Frequently Occurring Distributions. Here, we focus on the most often occurring distributions, i.e., when using the distribution-based estimator. Consider Table 3, in which we depict the number of times a given distribution was deemed the best fit for an activity-resource combination. Due to its relatively flexible nature, the beta distribution is most often used, i.e., in approximately $54,4\%$. In roughly 33%, the gamma distribution yields the best fit, and in 12.1%, the exponential distribution. Logically, the normal distribution rarely fits well, i.e., only in one case it returned the best fit. However, in some instances, limited training data may be available for the distribution fitting.

6   Conclusion

The application of scheduling often overlooks the availability of event data and does not recognize the vast potential such data can offer for an increased overall quality of generated schedules. At the same time, process-oriented research fields exploiting event data, i.e., process mining, tend to ignore the existence and importance of scheduling the to-be-executed process activities. In this paper, we proposed a novel event-data-driven schedule feasibility-checking framework to bridge the abovementioned gap. Our framework proposes to learn duration estimators based on event data, which are subsequently used to revise the duration of task allocations in a given schedule. Our initial results confirm the general applicability of our proposed framework and show that the proposed framework instantiations are computationally feasible.

As future work, we plan to conduct several case studies, enabling the use of more realistic schedules and corresponding event data. Secondly, we also aim to allow the replacement of scheduled tasks by shorter expected activity duration. We additionally aim to work with *buffers*, i.e., portions of idle time in which the scheduled activities are allowed to exceed their initially scheduled time.

References

1. van der Aalst, W.M.P.: Process Mining - Data Science in Action, 2nd edn. Springer, Heidelberg (2016). https://doi.org/10.1007/978-3-662-49851-4
2. Arias, M., Munoz-Gama, J., Sepúlveda, M., Miranda, J.C.: Human resource allocation or recommendation based on multi-factor criteria in on-demand and batch scenarios. Eur. J. Ind. Eng. **12**(3), 364–404 (2018)
3. Bala, S., Cabanillas, C., Mendling, J., Rogge-Solti, A., Polleres, A.: Mining project-oriented business processes. In: Motahari-Nezhad, H.R., Recker, J., Weidlich, M. (eds.) BPM 2015. LNCS, vol. 9253, pp. 425–440. Springer, Cham (2015). https://doi.org/10.1007/978-3-319-23063-4_28
4. Bellaaj, F., Sellami, M., Bhiri, S., Maamar, Z.: Obstacle-aware resource allocation in business processes. In: Abramowicz, W. (ed.) BIS 2017. LNBIP, vol. 288, pp. 207–219. Springer, Cham (2017). https://doi.org/10.1007/978-3-319-59336-4_15
5. Berkenstadt, G., Gal, A., Senderovich, A., Shraga, R., Weidlich, M.: Queueing inference for process performance analysis with missing life-cycle data. In: van Dongen, B.F., Montali, M., Wynn, M.T. (eds.) 2nd International Conference on Process Mining, ICPM 2020, Padua, Italy, 4–9 October 2020, pp. 57–64. IEEE (2020)

6. de Man, J.C., Strandhagen, J.O.: Spreadsheet application still dominates enterprise resource planning and advanced planning systems. IFAC-PapersOnLine **51**(11), 1224–1229 (2018). 16th IFAC Symposium on Information Control Problems in Manufacturing INCOM 2018
7. van Dongen, B.F.: BPI Challenge 2017 (2017). https://doi.org/10.4121/uuid: 5f3067df-f10b-45da-b98b-86ae4c7a310b.   https://data.4tu.nl/articles/dataset/ BPI_Challenge_2017/12696884
8. van Eck, M.L., Firat, M., Nuijten, W.P.M., Sidorova, N., van der Aalst, W.M.P.: Human performance-aware scheduling and routing of a multi-skilled workforce. Complex Syst. Informatics Model. Q. **12**, 1–21 (2017)
9. Havur, G., Cabanillas, C., Mendling, J., Polleres, A.: Resource allocation with dependencies in business process management systems. In: La Rosa, M., Loos, P., Pastor, O. (eds.) BPM 2016. LNBIP, vol. 260, pp. 3–19. Springer, Cham (2016). https://doi.org/10.1007/978-3-319-45468-9_1
10. Havur, G., Cabanillas, C., Polleres, A.: Benchmarking answer set programming systems for resource allocation in business processes. Expert Syst. Appl. **205**, 117599 (2022)
11. Ihde, S., Pufahl, L., Völker, M., Goel, A., Weske, M.: A framework for modeling and executing task-specific resource allocations in business processes. Computing **104**(11), 2405–2429 (2022)
12. Kinast, A., Doerner, K.F., Rinderle-Ma, S.: Combining metaheuristics and process mining: improving cobot placement in a combined cobot assignment and job shop scheduling problem. Procedia Comput. Sci. **200**, 1836–1845 (2022). 3rd International Conference on Industry 4.0 and Smart Manufacturing
13. Leung, J.Y. (ed.): Handbook of Scheduling - Algorithms, Models, and Performance Analysis. Chapman and Hall/CRC (2004)
14. Loeve, M.: Probability Theory, 3rd edn. Dover Publications, Mineola (2017)
15. Low, W.Z., van der Aalst, W.M.P., ter Hofstede, A.H.M., Wynn, M.T., Weerdt, J.D.: Change visualisation: analysing the resource and timing differences between two event logs. Inf. Syst. **65**, 106–123 (2017)
16. Mans, R., Russell, N.C., van der Aalst, W.M.P., Moleman, A.J., Bakker, P.J.M.: Schedule-aware workflow management systems. Trans. Petri Nets Other Model. Concurr. **4**, 121–143 (2010)
17. Mans, R.: Workflow support for the healthcare domain. Ph.D. thesis, Industrial Engineering and Innovation Sciences (2011)
18. Ouelhadj, D., Petrovic, S.: A survey of dynamic scheduling in manufacturing systems. J. Sched. **12**(4), 417–431 (2009)
19. Patel, J.K., Read, C.B.: Handbook of the Normal Distribution, 2nd edn. CRC Press, Boca Raton (1996)
20. Pinedo, M.L.: Scheduling - Theory, Algorithms, and Systems, 5th edn. Springer, Cham (2016). https://doi.org/10.1007/978-3-319-26580-3
21. Senderovich, A., Booth, K.E.C., Beck, J.C.: Learning scheduling models from event data. In: Benton, J., Lipovetzky, N., Onaindia, E., Smith, D.E., Srivastava, S. (eds.) ICAPS 2018, Berkeley, CA, USA, 11–15 July 2019, pp. 401–409. AAAI Press (2019)
22. Senderovich, A., et al.: Conformance checking and performance improvement in scheduled processes: a queueing-network perspective. Inf. Syst. **62**, 185–206 (2016)
23. Taha, H.A.: Operations Research: An Introduction, 10th edn. Pearson Education, Harlow, England and London and New York and Boston and Amsterdam and Munich (2017)
24. Winston, W.L., Goldberg, J.B.: Operations Research: Applications and Algorithms, 4th edn. Thomson Brooks/Cole Belmont (2004)

Comparing Trace Similarity Metrics Across Logs and Evaluation Measures

Christoffer Olling Back[1,2]([⊠]) [iD] and Jakob Grue Simonsen[1] [iD]

[1] University of Copenhagen, Copenhagen, Denmark
{back,simonsen}@di.ku.dk
[2] ServiceNow Denmark ApS, Copenhagen, Denmark

Abstract. Trace similarity is a prerequisite for several process mining tasks, e.g. identifying process variants and anomalies. Many similarity metrics have been presented in the literature, but the similarity metric itself is seldom subject to controlled evaluation. Instead, they are usually demonstrated in conjunction with downstream tasks, e.g. process model discovery, and often evaluated qualitatively or with limited comparison.

In this paper, we isolate similarity metrics from downstream tasks and compare them wrt. evaluation measures adapted from metric learning and clustering literature. We present a comparison of 18 similarity metrics across 4 evaluation measures and 12 event logs.

Friedman and Nemenyi tests for statistical significance show that certain similarity metrics consistently outperform on some evaluation measures, but their mean rank varies across evaluation measures. One similarity metric based on a weighted eventually-follows relation does stand out as consistently outperforming, and the simplest n-gram similarity metrics also perform well. Our results demonstrate that choice of evaluation measures will determine the contours of the metric that are revealed. This study may be harnessed as a baseline for benchmarking future work on trace similarity, and describes tools for quantitative evaluation that we hope will inspire empirical rigor in future work.

Keywords: Process Mining · Similarity Metric · Empirical Evaluation

1 Introduction

Similarity metrics lie at the foundation of many tasks in machine learning, pattern recognition and information retrieval; e.g. object recognition, ranking search results, even detecting malicious code [18]. In our collaborations with industry, information system stakeholders express strong interest in identifying sources of variation in process flows in large-scale systems – specifically enterprise resource planning systems – and exploring groups of similar process instances as captured by event traces. Their goal is to gain a high-level overview of system behaviour in general, and more specifically to identify causes of delay, poor outcomes, bottlenecks and inefficient use of resources. Outlier patterns often provide clues to

Supported by Innovation Fund Denmark as part of DIREC initiative.

hidden software inefficiencies, bugs or design flaws that cause inconsistencies in business documents, delaying process flows.

Yet, the precise definition of variation in terms of process traces is rarely given apriori. Within process mining, many similarity metrics defined on traces have been proposed, nearly always with clustering - and subsequent process discovery - as downstream tasks [30]. Evaluation is typically performed on the end result of the full process mining pipeline, most often the discovered process model.

However, in some cases, the end goal may not necessitate model discovery or even clustering as intermediate tasks (see Fig. 1). In interactions with industry, we have observed that many common end goals are tasks that could be tackled with the help of a similarity metric and standard data mining/machine learning techniques. Such end goals include identifying process variants, retrieving similar traces, classification, and detecting outliers/deviations. The variety of end goals and downstream tasks suggests the need to isolate the evaluation of trace similarity metrics, apart from confounding factors, and using methods not closely tied to process model evaluation measures.

We evaluate the most common trace similarity metrics across 12 event logs and 4 evaluation measures to determine whether any consistently outperform. This approach allows us to demonstrate empirically the variation in outcome resulting from the combination of similarity metric, event log, and evaluation measure. Furthermore, we show that some similarity metrics, in particular eventually-follows [7], consistently outperform; but also that the simplest n-gram based similarity metrics perform comparably to more sophisticated, computationally expensive alignment and edit-based similarity metrics. Maximal repeat alphabet based similarity metrics appear to underperform, but we speculate they may be best suited to be combined with other, e.g. n-gram, similarity metrics.

The paper is organized as follows: Sect. 3 introduces basic notation and definitions; Sect. 4 covers methodology, including sampling strategy, choice and definition of evaluation measures, similarity metrics; Sect. 5 describes data and experiments; Sect. 6 contains results which we discuss in Sect. 7 and Sect. 8 concludes.

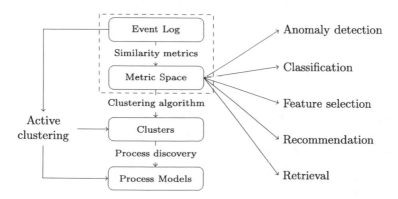

Fig. 1. Tasks downstream from similarity metrics. Left: process discovery chain. Right: other similarity metric-based applications. Dashed box: scope of study.

2   Related Work

Trace similarity metrics arose early in the development of process mining as a field [30], with most similarity metrics having been borrowed from other fields and adopted with little modification. For example, n-gram embeddings from natural language processing, edit distances from error correcting codes and spelling correction, and alignment from bioinformatics [10]. Some of these were extended based on specific insights from event logs, such as the maximal repeat alphabet embeddings [4], and generic edit distance [3]. Trace similarity metrics can take any trace attributes into account [26], but sequential activity ordering has clearly been the dominant approach in the literature.

By far the most prevalent use of trace similarity metrics is to cluster traces into sublogs which are mined separately in order to discover more succinct and precise models [3, 26]. Active clustering approaches bypass the notion of similarity entirely by iteratively clustering and fitting a model, similar to learning probability distributions on data with the Expectation-Maximization algorithm [6].

Finally, the field of similarity metric learning has seen growing interest over the past decade [2], and demonstrated that, rather than using predefined similarity metrics, transformations of data to embeddings and similarity metric spaces can be *learned*, e.g. via deep neural networks [17]. The first steps in learning representations for process mining have been taken in [5, 16].

3   Preliminaries

In this paper, the terms "metric" and "similarity metric" will refer to a binary function between traces that quantifies the similarity between them; the terms "measure" and "evaluation measure" will refer to a function defined on a similarity metric and an event log with a class partitioning; see formal definitions below. Not all similarity metrics under consideration strictly meet the 3 mathematical criteria of a metric: all are nonzero and symmetric, but some fail to satisfy the triangle inequality. This is not uncommon for similarity metrics used in practice, and does not prevent subjecting them to our evaluation procedure.

Any reference to the "performance" of a similarity metric refers to the value returned by a given evaluation measure taking that similarity metric and an event log as input. Furthermore, when stating than a similarity metric "outperforms", this refers strictly to its performance relative to the other similarity metrics under consideration in this study. In some cases, a similarity metric may outperform others despite the fact that the value returned by the given evaluation measure is low in absolute terms.

Just as in classical machine learning, we require the notion of a class label on data points, in our case: trace-level attributes. These attributes are defined on entire traces and given by the creator of the event log. They are not derived from the individual events in a trace, though this is possible.

When we refer to an embedding, this is defined as some function mapping traces (or any sequence of symbols) to a real-valued vector space.

3.1   Formal Definitions

For a finite alphabet of activity symbols Σ, we denote the set of finite activity sequences by $\Sigma^\star$. A log $L \equiv \{t_1, \ldots, t_N\}$ is a set of traces, where $t_i \equiv e_1 \ldots e_{n_i}$ i.e. sequences of events. Denote by $\mathcal{E}$ the universe of events with $e \in \mathcal{E}$. Events have an associated activity symbol: given sequence $e_1 \ldots e_n \in \mathcal{E}^\star$, the function $\sigma : \mathcal{E}^\star \to \Sigma^\star$ returns a sequence of activities, i.e. trace variants.

A similarity metric space M is an ordered pair (X, d) consisting of a set X with a similarity metric $d : X \times X \to \mathbb{R}$ defining pairwise distances between members of X. Denote by $\mathcal{D}$ a function space with $d \in \mathcal{D}$. The set of similarity metric spaces is thus given by $\{X\} \times \mathcal{D}$.

Denote by $P(X)$ the set of possible partitions of X and define a partitioned similarity metric space as an ordered triple (X, d, X') with X and d as above and $X' \subset P(X)$. An evaluation measure $E : \{X\} \times \mathcal{D} \times P(X) \to \mathbb{R}$ is thus a function from all partitioned similarity metric spaces resulting from X and $\mathcal{D}$ to the reals. In the context of logs, partitioning is based on a trace attribute $a \in A$. For convenience, define $\phi : L \to A$, i.e. a mapping of traces to attribute values. Write $L_a \equiv \{t \in L \mid \phi(t) = a\}$ to denote the set of traces with attribute value a.

4   Methodology

For each evaluation measure, we test whether any similarity metric outranks its competitors using a non-parametric Friedman test for significance, along with a post-hoc Nemenyi test. Below we describe sampling strategy, statistical tests, evaluation measures, and similarity metrics. The choice of event logs is based on criteria regarding trace attributes, and is described in Section 5.2.

4.1   Sampling Strategy

For most event log/similarity metric combinations, exhaustively computing an evaluation measure across all traces is practically intractable. This is due primarily to the minimum $\mathcal{O}(|L|^2)$ complexity of the evaluation measures; calculating the similarity metric itself also adds to the challenge for those that grow super-linearly wrt. trace length, e.g. edit and alignment distances. Therefore, we employed a sampling strategy in which a subset of traces is sampled randomly, in proportion to the original distribution across classes.

4.2   Significance Testing

We require statistical tests for comparing multiple similarity metrics across multiple domains (event logs). This is known as a complete block design, for which the appropriate test is the Friedman test for significance combined with a post-hoc Nemenyi test. These tests are based on the *ranking* of a similarity metric - wrt. an evaluation measure - on a given event log, allowing similarity metrics to be compared across logs. This addresses the fact that for some event logs, all similarity metrics achieve high (or low) values on the same evaluation measure.

The Friedman test establishes whether the difference in similarity metric rankings across logs is statistically significant *overall*. The post-hoc Nemenyi test compares similarity metrics *pairwise* to determine whether the difference in mean ranks between individual similarity metrics are statistically significant. We perform significance tests separately for the 4 evaluation measures.

4.3   Evaluation Measures

We reviewed 90 papers (the 35 most relevant in detail) from the similarity metric learning literature, relying heavily on existing surveys [2,17]. We identified those evaluation measures that meet our criteria of: 1) being quantitative, 2) not relying on downstream tasks, and 3) applicability to selected similarity metrics.

Qualitative approaches based on visualizations were precluded by 1), while normalized mutual information for cluster separability - a common method for evaluating clustering results wrt. true class labels - did not fulfill 2). Pair-based error, which constructs a set of similar and dissimilar pairs was abandoned due to 3), as it requires the added step of setting a cutoff threshold.

Four evaluation measures meet our criteria: nearest neighbor [8,9,12,13,15, 19,22,28,29], precision@10 [1,11,14,20,27,31], triplet [21,25], and silhouette [23].

Nearest Neighbor. This evaluation measure simply considers the expected ratio of traces whose nearest neighbor shares the same class label. Formally,

$$E_{\mathrm{NN}}(L, d) \equiv \frac{1}{|A|} \sum_{a \in A} \frac{1}{|L_a|} \sum_{t_i \in L_a} \mathbf{1}(t_i), \quad \mathbf{1}(t_i) \equiv \begin{cases} 1 & \text{if } \phi(\arg\min_{t_j \neq i \in L} d(t_i, t_j)) = \phi(t_i) \\ 0 & \text{otherwise} \end{cases}$$

As described in Sec 4.1, we sample traces from L_a rather than performing all $\mathcal{O}(|L|^2)$ comparisons, but for each $t \in L_a$, we iterate exhaustively over L to solve $\arg\min$ in $\mathbf{1}(t)$ exactly.

Precision@k. This evaluation measure captures the expected proportion of a trace's k nearest neighbors that share the same class label. Formally,

$$E_{\mathrm{prec@}k}(L, d) \equiv \frac{1}{|A|} \sum_{a \in A} \frac{1}{|L_a|} \sum_{t_i \in L_a} \frac{|\{t_j \in N_k(t_i) \mid i \neq j \wedge \phi(t_j) = \phi(t_i)\}|}{k}$$

where $N_k(t_i)$ denotes the k nearest neighbors of t_i. The sampling strategy is identical to that of nearest neighbor.

Triplet. This evaluation measure [24] frames similarity metric error by asking the question: given an anchor data point x, is a second data point y of the same class closer than a data point z belonging to a different class?

A margin ϵ represents a minimum level of discrimination between classes, defined by $\max(d(x, y) + \epsilon - d(x, z), 0)$, see Fig. 2a. Formally, the triplet error is defined as:

(a) Triplet evaluation uses the relative distance of an anchor point (x) to an in-class (y) and out-of-class (z) point.

(b) Silhouette evaluation contrasts mean in-class distance with minimum mean out-of-class distance (dashed).

Fig. 2. Illustrations of Triplet and Silhouette evaluation measures.

$$E_{triplet}(L,d) \equiv \frac{1}{|A|^2 - |A|} \sum_{a,b \in A} \frac{1}{|L_a|} \sum_{t_1 \in L_a} \frac{1}{|L_a|} \sum_{t_2 \in L_a} \frac{1}{|L_b|} \sum_{t_3 \in L_b} \mathbf{1}(t_1, t_2, t_3)$$

$$\text{where } a \neq b \text{ and } \mathbf{1}(t_1, t_2, t_3) \equiv \begin{cases} 1 & \text{if } d(t_1, t_2) + \epsilon < d(t_1, t_3) \\ 0 & \text{if } d(t_1, t_2) + \epsilon \geq d(t_1, t_3) \end{cases}$$

where a and b are attributes, t_1 is an anchor trace, t_2 an in-class trace distinct from t_1, and t_3 and out-of-class trace. For this study, we simply set ϵ to 0.

As described in Sect. 4.1, we sample a portion of the $\mathcal{O}(|L|^3)$ triplet permutations, preserving the original distribution of traces across class labels.

Silhouette. Originally an internal evaluation technique from cluster analysis, this evaluation measure captures the quality of a given clustering by comparing mean intra-cluster distance to (nearest) mean inter-cluster distance, see Fig. 2b.

Normally a similarity metric is fixed, and clusterings are under evaluation. In our adaptation of this evaluation measure, the true clusters are fixed, with distribution of traces wrt. different similarity metrics under evaluation.

Formally, define for trace $t_i \in L_a$ where $|L_a| > 1$, a mean intra-cluster distance f and nearest mean inter-cluster distance g:

$$f(t_i) = \frac{1}{|L_a| - 1} \sum_{t_j \in L_a, i \neq j} d(t_i, t_j), \qquad g(t_i) = \min_{b \in A, b \neq a} \frac{1}{|L_b|} \sum_{t_j \in L_b} d(t_i, t_j)$$

The silhouette value of $t_i \in L_a$ is defined as

$$s(t_i) = \begin{cases} \frac{g(t_i) - f(t_i)}{\max(f(t_i), g(t_i))} & \text{if } |L_a| > 1 \\ 0 & \text{if } |L_a| = 1 \end{cases}$$

and the mean silhouette value across sampled traces as

$$E_{silhouette}(L,d) \equiv \frac{1}{|A|} \sum_{a \in A} \frac{1}{|L_a|} \sum_{t_i \in L_a} s(t_i)$$

4.4   Similarity Metrics

We aimed to include a representative selection of those similarity metrics most widely referenced in the process mining literature. Most similarity metrics fall into the categories of vector-space *embeddings* and *syntactic* similarity metrics.

Embeddings. Formally, a trace embedding is a map from trace variants to a vector space $e : \Sigma^* \to \mathbb{R}^n$. Include a distance similarity metric $h : \mathbb{R}^n \to \mathbb{R}$, and the composition of the two gives the complete similarity metric $d : \Sigma^* \to \mathbb{R}; e \circ h$. We compose trace embeddings with cosine and Euclidean distances, except eventually-follows:

n-gram. The n-gram embedding [3, 26], is defined as a mapping $\Sigma^* \to \mathbb{Z}_+^{|\Sigma|^n}$ that takes a trace variant $\sigma(t)$ and returns a vector $\mathbf{v} = (v_1, \ldots, v_i, \ldots, v_{|\Sigma|^n})^T$ s.t. v_i represents the number of occurrences of the ith n-gram in Σ^n.

Eventually-Follows. This similarity metric, as proposed by Delias et al. [7] captures the eventually-follows relation between activities as a value between 0 and 1 using the inverse of the size of the interval between preceding and succeeding activities.

Furthermore, a boolean 1-gram embedding captures the presence or absence of activities in a trace. Cosine distance is defined on the two separate embeddings and a weighted mean of the two defines the final similarity metric.

Maximal Repeat Alphabets. The family of repeat alphabets [4], are defined using repetition and subsumption criteria on substrings in trace variants. A *maximal pair* is a pair of substrings $\alpha_i = \alpha_j$ in a trace, with starting positions i and j where $i \neq j$, such that concatenating any adjacent activity symbols $a\alpha_i$, $b\alpha_j$ similarly $\alpha_i a$, $\alpha_j b$ results in unequal strings, i.e. $a\alpha_i \neq b\alpha_j$ respectively $\alpha_i a \neq \alpha_j b$. Define the following sets in addition to the the the set of pairs (MR) defined above:

– *Near Super Maximal Repeats* ($NSMR$): MR with at least one occurrence in a trace where it does not occur as a substring of another maximal repeat
– *Super Maximal Repeats* (SMR): MR that do not occur anywhere in a trace as a substring of another maximal repeat

These feature sets are used to define embeddings $\Sigma^* \to \mathbb{Z}_+^{|MR|}$, $\Sigma^* \to \mathbb{Z}_+^{|NSMR|}$ and $\Sigma^* \to \mathbb{Z}_+^{|SMR|}$ reflecting occurrences of a given maximal repeat in a trace.

Syntactic. These similarity metrics are defined directly between strings without resorting to the composition of a vector-space embedding and distance similarity metric. The approaches proposed in the process mining literature fall into two categories: edit distance and alignment based approaches.

Edit distance - Levenshtein Raw and Normalized. The Levenshtein distance is defined as the number of insertions, deletions and substitutions of symbols needed to transform one string into another.

We also consider a normalized variant, which accounts for the number of edits relative to the worst-case, i.e. the length of the longest of the two strings.

Table 1. Log overview with trace and class statistics. Abbreviations in **boldface**.

Event Log	Activ.	Traces	Min.	Max.	Mean	Label	Count
			Trace Length			Classes	
Recomposing Conformance (**INS '18**)	230	45000	1	410	71.4	sublog	15
Logs to Test **Scalab.** of Disc. Alg	17	40000	1	53	6.8	sublog	4
Testing Representational **Bias**	8	4000	2	8	4.2	sublog	4
Business Process **Drift**	51	35000	14	50	21.0	variant	13
Artificial Digital **Photo**copier	68	100	43	2140	410.0	Class	2
Process Disc. Contest 2016 (**PDC '16**)	28	10000	1	84	12.9	sublog	10
Process Disc. Contest 2017 (**PDC '17**)	29	10000	4	59	13.3	sublog	10
Process Disc. Contest 2019 (**PDC '19**)	48	7000	1	31	13.0	sublog	10
Process Disc. Contest 2020 (**PDC '20**)	36	192000	3	344	26.9	sublog	192
Process Disc. Contest 2021 (**PDC '21**)	63	479000	1	330	17.5	sublog	479
Process Disc. Contest 2022 (**PDC '22**)	17	480000	1	65	5.6	sublog	480
Env. permit appl. process ('**WABO**')	465	4348	1	124	45.0	Muni	5

Edit Distance - Generic. Proposed in [3], this similarity metric is defined as above but edit operation costs are learned automatically based on symbol co-occurrence.

Alignment. Sequence alignment [10] is defined as a transformation of two sequences s_1 and s_2 by means of the insertion of a gap symbol, such that $|s_1| = |s_2|$ and a cost function over matches, mismatches and gaps is minimized. The cost function rewards matches and punishes mismatches, gaps, and runs of gaps.

The exact alignment is determined by costs and alignment algorithm, in our case the Needleman-Wunsch algorithm with default costs from examples in the codebase: rewards of 2 for matches and costs of 1 for mismatches, 2 for gaps.

We investigated two scoring functions on the resulting alignment: the raw matching pair count (write a_{raw}), and the full cost score described above (write a_{F1}). To transform these into valid distance similarity metrics, we performed the following normalization and logistic transformations:

$$\mathrm{Align}(t_1, t_2) = 1 - \frac{a_{raw}(\sigma(t_1), \sigma(t_2))}{\max(|t_1|, |t_2|)}$$

$$\mathrm{AlignF1}(t_1, t_2) = \frac{1}{1 + \exp(0.05 \cdot a_{F1}(\sigma(t_1), \sigma(t_2)))}$$

5   Experiments

We compare 18 similarity metrics across 12 log collections wrt. 4 evaluation measures and evaluate performance for each evaluation measure independently using a Friedman test for significance with a post-hoc Nemenyi test. We implemented the methodology described above in Java[1].

---

[1] https://github.com/backco/tracesim.

5.1 Sample Size

We set sample size to the highest value possible s.t. calculations were tractable across all logs and similarity metrics using a uniform sample size. For triplet evaluation sample size was set to 0.01% of the total number of possible triplets ($\mathcal{O}(|L|^3)$). For the 3 other evaluation measures, 1% of the log. One exception was the Photocopier log which is so small that the entire log was sampled.

For a handful of log/similarity metric combinations (marked with * in tables), it became apparent that a smaller sample was necessary to complete triplet evaluation. Determining after at least one hour of processing that runtime would exceed 24 h, we decreased sample size by an order of magnitude. Despite this discrepancy, we believe results to be representative, since the absolute sample size was nevertheless very large: these logs are an order of magnitude larger than others. They also have hundreds of classes (causing the combinatorial explosion), so we confirmed that the sample contained at least 10 traces per class.

We relied on implementations of several similarity metrics from the `ProM` suite (www.promtools.org) and `JAligner` for alignments (https://jaligner. sourceforge.net). We performed statistical analysis in R using the standard Friedman test and `tsutils` library for Nemenyi tests (https://github.com/trnnick/ tsutils).

5.2 Datasets

We performed a thorough cataloging of datasets from the process mining community, specifically in terms of trace-level attributes. We considered the attribute cardinality, and distribution wrt. traces. Since class labels are central to the evaluation measures in question, we elected to focus on a set of event logs with clearly distinguishable generating processes s.t. the distribution of traces across class labels can be reasonably assumed to correlated with differences in activity sequence structure that a useful similarity metric should capture.

These criteria resulted in synthetically generated event logs dominating the collection of suitable event logs since these have the advantage that they are generated from known process models. Differences between generating models are often variations on a similar theme s.t. activities are similar, allowing for comparison, but with known differences in control-flow or noise.

In particular, event logs from the annual Process Discovery Contest[2], make up 6 of 12 event logs since they fit our criteria well. One dataset (WABO) in our collection stems from a real-world process represents a collection of event logs stemming from 5 separate municipalities with variations in their procedure for a handling environment permitting. The remaining synthetic logs are all established in the literature for benchmarking process mining algorithms and happen to suit our criteria even if originally designed for other purposes.

Table 1 presents an overview of event logs with statistics regarding unique activities, trace length and distribution across class labels.

---

[2] https://www.tf-pm.org/competitions-awards/discovery-contest.

Table 2. Nearest neighbor evaluation measures for similarity metrics on logs. Highest value for each log is in **boldface**. Abbreviations in Table 1. Suffixes -C, -E denote cosine, Euclidean resp.; Edit{Gen—Lev—Nor}: generic, Levenshtein, normalized edit distances resp.; EvFollows: eventually follows; -Rep: maximal repeat alphabets.

METRIC	INS'18	Scalab.	Bias	Drift	Photo	PDC'16	PDC'17	PDC'19	PDC'20	PDC'21	PDC'22	WABO
					NEAREST NEIGHBOR							
1-gram-C	**1.00**	0.75	**1.00**	0.40	**1.00**	**1.00**	**1.00**	**1.00**	**0.18**	0.02	0.02	0.65
2-gram-C	**1.00**	0.69	**1.00**	0.55	**1.00**	**1.00**	**1.00**	0.98	0.13	**0.03**	0.02	0.81
3-gram-C	**1.00**	0.69	0.88	0.59	**1.00**	**1.00**	**1.00**	0.96	0.15	0.02	0.01	0.80
1-gram-E	**1.00**	0.75	**1.00**	0.41	**1.00**	**1.00**	**1.00**	0.97	0.16	0.02	0.02	0.73
2-gram-E	0.86	0.75	**1.00**	0.61	**1.00**	0.96	**1.00**	0.79	0.13	0.03	**0.02**	0.79
3-gram-E	0.68	0.75	**1.00**	0.63	**1.00**	0.88	0.96	0.59	0.14	0.02	0.02	0.76
Align	**1.00**	**0.76**	**1.00**	0.62	**1.00**	**1.00**	**1.00**	**1.00**	0.08	0.02	0.01	**0.98**
AlignF1	**1.00**	0.76	**1.00**	0.61	**1.00**	**1.00**	**1.00**	0.99	0.07	0.02	0.01	0.86
EditGen	**1.00**	0.76	**1.00**	0.63	**1.00**	**1.00**	**1.00**	**1.00**	0.11	0.02	0.02	0.82
EditLev	**1.00**	0.75	**1.00**	0.61	**1.00**	**1.00**	**1.00**	**1.00**	0.12	0.03	0.02	0.87
EditNor	**1.00**	0.76	**1.00**	0.62	**1.00**	**1.00**	**1.00**	**1.00**	0.12	0.02	0.02	0.85
EvFol	**1.00**	0.76	**1.00**	0.63	**1.00**	**1.00**	**1.00**	**1.00**	0.16	0.03	0.02	0.86
MaxRep-C	0.44	0.34	0.25	0.42	**1.00**	0.41	0.58	0.40	0.07	0.01	0.00	0.24
NSMRep-C	0.45	0.25	0.50	0.41	**1.00**	0.31	0.45	0.41	0.03	0.01	0.00	0.24
SMRep-C	0.40	0.25	0.50	0.41	0.67	0.42	0.63	0.43	0.04	0.01	0.00	0.20
MaxRep-E	0.44	0.32	0.50	0.42	**1.00**	0.38	0.67	0.40	0.07	0.01	0.00	0.18
NSMRep-E	0.39	0.25	0.50	0.41	0.85	0.32	0.56	0.39	0.03	0.00	0.00	0.18
SMRep-E	0.32	0.37	0.50	0.42	0.50	0.39	0.61	0.39	0.04	0.01	0.00	0.23

6 Results

We present results for nearest neighbor, precision@10, silhouette, and triplet evaluation measures in Tables 2,3,4,5, resp. The results of Friedman and Nemenyi tests for statistical significance are illustrated in four *Multiple Comparisons with Best (MCB)* plots in Fig. 3. These plots summarize the ranking of similarity metrics across logs for a given evaluation measure.

The differences between similarity metric rankings are statistically significant with 99% confidence for all of the 4 evaluation measures with Friedman p values of $2.2 \cdot 10^{-16}$ for all but silhouette, which has a p value of 0.00178. The Nemenyi post-hoc tests indicate how the mean ranks of individual similarity metrics compare to one another, whether the pairwise differences are statistically significant.

We see that *eventually-follows* consistently ranks higher than most similarity metrics across a majority of logs for all 4 evaluation measures, with the highest mean rank on all but silhouette. There is also a group of several similarity metrics whose mean rank is high and falls within the critical distance of eventually-follows: edit, alignment, and some n-gram similarity metrics.

Table 3. Precision@10 scores for similarity metrics on logs. The highest value for each log is shown in **boldface**. Abbreviations in Table 1.

METRIC	INS'18	Scalab.	Bias	Drift	Photo	PDC'16	PDC'17	PDC'19	PDC'20	PDC'21	PDC'22	WABO
						PRECISION@10						
1-gram-C	**1.00**	0.75	**1.00**	0.40	**1.00**	**1.00**	**1.00**	1.00	**0.16**	0.03	0.02	0.67
2-gram-C	**1.00**	0.70	**1.00**	0.55	**1.00**	0.99	**1.00**	0.96	0.12	0.02	0.02	0.72
3-gram-C	**1.00**	0.70	0.87	0.59	**1.00**	**1.00**	**1.00**	0.93	0.13	0.02	0.02	0.72
1-gram-E	**1.00**	0.75	**1.00**	0.41	0.98	**1.00**	**1.00**	0.96	0.15	0.02	**0.02**	0.67
2-gram-E	0.75	0.75	**1.00**	0.62	0.98	0.88	0.98	0.62	0.10	0.02	0.02	0.68
3-gram-E	0.62	0.75	**1.00**	0.63	0.98	0.75	0.92	0.47	0.11	0.02	0.02	0.62
Align	**1.00**	0.77	**1.00**	0.62	**1.00**	**1.00**	**1.00**	1.00	0.06	0.01	0.01	**0.81**
AlignF1	**1.00**	0.77	1.00	0.61	0.99	**1.00**	**1.00**	0.99	0.05	0.01	0.01	0.73
EditGen	**1.00**	0.77	0.99	0.63	**1.00**	**1.00**	**1.00**	1.00	0.10	0.02	0.02	0.75
EditLev	**1.00**	0.77	0.97	0.61	0.97	**1.00**	**1.00**	1.00	0.11	0.02	0.02	0.77
EditNor	**1.00**	0.77	0.99	0.61	**1.00**	**1.00**	**1.00**	1.00	0.10	0.02	0.02	0.72
EvFol	**1.00**	**0.78**	**1.00**	0.63	**1.00**	**1.00**	**1.00**	1.00	0.15	**0.03**	0.02	0.75
MaxRep-C	0.42	0.32	0.25	0.42	**1.00**	0.41	0.59	0.40	0.07	0.01	0.00	0.22
NSMRep-C	0.32	0.25	0.45	0.29	0.96	0.17	0.39	0.23	0.02	0.00	0.00	0.19
SMRep-C	0.25	0.25	0.51	0.41	0.60	0.40	0.65	0.43	0.04	0.01	0.00	0.16
MaxRep-E	0.43	0.33	0.50	0.42	0.97	0.38	0.67	0.40	0.06	0.01	0.00	0.18
NSMRep-E	0.21	0.25	0.45	0.27	0.66	0.21	0.39	0.18	0.02	0.00	0.00	0.17
SMRep-E	0.19	0.37	0.50	0.41	0.51	0.36	0.59	0.39	0.03	0.01	0.00	0.22

For 3 of the 4 evaluation measures, the similarity metrics based on maximal repeats alphabets (MRA) occupy the last 6 of 18 places in terms of mean rank, and by a significant margin – clearly influencing statistical significance tests.

7   Discussion

In interpreting our results, we can see patterns among similarity metrics as well as between the evaluation measures themselves. We propose some mechanisms underlying the observed results; discuss the costs, benefits and prerequisites in terms of data availability for specific similarity measures; and describe which evaluation measures are the most informative bases for comparing similarity metrics in typical application scenarios.

Similarity metrics We suspect the high mean rank of the eventually-follows similarity metric is due in part to its ability to quantify temporal relations: e.g. *when* – not just if – b follows a; as well as its being the only similarity metric under consideration to incorporate a second, boolean 1-gram embedding [7].

This similarity metric would likely be well-suited to a context in which timing characterizes the behavior of the software or user of interest, rather than simply control-flow. For example, the behavior of two different programs/agents in an IT system may display indistinguishable control-flow patterns, yet one be identifiable by a pronounced delay between two activities, e.g. b follows a after 1 occurrence of c, vs. b follows a after 10 occurrences of c.

Table 4. Silhouette scores for similarity metrics on logs. The highest value for each log is shown in **boldface**. Abbreviations in Table 1.

METRIC	INS'18	Scalab.	Bias	Drift	Photo	PDC'16	PDC'17	PDC'19	PDC'20	PDC'21	PDC'22	WABO
					SILHOUETTE							
1-gram-C	0.32	0.08	**0.75**	0.31	**0.90**	**0.51**	0.59	**0.42**	0.34	0.17	0.05	0.03
2-gram-C	0.23	0.05	0.41	**0.34**	0.84	0.27	0.31	0.16	0.12	0.12	0.06	0.04
3-gram-C	0.14	0.06	0.37	0.32	0.80	0.18	0.19	0.10	0.08	0.06	0.04	0.03
1-gram-E	0.18	0.14	0.70	0.21	0.46	0.42	0.42	0.24	**0.43**	0.20	0.09	0.03
2-gram-E	0.15	0.12	0.38	0.21	0.41	0.20	0.07	0.07	0.33	0.14	0.18	0.04
3-gram-E	0.12	0.13	0.36	0.18	0.38	0.15	0.00	0.03	0.32	0.15	0.09	0.02
Align	0.29	0.24	0.51	0.30	0.52	0.51	0.41	0.28	0.18	0.13	0.15	0.06
AlignF1	0.29	0.13	0.12	0.25	0.58	0.30	0.26	0.16	0.15	0.10	0.10	0.01
EditGen	**0.35**	0.27	0.43	0.22	0.53	0.28	0.26	0.31	0.11	0.15	0.00	0.09
EditLev	0.27	0.29	0.50	0.25	0.49	0.46	0.40	0.18	0.41	0.06	0.03	0.06
EditNor	0.23	0.16	0.44	0.28	0.50	0.38	0.36	0.25	0.14	0.15	0.06	0.06
EvFol	0.30	0.14	0.53	0.29	0.89	0.46	0.47	0.28	0.22	0.15	0.05	0.06
MaxRep-C	0.09	0.00	0.25	0.23	0.76	0.12	0.32	0.15	0.05	-0.01	0.02	0.03
NSMRep-C	-0.07	**0.63**	0.03	0.20	0.76	0.42	**0.78**	0.07	0.38	**0.46**	**0.42**	0.29
SMRep-C	-0.09	0.61	0.25	0.22	0.15	0.41	0.69	0.06	0.28	0.27	0.25	0.17
MaxRep-E	-0.33	0.55	0.25	0.12	0.39	0.41	0.63	0.08	0.41	0.42	0.38	0.18
NSMRep-E	-0.33	0.58	0.25	0.10	0.39	0.47	0.70	0.04	0.31	0.12	0.35	0.19
SMRep-E	-0.36	0.59	0.03	0.16	0.17	0.46	0.65	0.15	0.31	0.39	0.28	**0.34**

In a context where the simple presence/absence – or relative frequency – of certain activities is defining for behavior patterns, n-gram similarity metrics may be sufficient and has the advantage of being efficient to compute. We see this in the case of the Photocopier log. Another plausible scenario might be failing requests in a client-server scenario; the absolute number of retries being characteristic of poor server/database performance or even malicious client activity.

Edit and alignment-based similarity metrics will be able to capture more nuanced differences in local structure of traces, e.g. *abab* vs. *baba*, but suffer from being very expensive to compute.

We believe the low mean rank of the MRA similarity metrics is due in part to the sparsity of this embedding on many logs: many traces simply do not contain many examples of the patterns in a given repeat alphabet. Defining an embedding using these alphabets in a weighted combination with other embeddings, e.g. n-gram, would likely lead to better results.

Evaluation Measures. We also observe differences between evaluation measures themselves, except between nearest neighbor and precision@10, which largely agree. This is expected since precision@10 is based on nearest neighbors as well.

Silhouette stands out, revealing nuances not captured by the other evaluation measures. For example, performance on the Photocopier log in terms of nearest neighbor and precision@10 is 1.0 for nearly all similarity metrics, but for silhouette, scores range from 0.17 to 0.9. Similarly, triplet considers a broad sample of

Table 5. Triplet scores for similarity metrics on logs. The highest value for each log is shown in **boldface**. Abbreviations in Table 1. (*): see Sect. 5.1.

METRIC	INS'18	Scalab.	Bias	Drift	Photo	PDC'16	PDC'17	PDC'19	PDC'20	PDC'21	PDC'22	WABO
						TRIPLET						
1-gram-C	0.83	0.54	0.85	0.64	1.00	0.87	0.87	0.78	0.71	0.57	0.51	0.54
2-gram-C	0.89	0.23	0.53	0.75	1.00	0.82	0.86	0.64	0.64	0.47	0.40	0.54
3-gram-C	0.84	0.13	0.35	**0.78**	1.00	0.58	0.64	0.44	0.53	0.28	0.18	0.54
1-gram-E	0.82	0.55	**0.86**	0.64	0.86	0.87	0.89	0.84	0.67	0.54	0.48	0.53
2-gram-E	0.71	0.49	0.67	0.73	0.86	0.80	0.82	0.63	0.58	0.54	0.48	0.55
3-gram-E	0.63	0.47	0.68	0.75	0.82	0.69	0.69	0.56	0.54	0.51	0.45	0.51
Align	0.92	0.62	0.80	0.72	1.00	**0.94**	0.91	0.83	0.69	0.52	0.47	0.55
AlignF1	0.88	**0.70**	0.79	0.72	0.85	0.90	**0.92**	**0.86**	0.69	0.56*	0.50*	0.55
EditGen	0.90	0.62	0.77	0.75	0.98	0.92	0.90	0.82	0.73*	0.59*	0.50*	**0.58**
EditLev	0.86	0.62	0.73	0.72	0.87	0.90	0.88	0.79	0.64	0.54	0.46	0.54
EditNor	**0.92**	0.54	0.74	0.73	1.00	0.93	0.89	0.81	0.67	0.57	0.48	0.54
EvFol	0.89*	0.59	0.81	0.73	**1.00**	0.92	0.91	0.84	**0.74***	**0.60***	**0.51***	0.55
MaxRep-C	0.18	0.01	0.25	0.66	1.00	0.16	0.43	0.27	0.33	0.08	0.05	0.05
NSMRep-C	0.44	0.14	0.50	0.67	0.83	0.40	0.68	0.49	0.56	0.32	0.25	0.17
SMRep-C	0.28	0.13	0.50	0.68	0.59	0.35	0.56	0.51	0.30	0.20	0.18	0.14
MaxRep-E	0.42	0.08	0.52	0.65	0.83	0.41	0.64	0.46	0.51	0.32	0.24	0.27
NSMRep-E	0.40	0.15	0.50	0.67	0.54	0.41	0.63	0.46	0.49	0.31	0.25	0.16
SMRep-E	0.37	0.18	0.50	0.66	0.50	0.38	0.64	0.49	0.45	0.30	0.25	0.28

the similarity metric space, rather than just the nearest neighbors, and we see it returns values for the Photocopier log between 0.5 and 1.0.

While nearest neighbor, precision@10, and triplet focus on the local structure of a similarity metric space, silhouette captures how well separated entire clusters are, allowing it to capture that MRA similarity metrics may be more capable of separating entire trace classes than indicated by other evaluation measures.

The choice of evaluation measure will depend on the downstream task at hand: obviously for nearest neighbor based classification, nearest neighbor as well as precision@10 will be most relevant. For information retrieval – i.e. presenting a user with the most similar examples of process execution, based on some query or example – precision@10 is most relevant. For anomaly detection we expect silhouette would best capture whether a similarity metric places outlier traces far away from clusters of expected behavior, and also places normal traces close to one another. For feature extraction and variant analysis we expect that both silhouette and triplet would best capture the overall variability between traces, e.g. wrt. secondary trace attributes. When performing trace clustering prior to process model discovery, silhouette is likely the most appropriate evaluation measure. In this use case nearest neighbor and precision@10 will be too narrowly focused on local structure in the metric space, and fail to capture overall cluster separability, which is important for discovering succinct process models within each trace cluster.

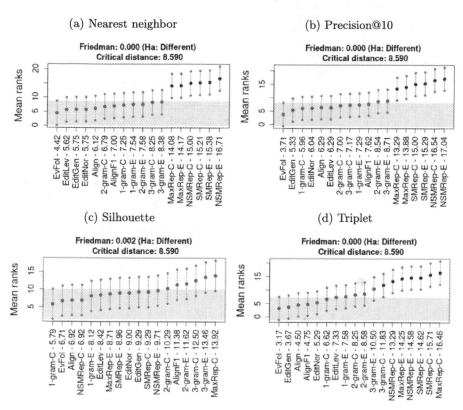

Fig. 3. *Multiple Comparison with Best* plots visualizing Friedman and Nemenyi post-hoc tests of statistical significance (confidence: 99%). Tests across rankings within event logs. Grey block indicates critical distance from the best performer.

Other practical considerations will motivate the choice of evaluation measure: in scenarios of very sparsely labelled data, triplet will likely be most appropriate. However, the distribution of labels across classes should also be considered: if a small number of labels are available for many classes, triplet is suitable, but if labeled traces are available only for a handful of classes – and many more are expected to exist – silhouette will better capture intra-inter cluster separability induced by a similarity metric. Finally, in scenarios where only relative rankings are available, triplet will be most appropriate. This is a standard scenario, e.g. in information retrieval tasks where a user clicks on the third, rather than the first, list of results to a query.

For some applications, such as classification or retrieval, the failure of nearest neighbor and precision@10 to reveal differences between similarity metrics will not be a shortcoming: the evaluation measures correctly indicate that these similarity metrics are most likely equally well-suited for identifying the nearest neighbors of a trace. For applications such as clustering and feature extraction/selection, silhouette is more informative since it captures the variance between many data points which may or may not include nearest neighbors. Similarly, triplet ensures the entire similarity metric space is sampled – though across all class pairings, which is in contrast to silhouette.

8   Conclusion and Future Work

We presented initial results for quantitative comparison of similarity metrics on event logs. This evaluation occurs prior to any downstream tasks, isolating it from confounding aspects. Our empirical results provide evidence that some similarity metrics, especially *weighted eventually-follows*, tend to outperform across logs, but also that choice of evaluation measures is crucial and reveals different contours of the resulting similarity metric space.

One clear direction for future work is to develop similarity metrics that take into account more semantic detail of activities, traces and event logs: e.g. that some activities are clearly more similar that others, as well as attributes on activities, and other relational information (e.g. that one event triggered another).

Learning based approaches for deriving a similarity metric space automatically from a specific event logs, are also a clear avenue to explore. Finally, our reliance on synthetically generated event logs, generated from a limited class of process models (workflow nets – a subclass of Petri nets), represents a threat to validity and speaks to the dearth of publicly available, real-world event logs amenable to standard, established evaluation procedures.

References

1. Bar-Hillel, A., Hertz, T., Shental, N., Weinshall, D., Ridgeway, G.: Learning a mahalanobis metric from equivalence constraints. JMLR. **6**(6) (2005)
2. Bellet, A., Habrard, A., Sebban, M.: A survey on metric learning for feature vectors and structured data. arXiv (2014)
3. Bose, R.P.J.C., Aalst, W.M.P.V.D.: Context aware trace clustering: Towards improving process mining results. In: Proceedings of 2009 SIAM International Conference on Data Mining, pp. 401–12. SIAM (2009)
4. Bose, R.P.J.C., van der Aalst, W.M.P.: Trace clustering based on conserved patterns: towards achieving better process models. In: Rinderle-Ma, S., Sadiq, S., Leymann, F. (eds.) BPM 2009. LNBIP, vol. 43, pp. 170–181. Springer, Heidelberg (2010). https://doi.org/10.1007/978-3-642-12186-9_16
5. De Koninck, P., vanden Broucke, S., De Weerdt, J.: act2vec, trace2vec, log2vec, and model2vec: representation learning for business processes. In: Weske, M., Montali, M., Weber, I., vom Brocke, J. (eds.) BPM 2018. LNCS, vol. 11080, pp. 305–321. Springer, Cham (2018). https://doi.org/10.1007/978-3-319-98648-7_18
6. De Weerdt, J., Vanden Broucke, S., Vanthienen, J., Baesens, B.: Active trace clustering for improved process discovery. IEEE Trans. Know. Data Eng. **25**(12), 2708–20 (2013)
7. Delias, P., Doumpos, M., Grigoroudis, E., Manolitzas, P., Matsatsinis, N.: Supporting healthcare management decisions via robust clustering of event logs. Knowl. Based Syst. **84**, 203–13 (2015)

8. Der, M., Saul, L.: Latent coincidence analysis: a hidden variable model for distance metric learning. Adv. Neural Inf. Process. Syst. **25** (2012)
9. Do, H., Kalousis, A., Wang, J., Woznica, A.: A metric learning perspective of SVM: on the relation of LMNN and SVM. In: AI and Statistics, pp. 308–17. PMLR (2012)
10. Evermann, J., Thaler, T., Fettke, P.: Clustering traces using sequence alignment. In: Reichert, M., Reijers, H.A. (eds.) BPM 2015. LNBIP, vol. 256, pp. 179–190. Springer, Cham (2016). https://doi.org/10.1007/978-3-319-42887-1_15
11. Fehervari, I., Ravichandran, A., Appalaraju, S.: Unbiased evaluation of deep metric learning algorithms. arXiv:1911.12528 (2019)
12. Globerson, A., Roweis, S.: Metric learning by collapsing classes. Adv. Neural Inf. Process. Syst. **18** (2005)
13. Goldberger, J., Hinton, G.E., Roweis, S., Salakhutdinov, R.R.: Neighbourhood components analysis. Adv. Neural Inf. Process. Syst. **17** (2004)
14. Hoi, S.C.H., Liu, W., Lyu, M.R., Ma, W.Y.: Learning distance metrics with contextual constraints for image retrieval. In: IEEE Computer and Social Conference, CVPR. vol. 2, pp. 2072–8. IEEE (2006)
15. Hong, Y., Li, Q., Jiang, J., Tu, Z.: Learning a mixture of sparse distance metrics for classification and dimensionality reduction. In: International Conference on CV, pp. 906–13. IEEE (2011)
16. Huo, S., Völzer, H., Reddy, P., Agarwal, P., Isahagian, V., Muthusamy, V.: Graph autoencoders for business process anomaly detection. In: Polyvyanyy, A., Wynn, M.T., Van Looy, A., Reichert, M. (eds.) BPM 2021. LNCS, vol. 12875, pp. 417–433. Springer, Cham (2021). https://doi.org/10.1007/978-3-030-85469-0_26
17. Kaya, M., Bilge, H.S.: Deep metric learning: a survey. Symmetry. **11**(9) (2019)
18. Li, Y., Gu, C., Dullien, T., Vinyals, O., Kohli, P.: Graph matching networks for learning the similarity of graph structured objects. In: International Conference on ML, pp. 3835–45. PMLR (2019)
19. Nguyen, N., Guo, Y.: Metric learning: a support vector approach. In: Daelemans, W., Goethals, B., Morik, K. (eds.) ECML PKDD 2008. LNCS (LNAI), vol. 5212, pp. 125–136. Springer, Heidelberg (2008). https://doi.org/10.1007/978-3-540-87481-2_9
20. Oh Song, H., Xiang, Y., Jegelka, S., Savarese, S.: Deep metric learning via lifted structured feature embedding. In: Proceedings of IEEE Conference on CVPR, pp. 4004–12 (2016)
21. Park, K., Shen, C., Hao, Z., Kim, J.: Efficiently learning a distance metric for large margin nearest neighbor classification. In: Proceedings of AAAI Conference on AI. vol. 25, pp. 453–458 (2011)
22. Ramanan, D., Baker, S.: Local distance functions: a taxonomy, new algorithms, and an evaluation. Trans. Pattern Anal. Mach. Intell. **33**(4), 794–806 (2010)
23. Rousseeuw, P.J.: Silhouettes: a graphical aid to the interpretation and validation of cluster analysis. J. Comput. Appl. Math. **20**, 53–65 (1987)
24. Schroff, F., Kalenichenko, D., Philbin, J.: Facenet: A unified embedding for face recognition and clustering. In: Proceedings of IEEE Conference on CVPR, pp. 815–23 (2015)
25. Schultz, M., Joachims, T.: Learning a distance metric from relative comparisons. Adv. Neural Inf. Process. Syst. **16** (2003)
26. Song, M., Günther, C.W., van der Aalst, W.M.P.: Trace clustering in process mining. In: Ardagna, D., Mecella, M., Yang, J. (eds.) BPM 2008. LNBIP, vol. 17, pp. 109–120. Springer, Heidelberg (2009). https://doi.org/10.1007/978-3-642-00328-8_11

27. Tarlow, D., Swersky, K., Charlin, L., Sutskever, I., Zemel, R.: Stochastic k-neighborhood selection for supervised and unsupervised learning. In: International Conference on ML, pp. 199–207. PMLR (2013)
28. Torresani, L., Lee, K.C.: Large margin component analysis. Adv. Neural Inf. Process. Syst. **19** (2006)
29. Weinberger, K.Q., Saul, L.K.: Distance metric learning for large margin nearest neighbor classification. J. ML Res. **10**(2) (2009)
30. Zandkarimi, F., Rehse, J.R., Soudmand, P., Hoehle, H.: A generic framework for trace clustering in process mining. In: ICPM, pp. 177–84. IEEE (2020)
31. Zhou, M., Niu, Z., Wang, L., Gao, Z., Zhang, Q., Hua, G.: Ladder loss for coherent visual-semantic embedding. In: Proceedings of AAAI Conference on AI, vol. 34, pp. 13050–13057 (2020)

Ontology and Knowledge
Representation

Where Are the Readings Behind Your Concept Maps? Annotation-driven Concept Mapping

Oscar Díaz[ID] and Xabier Garmendia[(⊠)][ID]

University of the Basque Country (UPV/EHU), San Sebastián, Spain
{oscar.diaz,xabier.garmendiad}@ehu.eus

Abstract. Concept maps are widely used in education and business. They are reckoned to stimulate the generation of ideas, facilitate requirement elicitation, and serve as the first step in ontology building, and as such, they are used by a wide variety of practitioners, including designers, engineers, instructors, and others, to organize and structure knowledge. However, the rationales that drive the creation of the map's concepts and relations are often implicit in the practitioners' heads. These rationales should be often sought in the reading material, provided by instructors or stakeholders, and 'processed' by the learners or designers to deliver the concept map. This poses a traceability issue where concepts can not always be traced back to the document excerpts that originated the concepts in the first place. However, the existence of such traces is envisioned to bring two major gains. Concept-to-excerpt traceability would facilitate third-party observers (e.g., stakeholders, instructors) checking out the source of possible misunderstandings in the concept map. Excerpt-to-concept traceability would enable document reading to be strategic, i.e., framed by the concept map. This work pursues the synergy between Concept Mapping and Strategic Reading by means of highlighted annotations. This results in *annotation-driven concept mapping*, a process where concept maps unfold in tandem with the annotations derived from the readings. Through the interplay of annotation and mapping, learners get a headstart on both activities. As mappers, learners no longer have to resort to their reminders but text annotations provide the raw material to build up the concept and relations. As readers, learners no longer wander around the readings but concepts and relations might serve as focus drivers. This work proves the feasibility of this vision by making a popular tool for concept mapping, *CmapTools*, annotation-driven. A focus group (n=5) is used to anticipate its utility. The results identified two moderating variables: the level of elaboration of the reading material and the degree of abstraction of the assignment topic.

Keywords: Concept maps · Knowledge Management · Web Annotation · Learning

1 Introduction

Concept maps are graphical tools for organizing and representing knowledge through nodes that represent concepts and links that represent relations between concepts. Its simplicity is both its strength and its weakness. Their visual appeal makes concept maps

© The Author(s), under exclusive license to Springer Nature Switzerland AG 2023
M. Indulska et al. (Eds.): CAiSE 2023, LNCS 13901, pp. 245–260, 2023.
https://doi.org/10.1007/978-3-031-34560-9_15

very popular among academics and practitioners alike to account for the early stages of domain analysis [7]. In education, concept maps help students perform at higher cognitive levels, help teachers explain complicated subjects, and assess students' understandings [29]. In product design, concept maps are considered excellent storytellers, helping in the ideation and inspiration phases [10]. Finally, implementation-wise, concept maps help with instruction, documentation, and communication [1]. On the downside, concept maps are criticized for their looseness and lack of replicable process construction [13]. While the former has to do with the expressiveness of concept maps as a representation tool, the second limitation concerns the unfolding of concept maps, i.e., concept mapping. This paper is about *concept mapping*, i.e., the process of developing a concept map.

Concept mapping is informed by Ausubel's Assimilation Theory of meaningful learning [2,29]. Ausubel emphasized the centrality of relating concepts within a cognitive structure in learning and thinking processes. Ausubel uses the term "assimilation" to describe learners' propensity to relate novel ideas to existing cognitive structures to reduce the meaning of the novel idea to that of the established one. Different assistance means are proposed for concept mapping: in dialogue with the instructor or stakeholder [8], through pair-mapping with peers [5], employing rules of association of data mining [4], or through text while reading [32]. We focus on the latter, where learners draw concept maps from their reading recalls. In this scenario, we identify two shortcomings:

- traceability. It is not easy to identify the readings behind the concepts and relations, hence hindering the diagnoses of learners' misunderstandings,
- symbiosis with strategic reading. Strategic reading aims at constructing meaning by interacting with text, where learners use their prior knowledge along with clues from the text. Concept maps might offer a powerful scaffold for strategic reading.

Different strategies are proposed for strategic reading. Setting a purpose helps focus reading by setting a specific goal for reading. Incomplete concept maps might play such a role, offering 'those clues' to drive the learner's readings to fill in the gaps. A second strategy is active learning, i.e., highlighting important information or taking notes [30]. Learners can analyze the author's arguments and assess their validity by taking notes and making comments. In this way, we can consider 'annotation' as a way of appropriating a document, i.e., passing the document content through the sieve of the reader's prior knowledge. If this prior knowledge is reflected in a concept map, then it can be conjectured that annotation is the prelude of concept mapping, with annotations as the manifestation of the reflective process of the learner. This vindicates concept mapping and reading to be tightly integrated, paving the way towards *annotation-driven concept mapping*.

Problem. IF annotation is to be integrated within concept mapping AND concept mapping is a gradual and iterative process, THEN the interplay between document reading and concept mapping should better be as seamless as possible. Unfortunately, document reading and concept mapping tend to be dissociated into separate tools (e.g., *Acrobat Reader* and *CmapTools*). This imposes an important burden on learners to keep track of what is being read when concept mapping, and the other way around, i.e., to maintain track of what concepts have been mapped when reading. The question then arises about

How could annotation-driven concept mapping get support in current tools?

We address this question using a Design Science Research (DSR) approach [22]. DSR does not stop at understanding a problematic reality (e.g., the decoupling between concept mapping and reading) but strives to impact this reality through an intervention (e.g., an IT artefact). Using DSR parlance, we aim at designing an intervention that assists users (i.e., learners) during concept mapping in close relationship with their readings. DSR underscores the importance of the IT artefact as a means to impact a practice (i.e., concept mapping) while being informed by existing theories.

Accordingly, we contribute by:

- introducing the notion of annotation-driven concept mapping (Sect. 3),
- developing a plug-in for *CmapTools* to develop annotation-grounded concept maps (Sect. 4),
- anticipating advantages for annotation-driven concept mapping through a focus group evaluation (Sect. 5).

We start framing concept mapping within other document-based knowledge acquisition practices.

2   The Practice: Concept Mapping

DSR is "not content to just describe, explain, and predict. It also wants to change the world, to improve it, and to create new worlds" [22]. Changing the world starts by understanding the current world, i.e., the state of the practice aimed to be upgraded. For our purposes, this practice is concept mapping. Thus, the question arises about what is to be improved about the current practice of concept mapping.

This section confronts concept mapping with other related practices. Though concept maps show up in various scenarios, we go back to the original setting as proposed by Novak and Ausubel where new concepts are constructed on top of existing learners' cognitive structures from the inside out [2,29]. The term 'learners' should not be mapped exclusively to students but to anyone who faces a learning experience. Requirement concept mappers, analysts, and decision-makers can be labeled as 'learners' insofar as they face an uncharted scenario with the assistance of their prior experiences.

Concept maps are graphical tools for organizing and representing knowledge through nodes representing concepts and links representing relations between concepts. The theory goes as new concepts are constructed on top of existing learners' cognitive structures from the inside out [2,29]. The term 'learners' should not be mapped exclusively to students but to anyone who faces a learning experience. Requirement concept mappers, analysts, and decision-makers can be labeled as 'learners' insofar as they face an uncharted scenario with the assistance of their prior experiences. When it comes to learning, concept maps allow instructors to identify missing or irrelevant concepts and trivial or incorrect linking phrases [29]. Hence, concept maps provide the basis for discussions between learners and instructors to better understand the subject matter. In so doing, they foster meaningful learning by favoring reflective thinking with a focus on what is relevant and important [2]. In contrast, **mind maps** favor a brainstorming way of thinking among peers. This setting finds the propositional structure of concept maps too rigid, and prefers a radial disposition of nodes with a central idea placed in the middle and associated ideas arranged around it. In both notations, there is no strict right or wrong but relies on the arbitrariness of mnemonic associations to aid people's information organization [13]. On the other hand, a **conceptual model** resorts to a precise *standardized* notation to aid the design of systems, typically based on a theory or model (e.g., an entity-relationship model). The aim: analyze a topic or situation through a proven analytic framework. Yet, early conceptual modeling techniques lacked an adequate specification of the semantics of the notation of the underlying models, leading to the use of ontologies [18]. Ontologies account for a more sophisticated representation of the domain being modeled, and a higher level of domain understanding by their modelers [16]. This sets the basis for supporting the analytic process of conceptual models, paving the way to transform conceptual models into knowledge graphs [31]. A **knowledge graph** is "a large network of entities, and instances for those entities, describing real-world objects and their interrelationships, with specific reference to a domain or an organization" [3]. In comparison with concept maps, knowledge graphs differ in size (huge w.r.t. concept maps), stability (often based on agreed ontologies), and pursued benefits (deriving new facts that are not explicit in the graph). Table 1 summarizes this comparison. For our purposes, we can conclude that what sets concept maps apart from other graphical representations of information is both the aim (i.e., learning) and the target audience (i.e., learners). Rather than the notation itself, the distinctive value rests on developing concept maps, i.e., concept mapping.

Table 1. Comparing concept maps within other graphical notations.

	Concept Maps	Mind Maps	Conceptual Models	Knowledge Graphs
Notation	Propositions	Ideas	Models	Entities & Instances
Aim	Learning	Brainstorming	Modeling	Reasoning
Audience	Learners	Peers	Analysts	Soft. Agents

Concept mapping is based on Ausubel's assimilation theory of cognitive learning [2]. Here, learning is conceived as a 'transformative' process fed by two inputs (i.e., the learner's prior knowledge and the reading material) that result in the learner's knowledge being enhanced. We can then characterize approaches to learning based on the learner's prior knowledge and the degree of elaboration of the reading material (see Fig. 1). First, the act of reading is certainly influenced by the reader's mindset, let this be a first-grade student, a college student, or a mature researcher. Even if the text is the same, the changes vary. The second factor is the degree of elaboration of the reading material. By 'elaboration' it meant the extent to which the text already holds the concept and the relations, or rather, just provides the raw data from where concepts need to be abstracted out. From this perspective, fairy tales might sit at the very bottom as they do not even represent real events, yet are effective in engaging first-grade students [27]. Next, interviews and transcripts in Qualitative Data Analysis (QDA) have low elaboration since they tend to represent individual experiences or events that need to be painstakingly distilled into theories, usually assisted by tools like *NVivo* [11]. By contrast, research articles, and even more so, textbooks, are highly elaborated with concepts and relations already being made explicit. Here, the effort goes not so much into coming up with the concepts/relations but integrating and selecting the concepts relevant to the question at hand, let this be a research question (e.g., in Systematic Mapping Studies with tools like *Buhos* [28]) or a focus question (e.g., in concept mapping with tools like *CmapTools*). Figure 1 arranges different knowledge-acquisition practices along with these two dimensions.

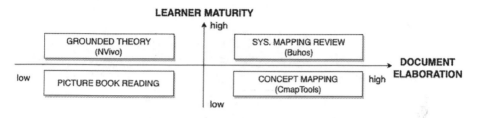

Fig. 1. A comparison framework for knowledge-acquisition practices.

Operationalization means turning abstract conceptual ideas into measurable observations. DSR underlines the importance of defining early on the metrics to assess an intervention's utility. What, then should be a metric to evaluate the goodness of concept mapping? A distinctive aspect of this practice is the role of the instructor. Unlike QDA or literature reviews, concept mapping is an *assisted* activity. There is no strict right or wrong concept map. Goodness is not set so much in terms of the output (i.e., the concept map) but how easy or difficult it is to understand the underlying learning process (i.e., concept mapping). As Cañas and Novak put it: "as a student is building a concept map, the teacher should probe the student to (a) find out how much the student knows about the topic and how his/her understanding evolves, and (b) help the student go deeper into understanding the subject and thereby improve, refine or expand the concept map" [6]. Thus, a metric for concept mapping quality would be in terms of the students' misunderstandings instructors can detect. Specifically, Concept Mapping is considered useful for the diagnosis of students' misunderstandings owing to their sensitivity to (i) the structure of knowledge, (ii) the intrusion or distortion of knowledge, and (iii) the omission of knowledge [33]. Hence, the challenge is to prove that annotation-driven concept mapping leverages traditional concept mapping in terms of the students' misunderstandings spotted by the instructor.

3   Changing the Practice: Introducing Annotation in Concept Mapping

In DSR, kernel theories are used throughout the design process for informing the intervention [22]. This section introduces the theoretical underpinnings that inform the introduction of annotation in concept mapping.

When it comes to the process of coming up with a concept map, we are not aware of full-fledged theories but just some guidelines. The most extensively cited reference is that of Novak's where five main steps are introduced [29]:

1. identify the focus question or main topic of the concept map to resolve,
2. identify all the key concepts that relate to the main idea you identified,
3. create a preliminary concept map linking the concepts together with linking words,
4. add cross-links to connect concepts in different domains,
5. continually revises your concept map as needed.

Notice that this description is still quite elusive: *how key concepts are identified* (step 2) or *how the concept map is revised* (step 5).

If concept mapping is based on reading, then strategic reading is another theory that comes into play. This term denotes the active engagement of students in reading. Process-wise, this engagement is achieved through seven reading strategies [26]:

1. *activating*, i.e., recalling relevant knowledge from long-term memory,
2. *inferring*, i.e., connecting the implicit and explicit meaning of the text to one's own experiences and knowledge. This may imply actively checking regularly if the text is fully comprehended (clarifying), and self-questioning and finding the answers to those questions in the text (i.e., questioning)
3. *annotating*, i.e., identifying samples in the text that answer these questions, solve problems, and define important terms,
4. *summarizing*, i.e., creating a "mental image", some graphical representation of the text, to elicit meaning from the text or a summary of the text in one's own words.

Specifically, highlighting annotation has been proven to be an effective way of aiding in the comprehension and interpretation of written information [23]. Because annotating slows the reading down, learners discover and uncover ideas that would not have emerged otherwise [30]. Different studies acknowledge annotation as a common practice among both academics and practitioners [15]. We then consider annotation as a means for Strategic Reading, and in doing so, a way of appropriating a document, i.e., passing the document content through the sieve of the reader's prior knowledge. If this prior knowledge is reflected in a concept map, then annotation is the prelude of concept mapping, with annotations as the manifestation of the reflective process of the learner.

Our main hypothesis is that concept mapping and strategic reading feedback each other. Specifically,

– Concept mapping might play the role of "the mental image" or "long-term memory" that sustains Strategic Reading. If what gets 'activated' is a concept map, then *inferring* might be referred to the concepts and relations of the concept map,
– Strategic reading might provide the evidence on which to feed concept maps out of "identifying samples in the text that define important terms". If what gets 'visualized' is a concept map, then *concept identification, concept ordering*, and *concept linking* are the means to abstract out what is being read.

This results in a gradual and iterative process where concept mapping and strategic reading interplay throughout.

On these premises, we introduce *annotation-based concept mapping* as a concept mapping process where concepts and relations are sustained and derived from annotations where the annotation process itself is driven by the concept map. This results in a continuous improvement loop where *annotation* events interplay with *mapping* events (i.e., creating concepts, relations, and links).

Figure 2 captures this vision as a state chart. Broadly, the learner can be in two states: *the map-visualization* state or *the document-visualization* state. Either of these states can be the entry point to the learning experience. The learner might already depart from a kick-off concept map that results from either his prior knowledge or an instructor-given head start. Alternatively, the learner might be provided with a set of documents to address the focus question. The exit point can be diverse, e.g. deadlines, stakeholder agreement, or some sort of 'conceptual saturation'. We do not develop this concern here. No matter the entry point, the concept map unfolds as the learner moves between these two states:

- when in *map-visualization*, the learner's self-question about the focus question, revising the map as appropriate (i.e., *Strategic Reading's mapping*),
- when in *document-visualization*, the learner connects the implicit meaning of the text to the concepts in the map through annotation (i.e., *Strategic Reading's inferring*).

On these grounds, and following the DSR mandate, we aim at impacting the practice of concept mapping by introducing an IT intervention that brings about annotation as part of concept mapping.

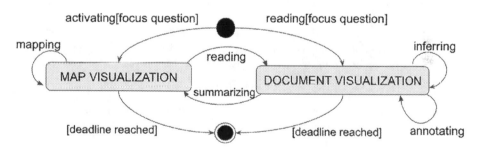

Fig. 2. State Transition Diagram for annotation-driven concept mapping

4   The Intervention: *Concept&Go*

We aim to impact the current practice of concept mapping. We do so by introducing *Concept&Go*, a mediator between *CmapTools* as the concept-map editor, and *Hypothes.is* as the annotation reservoir. *CmapTools* is a free software environment developed at the Institute for Human and Machine Cognition (IHMC) and used by thousands of individuals in schools and institutions all around the world [5]. On the other hand, *Hypothes.is* is an open-source software project that collaborates with a wide variety of organizations. By September of 2022, *Hypothes.is* reached over one million users in 2.3 million digital documents [21]. The bottom line is that both tools account for thousands of users each, making them appropriate choices to increase the eventual impact of this research.

Moreover, *Concept&Go* is supported as a browser extension for Chrome [12]. The use of a browser extension brings some benefits to our settings:

- easy to install (i.e., extension installation is commonly limited to a single click),
- familiarity (i.e., the odds are that concept mappers already enjoy some extensions in their browsers), and
- configurability (i.e., extensions are locally installed; should appropriate configuration parameters be defined, this permits tuning the behavior of the extension to the user preferences).

Concept&Go is available for download at the Chrome's Web Store[1], and its source code is publicly available under the MIT license on GitHub[2]. So far, a driver is available for *CmapTools*, and the one for *Sero!*[3] is on the way.

4.1 *Concept&Go* at Work

Figure 3(A) realizes the aforementioned state chart for the *CmapTool* case where events now denote the GUI interactions of the *CmapTools* canvas, and states include a *do* action to be executed on entering the state.

These *do* actions carry out the main functionality of *Concept&Go*, namely

- on entry the *CmapTools* state, *Concept&Go* retrieves existing annotations and attaches them as resources to their concept/relation counterparts in the *CmapTool* canvas,
- on entry the *DocumentVisor* state, *Concept&Go* retrieves the twin concept map, generates a highlighter out of its concepts/relations, and renders the highlighter as a lateral bar on top of the visor

Figure 3(B) provides a possible event trace along this transition diagram.

- (step 1) The instructor provides a focus question (*'What are the means and ends of the XML technology?'*) together with a head start regarding two notions involved in the focus question: *'ends'* and *'means'*.
- (steps 2 & 3) The student moves to Wikipedia where a highlighter shows up out of the kick-off map. The student starts identifying excerpts that account for means and ends, substituting the instructor's cues by their realization for the XML case: the concept 'end' is renamed as *'Interchange data'* while the concept *'means'* results in the concept *'Standard'*, and new concepts are introduced: *'AJAX message exchange'*. At this point, the student might collect a list of potentially interesting concepts, though they do not know yet how they will be related. This list is called 'a parking lot', as you will move the items into the map as you figure out where they fit in. Time to have a break.

---

[1] https://rebrand.ly/conceptAndGoWebStore.
[2] https://github.com/onekin/ConceptAndGo.
[3] https://serolearn.com/.

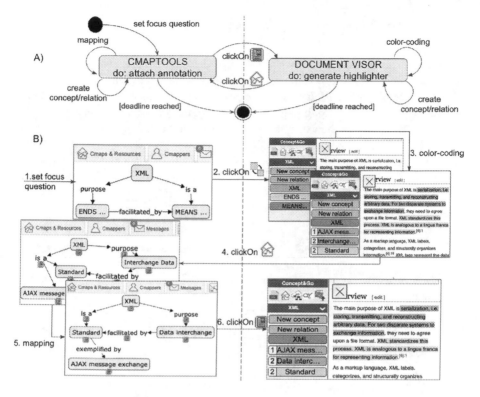

Fig. 3. Annotation-driven concept mapping in *Concept&Go*: state-transition diagram (A), and a possible path of events along the *Concept&Go* realization of this diagram (B).

- (steps 4 & 5) The next day, the student returns to *CmapTools*. At opening time, the twin concept map is displayed based on the annotations taken when in the *document-visualization* state. Some concepts might be renamed (e.g., *'Data interchange'* rather than *'Integrate data'*), new relations can be set (e.g., *'exemplified by'*), or even new concepts with no pair annotation can be added, if so, the student wishes.
- (steps 6) Time to go back to Wikipedia (or any other document) to search for paragraphs that sustain and leverage the twin concept map. New concepts/relations can be created as far as they are sustained by an annotation. Alternatively, annotations can be anchored to existing concepts through color coding (see next).

The next subsections delve into the details.

4.2   When in the *Map-visualization* State

A concept map is depicted by a labeled, directed graph with the vertices (nodes) representing concepts, and the directed and labeled edges (arcs) representing the relations that exist between those concepts. Nodes and arcs can now be attributed with annotations. Annotations depart from the reading realm, where they are born, to be arranged across the concept map where they are anchored. Hence, annotation portability is a must, and this mandates the use of standards.

The W3C's Annotation Model. The W3C provides a model for annotations, formalized in the 'Open Annotation' ontology. Figure 4 provides an example: *"oa:hasBody"* stands for comment *"Serialization"*; *"oa:hasTarget"* points to an *oa:hasSource* resource which is pinpointed through the quote (*"serialization ... arbitrary data"*) that appears in *Wikipedia*. In the example, the way to single this quote out is by indicating the text that precedes (*"XML is"*) and follows (*"For two"*) the text paragraph that is the focus of the annotation[45]. Figure 4 is realized as a JSON-formatted URL-addressable Web document. *Concept&Go* generates W3C-compliant annotations out of user highlights, which are stored in the *Hypothes.is* server.

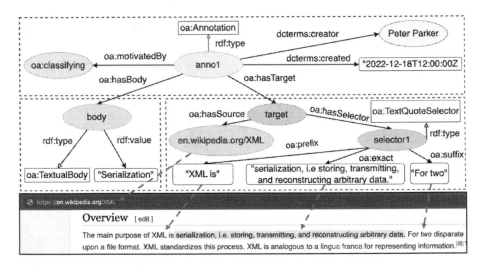

Fig. 4. A Web annotation sample using W3C's data model. The annotation classifies the highlighted text in the XML page (i.e. the target) as a case of the "Serialization" concept (i.e. the body).

Annotation Dereferencing. As other Web resources, annotations are amenable to be dereferenced, i.e., the act of retrieving a representation of a resource identified by a URI. Implementation-wise, this is achieved by clicking on the *resource* icon (▧) on the *CmapTools* canvas. This results in a transition to the *document-visualization* state: a new browser tab is shown up where the annotation is framed within the original document using *Concept&Go* side panel.

---

[4] In addition, W3C provides properties to indicate the annotation's provenance (*"dcterms:creator"*)(see footnote 5), when the annotation is created (*"dcterms:created"*) or the reasons why the annotation was created (*"oa:motivatedBy"*). W3C includes a predefined list of motivations, which is possible to extend with new, more precise motivation definitions.

[5] dcterms: This alias identifies the namespace of Dublin Core Schema. This schema defines a set of vocabulary terms that can be used to describe digital or physical resources.

4.3   When in the *Document-visualization* State

Traditionally, document visors permit a broad range of annotations, highlights included. *Concept&Go* replaces the visor's highlighter with a dedicated highlighter which is generated out of the concepts and relations of the twin concept map. This highlighter supports color coding. Color-coding is a common approach in QDA tools such as NVivo to extract and assign codes to excerpts by mapping colors to codes [11]. The highlighter is generated on the fly out of the twin concept map. Learners can now recognize the realization of the concepts in the document by highlighting the excerpt with the appropriate color. For relations, the tool also prompts the participating concepts. In addition, the sidebar allows for renaming or creating new concepts or relations. Learners can initially name the concept after the excerpt (sort of *in Vivo* coding) and decide later to rename it as they face new terminology. Throughout the reading session, *Concept&Go* generates the corresponding annotations that will later be mapped into the twin concept map, thus closing the loop.

This *modus operandi* resembles Thematic Analysis. Specifically, Cruces et al. distinguish three approaches [9]: deductive (i.e., starting with a provisional 'start list' of codes), inductive (i.e., codes emerge from highlighting and coding lines, paragraphs, or segments that illustrate the chosen concept), and integrated (i.e., a partway between the deductive and inductive approaches). The integrated approach is the one that better fits Ausubel's assimilation theory. Here, the learner approaches the documents with specific questions that she or he wishes to code according to existing concepts (i.e., strategic reading) while she keeps open to amending his mindset to the insights found in the documents (i.e., assimilation). These 'questions in mind' should be sought in the learner's prior knowledge, i.e. the transient concept map. Existing concepts and relations become the codes that guide the reading. According to the integrated approach, these codes are not fixed but are in flux as the learner contrasts his codes to the concepts that the authors of the documents have organized their findings around. As a result of this reflection, new codes (concepts, relations) might arise, be renamed, or be deleted in line with the focus question of the concept map. This outlines *Concept&Go*'s realization of annotation-driven concept mapping.

5   Evaluation

While characterizing the practice of concept mapping in Sect. 2, we argued about its role as an assisted activity. Consequently, we propose a goodness criterion based on the instructor's identification of students' misunderstandings. This introduces 'appreciation of misunderstandings' as a dependent variable to evaluate the effectiveness of 'annotation-driven concept mapping' compared to traditional concept mapping. The variable can be measured by the number of misunderstandings identified. However, due to the novelty of this approach, the selection of appropriate both control and moderating variables remains uncertain. Therefore, we turn to a focus group to gain insights into the contextual parameters that could affect the impact of annotation on the practice of concept mapping. We then state the purpose of this evaluation as

Identifying *the moderating variables for annotation-driven concept mapping*
with respect to *guiding future evaluations of Concept&Go*
from the point of view of *instructors*
in the context of *using CmapTools in a Computer Science degree course.*

Method We resort to a focus group [24]. A focus group is a group interview involving a few demographically similar participants with common traits or experiences. In Software Engineering, focus groups are proposed as an empirical approach for obtaining qualitative insights and feedback from practitioners, particularly during the early stages of research for identifying problems [24]. This is the case with *Concept&Go*. Group settings have the advantage of eliciting emerging ideas and opinions that may not emerge in individual interviews and that cannot be easily reduced to simple 'yes' or 'no' answers. This is particularly beneficial in novel practices like annotation-driven concept mapping.

Design We planned a single in-person focus group session. As highly diverse groups could result in a shallow discussion, participants were recruited along with the following criteria: familiarized with concept maps, knowledgeable about the domain sample, i.e., XML, and at least four-year experience in lecturing. We identified five potential participants from the University of the Basque Country.

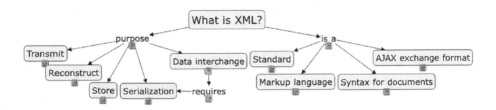

Fig. 5. Concept map using Wikipedia's XML entry page as the reading material.

Execution The focus group lasted for 107 min. It was moderated by the second author, while the first author attended the session as an observer and took notes. The session began with a presentation on the study's goals and an explanation of annotation-driven concept mapping. Then, the XML example introduced in Sect. 4.1 was used as the running example to explain the tool's functionalities. Next, the participants faced the annotation-grounded concept map in Fig. 5. We leave a computer for each participant with the annotation-grounded concept map opened in *CmapTools* to allow them to interact with it and its annotations. Before the discussion, the participants moved between the concept map and Wikipedia's XML entry and delved into the text fragments that derived the concepts and relations. This helped to pinpoint the origin of some misunderstandings. First, regarding knowledge structure, the student wrongly infers different rationales for a different rephrasing of the same notion, i.e., serializing. As for the distortion of knowledge, the student confuses XML (a syntax for markup language) with the markup language itself. Describing XML as a markup language rather than a meta-markup language might confuse when the student reads that XHTML is also a markup language, then setting XML and XHTML at the same level. Finally, concerning the omission of knowledge, the student might miss linking the means with the ends. At the end of the session, we gathered the participants to carry out an open debate about the extent to which annotation-driven concept mapping helps diagnose students' misunderstandings. The whole session was carried out in Spanish. The audio was recorded and then transcribed to be analyzed.

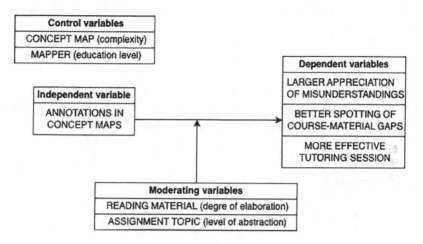

Fig. 6. Experiment Design derived from the focus group.

Data Analysis and Results. Participants found the approach of interest to detect omissions that might hinder understanding follow-on concepts. They observed that some misunderstandings might be rooted in the poor quality of the reading material. In this respect, objections were raised about Wikipedia's XML entry and its confusing wording. This led to an interesting observation about annotation-grounded concept maps used as an ACID test for course material. Participants also noticed that misunderstanding likelihood would also depend on the level of abstraction of the subject at hand. Participants teaching more abstract courses (e.g., software quality vs XML technology) conjectured this approach to be more appealing when more abstract concepts are involved. We coded these observations as two moderating variables: the degree of elaboration of the course material (e.g., Wikipedia entry, PPT slides, course book) and the topic's level of abstraction. Furthermore, the participants expressed concerns regarding the scalability of the approach to an entire class. Three participants observed that they could not afford it regularly. Instead, they suggested annotation-based concept mapping as a head-start for tutoring sessions. Here, students would be asked to prepare the annotation-grounded concept map to anchor the discussion during mentoring. Most of the participants were excited about this insight. Expected benefits include: (1) forcing students to self-reflect before tutoring and (2) providing a better framing for the discussion. Fig 6 depicts these insights as eventual dependent variables for future evaluations. This design framework will guide the future evaluation episodes of *Concept&Go*.

Threats to Validity. We consider threats for qualitative research as described in [25]. Regarding *Interpretive Validity*, i.e., how well researchers capture participants' meaning of events without imposing their perspective, we began the session with a brief presentation on the study's objectives and the proposed intervention. This presentation was aimed at establishing common terminology and avoiding misunderstandings. Moreover, the data analysis was made with the original Spanish version not to alter the participants' intended meaning. Another critical threat in focus groups is *Theoretical Validity* , i.e., the extent to which researchers provide an accurate and coherent explanation of the phenomena. The main threat to theoretical validity concerns the thematic analysis of the data. We tried to mitigate this threat by carrying out several iterations of coding, where themes were limited to the role played by the variable in the design experiment.

Strictly speaking, this evaluation leaves unanswered our initial RQ. Yet, this focus group provided the groundwork for the design of future evaluations and, in this way, achieves one of its primary purposes: "seeking directional information that will help uncover new questions or future research ideas" [17].

6   Conclusions

Highlight-based annotation and concept mapping are visible activities that sustain the invisible learning process. This work advocates for *annotation-driven concept mapping*. We expect this approach would help instructors trace concepts back to the reading sources and, in doing so, trace misunderstandings back to the reading sources. As proof of concept, we introduce *Concept&Go*, a mediator between *CmapTools* and Web-based document visors. The extent to which this intervention can achieve the stakeholders' goals (i.e., traceability & strategy reading) has not yet been proven. A focus group consisting of five teachers was conducted to inform subsequent evaluations. The results of this focus group identified two moderating variables: the level of elaboration of the reading material and the degree of abstraction of the assignment topic.

Besides further evaluation, the next follow-on includes extending annotation-driven concept mapping to domains other than education. Specifically, in Software Engineering, concept maps are proposed for providing a quick and low-cost process for the involvement of various stakeholders and target end users of the system, which is key in user-centered design [20]; for sense-making technique so that they give meaning to the requirements for specified tasks, which all the members of a team understand in a project [14] or for mapping across different views of software to enable a shared understanding between various stakeholders [19]. These activities might also benefit from the traceability and focus reading that annotation-driven concept mapping aims to bring about.

Acknowledgements. Research supported by MCIN/AEI/10.13039/501100011033 and the "European Union NextGenerationEU/PRTR" under contract PID2021-125438OB-I00. Xabier Garmendia enjoys a grant from the University of the Basque Country - PIF20/236.

References

1. Arnicans, G., Straujums, U.: Transformation of the software testing glossary into a browsable concept map. In: Sobh, T., Elleithy, K. (eds.) Innovations and Advances in Computing, Informatics, Systems Sciences, Networking and Engineering. LNEE, vol. 313, pp. 349–356. Springer, Cham (2015). https://doi.org/10.1007/978-3-319-06773-5_47
2. Ausubel, D.P., Novak, J.D., Hanesian, H., et al.: Educational Psychology: A Cognitive View, vol. 6. New York (1968)
3. Bellomarini, L., Fakhoury, D., Gottlob, G., Sallinger, E.: Knowledge graphs and enterprise AI: the promise of an enabling technology. In: ICDE, pp. 26–37. IEEE (2019). https://doi.org/10.1109/ICDE.2019.00011
4. Boguski, R.R., Cury, D., Gava, T.: Tom: an intelligent tutor for the construction of knowledge represented in concept maps. In: 2019 IEEE Frontiers in Education Conference (FIE), pp. 1–7. IEEE (2019). https://doi.org/10.1109/FIE43999.2019.9028615
5. Cañas, A.J., et al.: CmapTools: a knowledge modeling and sharing environment. In: Proceedings of the 1st International Conference on Concept Mapping, vol. 1, pp. 125–134 (2004)
6. Cañas, A.J., Novak, J.D.: Re-examining the foundations for effective use of concept maps. In: Proceedings of the 2nd International Conference on Concept Mapping, vol. 1, pp. 494–502 (2006)
7. Castro, A.G., Rocca-Serra, P., Stevens, R., Taylor, C., Nashar, K., Ragan, M.A., Sansone, S.A.: The use of concept maps during knowledge elicitation in ontology development processes-the nutrigenomics use case. BMC Bioinform. 7(1), 1–14 (2006). https://doi.org/10.1186/1471-2105-7-267
8. Chacón Ramírez, S.: La pregunta pedagógica como instrumento de mediación en la elaboración de mapas conceptuales. In: Proceedings of the 2nd International Conference on Concept Mapping. Universidad de Costa Rica (2006)
9. Cruzes, D.S., Dybå, T.: Recommended steps for thematic synthesis in software engineering. In: ESEM, pp. 275–284. IEEE Computer Society (2011). https://doi.org/10.1109/ESEM.2011.36
10. Daley, B.J., Lovell, M.R., Perez, R.A., Stern, N.E.: Using concept maps within the product design process in engineering: a case study. In: Applied Concept Mapping: Capturing, Analyzing, and Organizing Knowledge, pp. 317–326 (2011)
11. Dhakal, K.: Nvivo. J. Med. Libr. Assoc. 110(2), 270–272 (2022)
12. Díaz, O., Arellano, C.: The augmented web: rationales, opportunities, and challenges on browser-side transcoding. ACM Trans. Web (TWEB) 9(2), 1–30 (2015). https://doi.org/10.1145/2735633
13. Eppler, M.J.: A comparison between concept maps, mind maps, conceptual diagrams, and visual metaphors as complementary tools for knowledge construction and sharing. Inf. Vis. 5(3), 202–210 (2006). https://doi.org/10.1057/palgrave.ivs.9500131
14. Faily, S., Lyle, J., Paul, A., Atzeni, A., Blomme, D., Desruelle, H., Bangalore, K.: Requirements sensemaking using concept maps. In: Winckler, M., Forbrig, P., Bernhaupt, R. (eds.) HCSE 2012. LNCS, vol. 7623, pp. 217–232. Springer, Heidelberg (2012). https://doi.org/10.1007/978-3-642-34347-6_13
15. Franze, J., Marriott, K., Wybrow, M.: What academics want when reading digitally. In: ACM Symposium on Document Engineering, pp. 199–202. ACM (2014). https://doi.org/10.1145/2644866.2644894
16. Gemino, A., Wand, Y.: Complexity and clarity in conceptual modeling: comparison of mandatory and optional properties. Data Knowl. Eng. 55(3), 301–326 (2005). https://doi.org/10.1016/j.datak.2004.12.009

17. George, T.: What Is a Focus Group? — Step-by-Step Guide & Examples (2022). https://www.scribbr.com/methodology/focus-group/
18. Guarino, N., Guizzardi, G.: In the defense of ontological foundations for conceptual modeling. Scand. J. Inf. Syst. 18(1), 1 (2006). https://aisel.aisnet.org/sjis/vol18/iss1/1
19. Hubbard, T., Stafford, J.A.: Using concept maps to enhance system view navigation. In: Proceedings of the 3rd International Conference on Concept Mapping. Citeseer (2008)
20. Hughes, G., Hay, D.: Use of concept mapping to integrate the different perspectives of designers and other stakeholders in the development of e-learning materials. Br. J. Edu. Technol. 32(5), 557–569 (2001). https://doi.org/10.1111/1467-8535.00225
21. Hypothes.is project: We've Reached 40 Million Annotations (2022). https://web.hypothes.is/blog/celebrating-nearly-40-million-annotations/
22. Johannesson, P., Perjons, E.: An Introduction to Design Science. Springer, Cham (2014). https://doi.org/10.1007/978-3-319-10632-8
23. Kawase, R., Herder, E., Nejdl, W.: A comparison of paper-based and online annotations in the workplace. In: Cress, U., Dimitrova, V., Specht, M. (eds.) EC-TEL 2009. LNCS, vol. 5794, pp. 240–253. Springer, Heidelberg (2009). https://doi.org/10.1007/978-3-642-04636-0_23
24. Kontio, J., Bragge, J., Lehtola, L.: The focus group method as an empirical tool in software engineering. In: Shull, F., Singer, J., Sjoberg, D.I.K. (eds.) Guide to Advanced Empirical Software Engineering, pp. 93–116. Springer, London (2008). https://doi.org/10.1007/978-1-84800-044-5_4
25. Maxwell, J.: Understanding and validity in qualitative research. Harvard Educ. Rev. 62(3), 279–301 (1992). https://doi.org/10.17763/haer.62.3.8323320856251826
26. McEwan, E.K.: Seven strategies of highly effective readers: using cognitive research to boost K-8 achievement. Corwin Press (2004)
27. Murphy, P.: Using picture books to engage middle school students. Middle Sch. J. 40(4), 20–24 (2009). https://doi.org/10.1080/00940771.2009.11461677
28. Navarrete, C.B., Malverde, M.G.M., Lagos, P.S., Mujica, A.D.: BUHOS: a web-based systematic literature review management software. SoftwareX 7, 360–372 (2018). https://doi.org/10.1016/j.softx.2018.10.004
29. Novak, J.D., Gowin, D.B.: Learning How To Learn. Cambridge University Press (1984). https://doi.org/10.1017/CBO9781139173469
30. Porter-O'Donnell, C.: Beyond the yellow highlighter: teaching annotation skills to improve reading comprehension. The English J. 93(5), 82–89 (2004). https://doi.org/10.2307/4128941
31. Smajevic, M., Bork, D.: From conceptual models to knowledge graphs: a generic model transformation platform. In: MoDELS (Companion), pp. 610–614. IEEE (2021). https://doi.org/10.1109/MODELS-C53483.2021.00093
32. Soyibo, K.: Using concept maps to analyze textbook presentations of respiration. The American Biology Teacher, pp. 344–351 (1995). https://doi.org/10.2307/4450013
33. Surber, J.R.: Mapping as a testing and diagnostic device. In: Spatial Learning Strategies, pp. 213–233. Elsevier (1984). https://doi.org/10.1016/B978-0-12-352620-5.50016-3

Ontological Representation of FAIR Principles: A Blueprint for FAIRer Data Sources

Anna Bernasconi[1], Alberto García Simon[2]([✉]), Giancarlo Guizzardi[3],
Luiz Olavo Bonino da Silva Santos[3,5], and Veda C. Storey[4]

[1] Politecnico di Milano, Milan, Italy
anna.bernasconi@polimi.it
[2] Universitat Politècnica de València, Valencia, Spain
algarsi3@pros.upv.es
[3] University of Twente, Enschede, The Netherlands
{g.guizzardi,l.o.boninodasilvasantos}@utwente.nl
[4] Georgia State University, Atlanta, USA
vstorey@gsu.edu
[5] Leiden University Medical Center, Leiden, The Netherlands

Abstract. Guidelines to improve the Findability, Accessibility, Interoperability, and Reuse of datasets, known as FAIR principles, were introduced in 2016 to enable machines to perform automatic actions on a variety of digital objects, including datasets. Since then, the principles have been widely adopted by data creators and users worldwide with the 'FAIR' acronym becoming a common part of the vocabulary of data scientists. However, there is still some controversy on how datasets should be interpreted since not all datasets that are claimed to be FAIR, necessarily follow the principles. In this research, we propose the *OntoUML FAIR Principles Schema*, as an ontological representation of FAIR principles for data practitioners. The work is based on OntoUML, an ontologically well-founded language for Ontology-driven Conceptual Modeling. OntoUML is a proxy for ontological analysis that has proven effective in supporting the explanation of complex domains. Our schema aims to disentangle the intricacies of the FAIR principles' definition, by resolving aspects that are ambiguous, under-specified, recursively-specified, or implicit. The schema can be considered as a blueprint, or a template to follow when the FAIR classification strategy of a dataset must be designed. To demonstrate the usefulness of the schema, we present a practical example based on genomic data and discuss how the results provided by the OntoUML FAIR Principles Schema contribute to existing data guidelines.

Keywords: FAIR data · OntoUML FAIR Principles Schema · FAIRness guidance · Ontological Modeling Language · OntoUML

A. Bernasconi and A. García S.—should be regarded as Joint First Authors.

M. Indulska et al. (Eds.): CAiSE 2023, LNCS 13901, pp. 261–277, 2023.
https://doi.org/10.1007/978-3-031-34560-9_16

1   Introduction

Since the publication of the seminal paper in early 2016 [33], the FAIR principles gained significant attention. The principles have quickly been embraced by industry and academic communities, leading to several initiatives aiming at developing FAIR-compliant implementations. The implementation efforts can normally be classified into FAIRness assessment [1,6,34], FAIR tooling [30] and FAIR service support [20,28].

However, these initiatives quickly faced challenges to consistently interpret the principles in enough detail that could derive proper implementations. A possible consequence of inconsistent interpretations of the principles is the emergence of potentially incompatible implementations, defeating the original purpose of the FAIR principles. The difficulty in consistent interpretation can be traced to two aspects: (i) by design, principles do not provide specific implementation definitions; and (ii) the original FAIR paper did not explain in detail the intentions behind the principles and related consequences. Almost four years later, a subset of the original FAIR paper authors, together with other collaborators attempted to provide further explanations for the intended interpretations of the FAIR principles and implementation considerations related to each principle and sub-principle [19].

Once someone intends to adopt the FAIR principles to "make my data FAIR", three main questions need to be answered: (i) to what extent does my resource (e.g., dataset) currently follow the FAIR principles, i.e., what is its current FAIRness level?; (ii) what is the intended FAIRness level that I want it to reach?; and (iii) how can I improve from the current-level to the intended-level FAIRness? To answer these questions, one must hold a good understanding of the principles. Ontological models, traditionally employed to provide clear and precise explanations of a domain and enforce its shared understanding among stakeholders, are particularly suitable for representing the complex world of FAIR principles.

The objective of this research, therefore, is to propose the *OntoUML FAIR Principles Schema* resulting from an ontological analysis of the FAIR principles. OntoUML is an ontologically well-founded language for Ontology-driven Conceptual Modeling, which was built as a UML extension based on the Unified Foundational Ontology (UFO) [14]. This means that the modeling primitives of the language reflect the ontological distinctions put forth by the underlying foundational ontology. In other words, the modeling patterns constituting the language reflect the axiomatic micro-theories in UFO [27]. As a proxy for ontological analysis, OntoUML has proven to be a very effective support for the explanation of complex domains [3,9,16], because it can improve the understandability of technical concepts over traditional conceptual models [8,32].

Information integration and interoperability are important for the Information Systems domain. These aspects can be facilitated by applying the FAIR principles to both the data handled by information systems and the systems themselves. We aim to demonstrate that a clear and precise description leads to a more consistent interpretation of the FAIR principles and can contribute to the Information Systems domain by facilitating the development of more inter-operable information ecosystems.

The contribution of our work is to show how using a foundational ontology-based model to represent the FAIR principles can provide the following benefits: (a) Explicit representation of a particular shared interpretation of the principles in a concrete artifact; (b) Controlled vocabulary for use in semantic annotations of (meta)data entities; (c) Rationale for deriving FAIR evaluation metrics; (d) Prescriptive guidelines based on the metrics that operationalize the more abstract guiding principles. Moreover, the ontological schema also facilitates the use of its concepts and relations to semantically annotate metadata and data to make explicit, to machines and humans, their semantic commitments with the interpretation of the FAIR principles that our proposed schema represents.

The remainder of the paper is organized as follows. Section 2 provides an overview of the FAIR principles. Section 3 briefly describes the modeling language applied, OntoUML, the modeling method, and the resulting Schema (i.e., the main result of this paper addressing benefit (a) above). Section 4 shows one application in the genomics domain to illustrate how the schema can be used for semantic annotation (benefit (b)) and for deriving prescriptive operationalization guidelines (benefit (d)). Section 5 discusses the implications and Sect. 6 concludes the paper.

2   The FAIR Guiding Principles

FAIR Principles were first proposed by Wilkinson et al. [33] and further discussed and analyzed by the GO-FAIR initiative (https://www.go-fair.org/fair-principles/). The four FAIR principles are divided into the following sub-principles.

Findability. The utility of a dataset depends, to a large extent, on how easily its potential users can find it. The FAIR principles consider both humans and computers as potential users. Therefore, the means to uniquely identify a given digital object and the provision of rich enough metadata - so that potential (re)users can discover it - are the main targets of the findability sub-principles described below.

F1. (meta)Data are Assigned a Globally Unique and Persistent Identifier. Both metadata and data should be uniquely identified by persistent identifiers (e.g., a globally unique and persistent URI). To ensure uniqueness, once an identifier has been associated with a (meta)data, the same identifier should not relate to any other object. The persistence aspect relates to the identifier being associated with the same object over a period of time. F1 is one of the most relevant FAIR principles, because several others are built upon unique identifiers. Commonly, data repositories automatically assign globally unique identifiers for their hosted datasets. However, it is not always the case for the metadata records.

F2. Data are Described with Rich Metadata (defined by R1 below). Although the distinction between data and metadata is arbitrary, this principle attributes to metadata the specific role of describing other data with, for instance, the types of descriptors defined in the R1 sub-principles. The metadata should be "generous and extensive". The richer the metadata, the higher the chance that potential users find data based on the information provided in the metadata. Several types of metadata exist, including data about how a dataset was processed (e.g., the assembly used in a sequencing process); the context surrounding its acquisition (e.g., the protocol for obtaining a biological sample); device measurements (e.g., quality data for the devices used to extract a biological sample); or domain-specific information (e.g., the genes or proteins considered in a sequencing procedure).

F3. Metadata Clearly and Explicitly Include the Identifier of the Data it Describes. In some approaches or technologies metadata and data are stored in the same location (e.g., readme-files in the same folder as the described file) or even in the same file (e.g., EXIF metadata in image files). However, we cannot rely on file proximity to establish the connection between the metadata record and the object it describes. When someone discovers a given dataset through its metadata, the metadata record should explicitly contain the identifier of the dataset. Since a metadata record may contain a number of different identifiers (e.g., identifiers of other concepts and relations), the data identifier should be indicated with a relation/predicate that clearly communicates their connection (e.g., the isMetadataOf relation in our proposed schema).

F4. (meta)Data are Registered or Indexed in a Searchable Resource. Although rich metadata increases datasets' findability, it is insufficient to ensure it. If the existence of a dataset is unknown, users will not be able to use it, regardless of its metadata. Datasets and/or their corresponding metadata should be indexed in searchable engines. Principles F1, F2, and F3 establish the core requirements for findability and principle F4 indicates the finding mechanism.

Accessibility. When a user finds a (meta)data and, consequently its identifier, there should be a mechanism to access the (meta)data. Moreover, in many situations, data will cease to exist. Even then, it is relevant to keep their metadata accessible so the existence and characteristics of the data can still be known.

A1. (meta)Data are Retrievable by their Identifier Using a Standardized Communication Protocol. Datasets are retrieved with the support of a communication protocol. Among the several available ones, some are private, offer limited implementation capabilities, or are poorly documented. To address these cases, this FAIR principle requires the standardized communication protocol used to retrieve the (meta)data from its identifier to have the following properties: 1) the communication protocol should be open, free, and universally implementable; 2) the communication protocol should provide authentication and authorization procedures when required. FAIR does not require the data or metadata to be open or free; rather, it requires that the descriptions of the mechanism to retrieve the data and/or metadata be open and free (A1.1).

A2. Metadata are Accessible, Even when the Data are no Longer Available. The metadata associated with a dataset is a valuable resource *per se*. Data tend to become inaccessible over time for a variety of reasons, e.g., unsustainable maintenance costs. If a dataset becomes inaccessible, its corresponding metadata should remain accessible. In practice, metadata is much easier and cheaper to maintain accessible.

Interoperability. This principle considers the ability of (meta)data from one source to be connected in workflows with (meta)data from other sources for different purposes, such as analysis, storage, or processing.

I1. (meta)Data use a Formal, Accessible, Shared, and Broadly Applicable Language for Knowledge Representation. For data to be exchangeable, it should be in the same format, or appear in formats that can be parsed and interpreted by its corresponding parties. Therefore, this principle determines minimal requirements for the language used to represent the (meta)data.

I2. (meta)Data Use Vocabularies that Follow FAIR Principles. Another aspect to improve interoperability is the use of (commonly) employed vocabularies, ontologies, thesauri or data models. However, these vocabularies should also be findable, accessible, interoperable and reusable to a certain degree.

I3. (meta)Data Include Qualified References to Other (meta)Data. For links to be meaningful, references between entities must have a clear and informative semantics ('is regulator of' is better than 'is associated with'). This holds for both metadata elements and entire datasets. Datasets should be cited and the scientific links between them described.

Reusability. For optimizing the reuse, metadata and data should be well-described so their use in different settings can be assessed.

R1. Meta(data) are Richly Described with a Plurality of Accurate and Relevant Attributes. If deemed useful in a particular context, data should be reused. In order to support the potential (re)user to assess whether a particular data is relevant, rich and relevant metadata information should be provided. The R1 sub-principles provide 3 main categories of relevant metadata information to foster reuse as well as compose the rich metadata expected by principle F2. A non-exhaustive list of exemplar metadata properties is provided at (https://www.go-fair.org/fair-principles/r1-metadata-richly-described-plurality-accurate-relevant-attributes/).

R1.1. (meta)Data are Released with a Clear and Accessible Data Usage License. This sub-principle refers to the usage rights attached to a dataset, from which one can define the possible legal interoperability (licensing) of the data. Moreover, by defining reuse conditions, which include accessing the (meta)data, the license determines when the authentication and authorization procedures of the sub-principle A1.2. are required.

R1.2. (meta)Data are Associated with Detailed Provenance. This principle refers to the information about how the (meta)data came about, e.g., its origin and history, including who oversaw its generation and how it did so.

R1.3. (meta)Data Meet Domain-Relevant Community Standards. When (even minimal) information standards exist for a community, these should be employed to make similar (meta)data easier to be used together.

3   Ontological Modeling

3.1   OntoUML

The meta-model of the OntoUML language complies with the ontological distinctions and axiomatization of the well-grounded Unified Foundational Ontology (UFO [17]). Only the main concepts are presented here. The complete presentation of the language, the philosophical justifications, formal characterizations, and primitives are available in [14].

OntoUML includes the subcategory of *endurants*, i.e., entities that have essential and accidental properties and, hence, can change over time. Endurant types include *Kinds*, the fundamental types of objects that exist in a domain. Objects classified by a kind could not possibly exist without being of that specific kind. All objects necessarily belong to exactly one kind and cannot change kinds. There can be other static subdivisions of a kind, termed *Subkinds*. Object kinds and subkinds represent essential properties of objects (*rigid* types). There are, however, types that represent contingent or accidental properties of objects (*anti-rigid* types). These include *Phases* (properties that are intrinsic to entities: 'being a puppy' is being a dog in a particular developmental phase) and *Roles* (properties of entities within a relational context: 'being a husband' captures a cluster of contingent relational properties of a man participating in a marriage). Kinds, Subkinds, Phases, and Roles are categories of object *Sortals* (a type that provides a uniform principle of identity, persistence, and individuation for its instances).

Relators (such as enrollments, mandates, affiliations) represent clusters of relational properties that are kept together by a nexus. Relations (as classes of n-tuples) can be completely derived from relators [12]. Relators are existentially dependent entities that bind together entities (their relata) by the *mediation* relations, which is a particular type of *existential dependence* relation (A being existentially dependent on B means that B has to exist in all situations where A exists). Besides existential dependence, OntoUML countenances the relation of *external dependence*: an object A is externally dependent on an object B iff A is existentially dependent on B and B and A are mereologically disjoint (neither A is part of B nor B is part of A and they do not share any common part). Objects typically participate in relationships (relators) playing certain "roles". We call *RoleMixins* those role-like types that classify entities of multiple kinds.

Types that represent properties shared by entities of multiple kinds are called *Non-Sortals*. *Categories* are non-sortals that represent necessary properties shared by entities of multiple kinds.

Objects have parts (called components) that play different functional roles with respect to the whole. *Collectives* are entities that have a uniform structure, i.e., whose parts play the same role with respect to the whole.

Besides relator, another type of dependent endurant is a *mode*: an endurant that is existentially dependent on (inheres in) a singular individual.

3.2   OntoUML FAIR Principles Schema

Operationally, we first considered the FAIR principles as a whole, capturing the general spirit they convey. Then, we considered one sub-principle at a time, evaluating which OntoUML entity stereotypes are needed for representing the involved concepts and then connecting them with relationship stereotypes or generalization/compositions. In the following, we describe the OntoUML FAIR Principles Schema, representing the template of a world that more precisely instantiates FAIR choices within the context of the creation of a scientific dataset.

Findability and Interoperability. The excerpt of the schema related to these two highly interlinked principles is shown in Fig. 1. DATA is a *collective* of DATA ITEMS. One should notice that METADATA is DATA, namely, data that *refers to* (*is externally dependent of*) DATA. Metadata describes, puts into context, and informs the provenance of data. The recursive chain of reference here stops at what is termed GROUND DATA, i.e., data that cannot serve as metadata to other data. Metadata does not have to have metadata itself – otherwise, we would incur in a vicious regression. However, ground data must be described by metadata (see **F2**). Data can play the role of SEARCHABLE DATA (i.e., data with a metadata description) when it benefits from a REGISTRATION/INDEXING relator, within a SEARCHABLE RESOURCE (see **F4**). Data Items are, in turn, composed of ATTRIBUTES. Since metadata is data, METADATA ITEMS are those data items that compose metadata resources and, analogously, METADATA ITEM ATTRIBUTES are those attributes that compose metadata items. Note that (meta)data and their (meta)data item subparts (termed here simply DATA ENTITIES) must conform to a DATA MODEL, expressed by a REPRESENTATION LANGUAGE – which could be different for each of these (see **I1**). DATA MODELS and REPRESENTATION LANGUAGES are RESOURCES. Any resource can be considered as a COMMUNITY STANDARD. The acceptance of a resource as a community standard is given by the COMMUNITY CONSENSUS of a given COMMUNITY (a collective belief of a community, thus, modeled here as a *mode*), see **I1**. For example, Data could be instantiated with a textual genomic file, following an XML schema. Each item could be a genomic region following the simple schema <chromosome, start_coordinate, end_coordinate>. The linked Metadata could be another textual file – each referring to one data file – composed of <key,value> pairs items. Every attribute is composed of two essential and inseparable parts: an ATTRIBUTE KEY and an ATTRIBUTE VALUE. For both keys and values, the following principle holds: they can use a self-contained terminology (i.e., SELF-EXPLANATORY for keys or INTRINSIC for values), meaning that they only provide the information their name conveys, as opposed to linked terminology (i.e., EXPLAINED for keys or EXTRINSIC for values, termed here as QUALIFIED ATTRIBUTE ITEMS), so that the meaning they convey is enriched by the connection (*external dependence*) with another FAIR dataset (see **I3**). Qualified attribute items form parts of IDs, which are special types of attributes issued by an IDENTIFICATION SERVICE through an ID REGISTRATION relator (see **F1**).

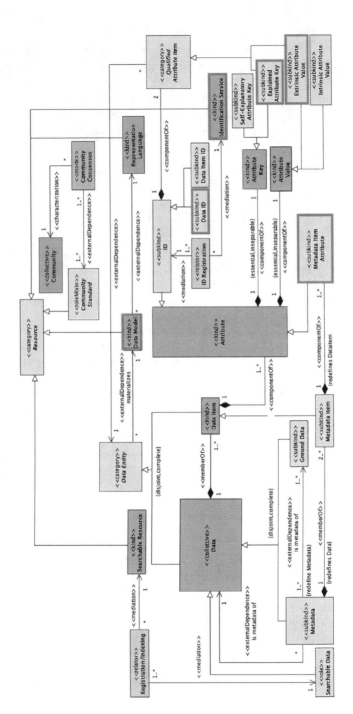

Fig. 1. OntoUML FAIR Principles Schema: module that represents Findability and Interoperability aspects.

Identifiers can then be used to identify (meta)data via these qualified references, thereby allowing data sources (through their metadata) to interoperate with (meta)data of other sources. This mechanism is made possible by means of explained keys and extrinsic values. The model contains a path that illustrates this recursive mechanism, which is left implicit in the FAIR principles (see **I3**). Note that, based on this representation, we do not need to explicitly model the 'controlled vocabularies' mentioned in **I2**, because they can be intended as represented by DATA sources themselves, referenced by metadata qualified attributes. IDs are specialized into DATA ID - identifiers of a dataset, as well as DATA ITEM IDs, i.e., not only the whole collective can have identifiers, but single items can as well. Furthermore, as mandated by **F3**, a data ID must be represented as a metadata item attribute. SEARCHABLE RESOURCE, DATA MODEL, REPRESENTATION LANGUAGE, and IDENTIFICATION SERVICE are all RESOURCES and, hence, consensus and community standards can be established for all these types of entities.

Accessibility. The excerpt of the schema related to this principle is shown in Fig. 2. The retrieval of metadata should always be possible, according to FAIR (**A2**). Depending on the choices and policies of the data-creators, data can be (contingently) ACCESSIBLE DATA, which in turn can either be OPEN DATA or DATA WITH RESTRICTED ACCESS. Data is accessible if it has an identification scheme (see ID) and explicitly prescribed DATA ACCESSIBILITY REQUIREMENTS defined as a contract (in the sense of [10]), but necessarily in a machine-readable format, i.e., as a machine-readable bundle of social and legal rights, obligations, powers, etc., connecting a given a data set with a COMMUNITY. When data has restricted access, we use the RESTRICTED DATA ACCESSIBILITY REQUIREMENTS. Data accessibility requirements demand DATA ACCESS PROTOCOL (see **A1.1**), which can be AUTHORIZATION PROTOCOLS or AUTHENTICATION PROTOCOLS, specifically included in restricted data accessibility requirements (see principle **A1.2**). PROTOCOLS (and specializations thereof) are RESOURCES and, once more, they can be subject to a COMMUNITY CONSENSUS and then accepted as COMMUNITY STANDARDS (see **A1**).

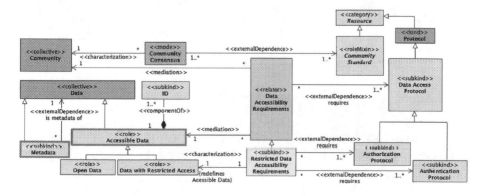

Fig. 2. OntoUML FAIR Principles Schema: module that represents Accessibility.

Reusability. The excerpt of the schema related to this principle is reported in Fig. 3. Here, a RICH METADATA is a collective of RICH METADATA ITEM ATTRIBUTES (**R1**). The latter is a role played by METADATA ITEM ATTRIBUTES when described following COMMUNITY STANDARDS for accuracy and relevance (see **R1** and **R1.3**). If a METADATA ITEM ATTRIBUTE describes provenance information then it is also a PROVENANCE METADATA ITEM ATTRIBUTE (see **R1.2**), and metadata containing PROVENANCE METADATA ITEM ATTRIBUTES are considered to be PROVENANCE METADATA. If a PROVENANCE METADATA ITEM ATTRIBUTE is richly described according to COMMUNITY STANDARDS then it is a RICH PROVENANCE METADATA ITEM ATTRIBUTE If all the constituents of a PROVENANCE METADATA collective are RICH PROVENANCE METADATA ITEM ATTRIBUTES, then we have a RICH PROVENANCE METADATA collective. One could argue that the above description does not fully characterize what is intended by 'rich' in this context. However, it does emphasize the role of community standards in this process. That is, the principles prescribed that - if COMMUNITY STANDARDS exist - they should be preferred to any other initiative with the same objective as the standard. Frequently, one standard does not cover all the needs for (meta)data, requiring the combination with other standards and/or approaches. (META)DATA is considered here to be REUSABLE DATA if it is described by RICH METADATA (including RICH PROVENANCE METADATA, see **R1.2** and **R1.3**) and if we have explicit DATA USAGE LICENCES associated to it (see **R1.1**). The latter is a contract (again, ideally in the sense of [10]) directed towards a target COMMUNITY.

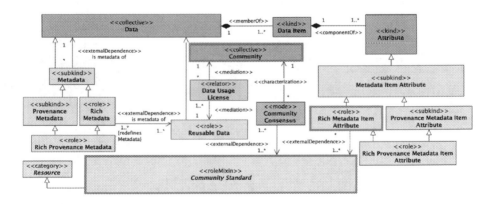

Fig. 3. OntoUML FAIR Principles Schema: module that represents Reusability.

The OntoUML FAIR Principles Schema as an ontology. The described artifact is a schema that results from a process of ontological analysis. We do not call it a FAIR ontology, to avoid terminological confusion. In the conceptual modeling literature, the term ontology is used in three different ways, which are briefly discussed in the sequel.

In the first sense, an 'ontology' is a theory about what is assumed to exist by a representation artifact [15]. The process of ontological analysis here reveals the ontology behind the original description of the FAIR principles. The result of this analysis is explicitly captured in an OntoUML model, whose primitives make explicit the ontological categories of the involved domain notions, as well as the so-called *truthmakers* of the propositions constituting that description [12]. This is a process of explanation (of the ontology underlying a certain description) that is called *ontological unpacking*. The process of unpacking that we have employed here is described in [3,9,16]. In this sense, our proposed schema is a representation of the data ontology behind the FAIR principles.

In the second sense, an 'ontology' is supposed to be a "formal, explicit specification of a shared conceptualization" [4]. Given that (1) the FAIR principles themselves represent a shared conceptualization of data management guidelines; (2) they are explicitly represented in the OntoUML model/specification; and (3) OntoUML has a formal semantics [14], then the proposed OntoUML schema can be termed an 'ontology' (in the second sense).

Finally, there is a third sense in which an ontology is taken to be "equivalent to a Description Logic knowledge base" [18]. This is typically represented in the Web Ontology Language (OWL). One of us has argued in depth elsewhere why this is a problematic interpretation of the term [15]. In any case, the OntoUML tool set includes a fully automated approach for generating OWL specifications from OntoUML models [13]. So, an 'ontology' in this third sense can be automatically generated from the proposed schema.

4 Example Implementations

To illustrate the usage of our proposed ontological schema, from the expected benefits mentioned in Sect. 1, we discuss an example of data annotation with the schema (Sect. 4.1) and the use of our model for deriving prescriptive guidelines that operationalize the principles in a specific case (Sect. 4.2):

4.1 Semantic Annotation

Here we present an example concerning the genomic information related to the BRCA1 gene, which produces proteins that help repair damaged DNA. Certain harmful mutations in this gene increase the risks of several cancers, most notably breast, and ovarian cancer. Its information can be obtained from the Gene Database of the RefSeq data source [24]. From https://www.ncbi.nlm.nih.gov/gene/672 we downloaded three files, whose partial information is represented in the Object Diagram in Fig. 4.

- the GROUND DATA instance `gene.fna`, i.e. a FASTA file storing DNA sequence stretches on different DATA ITEMS (rows), with two attributes: 1) a content-oriented ATTRIBUTE, with a SELF EXPLANATORY ATTRIBUTE KEY called 'sequence' and a very long INTRINSIC ATTRIBUTE VALUE starting with 'GCTGAGAC...'; 2) an identifying attribute (the DATA ITEM ID)

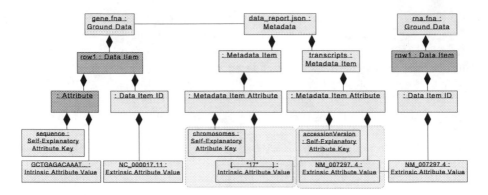

Fig. 4. Object Diagram of the OntoUML FAIR Principles Schema, for RefSeq data.

following the FAIR principle **F3**, holding an INTRINSIC ATTRIBUTE VALUE 'NC_000017.11'.

- the GROUND DATA instance `rna.fna`, containing RNA sequence stretches, with a DATA ITEM identified by the DATA ITEM ID 'NM_007297.4'.
- the METADATA instance `data_report.json`, with (1) atomic METADATA ITEMS with one JSON element (METADATA ATTRIBUTE), containing information, e.g., on the human organism to which the gene belongs (not shown in the diagram) or on the chromosome (key) and its number '17' (value). See Fig. 4 (purple background); (2) composite/nested METADATA ITEMS, e.g., about the transcripts of the gene. Each transcript item includes several METADATA ITEM ATTRIBUTES, e.g., name, length, ensemblTranscript (not shown), and accessionVersion. The accessionVersion is a SELF-EXPLANATORY ATTRIBUTE KEY corresponding to the 'NM_007297.4' EXTRINSIC ATTRIBUTE VALUE (see Fig. 4, orange background). This is a QUALIFIED ATTRIBUTE ITEM forming the ID of the `rna.fna` GROUND DATA mentioned above. It is important to note that the extrinsic 'NM_007297.4' value allows us to connect the data attributes of `rna.fna` with the metadata attributes of `gene.fna`.

4.2   Refining and Operationalizing Guidelines

The FAIR principles were originally defined in an abstract manner thus hampering its direct operationalization. The ontological analysis and resulting schema conducted here can be systematically employed to refine and propose concrete guidelines for the operationalization of principles. Due to space limitations, we will illustrate this process here by addressing only certain aspects of a few principles.

First, consider **R1.3**. The model of Fig. 3 makes it explicit that community standards are established by the collective belief of a community (a community consensus). This consensus can be established with respect to resources in general, not only with respect to the rich description of metadata and metadata item attributes (see Figs. 1–2); for example, data models, representation languages, as well as data access protocols. In fact, this notion of employing resources that are deemed consensual in the collective belief of a community, also appears in a less obvious way when referring to protocols (see "standardized communication protocols" in **A1**), to representation languages ("broadly applicable languages" in **I1**), and to data models ("vocabularies that follow FAIR principles" in **I2**) - the original proposal explicitly refers to these as "community-endorsed vocabularies" [33], for example. Moreover, the community whose consensus one needs to follow is the target community towards which Data Accessibility Requirements and Data Usage Licenses are directed by Data entity creators. In fact, our analysis makes the centrality of communities and their collective beliefs clear, despite the fact that the term community is used only once in the description of the principles (**R1.3**).

As a result of this analysis, one can refine the aforementioned principles. It is important to make explicit that, when creating data entities, data creators must identify target communities to which accessibility requirements and usage licenses shall be directed, and which standards regarding protocols, data models, representation languages, and approaches for metadata description need to be properly identified and adopted.

5   Discussion

Several aspects of our work require discussion. First, selected aspects of the FAIR principles need additional effort to achieve a more precise specification. We highlighted the corresponding areas in Figs. 1- 3 with a light-blue outline. Second, the FAIR principles, as currently stated [33], provide asymmetric definitions. Third, there is a need for the identification of communities before community standards can be created and applied. Finally, the term 'rich' seems too broad to be interpreted properly within a scientific context.

1) Under-specified areas.
In Fig. 1, we highlight that the IDENTIFICATION SERVICE shows another crucial part of the FAIR ecosystem, as mandated by principle **F1**. Schwanitz et al. [29] reviewed 80 representative databases employed in research on low carbon energy using the automatic evaluation framework proposed by proponents of FAIR principles [34]. However, none of these databases complied with **F1**, which means that data identifiers are not persistent in any of these cases.

The DATA ID should be represented as a METADATA ITEM ATTRIBUTE according to **F3**. While this is currently implemented by some genomic data sources (see [2,5,11]), it is less apparent in others [21,25].

The DATA MODEL is a fundamental entity to comply with principle **I1**. Data models currently face many challenges, as highlighted in the Dutch initiative on FAIR Genomes [31]. This includes the non-negligible problem of dealing with the updating strategy of data models, which must remain compliant with the domain to be represented as well as with the followed principles.

Moreover, the presence of EXPLAINED ATTRIBUTE KEYS and EXTRINSIC ATTRIBUTE VALUES is tightly related to principles **I2** and **I3**. This highlights a very important requirement that is not yet broadly accepted in scientific data sources. For example, in The Cancer Genome Atlas (part of Genomic Data Commons [11]), clinical and biospecimen metadata are arranged according to a complex XML schema that contains self-explanatory keys of difficult interpretation, without following a controlled vocabulary. Examples include the: 'clinical.ablation.ablation_performed_indicator' or 'biospecimen.bio.bcr_analyte_barcode'. Instead, in Roadmap Epigenomics [21], tissues are described with values decided in-house by the data curation team of the source (see https://www.roadmapepigenomics.org/data/tables). Possible values include 'GI-COLON' or 'MUSCLE-Adult', which can lead to different interpretations when the corresponding genomic data is integrated with similar datasets, thereby hindering the possibility of their joint use. Such intrinsic attributes would clearly benefit from becoming extrinsic, using, for example, well-recognized ontologies for Anatomic sites (e.g., UBERON [22]).

According to the **A2** principle and, as observed in Fig. 2, when data is inaccessible (i.e., the complement class of ACCESSIBLE DATA in that model), METADATA should be accessible through the corresponding event. However, there are still several examples in the literature where this does not occur; e.g., in the energy domain [29] or the genomics domain [23].

Figure 3, highlights COMMUNITY STANDARDS (discussed by **R1.3**). This is still a controversial concept because, in a given well-defined domain, it is not clear who should define the community standards for that domain. Large initiatives are starting to recognize these issues. For instance, Uniprot [26] claims to be FAIR for all other principles except R1.3, because the recognized authority is not known within the field of proteins [7]). Similarly, this aspect also remains unresolved in the field of low carbon energy data after a systematic assessment [29].

2) Asymmetric definitions. There is an asymmetry in the 4 letters inherent in FAIR. Findable (F) is fundamentally based on technology, whereas Interoperability (I) is very conceptual. In OntoUML we had difficulties modeling interoperability, highlighting that it is highly under-specified or under-formalized in the current FAIR principles.

3) Unclear community roles. In OntoUML, we modeled COMMUNITY STANDARD as a role played by resources of different kinds when enriching data item attributes (turning them into RICH METADATA ITEM ATTRIBUTE, i.e., a metadata attribute that is complete, generous, and explanatory enough to be adopted and reused by anyone in the COMMUNITY). Our representation should facilitate a discussion on the characteristics of a good community standard: *Who should define it? How should it be formalized, communicated, and enforced?*

4) How rich is 'rich'? The 'rich' adjective could refer to a property of the meta-schema or something assigned with a relationship to the community that defines or uses the metadata. If a rich metadata attribute is shared by multiple communities, is it more relevant than one that is only considered by one? A challenge is how to deal with discrepancies between communities from the same domain.

Aspects 3) and 4) are tightly related. We consider an 'unfair' situation to be one in which there are no community standards or it is not possible to clearly and unambiguously identify them. As a result, it might not be possible to define rich metadata attributes. Consequently, it becomes difficult to ensure that metadata has the required minimum quality for FAIR (specifically, for R1.3, but also for Findability and Interoperability-related principles). Overall, our results suggest the need for more efforts to define and agree upon community standards.

6   Conclusion

The adoption of FAIR principles for datasets is important and well-recognized by data scientists. In this research, we proposed an OntoUML FAIR Principles Schema to extend work on the adoption of FAIR principles by providing an ontologically grounded schema. The schema was applied, and its results shown to be effective, thereby establishing support for the implementation of FAIR principles. Further research is needed to apply this schema to other applications and refine it to support all aspects of the FAIR principles.

Acknowledgements. A.G.S. was supported by the Valencian Innovation Agency and Innovation through the OGMIOS project (INNEST/2021/57), the Generalitat Valenciana through the CoMoDiD project (CIPROM/2021/023), and the Spanish State Research Agency through the DELFOS (PDC2021-121243-I00,MICIN/AEI/10.13039/501 100011033) and SREC (PID2021-123824OB-I00) projects, and co-financed with ERDF and the European Union Next Generation EU/PRTR.

References

1. Ammar, A., et al.: A semi-automated workflow for FAIR maturity indicators in the life sciences. Nanomaterials **10**(10), 2068 (2020)
2. Bernasconi, A., et al.: META-BASE: a novel architecture for large-scale genomic metadata integration. IEEE/ACM Trans. Comput. Biol. Bioinf. **19**(1), 543–557 (2022)
3. Bernasconi, A., et al.: Semantic interoperability: ontological unpacking of a viral conceptual model. BMC Bioinform. **23**(11), 491 (2022)
4. Borst, P., et al.: Engineering ontologies. Int. J. Hum Comput. Stud. **46**(2–3), 365–406 (1997)
5. Buniello, A., et al.: The NHGRI-EBI GWAS catalog of published genome-wide association studies, targeted arrays and summary statistics 2019. Nucleic Acids Res. **47**(D1), D1005–D1012 (2018)
6. Devaraju, A., et al.: An automated solution for measuring the progress toward FAIR research data. Patterns **2**(11), 100370 (2021)
7. Garcia, L., et al.: FAIR adoption, assessment and challenges at UniProt. Sci. Data **6**, 175 (2019)

8. García S, A., et al.: An initial empirical assessment of an ontological model of the human genome. In: Guizzardi, R., Neumayr, B. (eds.) Advances in Conceptual Modeling. ER 2022. LNCS, vol. 13650, pp. 55–65. Springer, Cham (2022). https://doi.org/10.1007/978-3-031-22036-4_6

9. García S. A. et al.: An ontological characterization of a conceptual model of the human genome. In: De Weerdt, J., Polyvyanyy, A. (eds.) Intelligent Information Systems. CAiSE 2022. LNBIP, vol. 452, pp. 27–35. Springer, Cham (2022). https://doi.org/10.1007/978-3-031-07481-3_4

10. Griffo, C., Almeida, J.P.A., Guizzardi, G.: Conceptual modeling of legal relations. In: Trujillo, J.C., Davis, K.C., Du, X., Li, Z., Ling, T.W., Li, G., Lee, M.L. (eds.) ER 2018. LNCS, vol. 11157, pp. 169–183. Springer, Cham (2018). https://doi.org/10.1007/978-3-030-00847-5_14

11. Grossman, R.L., et al.: Toward a shared vision for cancer genomic data. N. Engl. J. Med. **375**(12), 1109–1112 (2016)

12. Guarino, N., Guizzardi, G.: We need to discuss the relationship: revisiting relationships as modeling constructs. In: Zdravkovic, J., Kirikova, M., Johannesson, P. (eds.) CAiSE 2015. LNCS, vol. 9097, pp. 279–294. Springer, Cham (2015). https://doi.org/10.1007/978-3-319-19069-3_18

13. Guerson, J., et al.: Onto UML lightweight editor: a model-based environment to build, evaluate and implement reference ontologies. In: IEEE EDOCW 2015 (2015)

14. Guizzardi, G.: Ontological foundations for structural conceptual models. CTIT, Centre for Telematics and Information Technology (2005)

15. Guizzardi, G.: Ontology, ontologies and the "I" of fair. Data Intell. **2**, 181–191 (2020)

16. Guizzardi, G., Bernasconi, A., Pastor, O., Storey, V.C.: Ontological unpacking as explanation: the case of the viral conceptual model. In: Ghose, A., Horkoff, J., Silva Souza, V.E., Parsons, J., Evermann, J. (eds.) ER 2021. LNCS, vol. 13011, pp. 356–366. Springer, Cham (2021). https://doi.org/10.1007/978-3-030-89022-3_28

17. Guizzardi, G., et al.: UFO: unified foundational ontology. Appl. Ontol. **17**(1), 167–210 (2022)

18. Horrocks, I., et al.: From SHIQ and RDF to owl: the making of a web ontology language. J. Web Semant. **1**(1), 7–26 (2003)

19. Jacobsen, A., et al.: FAIR principles: interpretations and implementation considerations. Data Intell. **2**(1–2), 10–29 (2020)

20. Kersloot, M.G., et al.: Perceptions and behavior of clinical researchers and research support staff regarding data FAIRification. Sci. Data **9**, 241 (2022)

21. Kundaje, A., et al.: Integrative analysis of 111 reference human epigenomes. Nature **518**(7539), 317–330 (2015)

22. Mungall, C.J., et al.: Uberon, an integrative multi-species anatomy ontology. Genome Biol. **13**, R5 (2012)

23. Nayar, P.G., et al.: CardioGenBase: a literature based multi-omics database for major cardiovascular diseases. PLoS ONE **10**(12), e0143188 (2015)

24. O'Leary, N.A., et al.: Reference sequence (RefSeq) database at NCBI: current status, taxonomic expansion, and functional annotation. Nucl. Acids Res. **44**(D1), D733–D745 (2016)

25. 1000 Genomes Project Consortium: A global reference for human genetic variation. Nature **526**(7571), 68 (2015)

26. The UniProt Consortium: UniProt: the universal protein knowledgebase in 2021. Nucl. Acids Res. **49**(D1), D480–D489 (2021)

27. Ruy, F.B., et al.: From reference ontologies to ontology patterns and back. Data Knowl. Eng. **109**, 41–69 (2017)

28. Sansone, S.A., et al.: FAIRsharing as a community approach to standards, repositories and policies. Nat. Biotechnol. **37**(4), 358–367 (2019)

29. Schwanitz, V.J., et al.: Current state and call for action to accomplish findability, accessibility, interoperability, and reusability of low carbon energy data. Sci. Rep. **12**, 5208 (2022)

30. Bonino da Silva Santos, L.O., et al.: FAIR data point: a FAIR-oriented approach for metadata publication. Data Intell. (2022)

31. van der Velde, K.J., et al.: FAIR genomes metadata schema promoting next generation sequencing data reuse in Dutch healthcare and research. Sci. Data **9**, 169 (2022)

32. Verdonck, M., et al.: Comparing traditional conceptual modeling with ontology-driven conceptual modeling: an empirical study. Inf. Syst. **81**, 92–103 (2019)

33. Wilkinson, M.D., et al.: The FAIR guiding principles for scientific data management and stewardship. Sci. Data **3**, 160018 (2016)

34. Wilkinson, M.D., et al.: Evaluating FAIR maturity through a scalable, automated, community-governed framework. Sci. Data **6**, 174 (2019)

Enabling Representation Learning in Ontology-Driven Conceptual Modeling Using Graph Neural Networks

Syed Juned Ali[1]([⊠]) , Giancarlo Guizzardi[2] , and Dominik Bork[1]

[1] Business Informatics Group, TU Wien, Vienna, Austria
{syed.juned.ali,dominik.bork}@tuwien.ac.at
[2] University of Twente, Enschede, The Netherlands
g.guizzardi@utwente.nl

Abstract. Conceptual Models (CMs) are essential for information systems engineering since they provide explicit and detailed representations of the subject domains at hand. Ontology-driven conceptual modeling (ODCM) languages provide primitives for articulating these domain notions based on the ontological categories put forth by upper-level (or foundational) ontologies. Many existing CMs have been created using ontologically-neutral languages (e.g., UML, ER). Connecting these models to ontological categories would provide better support for meaning negotiation, semantic interoperability, and complexity management. However, given the sheer size of this legacy base, manual stereotyping is a prohibitive task. This paper addresses this problem by proposing an approach based on Graph Neural Networks towards automating the task of stereotyping UML class diagrams with the meta-classes offered by the ODCM language OntoUML. Since these meta-classes (stereotypes) represent ontological distinctions put forth by a foundational ontology, this task is equivalent to ontological category prediction for these classes. To enable this approach, we propose a strategy for representing CM vector embeddings that preserve the model elements' structure and ontological categorization. Finally, we present an evaluation that shows convincing learning of OntoUML model node embeddings used for OntoUML stereotype prediction.

Keywords: Ontology-Driven Conceptual models · Graph Neural Networks · Representation Learning

1 Introduction

Conceptual Models (CMs) are essential for information systems engineering in complex domains since they provide explicit and detailed representations of the subject domains. Ontology-driven conceptual modeling languages provide primitives for articulating these domain notions based on the ontological categories put forth by upper-level (or foundational) ontologies. These Ontology-Driven Conceptual Models (ODCMs) are believed to provide better support for semantic

M. Indulska et al. (Eds.): CAiSE 2023, LNCS 13901, pp. 278–294, 2023.
https://doi.org/10.1007/978-3-031-34560-9_17

interoperability of the systems as shown in [13] that methodologies and modeling languages based on theoretically principled foundational ontologies can mitigate a number of semantic interoperability problems that arise in concrete application scenarios. The fundamental ontological distinctions embodied in a foundational ontology have been used a conceptual toolbox for supporting ontological analysis, meaning explication and negotiation, and conceptual clarification [2]. ODCM has been further applied for more sophisticated conceptual model modularization mechanism for complexity management [14] and database design [3].

There exist, however, many CMs that have been created using ontologically-neutral languages (e.g., UML, ER). Connecting models created with these languages to ontological categories would bring the aforementioned benefits to them. However, given the sheer size of this legacy base, manually doing this is a prohibitive task. For this reason, an automated approach for suitably addressing this task would significantly advance the state of the art in the field.

Recently, advanced Artificial Intelligence approaches based on deep learning (DL) and Natural Language Processing (NLP) techniques have been used in conceptual modeling to support intelligent modeling assistants [24], model transformation [8], and metamodel classification [35]. However, these approaches limit the CM representation to the CM elements' labels and do not sufficiently exploit the CM structure and real-world semantics to learn the vector representation of these models. For example, Weyssow et al. [35] transform a CM into a tree-based structure where each class has its attributes and associations as children. As a result, they cannot capture the model's graph structure. Konick et al. [20] limit the representation learning of CM to labels. Due to the lack of such knowledge transfer from a CM to its encoding prior to training, the learned ML models do not generalize well to be used as a more robust vector representation of a CM.

To address the problem of predicting the ontological categorization of a CM, we need semantically richer representations of these models. For that, we need encodings that make the semantics of these models and their constituents accessible to the representation learning algorithms. Knowledge Graphs (KG) can effectively organize and represent knowledge to be efficiently utilized in advanced applications by applying different kinds of reasoning (e.g., rule-based and ML-based). KG representation of CMs can comprehensively capture the CM's graph structure and relations between model elements. Therefore, instead of extracting the information from CMs and applying ML algorithms to the extracted data, we can use an intermediary KG representation of models and apply AI techniques to learn their semantically richer representations. In particular, we propose a type of KG that captures the ontological categorizations of the elements constituting an ODCM. This is termed in the following a *Conceptual Knowledge Graph (CKG)*. CKGs embeddings preserve both the model's original structure and its elements' ontological categorization (*Contribution 1*). We then employ these embeddings to enable a Graph Neural Network (GNN)-based approach for automating the task of stereotyping UML CMs (class diagrams) with the meta-classes offered by the ODCM language OntoUML [15] (*Contribution 2*). Since these meta-classes (stereotypes) represent ontological distinctions put forth by the Unified Foundational Ontology (UFO) [15], this task is equivalent to a task of ontological category attribution for these classes.

We employ our representation learning approach to learn the model nodes' vector-based representation (embeddings). These embeddings can assist modelers with intelligent conceptual modeling tasks, like ontology mapping, model auto-completion, and model search. Since OntoUML and UFO are, respectively, among the most used modeling languages and foundational ontologies in ODCM, our proposal makes a clear contribution in advancing the state of art in this field. We present an experimental evaluation to validate our approach and provide a detailed comparative impact analysis of various design choices in our solution architecture. We use the OntoUML FAIR model dataset described in [3].

The remainder of the paper is structured as follows: Sect. 2 briefly presents relevant background, including a brief discussion about UFO/OntoUML, Knowledge Graphs, (Graph) Representation Learning, and GNNs. Section 3 discusses how our proposals for i) CM vector representations (embeddings), and ii) ontological categorization prediction advance the state of art in these two enterprises. Section 4 presents the two contributions of this paper, namely, i) an approach for transforming OntoUML models to CKGs; and ii) an approach for using GNN-based representation learning that employs these CKGs for OntoUML stereotype prediction. Section 5 reports the results of an experimental evaluation of our approach. Section 6 discusses the obtained results and their implications, as well as threats to validity. Section 7 concludes the paper.

2   Background

In the following, we provide a brief background on conceptual modeling, ontologies, knowledge graphs, and graph-based machine learning.

Conceptual modeling is the activity of representing aspects of the physical and social world for communication, learning, and problem-solving among human users [34]. Conceptualizations are entities that are abstractions (of a part) of reality. A modeling language provides a set of modeling primitives that can represent these conceptualizations. CMs represent abstractions using CML primitives, and ontologies define the conceptualizations. An **Ontology** makes the structure of domain conceptualization accessible through an explicit and formal description. **ODCM** extends or supports conceptual modeling techniques by ontological theories that further formalize the conceptual modeling grammars [34], thereby strengthening the ontological commitment of these languages and thus improving the semantic quality of the CML.

Knowledge Graphs (KGs) represent a collection of interlinked descriptions of entities – e.g., objects, events, and concepts. KGs provide a foundation for data integration, fusion, analytics, and sharing [29] based on linked data and semantic metadata. KGs have been recently used for the representation [30,32] of CMs. Such KG-based representations can act as the intermediary representation of CMs to enable ML-based applications on CMs. Existing works (cf. [28]) for creating KGs from structured and semi-structured data exist. Recently, a generic approach has been proposed that is able to transform arbitrary CMs into CKGs called *CM2KG* [30]. However CM2KG focuses only on the element labels and metamodel information. We define the notion of Conceptual Knowledge Graphs (CKGs) as follows: *Conceptual Knowledge Graphs* (CKG) are ontologically enriched KGs representing CMs. KGs are a suitable representation for applying ML and solving question answering, recommendation, and information retrieval. With CKGs, we aim to enable AI-based applications that exploit the full semantic richness of ontologically enriched conceptual models.

Representation learning makes learning algorithms less dependent on manual feature engineering by using DL methods to learn the underlying explanatory factors hidden in the low-level sensory data [4]. In NLP, representation learning is applied to learn natural language (NL) words' representations and then use these representations in various tasks, e.g., sentence sentiment analysis. *Language models* (LM) are trained to learn the vector representations of NL words. Initial works in LMs include GloVe [25], which learns non-contextual word embeddings by learning a global (context-free) embedding for each word. Pre-trained transformer-based LMs such as BERT [10] can learn robust contextual text embeddings and perform better than traditional non-contextual LMs. Moreover, LMs such as BERT apply a masked language modeling approach, where a language model is trained to predict missing words in a text based on the surrounding context. The model is presented with text with some words randomly masked (or hidden) out, and it must generate the missing words based on the remaining words in the sentence.

Graph representation learning (GRL) creates a mapping that represents nodes or entire (sub)graphs as points in a low-dimensional vector space that reflects the original graph's structure, like global positions of nodes in the graph and the structure of local graph neighborhoods [17]. Graph representation techniques for an Encoder-Decoder framework [17] involve two key mapping functions: an *encoder* function, which maps each node to a low-dimensional vector, and a *decoder* function, which decodes the graph information from the learned embeddings. E.g., the decoder might predict an edge between nodes or a node class. GRL optimizes the encoder and decoder mappings to minimize the error between the decoder mapping node embedding from the encoder and the expected statistic value. E.g., if a decoder maps the node embedding to node degree, then GRL minimizes the error between the decoder predicted degree and the node's degree in the initial graph.

The quality of the learned representation, i.e., how well it encodes the intended *meaning* of the data, depends upon the data quality, the architecture of the DL model, and the learning objectives. E.g., different descriptors of a graph element, e.g., label, degree, and node type, will learn node representations to different extents. Different approaches like node2vec [12] and random walk [26] focus on node-level representation learning and graph representations [17].

Graph Neural Networks are neural models that learn graph representations via *message passing* between graph nodes by information aggregation of a node from its neighborhood. In recent years, variants of GNNs such as Graph Convolutional Networks (GCN), Graph Attention Networks (GAT), and Graph Recurrent Networks (GRN) have demonstrated good performance on many DL tasks. GraphSAGE [16] generalized the aggregation function (compared to GCN, which uses "mean" as the aggregation function) that generates node embeddings by sampling and aggregating features from a node's local neighborhood. Once the representations are learned, GNNs achieve state-of-the-art performance in link prediction, node classification, graph classification, and graph mining [36].

3   Related Work

Several works have recently proposed ML-based solutions for various conceptual modeling tasks (cf. [6,7]). To use ML, CMs need to be transformed into vectors. In the following, we provide an overview of the existing means to represent CMs in a vector. We thereby mainly focus on encoding the conceptual model characteristics (see Table 1).

Koninck et al. [20] present representation learning techniques for BPMN business processes. They use BPMN model elements' label information and apply doc2vec-like [21] vector representations of activities, traces, and logs and finally aggregate these representations to produce the entire model's vector representations. Luettgen et al. [23] present a similar representation learning technique using word embeddings for business processes' data to improve the encoding. In their work, they add contextual information using the attributes of the activities instead of only the BPMN elements' labels. Both presented works use the learned representations for model discovery, trace clustering, process model selection, and process monitoring.

Burgueno et al. [8] present a Long Short Term Memory Neural Networks (LSTM)-based approach to infer model transformations from UML class diagrams to ER models. Before feeding the models into LSTM, they transform the input CM into a tree-based representation to capture the model elements (e.g., classes, attributes) and their associations. Their approach also captures contextual information and hierarchy, which is not preserved by using only the object's labels and attributes. Similarly, Weyssow et al. [35] present a meta-model concepts recommendation system. They use the data from a dataset of Ecore-based metamodels and train language models over the model elements' data (name and attributes) to learn the word embeddings of the words present in the metamodels. These learned word embeddings are then used to learn the model representations.

Huo et al. [18] propose an approach to detect business process anomalies using graph encodings of process event log data coupled with graph autoencoders. The authors choose GNNs to improve the encoding of the business process's graph structure during representation learning. Berquand et al. [5] present a KG-based approach to enhance data linkage, reusability, and interpretability of engineering models. Furthermore, they augment the KG with a reasoner, an inference engine, and an NLP layer to apply logical reasoning and extract crucial insights.

Table 1. Comparison of related works proposing an encoding for CM knowledge

Work	CML	MP	GS	OS
[20]	BPMN	†	✗	✗
[23]	BPMN	✓	✗	✗
[8]	UML, ER	✓	†	✗
[35]	ECore	✓	†	✗
[18]	BPMN	†	✓	✗
Ours	OntoUML	✓	✓	✓

✓ Captured ✗ Not Captured † Partially captured
MP: meta-properties, GS: graph structure, OS: ontological semantics

Table 1 shows that the ontological semantics are not considered in the CM's transformation into a vector-based representation. All presented works focus on using labels and attribute data to create a model's vector representation. Moreover, a tree-based structure only partially captures the structural information of the CMs graph structure and does not capture longer dependencies, i.e., dependencies exceeding each element's direct neighbors, whereas GNNs allow capturing such information to larger depths.

Existing works align or map foundational ontologies with domain ontologies [33]. Felipe et al. [22] propose mapping rules between the noun synsets of Wordnet and the top-level constructs of UFO. Several works use representation learning on ontologies as graphs to achieve ontology mapping [31]. RDF2Vec [27] considers entities' lexical terms for learning node embeddings; however, they treat an entity composed of multiple words as a single entity, which limits generality. OWL2Vec [9] considers word compositions and adds OWL constraints. Junior et al. [19] propose a DL approach that automatically classifies domain entities into top-level concepts using their informal definitions and the word embedding of the terms. However, their work does not consider graph structure contextual information and only relies on textual labels associated with each entity to predict the foundational ontology concept. Graphmatcher [11] is an ontology matching system that uses a graph attention approach to compute a higher-level representation of a class together with its surrounding terms. Regarding representation learning, [11] is similar to our approach, however, their work does not consider ontological semantics from foundational ontologies.

Therefore, in this work, we present a GNN-based representation learning approach for OntoUML models that not only captures the elements' label and attribute information but also considers the CM's ontological semantics from a foundational ontology, CML's meta-properties and the graph structure information of the model.

4   OntoUML Embeddings and Stereotype Prediction

This section presents the two contributions this paper aims to make. In Sect. 4.1 we present an approach to transform OntoUML models into Conceptual Knowl-

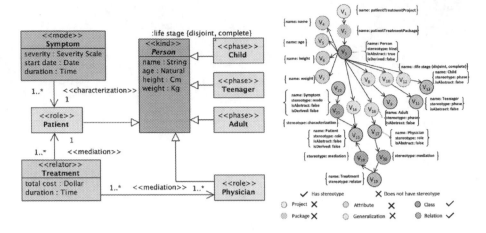

Fig. 1. An example OntoUML model (left) and transformed CKG (right)

edge Graph embeddings. Section 4.2 then discusses how the learned embeddings can be used for OntoUML stereotype prediction.

4.1   Transforming OntoUML Models into CKGs Embeddings

We will now describe the *OntoUML2CKG* transformation that aims to bridge the CM knowledge encoding gap by incorporating ontological knowledge and graph-structural knowledge in CKG creation – a prerequisite for the GNN-based node embedding learning (see Sect. 4.2). The transformation is composed of two sequential steps (cf. Fig. 2): *i) knowledge encoding* by transforming an input OntoUML model into a CKG; and *ii)* transforming the CKG into a vector space to enable GNN-based processing of the CKG.

We will use the example OntoUML model in Fig. 1 to illustrate our approach. The example shows classes and relations with ontological semantics from UFO captured by the stereotype attribute of the classes and relationships, e.g., *kind*, *role*, and *mediation*. In this step, we transform an input OntoUML model into a CKG as shown on the right of Fig. 1. A CKG is a directed graph that consists of nodes and edges. Each node consists of multiple attributes, and each attribute is associated with its value. The attributes capture the *label* information, meta-properties like *isAbstract*, *isDerived*, and the *stereotype* meta-attribute, which captures UFO-based ontological information for an element. Note that there will, of course, be many more meta-properties present; however, we show only *isAbstract* and *isDerived* for simplicity.

Serialized OntoUML models are structured into *projects*, which contain *packages*, and each package has OntoUML *classes*. OntoUML classes are related to each other by *generalization* relationships, which connect abstract to concrete classes and *relation* relationships of different types, namely, *association*, *composition*, and *aggregation*. Each class further contains *attributes*. The stereotype meta-attribute is associated with *class* and *relation*. To transform the input model into a CKG, we create a graph from the model's JSON serialization. During our transformation, we consider the six different structures as nodes as shown in Fig. 1, for e.g., *project* as V_1, *package* as V_2 and *class* V_3. We consider *project* and *package* as a node in our transformation because these structures link multiple models present in a project. We model *generalization* and *relation* relationships also as nodes because this allows us to associate each element in the input model with its attributes. E.g., treating the *mediation* relation between "Treatment" and "Physician" classes as a node allows us to separately add properties to the node as shown for node V_{21} in Fig. 1. Furthermore, this makes our approach suitable for stereotype prediction on the classes and relations. Each relationship is associated with a source and a target class. To model relationships as nodes, we create connections from the source class to the relationship node and from the relationship node to the target class.

Once we have transformed the input model into a CKG, we need to initialize a feature vector for each node in the CKG that will be trained using GNNs to capture the node's semantics. We consider each node's semantics from its NL *label*, its meta-properties, and its associated *stereotype*. Figure 1 shows a class with the label "Symptom", *stereotype* "mode" and meta-properties associated with this class like "isDerived" and "isAbstract". The GNN algorithm captures the graph structure properties (e.g., node degree) during training of the node embeddings.

The label of each node can contain ontological semantics encoded in NL words. We need a vector representation of a word that captures its contextual information, which can further support predicting the ontological stereotype associated with the label. Therefore we choose BERT as the language model that learns robust contextual word embeddings. However, BERT is a pre-trained model on a large corpus of domain-independent data and, therefore, lacks any OntoUML-specific semantics. To produce domain-specific word embeddings, we therefore also use a GloVe-based language model trained on OntoUML model data exclusively. To that end, we extract all the node and attribute labels data from each OntoUML model in our data set [3], create a data corpus from all the models, and use this corpus to train a GloVe model to learn OntoUML models-specific node label embeddings. To transform the meta-properties into a numerical vector, we create a vector with a set of meta-properties. We then assign a binary value for each meta-property, indicating the presence of that meta-property in a CKG node. We concatenate the two vectors (label and meta-properties, see Fig. 2), and use it as the initial representation of a CKG node. This vector-based representation is still incomplete because it does not yet capture the graph structure and information contributed by the node's neighbors. Once each node in the CKG is associated with a feature vector, each node is also associated with its stereotype label information. We need to train the graphs for a node classification task that predicts the correct OntoUML stereotype for each node. Therefore, we mask (i.e., hide) the stereotype label for 20% of the nodes.

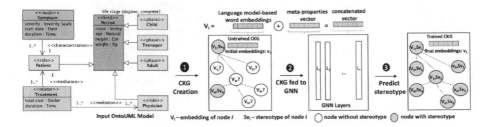

Fig. 2. OntoUML Node Representation Learning Architecture

A transformed CKG with masked labels is shown in Fig. 2 with the nodes as V_i, S_{V_i}. We train the GNN to predict the masked label for each node correctly.

4.2   Using GNN for OntoUML Stereotype Prediction

In the following, we will explain the GNN-based training phase of the CKG nodes' vector embeddings which produces OntoUML node and edge embeddings. Figure 2 shows all the steps that lead to GNN-based representation learning of OntoUML CMs. Steps 1 and 2, described in Sect. 4.1, produced GNN suitable representation of the OntoUML CKG.

The CKG is fed to several GNN layers. These layers are responsible for updating or optimizing and thereby "learning" the embeddings. The GNN captures the structure and semantics of the involved nodes, edges, and even entire graphs by aggregating contextual information between neighboring nodes. Figure 2 shows multiple layers which propagate information in each layer and extract high-level information about the nodes. These layers are usually stacked to obtain better representations [37]. Based on the information aggregation, the GNN model predicts a node's stereotype (class label). The objective function tries to minimize the error in each node between the predicted stereotype label and the true stereotype label. The error is measured by evaluating the binary cross-entropy loss as follows:

$$L = -\frac{1}{N}(\Sigma_{i=1}^{N} y_i.log(\hat{y}_i) + (1 - y_i).log(1 - \hat{y}_i)) \tag{1}$$

where N represents the number of nodes in the CKG while y_i and $\hat{y}_i$ represent the ground truth, and GNN predicted stereotype of the node, respectively. The error is then used to update the node embeddings. Once the training is completed, the final updated embeddings form the learned node embeddings of the CKG, and the stereotype label predicted based on the final learned embeddings forms the final predicted node label as shown in Fig. 2. The results of the training are saved, and test accuracy provides an estimate of the quality of learned node representations. We used a batched graph approach for training the model. However, the model can be trained on each graph with a batch size of 1. Depending upon the batch size, the GNN model can learn model-specific or model-agnostic patterns. We will describe the different configurations in detail in Sect. 5.

5   Experimental Evaluation

A commonly-agreed encoding for ODCM models like OntoUML is missing. In the following experimental evaluation, we account for this research gap by comprehensively discussing and comparing alternative configurations of the GNN architecture and the impact of incorporating specific aspects of the CKG during the training on the model quality. Eventually, we will report on the results of the best-performing configurations when using the trained GNN model for OntoUML stereotype prediction of a partial OntoUML model.

By transforming the models of our OntoUML dataset [3] into CKGs, we produced a CKG dataset composed of 131 models with **32492** nodes and **287259** edges[1] (cf. Table 2). Each OntoUML class and relationship can have properties connected by edges to the corresponding node. Therefore we see a larger number of edges in Table 2.

Table 2. Dataset statistics

Attribute Nodes (PN)	FSF	# models	# nodes	# edges	# labeled nodes
With PNs	Unfiltered	131	32492	287259	10400
	FSF 100	101	26472	267199	8982
	FSF 1000	40	12720	200913	3027
Without PNs	Unfiltered	131	19872	250086	10400
	FSF 100	113	18006	243159	9479
	FSF 1000	72	12127	202562	4052

Table 3. Stereotypes with a frequency greater than 100

Stereotype	Frequency	Stereotype	Frequency	Stereotype	Frequency
subKind	1460	category	412	derivation	184
kind	1155	event	384	participation	170
mediation	1151	roleMixin	337	datatype	126
role	1030	mode	316	type	118
relator	694	characterization	287	collective	113
material	524	phase	267	quality	105
componentOf	436	formal	218	memberOf	101

Each model has a fraction of the total nodes with a stereotype label. After doing a frequency analysis of each stereotype, we selected stereotypes with more

---

[1] Note that the edges in Table 2 do not denote the OntoUML relations as they were transformed into CKG nodes to enable their prediction.

than 100 occurrences over all models. We call the stereotypes in this set *frequent stereotypes*. During training, we consider only the nodes associated with a frequent stereotype. We call this node filtering frequent stereotype filtering (FSF). FSF with value N implies selecting nodes with a stereotype with stereotype frequency more than N., E.g., FSF 1000 implies nodes with stereotype frequency more than 1000, e.g., "kind" in Table 3 will be selected. The stereotypes form the different labels that the GNN needs to predict. Note that the connections of nodes without stereotypes with the labeled nodes can still provide crucial semantics. We only mask these nodes, so they are not considered for stereotype prediction. After FSF, we further filter the graphs if less than 20% of the total nodes have a frequent stereotype. We consider FSF 100, which gives 21 different classes, and FSF 1000, which gives four different classes.

In OntoUML models, a stereotype is not defined for nodes of type "Attribute", which reduces the number of nodes with frequent stereotypes. Therefore we distinguish the cases of training the GNN model with and without attribute nodes (AN). Table 2 shows the dataset statistics with a total number of nodes with stereotype labels based on attribute nodes consideration and FSF. Our dataset has around 9000 labeled nodes for classifying nodes in 21 classes and around 4000 for classifying nodes in four classes.

We explained that the textual data is transformed into vectors using two different language models, i.e., GloVe and BERT; therefore, we compare the effect of both LMs on prediction accuracy. Moreover, we also analyze the effect of incorporating the meta-properties on stereotype prediction accuracy by training the GNN, with and without the meta-properties vector. We used a batched training approach that trains the GNN model over batches of CKGs of models. Deep Graph Library[2] provides a way to combine a set of the graph in a batch of fixed size from a set of graphs; therefore, we use two different batch sizes, once with each graph individually and once with all the graphs together (batch size 40, 72, 101, and 131). Note that the different batch sizes result from different configurations, as in Table 2. We use two different variants of GNN models, i.e., Graph Convolution Network (GCN) and GraphSage with max pooling as the aggregation function[3] for GraphSage. GCN uses a weighted sum of the information from all node's neighbors. We train our models with two hidden layers, each of size 128. Therefore, we treat *i*) the GNN model, *ii*) the language model, *iii*) meta-properties, *iv*) attribute nodes, and *v*) batch size as the different configuration parameters. Next, we present the best-performing configurations and then elaborate on the impact of different configuration parameter values.

5.1   Stereotype Prediction Accuracy

We evaluate the prediction accuracy individually using the percentage of correctly predicted stereotypes for each of the discussed configurations.

---

[2] Deep Graph Library: https://www.dgl.ai/.
[3] This function aggregates the information from a sample of node's neighbors.

Table 4. OntoUML representation learning results

GNN Model	LM	MP	AN	BS	Accuracy
Node classification in four classes (Case 1)					
GraphSage	BERT	Yes	No	1	94.06%
GraphSage	GloVe	Yes	No	1	93.88%
GraphSage	BERT	Yes	Yes	1	93.81%
GraphSage	GloVe	Yes	Yes	1	93.15%
GraphSage	GloVe	Yes	Yes	40	90.20%
Node classification in 21 classes (Case 2)					
GraphSage	GloVe	Yes	Yes	1	67.05%
GraphSage	GloVe	Yes	No	1	61.59%
GraphSage	GloVe	Yes	Yes	101	59.70%
GraphSage	GloVe	Yes	No	113	59.10%
GraphSage	GloVe	No	No	1	44.85%

LM: Language model MP: meta-properties AN: Attribute Nodes BS: Batch Size

Table 5. Configuration parameter impact analysis

Variable	Case 1 Δ Accuracy*	Case 2 Δ Accuracy*
GNN Model	27.45% points ↑ GCN → GraphSage	22.57% points ↑ GCN → GraphSage
Metamodel Properties	21.17% points ↑ No → Yes	18.34% points ↑ No → Yes
Language Model	3.74% points BERT → GloVe	29.91% points ↑ BERT → GloVe
Attribute Nodes	0.49% points ↑ No → Yes	4.80% points ↓ No → Yes
Batch Size	9.78% points ↑ 72 → 1	3.48% points ↑ 113 → 1

Table 4 shows the best five configurations with their accuracy values, once with four classes and once with 21 classes corresponding to FSF 1000 (Case 1) and FSF 100 (Case 2). We get a maximum accuracy of 94% with four classes and 67% with 21 classes, and we see that GraphSage outperforms GCN in both cases for all top five configurations.

5.2   Configuration Impact Analysis

Besides the overall accuracy, we are interested to learn how the individual configuration parameters influence the prediction accuracy. Table 5 shows the average change in accuracy of the learned GNN model on the best five configurations, going from one parameter value to another for case 1 and case 2. We find that the choice of the GNN model, the language model, and using meta-properties (in the feature vector) impact the accuracy more than adding attribute nodes. The accuracy increases by 27.45% points for Case 1 and 22.57% points for Case 2, going from GCN to GraphSage. This increase can be attributed to the pooling aggregation of GraphSage, which uses the information only from the most relevant neighbor to learn a node's embedding, thereby reducing the noise in the embedding. Similarly, using the meta-properties also increases the accuracy by more than 18% points in both cases. Meta-properties seem to add more representational semantics to the nodes. Using GloVe over BERT slightly improves the accuracy for Case 1. However, for Case 2, GloVe outperforms BERT by around 29% points. The training of GloVe-based word embeddings using the OntoUML-specific domain semantics seems to impact the accuracy positively. Adding attribute nodes has a poor impact on accuracy, in case 2, almost $-5\% points$. This may be because they add noise during training to the labeled nodes and do not carry enough relevant information to contribute towards the representation of the nodes connected to them. Finally, training the model on individual graphs using a batch size of 1 rather than a single huge graph increases the accuracy. It seems the GNN model is better capable of learning individual model patterns instead of identifying patterns across multiple non-related models. Due to lack of space, we provide details and comparison plots of all configuration parameters in our drive repository [4].

6   Discussion

In the previous section, we presented the performance results of the GNN model for a node stereotype prediction task in OntoUML models. We showed the different possible training configurations and the impact of individual parameters on the prediction accuracy of the GNN model. We trained the GNN Graph-Sage model to predict the stereotype of an OntoUML model element from four classes and 21 classes with 94% and 67% accuracy, respectively. These results are very promising. The embeddings are learned using message passing in GNN, which implies that the representation of each node reflects its semantics and its relationship with the neighboring nodes. Moreover, the embeddings capture the graph's structural features and stereotype-based ontological semantics, which supports the model in predicting the correct stereotype of the model elements with good accuracy. The stereotype of an OntoUML model element carries rich ontological semantics, and a representation that captures such semantics can be applied in various conceptual modeling tasks where model semantics are crucial. Therefore, the node embeddings learned using the stereotype prediction can now be used for tasks like OntoUML model completion or model search by applying graph-similarity metrics. E.g., cosine similarity between the representation of two graphs can provide an estimate of model similarity, which can be further used to search for similar models or detect model clones. An accuracy of 94% without any hyperparameter tuning of the GNN model shows sufficient potential to be improved using different graph encodings that better capture the ontological semantics and more advanced variants like Graph Attention Transformer.

Of course, this research is not free from threats to validity.

Dataset size – The training dataset for the experiment consists only of 131 OntoUML models. Each model belongs to a specific domain, and the labels

---

[4] http://shorturl.at/EHKNT.

consist of domain-specific information, which makes it difficult for the model to learn generalized patterns. We mitigated this by training the OntoUML models over the entire batch of models such that the GNN model learns general patterns and not domain-specific ones. Our batch approach further mitigates this issue as the batch of all the graphs consists of more than 30000 nodes and 10000 labeled nodes.

Labels distribution – Each model consists of nodes with labels; however, certain node types (e.g., Generalization and Attribute) do not have any stereotype, which makes up for about 50% of the nodes. Moreover, the stereotype distribution (see Table 3) shows that the top four stereotypes make up about 21% of the nodes in the dataset. This leads to an uneven distribution of the node classes and affects the classifier model during training. We mitigated this by first training the model on classes with higher frequency, i.e., top four stereotypes, and then training the model on the top 20 classes with at least 100 nodes having that stereotype.

Validation with Pure UML models - We validated our approach on OntoUML models using a fraction of our dataset as a test set. We followed a masked label prediction approach due to which, OntoUML models were suitable for training our GNN models because we could mask a node's stereotype and train the GNN model to predict the masked node, which will not be possible with pure UML models. However, UML models can also be transformed into CKG as our CM to CKG approach is modeling language agnostic and therefore can be used to test on our framework but therefore, testing our approach on pure UML models is part of our future work.

7 Conclusion

In this work, we presented an OntoUML model representation learning approach using an OntoUML to CKG transformation. This transformation encodes the model knowledge, including not only the model elements labels but also UFO-based foundational semantics from the elements' stereotype, meta-properties, the metamodel information, and it preserves the model's graph structure. Our work contributes toward learning semantically richer CMs' embeddings that elevate ML-based conceptual modeling tasks. In our approach, a GNN learns model primitives' vector embeddings trained on a node classification task to classify the stereotype of the CKG node. We achieved this representation learning using an open OntoUML models dataset. We exhaustively explored the dependence on different parameters related to the encoding of knowledge, i.e., meta-properties, attribute nodes, and language model, to understand the impact of these parameters on GNN model training. In the future, we plan to extend our approach towards a larger dataset of the model and use the learned representations on applications like a CMs search [1] where the model similarity is not restricted to the model labels but extends to graph structure information, ontological, and metamodel semantics. Finally, we plan to explore different GNN variants suitable for representation learning of conceptual modeling language primitives.

Acknowledgements. This work has been partially funded through the Austrian Research Promotion Agency (FFG) via the Austrian Competence Center for Digital Production (CDP) under the contract number 854187.

References

1. Ali, S.J.: Knowledge graph-based conceptual models search. In: Proceedings of the ER Forum and PhD Symposium 2022 (ER 2022). CEUR Workshop Proceedings, vol. 3211 (2022)
2. Amaral, G., Baião, F., Guizzardi, G.: Foundational ontologies, ontology-driven conceptual modeling, and their multiple benefits to data mining. Wiley Interdisc. Rev. Data Min. Knowl. Discov. **11**(4), e1408 (2021)
3. Barcelos, P.P.F., et al.: A FAIR model catalog for ontology-driven conceptual modeling research. In: Ralyté, J., Chakravarthy, S., Mohania, M., Jeusfeld, M.A., Karlapalem, K. (eds.) ER 2022. LNCS, vol. 13607, pp. 3–17. Springer, Cham (2022). https://doi.org/10.1007/978-3-031-17995-2_1
4. Bengio, Y., Courville, A., Vincent, P.: Representation learning: a review and new perspectives. IEEE Trans. Pattern Anal. Mach. Intell. **35**(8), 1798–1828 (2013)
5. Berquand, A., Riccardi, A.: From engineering models to knowledge graph: delivering new insights into models. In: 9th International Systems & Concurrent Engineering for Space Applications Conference (SECESA 2020) (2020)
6. Bork, D.: Conceptual modeling and artificial intelligence: mutual benefits from complementary worlds. CoRR abs/2110.08637 (2021). https://arxiv.org/abs/2110.08637
7. Bork, D., Ali, S.J., Roelens, B.: Conceptual modeling and artificial intelligence: a systematic mapping study. CoRR abs/2303.06758 (2023). https://doi.org/10.48550/arXiv.2303.06758
8. Burgueño, L., Cabot, J., Gérard, S.: An LSTM-based neural network architecture for model transformations. In: ACM/IEEE 22nd International Conference on Model Driven Engineering Languages and Systems (MODELS), pp. 294–299 (2019)
9. Chen, J., Hu, P., Jimenez-Ruiz, E., Holter, O.M., Antonyrajah, D., Horrocks, I.: OWL2Vec*: embedding of OWL ontologies. Mach. Learn. **110**(7), 1813–1845 (2021). https://doi.org/10.1007/s10994-021-05997-6
10. Devlin, J., Chang, M.W., Lee, K., Toutanova, K.: BERT: pre-training of deep bidirectional transformers for language understanding. arXiv preprint arXiv:1810.04805 (2018)
11. Efeoglu, S.: GraphMatcher: a graph representation learning approach for ontology matching (2022)
12. Grover, A., Leskovec, J.: node2vec: scalable feature learning for networks. In: Proceedings of the 22nd ACM SIGKDD International Conference on Knowledge Discovery and Data Mining, pp. 855–864 (2016)
13. Guizzardi, G.: The role of foundational ontologies for conceptual modeling and domain ontology representation. In: 2006 7th International Baltic Conference on Databases and Information Systems, pp. 17–25. IEEE (2006)
14. Guizzardi, G., Prince Sales, T., Almeida, J.P.A., Poels, G.: Relational contexts and conceptual model clustering. In: Grabis, J., Bork, D. (eds.) PoEM 2020. LNBIP, vol. 400, pp. 211–227. Springer, Cham (2020). https://doi.org/10.1007/978-3-030-63479-7_15

15. Guizzardi, G., Wagner, G., Almeida, J.P.A., Guizzardi, R.S.: Towards ontological foundations for conceptual modeling: the unified foundational ontology (UFO) story. Appl. Ontology **10**(3–4), 259–271 (2015)
16. Hamilton, W., Ying, Z., Leskovec, J.: Inductive representation learning on large graphs. In: Advances in Neural Information Processing Systems, vol. 30 (2017)
17. Hamilton, W.L., Ying, R., Leskovec, J.: Representation learning on graphs: methods and applications. arXiv preprint arXiv:1709.05584 (2017)
18. Huo, S., Völzer, H., Reddy, P., Agarwal, P., Isahagian, V., Muthusamy, V.: Graph autoencoders for business process anomaly detection. In: Polyvyanyy, A., Wynn, M.T., Van Looy, A., Reichert, M. (eds.) BPM 2021. LNCS, vol. 12875, pp. 417–433. Springer, Cham (2021). https://doi.org/10.1007/978-3-030-85469-0_26
19. Junior, A.G.L., Carbonera, J.L., Schimidt, D., Abel, M.: Predicting the top-level ontological concepts of domain entities using word embeddings, informal definitions, and deep learning. Expert Syst. Appl. **203**, 117291 (2022)
20. De Koninck, P., vanden Broucke, S., De Weerdt, J.: act2vec, trace2vec, log2vec, and model2vec: representation learning for business processes. In: Weske, M., Montali, M., Weber, I., vom Brocke, J. (eds.) BPM 2018. LNCS, vol. 11080, pp. 305–321. Springer, Cham (2018). https://doi.org/10.1007/978-3-319-98648-7_18
21. Lau, J.H., Baldwin, T.: An empirical evaluation of doc2vec with practical insights into document embedding generation. arXiv preprint arXiv:1607.05368 (2016)
22. Leão, F., Revoredo, K., Baião, F.: Extending wordnet with UFO foundational ontology. J. Web Semant. **57**, 100499 (2019)
23. Luettgen, S., Seeliger, A., Nolle, T., Mühlhäuser, M.: Case2vec: advances in representation learning for business processes. In: Leemans, S., Leopold, H. (eds.) ICPM 2020. LNBIP, vol. 406, pp. 162–174. Springer, Cham (2021). https://doi.org/10.1007/978-3-030-72693-5_13
24. Mussbacher, G., et al.: Opportunities in intelligent modeling assistance. Softw. Syst. Model. **19**(5), 1045–1053 (2020). https://doi.org/10.1007/s10270-020-00814-5
25. Pennington, J., Socher, R., Manning, C.D.: GloVe: global vectors for word representation. In: Proceedings of the 2014 Conference on Empirical Methods in Natural Language Processing (EMNLP), pp. 1532–1543 (2014)
26. Perozzi, B., Al-Rfou, R., Skiena, S.: DeepWalk: online learning of social representations. In: Proceedings of the 20th ACM SIGKDD International Conference on Knowledge Discovery and Data Mining, pp. 701–710 (2014)
27. Ristoski, P., Rosati, J., Di Noia, T., De Leone, R., Paulheim, H.: RDF2Vec: RDF graph embeddings and their applications. Semant. Web **10**(4), 721–752 (2019)
28. Ryen, V., Soylu, A., Roman, D.: Building semantic knowledge graphs from (semi-) structured data: a review. Future Internet **14**(5), 129 (2022)
29. Sequeda, J., Lassila, O.: Designing and building enterprise knowledge graphs. In: Synthesis Lectures on Data, Semantics, and Knowledge, vol. 11, no. 1, pp. 1–165 (2021)
30. Smajevic, M., Bork, D.: Towards graph-based analysis of enterprise architecture models. In: Ghose, A., Horkoff, J., Silva Souza, V.E., Parsons, J., Evermann, J. (eds.) ER 2021. LNCS, vol. 13011, pp. 199–209. Springer, Cham (2021). https://doi.org/10.1007/978-3-030-89022-3_17
31. Sousa, G., Lima, R., Trojahn, C.: An eye on representation learning in ontology matching (2022)
32. Sun, S., Meng, F., Chu, D.: A model driven approach to constructing knowledge graph from relational database. In: Journal of Physics: Conference Series, vol. 1584, p. 012073. IOP Publishing (2020)

33. Trojahn, C., Vieira, R., Schmidt, D., Pease, A., Guizzardi, G.: Foundational ontologies meet ontology matching: a survey. Semant. Web **13**(4), 685–704 (2022)
34. Verdonck, M., Gailly, F., Pergl, R., Guizzardi, G., Martins, B., Pastor, O.: Comparing traditional conceptual modeling with ontology-driven conceptual modeling: an empirical study. Inf. Syst. **81**, 92–103 (2019)
35. Weyssow, M., Sahraoui, H., Syriani, E.: Recommending metamodel concepts during modeling activities with pre-trained language models. Softw. Syst. Model. **21**(3), 1071–1089 (2022). https://doi.org/10.1007/s10270-022-00975-5
36. Xu, K., Hu, W., Leskovec, J., Jegelka, S.: How powerful are graph neural networks? arXiv preprint arXiv:1810.00826 (2018)
37. Zhou, J., et al.: Graph neural networks: a review of methods and applications. AI Open **1**, 57–81 (2020)

Model-Driven Approaches

DOML: A New Modelling Approach to Infrastructure-as-Code

Michele Chiari[1] , Bin Xiang[2(✉)] , Galia Novakova Nedeltcheva[2] ,
Elisabetta Di Nitto[2] , Lorenzo Blasi[3] , Debora Benedetto[3],
and Laurentiu Niculut[3]

[1] TU Wien, Treitlestraße 3, Vienna, Austria
michele.chiari@tuwien.ac.at
[2] Politecnico di Milano, Piazza Leonardo Da Vinci 32, Milano, Italy
{bin.xiang,galia.nedeltcheva,elisabetta.nitto}@polimi.it
[3] Hewlett Packard Italiana s.r.l., Via Giuseppe Vittorio, Cernusco sul Naviglio, Italy
{lorenzo.blasi,debora.benedetto,laurentiu.niculut}@hpe.com

Abstract. One of the main DevOps practices is the automation of
resource provisioning and deployment of complex software. This automation is enabled by the explicit definition of *Infrastructure-as-Code* (IaC),
i.e., a set of scripts, often written in different modelling languages, which
defines the infrastructure and applications to be deployed.

We introduce the DevOps Modelling Language (DOML), a new Cloud
modelling language for infrastructure deployments. DOML is a modelling
approach that can be mapped into multiple IaC languages, addressing
infrastructure provisioning, application deployment and configuration at
once. The idea behind DOML is to use a single modelling paradigm which
can help to reduce the need of deep technical expertise in using different
specialised IaC languages.

We present the DOML's principles and discuss the related work on
IaC languages. We demonstrate the DOML advantages for the end-user
in comparison with state-of-the-art IaC languages such as Ansible, Terraform, and Cloudify, and show its effectiveness through an example.

Keywords: Infrastructure-as-Code · DevOps · IaC Modelling
languages · Multi-layer approach · Evaluation

1 Introduction

Employing Infrastructure-as-Code (IaC) means creating and managing an IT
infrastructure, typically composed of computational resources and multiple software layers, by defining and executing code written in some special-purpose
programming languages [20].

Defining a whole IT infrastructure deployment through IaC introduces several advantages in terms of repeatability of actions, reusability, and speed. However, it requires deep knowledge of multiple IaC languages and frameworks, since
each specific framework is covering a specific aspect of the whole problem [5].

© The Author(s) 2023
M. Indulska et al. (Eds.): CAiSE 2023, LNCS 13901, pp. 297–313, 2023.
https://doi.org/10.1007/978-3-031-34560-9_18

This causes a steep learning curve for non-technical users and even for expert practitioners migrating from other technologies. Moreover, the selection of a specific set of IaCs, given the peculiarities of each individual language, tends to foster vendor lock-in.

In this paper, we propose a low-code approach to IaC, which makes the creation of infrastructural code more accessible to the designers, developers and operators. We present the DevOps Modelling Language (DOML), which hides the specificity and technicalities of the current IaC solutions.

The DOML allows for a complete specification of a deployment from its applications and software services to the infrastructural components and services supporting them. DOML models are mainly structured in three layers. Specifically, software components (e.g., web servers, databases, etc.) are described in the *application layer*, abstracting away from the infrastructure on which they are supposed to run. Infrastructure components are specified in the *abstract infrastructure layer*, and then linked to the applications they are supposed to host. This layer models infrastructural facilities, such as virtual machines, networks, containers, etc., without referring to their actual concretization in specific technologies (e.g., AWS or OpenStack VMs, Docker containers). This aspect is tackled by the *concrete infrastructure layer*, where the user specifies the infrastructure components offered by the Cloud Service Provider (CSP).

This modelling approach comes out from a careful analysis of related works concerning IaC languages, as well as other Cloud modelling approaches [5] and a critical review of the requirements for the DOML, provided by practitioners from several companies (HP Enterprise, Ericsson and Prodevelop).

Following the idea of generating code from an abstract model that is at the heart of Model Driven Development (MDD) [24], DOML models are turned into actual deployments by the Infrastructural Code Generator (ICG), which produces IaCs executable in the existing and well-supported frameworks. Our first target IaCs are Terraform and Ansible. Nevertheless, the same ICG could be extended to generate other IaC languages to target more applications and CSPs.

In this paper, we present the DOML language and its advantages, and show its effectiveness through case studies. We evaluate our approach by comparing its usage with the direct use of IaC languages such as Terraform and Cloudify. We show that the DOML is complete enough to model a whole deployment by itself, while the other approaches require the simultaneous use of more than one IaC language. Moreover, we show that DOML is generally more concise than the competing approaches.

Paper Structure. In Sect. 2 we review some state-of-the-art IaC approaches, highlighting the motivation behind ours. Section 3 presents a simple case study that will be used as running example. Section 4 outlines the principles behind the DOML, while Sect. 5 defines its modeling abstractions; Sect. 6 presents the IaC generation mechanism. Section 7 compares the DOML with state-of-the-art IaC approaches, and Sect. 8 discusses this evaluation. Finally, Sect. 9 concludes the paper.

2   Related Work

Choosing the right approach for automating the provisioning of computational resources and deployment of application components is not an easy task. In fact, each of the available IaC frameworks covers different parts of the whole problem. As a result, multiple frameworks must be combined, resulting in the need for the DevOps teams to understand all such frameworks. IaC frameworks can be divided into the following four categories.

– *Deployment and configuration management* frameworks focus on automating the installation, setup and life cycle of software applications deployed on top of an existing infrastructure. Examples of such tools are Chef [8], Puppet [22] and Ansible [23]. While they have similar purposes, they are quite different from each other in terms of the defined IaC language and of the corresponding execution semantics.
– *Infrastructure provisioning* frameworks focus on describing the infrastructural topology, defining the virtual or physical infrastructural elements and their configurations, and providing automated means of managing their life cycles. For example, Terraform [16] is a proprietary language with an associated executor. It allows users to define an infrastructure configuration; it keeps track of the actual configuration of the managed infrastructure and, when needed, aligns it with the defined configuration. TOSCA [21], instead, is an OASIS standard modelling language that aims at allowing users to specify any type of IT system through powerful abstraction mechanisms, consisting of abstract *node templates* that can be combined through inheritance. The TOSCA language is adopted by a variety of executors that define its operational semantics in different ways [5,10].
– *Virtualization/Containerization* tools provide automation in building and managing VM or container images. An example of such tools is Docker [11] that has become the de-facto standard for running container-based applications on-premises, in public and private cloud providers [18]. Docker solves issues related to application portability, as containerised applications carry on their dependencies. It lets users define the recipe to build a container image using a custom, domain-specific language.
– *Runtime Orchestration* tools automate the whole life cycle of container-based deployments, including scaling and other management operations. An important representative of this category is Kubernetes [9], which also provides its own IaC language.

In general, managing a complex application, multiple of the mentioned frameworks must be used. For instance, the infrastructure to be provisioned (VMs, network elements, firewalls, etc.) could be modeled and then created with Terraform or TOSCA plus its executors. Ansible (or Chef/Puppet) playbooks could be executed to deploy and configure applications on top of the created infrastructure. Given that most of the application components rely on external preexisting software layers, it is typically advisable to embed all needed elements within some containers. This calls for the usage of Docker or of a similar approach. Finally, if the user wants to have a dynamic management of the application at runtime, an orchestration framework will have to be adopted.

This scenario clearly requires the experienced users who are proficient with multiple IaC languages and tools, and that are able to take advantage of the ample and scattered offers. An initial approach that aims at reducing the learning curve in adopting any DevOps-relevant platform is presented in [10]. The basic idea is to model DevOps processes, platforms and languages and to exploit these models within the context of low-code environments to let non-experienced users to exploit the defined platforms and languages. Other approaches exploit model-driven engineering in the specific context of IaC development. For example, DICER [4] is focusing on deployment and operation of big data applications. It consists of a UML-based Domain-Specific Language (DSL) and a generator to derive TOSCA code from it. The limit of this approach is that it assumes the existence of additional low level scripts (in Chef or Ansible) taking care of the configuration of applications. Such scripts work underneath and are not exposed to nor modifiable by the DevOps team through the DICER modelling framework. SODALITE [25] is another framework based on TOSCA. Its aim is to offer the support and guidance in the creation of TOSCA blueprints through the usage of its defined DSL. Additionally, it supports the creation of Ansible scripts for deployment and configuration, and exploits semantics reasoning to help the users in the modelling task. Despite this, the SODALITE approach still requires users to be proficient in both Ansible and TOSCA.

A more sophisticated approach is EDMM [30], an Essential Deployment MetaModel. It defines the main concepts that are common to multiple deployment and configuration management frameworks and allows users to exploit such concepts to define application models. Then, through some transformators, EDMM supports the generation of codes in various IaC languages.

In the DOML approach proposed in this paper, we follow the EDMM idea of targeting multiple IaC languages, but we try to extend the scope of the approach beyond deployment and configuration. In particular, at the moment, we are also able to handle infrastructure provisioning, and we plan to support both containerization and runtime orchestration in the next releases of the approach. We offer a single modelling language and a smart IaC generation approach allowing inexperienced DevOps teams to manage all aspects of deployment and operation on different types of infrastructures. So, from the same model we are able to produce IaC code in multiple pre-existing languages.

3   Running Example

To illustrate our approach, we use a simple deployment as a case study. It consists of a website hosted by an instance of the NGINX web server [15] deployed on a VM. A more sophisticated example involving more components will be demonstrated in Sect. 7. This example, though, is representative of typical deployments, because it contains some of the most common components (see Fig. 1 for a component diagram representation). The NGINX server instance is the execution

Fig. 1. Component diagram of the NGINX case study.

environment for the website and runs on a VM with a GNU/ Linux-based operating system (Ubuntu 20.04). To ensure the website scalability with respect to the number of connected users, multiple instances of the VM are spawned and managed by an auto-scaling group. The network interface that links the VMs to the Internet is managed by a security group, containing the security rules that enable HTTP, HTTPS and ICMP network traffic. The standard SSH port is enabled, enabling the direct access to the VMs, protected by an RSA key pair for authentication.

An infrastructure like this can be implemented by relying either on a private cloud or on public cloud providers, such as Amazon Web Services, Google Cloud Platform, Microsoft Azure, etc. Initially, in our case study we choose to deploy the application on OpenStack [26], which is an open source industry standard. Further on, in Sect. 7 we show how we can change the underlying provider.

4   DOML Design Principles

In this section, we present the principles underneath the definition of DOML.

4.1   A Single Model for Multiple IaC Fragments

The DOML is defined to support the creation of models resulting in IaC codes written in different languages and dedicated to different operations. For instance, let us consider the system outlined in Fig. 1. The following steps must be performed to deploy the modeled system:

1. A VM with the correct OS must be retrieved if preexisting, or created;
2. The VM must be set up for access through SSH;
3. The NGINX server with the website sources must be installed on the VM;
4. The autoscaling group must be set up with the VM image;
5. The network must be configured with the required security rules;
6. The deployment process must be planned and executed.

To execute the above listed steps adopting the current technologies, we would need some Ansible playbooks or other scripts executing steps 2 and 3, together with a Terraform or TOSCA blueprint to orchestrate all other steps. Such scripts have their inherent complexities, and they are all written in different languages featuring different programming models. With the DOML approach, we aim to derive such scripts from a high-level model, and to reduce the need for the end users to work with the low-level target languages as much as possible.

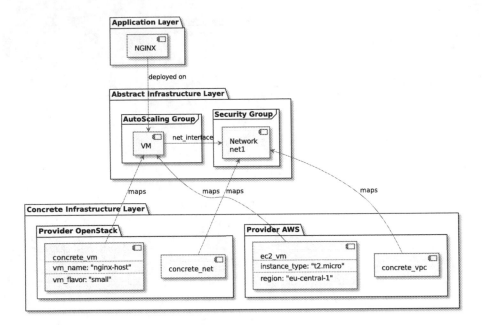

Fig. 2. The NGINX case study represented as different DOML layers.

4.2   Multiple Modeling Layers

Another objective we target is to support separate modeling of the application-level components from their execution environments (e.g., containers, VMs, etc.). In fact, we argue that different users, with different skills and roles, should focus on the specific aspects that fall within their expertise. Typically, the application designer will focus on the application structure definition in terms of software components and their connections, while an operations expert will oversee the allocation of software components within proper computing nodes.

Furthermore, multiple providers and technologies offering the same IaaS (Infrastructure-as-a-Service) and in some cases, compatible PaaS (Platform-as-a-Service) solutions are available. Thus, we want to offer the possibility to provide an abstract definition of the infrastructure to be used to run an application, and then to define different concretisations, so as to support deployment and execution of applications into multiple contexts.

Referring to the example of Fig. 1, Fig. 2 shows a distribution of components into three layers: one describes the application, and the remaining two layers describe the infrastructure at different levels. In particular, the same *abstract* infrastructure can be implemented by two different *concrete* infrastructures, respectively based on OpenStack and AWS.

5 DOML Language

The DOML language implementation consists of two parts: the DOML meta-model, described using Ecore from the Eclipse Modeling Framework (EMF) [13], and the textual syntax used to create models, based on Xtext [14].

We organize all modeled entities in the following layers, which aggregate the modeling abstractions in coherent groups:

- *Application Layer (AL)*: concepts required to define an application, e.g., software components, interfaces, connectors between components, services, and specific subcategories thereof.
- *Abstract Infrastructure Layer (AIL)*: concepts associated to the definition of the infrastructure (e.g., computing nodes) without referencing a specific provider.
- *Concrete Infrastructure Layer (CIL)*: concepts associated to the definition of infrastructure elements within a specific provider, e.g., a Docker container or an Amazon VM.

In Sect. 5.1, we describe the components that can be defined in each layer. We do not include the complete definition of DOML concepts, which is available in [29, 31], due to page limits, but we illustrate it in Sect. 5.2 through an example.

5.1 Components of DOML Layers

A *DOMLModel* is composed of an AL, an AIL, one or more CILs, and a *Configuration*. A *Configuration* is a list of one or more *Deployments* that consist of the associations between *ApplicationComponents* (from the AL) and *InfrastructureElements* (from the AIL) on which they are deployed. Only one *Deployment* can be active at a time. All other components derive from a base *DOMLElement* class, which gives them the ability to have custom *Properties* encoding some of their features.

Application Layer (AL). The *ApplicationLayer* is composed of many *ApplicationComponents*, which can be *SoftwareComponents*, *SoftwareInterfaces*, or *SaaS* (Software-as-a-Service) components. A *SaaS* can be, e.g., a *SaaSDBMS* if it implements a database. *ApplicationComponents* may expose or consume different *SoftwareInterfaces*, providing or requiring services from other *ApplicationComponents*. For instance, a database *SoftwareComponent* can expose a SQL-based interface, and a web application component can consume it, meaning that the latter will communicate with the former to retrieve and write data.

Abstract Infrastructure Layer (AIL). The *InfrastructureLayer* is composed of *ComputingNodes*, *Networks*, *SceurityGroups*, and *AutoScalingGroups*. A *ComputingNode* models any infrastructure element that can run software: it can be a *Container*, a *Physical ComputingNode* or a *VirtualMachine*. *ComputingNodes* can have multiple *NetworkInterfaces* that link them to a network. A *Container* can be generated from a *ContainerImage*, and a *VirtualMachine* from a *VMImage*. A *Network* can have many *Subnets*, and its configuration is represented by a *SecurityGroup* containing firewall rules.

Concrete Infrastructure Layer (CIL). This layer provides the *concretizations* for the AIL, mapping the abstract infrastructure elements to the concrete ones from the supported cloud service providers. In general, each element of the AIL has a corresponding "concrete" version. The CIL contains one or more *Runtime-Providers*, e.g., Amazon AWS, OpenStack, etc. Each *RuntimeProvider* contains the concrete elements which are linked to the AIL elements via the *maps* association. For instance, an OpenStack provider could provide *VirtualMachines*, *Networks*, *Containers*, etc.

5.2 DOML Model of the Running Example

To illustrate the syntax of the DOML, we show and comment the DOML model of the case study of Sect. 3. The entire model can be found in [28].

Application Layer. In Listing 1.1 we show the AL of the DOML model for the deployment of Fig. 1. It only contains a *SoftwareComponent* for the NGINX server, with a *Property* indicating the website's sources.

Listing 1.1. DOML Application Layer

```
application app {
  software_component nginx {
    properties { source_code="/.../html/index.html"; }
  }
}
```

Abstract Infrastructure Layer. The AIL is partially shown in Listing 1.2. It defines the infrastructure topology that supports the execution of application components. We define the VM that hosts the NGINX instance in the autoscaling group that manages it. We declare its guest operating system, its credentials, and its network interface, which is linked to a network called `net1` and controlled by a security group called `sg` (we do not show all components here for space constraints, but they are defined in this layer too [28]).

The *deployment configuration*, at the bottom of Listing 1.2, provides the link between the AL and AIL: it assigns the NGINX instance to the VM.

Concrete Infrastructure Layer. The last step needed to make this DOML model functional is to assign all components in the AIL to a cloud service provider. This is done by defining one or more CILs (only one of which will be active at a time). To simplify the presentation, in Listing 1.3 we show only one of such layers, and only for the VM.

Listing 1.2. Autoscaling group in the AIL, and deployment configuration.

```
infrastructure infra {
   ...
   autoscale_group ag {
     vm vm1 {
       os "ubuntu-20.04.3"
       iface i1 {
         address "10.0.0.1"
         belongs_to net1
         security sg
       }
       credentials ssh_key
     }
   }
}
deployment config {
   nginx -> vm1
}
```

Listing 1.3. Part of the concrete infrastructure layer.

```
concretizations {
   concrete_infrastructure con_infra {
     provider openstack {
       vm concrete_vm {
         properties {
           vm_name = "nginx-host";
           vm_flavor = "small";
           vm_key_name = "user1";
         }
         maps vm1
       }
       ...
     }
   }
   ...
   active con_infra
}
```

We create a concrete infrastructure configuration called con_infra. We could assign different components of the AIL to different providers. For the sake of space, in this section we use only OpenStack. Thus, we create a block for the OpenStack provider containing a component for each of the abstract infrastructure elements. In Listing 1.3 we show the VM concretization. Its maps attribute links it to the appropriate VM component in the AIL. Moreover, in the CIL we can customize aspects that cannot be described in the AIL because they are provider-specific. Here we choose the name and size of the VM.

The information in this model is enough for the ICG to produce IaC scripts that can create VMs on OpenStack, the autoscaling group and all other required features and installs NGINX on top of such infrastructure.

6   IaC Generation Mechanism

To generate executable IaC code from DOML, we have built a tool named Infrastructural Code Generator (ICG). The ICG receives a DOML model as input and generates IaC code like Terraform, Ansible, etc., as output.

The generation of code from an abstract model is one of the main advantages of MDD [24], but the benefit is real when the generated code is complete and executable, i.e., not just a skeleton or something that needs manual editing. Generating code from a model can be done using Template-Based Code Generation (TBCG), a technique that transforms input data into structured text by using templates [7]. The process is simple: our template engine uses templates that contain code in the target language and substitutes values taken from the input for placeholders. Each template has a static part, that is transferred as-is in the output, and a dynamic part whose result depends on the input. Most template engines support control structures in the dynamic part of their templates, which allows part of the transformation logic to be embedded in the template itself.

Template engines can be classified according to the input they rely on: according to Luhunu [17], there are model-based engines, such as Acceleo [12], that are

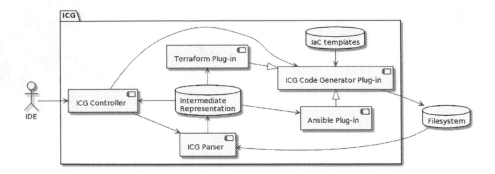

Fig. 3. Infrastructural Code Generator Architecture.

based on an input metamodel, and code-based tools, such as Velocity [3], which rely on a DSL to express the dynamic part of their templates. In our case, the structured text generated is the IaC in languages that can be executed by the most used IaC tools, e.g., Terraform and Ansible. The ICG is based on the DOML metamodel but uses the code-based Jinjia2 library [27]. Jinjia2 is a simple but powerful template engine that supports plain placeholder substitution, and also several control structures, such as loops, conditionals and functions, to build dynamic templates (see Listing 1.4).

We implemented the ICG in Python. Its internal architecture, represented in Fig. 3, is inspired by the classic structure of a compiler (see e.g. [1]) and consists of separate modules for parsing the input and for generating the output, with an Intermediate Representation (IR) in between. The parser reads the DOML model using the PyEcore library [19] and generates an IR as a JSON document. Then, different Code Generator plug-ins, one for each language to be generated, read the input data from the IR and substitute values in the templates. The whole flow is driven by the Controller, that selects the right templates and activates the corresponding plug-in, depending on the information included in the IR itself.

The IR created by the Parser is structured as a sequence of steps, representing the main code blocks to be generated. Each step includes general information, such as the target language, the target cloud provider, the type of DOML object for which code should be generated, and attributes specific to the target DOML object, in the form of key/value pairs, to be substituted in the template for the corresponding placeholder.

The Controller selects the template to be used depending on the information indicated above (target language, cloud provider, and type of DOML object), and then activates the Code Generator plug-in specific to the desired target language. Template selection and plug-in activation are repeated for each one of the steps in the IR. Thus, the ICG starts creating IaC code for the elements in the CIL and navigates up in the model to find other resources for which there is enough information for generating the related code.

When generating code for the example of Fig. 1, the ICG first learns from the CIL of Listing 1.3 that the VM should be deployed on OpenStack. Thus, it

Listing 1.4. ICG template for OpenStack VMs.

```
resource "openstack_compute_instance_v2" "{{␣infra_element_name␣}}" {
    name        = "{{␣name␣}}"
    image_name  = "{{␣os␣}}"
    flavor_name = "{{␣vm_flavor␣}}"
    key_pair    = openstack_compute_keypair_v2.{{ credentials }}.name
    network { ... }
}
```

selects the template shown in Listing 1.4, and populates the fields it finds in the CIL (e.g., name with the value of vm_name, etc.). The remaining fields (network and key-pair) are populated by looking at the AIL.

The generated IaC code is intended to create an infrastructure in the selected provider or to configure it in some way, in short to modify the target environment. Our aim is to create a stateless code generator, i.e., one that does not take into consideration the current status of the target environment. This works well when the target language is declarative, such as Terraform, but it is not the case when generating code for an imperative language. In this last case, the target code (its template actually) should be idempotent, i.e., such that the status of the target system does not change even if the code is run multiple times.

The current version of the ICG can generate both Terraform and Ansible code, depending on the specific activity that is intended to be performed. We use Terraform for provisioning and Ansible for configuration. The aim is to have a code generator that can be configured to produce code also for other IaC tools, and can be extended also to support new model abstractions: this is partially true for the current version, and will be one of the main targets for the future versions.

7   Evaluation

We evaluate the DOML against other state-of-the-art IaC approaches to demonstrate its capabilities and shortcomings. We provide a discussion of the evaluation in Sect. 8. We identify the following two research questions (RQs):

- RQ1: Can a DOML model represent the information required to generate executable IaC tackling both provisioning and configuration? Is a DOML model more readable and easier to use than the state-of-the-art approaches?
- RQ2: Is a DOML model able to target multiple execution platforms?

We answer these questions by comparing different representations of system larger than the NGINX example and taken from previous literature. The example has been introduced in [6] and is described in the component diagram of Fig. 4.

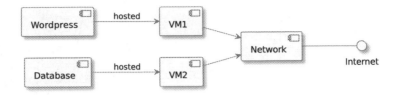

Fig. 4. Component diagram of the Wordpress application deployment from [6].

The application to be deployed is the Wordpress content management system, which runs on a VM. Wordpress depends on a database hosted on a separate VM. The two VMs communicate with each other as well as with the Internet through a common network.

7.1 RQ1: Ability to Generate Executable IaC and Comparison

We answer RQ1 by writing a DOML specification of the Wordpress deployment from Fig. 4 targeting OpenStack as the CSP and successfully running the corresponding IaC code generated by the ICG.

Next, we compare the DOML specification with two equivalent specifications in state-of-the-art languages: the Terraform and Cloudify implementations written by the authors of [6].

DOML. We do not show the whole DOML model for the Wordpress deployment due to the page limits, but it is available in [28]. Similarly to the NGINX example, this DOML model closely resembles the diagram of Fig. 4. The model is small enough to be represented in a single file, and its subdivision into components is very natural: roughly, two components in the application layer for the Wordpress and database, two corresponding VMs and one network in the abstract infrastructure layer, etc.

An advantage brought by the DOML is that the ICG is capable of automatically generating certain common components from its templates, so that they need to be specified in the DOML only if a non-default configuration is required. One of such components is the Security Group: in this Wordpress case study, the ICG creates it automatically thanks to the information included in the AL, so it is not necessary to include it in the DOML model. In fact, the Wordpress component has to be exposed to the Internet by default, and the AL states that it needs to be able to communicate with the database: the security group is created accordingly.

Terraform [6]. The Terraform definition of the deployment is centered around the provisioning of VMs. First, the provider is set, in this case AWS. This enables the use of AWS-specific components, such as `aws_instance` to define the VMs. The VMs are defined in this way, with their features set as properties (e.g., size, image to be run, etc.); the network to which VMs are attached is defined similarly. The applications (Wordpress and the database) need to be deployed

Table 1. Metrics on the IaC in Sect. 7.1.

Approach	#LOC	# Files	# Languages	Available at
DOML	103	1	1	[28]
Terraform + Shell	305	3	2	[6]
Cloudify + Ansible	506	9	2	[6]

to their respective VMs. Terraform does not support application deployment directly, but a configuration language—Bash scripts in this case—is needed. The two bash scripts, one for Wordpress and one for the database, are stored as templates, that are instantiated, sent to the VMs through SSH, and automatically executed during deployment.

Cloudify [6]. The Cloudify definition of the deployment starts by importing plugins related to the targeted cloud platform. These allow to use provider-specific node types to define the VMs and the networks. Again, the Ansible configuration language is needed to deploy applications to the VMs.

In Table 1 we provide a summary of the objective metrics we have collected.

7.2   RQ2: Targeting Multiple Execution Platforms

DOML supports multi-platform deployment and operation. We show this by modifying the OpenStack-based Wordpress DOML model to incorporate a new deployment on AWS EC2 [2].

The differences in modelling the deployment on AWS EC2 only occur in the CIL and concern the definitions of the VM and the network. In the CIL, the VM image name is specified by the Amazon Machine Images (AMI) format, e.g., `name ="ami-xxx"`, which provides the information required to launch a VM instance. In the VM block, we specify other vendor-specific settings, such as the location information (e.g., `region = "eu-central-1"`) and the `instance_type`. These parameters are optional, and the ICG chooses default values if they are not specified. Another issue caused by switching to AWS concerns the network. Amazon provides Virtual Private Cloud (VPC) for controlling the virtual networking environment, which requires defining a subnet into any network. If no subnet has been defined in the AIL, the ICG creates a default one. This way, a user not familiar with AWS requirements can still create a working deployment.

Listing 1.5 shows the new CIL, while everything else is unchanged. Providers can be switched by just changing the active one.

Listing 1.5. VM definition in the concrete infrastructure layer.

```
concrete_infrastructure
    ⤳ con_aws_infra {
  provider aws {
    properties { }
    vm concrete_vm1 {
      properties {
  maps vm2
    }
    net concrete_net {
      properties {}
      maps net1
```

```
      vm_flavor = "t2.micro";
    }
    maps vm1
  }
  vm concrete_vm2 {
    properties {
      vm_flavor = "t2.micro";
    }

  }
}
active con_aws_infra
}
```

8   Discussion

The experiments in Sect. 7 show that DOML and the other languages have a few important differences in their modelling approach.

Firstly, in Terraform and Cloudify everything depends on the chosen cloud provider. Each provider brings in a custom set of resources that define different pieces of the infrastructure, but there is no way of abstracting over them. Thus, when changing the provider, the user must learn the components offered by the target provider and its features, and rewrite most of the deployment configuration. Conversely, in DOML the infrastructure description is completely decoupled from providers, and users need not be familiar with what a specific provider offers. The ICG gathers the information needed to deploy an infrastructure configuration on a specific provider, still allowing for customization in the CIL. This also improves reusability of infrastructure components.

Moreover, Terraform and Cloudify are centered around infrastructure components, while in DOML applications have a central role. In languages other than DOML, the fact that Wordpress is deployed on the VM can only be inferred by reading an Ansible or shell script. In DOML, Wordpress is a first-class component, and it is up to the ICG to ensure that it is correctly deployed on a VM, instead of the user. This makes the whole deployment more robust.

Table 1 shows the size of the considered deployment specifications. The one in DOML is significantly more compact in terms of number of lines of code and files. All other approaches require the use of two languages, one for infrastructure definition and one for configuration management. The DOML, on the contrary, can handle both.

Finally, in Sect. 7.2 we show that the abstraction mechanisms offered by the DOML allow for changing the target cloud platform by just adding and activating a new concrete infrastructure. In Terraform and Cloudify all components are defined in a different way based on the target cloud provider, so changing it requires rewriting most of the specification.

Limitations and Threats to Validity. The experimental evaluation we conducted still has some limitations that will be addressed through further research.

In particular, we compared the DOML definition of the Wordpress deployment with some specific definitions. The main conclusion we inferred from the evaluation is that such definitions are more concise than the DOML-based one. This represents a threat to internal validity, because the analysis of a few specifications does not allow us to exclude the possibility of making more concise ones. Nonetheless, such specifications were written by experts, and we argue that it is unlikely that such a large conciseness gap can be recovered.

Another threat to internal validity is that we only compare metrics concerning code size as a proxy of both ease of writing and maintaining code. However, a proper evaluation of such features would require an empirical study.

The main threat to external validity is that the evaluation is performed on a single application deployment, so the claims we make could not be generalized to the other more complex cloud applications. One of our next research steps will be the evaluation on a larger benchmark suite.

9   Conclusion

We have presented the DOML, a novel approach to cloud deployment modelling. We have shown that the approach works for relatively simple but complete systems with practical significance.

Our next challenge is to check whether the approach is usable and works with more complex case studies, including applications with multiple components that rely on different computational resources and middleware layers.

Our ultimate aim is to be able to write the DOML model only once and then use it to deploy the same complex system on different cloud service providers or physical machines. This has resulted in the definition of the DOML as a multi-layer modelling language, where the application and abstract infrastructure layers include a platform-independent specification of the application and its underlying infrastructure, while the concrete infrastructure layer specifies the details associated to the actual deployment on a specific platform.

The DOML has been developed keeping in mind the need for extensibility, and includes an extension mechanism called DOML-E, which will be analysed in detail in a future work.

Acknowledgments. This work has been funded by the EU Commission in the Horizon 2020 research and innovation programme under grant agreement No. 101000162 (PIACERE project), and partially funded by the Vienna Science and Technology Fund (WWTF) [10.47379/ICT19018].

References

1. Aho, A.V., Lam, M.S., Sethi, R., Ullman, J.D.: Compilers: Principles, Techniques, & Tools. Pearson Education India, Noida (2007)
2. Amazon Web Services Inc: AWS EC2 (2022). https://aws.amazon.com/ec2/
3. Apache software foundation: the apache velocity project (2022). https://velocity.apache.org/

4. Artac, M., Borovšak, T., Di Nitto, E., Guerriero, M., Perez-Palacin, D., Tamburri, D.A.: Infrastructure-as-Code for data-intensive architectures: a model-driven development approach. In: Proceedings ICSA 2018, pp. 156–165 (2018)
5. Bergmayr, A., et al.: A systematic review of cloud modeling languages. ACM Comput. Surv. **51**(1) (2018). https://doi.org/10.1145/3150227
6. Rebouças de Carvalho, L., Favacho de Araújo, A.P.: Performance comparison of terraform and cloudify as multicloud orchestrators. In: Proceedings CCGRID 2020, pp. 380–389. IEEE (2020). https://doi.org/10.1109/CCGrid49817.2020.00-55
7. Chared, Z., Tyszberowicz, S.S.: Projective template-based code generation. In: CAiSE Forum, pp. 81–87 (2013) https://doi.org/10.1109/ACIT-CSII-BCD.2016.023
8. Chef: Chef infra: powerful policy-based configuration management system software (2022). https://www.chef.io/products/chef-infra
9. CNCF: Kubernetes (2022). https://kubernetes.io/
10. Colantoni, A., Berardinelli, L., Wimmer, M.: DevOpsML: towards modeling DevOps processes and platforms. In: Proceedings. MODELS 2020, ACM (2020)
11. Docker: docker (2022). https://www.docker.com/
12. Eclipse foundation: acceleo home page (2022). https://www.eclipse.org/acceleo/
13. Eclipse foundation: eclipse modeling framework (EMF) (2022). https://www.eclipse.org/modeling/emf/
14. Eclipse foundation: Xtext (2022). https://www.eclipse.org/Xtext/
15. F5 Inc: nginx (2022). https://www.nginx.com/
16. HashiCorp Inc: Terraform documentation (2022). https://www.terraform.io/docs
17. Luhunu, L., Syriani, E.: Comparison of the expressiveness and performance of template-based code generation tools. In: Proceedings SLE 2017, pp. 206–216. ACM (2017)
18. Miell, I., Sayers, A.: Docker in Practice. Simon and Schuster, New York (2019)
19. Pagel, M., et al.: PyEcore/PyEcore: a Python(NIC) implementation of EMF/Ecore (Eclipse Modeling Framework) (2022). https://github.com/pyecore/pyecore
20. Morris, K.: Infrastructure as Code. O'Reilly Media, Sebastopol (2016)
21. OASIS standard: topology and orchestration specification for cloud applications version 1.0 (2013)
22. Puppet Inc: puppet (2022). https://puppet.com/
23. Red Hat Inc: ansible documentation (2022). https://docs.ansible.com/
24. Selic, B.: The pragmatics of model-driven development. IEEE Softw. **20**(5), 19–25 (2003)
25. SODALITE Consortium: SODALITE: software defined application infrastructures management and engineering (2022). https://sodalite.eu/
26. The OpenStack project: OpenStack (2022). https://www.openstack.org/
27. The pallets project: Jinja (2022). https://jinja.palletsprojects.com/
28. The PIACERE Project: IaC artefacts repository (2022). https://github.com/michiari/DOML-case-study
29. The PIACERE project: PIACERE DevSecOps modelling language (DOML) (2022). https://www.piacere-doml.deib.polimi.it/
30. Wurster, M., et al.: The EDMM modeling and transformation system. In: Yangui, S., et al. (eds.) ICSOC 2019. LNCS, vol. 12019, pp. 294–298. Springer, Cham (2020). https://doi.org/10.1007/978-3-030-45989-5_26
31. Xiang, B., Di Nitto, E., Nedeltcheva, G.N.: Deliverable D3.2 PIACERE abstractions, DOML and DOML-E - v2 (2023). https://doi.org/10.5281/zenodo.7645687

Task Completeness Assessments in the Evolution of Domain-Specific Modelling Languages

Vijanti Ramautar$^{(\boxtimes)}$, Sergio España, and Sjaak Brinkkemper

Department of Information and Computing Sciences, Utrecht University,
Princetonplein 5, Utrecht 3584 CC, The Netherlands
{v.d.ramautar,s.espana,s.brinkkemper}@uu.nl

Abstract. [**Background**] Domain-specific modelling languages (DSMLs) are tailored to particular application domains and are common in model-driven information system engineering. To support new modelling requirements, increase the maturity of the languages, and keep them relevant to their domain, DSMLs need to be evolved. [**Aims**] Since little is known regarding the complexity of the evolution process, in this paper, we investigate which incompletions are prevalent in each DSML evolution activity. [**Method**] We conduct a quantitative empirical study where the object of study, a DSML in the domain of ethical, social and environmental accounting, is supported by a metamodel in UML and a textual grammar in Xtext. Ninety-two participants grouped in 25 teams have evolved the DSML based on a set of new requirements, updating the metamodel and the grammar. We assess the completeness of each evolution activity and identify incompletions per artefact. We have also enquired the participants about their perceptions of the evolution process. [**Results**] The completeness of the metamodel evolution activity is about 1.25 times higher than it is for the grammar. The metamodelling primitives that are more likely to cause problems are relationships and enumerations. With respect to the Xtext grammars most incompletions are localised in rule calls, cross references and cardinalities. This is consistent with the participants' perceptions about the difficulty of each activity and primitive. [**Contribution**] Our findings are relevant for the design and testing of DSMLs, as well as for education on DSMLs.

Keywords: Model-driven information systems engineering ·
domain-specific modelling language · evolution · Xtext grammar ·
metamodel

1 Introduction

Model-driven information systems engineering (MDE) aims at decreasing the developer effort, reducing time-to-market, and reducing development complexity [14,37]. In some project situations, creating a domain-specific modelling language (DSML) is a convenient approach [25]; for instance, when engineering

© The Author(s), under exclusive license to Springer Nature Switzerland AG 2023
M. Indulska et al. (Eds.): CAiSE 2023, LNCS 13901, pp. 314–329, 2023.
https://doi.org/10.1007/978-3-031-34560-9_19

a software product line where a family of related information systems (ISs) is developed, or when user-modelling is intended. DSMLs are one family of domain-specific languages (DSL), where the goal leans towards modelling rather than programming. DSLs can be designed in many application domains, and in contrast to general-purpose languages, DSLs provide the right level of abstraction and expression for the problem domain, while providing critical domain properties [20]. DSML and DSL engineering methodology has garnered much attention from practitioners and academia and several development methods exist (e.g. in [5]). DSMLs are expressed by several types of formalisms, where metamodels and textual grammars are two common artefacts, the former often specifying the abstract syntax and the latter often specifying the concrete syntax of the DSML [13]. Visual notations are another approach to concrete syntaxes [22]. In such project situations, a DSML evolution will require interrelated activities to update the metamodel and the grammar or visual notation. In this paper, we focus on metamodels and grammars.

While DSL evolution and maintenance have been the focus of several investigations [38], this practice has received less attention in the case of DSMLs. Moreover, we miss insights on the degradation of DSMLs due to evolution activities. The introduction of incompletions in the DSML artefacts is likely to affect the process of the underlying IS engineering endeavours, as well as the quality of the resulting system. Understanding, anticipating, preventing, and resolving incompletions in the DSML artefacts that arise as a result of an evolution process becomes paramount for the overall success of IS engineering practices involving DSMLs.

This paper aims to investigate which incompletions are prevalent in each DSML evolution activity. We conduct an empirical study where teams of participants are requested to evolve a given DSML based on a set of new requirements, and then asked about their perceptions of the process. Following the traditional metrics of task completeness in usability studies [36], we define (task) incompletion as the lack of an element that should have been added, updated or deleted to implement the requirement.

The main contributions are: (i) an assessment of the prevalence of incompletions in each DSML evolution activity (and its corresponding artefact), (ii) an analysis of how the incompletions are located in the primitives of the metamodel and the grammar, (iii) an analysis of the perceptions of the participants, also in relation to their performance. We analyse whether there is a relationship between problems that arise during metamodel evolution and issues that arise during grammar evolution. The scientific contributions can be employed by DSML engineers and teachers to identify where to put emphasis (e.g. elaborate explanations, training, and documentation) during DSML development and evolution. Moreover, the results can provide the focus for DSML testing to discover whether DSML evolution is likely to be problematic. Lastly, DSML engineers and researchers can use our results to prevent complications during model-driven information systems engineering projects.

The paper is structured as follows. Section 2 presents background information. The empirical study design is explained in Sect. 3. We present and discuss the results of the empirical study in Sect. 4. In Sect. 5 we address threats to validity and formulate our conclusions.

2   Background

2.1   Related Work

One of the most common MDE approaches entails transforming a model, using model transformation technologies to derive a software product [30]. The models that provide the input for MDE are created with a DSL. Mernik et al. [25] define four types of DSLs: i) DSLs with well-defined execution semantics, (ii) input languages of an application generator, (iii) DSLs not primarily meant to be executable but nevertheless useful for application generation, and (iv) DSLs not meant to be executable, for instance, domain-specific data structure representations. Examples of approaches for DSL implementation are using an interpreter or a compiler. In this article, we focus on a DSL of the fourth type (referred to as DSML), which is later interpreted in runtime.

Typical artefacts in DSML engineering are metamodels for specifying the abstract syntax of the DSML [13], and textual grammars for specifying its concrete syntax. Frank emphasises the importance of selecting a suitable meta-modelling language [11]. Moreover, he describes DSML development as a major effort that requires a clear division of labour. The tasks can be divided over roles including domain expert, user, business analyst, language designer, tool expert, graphic artist, etc [11]. Herrmannsdoerfer et al. researched motivations behind language evolution and found that metamodels evolve due to user requests and technological changes [15]. Furthermore, metamodel changes are very likely to impact artefacts which are directly related to them (e.g. models and transformators). They conclude that language evolution is similar to software evolution.

We found that in the literary body DSL evolution is often understood as the co-evolution of parsers, textual syntax and graphical syntax editors, compilers, code generators, etc. In this article, we focus on metamodel and textual grammar evolution. DSL studies mainly focus on the domain analysis, design and implementation phases, conclude Kosar et al. [19]. They found that DSL maintenance/evolution is insufficiently investigated. Another systematic mapping study on DSL evolution, specifically, concludes that DSL evolution is a topic of increasing relevancy [39].

Scientific literature on approaches for DSL evolutions states that the usability of a DSL is crucial for its maintainability and adaptability [1], discusses the challenge of integrating several existing DSLs into one single and provides tools for automated DSL integration [7,18,24,26,28], explores the possibility of improving DSL evolution through composition [4,34], proposes community-driven language development [16], and weighs the costs and benefits of developing a DSL [6]. The typical activities known from software maintenance also apply to metamodel maintenance [15,23]. Other related work presents high-level insights gained by analysing a case of DSML evolution [2]. Our work contributes to the body of knowledge by pinpointing more exactly where challenges in DSL evolution occur.

2.2 The Application Domain of Ethical, Social Environmental Accounting

The approach studied in this article entails that the models are interpreted by an interpreter. The interpreter recognises constructs in the model and interprets these using an instruction cycle [25]. Our empirical study uses a DSML in the application domain of ethical, social and environmental accounting (ESEA). ESEA is the process of assessing and reporting on an organisation's ethical, social and environmental (ESE) performance [12]. ESEA methods provide guidelines on how to perform the accounting. The accounting results are typically published in an annual sustainability (or non-financial, or integrated) report.

The models created with our DSML contain information on the ESEA method (e.g. the name of the method, the topics assessed, and the indicators used to measure the ESE performance). We refer to this DSML as the openESEA DSML. The models produced with the DSML can be uploaded to an open-source interpreter, also called openESEA[1] [33]. The interpreter parses the models and reacts by activating the appropriate features and displaying the contents of the model. The openESEA DSML consists of a metamodel, which is a UML Class Diagram [29] and a textual Xtext grammar [3]. We use a metamodel as part of our DSML, given that metamodelling is a commonly used approach to capture the abstract syntax of a domain [10,17]. We follow [8] to conceptualise the domain, and express the concrete syntax with a textual grammar. In our approach, we always first evolve the metamodel and document the changes, only then we evolve the textual grammar based on the changes in the metamodel. We do not prescribe this specific approach for evolving DSMLs. However, most DSMLs have at least a metamodel or textual grammar. Hence our results are insightful in the contexts of DSMLs that are specified exclusively with a metamodel or grammar, and for DSMLs specified with both.

3 Quantitative Empirical Study Design

3.1 Research Questions and Objective

The aim of our research is to find out which problems arise during DSML evolution, hence we formulate the following research questions.

MRQ: Which incompletions are prevalent in DSML evolution activities?

RQ1.1: What is the task completion of DSML evolution activities?

RQ1.2: Which primitives of the metamodel and grammar specification languages are more likely to result in incompletion?

---

[1] https://github.com/sergioespana/openESEA.

We run a quantitative empirical study [41] to identify incompletions in DSML evolution. The objective, expressed with the Goal/Question/Metric method [40], is to (i) analyse incompletions that arise during DSML evolution activities, and (ii) to discover how the process of DSML evolution can be improved. The purpose of our study is to identify which aspects of DSML evolution require emphasis in DSML education and DSML testing. We do this by measuring the completeness of the models constructed, from the point of view of DSML engineers, in the context of extending the openESEA DSML.

3.2   DSML Evolution Process

The DSML evolution process, shown in Fig. 1 is based on earlier research in DSML development and evolution [8,9,33]. This process comprises six activities. During the first activity, new requirements are elicited (A1), previously implemented and backlogged requirements can provide input for this activity. The output is a collection of new requirements that will provide the backbone for the DSML evolution. Next, in A2, the metamodel is evolved, resulting in a new version of the metamodel. The corresponding documentation, explaining each element of the DSML, is updated (A3) to reflect the changes. In A4, the Xtext grammar is evolved, so it corresponds to the new version of the metamodel. Then, the interpreter is updated (A5), to ensure that it can parse and interpret the models that comply with the new grammar version. Lastly, the model is updated (A6) so that it adheres to the grammar. We investigate incompletions in activities A2, A3, A4, and A6. Strictly speaking, activities A2, A3, and A4 are performed by DSML engineers, whereas activity A6 is performed by the DSML users (i.e. IS engineers, domain modellers, etc.).

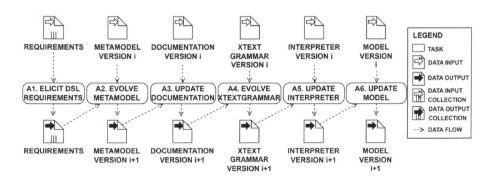

Fig. 1. The DSML evolution process

3.3   Object of Study: openESEA DSML

Every DSML engineering project can have a different infrastructure, but we consider an infrastructure such as in Fig. 2. This figure is a metamodel of DSMLs and details the deliverables involved in the DSML evolution process as seen in Fig. 1.

For simplification purposes, we left out the documentation, models, and interpreter. The **object of study** is the openESEA DSML, which is specified with a metamodel, and an Xtext grammar. All changes to the DSML are documented in an openESEA DSML manual. New requirements lead to a metamodel and grammar change. In case of a metamodel change, a metamodel element has to be changed. Metamodel elements are common primitives, used in UML class diagrams [29]. In case of a grammar change, the changes affect grammar elements, which can either be rules or elements of rules. Our Xtext grammar comprises standard Xtext prmitives [3].

The users of the openESEA technology use the DSML to specify ESEA methods which will later be supported by the interpreter. The metamodel is shown in Fig. 3, and the grammar can be found in a technical report [32]. `ESEA methods` typically consist of a set of `Topics` (e.g. gender diversity and greenhouse gas emission), the topics are measured using `Direct indicators` (e.g. number of non-binary employees) and `Indirect indicators` (e.g. non-binary to male ratio). Data is collected using `Surveys`, which consist of `Sections` and `Questions`. In case of a multiple choice question, `Answer options` can be defined. Some methods issue certification, if the certification requirements are met. Multiple `Certification levels` can be obtained (e.g. bronze, silver, or gold certification). To automatically validate the data, `Validation rules` can be defined. A validation rule can, for instance, state that the number of women in executive positions cannot be greater than the number of women staff.

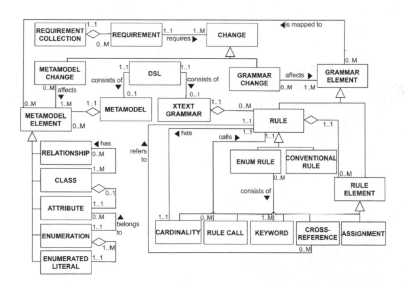

Fig. 2. Metamodel of the deliverables involved in the DSML evolution process

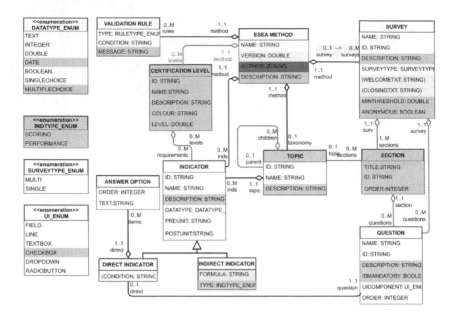

Fig. 3. The openESEA metamodel, with colour-coded changes required of study participants: green depicts additions, yellow updates and red deletions (Color figure online)

3.4   Subjects

We selected subjects using convenience sampling [41]. The subjects are students of the Business Informatics master's programme from Utrecht University (the Netherlands). The empirical study is performed as part of a course on Responsible ICT and is repeated over two years (2021 and 2022). In 2021 45 students, divided over 12 teams, participated; in 2022, 47 students divided over 13 teams participated. The students are educated in method engineering, but prior to the study, they had no knowledge of DSML development and ESEA.

3.5   Empirical Study Protocol

In the empirical study, the participants are asked to perform activities A2, A3, A4, and A6 of the DSML evolution process (see Fig. 1). Before they start the evolution process, they receive training, during which they are familiarised with DSML development, including metamodelling and Xtext grammar development. After the training, they receive an initial metamodel, initial documentation and 16 requirements. Two examples of requirements can be found in Table 1. Based on the requirements, they have to evolve the metamodel and update the documentation accordingly. The requirements can be implemented by adding, updating or removing attributes, relationships, cardinalities, and classes. If all requirements are implemented correctly the metamodel should resemble the reference model in Fig. 3. Next, the participants evolve the Xtext grammar based on the

Table 1. Two examples of requirements (full list in the technical report [32])

ID	Requirement
R5	Right now, the topics are just a flat list. There is also the need to convert that into a taxonomy; that is, a tree of topics. This way, the information is more structured
R14	Based on conversations with a network that could become a future client, we have discovered that their method has indicators whose datatype is a date. We would like to support this in the next version, so we have better chances of convincing them to use our tool

Table 2. The number of metamodel and grammar elements that are necessary to implement each of the requirements.

	Requirement ID																
	R1	R2	R3	R4	R5	R6	R7	R8	R9	R10	R11	R12	R13	R14	R15	R16	Total
Metamodel element																	37
Class	-	-	-	-	-	-	-	-	1	-	-	-	-	-	-	1	2
Attribute	1	5	1	1	-	-	1	1	2	-	1	1	-	-	1	4	19
Relationship	-	-	-	-	1\2	1	-	-	3	1	-	-	-	-	-	2	8\9
Enumeration	-	-	-	-	-	-	-	-	-	-	-	-	-	-	1	-	1
Enumerated literal	-	-	-	-	-	-	-	-	-	-	-	-	1	3	2	-	6
Grammar element																	34
Cross-reference	-	-	-	-	1	-	-	-	-	1	-	-	-	-	-	1	3
Keyword	1	5	1	1	-	-	1	1	2	-	1	-	1	-	1\0	4	19\18
Rule call	-	-	-	-	0\1	1	-	-	3	-	-	-	-	2	-	1	7\8
Enum rule	-	-	-	-	-	-	-	-	-	-	-	-	1	-	0\1	-	1\2
Assignment	-	-	-	-	-	-	-	-	1	-	-	-	-	-	-	1	2
Cardinality	-	-	-	-	-	-	-	-	-	-	-	1	-	-	-	-	1

same set of requirements. They receive the reference solution of the metamodel and documentation in advance. This prevents them from making mistakes in their Xtext grammar evolution due to a mistake in their metamodel and documentation solutions. Table 2 shows how each of the requirements can be implemented in the metamodel and grammar. For instance, implementing requirement 5 (R5) requires the participant to add a relationship in the metamodel, and one cross-reference in the grammar. R15 and R5 can be implemented in multiple ways. In R5, another relationship can be updated and a rule call can be added. R15 requires either adding a keyword or an enum rule in the grammar. To assess artefacts created by the participants, we have created a template where, for each requirement, we have listed all the implementations we had conceived beforehand. This acted as a completeness benchmark. We then systematically checked whether the participant had implemented each requirement and; if so, which solution they had opted for, and whether they implemented it correctly.

While we were prepared to extend our list of possible implementations in case they had come up with one that we had not conceived, this did not happen.

After updating the Xtext DSML, the participants should update a model of an ESEA method to make it compliant with the new version of the DSML and showcase the changes they made in the grammar. The DSML evolution activities are performed in groups of four participants, with a couple of teams having fewer participants to accommodate course-related exceptional circumstances. After the DSML evolution tasks, the participants are asked to fill in an extended version of the Method Evaluation Model (MEM) questionnaire [27] where they reflect on the evolution process.

3.6   Variables

For each participant team, we inspect the four evolved DSML artefacts (i.e. metamodel, documentation, Xtext grammar, and model) to identify incompletions. That is, elements that should have been added, updated or deleted to implement the requirements, but the team failed to. This allows us to measure their *completeness* by dividing the number of correctly implemented changes per primitive or artefact by the number of required changes per primitive or artefact.

Apart from completeness, we measured the *perceived ease of use*, *perceived usefulness*, and *intention to use* by deploying a 5-point Likert scale based on the MEM questionnaire. Moreover, we asked the participants to indicate their perceived difficulty of the metamodel and grammar elements, and to reflect on the evolution process in an open question.

3.7   Analysis Procedure

We analyse the task completeness per metamodel and grammar primitive. Moreover, we know the mapping between elements of the metamodel and elements of the grammar; this relationship is labelled "is mapped to" in Fig. 2 and quantified in Table 2. This allows us to also analyse which metamodel primitives suffer from more incompletions when implemented in the grammar. The MEM questionnaire responses are quantitatively analysed and illustrated in box plots. Regarding the open question, we used Nvivo [31] to analyse the responses by creating a taxonomy of codes (e.g. a code for each metamodel primitive) and mapping the part of the response that discusses the code.

4   Results

4.1   Metamodel and Documentation Completeness

The completeness of the evolution activities of the metamodel and documentation is shown in Table 3. The completeness is the lowest for the *enumeration* and the *relationship* elements. Requirements related to the enumeration element entailed creating new enumerations, including the enumerated literals. The

Table 3. The completeness percentages for the metamodel (Meta) and documentation (Docu), aggregated per metamodel primitive (Meta primitive)

		2021 (n=12)		2022 (n=13)	
		Meta	**Docu**	**Meta**	**Docu**
Meta primitive	Class	100.0%	98.1%	100.0%	100%
	Attribute	92.6%	93.6%	95.5%	98.3%
	Enumeration literal	82.3%	73.1%	87.7%	72.4%
	Enumeration	61.5%	69.2%	84.6%	46.2%
	Relationship	64.5%	74.6%	70.2%	77.5%

Table 4. Left, the initial metamodel and grammar fragments for R5, and right their solutions.

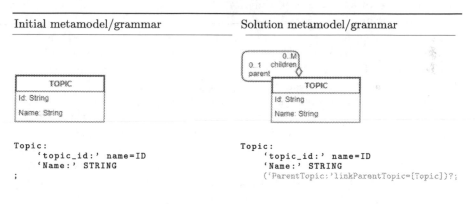

```
Topic:                                  Topic:
    'topic_id:' name=ID                     'topic_id:' name=ID
    'Name:' STRING                          'Name:' STRING
;                                           ('ParentTopic:'linkParentTopic=[Topic])?;
```

relationship-related tasks entailed adding or deleting relationships and updating cardinalities. As an example, implementing requirement 5 entailed adding a reflective relationship to the Topic class to support a taxonomy of topics. The initial metaclass and metaclass in the reference solution are shown in Table 4. Evidently, these types of evolution activities resulted in the most incompletions. The overall completeness for the metamodel and documentation evolution, shown in Fig. 4, is quite high (>80%). Strikingly, in some cases, the completeness is higher for the documentation evolution than for the metamodel evolution. This indicates that the participants were able to document the required change well, but they did not implement them correctly in the metamodel. Strictly speaking, when following the sequence of activities as described in Fig. 1 this should not be possible.

4.2 Grammar and Model Completeness

The task completeness of the grammar and model yields Table 5. The left table shows the grammar and model task completeness per grammar element, whereas the right depicts the grammar task completeness per metamodel element. We express the grammar completeness also in terms of metamodel elements because metamodel elements are commonly known and intuitive. This analysis shows that implementing relationships in Xtext caused most incompletions, which is in line with our findings presented in Sect. 4.1. When examining the table on the left, the overall completeness of the metamodel solutions is 1.25 times higher than that of the grammar solutions, and Fig. 4 shows that the completeness of the grammar evolution activity is the lowest of all artefacts. *Cross-references*, *cardinalities*, and *rule calls* are the source of most incompletions. To provide an example of what a cross-reference entails, we present the example in Table 4, which shows the initial and solution grammar fragments related to requirement 5. The requirement can be implemented in Xtext by adding a cross-reference, which links a parent topic to a subtopic, using the parent topic ID. Such cross-references have proven to be difficult for the participants. The other element that causes incompletions is the rule call, which is a rule that calls on another rule. For implementing requirement 14, the participants had to create a new rule named `MultipleChoice`, comprising of two keywords and one rule call to the rule `AnswerOption`. Moreover, they had to create a call to the rule `MultipleChoice` in the `Datatype` rule. Such tasks resulted in low completeness. The other element with low overall task completeness is *cardinality*. Rule calls, cardinalities, and cross-references generally refer to relationships in the metamodel. Given that participants had problems modelling relationships in the metamodel, it seems rather logical that these primitives resulted in incompletions. The participants also updated a model to reflect the grammar changes. In some cases, the model task completeness is higher than the grammar completeness. In practice, this is an invalid outcome since the model has to adhere to the grammar rules. However, we noticed that participants divided tasks among the members of their group, where some group members only evolved the grammar, whereas others only updated the model, resulting in models that do not adhere to the team's grammar.

Table 5. Left, the task completeness of the grammar per grammar primitive. Right, the task completeness of the grammar per metamodel primitive.

		2021 (n=12)		2022 (n=13)	
		Gram.	Model	Gram.	Model
G. primitive	Keyword	93.6%	84.6%	94.0%	80.1%
	Assignment	82.1%	87.5%	100.0%	82.1%
	Enum rule	87.5%	33.3%	98.2%	35.7%
	Cardinality	39.3%	80.6%	65.2%	73.2%
	Rule call	43.1%	29.2%	40.0%	59.6%
	Cross-reference	22.3%	43.8%	39.3%	50.0%

		2021	2022
		n= 12	n=13
		Gram.	Gram.
M. primitive	Class	82.1%	100.0%
	Attribute	97.4%	98.9%
	Enumeration literal	98.2%	100.0%
	Enumeration	75.0%	96.4%
	Relationship	43.4%	51.1%

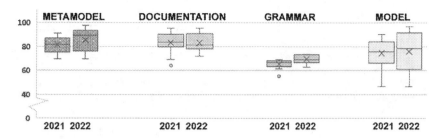

Fig. 4. The completeness per artefact

4.3 Participant Perceptions

The responses to the extended MEM questionnaire reveal the participants' perceptions about three aspects of DSML evolution.

Aspect 1: Difficulty Per Element. In general, the participants perceived evolving the metamodel as quite easy. They described the task as "doable", "intuitive", and "not too difficult". They found updating the documentation rather dull and repetitive, but they understood the necessity for it and acknowledged that it helped them understand the requirements better.

The majority of the students perceived evolving the Xtext grammar as the most difficult step in the evolution process. They found the Xtext framework difficult to work with and the rules were hard to grasp. They described the Xtext grammar as somewhat abstract, and expressed that they were having trouble staying consistent in their application of the rules. Moreover they expressed that they were often able to pinpoint which lines had to be edited, but it was hard to figure out how the lines had to be edited.

In the questionnaire we asked the students to indicate how difficult they found each of the metamodel and grammar primitives, the results are presented in Fig. 5. The perceived difficulty seems to align with the task completeness. The students indicated that they found *relationships* in metamodels and *cardinalities*, *rule calls*, and *cross-references* in grammars the most difficult. The task completeness is the lowest for these elements. There seems to be a correlation between the perceived difficulty of elements and the task completeness of those elements. However, more data points are needed to prove such a relationship.

Aspect 2: Sequence of Activities. The participants were positive about the sequence of evolution activities. They stressed that the metamodel was essential for evolving the Xtext grammar. A quote by a student that emphasises this reads: *"While reading the metamodel I figured [out how] some parts of the grammar should look and operate. Without the metamodel, the grammar alone would be dramatic to understand. The documentation helped in understanding the metamodel itself since [it] showed what the classes in the metamodel did and what attributes they consisted of"*.

Aspect 3: Perceived Efficacy and Intention to Use. The results of the MEM questionnaire are shown in Fig. 6. Five is the highest score, indicating

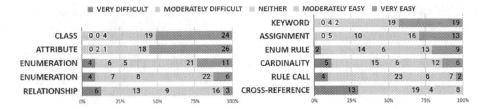

Fig. 5. The perceived difficulty of the metamodel primitives (left) and the grammar primitives (right) for the 2022 edition

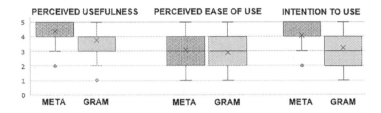

Fig. 6. The results of the Method Evaluation Model questionnaire (2022 edition)

that the participants found evolving the artefact useful and easy to use, and that they intend to use the artefact in the future. As for usefulness, the metamodel is perceived as more useful than the grammar, although they are generally both perceived as useful. Interestingly, the perceived ease of use for the grammar and metamodel is similar. Almost half of the participants expressed that they do not intend to use Xtext grammars in the future.

5   Discussion, Validity and Conclusions

Discussion. When reflecting on the evolution process, the participants expressed the need for longer training sessions with more guidance and literature they could refer back to. They expressed that they found using and evolving the metamodel easier due to their prior training in method engineering. Based on the numerous suggestions by students we conclude that training is a crucial part of DSML evolution. We improved the training in 2022, hoping that it would improve the results. Generally, the results are better in the second edition of the study. In the first year, the training did not include the openESEA DSML, instead, the participants were trained on DSMLs in different domains. The participants were only confronted with the openESEA DSML during the empirical study. In the second year, the training included an explanation of each of the openESEA metamodel and grammar primitives. Additionally, in the second year, the students were provided with self-paced learning material on Xtext.

We use completeness to refer to task completeness of the evolution activities; that is, the extent to which the team evolving the DSML successfully made all the changes that were required to implement the requirements in each DSML artefact, as is typical in usability studies [36]. Therefore, completeness should not be understood in the same way as it is defined by SEQUAL [21]. Task completeness aggregates both dimensions of SEQUAL's semantic quality: completeness and validity. Moreover, we solely focus on DSML evolution based on functional requirements. To limit the scope we have purposely left out quality requirements.

Validity. Regarding construct validity, we use the MEM questionnaire to analyse the participants' perceptions, since the MEM has been validated thoroughly [27]. We analyse incompletions in DSML evolution by calculating completeness of the DSML evolution activities. Variables, such as efficiency and consistency were left for future studies. Concerning external validity, we expect that our results can be generalised outside the setting of our study since we present our results in the context of commonly used UML and Xtext primitives. However, we acknowledge that there are other factors that influence the DSML evolution process, such as the usability of the DSML [1], or the participants' knowledge of the ESEA domain. Although we have opted for an approach that seems intuitive to us (i.e. first evolving the metamodel, then involving the grammar), and we tried to ensure human readability in the grammar, we cannot assess the usability of our DSML. Thus, we cannot identify the effect of the usability of our DSML on the incompletions witnessed in our study. Given that the study only assesses task completeness, there might be a threat to content validity. Nonetheless, we deem our results valuable in the evolution of domain-specific modelling languages, to prevent complications during MDE projects. To mitigate another content validity threat, we built upon an existing reengineering framework, and used the conceptual model evolution traces defined in [35]; this is reflected in 3, where we show model element additions, updates and deletions with green, yellow and red, respectively.

Next Steps. Regarding the evolution of the DSML, our next steps involve extending the language to support more aspects of ethical, social and environmental accounting. We would, for instance, like to include classes and primitives that allow for auditing and visualising accounts. With regards to our research on DSML evolution, the next steps could entail measuring additional variables such as the efficiency of DSML evolution and studying which cognitive aspects are related to the various artefacts.

Conclusion. In summary, we presented an empirical study that analyses which incompletions are prevalent in DSML evolution activities. Our results reveal that the completeness of the metamodel evolution activity is about 1.25 times higher than it is for the grammar. The metamodelling primitives that are more likely to cause problems are relationships and enumerations. With respect to the Xtext grammars, most incompletions are localised in rule calls, cross references and cardinalities. We also found that the metamodel is perceived as an important artefact to understanding and evolving the DSML. Additional training with emphasis on the problematic elements may result in fewer incompletions in DSML evolutions.

References

1. Albuquerque, D., Cafeo, B., Garcia, A., Barbosa, S., Abrahão, S., Ribeiro, A.: Quantifying usability of domain-specific languages: an empirical study on software maintenance. JSS **101**, 245–259 (2015)
2. Aschauer, T., Dauenhauer, G., Pree, W.: A modeling language's evolution driven by tight interaction between academia and industry. In: ICSE, IEEE (2010)
3. Behrens, H., et al.: Xtext user guide. Eclipse Foundation (2010)
4. Cazzola, W., Poletti, D.: DSL evolution through composition. In: RAM-SE (2010)
5. Ceh, I., Crepinšek, M., Kosar, T., Mernik, M.: Ontology driven development of domain-specific languages. Comput. Sci. Inf. Syst. **8**(2), 317–342 (2011)
6. Cook, S., Jones, G., Kent, S., Wills, A.C.: Domain-Specific Development with Visual Studio dsl tools. Pearson, London (2007)
7. De Geest, G., Vermolen, S., Van Deursen, A., Visser, E.: Generating version convertors for domain-specific languages. In: WCRE, pp. 197–201. IEEE (2008)
8. España, S., Bik, N., Overbeek, S.: Model-driven engineering support for social and environmental accounting. In: RCIS, pp. 1–12. IEEE (2019)
9. España, S., Ramautar, V., Overbeek, S., Derikx, T.: Model-driven production of data-centric infographics: an application to the impact measurement domain. In: Guizzardi, R., Ralyté, J., Franch, X. (eds.) Research Challenges in Information Science. RCIS 2022. Lecture Notes in Business Information Processing, vol. 446, pp 477–494. Springer, Cham (2022). https://doi.org/10.1007/978-3-031-05760-1_28
10. Falazi, G., Breitenbücher, U., Daniel, F., Lamparelli, A., Leymann, F., Yussupov, V.: Smart contract invocation protocol (SCIP): a protocol for the uniform integration of heterogeneous blockchain smart contracts. In: Dustdar, S., Yu, E., Salinesi, C., Rieu, D., Pant, V. (eds.) CAiSE 2020. LNCS, vol. 12127, pp. 134–149. Springer, Cham (2020). https://doi.org/10.1007/978-3-030-49435-3_9
11. Frank, U.: Domain-specific modeling languages: requirements analysis and design guidelines. In: Reinhartz-Berger, I., Sturm, A., Clark, T., Cohen, S., Bettin, J. (eds.) Domain Engineering, pp. 133–157. Springer, Berlin (2013). https://doi.org/10.1007/978-3-642-36654-3_6
12. Gray, R., Adams, C.A., Owen, D.: Accountability, social responsibility and sustainability. Pearson, London (2014)
13. Gronback, R.C.: Eclipse Modeling Project: a Domain-Specific Language (DSL) Toolkit. Pearson Education, London (2009)
14. Hailpern, B., Tarr, P.: Model-driven development: the good, the bad, and the ugly. IBM Syst. J. **45**(3), 451–461 (2006)
15. Herrmannsdoerfer, M., Ratiu, D., Wachsmuth, G.: Language evolution in practice: the history of GMF. In: van den Brand, M., Gašević, D., Gray, J. (eds.) SLE 2009. LNCS, vol. 5969, pp. 3–22. Springer, Heidelberg (2010). https://doi.org/10.1007/978-3-642-12107-4_3
16. Izquierdo, J.L.C., Cabot, J.: Community-driven language development. In: MISE, pp. 29–35. IEEE (2012)
17. Jazayeri, B., Schwichtenberg, S., Küster, J., Zimmermann, O., Engels, G.: Modeling and analyzing architectural diversity of open platforms. In: Dustdar, S., Yu, E., Salinesi, C., Rieu, D., Pant, V. (eds.) CAiSE 2020. LNCS, vol. 12127, pp. 36–53. Springer, Cham (2020). https://doi.org/10.1007/978-3-030-49435-3_3
18. Juergens, E., Pizka, M.: The language evolver lever-tool demonstration-. Electron. Notes Theor. Comput. Sci. **164**(2), 55–60 (2006)

19. Kosar, T., Bohra, S., Mernik, M.: Domain-specific languages: a systematic mapping study. IST **71**, 77–91 (2016)
20. Kosar, T., et al.: Comparing general-purpose and domain-specific languages: an empirical study. Comput. Sci. Inf. Syst. **7**(2), 247–264 (2010)
21. Krogstie, J.: Model-based Development and Evolution of Information Systems: A Quality Approach. Springer, New York (2012). https://doi.org/10.1007/978-1-4471-2936-3
22. Kulkarni, V., Reddy, S., Clark, T.: Advanced Digital Architectures for Model-Driven Adaptive Enterprises. IGI Global, Hershey (2020)
23. Lientz, B.P., Swanson, E.B.: Software Maintenance Management. AW, Boston (1980)
24. Mayer, P., Schroeder, A.: Towards automated cross-language refactorings between Java and DSLs used by Java frameworks. In: WRT (2013)
25. Mernik, M., Heering, J., Sloane, A.M.: When and how to develop domain-specific languages. CSUR **37**(4), 316–344 (2005)
26. Meyers, B., Vangheluwe, H.: A framework for evolution of modelling languages. Sci. Comput. Program. **76**(12), 1223–1246 (2011)
27. Moody, D.L.: The method evaluation model: a theoretical model for validating information systems design methods (2003)
28. Nikolov, N., Rossini, A., Kritikos, K.: Integration of DSLs and migration of models: a case study in the cloud computing domain. Procedia CS **68**, 53–66 (2015)
29. OMG: Unified Modeling Language, Version 2.5.1 (2017)
30. Pastor, Ó., España, S.: Full model-driven practice: from requirements to code generation. In: Ralyté, J., Franch, X., Brinkkemper, S., Wrycza, S. (eds.) CAiSE 2012. LNCS, vol. 7328, pp. 701–702. Springer, Heidelberg (2012). https://doi.org/10.1007/978-3-642-31095-9_48
31. Phillips, M., Lu, J.: A quick look at NVivo. J. Electron. Resour. Librariansh (2018)
32. Ramautar, V., España, S.: Evolution of the openESEA DSL. Technical Report (2022). https://doi.org/10.17632/2xjbs6x6bp.1
33. Ramautar, V., España, S.: Managing the complexity in ethical, social and environmental accounting: engineering and evaluating a modelling language. In: ManComp (2022)
34. Rieger, C., Westerkamp, M., Kuchen, H.: Challenges and opportunities of modularizing textual domain-specific languages. In: MODELSWARD, pp. 387–395 (2018)
35. Ruiz, M., España, S., Pastor, Ó., Gonz, A., et al.: Supporting organisational evolution by means of model-driven reengineering frameworks. In: IEEE 7th International Conference on Research Challenges in Information Science (RCIS), pp. 1–10. IEEE (2013)
36. Seffah, A., Kececi, N., Donyaee, M.: Quim: a framework for quantifying usability metrics in software quality models. In: APSEC, IEEE (2001)
37. Sendall, S., Kozaczynski, W.: Model transformation: the heart and soul of model-driven software development. IEEE Softw. **20**(5), 42–45 (2003)
38. Strembeck, M., Zdun, U.: An approach for the systematic development of domain-specific languages. Softw. Pract. Experience **39**(15), 1253–1292 (2009)
39. Thanhofer-Pilisch, J., Lang, A., Vierhauser, M., Rabiser, R.: A systematic mapping study on DSL evolution. In: Euromicro, pp. 149–156. IEEE (2017)
40. Van Solingen, R., Basili, V., Caldiera, G., Rombach, H.D.: Goal question metric (GQM) approach. Encyclopedia of software engineering (2002)
41. Wohlin, C., Runeson, P., Höst, M., Ohlsson, M.C., Regnell, B., Wesslén, A.: Experimentation in Software Engineering. Springer, New York (2012). https://doi.org/10.1007/978-3-642-29044-2

Lessons Learned in Model-Based Reverse Engineering of Large Legacy Systems

Laura García-Borgoñón[1]([⊠])(iD), Miguel Angel Barcelona[1](iD), Armando J. Egea[2], German Reyes[2], Alejandro Sainz-de-la-maza[2], and Adolfo González-Uzabal[2]

[1] Instituto Tecnológico de Aragón, Av/ María de Luna 7, 50018 Zaragoza, Spain
{laurag,mabarcelona}@itainnova.es
[2] NTT Data Spain Soluciones Tecnológicas SLU, Pl. de Antonio Beltrán Martínez 1, 50002 Zaragoza, Spain
{armando.javier.egea.moneva,german.reyes.munoz,
alejandro.sainz.de.la.maza.sainz.de.la.maza,
adolfo.gonzalez.uzabal}@nttdata.com

Abstract. Large technologies companies that offer software modernization and maintenance services for legacy software applications in diverse
sectors such as banking, insurance, healthcare and public sector, face
a significant challenge. Legacy systems were usually developed in old
programming languages, often have outdated documentation and the
processes used for software development were immature. Modernization
and maintenance projects include tasks such as source code analysis with
high effort and time costs, and an important risk of misunderstanding.
In the literature, model-driven reverse engineering (MDRE) approaches
promise to address these challenges successfully, but most of existing
proposals are focused on a concrete technological stack. This paper aims
to present the preliminary results and lessons learned when adopting
MDRE in a large multinational company, providing a series of reflections and open issues to reduce the gap between academia and industry.
It introduces STRATO, a corporate solution that proposes a MDRE
approach focused on a high flexibility to incorporate new programming
languages. It reads source code and through model-to-model transformations convert it into platform independent conceptual, persistence and
business logic models. Preliminary outcomes, lessons learned and open
issues concerning MDRE industry adoption are presented.

Keywords: Model Based Reverse Engineering · Large Legacy
Systems · Industrial application

1 Introduction

NTT Data is a large multinational technology company that offers to its clients
comprehensive business solutions covering all aspects of the value chain, from
business strategy to systems implementation. It operates in the Telecommunica-
tions, Banking, Healthcare, Industry, Insurance, Media, Public Sector and Utilities sectors. Within its activities, the maintenance of legacy information systems

M. Indulska et al. (Eds.): CAiSE 2023, LNCS 13901, pp. 330–344, 2023.
https://doi.org/10.1007/978-3-031-34560-9_20

is an important line of business due to enterprises from all sectors have many applications which were developed in the past and are still operated today. Modernization and maintenance tasks of such legacy systems are complex because the applications were usually developed in old programming languages, documentation is often outdated and poor, and software processes used to develop them are not easily repeatable. That is the reason many organizations outsource modernization and maintenance services.

Model-driven engineering (MDE) is a development paradigm that uses high-level models and model transformations in order to produce software applications [1]. The Object Management Group (OMG) [2] establishes that "a model of a system is a description or specification of that system an its environment for certain purpose". MDE is the general term for all model-based principles and techniques that can be applied to both forward and reverse engineering [3]. In [4] authors define reverse engineering as the process of comprehending software and producing a model of it at a higher abstraction level than source code. The application of MDE principles and techniques in reverse engineering is called Model-Driven Reverse Engineering (MDRE) [4].

This paper aims at sharing our experience by creating and using a MDRE approach to systematize the modernization and maintenance services. After analyzing existing solutions and considering the needs of a multinational company that must cover a wide technological spectrum, we have developed a corporate solution, called STRATO, which focuses on facilitating extensibility when incorporating new programming languages. As a proof of concept we have evaluated it on real customer legacy systems. The main contribution of this article is to present the preliminary results and lessons learned when adopting MDRE in a large multinational company, providing a series of reflections and open issues to reduce the gap between academia and industry.

The paper is organized as follows. Section 2 reports the motivation of facing to the challenge of the MDRE in NTT Data real environments. Section 3 shows the related work and background in this research. Section 4 describes the conceptual approach proposed. STRATO platform as a tool is shown in Sect. 5. Section 6 exposes results with real legacy systems as a proof of concept evaluation. Section 7 summarizes lessons learned. Finally, Sect. 8 presents conclusions and future work.

2   Motivation

One of the business areas of the multinational NTT Data is the maintenance of large legacy applications, accounting for up to 40% of the business volume. Although the service offering covers all sectors, banking and utilities are the main ones in which there is a group of clients that maintain the core of their business with software developed decades ago. Sometimes these systems have gone through evolutions, carried out by various companies over the years, so estimating the effort required to understand and know how to evolve or correct these systems is a very complex task without having time to evaluate its source code.

Generally, these systems were developed with old technological stacks and the associated documentation is either non-existent or is not a true reflection of how the software has evolved, so the first task of the maintenance team is to be able to understand how a system was built by reading the source code. This work, although it is carried out by technical experts in the specific technologies, requires a great effort and entails a time period of several weeks and, in turn, is subject to potential errors caused by the manual work of reading, interpreting and documenting the software.

From the Innovation and Strategic Investments (ISI) area, in charge of leading corporate assets that allow the company to innovate and change the business, we have set ourselves the challenge of automating this first phase of discovering large legacy systems, based on MDRE principles, working on abstract models instead on source code. For this reason, we consider the creation of a technological platform that automates parsing source code and transforming it into models, to improve the productivity of technical teams during early stages of large legacy systems maintenance projects.

Although there may be some specific solutions that perform automatic code conversion from one language to another, this scenario is in practice very little demanded by clients, since in the modernization process there are always changes in functionality or change requests not to drag errors accumulated in the evolution of code for years. Additionally, our approach must meet two characteristics: i) be easily extensible to several languages, due to the great variability of clients and sectors that means that even for the same programming language we find more than 10 versions, and; ii) be a web-based collaborative platform in which large teams can work simultaneously on the same project.

Consequently, our hypothesis is that through an MDRE solution, we will be able to improve early stages of maintenance or modernization projects of large real legacy systems in a practical way, automating acquisition, generating technical documentation and guiding the team to identify problems and propose solutions. In this way we could reduce the effort and time required to maintain an existing system, increasing our competitiveness and being proactive in reducing its technical debt, which sums up our motivation from a business perspective.

3   Background and Related Work

In the field of MDRE there are some initiatives aimed at obtaining descriptive models from existing systems that have previously been developed [5], generally structured in two steps: i) obtaining a view, a model, of the legacy system analyzed from source artifacts, and; ii) the exploitation of the model to achieve a specific objective, for example, to document or re-engineer a system.

Regarding languages for reverse engineering, OMG Architecture-Driven Modernization (ADM) [6] initiative defined different models with the aim of supporting reverse engineering activities: i) the knowledge discovery metamodel (KDM) [7], which aims to define a shared and complete representation experience capable of guaranteeing the interoperability of different tools, efficiently supporting maintenance, evolution, evaluation and activities of modernization; ii) the Abstract Syntax Tree (AST) Metamodel (ASTM) [8], which represents the AST of virtually any programming language, allowing parsing tools to target the metamodel rather than the specific language AST. The metamodel defines the generic AST, with definitions that can be applied recurrently to most programming languages, but also allows extensions, known as specialized ASTM, to be able to include the specific characteristics of a specific programming language; iii) the Consortium for Information and Software Quality contributed to the definition of metamodels integrated with ADM standards, adding the representation of different quality measures, for example, maintainability with the Automated Source Code Maintainability Measure (ASCMM) [9]; iv) the metamodel for the definition and description of patterns as used in the architecture, design and implementation of software systems, working with software flaws or security problems, and any situation in which a pattern is appropriately applied, known as Structured Patterns Metamodel Standard (SPMS) [10], and; iv) the metamodel to support the representation of software metrics applied to existing models (Structured Metrics Metamodel, SMM) [11], which defines the way to represent measurement information related to any structured information model, being extensible to exchange both measurements as measurement information about artifacts contained or expressed by structured models. In 2017 a systematic literature review (SLR) [3] of MDRE presented 15 different initiatives, supporting several programming languages (*java, cobol, structured query language (SQL), javascript, php* or *delphi* among others), as well as metamodels and tools created from scratch or extending existing frameworks as MODISCO [12].

Regarding case studies, in 2007 Tonella et al. [13] performed a review of empirical studies in reverse engineering and identified the need to adopt a common framework for the execution of experiments. In 2019 Pa Pascal developed a study on the practical adoption of MDRE approaches [14] with these conclusions: i) MDRE for general purpose languages such as *java* was currently still a myth, and; ii) even when there were generic tools such as MODISCO, they were far from being able to raise understanding to an abstract level such as architecture. A SLR of automatic software refactoring was conducted in 2019 by Baqais and Alshayeb [15] including 41 primary studies with these conclusions: i) most research was done at code level (78%) so they encourage to do more research at model level; ii) there was a lack of tool support (only 29% of studies included a tool chain).

Regarding existing tool chains, there are several with a MDRE approach that proposes their own metamodels: i) Spoon [16] is an open source library for parsing, rewriting, and transforming *java* source code; ii) COALA with its CoAST (Universal and language-independent abstract syntax tree) metamodel [17] is a universal AST that makes it easy to analyze every programming language, and; iii) Grammar to Model Language (Gra2Mol) [18] is a domain-specific transformation language for defining relationships between grammar elements and metamodel elements. To build an MDRE solution from the definition of domain-specific languages, whether textual or graphical, we have also reviewed the existing tools. Iung et al. conducted a systematic mapping study in 2020 [19] where 59 tools were exposed. To support web based interaction we have developed some proof of concepts using Web Generic Modeling Environment (WebGME) tool [20], AToMPM [21], Pyro [22], EMF in cloud [23] with different graphical modeling extensions like Sirius [24] or Graphical Language Server Platform (GLSP) [25], and finally using Theia [26] or reproducing existing solutions for data modeling [27]

After analyzing the state of the art we have evidenced that: i) there is no solution to automate reverse engineering for any programming language; ii) there are several metamodel proposals to follow an MDRE approach; iii) ASTM seems to be the OMG standard that would allow to cover the platform independent perspective we are pursuing; iv) there is not much practical evidence of the application of reverse engineering in industry in real cases to compare with.

4   Conceptual Approach

This section introduces conceptual MDRE approach proposed. Figure 1 shows a schematic of the general reverse engineering process, according to a bottom-up approach, in which top services are based on platform independent models, reducing the effort required to incorporate new languages. The new solution must be applied to various programming languages and technologies, but we have started with *java*, *cobol* and relational databases due to the volume of existing maintenance legacy systems in our business.

At the bottom there is the **legacy systems layer**. The information available from the legacy systems is used, whether they are *java* or *cobol* solutions, which can be accessed via a local folder, a compressed file with the sources, git repository credentials, or compiled code. Additionally, if the system stores persistent data, the Open Database Connectivity (ODBC) connection or the SQL of the relational database schema may be provided.

Then there is the **discovery layer**. In this phase, the source code is parsed using lexical and syntactic analyzers, according to concrete programming languages grammars, and their respective ASTs are obtained. Next, a model-to-model (M2M) conversion is carried out towards a platform independent AST model (PIM ASTM) that allows the rest of the functionalities and transformations to be reused independently of the Platform Specific Models (PSM). This way, the possibility of extending the MDRE coverage towards new languages is simplified because the rest of the upper layers would not require modifications.

The objective of the **understanding layer** is to transform the information from the ASTM to a set of more representative models of an information system. The solution includes three PIM metamodels: i) the domain model includes conceptual elements with attributes and relationships; ii) the persistence model includes the relational database schema with tables, columns and relationships; iii) the business logic model includes functions, services, their statements and relations to domain and persistence models.

At the top there is the **diagnostic and transformation services layer**. Once all the information of a legacy system is defined in the domain, persistence and business logic metamodels, there are services for technological debt diagnosis and automatic M2M transformation to reduce it.

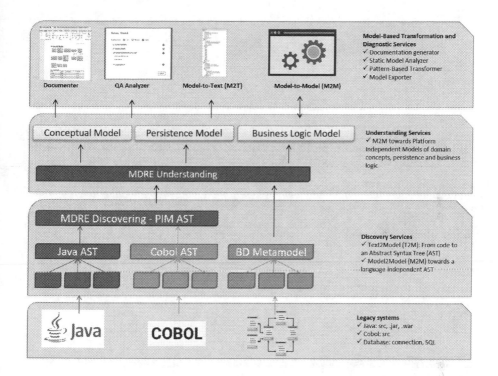

Fig. 1. Conceptual architecture for reverse engineering process

5   STRATO Platform

This section exposes the new corporate platform that, following MDRE principles, automates the discovery and understanding of legacy systems. At technical level, it is created as an extension on top of WebGME. The solution is composed by new metamodels and services for discovery, understanding, diagnosis, documentation and technical debt reduction. WebGME tool has been extended in functionality, some plugins have been developed and a new system architecture based on micro-services has been created as it is shown in the Fig. 2.

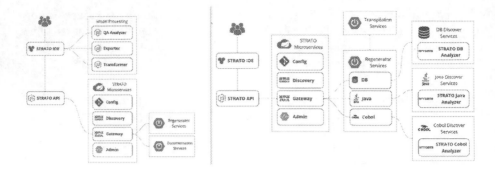

Fig. 2. Technical architecture of services

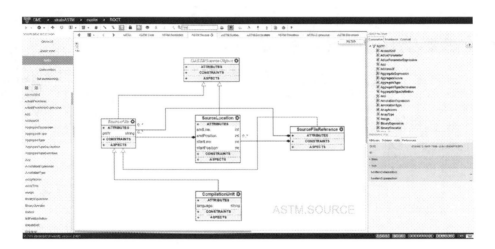

Fig. 3. View of ASTM meta visualizer in WebGME

The conceptual approach requires the generation of four platform independent metamodels: i) a domain conceptual metamodel for complex data structures, composed by 35 elements; ii) a persistence metamodel for relational databases that includes 39 metaelements; iii) a business logic metamodel for actions, services, statements and expressions, formed by 81 elements and; iv) an extension of the OMG ASTM standard composed by 196 metaelements. As the size of the metamodels is large and with WebGME we experienced problems when applying changes, we decided to create them using Essential Meta Object Facility (EMOF) [28]. We developed a tool to automate their transformation from ecore to WebGME. Figure 3 shows a view of ASTM source package metaelements into meta visualizer of WebGME.

Discovery services are responsible for parsing source code and convert it to ASTM model. It is the architecture layer closest to the concrete technology and the one that requires specific adaptation for each possible programming language. These services are built from the AST obtained after parsing the specific grammar of each language, using the *antlr4* tool [29], as Spring Boot based *java* services. When we want to include a new programming language, we need to have its grammar and build the service that reads its AST and transforms it into the ASTM model.

Once the ASTM model is filled, all transformations and analysis are done on top of abstract models, so that adding new languages requires no changes. Understanding services are in charge of transform ASTM information into domain, persistence and business logic models. At the beginning they were developed using WebGME plugins, but due to the huge size of ASTM models, we experienced performance and memory issues, so that they were developed in *java* and interacts with models using a new Representational State Transfer (REST) Application Program Interface (API) created on top of existing core API [30]. Since ASTM is an intermediate step between the code and the abstract models, we implemented its integration into the platform for demonstration purposes, but in its current version the transformation is performed without the need to dump the extensive information into MongoDB which is used by WebGME.

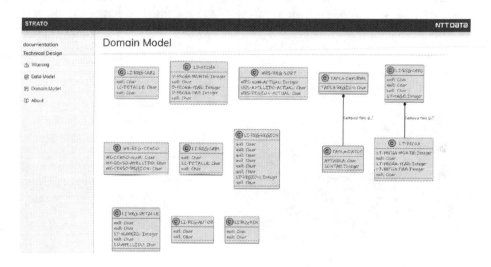

Fig. 4. Auto-generation of technical documentation from persistence model

The rest of features are implemented on the diagnostic and transformation services layer, launched by user as *javascript* plugins but all logic is included in external micro-services, so that we reduce the coupling with the WebGME tool and these services may be reused from different client tools. The first functionality is focused on the automated generation of technical documentation that allows visualizing the internal structure of a system and its call map, as an agile way of navigating between the components visually, but being able to access the developed code at the same time. This documentation may be generated in several formats like word, powerpoint, pdf or html, and there are templates for analysis and design. Figure 4 shows an example of documentation design profile which is created from the domain model in html.

The second feature is a system quality analyzer service that identifies technological debt based on unused variables, repeated code blocks, lack of control in the possible passage of null parameters or exception handling blocks without content, among others. This detail of the quality is extended through a static analyzer of a system, always based on the models and not from the source code, which allows to graphically analyze how maintainable a system is and the main risks detected in the face of evolution or modernization, creating the equivalent to a model-based Sonarqube [31] dashboard panel. Figure 5 shows an analysis model with hyperlinks to the erroneous elements as well as a dashboard panel to quickly get an idea of its technological debt.

The third functionality is a technical debt reduction service that realizes a set of changes on business logic model according to various transformation patterns that can help to maintain the system more easily, among others: i) deletion of unused variables, function blocks, domain or persistence elements; ii) control of datatypes in parameter binding; iii) normalization of naming; iv) initialization of variables, and; v) conversion from complex data structures to equivalent domain model elements. Finally there is a service to export all models to *json* so that this models may be used by external code generators.

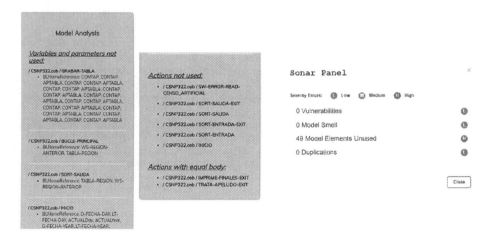

Fig. 5. Model based sonar and QA diagnosis from models

6   Evaluation

For the development of the platform we have followed an iterative and incremental methodology. We have started from a simplified set of legacy systems from real clients to validate each of the stages of the MDRE cycle during its development. According to the different potential purposes of a reverse engineering empirical study [13], our main motivation was to evaluate the feasibility of the technical proposal with real large legacy systems, so that our evaluation method is a proof of concept. To validate the proposal, a set of real maintenance projects of large legacy systems have been used. In some of them we have not achieved 100% coverage of the source code because discovery services have limitations such as: i) Spring framework annotations are ignored ; ii) third party libraries are parsed only when included in maven pom.xml and accessible by maven central repository, or; iii) cobol code cannot include sql sentences. This way we only expose a summary of relevant pilot projects in which reverse engineering coverage was 100% without manual work and are shown in Table 1:

Table 1. Most relevant real projects used for validation.

Project	Legacy	Source	Size
P1	Banking transactional	Cobol	636 lines
P2	Banking batch	Cobol Micro Focus	603 lines + 17 functions
P3	Integration platform	Java 6	400 classes
P4	Online ecommerce	Java 6	110 classes
P5	Management system	Dump script SQL	1379 tables

Table 2 shows a summary of the reverse results obtained. The process time is detailed, which includes the reading and parsing of the grammar, its conversion to ASTM and its subsequent conversion to the domain, business logic and persistence models. Additionally, figures of the size of these models, expressed in metaelements, including all the nodes and the connections between them, are shown.

Table 2. Process time and model size generated from source code.

Project	Reverse process time	Domain Size	Business Logic Size	Persistence Size
P1	0:00:59	864	71283	0
P2	0:01:06	1062	92693	0
P3	0:04:39	444080	5124307	0
P4	0:03:09	1400	1319600	0
P5	0:02:08	0	0	1612781

Once the transition to technology independent models has been made, in all of them we have been able to: i) perform automatic generation of documentation in less than one minute in any format; ii) perform the analysis of the technological debt, both detailed and sonar panel, in less than two minutes; iii) generate a new model that reduces the technological debt in less than three minutes. Due to confidentiality agreements with clients, we do not include details on the existing technical debt in the projects, but we do include details on the value that the solution provides to our maintenance teams. To this end, we have performed an analysis of the reduction in time and effort required to understand and document a legacy system, comparing it with the historical data available at the corporate level, as it is shown in Table 3:

Table 3. Summary of the effort and time reduction obtained.

KPI	Method	Average Value
Reduction of effort in analyzing a legacy system	Person hours required with STRATO vs Person hours required in historical data for similar size and complexity projects	75%
Reduction of time in analyzing a legacy system	Working period (days) required with STRATO vs Working period (days) required in historical data for similar size and complexity projects	87%
Reduction of effort for generating technical documentation	Person hours required with STRATO vs Person hours required in historical data for similar size and complexity projects	99%

7   Lessons Learned

In this section we are going to share some of the lessons learned when running this applied research project in a corporate environment with large real legacy systems. These thoughts are divided into four perspectives: industrial, technological, academic and finally we write down some reflections and open questions for the MDE community.

From a business perspective: 1) pilot projects have validated there is immediate business value when maintaining the same code base and a potential differential factor in the market: i) an average saving of 75% of the effort needed to understand how a legacy system is built and technological debt analysis, compared to historical maintenance team data; ii) elimination of interpretation errors when creating the legacy system documentation, which reduces the risk of misinterpretation when creating the work plan; iii) more than 40% of clients interviewed perceive added value in maintaining their legacy systems using these kind of automation tools, especially in banking sector. 2) the proposal is valid for any technology but depending on the project it may not be profitable. It is necessary to evaluate the cost of developing the discovery service of a technology stack when not only the grammar changes but also when there are proprietary libraries that condition the technical debt analysis. For example, when there is a proprietary library that manages a transactional and should only be used from certain components. This requires new validation rules beyond the interaction between logical blocks and requires changes on current analyzers; 3) customers interviews have confirmed that business case for reverse engineering is not in automating technology modernization. They want to know how a legacy system was built so they can best incorporate it when building a new solution, not simply transform a system from one programming language to another, and; 4) in some projects a static analysis of the code is not enough, it is necessary to combine it with usage based logs to understand and improve its dynamic behavior. The lack of this functionality has been a barrier to its use in some pilots.

From a technological perspective: 5) we believe that it is feasible to perform a layered MDRE process using PIM ASTM, although it is necessary to perform a set of interpretations of how to map certain elements of each specific language, for example a Cobol *DISPLAY* statement, to the ASTM metaelements. We have not found a standard guide on how to map PSM AST to PIM ASTM; 6) although there are web-based MBSE tools like WebGME, their mechanisms for M2M transformations are not valid for very large systems. We have experienced memory or timeout issues when processing models with hundreds of thousands of nodes, so we have modified the architecture adding external services outside of the tool to ensure its scalability, and; 7) the effort to adapt the solution to new grammars is assumable, but to be able to analyze the technical debt at the architecture level, it is necessary to extend the business logic metamodel to be able to characterize the semantics of certain blocks, their relationships and constraints, as well as to be able to analyze runtime data or functional programming languages. We have not found any standard or existing technical approach for these needs.

At an academic level, understood by the ability to understand and reuse research results: 8) although we have extended the OMG ASTM standard, its formal specification in XSD format contains form errors and is not consistent with the official document specification, which has led us to question whether we are the first company to approach a real project with all the metaelements of the standard without reducing its scope; 9) one of the conclusions of the review done by Tonella et al. [13] was the need to adopt a common framework for the execution of experiments in reverse engineering. Many years later, we have not found a way to analyze and measure the value of reverse engineering or to compare with other academic or industry initiatives; 10) we have detected a gap between academia and industry, in the sense that many of the publications or open research projects are far from the possibility of being used in a practical way for real cases, due to the fact that the scope of the investigations is generally limited. As an example, we have not been able to parse complex *java* expressions with most of the existing proposals reviewed in the state of the art, and; 11) the existence of research articles that summarize and systematically analyze the publications or tools has allowed us to quickly obtain a global vision of the state of the art, so from the industry we highly value this type of contributions that allow us to identify research status and pending challenges. We have not been able to find the same level of reviews at a practical level, who has tested what, how they have done it and what they have obtained, in order to have a summary at the level of research projects applied to the industry.

Finally, we write down a series of open questions for the community: 10) in our platform the code is transformed to models under three perspectives, the business logic, the database and the domain model, but the interactions among them are shown by the interconnections between metaelements. The component or block diagrams that can represent an architecture are not applicable to these monolithic systems either, so this question arises: what is the best graphic representation to express how a legacy system is built?; 11) at academic level there are many publications on the subject but they generally do not use real scenarios and the scope of the proposals is generally limited to hypothetical situations that are far from the problems that occur in the industry, so we ask ourselves: why validation cases in scientific publications are far from real scenarios? How can the industry contribute to raising the problems and needs to align the research results to the industry?; 12) at the standards level, OMG ASTM seems to be the most ambitious proposal to propose a systematic way for reverse engineering, but in our opinion it has remained at a theoretical level. In other areas, such as the specification of REST services, there are standards such as openAPI [32] that are complemented by a set of tools [33] that facilitate their practical adoption. Would it make sense that standards were complemented by the industry and the academy with tools that facilitate their use at a practical level?; 13) there are three areas in which we have not found any existing metamodel standard: i) is there any initiative to describe visual elements of interaction with the user independently of the technology?; ii) just as there are class diagrams for domain or relational diagrams for persistence, is there any standard to describe business logic independently of technology?, and; iii) is there any way to describe architectural constraints for a technological debt analysis?.

8   Conclusion and Future Work

In this article we have presented the experience of a multinational when addressing the technical approach to resolve the need to automate the process of understanding and maintaining large legacy systems. After analyzing the research results published by academia and the existing tools, we have concluded that there was no MDRE solution that can cover a variety of technology stacks and was designed for extensibility.

For this reason we have developed our own solution, created on top of WebGME but with an external micro-services architecture for transformations, which incorporates platform independent domain, persistence and business logic metamodels. Additionally, our proposal differs from other existing tools because the usage of an extension of the OMG ASTM standard, which allow us to separate the discovery phase from the rest of the layers to facilitate the future extension to new languages and technology stacks.

The use of this proposal in real projects has allowed us to confirm that: i) we can reduce the effort and time needed to understand a legacy system, by automating the generation of documentation; ii) we are able to improve system maintenance by automatically detecting optimizations and improvements; iii) it allows us to approach technological transformation processes in a systematized and model-based manner, with a higher level of abstraction than code, and; iv) at the business level, clients have shown their interest in being able to undertake more ambitious modernization projects by being able to shorten deadlines and costs.

'As lines of future work we have identified: i) the extension of the coverage of languages supported in the discovery layer, including new grammars and their transformation to the ASTM; ii) the inclusion of automatic code generation services to regenerate the code in various technologies based on the modified models, closing a technological modernization service; iii) the integration of code related to interaction with the user or semantics for architectural debt analysis; iv) the application of artificial intelligence techniques to automatically obtain a textual description of what a functional block does from its source code or its ASTM representation, and; v) the potential usage of software experimentation methods [34] to achieve a systematic evaluation of its value in real projects.

Acknowledgements. This work was supported in part by Centro para el Desarrollo Tecnológico Industrial (CDTI) under Grant IDI-20210948 (STRATO, nuevaS herramienTas para la modeRnizAción de sisTemas heredadOs).

References

1. Ruiz, F.: An approach for model-driven data reengineering (Doctoral dissertation, PhD dissertation, University of Murcia) (2016)
2. Object Management Group, Inc. Object Management Group (2012). http://www.omg.org
3. Raibulet, C., Fontana, F.A., Zanoni, M.: Model-driven reverse engineering approaches: a systematic literature review. IEEE Access **5**, 14516–14542 (2017)
4. Rugaber, S., Stirewalt, K.: Model-driven reverse engineering. IEEE Software **21**(4), 45–53 (2004)
5. Favre, J.M.: Foundations of model (Driven)(Reverse) engineering: models-Episode I: stories of the fidus papyrus and of the solarus. In Dagstuhl Seminar Proceedings. Schloss Dagstuhl-Leibniz-Zentrum für Informatik (2005)
6. Object Management Group, Inc. Arquitecture Driven Modernization Task Force (2022). https://www.omg.org/adm/
7. Pérez-Castillo, R., de Guzmán, I.G.-R., Piattini, M.: Knowledge discovery metamodel-ISO/IEC 19506: a standard to modernize legacy systems. Comput. Stand. Interf. **33**(6), 519–532 (2011)
8. Object Management Group, Architecture-Driven Modernization: Abstract Syntax Tree Metamodel (ASTM), OMG document number: formal/2011-01-05 (2011)
9. Object Management Group, Automated Source Code Maintainability Measure TM (ASCMM TM), OMG document number: formal/2016-01-01 (2016)
10. Object Management Group, Structured Patterns Metamodel Standard (SPMS), OMG document number: formal/2011-01-05 (2017)
11. Object Management Group, Structured Metrics Metamodel (SMM), OMG document number: formal/2018-03-01 (2018)

12. Bruneliere, H., Cabot, J., Dupé, G., Madiot, F.: Modisco: a model driven reverse engineering framework. Inf. Softw. Technol. **56**(8), 1012–1032 (2014)
13. Tonella, P., Torchiano, M., Du Bois, B., Systä, T.: Empirical studies in reverse engineering: state of the art and future trends. Empirical Softw. Eng. **12**, 551–571 (2007)
14. Pascal, A.: Case studies in model-driven reverse engineering. In: Proceedings of the 7th International Conference on Model-Driven Engineering and Software Development, pp. 256–263. SCITEPRESS-Science and Technology Publications, Lda (2019)
15. Baqais, A.A.B., Alshayeb, M.: Automatic software refactoring: a systematic literature review. Softw. Q. J. **28**(2), 459–502 (2020)
16. Pawlak, R., Monperrus, M., Petitprez, N., Noguera, C., Seinturier, L.: Spoon: a library for implementing analyses and transformations of java source code. Softw. Pract. Experience **46**(9), 1155–1179 (2016)
17. coAST coala Abstract Syntax Tree https://github.com/coala/coAST
18. Izquierdo, J.L.C., Cuadrado, J.S., Molina, J.G.: Gra2MoL: a domain specific transformation language for bridging grammarware to modelware in software modernization. In: Workshop on Model-Driven Software Evolution, pp. 1–8 (2008)
19. Iung, A., et al.: Systematic mapping study on domain-specific language development tools. Empirical Softw. Eng. **25**(5), 4205–4249 (2020). https://doi.org/10.1007/s10664-020-09872-1
20. Maróti, M., et al.: Next generation (meta) modeling: web-and cloud-based collaborative tool infrastructure. MPM@ MoDELS **1237**, 41–60 (2014)
21. AToMPM: a tool for multi-paradigm modeling. (n.d.). https://atompm.github.io/
22. Pyro: a collaborative, meta-model-driven, Web-based and graphical modeling environment. (n.d.). https://pyro.scce.info/
23. Eclipse foundation. (n.d.). Eclipse modeling framework in cloud. https://www.eclipse.org/emfcloud/
24. Eclipse foundation. (n.d.). Sirius web. https://www.eclipse.org/sirius/sirius-web.html
25. Eclipse foundation. (n.d.). Graphical language server platform for building web-based diagram editors. https://github.com/eclipse-glsp/glsp
26. Theia - cloud and desktop IDE platform. (n.d.). https://theia-ide.org/
27. Glaser, P.L.: Developing sprotty-based modeling tools for VS code (2022)
28. Object management group, Meta object facility (MOF) Core specification, version 2.5.1. OMG document number: formal/2019-10-01 (2016)
29. Parr, T.: The definitive ANTLR 4 reference. In: The Definitive ANTLR 4 Reference, pp. 1–326 (2013)
30. ISIS/Vanderbilt university, WebGME Documentation, Release 1.0.0 (2022)
31. Campbell, G.A., Papapetrou, P.: SonarQube in action. Manning Publications Co, Shelter Island (2013)
32. OpenAPI initiative, OpenAPI specification v3.1.0 (2021). https://spec.openapis.org/oas/v3.0.1
33. OpenAPI initiative, OpenAPI tools (2022). https://openapi.tools/
34. Juristo, N., Moreno, A.M.: Basics of Software Engineering Experimentation. Springer Science & Business Media (2013)

Process Monitoring

Design and Evaluation of a User Interface Concept for Prescriptive Process Monitoring

Kateryna Kubrak[1], Fredrik Milani[1], Alexander Nolte[1,2], and Marlon Dumas[1]($\boxtimes$)

[1] University of Tartu, Tartu, Estonia
{kateryna.kubrak,fredrik.milani,alexander.nolte,marlon.dumas}@ut.ee
[2] Carnegie Mellon University, Pittsburgh, PA, USA

Abstract. Prescriptive process monitoring methods recommend interventions during the execution of a process to maximize its success rate. Current research in this field focuses on algorithms to learn intervention policies that maximize the expected payoff of the interventions under certain statistical assumptions. In contrast, there has been limited attention on how to aid process stakeholders in understanding the outputs of these algorithms. In this research, we set to develop an interface to provide end users with relevant information to guide the decision on where and when to trigger interventions in a process. We draw upon an analysis of existing solutions and a review of the literature to elicit information items for a user interface for prescriptive process monitoring. Thereon, we develop a user interface concept and evaluate it with experts. The evaluation confirms the informational needs covered by the user interface concept. In addition, the evaluation shows that different end-user groups (operational users, tactical managers, and process analysts) can benefit from the information items included in the interface.

Keywords: Process Mining · Prescriptive Process Monitoring · User Interface

1 Introduction

Prescriptive process monitoring methods recommend runtime interventions that optimize the performance of a process with respect to one or more performance measures, such as the success rate – the percentage of cases of a process that end in a positive outcome [15]. For example, prescriptive process monitoring methods may recommend the next task to execute or the resource to assign a task to.

Prior work on prescriptive process monitoring focuses on developing algorithms to learn intervention policies from execution data based on process mining [12,28], machine learning [8,20,26], or causal inference [3,24] methods. In contrast, little attention has been given to ensuring that the outputs of these techniques are understandable and useful, although this has been highlighted as one of the challenges of applying process mining in organizations [17]. Only a handful of studies discuss the understandability or usefulness of prescriptive

© The Author(s) 2023
M. Indulska et al. (Eds.): CAiSE 2023, LNCS 13901, pp. 347–363, 2023.
https://doi.org/10.1007/978-3-031-34560-9_21

process monitoring outputs [6,19] or include an interface for end users [12,28]. However, in all cases, information needs of end users, such as process workers, were not explicitly analyzed nor evaluated. Previous research highlights the need of providing end users with suitable information to facilitate technology acceptance, with examples in expert systems [29] and, more recently, recommender systems [1]. Cases in manufacturing [5] and construction [16] exemplify that information provided to end-users should be comprehensible and supportive of the task at hand in order to be useful. In the context of prescriptive process monitoring, it has been shown that users sometimes do not follow recommendations produced by such solutions even if they understand them [6].

In light of this, our research objective (RO) is *to develop an interface that provides end users with relevant information items generated by prescriptive process monitoring methods.* To pursue this objective, we follow a design science methodology [11]. We first analyze existing prescriptive process monitoring methods and tools to elicit common information items. We then create a user interface concept, realized as a wireframe, and evaluate it with experts. Based on the feedback, we refine the wireframe. The evaluation shows that different end-user groups (operational users, tactical managers, and process analysts) could benefit from the information items included in the interface.

The contributions of the paper are a wireframe for a prescriptive process monitoring interface and an evaluation of information items that may help users to decide where and when to trigger interventions in a process. These contributions are relevant for developers of process mining tools and researchers. Developers benefit from a better understanding of end users' informational needs, and researchers gain insights into possible avenues for future work.

2 Background and Related Work

Prescriptive process monitoring methods recommend interventions to optimize performance measures, such as success rate (percentage of cases that end in a positive outcome) [7,24], on-time completion rate [26], cycle time [3], or processing time [20]. In the past five years, the variety of methods has grown and new methods are being proposed [15]. Existing methods differ w.r.t. the interventions they prescribe, such as the next task in a case [26] or the resource to assign a task to [27], and w.r.t. the basis of these prescriptions. Along the latter dimension, methods can be correlation-based or causality-based. For example, the authors of [13] and [7] propose methods that prescribe interventions based on correlation-based predictions of case outcomes. Causality-based methods estimate the effect of an intervention, in addition to predicting the case outcome. For example, several methods [3,24] estimate the CATE (Conditional Average Treatment Effect) of an intervention at each point during the execution of a case to recommend interventions that maximize a performance measure.

While there is a substantial body of techniques for generating recommendations for prescriptive process monitoring, only a handful of studies consider the design of user interfaces to communicate these recommendations. In this respect, one study proposes an interface for a tool that allows for discovering and visualizing treatment rules that increase the probability of positive case outcomes based on causal machine learning [2]. In [28], the authors propose a UI to recommend a process trace (representing a treatment) in the medical domain. In [12], the authors provide a UI to review case goals, predictions, and recommendations. However, these interfaces center around technological capabilities of introduced methods and not on the end-users. For instance, visualizations such as confusion matrix, scatter plot for clusters, bar charts for attributes are used in [2,28]. However, even end-users with knowledge of BPM and ML struggle with comprehending plots used for explainability [22]. In this paper, we analyze both the technical capabilities of existing methods and the needs of end-users to ensure that information items presented to them serve their needs.

Commercial process mining tools also consider the design of interfaces for predictive and prescriptive functionalities. For instance, Apromore[1] and Appian (formerly Lana)[2] include predictive process monitoring interfaces that highlight cases with a high probability of leading to a negative outcome. Other tools, such as ABBYY Timeline[3] provide the functionality to prevent deviating process flows. Celonis Action Engine[4] generates suggestions for continuous improvement based on data. In summary, these tools generate alert-based recommendations [7] based on predictions or correlations. In contrast, in this paper, we consider information items that are applicable to a broader set of prescriptive methods, also including causality-based methods and user guidelines [15].

3   Research Method

The aim of this study was to develop an interface that provides users with relevant information items generated by prescriptive process monitoring methods. We followed the design science methodology (DSM) [11] to achieve this aim. The design science methodology prescribes beginning with exploring the problem relevance and defining the objectives. In our case, the problem identified from prior work is related to defining relevant information items for users of prescriptive process monitoring outputs (sect. 2). In the next phase of DSM, we identified our objectives. To do that, we analyzed tools and conducted a domain analysis to elicit information items for our interface. This corresponds to step 1 in Fig. 1 (Sect. 3.1). The next phase of DSM is Design & Development of an artifact. We developed an initial wireframe for prescriptive process monitoring (step 2.1, Sect. 3.2). In the next phase, Evaluation & Refinement, we evaluated the wireframe with experts and refined it based on the feedback we received (steps 2.2, 2.3, Sect. 3.2). This paper communicates our findings. In the future, we aim to conduct one more iteration of the phases of Design & Development, and Evaluation & Refinement by implementing an interactive prototype and conducting a usability evaluation (step 3). This step is outside of the scope of this paper.

---

[1] https://apromore.org/.
[2] https://appian.com/.
[3] https://www.abbyy.com/timeline.
[4] https://www.celonis.com/.

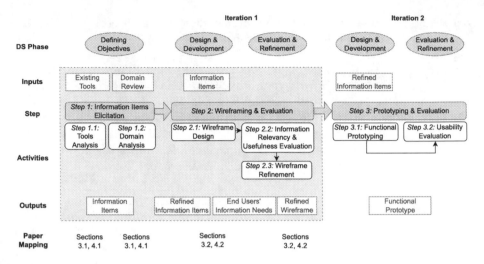

Fig. 1. Research process (steps in the scope of this paper are in blue dotted box). (Color figure online)

3.1   Step 1: Information Items Elicitation

We analyzed existing prescriptive monitoring tools to identify information items to include in a prescriptive process monitoring interface. By tools we refer to academic and commercial solutions based on prescriptive process monitoring algorithms. We also drew insights from literature using the prescriptive process monitoring framework presented in [15]. The aim of these analyses was to identify the capabilities of existing prescriptive process monitoring methods.

***Step 1.1*: Tools Analysis.** First, we analyzed commercial process mining solutions based on the survey of 17 process mining tools [25][5]. We reviewed the list to identify tools that provide "recommendations (prescriptive analytics)". According to the list, only Celonis has prescriptive functionality. We also manually examined each of the listed solutions since new features could have been introduced since the survey was conducted. Thus, we also added SAP Signavio and ABBYY Timeline to the analysis. Next, we included academic solutions that propose an interface for the prescriptive method ([12,28]). Selection of these tools is based on the review of prescriptive process monitoring methods [15]. In total, five solutions that provide interfaces were identified.

We analyzed the selected tools using a visual analytics framework [18]. More specifically, we extracted how each tool corresponds to the questions "What?" (items and attributes), "Why?" (performed task, usually expressed as a verb and a noun), and "How?" (visualization elements) as prescribed by the framework [18,21]. For example, one tool [28] presented a statistical analysis (what) to explaine the calculation (why) using a heatmap (how).

We clustered the results and elicited four main tasks ("whys") as per the visual analytics framework: (i) Describe Case, (ii) Describe Recommendation,

---

[5] https://www.processmining-software.com/tools/.

(iii) Explain Recommendation, and (iv) Assign Resource. These tasks served as the base for groups of information items for the interface. For example, we refined the first task into a group of information items "Case Description" which includes information items related to describing the ongoing case.[6]

Step 1.2: **Domain Analysis.** In this step, we analyzed the prescriptive process monitoring framework presented in [15]. In this framework, existing methods are categorized according to their objective, intervention types, modeling technique, and policy. We created a UML domain model [23] for prescriptive process monitoring based on the framework. Then, we drew insights related to information items to be additionally added. Such items include, for instance, the type of an intervention and its frequency (see Sect. 4.1 for elicited information items).

3.2   Step 2: Wireframing & Evaluation

Step 2.1: **Wireframe Design.** Using Figma[7], we created a simple wireframe [9] that the experts would use during the evaluation. We used a loan application process to exemplify included information items since it is one of the most known and used event logs in the community[8].

Step 2.2: **Information Relevancy & Usefulness Evaluation.** Finally, we conducted an evaluation of the initial wireframe to assess the information included in the wireframe at an early stage before investing resources into developing a working prototype. We particularly focused on assessing the relevancy and usefulness of the information items. For this, we recruited 13 process mining experts from different consultancies and companies that conduct process improvement projects (Table 1). The aim was to recruit individuals that have an overview of the needs of different end users. Our participants had seven years of experience with process mining on average. Ten participants represented consulting domain, and three were from product-oriented companies.

We conducted semi-structured interviews with the participants. This approach is suitable because we wanted the participants to be able to discuss their own perspective [10]. During interviews, we showed the wireframe and described the visualized information items using the example of the aforementioned loan application process. More specifically, we explained that the interface would allow the user to gain an overview of open loan applications and optimize ongoing cases. To add focus, we asked the participants to think about a recent situation where a similar interface could be used. This allowed us to discuss a specific situation instead of collecting scattered opinions from different contexts. After introducing the information, we asked the participant three questions based on our research objective. Namely, the first question aimed at evaluating the relevancy of each group of information items to the task of optimizing ongoing cases: *"Which information do you find most/least relevant and why?"* With the second question, the interviewee was asked to evaluate the usefulness of the information w.r.t. recommendations in the ongoing case: *"Which information do you*

---

[6] Full analysis is available at https://doi.org/10.6084/m9.figshare.21629615.v1.

[7] We utilized a free wireframe kit https://bit.ly/3ERovZU to design the wireframe.

[8] https://doi.org/10.4121/uuid:3926db30-f712-4394-aebc-75976070e91f.

Table 1. Evaluation interviews participants.

Code	Domain	Experience
I-01	Real Estate	12 years
I-02	Banking	7 years
I-03	Consulting (Process Mining & Data Analytics)	2 years
I-04	Consulting (Process Mining)	8 years
I-05	Consulting (Process Mining & Data Science)	5 years
I-06	Consulting (Process Mining)	7 years
I-07	Consulting (Process Mining)	7 years
I-08	Consulting (Process Mining)	9 years
I-09	Consulting (Process Mining)	18 years
I-10	Consulting (Process Mining & BPM)	2 years
I-11	Online Retail	4 years
I-12	Consulting (Process Mining)	6 years
I-13	Consulting (Process Mining)	6 years

find most/least useful and why?" Finally, with the third question, the participant provided suggestions on crucial information items not included: *"What information do you think is missing?"*

The interviews lasted between 14 and 25 min. We recorded the interviews, transcribed the audio files with Otter.ai[9], and manually corrected the transcripts. Then, we used thematic analysis [4] to analyze the interviews. We combined deductive and inductive coding. Namely, one researcher first familiarized themselves with the interviews and created the first set of codes based on our research objective. The first set included codes related to information items elicited in Sect. 3.1. For instance, we tagged *"Effect of recommendation"* on parts of the interviews that referred to information included in the group Recommendation Explanation, and *"Process model is relevant"* to comments about the process model included in Case Description. When conducting the coding, we noticed the need to add additional codes, such as *"End user"* that related to comments the interviewees made about information being relevant for different user groups. Thus, we added this code to the list. We discussed the codes inside the research team and refined them by marking to which group of information items the code related to and iterated the coding procedure. For example, *"Effect of recommendation"* was refined into *"Recommendation explanation: Effect of recommendation"*. We then clustered the codes into themes. We identified seven themes in total: one for each group of information item (e.g., *"Case Description"* and the additional themes *"End User"*, *"Cases Prioritization"*, and *"Overview (Multiple Cases)"*. For example, the theme *"End User"* captured comments about the information needs of different user groups, and the theme of *"Cases Prioritization"* described the importance of prioritizing ongoing cases according to different criteria.[10]

---

[9] https://otter.ai/.

[10] Coding scheme is available at https://doi.org/10.6084/m9.figshare.21629615.v1.

Step 2.3: Wireframe Refinement. Finally, we summarized the findings from the evaluation. Utilizing the findings about relevant information items, we adapted the wireframe (see Sect. 4.2).

4   Results

This section is organized along the methodological steps described in Fig. 1. We first elaborate on information items to be included in the interface (step 1, Sect. 4.1). Then, we describe the wireframe design, the findings from the wireframe evaluation, and the refinement based on the evaluation results (step 2, Sect. 4.2).

4.1   Step 1: Information Items Elicitation

Step 1.1: Tools Analysis & Step 1.2: Domain Analysis. As to the information items required in a prescriptive process monitoring interface (*RO*), we elicited four groups. Case Description (i) includes items describing the general attributes of an ongoing case. The second group, Recommendation Description (ii), describes basic information about the prescribed recommendations. The third is Recommendation Explanation (iii) which elaborates on how a recommendation is calculated. Finally, Resource Assignment (iv) provides an overview of resources, facilitating assigning of a suitable resource for the recommendation.

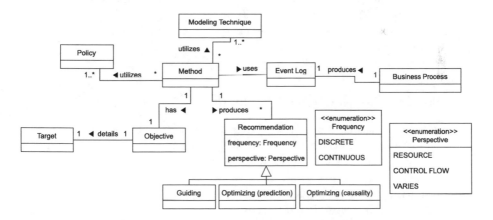

Fig. 2. Domain model for prescriptive process monitoring (based on [15]).

In addition, we categorized specific information items for each group. For example, the information item "process visualization" (process model) is included in the group Case Description because it provides general information about an ongoing case. Similarly, remaining time, impact, and statistical analysis are parts of the group Recommendation Explanation (see Table 2). Furthermore,

Table 2. List of elicited information items. Screen numbers and information items numbers correspond to the wireframe in Fig. 3.

Insights from Tools Analysis	Insights from Domain Analysis (Domain Model)	Information Items (Wireframe Mapping)
(i) Case Description (screen #2)		
(T1) Process visualization		Process model (2.2)
(T2) KPI-dependent performance data	(D1) Domain-related information (D2) Objectives	KPI status, Case-specific attributes (2.1, 1.2)
(T3) Affected KPI		
(T4) Case details		
(ii) Recommendation Description (screen #3)		
(T5) Recommendation name	(D3) Type	Type (3.2)
	(D4) Recommendation perspective	Process Aspect (3.3)
	(D5) Recommendation frequency	Frequency (3.1)
(iii) Recommendation Explanation (screen #3)		
(T6) Remaining time, impact, statistical analysis		Prediction description (3.4)
(T7) Confusion matrix, model accuracy, attributes contribution		Calculation description (3.5)
(iv) Assign Resource (screen #4)		
(T8) Assignee		Resource availability (4.1), Last update (4.2), Role (4.3)

we created a domain model (Fig. 2) derived from the prescriptive process monitoring framework [15] to add additional input to groups (i), (ii), and (iii). For instance, we included intervention frequency, which can be discrete or continuous, in the Recommendation Description (iii) group. The elicited information items are summarized in Table 2.

4.2   Step 2: Wireframing and Evaluation

***Step 2.1*: Wireframe Design.** We designed a wireframe based on the information items elicited from the tools review and the domain model in the first step of our study (Table 2). The wireframe represented a loan application process. A case in this process is a loan application, and case attributes are the requested amount, purpose, and applicant.

For the wireframe, we followed the common interface layout of process mining tools, e.g., including tabs for different categories, such as Cases and Resources. The wireframe consists of four screens (Fig. 3)[11]. The groups of information items from Table 2 refer to one individual ongoing case. However, in a process, there are multiple concurrent cases being executed. Therefore, screen #1 refers to a group of ongoing cases (loan applications) and shows an overview of case attributes. The next screens refer to a single ongoing case. Screen #2 covers information items categorized under Case Description (i in Table 2), whereas

---

[11] The full version of the wireframe can be found at https://bit.ly/3gFBDsL.

Screen #3 incorporates information items of the Recommendation Description (ii) and Recommendation Explanation (iii). Last, screen #4 refers to information items of Resource Assignment (iv).

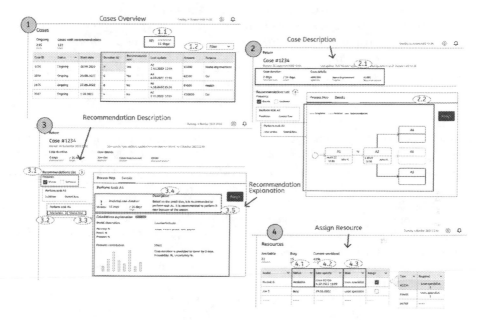

Fig. 3. Initial wireframe for prescriptive process monitoring interface. Screen numbers and information items numbers correspond to Table 2.

***Step 2.2*: Information Relevancy & Usefulness Evaluation.** In this section, we present the results of the expert evaluation (see summary in Table 3). Our findings indicate that the majority of interview participants (8) pointed towards different information needs for different end-user groups. This is evident by a comment from an interviewee: *"But what I would really define upfront is, who is going to be your consumer of the information. Because for me, these are different levels of abstraction."* (I-04). As another interviewee put it, *"I was thinking, am I looking at this strategically or operationally? What I'm seeing might change on that basis."* (I-10). More specifically, in its current state, the participants found different information items to be relevant and useful for different end-user groups. As such, our evaluation indicates three distinct groups of end users: operational, tactical manager, and process analyst. The operational user is concerned with processing the ongoing case. Next, the tactical manager is interested in optimizing the resource allocation. Finally, process analysts seek to identify improvement opportunities for the business process. In the following paragraphs, we detail the information items for different user groups.

Operational User. Interview participants expressed that operational users should focus on their main task, i.e., case processing. Therefore, they should not be overloaded with information items. As one participant expressed it: *"They [operational users] always need to stay focused, otherwise, they are lost."* (I-06). Similarly, another interviewee said that *"the user who's only doing [processing work] should be fast, and s/he should concentrate on doing task after task; something like this [looking at all screens] would be getting out of this flow."* (I-01).

Seven participants found the recommendation explanation (Fig. 3, screen #3) too complex for operational users. One interviewee exemplified by stating that *"... usually talking about the prediction accuracy, these people [operational workers] don't understand. Or have any clue about that."* (I-13). At the same time, the majority of the participants (9) considered it important for the operational user to understand the predicted effect a recommendation could have on an ongoing case. As one interviewee expressed it, *"I think it would be much more about knowing the outcome of the action rather than suggesting the action. [...] Really, rather to evaluate the impact of the action."* (I-08).

Half of the participants (6) proposed to introduce the history of following a recommendation. This would help in evaluating whether the recommendation brought the desired effect in the past: *"The next question would be also, if this is completed, did it help? If I follow the recommendation, did I achieve what was predicted, what was in the recommendation as the effect?"* (I-06). As another interviewee described, such a history *"gives me reassurance."* (I-11).

Furthermore, half of the participants (6) suggested making explanations available on demand. In this way, the user could learn about the calculation details when needed but would not be part of the information items. As described by one interviewee, *"And if s/he [user] wants to, s/he can drill down to the information about why is this recommendation. So drill down should be optional. Not mandatory for the whole process."* (I-02).

As to the group of cases (Fig. 3, screen #1), the participants found it relevant for operational users to know which cases are assigned to them. As one interviewee put it, *"So it is important for me to have an overview, how many cases do I need to action on? What are the cases that are most important? Because that gives me an idea of my workload."* (I-11). Moreover, the majority of participants (8) expressed that cases should be prioritized based on the process objective, and the user should be presented with attainable cases. In this way, *"everything which is one day late can maybe still be on time if we pick it up now."* (I-07).

In summary (Table 3), according to the experts we interviewed, the most relevant information about the recommendation for operational users is the predicted effect of the recommendation and examples of similar past instances where the recommendation was followed. The explanations should be presented to the user on demand. Furthermore, the operational user should have an overview of the cases they are responsible for and know which are prioritized based on the process objectives and the possibility of influencing the ongoing case.

Tactical Manager. According to our interviews, information about resource assignment (Fig. 3, screen #4) can be considered to be most relevant for tactical managers, i.e., those responsible for managing a group of resources. Several participants (4) consider information items on resource performance and workload as required for tactical managers to ensure efficient resource assignment: *"And that will be interesting, if I have several loan specialists, how quickly are they typically processing a car loan versus a home improvement? So, can I get a KPI for that specific case that tells me: this person is typically better in handling these type of cases."* (I-04). In addition, according to the participants, the tactical manager might be interested in an overview of cases allocated to different teams to *"see how many open cases per team member or per department, or is there a significant difference between my teams."* (I-08). In conclusion, the participants of our study perceived recommendations from the resource perspective to be the main interest of tactical managers (Table 3).

Process Analyst. Our participants perceived process analysts to be interested in analyzing recommendations prescribed for cases to elicit policies that improve the overall performance of the business process. One interviewee expressed that *"if the user is improving the processes, and s/he needs some kind of recommendation to improve it, it's the way to go."* (I-01). According to four participants, a process map (Fig. 3, screen #2) is relevant for process analysts, but would not be valuable to the other two user groups: *"I think that this part [process map], although very nice to have for analytics, is not necessary for guys who are you know, relocate resources and do day to day jobs."* (I-02). In addition, detailed explanations of recommendation calculations could help to understand their background and thus, deciding on new policies: *"And a huge level of detail of why such a recommendation is done or what is the base, it is interesting for someone that's doing process mining, but for someone that's doing operational work, it can be overwhelming."* (I-11). Therefore, in the context of our study, the most relevant information for a process analyst is a process map and a detailed explanation of recommendation calculation.

In conclusion, the evaluation provided an indication that, although the information included in the original wireframe was mostly relevant, different items were relevant for different end-user groups. Namely, an operational user responsible for ongoing cases might require information on cases assigned to them, as well as a specific recommendation on how to improve them and the estimated effect of the recommendation. A tactical manager, in addition to the overview of ongoing cases and recommendations, might require information on resources that could be assigned to the recommendations. The information relevant for a process analyst involved in improving the process should include a process model and a detailed explanation of recommendation calculation for the reasoning behind the improvement policies. Thus, with regard to the RO, an interface for prescriptive process monitoring outputs could be used by different end-user groups. It should, therefore, be adjusted depending on the target user.

***Step 2.3*: Wireframe Refinement.** We used evaluation results to refine the information items included in the wireframe (Fig. 4). According to the evaluation, no new information items had to be added. Rather, existing information items had to be adjusted. The evaluation indicated that information needs differ

Table 3. Summary of end users' information needs.

Information Items Groups	Operational User	Tactical Manager	Process Analyst
(i) Case Description	* KPI status * Case-specific attributes	* KPI status * Case-specific attributes	* Process model * KPI status * Case-specific attributes
(ii) Recommendation Description	* List of options	* List of options	* List of options * Recommendation characteristics
(iii) Recommendation Explanation	* Effect * History of past recommendations * Other details on demand	* Effect * History of past recommendations * Model description	* Effect * History of past recommendations * Model description * Original data
(iv) Resource Assignment	Not relevant	* Information on resources	No information

for different user groups. We refined the wireframe according to the needs of the operational worker. Operational users can be expected to benefit the most from using the interface as they are responsible for optimizing ongoing cases. To achieve this, we used the summary of information needs of operational workers from Table 3. As such, we added prioritization to the current duration column on screen #1 as it refers to ongoing cases. In screen #2, we removed the process map as the evaluation showed it to be less relevant for operational users. In its place, we added information items from the Recommendation Explanation group (iii), making them available on demand. For the explanations, we highlighted the effect of the proposed recommendation and added similar cases. Thus, screen #3, which initially contained the Recommendation Explanation group (iii) was removed. We also removed screen #4 with the Resource Assignment group (iv) since its items were found to be more relevant for tactical managers.

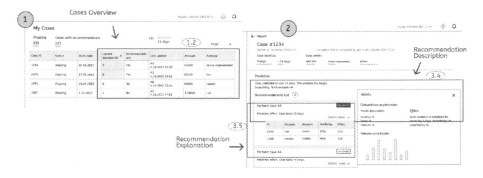

Fig. 4. Refined wireframe for prescriptive process monitoring interface. Screen numbers and information items numbers correspond to Table 2.

5   Discussion

In this section, we discuss information items for a prescriptive process monitoring interface (RO). We draw implications for research (Sect. 5.1) and practice (Sect. 5.2) and highlight the limitations of our study (Sect. 5.3).

5.1   Implications for Research

Our findings indicate that end users of prescriptive process monitoring methods are not homogeneous. We identified three distinct user groups (operational users, tactical managers, and process analysts) that could benefit from prescriptive process monitoring outputs. We also found that each user group might consider different information items as relevant and useful. For instance, our evaluation indicated a potential need for explanations of how recommendations are calculated, but – depending on the user group – at different levels of detail.

Process analysts will likely seek detailed explanations for recommendation to understand why and how to improve the business process. Thus, detailed explanations and process models might be more useful for process analysts. This finding is aligned with [14] that reports on process analysts using process maps and advanced views into the data as a starting point for process improvement. This might be also be one of the reasons for the emergence of research on explainable prescriptive process monitoring ([19]). Such works focus on information items that, according to our evaluation, would best be suited for process analysts. However, operational users might consider explainability differently. Operational users – according to our findings – consider information items about the effect and historical evidence of following the same recommendations as most relevant and useful. This is confirmed by [22], who found information about past actions for similar cases valuable for decision making. Explainability is thus relevant for both operational users and process analysts, but in a different way.

In light of this, operational users seem to require an estimate of the effect of the recommendation on the outcome (e.g., [3,24]). However, most existing methods rely on correlations between case characteristics and the probability of a given case outcome. In other words, they are correlation-based [15]. Thus, a possible venue for future research could be developing causality-based methods that can estimate the effect of a proposed intervention using causal models.

Existing studies focus on what can be communicated based on the prescriptive method rather than which user group to target or their information needs. For instance, in [2], the authors present a tool that allows for discovering and visualizing treatment rules that increase the probability of positive case outcomes, but the intended user is not discussed. Likewise, prescriptive methods that prescribe next actions, such as [12,28], also include information items that could be more suitable for process analysts. Thus, the effectiveness of prescriptive methods might be limited if the needs of the intended user group are not considered. Therefore, another direction of future work is customization of interfaces based on the information needs of the end users.

5.2   Implications for Practice

Our findings indicate that it is helpful to consider the information items that intended end users consider relevant. However, existing tools providing prescriptive process monitoring functionality (e.g., Celonis) focus predominantly on process analysts, although some parts are better suited for tactical managers (e.g., resource assignment). When commercial tools are enhanced to support operational users, it will be necessary to consider their informational needs. Our findings indicate that operational users might require less information than tactical managers or process analysts. Rather, operational users focus on relevant information to execute a recommendation, such as cases assigned to them, the recommendation, and its predicted effect.

We also found that prioritizing ongoing cases can be also relevant and useful. In other words, when starting to optimize ongoing cases, it is not feasible to address all cases at once. Therefore, ongoing cases could be assigned a priority to help operational users determine which case to work on next. Prioritization can be based on process objectives or specific organizational criteria.

5.3   Limitations

For our study, we applied the design science research methodology [11]. There are several limitations associated with different stages of the approach. First, when eliciting information items to include in the interface, we began by analyzing existing tools and reviewing the outputs of existing methods. This could lead to missing information items required by end users. We mitigated this threat by conducting an evaluation with 13 experts from different domains and backgrounds. Second, it is possible that conducting the evaluation with different experts from different domains might have yielded different results. Using examples of other processes in the wireframe might have also yielded different results. However, we evaluated the information items and not the particular process attributes. Third, we opted to conduct the evaluation with experts and not end users, which poses an additional limitation. This limitation is acceptable because our aim was to get a broad perspective about the interface. Another limitation is associated with only evaluating the wireframe concept. We acknowledge this limitation for this study. However, we plan to conduct a second evaluation on an interactive prototype using a real-life scenario. Next, when analyzing qualitative data, there is a threat of misinterpreting the data due to bias or subjectivity. To reduce this threat, we discussed the data collected and analyzed within the research team. Finally, we abstain from making causal claims and prioritizing specific findings. Instead, we describe the observations made and discuss differences in the information items required by different end-user groups.

6   Conclusion

In this paper, we aimed to develop an interface that provides end users with relevant information items from prescriptive process monitoring methods. To achieve this objective, we analyzed existing tools and research to elicit information items to include in an interface. We elicited four main groups of information items: Case Description, Recommendation Description, Recommendation Explanation, and Resource Assignment. We then developed the first version of the interface and evaluated it with experts. The results indicate that the included information items are relevant. However, we also observed that prescriptive monitoring outputs are of interest to three distinct user groups (operational worker, tactical manager, and process analyst). Thus, certain information items are more relevant for one user group as compared to another. The contribution of this paper is an initial version of an interface and a summary of information items relevant to each of the three user groups when working with prescriptive process monitoring outputs. We also formulate implications for practice, in particular, for developers of process mining tools, and provide insight into directions for further academic research. For future work, we aim to implement the wireframe for operational users and evaluate its usability and usefulness with the users on a real-life scenario.

Acknowledgements. This research is supported by the Estonian Research Council (PRG1226) and the European Research Council (PIX Project).

References

1. Afolabi, A.O., Toivanen, P.: Improving the design of a recommendation system using evaluation criteria and metrics as a guide. J. Syst. Inf. Technol. **21**(3), 304–324 (2019)
2. Bozorgi, Z.D., Kopolov, A., Dumas, M., Rosa, M.L., Polyvyanyy, A.: Prolift: automated discovery of causal treatment rules from event logs (extended abstract). In: ICPM Doctoral Consortium / Demo. CEUR Workshop Proceedings, vol. 3299, pp. 108–112. CEUR-WS.org (2022)
3. Bozorgi, Z.D., Teinemaa, I., Dumas, M., Rosa, M.L., Polyvyanyy, A.: Prescriptive process monitoring for cost-aware cycle time reduction. In: ICPM, pp. 96–103. IEEE (2021)
4. Braun, V., Clarke, V.: Using thematic analysis in psychology. Qualit. Res. Psychol. **3**(2), 77–101 (2006)
5. Colceriu, C., Leichtmann, B., Brell-Cokcan, S., Jonas, W., Nitsch, V.: From task analysis to wireframe design: An approach to user-centered design of a GUI for mobile HRI at assembly workplaces. In: RO-MAN, pp. 876–883. IEEE (2022)
6. Dees, M., de Leoni, M., van der Aalst, W.M.P., Reijers, H.A.: What if process predictions are not followed by good recommendations? In: BPM (Industry Forum). CEUR Workshop Proceedings, vol. 2428, pp. 61–72. CEUR-WS.org (2019)
7. Fahrenkrog-Petersen, S.A., et al.: Fire now, fire later: alarm-based systems for prescriptive process monitoring. Knowl. Inf. Syst. **64**(2), 559–587 (2022)
8. Galanti, R., Coma-Puig, B., de Leoni, M., Carmona, J., Navarin, N.: Explainable predictive process monitoring. In: ICPM, pp. 1–8. IEEE (2020)
9. Hamm, M.J.: Wireframing Essentials. Packt Publishing Ltd, Birmingham (2014)

10. Harrell, M.C., Bradley, M.A.: Data collection methods. semi-structured interviews and focus groups. Technical Report, Rand National Defense Research Institute, Santa Monica, USA (2009)
11. Hevner, A.R., March, S.T., Park, J., Ram, S.: Design science in information systems research. MIS Q. **28**, 75–105 (2004)
12. Huber, S., Fietta, M., Hof, S.: Next step recommendation and prediction based on process mining in adaptive case management. In: S-BPM ONE, pp. 3:1–3:9. ACM (2015)
13. Khan, A., et al.: DeepProcess: supporting business process execution using a MANN-based recommender system. In: Hacid, H., Kao, O., Mecella, M., Moha, N., Paik, H. (eds.) ICSOC 2021. LNCS, vol. 13121, pp. 19–33. Springer, Cham (2021). https://doi.org/10.1007/978-3-030-91431-8_2
14. Kubrak, K., Milani, F., Nolte, A.: Process mining for process improvement - an evaluation of analysis practices. In: Guizzardi, R., Ralyté, J., Franch, X. (eds) Research Challenges in Information Science. RCIS 2022. LNBIP, vol. 446, pp. 214–230. Springer, Cham (2022). https://doi.org/10.1007/978-3-031-05760-1_13
15. Kubrak, K., Milani, F., Nolte, A., Dumas, M.: Prescriptive process monitoring: quo vadis? PeerJ Comput. Sci. **8**, e1097 (2022)
16. Makarov, D., Vahdatikhaki, F., Miller, S., Mowlaei, S., Dorée, A.: Usability assessment of compaction operator support systems using virtual prototyping. Autom. Constr. **129**, 103784 (2021)
17. Martin, N., et al.: Opportunities and challenges for process mining in organizations: Results of a delphi study. Bus. Inf. Syst. Eng. **63**(5), 511–527 (2021)
18. Munzner, T.: Visualization Analysis and Design. A.K. Peters visualization series, A K Peters (2014)
19. Padella, A., de Leoni, M., Dogan, O., Galanti, R.: Explainable process prescriptive analytics. In: ICPM. IEEE (2022)
20. Park, G., Song, M.: Prediction-based resource allocation using LSTM and minimum cost and maximum flow algorithm. In: ICPM, pp. 121–128. IEEE (2019)
21. Raimbaud, P., Espitia Castillo, J.C., Guerra-Gomez, J.A.: A visual analytics framework case study: understanding Colombia's national administrative department of statistics datasets. In: Ruiz, P.H., Agredo-Delgado, V. (eds.) HCI-COLLAB 2019. CCIS, vol. 1114, pp. 57–72. Springer, Cham (2019). https://doi.org/10.1007/978-3-030-37386-3_5
22. Rizzi, W., et al.: Explainable predictive process monitoring: a user evaluation. CoRR abs/2202.07760 (2022)
23. Selic, B.: A systematic approach to domain-specific language design using UML. In: ISORC, pp. 2–9. IEEE Computer Society (2007)
24. Shoush, M., Dumas, M.: Prescriptive process monitoring under resource constraints: a causal inference approach. In: Munoz-Gama, J., Lu, X. (eds.) ICPM 2021. LNBIP, vol. 433, pp. 180–193. Springer, Cham (2022). https://doi.org/10.1007/978-3-030-98581-3_14
25. Viner, D., Stierle, M., Matzner, M.: A process mining software comparison. CEUR Workshop Proceedings, vol. 2703, pp. 19–22. CEUR-WS.org (2020)
26. Weinzierl, S., Dunzer, S., Zilker, S., Matzner, M.: Prescriptive business process monitoring for recommending next best actions. In: Fahland, D., Ghidini, C., Becker, J., Dumas, M. (eds.) BPM 2020. LNBIP, vol. 392, pp. 193–209. Springer, Cham (2020). https://doi.org/10.1007/978-3-030-58638-6_12

27. Wibisono, A., Nisafani, A.S., Bae, H., Park, Y.-J.: On-the-fly performance-aware human resource allocation in the business process management systems environment using naïve bayes. In: Bae, J., Suriadi, S., Wen, L. (eds.) AP-BPM 2015. LNBIP, vol. 219, pp. 70–80. Springer, Cham (2015). https://doi.org/10.1007/978-3-319-19509-4_6

28. Yang, S., et al.: A data-driven process recommender framework. In: KDD, pp. 2111–2120. ACM (2017)

29. Ye, L.R., Johnson, P.E.: The impact of explanation facilities on user acceptance of expert systems advice. Mis Q. **19**, 157–172 (1995)

Learning When to Treat Business Processes: Prescriptive Process Monitoring with Causal Inference and Reinforcement Learning

Zahra Dasht Bozorgi[1], Marlon Dumas[2], Marcello La Rosa[1],
Artem Polyvyanyy[1], Mahmoud Shoush[2], and Irene Teinemaa[1,2(✉)]

[1] University of Melbourne, Parkville, VIC 3010, Australia
zahra.dashtbozorgi@student.unimelb.edu.au,
{marcello.larosa,artem.polyvyanyy}@unimelb.edu.au,
irene.teinemaa@gmail.com
[2] University of Tartu, Narva Mnt 18, 51009 Tartu, Estonia
{marlon.dumas,mahmoud.shoush}@ut.ee

Abstract. Increasing the success rate of a process, i.e. the percentage of cases that end in a positive outcome, is a recurrent process improvement goal. At runtime, there are often certain actions (a.k.a. treatments) that workers may execute to lift the probability that a case ends in a positive outcome. For example, in a loan origination process, a possible treatment is to issue multiple loan offers to increase the probability that the customer takes a loan. Each treatment has a cost. Thus, when defining policies for prescribing treatments to cases, managers need to consider the net gain of the treatments. Also, the effect of a treatment varies over time: treating a case earlier may be more effective than later in a case. This paper presents a prescriptive monitoring method that automates this decision-making task. The method combines causal inference and reinforcement learning to learn treatment policies that maximize the net gain. The method leverages a conformal prediction technique to speed up the convergence of the reinforcement learning mechanism by separating cases that are likely to end up in a positive or negative outcome, from uncertain cases. An evaluation on two real-life datasets shows that the proposed method outperforms a state-of-the-art baseline.

Keywords: prescriptive process monitoring · causal inference · reinforcement learning

1 Introduction

Prescriptive process monitoring is a family of techniques to recommend actions (herein called *treatments*) that, if executed, are likely to optimise a process with respect to one or more process performance indicators [10]. For example, in a

---

I. Teinemaa—Now at DeepMind.

M. Indulska et al. (Eds.): CAiSE 2023, LNCS 13901, pp. 364–380, 2023.
https://doi.org/10.1007/978-3-031-34560-9_22

loan origination process, a treatment could be to send an additional loan offer with better conditions to a customer who is hesitating to accept a loan. This treatment is intended to increase a performance indicator known as the success rate – the percentage of cases that end in a positive outcome, which in this context means ending in an accepted loan offer.

Each treatment has a cost. This cost is often sufficiently high to make it impractical to treat every case. Furthermore, the effect of the treatment might be different across cases. A treatment that works well for one case, might be ineffective on others. Another important aspect of applying treatments is their timing. Coming back to the loan origination example, sending an additional offer later in the process might be less effective than sending it earlier.

Previous studies on prescriptive process monitoring propose to produce treatment recommendations by using machine learning models – trained on historical execution data – to predict the outcome of each case [7,25]. In particular, recommending treatments using online reinforcement learning (RL), combined with predictive models, has shown promising results [12]. However, this prior approach has two key limitations. First, given that it makes recommendations based on outcome predictions, it tends to treat cases that are likely to end up in a negative outcome, even when treating a case is unlikely to switch its outcome from negative to positive [4]. In other words, this prior approach does not consider the effectiveness of the treatments. The second limitation is concerned with the use of online RL, which requires learning through trial and error. This means that the RL agent makes mistakes until it eventually learns to perform well. In addition, the convergence of the agent may be slow, e.g. the RL agent may need to see hundreds of cases before converging to a satisfactory treatment policy.

Given the limitations discussed above, in this paper we study the problem of when-to-treat policies for business processes, where a decision maker-maker decides, on the fly, *when*, if at all should a process case receive an outcome-improving treatment.

This paper proposes an RL method for learning treatment policies for prescriptive process monitoring, which addresses the above problem as follows:

- To take into account the effectiveness of the treatments, it incorporates causal effect estimations into the RL process.
- To train the RL agent offline, it enhances the available dataset with so-called *alternative outcomes*. The enhanced dataset simulates a realistic environment, so that the RL agent can get feedback on its choices offline.
- To speed up the convergence of the RL agent, it leverages a method called conformal prediction – a predictive modeling method that segregates cases that are almost certain to finish in a positive class, from uncertain cases. Armed with this information, the RL agent is able to avoid treating cases that most likely will end up in a positive outcome anyway.

The rest of this paper is organised as follows. Section 2 reviews related work. Section 3 introduces relevant concepts and notations. The proposed method is discussed in Sect. 4, while an experimental evaluation is reported in Sect. 5. Finally, Sect. 6 draws conclusion and discusses future work.

2   Related Work

2.1   Prescriptive Process Monitoring

Kubrak *et al.* [10] present a survey of prescriptive monitoring methods. This survey classifies prescriptive process monitoring approaches into two groups. The first group aims to reduce the defect rate, while the second optimizes quantitative case performance. This paper falls in the first group since we aim to optimise a binary process outcome. In addition, existing methods can be classified by their perspective. Most prescribed treatments relate to the resource or control perspective, but other treatments are also considered. Treatments can be binary, discrete, or real-valued. This paper abstracts from the type of treatment as long as it can be represented as a binary variable.

Teinemaa *et al.* [25] propose a prediction-based system that uses empirical thresholding to fire alarms when treatment is needed. This work was later extended by Fahrenkrog-Petersen *et al* [7], who discovered that firing the treatment later some time after the threshold is reached may improve the outcome at lower cost. Metzger *et al.* [12] use online RL to learn the best time for triggering treatments. They show that RL outperforms empirical thresholding. These methods, however, do not address the effectiveness of the treatment or make simplistic assumptions about effectiveness. In this paper, we address these limitations.

In another line of work, prescriptive methods are used to recommend the next best activity. De Leoni *et al.* [11] prescribe the next tasks to the process workers helping clients with a job search. Weinzierl *et al.* [28] prescribe the next activity predicted to maximize the chance of a positive outcome. In a study by Batoulis [2], a proactive decision support framework is proposed that forecasts events and suggests the best action to execute. Another next activity recommender proposed by Nakatumba *et al.* [13] is based on predictions obtained from similar cases. Padella *et al.* [16] provided an explainability framework for prescriptive analytics of business processes. These works differ from ours in that the next best action is not a special treatment, only applied when the case is in a negative state. But the actions are part of the normal process execution.

2.2   Causal Inference in Process Mining

A number of studies in the field of process mining are concerned with discovering and estimating causal effects in processes. Koorn *et al.* [9] discover the cause-effect relationship between a worker's response to aggressive situations and their effectiveness. In subsequent work, they account for possible confounding variables [8]. Some approaches use structural equation models to discover root causes and answer counterfactual questions about undesired outcomes [17,18]. These methods are concerned with discovering causal effects, while we use causal effect estimation for outcome improvement. Our previous work proposes a rule-based recommendation method based on causal effects to improve process outcomes [3]. In another work, we use causal effects to address process duration reduction at runtime [4]. While our previous studies focus on finding the best cases to treat, in this work, we study when to treat a case. Shoush & Dumas [22] proposed a prescriptive approach based on both predictive and causal estimates while considering resource constraints. However, they do not address the when-to-treat problem based on the uncertainty of the underlying models.

3   Background

This section introduces process mining-related definitions used in the rest of the paper and introduces causal inference, reinforcement learning, and conformal prediction concepts upon which the proposal relies.

3.1   Process Mining

Definition 1 (Event, Trace, Event Log). An *event* is a tuple $(a, c, t, (d_1, v_1), \ldots, (d_m, v_m))$, $m \in \mathbb{N}_0$, where a is an activity name, c is a case identifier, t is a timestamp, and $(d_1, v_1), \ldots, (d_m, v_m)$ are attribute-value pairs. A *trace* is a finite sequence $\sigma = \langle e_1, \ldots, e_n \rangle$, $n \in \mathbb{N}$, of events with the same case identifier in ascending timestamp order. An *event log*, or *log*, is a multiset of traces.

Definition 2 (k-Prefix). A *k-prefix* of a trace $\langle e_1, \ldots, e_n \rangle$, $n \in \mathbb{N}_0$, is a sequence $\langle e_1, \ldots, e_k \rangle$, $0 \leq k \leq n$.

Definition 3 (Sequence encoder). A sequence encoder $f : S \to X_1 \times \cdots \times X_p$ is a function that takes a (partial) trace σ and transforms it to a feature vector X in the p-dimensional vector space $X_1 \times \cdots \times X_p$ with $X_i \subseteq \mathbb{R}, 1 \leq i \leq p$.

3.2   Causal Inference

We use the *Neyman-Rubin Potential Outcomes Framework* [20] for causal inference. An *intervention*, or a **treatment** is an action that can be done during the execution of a process to optimise the outcome of the case. In this paper, we consider the binary treatment setting where the treatment is denoted by a binary variable $T \in \{0, 1\}$, with $T = 1$ denoting when the treatment is applied to a case and $T = 0$ otherwise. According to the potential outcomes framework, each case has two potential outcomes: $Y(1)$ denoting the outcome under treatment and $Y(0)$ the outcome under no treatment. The effectiveness of the treatment is not constant across cases and throughout different points in the case. To measure the effectiveness of the treatment, we use the *Conditional Average Treatment Effect* (CATE):

Definition 4 (Conditional Average Treatment Effect). Let X be a set of attributes that characterize a case. Then, the *conditional average treatment effect* (CATE) of the case is defined as follows:

$$CATE : \theta(x) = \mathbb{E}[Y(1) - Y(0) \mid X = x].$$

To identify causal effects, we make the four standard assumptions in the potential outcomes framework: positivity, ignorability, consistency, and no-interference.

Assumption 1 *(Positivity)*. Every case has the potential to be selected for treatment, that is, $P(T = t \mid X = x) > 0$, for every treatment t and every vector x representing a prefix.

Assumption 2 *(Ignorability)*. Treatment assignment is independent of the potential outcomes conditioned on pre-treatment confounders X: $Y(1), Y(0) \perp\!\!\!\perp T \mid X$.

Assumption 3 *(Consistency)*. Observations of outcome after treatment selection are consistent with potential outcomes: $Y = Y(t)$ if $T = t$ for all t.

Assumption 4 *(No-interference)*. Treatment decision for one case does not affect treatment decisions for other cases.

Many approaches for estimating the CATE have been proposed in the literature. One such method that we use in this work is Causal Forest.

Causal Forest is a causal estimator proposed by Athey *et al.* [27]. It is an ensemble of causal trees [1]. Causal trees are a modification of decision trees that make them suitable for estimating causal effects. In decision trees, the splits aim to separate classes, but in causal trees, they aim to increase the expected causal effect. One major difference that distinguishes causal trees from decision trees is *honest splitting*. It means that during training, the data is divided into two sets: one for building the tree and the other for the estimation of the treatment effect after the split. A Causal Forest is constructed by aggregating the results of many honest causal trees using the subsampling method.

Realcause [14] is a method for generating realistic data with two potential outcomes. In this paper we keep the prefixes real and only generate two potential outcomes. Figure 1 describes the architecture of Realcause. First, a neural network is trained using all of the data (i.e., prefixes) to get a hidden representation.

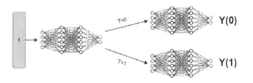

Fig. 1. Realcause potential outcome generation architecture

Then samples under treatment and no treatment are separated and two neural networks are trained for each group. The activation functions of the latter neural networks are used to parameterise distributions, which can then be sampled to generate both potential outcomes for each input sample.

3.3   Reinforcement Learning

Reinforcement learning is a branch of machine learning to train models that make a sequence of decisions. Typically, an agent is placed in an environment. It observes a state s and performs an action a from a set of actions in the action space, then observes a reward r and the next state s' as a response to a. The goal of the agent is to maximise the total cumulative reward. The agent typically starts by randomly selecting actions and receiving rewards for those actions. Through trial and error, it will figure out which actions in which conditions produce more reward. One of the main problems that the agent faces while learning is finding a good trade-off between exploration and exploitation. Exploitation means that the agent uses the knowledge already acquired to perform actions that are guaranteed to produce a lot of reward. Exploration means that the agent tries new actions to find other potentially rewarding actions. A good balance between exploration and exploitation is essential for the agent to discover all the rewarding actions.

3.4   Conformal Prediction

Conformal prediction is a method to generate prediction sets for any prediction model [19]. Given an uncertainty score by a prediction model, conformal prediction outputs a set of classes that covers the true class with mathematical guarantees. Below we describe how to construct these prediction sets and what guarantees they will have.

Suppose we have trained a prediction model $\hat{f}$ that outputs probabilities for each prediction class. We use a small set of unseen calibration data of size n to construct *conformal scores* $s_i = 1 - \hat{f}(x_i)_{Y_i}$ where $\hat{f}(x_i)_{Y_i}$ is the predicted probability of the true class. Score s_i is high if the model is very wrong, meaning that i does not conform to the training data. Next, given $s_1, \ldots, s_n$ we define $\hat{q} = \lceil (n+1)(1-\alpha) \rceil / n$ where $\lceil . \rceil$ is the ceiling function and α is a user-defined error tolerance threshold. Finally, using a separate test set X_{test}, we define the conformal prediction set as $C(X_{test}) = \{y : s(X_{test}) \leq \hat{q}\}$. In [19], it is shown that the prediction set is guaranteed to contain the true class with probability $1 - \alpha$.

4   Methodology

Suppose agent $\mathcal{A}$ is responsible for making decisions about treating ongoing cases. $\mathcal{A}$'s job is to consider each case after each event and decide whether to treat that case or not. At each decision point (after each event), $\mathcal{A}$ needs to answer the following two questions: Will applying the treatment now change the outcome of the case from negative to positive? How confident am I about the outcome of the case, regardless of treatment? To help $\mathcal{A}$ answer these questions, we train two machine learning models using past process executions: a predictive model estimating probabilities of each possible outcome and a causal model estimating the CATE of the chosen treatment. This is the first phase of the approach. In the second phase, we create a realistic environment for $\mathcal{A}$ to try different treatment policies and learn the best one. To do that, we use a generative model to generate potential outcomes for each prefix length in such a way that they are statistically indistinguishable from the actual outcomes. Finally, in the third phase, we let $\mathcal{A}$ learn the best treatment policy through trial and error. We design a reward function to guide $\mathcal{A}$ about when it makes correct or incorrect decisions. Figure 2 provides an overview of our approach. We explain each of the phases below.

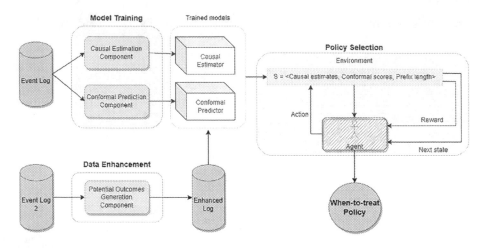

Fig. 2. Overview of the proposed approach

4.1   Model Training

Causal Effect Estimation. To answer $\mathcal{A}$'s first question, we train a causal estimator. Different from prediction methods that seek to estimate $P(Y|X)$, causal estimators estimate $CATE : P(Y(1) - Y(0)|X)$. Typically in the causal estimation literature, cases are divided into four groups: (a) Persuadables, (b) Do Not Disturbs, (c) Lost Causes, (d) Sure Things (See Fig. 3). Using causal estimation, we can separate cases into these groups. $CATE > 0$ describes the persuadables, $CATE < 0$ the do not disturbs, and $CATE = 0$ the sure things and the lost causes.

Since causal estimators are difficult to evaluate, a point estimate of the CATE may not be reliable enough to base treatment decisions on. Instead, we train the model to compute confidence intervals for CATE. The model takes a prefix σ_k with $k \leq n$ where n is the total length of the case and returns $\theta_{u,k}$ and $\theta_{l,k}$ which are the upper and lower bound for the estimated causal effect, respectively, for a prefix of length k. We use Causal Forest [27] to get these confidence intervals. Causal Forest and orthogonal random forest (ORF) [15] are two causal estimators that can produce valid confidence intervals.

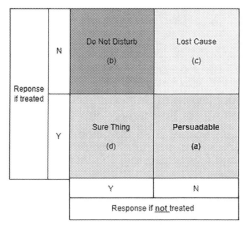

Fig. 3. Grouping of cases according to their response to treatment

We chose causal forest as we have found that it is quicker to train while having similar performance to ORF when both treatment and outcome are binary. But generally, our framework is independent of the chosen causal estimator, as long as it can produce confidence intervals.

Conformal Prediction. Having a CATE confidence interval allows agent $\mathcal{A}$ to converge to a good policy. Still, there can exist prefixes that the causal estimator is unsure about. For example, when $\theta_{u,k} > 0$ and $\theta_{l,k} < 0$. So we hypothesise that if we add an additional rigorous notion of uncertainty, such as conformal prediction, we can help the agent converge faster. Recall that with conformal prediction, we can construct prediction sets that are mathematically guaranteed to contain the true class. For binary outcome prediction, these sets will be one of the following: (a) {}, (b) {0, 1}, (c) {0}, and (d) {1}. In (a) and (b), the model is unsure about the outcome. But in (c) and (d), we have a rigorous guarantee that the case will end up with a negative and positive outcome, respectively. These correspond to the lost causes and the sure things. Because conformal prediction tells us that we are confident of the outcome based on the information in the prefix. So, showing these prediction sets to agent $\mathcal{A}$ should help it prune the search space for prefixes that need treatment because it will be sure not to treat the lost causes and the sure things that conformal prediction has identified.

To use conformal prediction, we need to train a predictive model first. This model is a function learned from the data that takes a prefix σ_k and returns two probabilities: $p_k(1)$, the probability of a positive outcome at prefix length k, and $p_k(0)$, the probability of a negative outcome. The predicted class is defined as the class with the highest probability:

$$p(\sigma_k) = Argmax(p_k(1), p_k(0)) \tag{1}$$

We use Catboost [6] to train the predictive model as it has been shown to perform well in recent works [16]. We then apply the conformal prediction algorithm as described in Sect. 3.4 to get the prediction sets. Then, we encode the prediction sets as the confidence measure ρ_k that the case will have a positive outcome. If the prediction set is (c) then $\rho_k = 0$, if the prediction set is (d) the $\rho_k = 1$, and if the prediction set is either (a) and (b) then $\rho_k = 0.5$.

4.2   Data Enhancement

In online RL, agent $\mathcal{A}$ must try different actions in different states to learn the optimal policy. But since we seek to find this policy using data, we need to simulate the environment in which the agent learns. This environment needs to be realistic enough to reflect the information in the data. In this phase, we seek to generate alternative outcomes that $\mathcal{A}$ can later use during learning to evaluate its knowledge and make decisions accordingly.

In real-world data, we only observe one of the potential outcomes in the Neyman-Rubin framework. Therefore, we cannot know the true unit-level causal effect. Recently, one solution has been to use generative machine learning to produce realistic data that is statistically indistinguishable from the original data. We can then use these generative

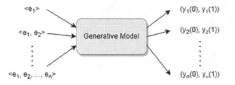

Fig. 4. Potential outcomes generation using generative machine learning

models to get two outcomes for the same feature vector describing a prefix: one outcome if $T = 1$ and another if $T = 0$. One such method is called Realcause [14] which uses a generative machine learning model to generate realistic data including the true causal effect. In our previous work [5] we successfully applied the Realcause method to generate encoded feature vectors describing cases. In this paper, however, we would like to keep agent $\mathcal{A}$'s environment as realistic as possible. Thus, we use Realcause to only generate potential outcomes for each prefix of each case (See Fig. 4).

Realcause is originally designed to handle independent data points. But in our method, each data point is a prefix and prefixes are parts of cases. So, to guide the generative model to discover this dependency, we take the following steps: we include the prefix number as a feature where for each case, this feature describes k for each prefix σ_k. Next, we convert the case identifiers to numeric values. We then include the numeric case ID and prefix numbers in model training. As Realcause directly learns the data-generating distribution, it will discover the relationship between the prefix numbers $1 \ldots n$ having the same numeric case ID. We use two multi-layer perceptrons with two hidden layers to model the treated and untreated groups. We assume a Bernoulli distribution to model the process outcome. Once the generative model is trained, we can generate an enhanced event log by sampling the outcome model under both treatment and no-treatment conditions, giving us both potential outcomes for each prefix. We use the enhanced version of the log in the policy selection phase.

4.3   Policy Selection

With two potential outcomes to create the learning environment for $\mathcal{A}$, the next step is to let $\mathcal{A}$ map its knowledge into actions by learning a treatment policy. A policy is a function π that maps a prefix σ_k to an action t. Our goal is to find a policy that maximises a net gain function. To find such a policy we use reinforcement learning. Specifically, we use the *policy-based* RL framework proposed in [12]. Below, we formulate the learning problem using RL.

As mentioned in Sect. 3.3, in reinforcement learning, an agent is placed in an environment and observes states s_k which describes the environment at each prefix length k. The agent selects an action t from action space $\mathcal{T}$ and observes: the reward r and the next state s_{k+1}. The agent then learns the best behaviour by trial and error until it reaches the optimal policy for selecting actions. To translate this learning problem into prescriptive monitoring, we modify the RL-based approach proposed by Metzger *et al.* [12]. Similar to them, we define a binary action space $\{0,1\}$ with $t = 1$ as applying the treatment and $t = 0$ as not applying it. Metzger *et al.* describe the state s to the agent as a tuple $s = (\delta_k, \gamma_k, k)$, where δ_k is the predicted deviation from a positive outcome, γ_k is a reliability score for the prediction, and k is the prefix length. We propose to modify s to contain the estimated CATE interval and the conformal prediction score: $s = (\theta_{u,k}, \theta_{l,k}, \rho_k, k)$.

One important aspect of the learning problem is defining a suitable reward function. The goal of agent $\mathcal{A}$ in RL is to maximise cumulative rewards. Since we consider the best policy to be one that maximises net gain, the most straightforward reward is the gain or loss that we get at the end of each case. So, we have decided to incorporate the treatment cost and the benefit of a positive case into the reward function. The intuition behind this design choice is that the treatment policy is directly related to the ratio between this cost and benefit. For example, if we have a cheap treatment and a high benefit, we can afford to apply the treatment more frequently, even if we are not certain about its effectiveness. But with an expensive treatment, it becomes more important to carefully select the cases and times of treatment, and only treat if the agent is sure that the treatment is necessary and effective.

The reward function also needs to contain information about the effectiveness of the treatment at each decision point. Recall that in the data enhancement phase, we generated $Y(1)$ and $Y(0)$ for each prefix length of each case. We can compute $Y(1) - Y(0)$ for each prefix to obtain the true treatment effect at each decision point. We include this true effect in the reward function to guide the agent about the effectiveness of the treatment. We provide the details of the reward function in Table 1.

Table 1. The proposed reward function

	True Treatment Effect		
Agent's Treatment	Positive	Negative	Zero
Yes	Gain - Cost	-Cost-Gain	Negative Outcome: -Cost Positive Outcome: -Cost
No	-Gain	Gain	Negative Outcome: 0 Positive Outcome: Gain

When the agent treats, if the treatment effect is positive, we give a reward of $r = Gain - Cost$, since we receive the gain of a positive outcome while paying the cost of treating. If the treatment effect is zero, we penalise the agent by giving it a negative reward of $r = -Cost$, since the agent wasted the cost of the treatment and it was ineffective. If the treatment effect is negative, we penalise the agent by giving it an even lower negative reward $r = -Cost - Gain$. We chose this reward because not only did the agent waste the cost of the treatment, but also caused further damage by treating when it hurt the outcome.

When the agent does not treat, if the treatment effect was positive, we penalise it by giving the reward $r = -Gain$ because the agent failed to act when necessary. If the treatment effect is zero, we look at the outcome. If the outcome is positive, the agent correctly decided not to apply the treatment and saved the cost of treatment, so $r = Gain$. If the outcome is negative, it means that the case is a lost cause and even treating it would not have changed anything. So, although the agent was correct in not treating, we give it $r = 0$ because there was no gain. Finally, if the treatment effect was negative, we give it a strong positive reward $r = Gain$ because choosing not to treat when the treatment hurt the outcome caused a positive outcome.

This reward function closely models the net gain achieved by following the agent's policy, except in three situations. First, if the agent does not treat when it would have been effective, the actual gain is 0, but we penalise the agent with $-Gain$. Second, if the agent treats when its effect is negative, we lose the cost of the treatment, so net gain is $-Cost$, but the reward is $-Cost - Gain$. Third, if the agent treats, and the treatment is ineffective, and outcome is positive, the net gain is $Gain - Cost$, but we give $r = -Cost$. We added these extra *punishments* to signal to the agent that it made incorrect decisions. According to [23], reward functions often need to be tweaked to speed up learning and convergence, and to avoid getting stuck in local optima. We found these further punishments are necessary to speed up the learning process.

We use a separate set of cases for the policy selection phase with timeframes later than the cases used for model training. The agent learns through a series of episodes. Each episode corresponds to one case. During each episode, the events are presented to the agent in the ascending order of their timestamps. At the end of each episode, we reveal the cumulative reward to the agent. Similar to [12], we use proximal policy optimization (PPO) [21] as our RL algorithm. We also represent the policy as a multi-layer perceptron. This network can be used later as a starting point in real-life situations. Since it has been trained on data with potential outcomes that are statistically similar to their real counterparts, it will make fewer mistakes than if the agent starts from scratch.

5   Results

In this section, we explain our experimental setup and report our results. Our method was developed in Python 3.8. We used the Catboost library for our predictive model and EconML for the causal forest. The generative model was developed using Pytorch.

For similar reasons as in predictive process monitoring [26], we use temporal splitting to simulate the real-life scenario where prediction models are trained on historical data and then an RL agent learns the best policy by applying interventions on running cases. We split the data into $50\% - 50\%$. The first half is used for training the predictive and causal models, and the second is used for policy selection using reinforcement learning. We used a temporal splitting, ensuring that the cases in the model training set whose timeframe overlaps the timeframe of the policy selection set are removed. The policy selection set was further split 50%–50%, with the first half being used to train the Realcause model and the second half as direct input to the reinforcement learning component.

We follow the same pre-processing and feature engineering steps for the predictive, causal, and generative models. We one-hot encode the categorical attributes. For encoding timestamp information, we create the following temporal features: 'time since case start', 'time since last event', 'time since midnight', 'month', 'weekday', and 'hour'. Also, to capture the temporal relationship between cases, we create a feature 'time since first case', which is a case attribute denoting the distance between the start of the case and the start of the first case. These temporal and inter-case features are added because they have been shown to increase performance in prediction models and are common practice in both predictive and prescriptive monitoring [10,24]. To pre-process the data, we standardize the features.

5.1 Datasets

We performed our experiments on two publicly available datasets, namely BPIC12 and BPIC17, and compare our approach with the state-of-the-art method in prescriptive process monitoring [12]. We chose these two datasets because, to the best of our knowledge, they are the only publicly available datasets with a treatment present in the log that can affect the process outcome. Both these logs contain traces of a loan origination process. We consider the process outcome to be positive if the customer accepts the loan offer. Also, usually one loan offer is made to each customer. But we observe cases where more than one offer is made to the same customer. We observe that the rate of success is higher for such cases. Hence, we consider multiple loan offers to one customer as a possible treatment. Although these two logs refer to the same process, they have some differences. The BPIC17 log has a considerably larger number of cases and contains more features. We provide a summary of the log sizes in Table 2.

Table 2. Number of cases in the event logs before and after data splitting.

Log	Total Cases	Cases in Model Training Set	Cases in Realcause Component	Cases in RL Component
BPIC12	5015	1967	900	1608
BPIC17	31413	13193	14789	8444

5.2   Performance Measure

In this experiment we evaluate the success of each component of our approach by measuring the following gain function:

$$NetGain = Y(t) * gain - t * cost,   \tag{2}$$

where $t \in \{0, 1\}$ is the treatment option the agent recommended. The net-gain measures the amount of money that we gain from each case. Negative net-gain represents loss. We first run our experiment only giving the CATE estimates $\theta_{u,k}$ and $\theta_{l,k}$ to the agent. In the second experiment, we give both the CATE estimates and the conformal prediction scores ρ_k to the reinforcement learning agent. We also compare our approach with the one proposed in [12] as it is state-of-the-art in addressing the when-to-treat problem. Figure 5 describes the results for both datasets.

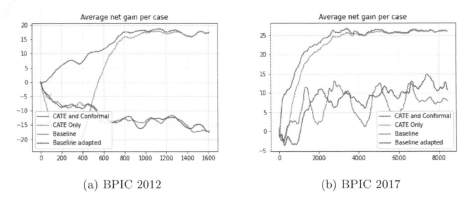

(a) BPIC 2012   (b) BPIC 2017

Fig. 5. Average net-gain of cases.

In the figures above, we consider an expensive treatment. Specifically, we suppose that the benefit of a positive outcome is $50 and the cost of the treatment is $25. We also experimented with cheap treatments (e.g., $1). But since cheap treatments do not require a strict policy, we include those results in the supplementary materials. The x-axis in Fig. 5 refers to the cases the agent decides on, and the y-axis is the net gain for each case. We can see that the agents using the CATE upper and lower bounds outperform the agents that use predictions about the case outcome. This result is because the agents using predictions, target cases that end up with a bad outcome. But the agents using CATE have information about the effectiveness of the treatment. They only treat if they are confident it will turn a negative outcome into a positive one. In other words, they target the persuadables in Fig. 3. Also, we observe that the agent using both conformal prediction score and CATE estimates, converges faster, empirically proving our hypothesis that conformal prediction can detect the sure things and the lost causes, thereby pruning the search space for the agent and helping it make fewer mistakes. This is important if RL is applied online in a real environment because, without conformal prediction, we observe that the net gain is negative for the first few hundred cases.

We ran two versions of the baseline. The first (shown in green) uses the reward function proposed in [12]. In the second version (shown in red), we adapt the baseline to use our proposed reward function (Table 1). We can see that in the BPIC17 dataset, the baseline is unstable. This is because in some cases, the predictive information that the agent has matches the effectiveness of the treatment, so the agent correctly decides to treat. But other times, it treats when the treatment is needed but ineffective. But when using our proposed reward function, we see a slow improvement in performance. This is because the agent is slowly learning to be more selective about when to apply the treatment through the reward function. But the description of its environment (the prediction and its reliability) does not have enough signal to converge faster. In the BPIC12 dataset, both versions of the baseline produce negative net gain. This is because this log is considerably smaller than the BPIC17 log. So the agent does not see enough samples to discover a policy producing a positive net gain.

We also experimented with the intuitive reward function that does not contain any further punishments for the agent's wrong decisions (see Sect. 4.3). However, we found that this reward function does not produce good results. This is because this reward function does not have enough signal for the agent to distinguish between correct and incorrect decisions, leading the agent to treat unnecessarily. This problem can be addressed by adjusting the exploration/exploitation rate of the agent. That said, since we are using an algorithm (PPO) that does not allow manual adjustment of this rate, we leave that for future work. The results of this experiment and the specifications of the alternative reward function can be found in the supplementary materials.

5.3   Statistical Tests on Enhanced Logs

In this section, we evaluate the quality of our generated potential outcomes. To this end, we ran a few statistical two-sample tests. We tested the hypothesis that the generated and real outcomes come from different distributions and report the p-values. Any p-value above 0.05 indicates that the test cannot conclude that the two samples come from different distributions. We use the same tests that we did in [5] and report the results in Table 3. It can be seen that all p-values are above the 0.05 threshold, meaning that none of the tests can detect that the enhanced and real outcomes come from different distributions.

Table 3. Table of p-values for statistical tests

	Kolmogorov Smirnov	Epps Singleton	Friedman Rafsky	k-Nearest Neighbor	Energy	Wasserstein 1	Wasserstein 2
BPIC12	0.244	0.311	0.109	0.088	0.228	0.323	0.329
BPIC17	1.0	0.996	0.647	0.359	0.92	0.916	0.87

5.4   Threats to Validity

The use of only two datasets in the experiments poses threats to external validity. While both datasets come from real-life sources, they both relate to the same type of process (loan origination). It may be that the proposed technique performs differently on less structured processes, for example, in healthcare processes. A threat to internal validity is that we synthetically enhanced the logs with potential outcomes. The quality of these potential outcomes depends on the quality of the input data. We mitigated this threat by applying statistical tests on the enhanced logs as reported above. Another internal validity threat stems from the fact that we treat cases as independent entities, while cases are inter-dependent due to shared resources. We mitigated this threat by including inter-case features in the predictive and causal estimators, but there may still be inter-case dependencies between not captured by these features. The use of observational data to estimate CATEs creates a threat to construct validity. When some confounders are not present in the dataset, CATE models reduce bias compared to purely correlation-based methods, but they do not eliminate it. Another threat to construct validity stems from the fact that we run one RL episode per case. At each step in a case, we use information about the case outcome to reward the agent. Thus, in the presence of long cases in the log, the agent gets exposed to information about the future. To mitigate this threat, we sorted the cases by their end timestamp to reduce data leakage. Also, we excluded any case information in the description of the environment. The agent only sees CATE estimates, conformal prediction scores, and prefix numbers. However, since these estimates and scores are derived from models using case information, the agent might still be indirectly exposed to future information.

6   Conclusion

This paper introduced a method to learn policies to prescribe treatments to cases of a business process to maximize the net gain generated by such treatments. The proposed method enhances an existing online RL method by: i) feeding causal effect estimates to obtain a higher net gain to prevent ineffective treatments; ii) using conformal predictions to speed up the convergence of the RL agent; and iii) using a causal dataset enhancement method to simulate an environment where the RL agent can be trained offline.

In the proposed method, each learning episode is one case. This approach potentially exposes the agent to information that is only known in the future, since cases may overlap in time (data leakage). A natural improvement of this work would be to change the notion of episodes to prevent such leakage. For instance, each episode could be all the events across multiple cases that occur on the same day. The difficulty here is finding a suitable time-step to make good use of the available dataset. Further directions for future work include expanding this approach to optimise continuous targets such as cycle time and considering resource availability when recommending treatments. Another direction is to investigate other RL algorithms and their potential advantages/disadvantages over PPO. One can also investigate different exploration/exploitation rates to measure their impact on performance.

Reproducibility The source code of our tool, the datasets, and the experiment results can be found at https://github.com/zahradbozorgi/WhenToTreat.

Acknowledgments. Research funded by the Australian Research Council (grant DP180102839), the European Research Council (PIX Project), and the Estonian Research Council (grant PRG1226).

References

1. Athey, S., Imbens, G.: Recursive partitioning for heterogeneous causal effects. In: Proceedings of the National Academy of Sciences (2016)
2. Batoulis, K.: Proactive decision support during business process execution. In: 1st International Workshop on Modeling Inter-Organizational Processes and 1st International Workshop on Event Modeling and Processing in BPM co-located with Modellierung (2014)
3. Bozorgi, Z.D., Teinemaa, I., Dumas, M., Rosa, M.L., Polyvyanyy, A.: Process mining meets causal machine learning: discovering causal rules from event logs. In: 2nd ICPM (2020)
4. Bozorgi, Z.D., Teinemaa, I., Dumas, M., Rosa, M.L., Polyvyanyy, A.: Prescriptive process monitoring for cost-aware cycle time reduction. In: 3rd ICPM (2021)
5. Bozorgi, Z.D., Teinemaa, I., Dumas, M., Rosa, M.L., Polyvyanyy, A.: Prescriptive process monitoring based on causal effect estimation. Inf. Syst. (2023)
6. Dorogush, A.V., Ershov, V., Gulin, A.: Catboost: gradient boosting with categorical features support. In: Workshop on ML Systems at NIPS (2017)
7. Fahrenkrog-Petersen, S.A., et al.: Fire now, fire later: alarm-based systems for prescriptive process monitoring. Knowl. Inf. Syst. 1–29 (2021). https://doi.org/10.1007/s10115-021-01633-w
8. Koorn, J.J., Lu, X., Leopold, H., Martin, N., Verboven, S., Reijers, H.A.: Mining statistical relations for better decision making in healthcare processes (2022)
9. Koorn, J.J., Lu, X., Leopold, H., Reijers, H.A.: Looking for meaning: discovering action-response-effect patterns in business processes. In: BPM Proceedings (2020)
10. Kubrak, K., Milani, F., Nolte, A., Dumas, M.: Prescriptive process monitoring: quo vadis? PeerJ. Comput. Sci. **8**, e1097 (2022)
11. de Leoni, M., Dees, M., Reulink, L.: Design and evaluation of a process-aware recommender system based on prescriptive analytics. In: 2nd ICPM (2020)
12. Metzger, A., Kley, T., Palm, A.: Triggering proactive business process adaptations via online reinforcement learning. In: BPM Proceedings (2020)
13. Nakatumba, J., Westergaard, M., van der Aalst, W.M.: A meta-model for operational support. BPM Center Report BPM-12-05, BPMcenter.org (2012)
14. Neal, B., Huang, C.W., Raghupathi, S.: Realcause: realistic causal inference benchmarking (2021)
15. Oprescu, M., Syrgkanis, V., Wu, Z.S.: Orthogonal random forest for causal inference. In: Proceedings of the 36th ICML (2019)
16. Padella, A., de Leoni, M., Dogan, O., Galanti, R.: Explainable process prescriptive analytics (2022)

17. Qafari, M.S., van der Aalst, W.M.P.: Root cause analysis in process mining using structural equation models. In: BPM International Workshops, Revised Selected Papers (2020)
18. Qafari, M.S., van der Aalst, W.M.P.: Case level counterfactual reasoning in process mining. In: CAiSE Forum Proceedings (2021)
19. Romano, Y., Sesia, M., Candes, E.: Classification with valid and adaptive coverage. In: NeurIPS (2020)
20. Rubin, D.B.: Estimating causal effects of treatments in randomized and nonrandomized studies. J. Educ. Psychol. **66**(5), 688 (1974)
21. Schulman, J., Wolski, F., Dhariwal, P., Radford, A., Klimov, O.: Proximal policy optimization algorithms. arXiv preprint arXiv:1707.06347 (2017)
22. Shoush, M., Dumas, M.: When to intervene? prescriptive process monitoring under uncertainty and resource constraints. In: BPM 2022 Forum (2022)
23. Sutton, R.S., Barto, A.G.: Reinforcement Learning: an Introduction. MIT Press, Cambridge (2018)
24. Teinemaa, I., Dumas, M., Rosa, M.L., Maggi, F.M.: Outcome-oriented predictive process monitoring: review and benchmark. ACM Trans. Knowl. Discov, Data **13**(2), 1–57 (2019)
25. Teinemaa, I., Tax, N., de Leoni, M., Dumas, M., Maggi, F.M.: Alarm-based prescriptive process monitoring. In: BPM Forum (2018)
26. Verenich, I., Dumas, M., Rosa, M.L., Maggi, F.M., Teinemaa, I.: Survey and cross-benchmark comparison of remaining time prediction methods in business process monitoring. ACM Trans. Intell. Syst. Technol. **10**(4), 1–34 (2019)
27. Wager, S., Athey, S.: Estimation and inference of heterogeneous treatment effects using random forests. J. Am. Stat. Assoc. **113**(523), 1228–1242 (2018)
28. Weinzierl, S., Dunzer, S., Zilker, S., Matzner, M.: Prescriptive business process monitoring for recommending next best actions. In: BPM Forum (2020)

Model-Agnostic Event Log Augmentation
for Predictive Process Monitoring

Martin Käppel[(✉)] and Stefan Jablonski

Institute for Computer Science, University of Bayreuth, Bayreuth, Germany
{martin.kaeppel,stefan.jablonski}@uni-bayreuth.de

Abstract. Predictive process monitoring aims to predict how the execution of a running process instance will evolve until its completion. Deep learning techniques have been shown to perform well for various prediction tasks, such as next activity prediction, remaining time prediction, or outcome prediction. However, the quality and performance of these models is highly dependent on the available amount of training data, as deep learning models require a lot of data to generalize well. In practice, the available event logs usually contain only a few thousand records with more or less redundancy, which is insufficient with respect to the large number of parameters that need to be estimated during training. For this reason, data augmentation is often used in machine learning research to increase the amount of available training data by applying transformations to them and create new samples synthetically. Since data augmentation is still largely unexplored in predictive process monitoring, this paper proposes an initial set of simple noise-based transformations that could be applied to any event log and boosts the performance of existing predictive process monitoring approaches. Our experimental evaluation shows that predictive process monitoring approaches for predicting the next activity benefit from this data augmentation technique in terms of performance and stability of the training process.

Keywords: Predictive Process Monitoring · Data Augmentation · Data Scarcity

1 Introduction

Predictive Process Monitoring [17] is a subfield of process mining that aims to predict how an ongoing process execution will unfold up to its completion. The ability to predict the further process execution in advance adds considerable value in various domains and scenarios, as potential problems can be identified early so that appropriate preventive measures can be taken in time [9].

For different prediction problems, such as outcome prediction [16], remaining time prediction [3,4], or next event prediction [3,4,8,15,24] various machine learning techniques and more recently deep learning methods have been used that are

Our work is supported by the Bavarian Research Foundation (grant no. AZ-1390-19).

trained on records of already completed process executions. In this paper, we are specifically interested in predicting which activity will be executed next.

The quality and performance of these models strongly depends on the amount and quality of training data available. In particular, deep learning methods require a lot of data to generalize well and learn salient patterns, as they need to estimate several thousands or even millions of parameters during training [10]. Therefore, a frequently propagated estimate recommends at least one unique training sample for each parameter to be determined to ensure stable training [10]. However, this basic prerequisite is often not met, because the event logs available in practice usually contain only a few thousand, often redundant samples [25].

Consequently, there is a strong interest in taking appropriate measures to automatically increase the amount of available data. In the context of machine learning, this is called *data augmentation*. In other research areas such as computer vision and NLP, automatic data augmentation is often used successfully and helps improve the performance and robustness of trained models, especially when using small datasets [22,27]. However, in predictive process monitoring data augmentation techniques are still neglected.

In this paper, we propose a set of simple noise-based data augmentation techniques that can be applied to any event log and boosts the performance of existing predictive process monitoring approaches regardless of their individual characteristics, such as network architecture or input encoding. We provide a profound evaluation of our approach and show that existing predictive process monitoring approaches for predicting next activity benefit from data augmentation. Therefore, we evaluated against a baseline that uses no data augmentation. The rest of the paper is structured as follows. Section 2 provides the necessary background on predictive process monitoring, including basic terminology. Section 3 discusses related work and delimits our work from it. In Sect. 4, we propose our approach to augment event log data, while in Sect. 5, we systematically evaluate our approach from different angles. Finally, we provide some possible limitations concerning validity and concluding remarks.

2   Preliminaries

The main input for process mining techniques is a (process) event log, i.e. a set of traces belonging to the same process. A trace (also called a *case*) is a temporally ordered sequence of events related to the same process execution. An event encapsulates the execution of an activity (i.e. a well-defined step in a process) and is described by event attributes. Each event contains at least three event attributes: a case identifier, an activity, and a timestamp. We define these terms formally, according to the standard literature [1, 20] as follows:

Definition 1 (Event). *Let A be the set of potential activities in a business process, C the set of case identifiers, T the time domain, and $D_1, ..., D_m$ the domains of additional event attributes (so called data payload) with $m \geq 0$. An* ***event*** *e is a tuple $(a, c, t, d_1, ..., d_m)$ where $a \in A$, $c \in C$, $t \in T$, and $d_i \in D_i$.*

Definition 2 (Event Attributes). *For each event attribute p of an event e, we define a function π_p, that assigns a value of the corresponding domain of p to an event. Hence, for activity, case identifier, and timestamp we get functions π_A, π_C, and π_T, with $\pi_A(e) = a$, $\pi_C(e) = c$, and $\pi_T(e) = t$.*

Definition 3 (Trace, Event Log). *A **trace** is a non-empty finite sequence of events $\sigma = \langle e_1, ..., e_n \rangle$ such that for $1 \leq i < j \leq n$ holds: all events $e \in \sigma$ are ordered by their timestamp, i.e. $\pi_T(e_j) \geq \pi_T(e_i)$ and belong to the same process instance, i.e. $\pi_C(e_j) = \pi_C(e_i)$. We say a trace $\sigma = \langle e_1, ..., e_n \rangle$ has length n, denoted as $|\sigma|$. An **event log** L is a set of traces $L = \{\sigma_1, \sigma_2, ...\sigma_l\}$ with size l, denoted as $|L|$.*

Predictive process monitoring approaches partition traces into sets of prefixes:

Definition 4 (Event Prefix). *Let $\sigma = \langle e_1, ..., e_n \rangle$ be a trace and $r \in \{1, ..., n-1\}$. We define the function hd which returns the **event prefix** of length r (i.e. the first r elements of a trace) as follows: $hd(\sigma, r) = \langle e_1, e_2, ..., e_r \rangle$.*

Given a certain prefix of an ongoing process execution, predictive process monitoring aims at predicting how this execution will unfold until the end of the case. For the scope of our paper, we can formally define the prediction of the next activity as follows:

Definition 5 (Next Activity Prediction). *Let $\sigma = \langle e_1, ..., e_n \rangle$ be a trace and $hd(\sigma, r)$ a prefix of length $r \in \{1, ..., n-1\}$ of σ. Then **next activity prediction** is defined as a function Ω_a that takes $hd(\sigma, r)$ and predicts the next activity, i.e.. $\Omega_a(hd(\sigma, r)) = \pi_A(e_{r+1})$.*

A predictive process monitoring approach tries to learn the function Ω_a with help of a given event log. In this paper this function is always represented by a neural network, since we are focused on deep learning techniques.

3   Related Work

Data scarcity is a well-known and critical problem in machine learning (ML) research and is considered as one of the major obstacles in deep learning research [18]. For a long time, this problem has been largely neglected in process mining research, in contrast to other research areas such as Natural Language Processing (NLP) [6] and Computer Vision [22]. Various manifestations and symptoms of data scarcity have been mentioned in passing rather than systematically (e.g. class imbalance in [19], number of trainable parameters in [25]). This problem was first discussed systematically in [14], where possible benefits of adapting Small Sample Learning (SSL) [23] techniques to the specifics of business process management are discussed. SSL subsumes a plethora of different techniques, such as data augmentation, to enable ML with only a limited amount of training data. An empirical study of the data hungriness of predictive process monitoring approaches conducted in [13] revealed that real-life event logs often exhibit less variance, such that 70–80% of the training data has no value for training. In line with that [21] proposes sub-sampling strategies to select those traces that have the most value for training. However, since the network architecture kept the same (in particular, the number of parameters to be trained), this only leads to more efficient training, but does not improve model performance.

Due to the learning capabilities of neural networks, they have become state-of-the-art in predictive process monitoring. A milestone was the work of Evermann et al. [8] who successfully applied Long-Short-Term-Memory (LSTM) networks for predicting the next event. A similar approach was explored by Tax et al. [24] to predict the remaining time and the next activity with its associated timestamp. This approach was extended by Camargo et al. [4] at two ends: a composition of LSTMs allows to process both categorical and numerical features and an embedding mechanism reduces the input dimension to better handle high-dimensional inputs. Although LSTMs are a popular choice due to the sequential structure of traces, other architectures have been explored recently. For instance, Mauro et al. [7] and Pasquadibisceglie et al. [19] leverage Convolutional Neural Networks (CNN), while Khan et al. [15] use Memory Augmented Neural Networks to process the same inputs as [24]. To improve the performance of the model, several approaches include either additional data sources, such as mined process models [26], clusters of event attributes [11], or incorporate a hyperparameter optimization [7]. More recently, the emergence of the groundbreaking transformer architecture led to the process transformer approach proposed by Buhksh et al. [3]. A comprehensive survey on all predictive process monitoring approaches can be found in [20]. To circumvent insufficient training data, Taymouri et al. [25] propose an adapted Generative Adversarial Neural Network (GAN) to predict the next event. Here, a generator component generates next events for an event prefix until a discriminator component can no longer distinguish it from the ground truth real next event. However, it is not used to create new training samples that can be used by other approaches to compensate for a lack of data. Thus, it is a new prediction technique rather than a data augmentation technique. Deep learning models such as [4] and [25] are used in process simulation [5] as generative models for event log generation. Therefore, they should replicate the as-is behavior of the process recorded in the event log as closely as possible. Thus, the goal of process simulation is fundamentally different from that of data augmentation. Moreover, they require a sufficient amount of initial training data and do not capture nuances in event logs [5]. Consequently, data augmentation is more of an upstream step that could help these approaches to perform better.

Although data augmentation is a proven technique in ML, it is largely ignored in process mining. In NLP research, a set of noise-based augmentation techniques is proposed in [27] that achieve performance gains of about 3% on different datasets. In [6] more than 100 augmentation techniques for natural texts (e.g. back-translation, paraphrasing) are collected and reviewed. Noise-based augmentations, such as flipping, rotating, or cropping, have also been used successfully in computer vision [22], as well as advanced techniques such as neural style transfer [22]. The ideas behind these techniques seem promising for other research areas such as BPM, but require adaptation to the specifics of the domain.

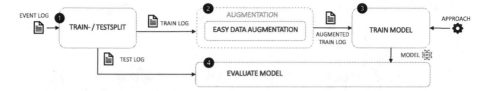

Fig. 1. Adapted machine learning pipeline for predictive process monitoring. The injected augmentation step is visualized by a dashed border.

4 Augmentation Approach

In general, *data augmentation* means the application of random (but more or less realistic) transformations (also called *augmentors*) to the original training data and the synthesis of new samples [2, 23]. Thus, it acts as a regularizer to overcome data scarcity, introduce more variability into the data (i.e. make the dataset more diverse), and reduce the risk of overfitting. Here, the *augmentation factor* indicates the strength of the augmentation, i.e. by what factor the existing dataset is increased. For example, an augmentation factor of 2 means that the existing amount of data is doubled (an augmentation factor of 1 means there is no augmentation). It is important to augment only the training data, otherwise the performance of the model would be evaluated on augmented (i.e. synthesized data) and thus possibly incorrect data. This is because the generated traces do not necessarily represent a real and valid state of the underlying process. However, to meet the definition of trace, the transformations are designed to maintain the temporal order of events, i.e. the timestamps within a trace are in ascending order (see more details at end of Sect. 4.2).

4.1 Augmentation Pipeline

To boost predictive process monitoring approaches through data augmentation, we inject an augmentation step into the classical predictive process monitoring pipeline. This step is applied to the training data before the data is used to train the model. The pipeline is shown in Fig. 1. The augmentation step receives the training data in form of an event log, applies various transformations (see Sect. 4.2), and in turn returns an (augmented) event log. Since we work directly with the event log and not with approach-specific encoded and preprocessed training data, augmentation is completely decoupled from any approach. It can therefore be applied to any process monitoring approach without modifying the approach.

4.2 Transformations

This section presents the core of our contribution by proposing several transformations. These are inspired by noise-based transformations from computer vision [22] and NLP [27] research, and are adapted to the specific needs of BPM. Our transformations modify three event attributes: the name of the activity, the execution timestamp, and the executing unit. This choice is guided by two

Table 1. Applying Random Deletion (RD) and Rework Activity (RW) to σ

σ	$\langle$(A, 12, 12/10/21, Pete), (B, 12, 12/11/21, Max), (D, 12, 12/14/21, Sys3)$\rangle$
RD:	$\langle$(A, 13, 12/10/21, Pete), (D, 13, 12/14/21, Sys3)$\rangle$
RW:	$\langle$(A, 18, 12/10/21, Pete), (B, 18, 12/11/21, Max), (B, 18, 12/12/21, Max), (D, 18, 12/14/21, Sys3)$\rangle$

aspects: First, activity and timestamp are mandatory event attributes and therefore present for every event. Second, activity and timestamp are those attributes
that are used as model inputs by all approaches. The resource attribute was
included only because the LSTM state-of-the-art approach of Camargo et al. [4]
requires it. There would be no benefit to modifying further event attributes since
most approaches do not use them as features (primarily because such attributes
would require an individual treatment for the particular event log). We randomly
select traces from the training data and randomly perform one of the following
transformations to create a new sample (a concrete sample is shown in Table 1):

- Random Insertion: Insert a randomly generated event into the trace (at a
  randomly chosen position but not at the first or last position).
- Random Deletion: Removes an event from a random position in the trace.
- Fragment Augmentation: Randomly extract a consecutive subsequence of the
  trace.
- Rework Activity: Execute a randomly chosen activity that is executed in the
  trace a second time right after the first execution (so called *rework activity*).
- Delete Rework Activity: If a trace contains a rework of an activity (i.e. the
  same activity is executed two times in sequence) then remove one execution.
- Random Replacement: Replace an event by a randomly generated event.
- Parallel Swap: Swap the execution order of two consecutive events if they
  have the same timestamp (so-called *parallel events*).
- Random Swap: Swap the execution order of two consecutive events.
- Loop Augmentation: If a trace contains a loop, execute the body of the loop
  at least once more. In this context, a loop means a repetition of a sequence
  of activities with length greater or equal one (i.e. the rework of an activity is
  also seen as a loop). The detection mechanism for loops acts on single trace
  level, i.e. it only analyses the trace selected for augmentation.

Before applying the transformation, we must check whether the transformation can be applied to the selected trace. For example, if a trace contains no parallel events or no loops, we cannot perform a Parallel Swap or a Loop Augmentation respectively. If a transformation is not applicable, we choose both another
transformation and another trace. After a successful transformation, we add the
created trace directly to the event log. In this way we offer the possibility to perform multiple transformations, i.e. to create new samples even from already augmented traces. Assume we created a new trace by applying a Random Insertion
to a trace. Later, another trace is created from this new trace by applying a Loop
Augmentation. Such *multiple augmentation* ensures that even more altered traces

can be created that differ quite clearly from the original traces. The procedure of selecting and transforming traces is repeated until the event log is enlarged by the desired augmentation factor. By randomly selecting transformations, they are used approximately the same number of times, unless the properties of the event log prevent this (e.g. no or not enough parallel events).

To satisfy the definition of a trace, we must ensure that a transformation preserves the temporal order of events, i.e. the events are ordered ascending in time by their timestamp. Therefore, we either swap the timestamps of the events (Parallel Swap, Random Swap) or in the case of insert operations (Loop Augmentation, Random Insertion, Rework Activity) by assigning appropriate timestamps. In concrete terms, this means that for insertions at position i, we choose timestamps that lie between the timestamp of the event at position $i-1$ and that of the event at position $i + 1$ (Random Insertion, Rework Activity) or shift up-following events into the future (Loop Augmentation). In the case of deletion operations (Random Deletion, Delete Rework), we do not change any timestamps and accept that within the trace there may remain a larger period of time without an execution of an activity. Maintaining the temporal order is essential, since most approaches derive different features from the timestamp (e.g. event duration, hours since midnight) and rely on the assumption of increasing timestamps.

4.3   Intent Behind the Transformations

Essentially, the transformations pursue two goals: *(i)* introducing minor perturbations that help the model become more robust, and *(ii)* adding traces that capture possible but not yet recorded behavior. However, it is crucial that these transformations do not confuse the model too much and prevent it from learning spurious patterns, i.e. patterns introduced through augmentation. Therefore, both the transformations themselves and the augmentation factor must be chosen appropriately. In the following, we briefly explain the intent behind the above transformations, which take into account both the process specific requirements and the particularities of different deep learning architectures:

- The Parallel Swap augmentation compensates for an ambiguity in the representation of a trace that arises from the fact that the order of two parallel events in the trace can be chosen arbitrarily. The Parallel Swap supports the predictive model in learning both representations.
  Often, certain activities need to be re-executed (rework), whether due to an error or a four-eye principle that applies to certain executing entities. The Rework Transformation simulates and captures such situations. In contrast, Delete Rework undoes such rework.
- Fragment Augmentation (inspired by cropping in computer vision) highlights parts of a trace. This is motivated by several points: *(i)* most approaches process a trace (or more concretely the prefix of a trace) not as a whole, but in parts (e.g. with time windows or n-grams of limited size), *(ii)* in the case of long prefixes, early events of that prefix fade away in LSTM architectures (i.e. they are not completely forgotten or ignored, but hardly affect the prediction),

(iii) the limited receptive field in CNN architectures allows to consider only parts of the trace, and *(iv)* approaches that process a trace as a whole are supported to focus on the relevant parts of the trace and not to get confused by irrelevant events.

- If a loop has already been run several times, there is a certain probability that the process will allow further iterations. The Loop Augmentation attempts to cover such executions. In addition traces with loops are often longer than the average trace length. Since, long sequences are difficult for LSTMs to learn, more training instances are needed for such cases.
- Swapping two successive events (Random Swap) supports learning in situations where little time elapses between events and thus the model mistakenly believes them to be simultaneous.
- Random Insertion and Random Deletion aim to insert small perturbations without altering the trace too much to improve robustness. Sometimes these transformations also cover situations where an activity can be optionally executed (Random Insertion) or skipped (Random Deletion).

It should be noted that a transformation is randomly selected for the trace to be augmented, rather than the one that may best fit the particular characteristics of the trace or the approach used. That ensures that the augmentation is independent of a particular approach.

5   Evaluation

We implemented our approach as a protoypical Python framework that includes the data augmentation technique and all methods required for reproducible evaluation[1] To test the effectiveness of data augmentation, we examined its impact on seven approaches using seven real-life event logs with diverse characteristics. In selecting the approaches, we relied on the results of the rigorous systematic literature review conducted in [20] and used all approaches with executable publicly available source code. In addition, we included the approach of Bukhsh et al. [3] which was published after conducting the literature review. An overview of the approaches including their main characteristics is shown in Table 3.

Experiments were run on a Dell PowerEdge R7525 server equipped with two AMD CPUs á 16 cores at 3,0 GHz, 256 GB RAM and an NVIDIA Ampere A40 with 48 GB of memory. For reliable time measurements, we ensured that no parallel experiments were run on the workstation.

5.1   Experimental Setup

Benchmark Datasets: We used event logs from different domains (healthcare, finance, public administration, customer service, and software) obtained from the *4TU Center for Research Data*[2]. Table 2 shows the characteristics of these logs, while the description of the process covered can be found below:

---

[1] Our code and detailed results can be found in the supplementary material at https://github.com/mkaep/pbpm-ssl-suite.

[2] https://data.4tu.nl/.

Table 2. Statistics of the event logs ($|\sigma|$ is the trace length, $\Delta_E t$ is the time difference between two successive events). All time related measures are shown in days.

	Helpdesk	Sepsis	BPIC13-c	BPIC13-i	BPIC15-1	BPIC12	NASA
#Cases	4580	1050	1487	7554	1199	13087	2566
#Events	21348	15214	6660	65533	52217	262200	73638
#Activities	14	16	4	4	398	24	47
AVG $|\sigma|$	4.66	14.49	4.48	8.68	43.55	20.04	28.7
Max. $|\sigma|$	15	185	35	123	101	175	50
Min $|\sigma|$	2	3	1	1	2	3	12
AVG $\Delta_E t$	40.86	28.47	178.88	12.08	95.72	8.62	0.0
Max $\Delta_E t$	59.92	417.26	2254.84	722.25	973.49	102.85	0.0
Min $\Delta_E t$	0.0	0.0	0.0	0.0	0.0	0.0	0.0
#Variants	226	846	183	1511	1170	4366	2513

Table 3. Considered approaches (ACT: activity, TIME: timestamp, RES: resource, PM: process model, NT: next timestamp, RT: remaining time, SFX: suffix prediction, RLSFX: role suffix)

Approach	Network Type	Input Features	Prediction	Hyper. Opt.
Bukhsh [3]	Transformer	ACT	ACT	-
Camargo [4]	LSTM	ACT, TIME, RES	ACT, Role, NT, RT, SFX, RLSFX	($\checkmark$)
Khan [15]	DNC	ACT, TIME	ACT, NT	-
Mauro [7]	CNN	ACT, TIME	ACT	$\checkmark$
Tax [24]	LSTM	ACT, TIME	ACT, NT, RT, SFX	-
Theis [26]	DFNN	ACT, PM, TIME	ACT	-
Pasquadibisceglie [19]	CNN	ACT, TIME	ACT	-

- *BPI12*: This event log contains records of a loan application process (consists of three subprocesses) of a German financial institute.
- *BPIC13 Closed* and *BPIC13 Incidents* are two event logs extracted from Volvo's IT incident and problem management system.
- *BPIC15-1*: This event log contains records of the execution of a building permit application process from a Dutch municipality.
- *Helpdesk* is an event log from a ticketing management process of the help desk of an Italian software company.
- *NASA* is an event log where the traces represents the method-call hierarchy of a unit test suite for the Crew Exploration Vehicle.
- *Sepsis*: This event log contains anonymized records of the treatment of sepsis cases in a hospital.

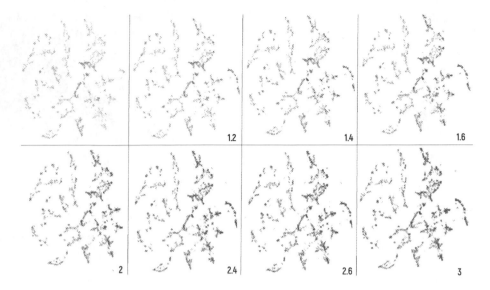

Fig. 2. t-SNE visualization of the Helpdesk log with different augmentation factors (green: non-augmented data, blue: test data, violet: augmented data) (Color figure online)

Training Setting: We used a temporal split to divide the event logs into training and test cases. Therefore, the traces in the event log were ordered by their start time (i.e. the timestamp of the first event). Then, the first 70% were used as training data, while the remaining 30% were used as test data. This method is in line with that of [3,4,15,24]. We created concrete test samples by extracting all prefixes with a minimum length of 2 from the traces in the test data.

To obtain a baseline against which we can evaluate, each approach was trained with the training data and evaluated with the test samples. We then created augmented training datasets of varying sizes by applying our data augmentation technique to the original training data. To do this, we used the following augmentation factors: 1.2, 1.4, 1.6, 2, 2.4, 2.6, and 3. Then, we trained all approaches on each of the augmented event logs. Finally, the resulting models were evaluated with all the test samples extracted at the beginning to ensure comparability.

For configuring the approaches, we used the default hyperparameters as they were recommended by their authors. Hyperparameter optimization was only performed if it was an integral part of the approach (this only was true for Mauro et al. [7]). Since hyperparameter optimization is very computational intensive, this assumption allowed us to consider more approaches on multiple event logs rather than just optimizing a few, even though this might mean further improvement.

5.2   Results

We evaluate three different aspects: *(i)* the quality of the generated traces and how much they differ from the non-augmented ones, *(ii)* the impact of data augmentation on the model performance, and *(iii)* the training process of the model using augmented and non-augmented training data.

Examining the Quality of the Generated Data: To compare augmented and non-augmented training data, we chose a visualization approach to provide a holistic view rather than picking out individual features in isolation[3]. Therefore, we used *t-distributed stochastic neighbor embedding* (also called *t-SNE*) [12], which allows visualization of high-dimensional data in a low-dimensional space. Note that the dimensions of the low-dimensional space have no concrete meaning, but the mapping is done in such a way that similar objects are more likely to be mapped closer together than dissimilar objects [12]. For our purpose of studying the similarity of augmented and non-augmented traces, this is sufficient.

We visualized the traces of the original training data (i.e. the non-augmented data), the test data, and the respective augmented data. Therefore, we encoded the traces using only the event attributes affected by the augmentation (i.e. activity, resource, and timestamp). We converted activity name and resource to numeric features and encoded the timestamps by calculating the difference between the timestamps of consecutive events. This allows us to observe how similar they are and how the augmented data covers the training and test data in dependency of the augmentation factor (exemplarily shown for the Helpdesk log in Fig. 2). We found that the resulting representations for the augmented traces closely surrounds those of the original traces most of the time. Thus, we conclude that our transformations largely preserve the semantics of the traces. We also found that the augmented traces are indeed distinct from the original traces in the event log and that conflicting transformations (e.g. Rework Activity and Delete Rework Activity) do not cancel each others effect. Moreover, we find that in some cases, data augmentation succeeds in interpolating previously unseen data from the test data. However, in a very small number of cases, we can also observe outlier behavior of the augmented traces, i.e. neither an original trace nor traces of the test data can be found in the immediate surrounding. These traces are thus significantly different from the non-augmented data, which basically means that the applied transformation(s) have changed the trace very much.

Performance Evaluation: For consistency, we score a model by its accuracy, i.e. the fraction of correct predictions to the total number of predictions, to evaluate its ability to predict the next activity. In addition to overall performance, we also analyzed the impact of prefix length. To do this, we divided our samples into bins according to the prefix length. We then calculated the accuracy for each bin in the same way as for the entire dataset. In a second analysis, we divided our samples according to the ground truth activity. This allows us to determine, whether the data augmentation helps to cope with imbalance. To investigate the

---

[3] We do not apply the commonly used edit distance metrics such as the Damerau-Levenshtein distance, since they would not provide much insight in our case. The reason is that these metrics cannot handle timestamps and the number of edits required for activity and resource attributes is obvious in most cases (with the exception of loop and fragment augmentation each transformation requires one edit for each attribute).

Table 4. Accuracy values achieved by baseline models (base) and best performing augmented models (best) with p-values (-: approach could not be run on this dataset due to missing or partially missing resource attribute (in case of Camargo) or limitations in the available source code (Khan), r: perfect agreement between the models).

Approach		BPIC12	BPIC13-c	BPIC13-i	BPIC15-1	Helpdesk	NASA	Sepsis
Bukhsh	base	83.43%	52.41%	**59.56%**	30.86%	62.09%	88.45%	52.89%
	best	**83.97%**	**53.81%**	59.33%	**37.25%**	**71.95%**	88.45%	**62.00%**
	p-value	≈ 0.00	≈ 0.00	≈ 0.00	≈ 0.00	≈ 0.00	≈ 0.00	≈ 0.00
Camargo	base	-	31.60%	28.35%	2.26%	51.93%	9.80%	-
	best	-	**53.55%**	**58.75%**	**4.63%**	**57.33%**	**12.47%**	-
	p-value	-	≈ 0.00	≈ 0.00	≈ 0.00	≈ 0.00	≈ 0	-
Khan	base	-	-	-	-	1.855%	-	-
	best	-	-	-	-	**39.657%**	-	-
	p-value	-	-	-	-	≈ 0.00	-	-
Mauro	base	1.60%	31.60%	40.72%	1.94%	38.16%	5.67%	5.18%
	best	**2.45%**	31.60%	**42.04%**	**2.08%**	**55.00%**	**11.49%**	**8.84%**
	p-value	≈ 0.00	r	≈ 0.00	≈ 0.00	≈ 0.00	≈ 0.00	≈ 0.00
Pasquadibisceglie	base	82.70%	52.03%	59.67%	16.77%	68.35%	85.33%	59.19%
	best	**83.12%**	**53.17%**	**59.95%**	**40.64%**	**69.65%**	**87.77%**	**62.11%**
	p-value	≈ 0.00	0.002	≈ 0.00	≈ 0.00	≈ 0.00	≈ 0.00	≈ 0.00
Tax	base	0.40%	38.83%	26.55%	0.21%	67.54%	**28.08%**	22.86%
	best	**23.90%**	**56.35%**	**56.80%**	**0.70%**	**68.62%**	19.18%	**24.08%**
	p-value	≈ 0.00	≈ 0.00	≈ 0.00	≈ 0.00	≈ 0.00	≈ 0.00	≈ 0.00
Theis	base	73.39%	53.68%	**59.41%**	7.51%	66.44%	79.18%	44.45%
	best	**74.67%**	**54.32%**	59.08%	**9.66%**	**68.87%**	**80.55%**	**44.88%**
	p-value	≈ 0.00	0.04	≈ 0.00	≈ 0.00	≈ 0.00	≈ 0.00	≈ 0.00

extent to which the approaches benefit from data augmentation, we determine the *accuracy gain* by calculating the difference between the accuracy of the models trained on augmented data, and the baseline models trained on data without augmentation. We found that for nearly each approach, for each event log, we were able to identify at least one configuration (i.e. augmentation factor) that had a positive impact on accuracy (i.e. an accuracy gain > 0). This observation is statistically significant in all cases (i.e. we can reject the null hypothesis that assumes that there is no difference between the models), as confirmed with the Stuart-Maxwell-Test[4] (see Table 4 for the p-values, p-values close to zero indicate a strong significance). However, the most appropriate augmentation factor varies depending on the architecture and/or event log, and in any case must be determined by experiment.

When we relate the accuracy gain to the number of parameters to be trained (see Fig. 3), we find that models with a large number of trainable parameters (LSTMs and DNC) benefit more from the data augmentation. Looking at the evolution of the accuracy as a function of augmentation factor (see Fig. 4), we find

---

[4] https://search.r-project.org/CRAN/refmans/DescTools/html/StuartMaxwellTest.html.

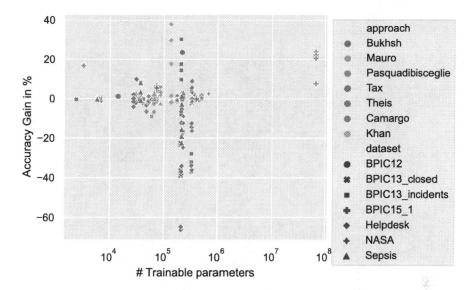

Fig. 3. Accuracy gain in relation to the number of trainable parameters (accuracy gain > 0 indicates a positive effect)

that some fluctuations occur for models with a large number of parameters (Tax, Camargo, Khan). This is due to the fact that the overparameterization (i.e. the amount of trainable parameters far out-weights the number of training samples) leads to unstable training of these models (less so in the case of Camargo than in the case of Tax due to the improvements mentioned in Sect. 3). As a result, it happens from time to time that a model hardly learns the patterns in the data, i.e. it can predict only a few classes (so-called no-skill models). This instability of the training process also explains the larger variance of the accuracy gain of these models (cf. Fig. 3). Ultimately, we can conclude that data augmentation helps to stabilize the training process and reduces the risk of no-skill models. In contrast, models with a comparatively small number of parameters to be trained (Bukhsh, Mauro, Theis, Pasquadibisceglie) benefit less from data augmentation, even though a slight to moderate gain in accuracy is observed. This is particularly evident for very complex event logs (Sepsis and BPIC15-1), which have a high number of variants relative to the total number of traces (in the case of the BPIC15-1 log this is exacerbated by the high number of activities). Moreover, the training process for these models can be considered more stable, as we can see from the fact that there is little fluctuations across different augmentation factors. In the case of the BPIC15-1 log the Pasquadibisceglie approach shows an outlier behavior in terms of the number of trainable parameters (it increases to several millions) due to the encoding of the activities. As we can see in Fig. 4 for this particular case, data augmentation yields a significant performance gain regardless of the augmentation factor. The described effects could be observed in the same way when analyzing the accuracy in dependency of the prefix length. Our analysis of performance per activity shows that data augmentation improves overall

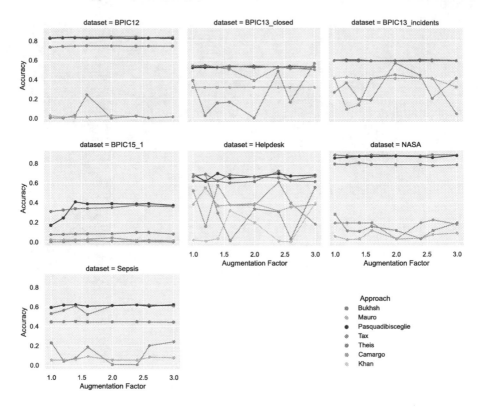

Fig. 4. Overview of the achieved accuracy values in dependency of different augmentation factors. Note that an augmentation factor of 1 means that there is no augmentation.

performance and stabilizes the training process, but does not solve the problem of poor prediction of rare activities. This was not to be expected, however, as this is due to the poor separability of the classes rather than imbalance [13]. This and further results can be found in the supplementary material.

Training Behavior: The increase in the amount of training data is accompanied by an increase in the computational effort, which includes both the training time and memory required. Figure 5 illustrates this trend. Despite the increase in training times due to data augmentation, they are still in a range that is not problematic in practice and would allow determining the most appropriate augmentation factor for a given event log.

6   Limitations

The experimental setting is limited to seven event logs and seven approaches. While the selection of the approaches are based on a systematic literature review, the selection of event logs is potentially biased. Although these event logs are

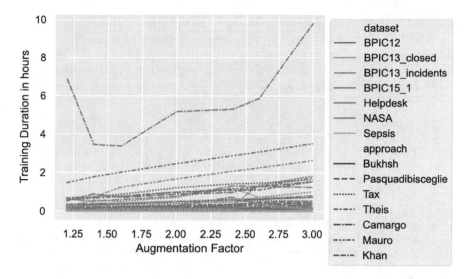

Fig. 5. Training duration for different event logs and approaches in dependency of the augmentation factor.

from different domains and have different characteristics, it is possible that the results would be different if other event logs were used. This flaw is mitigated by our implementation, which allows for the inclusion of other event logs and approaches. Since our transformations are random, it is not unlikely that using other seeds would produce different results. However, due to the use of the significance test, the uncertainty relates solely to the magnitude of the benefit, and not whether the data augmentation is useful at all. Future work should investigate how the individual transformations affect the overall results. Since these are sometimes contradictory (e.g. Delete Rework and Rework Activity) and not free of side effects, we theoretically need to examine all possible subsets of the transformations (i.e. 2^9 possibilities). This is unfeasible and sophisticated pruning strategies (similar to hyperparameter optimization algorithms) are required to find an optimal (weighted) combination of these transformations.

7   Conclusion and Future Work

This paper investigates noise-based data augmentation to improve the performance of predictive models for the next activity. Our evaluation highlights the merits of our approach, which helps stabilize the training procedure and leads to a slight to moderate performance gain in terms of accuracy, depending on the number of parameters to be trained. Since data augmentation in predictive process monitoring is still largely unexplored, we plan to develop additional, more sophisticated data augmentation techniques. Since our paper was limited to predicting the next activity, we intend to investigate in the future the impact of such simple data augmentation on other prediction problems, like remaining time, next time, or case outcome. The latter is of particular interest, since it is crucial here that the outcome-labels be preserved as much as possible. In addition, it should be investigated how this augmentation strategy can be used more specifically for certain problems, such as the class imbalance (here the challenge would be to predominantly augment non-frequent process variants).

References

1. van der Aalst, W.M.P.: Process Mining: Data Science in Action, 2nd edn. Springer, Heidelberg (2016). https://doi.org/10.1007/978-3-662-49851-4
2. Adadi, A.: A survey on data-efficient algorithms in big data era. J. Big Data **8**(1), 1–54 (2021)
3. Bukhsh, Z.A., Saeed, A., Dijkman, R.M.: Processtransformer: predictive business process monitoring with transformer network (2021)
4. Camargo, M., Dumas, M., González-Rojas, O.: Learning accurate LSTM models of business processes. In: Hildebrandt, T., van Dongen, B.F., Röglinger, M., Mendling, J. (eds.) BPM 2019. LNCS, vol. 11675, pp. 286–302. Springer, Cham (2019). https://doi.org/10.1007/978-3-030-26619-6_19
5. Camargo, M., Dumas, M., González-Rojas, O.: Learning accurate business process simulation models from event logs via automated process discovery and deep learning. In: Franch, X., Poels, G., Gailly, F., Snoeck, M. (eds.) CAiSE 2022. LNCS, vol. 13295. Springer, Cham (2022). https://doi.org/10.1007/978-3-031-07472-1_4
6. Dhole, K., et al.: NL-augmenter: a framework for task-sensitive natural language augmentation (2021)
7. Di Mauro, N., Appice, A., Basile, T.M.A.: Activity prediction of business process instances with inception CNN models. In: Alviano, M., Greco, G., Scarcello, F. (eds.) AI*IA 2019. LNCS (LNAI), vol. 11946, pp. 348–361. Springer, Cham (2019). https://doi.org/10.1007/978-3-030-35166-3_25
8. Evermann, J., Rehse, J.R., Fettke, P.: Predicting process behaviour using deep learning. Decis. Support Syst. **100**, 129–140 (2017)
9. Francescomarino, C.D., Ghidini, C.: Predictive process monitoring. In: van der Aalst, W.M.P., Carmona, J. (eds.) Process Mining Handbook, vol. 448, pp. 320–346. Springer, Cham (2022). https://doi.org/10.1007/978-3-031-08848-3_10
10. Goodfellow, I., Bengio, Y., Courville, A.: Deep Learning. MIT Press, Cambridge (2016)
11. Hinkka, M., Lehto, T., Heljanko, K., Jung, A.: Classifying process instances using recurrent neural networks. In: Business Process Management Workshops (2018)
12. Hinton, G.E., Roweis, S.: Stochastic neighbor embedding. In: Advances in NIPS, vol. 15. MIT Press, Cambridge (2002)
13. Käppel, M., Jablonski, S., Schönig, S.: Evaluating predictive business process monitoring approaches on small event logs. In: Paiva, A.C.R., Cavalli, A.R., Ventura Martins, P., Pérez-Castillo, R. (eds.) QUATIC 2021. CCIS, vol. 1439, pp. 167–182. Springer, Cham (2021). https://doi.org/10.1007/978-3-030-85347-1_13
14. Käppel, M., Schönig, S., Jablonski, S.: Leveraging small sample learning for business process management. Inf. Softw. Technol. **132**, 106472 (2021)
15. Khan, M.A., et al.: Memory-augmented neural networks for predictive process analytics (2018)
16. Kratsch, W., Manderscheid, J., Röglinger, M., Seyfried, J.: Machine learning in business process monitoring: a comparison of deep learning and classical approaches used for outcome prediction. BISE **63**, 261–276 (2020)

17. Maggi, F.M., Di Francescomarino, C., Dumas, M., Ghidini, C.: Predictive monitoring of business processes. In: Jarke, M., et al. (eds.) CAiSE 2014. LNCS, vol. 8484, pp. 457–472. Springer, Cham (2014). https://doi.org/10.1007/978-3-319-07881-6_31

18. Marcus, G.F.: Deep learning: a critical appraisal. arXiv (2018)

19. Pasquadibisceglie, V., Appice, A., Castellano, G., Malerba, D.: Using convolutional neural networks for predictive process analytics. In: ICPM 2019. IEEE (2019)

20. Rama-Maneiro, E., Vidal, J.C., Lama, M.: Deep learning for predictive business process monitoring: review and benchmark (2020)

21. Sani, M.F., Vazifehdoostirani, M., Park, G., Pegoraro, M., van Zelst, S.J., van der Aalst, W.M.P.: Event log sampling for predictive monitoring (2022)

22. Shorten, C., Khoshgoftaar, T.M.: A survey on image data augmentation for deep learning. J. Big Data 6(1), 1–48 (2019)

23. Shu, J., Xu, Z., Meng, D.: Small sample learning in big data era (2018)

24. Tax, N., Verenich, I., Rosa, M.L., Dumas, M.: Predictive business process monitoring with LSTM neural networks. arXiv (2017)

25. Taymouri, F., Rosa, M.L., Erfani, S., Bozorgi, Z.D., Verenich, I.: Predictive business process monitoring via generative adversarial nets: the case of next event prediction. In: Fahland, D., Ghidini, C., Becker, J., Dumas, M. (eds.) BPM 2020. LNCS, vol. 12168, pp. 237–256. Springer, Cham (2020). https://doi.org/10.1007/978-3-030-58666-9_14

26. Theis, J., Darabi, H.: Decay replay mining to predict next process events. IEEE Access 7, 119787–119803 (2019)

27. Wei, J., Zou, K.: EDA: easy data augmentation techniques for boosting performance on text classification tasks. In: Proceedings of EMNLP-IJCNLP. ACL (2019)

Conformance, Compliance
and Workarounds

Detecting Deviations Between External and Internal Regulatory Requirements for Improved Process Compliance Assessment

Catherine Sai[✉], Karolin Winter, Elsa Fernanda, and Stefanie Rinderle-Ma[iD]

TUM School of Computation, Information and Technology,
Technical University of Munich, Garching, Germany
{catherine.sai,karolin.winter,elsa.fernanda,stefanie.rinderle-ma}@tum.de

Abstract. In order to assure process compliance, a wide range of regulatory requirements from various documents must be considered. These external requirements are typically transformed into internal requirements such as policies or handbooks for process compliance in an organization. The transformation is mostly done manually, without the ability of a digitalized quality check. To support users, this work provides a semi-automatic approach based on state-of-the-art NLP algorithms. We first provide a list of Regulatory Compliance Assessment Solution Requirements (RCASR) based on which deviations between external and internal textual requirements can be detected and the root cause of the deviations can be identified. This detailed analysis helps to find mitigation actions in order to improve process compliance. The proposed approach is evaluated based on two Case studies with greatly varying regulatory documents and their realizations by companies. The evaluation demonstrates the feasibility of the approach and provides further insights into the applicability of NLP-based automation techniques in the field of process compliance assurance and management.

Keywords: Regulatory Compliance · Natural Language Processing · Alignment Support · Process Conformance

1 Introduction

Implementing regulatory documents is an expensive and cumbersome task for all companies, with severe consequences if their processes turn out to be noncompliant. *"Since the fall of 2021, Ireland's DPC has slapped Meta with 912 million euros in fines, [...] for alleged violations of Europe's signature data privacy law, known as the General Data Protection Regulation (GDPR)."*[1]. Complex regulations such as the GDPR require a lot of expert knowledge to read, understand and finally implement them which is still mostly done manually [15]. An increasing flood of regulatory documents, makes the system-supported implementation

---

[1] https://edition.cnn.com/2022/11/28/tech/meta-irish-fine-privacy-law/.

M. Indulska et al. (Eds.): CAiSE 2023, LNCS 13901, pp. 401–416, 2023.
https://doi.org/10.1007/978-3-031-34560-9_24

of regulatory documents more essential for companies than ever. Existing work in this research area has by now mostly focused on, e.g., deriving formalized constraints (cf., e.g., [4]) or process models from natural language text (cf., e.g., [1,12,31]). A recent approach assesses compliance between regulatory documents and process models [29]. However, regulatory documents usually need to be contextualized and adapted to a company's environment. For this purpose realizations of regulatory documents, i.e., internal documents such as handbooks or policies are distributed among employees setting out guidelines that need to be adhered to [15]. The goal is to combine the compliance requirements with company specific requirements. Realizations are often the intermediate step between external regulatory requirements and business processes. By ensuring that the formulation in corporate language, i.e. the realization, correctly reflects the external requirements, one lays the foundation that the business processes (which in turn are often aligned with the realization) are also compliant. Although this plays a crucial role for compliance management, machine learning assisted techniques for a compliance degree assessment between regulatory documents and their realizations are currently missing. Hence, this paper aims at providing an approach for this challenging task. As stated in [29], constraints, i.e., sentences containing signal words like "shall, should, must", offer the right level of abstraction to represent the semantics of regulatory documents. By operating on this constraint level, the approach also becomes independent of the order in which constraints are contained in the document. The challenge is to assess *coverage* and at the same time *deviations* between regulatory and realization constraint sets. For this, at first, *Regulatory Compliance Assessment Solution Requirements (RCASRs)* are elicited based on existing work (cf. Sect. 2). Based on the RCASRs, we present a compliance assessment approach (cf. Sect. 3). The first step is to map constraints from regulatory documents with their presumed counterparts from the realization, resulting in a set of constraint pairs. The constraint pairs are analyzed for different deviations, e.g., responsibility deviations, i.e., whether a task is executed by the correct resource. The results of this deviation analysis are aggregated in order to derive an overall compliance degree between a regulatory document and a realization. The approach is implemented and evaluated based on two real-world case studies with the GDPR and an ISO Norm (cf. Sect. 4). A discussion of limitations is outlined in Sect. 5. Related work is discussed in Sect. 6, a summary and outlook in Sect. 7 conclude the paper.

2 Regulatory Compliance Assessment Solution Requirements

Comparing regulatory documents and their realizations in a meaningful way is challenging w.r.t. granularity and significance of the comparison. Regarding the granularity, analogously to [29], we operate on *constraints* which constitute an adequate level of abstraction to represent semantics of regulatory documents. Regarding the significance, in the following, we elicit 13 *Regulatory Compliance Assessment Solution Requirements (RCASRs)* (cf. Table 1) for a (quantifiable) comparison. The RCASRs break the task of regulatory compliance assessment down into

Table 1. Regulatory Compliance Assessment Solution Requirements (RCASRs)

RCASR #: name	explanation	example
1: regulatory document relevance	companies and organizations have to identify the various regulatory documents they need to comply with	an international company must comply with regulatory documents from different regions (e.g. EU regulations)
2: content relevance	within the identified documents of RCASR1, the conformance relevant parts for a given company need to be identified	EU GDPR, Chap. 7 is not relevant for company x
3: constraint coverage	evaluation, if all constraints from regulatory documents are mentioned in a realization	20 relevant constraints from the EU GDPR are not mentioned in the data protection policy of a company
4: severity deviation	evaluation, if a realization is over-compliant, meaning it is stricter about aspects of constraints or includes constraints that are not required by the regulatory document	the data protection policy of a company states to inform a data subject within 24h, while the GDPR only requires to inform within 72h
5: execution style deviation	within the covered constraints from RCASR3, the phrase referring to how something is supposed to be done deviates between the regulatory document and its realization	the regulatory document requires gluing parts together, the realization states to weld the parts
6: negation deviation	evaluation if the constraint aspects (RCASR5, RCASR7 and RCASR8-10) are similar but negated	the regulatory document requires informing the customer via phone call, the realization states not to reach out via phone.
7: responsibility deviation	within the covered constraints from RCASR3, the phrase referring to who is supposed to be doing something deviates between the regulatory document and its realization	the regulatory document specifies that resource A must execute task t but in the realization, resource B is specified
8: data deviation	within the covered constraints from RCASR3, the phrase referring to what is supposed to be done deviates between the regulatory document and its realization	the regulatory document specifies to consider something as private data, the realization considers it as public data
9: time deviation	within the covered constraints from RCASR3, the time something is allowed to take deviates between the regulatory document and its realization	the regulatory document states a task must be finished within one day, the realization states it must be finished within two days
10: task execution order deviation	within the covered constraints from RCASR3, the order in which actions must be taken deviates between the regulatory document and its realization	the regulatory document states the order of events A-B-C, the realization states the order must be B-A-C
11: constraint duplicates	evaluation, if the same constraint appears multiple times in a realization	the constraint "the data subject needs to be informed of a data breach within 72h by the processor" appears 3 times in a realization
12: overall regulatory compliance	weighted aggregation of the coverage and deviation findings to enable a quantifiable degree of compliance between a regulatory document and its realization	80% of the EU GDPR is correctly covered by the data protection policy of an EU company
13: mitigation actions	provision of recommendations for improving regulatory compliance of a realization	change the order of events to A-B-C as stated in constraint x of the regulatory document

the steps, necessary to assure quality. Recent solutions comprise [10,20,21], comparing regulatory documents and realizations on a document or segment level. Especially in light of explainability and mitigation actions, we aim at a much deeper level of comparison between parts of constraints. This way our solution does not only indicate a deviation on, e.g., chapter level but identifies exactly which part of a constraint sentence deviates. The RCASRs are particularly suited for monitoring compliance, i.e., we do not target the initial modeling of a realization from a regulatory document, but the (continuous) compliance assessment of already modeled realizations for, e.g., checking whether a regulatory document and its realization still comply after changes.

The RCASRs are inspired and extended, based on the work from [3,19,29,30]. [29] compare requirements imposed by regulatory documents to business process models. They propose a cost score containing 3 types of violation that can be observed: 1) missing obligatory activity (compare RCASR 3); 2) wrong resource performing the activity (compare RCASR 7); 3) wrong order of activities (compare RCASR 10). [19] describe 10 compliance monitoring functionalities (CMFs) a holistic approach should address. For our application we found CMF 1–3, as well as CMF 9 and 10 to be relevant: CMF 1: Constraints referring to time (compare RCASR 9); CMF 2: Constraints referring to data (compare RCASR 8); CMF 3: Constraints referring to resources (compare RCASR 7); CMF 9: Ability to explain the root cause of a violation (compare RCASR 13); CMF 10: Ability to quantify the degree of compliance (compare RCASR 12). Finally, [3] introduces the phases of a compliance requirements assessment, starting with the discovery of relevant regulatory documents (compare RCASR 1). We further break this step down in not only identifying the relevant documents (RCASR 1) but also the relevant sections within a document (RCASR 2) and the extraction and completeness assessment of the constraints within the Sections (RCASR 3). [30] present an approach to identify redundant (compare RCASR 11), subsumed (RCASR 4) and in general conflicting (compare RCASR 5–6) constraints in text.

We combine these finding to allow a holistic and more detailed understanding of deviations. RCASR 4 and 11 are concerned with deviations that do not necessarily result in a violation, like a realization containing duplicate mentions of a constraint (RCASR 11), which might not be necessary, or a realization being unintentionally more strict about a constraint than the corresponding regulation (RCASR 4). Such an over-compliance can lead to higher costs and should thus be detected. RCASR 5 is concerned with deviations in how something is supposed to be done. The negation deviation RCASR 6 could have been integrated into RCASR 5, 7, 8–10 but as it is a challenging task to reliably identify the correct relation of a negation, we decided to leave it as a separate deviation to identify. This paper addresses RCASR2 – RCASR8 by constraint extraction, determination of constraint coverage and decomposition of a constraint into three parts reflecting the responsibility, task and data aspects. RCASR11 – RCASR13 are partly addressed and RCASR9 and RCASR10 require more complex means, i.e., time aspects need to be determined which is not a trivial task and in order to extract a control-flow from text we cannot consider constraints isolated from each other [31].

3   Compliance Degree Assessment Approach

As depicted in Fig. 1 the approach takes a regulatory document and its realization as input. The final outcome is a detailed assessment of the overall compliance degree based on constraint coverage and constraint deviation findings (post-processing). For those steps marked with grey boxes (*Relevance Identification, 1st Step Constraint Coverage*) we provide several options for implementing them in order to cope with, e.g., different styles of realizations. Note that a manual refinement of results is constantly possible, leaving room for incorporating users in the overall compliance degree assessment during each step.

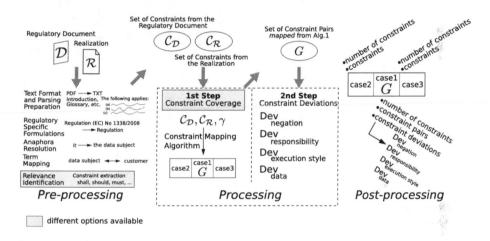

Fig. 1. Overview of Compliance Degree Assessment Approach

3.1   Pre-processing

The pre-processing is performed in a semi-automated manner with multiple cyber-human interaction options. As initial step, we automate the PDF to plain text transformation but strongly encourage a manual review in order to comprehensively tackle the challenge of sentence boundary detection, cf., e.g., [26]. Fully automated components are the anaphora resolution to enhance that sentences are self-contained and the identification of relevant sentences. For the regulatory document relevance is identified by signal words, concerning the realization, the user can choose to do the same or include all sentences in the assessment. The responsibility mapping again allows for human intervention: an automated extraction of entities facilitates a manual mapping inspection for responsibility terms from a realization and a regulatory document.

3.2   Processing

The processing phase consists of 2 steps. In step 1, we map similar constraints from realization and regulatory document by 5 different options. For the 2nd step, a decomposition of constraints into parts containing the responsibility information, execution style, data and negation is carried out (a) and the parts similarity is computed (b).

1st Step – Constraint Coverage The pre-processing resulted in the identification of relevant content in form of constraints (**RCASR2**). In the following, let $\mathcal{C}_\mathcal{D}$ be the set of constraints from regulatory document $\mathcal{D}$ and $\mathcal{C}_\mathcal{R}$ the set of constraints from the realization $\mathcal{R}$ respectively. In order to assess the compliance degree, associated constraints must be identified first which is a challenging task since regulatory documents and their realizations can be complex. Yet, only if constraints are correctly mapped, we can draw conclusions about constraint deviations in the latter. Algorithm 1, describes the constraint mapping. It takes as input $\mathcal{C}_\mathcal{D}, \mathcal{C}_\mathcal{R}$ and a threshold γ and first of all creates all possible pairs $(c_d, c_r) \in \mathcal{C}_\mathcal{D} \times \mathcal{C}_\mathcal{R}$ ($\mapsto$ line 1). Afterwards, in lines 4–15 those pairs are checked for whether their similarity $sim(c_d, c_r)$ is above threshold γ and if so, the pair is added to the list of mapped pairs.

Algorithm 1. Constraint Mapping Algorithm

    Input: $\mathcal{C}_\mathcal{D}, \mathcal{C}_\mathcal{R}, \gamma$
    Output: not_mapped, mapped
1: $pairs = \text{create\_pairs}(\mathcal{C}_\mathcal{D}, \mathcal{C}_\mathcal{R})$
2: mapped = {}
3: not_mapped = {}
4: **for** pair in $pairs$ **do**
5:     **if** sim(pair) $< \gamma$ **then**
6:        continue
7:     **end if**
8:     **if** mapped[pair[0]] == None **then**
9:        mapped[pair[0]] = { *"realization"*: pair[1], *"sim"*: sim(pair)}
10:    **else**
11:      **if** sim(pair) > mapped[pair[0]].sim **then**
12:         mapped[pair[0]] = { *"realization"*: pair[1], *"sim"*: sim(pair)}
13:      **end if**
14:    **end if**
15: **end for**
16: **for** pair in $pairs$ **do**
17:    **if** pair[0] not in mapped.keys **then**
18:      not_mapped[*"regdoc"*] << pair[0]
19:    **end if**
20:    **if** pair[1] not in mapped.values.map(val $\rightarrow$ val[*"realization"*]) **then**
21:      not_mapped[*"realization"*] << pair[1]
22:    **end if**
23: **end for**

Next, new pairs are filtered such that one constraint from the realization can have multiple counterparts in a regulatory document, but one constraint from a regulatory document can only have one counterpart within the realization by only retaining pairs with maximal similarity. The last part of the algorithm, lines 16–23, determines all components of pairs that were not mapped at all whereas we distinguish between not mapped constraints from a regulatory document and the ones not mapped from a realization. For the mapping, i.e., calculating the similarity of constraint pairs ($sim(pairs)$), the natural language text is first transformed in a mathematical representation, called vector or embedding. The similarity between these embeddings can be calculated by various approaches, the cosine similarity being most commonly used. The cosine similarity is based on the cosine of the angle between two vectors [14]. We provide the following five options of embedding methods for the implementation.

S-BERT sentence transformer embeddings and cosine similarity [2]: chosen as transformers are state-of-the art in NLP since their introduction in 2017 [13]. S-BERT is a transformer model specifically trained on estimating the similarity of sentences and comes with a significant performance increase compared to using BERT for the same task [22].

Legal-S-BERT legal sentence transformer embeddings and cosine similarity [8]: implemented to evaluate how a transformer model trained on the same domain as the application will affect the results. Legal-BERT is a transformer model trained on a wide span of legal texts [8]. In order to apply Legal-BERT as Legal-S-Bert, we performed a domain adaption [23], training a new model with Legal-BERT as pre-training on the target domain and the Natural Language Inference (AllNLI) dataset [5,28] for fine-tuning on labeled data.

TM topic modeling, word2vec and cosine similarity [32]: with this approach we test the hypothesis, that first clustering the constraints will improve the similarity identification. Within clusters including both regulatory and realization constraints, we calculate the similarity of the pairs as described in Algorithm 1. For Topic Modeling we use Gibbs Sampling Dirichlet Multinomial Mixture (GSDMM) which is a topic modeling approach with the underlying assumption of one topic per document [32]. This makes it especially useful for short documents or single sentences as we consider in this case.

k-means k-means, word2vec and cosine similarity: this approach is similar to **TM** as it groups the constraints before calculating similarity between the constraints in one group. Clustering is performed by first embedding the constraints as vectors by means of the sentence transformer model and then applying k-means to assign each constraint to a cluster.

key phrases key phrase extraction, S-BERT embedding and cosine similarity [24]: in contrast to the other approaches, here we do not compare the whole constraint text but extract key phrases from the text and section title to calculate the similarity between these key terms of the regulatory and realization constraints. The key phrase extraction is implemented with RAKE (Rapid Automatic Keyword Extraction) algorithm [24].

Based on the result of Algorithm 1 we can distinguish three cases. Case 1 is a set of constraint pairs which were mapped (**RCASR3**). Case 2 is a set of constraints from the regulatory document having no counterpart in the realization and case 3 the set of constraints within the realization having no counterpart in the regulatory document. Case 2 is particularly interesting because it could be an evidence that the realization is missing out some regulatory document parts. However, only a manual inspection can reveal whether these parts should have been included. Therefore, they will be extracted for a stakeholder review and we will not consider these constraints when determining constraint deviations. Case 3 indicates that the realization contains company specific parts that are not relevant in the regulatory context. We do not consider those constraints further, but they do give an indication as to topics the company is executing more severely than they are required to (**RCASR4**). Based on these observations, a notion for the **constraint coverage degree** is given as follows:

- Full constraint coverage of a regulatory document and a realization holds if all constraints were mapped by Algorithm 1.
- Partial constraint coverage of a regulatory document and a realization holds if *not_mapped* is not empty after applying Algorithm 1
- No constraint coverage of a regulatory document and a realization holds if *mapped* is empty after Algorithm 1

2nd Step – Constraint Deviations In the second step of the processing phase, we address determining constraint deviations. As already stated, for the compliance degree assessment only constraint pairs from case 1 can be considered for a deviation analysis. Let in the following G denote the set of all constraint pairs in *mapped* after applying Algorithm 1. In order to derive deviations, we decompose each constraint by utilization of custom built functions in combination with the "Part of Speech" (POS) information, specific occurrence matching, as well as position (e.g. subtree) and dependencies of a word in its constraint context. The outcome are phrases reflecting the *responsibility*, *task* and *data* parts, e.g., $c = $ "A data officer must glue all product parts." is decomposed into $c|_{res} = $ "data officer", $c|_{task} = $ "glue", $c|_{data} = $ "all product parts". Let $c|p$ denote the decomposition of $c \in \mathcal{C_D} \cup \mathcal{C_R}$ onto its part $p \in \{res, task, data\}$. Based on this decomposition the deviations for RCASR 5–8 can be defined using again the cosine similarity for comparing the parts as follows.

Definition 1 (execution style deviation – RCASR5). *An execution style deviation for a constraint pair* $(c_d, c_r) \in G$ *occurs if for thresholds* $\gamma_i \in [-1, 1], i = 1, 2, 3$:

$$sim(c_d|_{res}, c_r|_{res}) \geq \gamma_1 \wedge sim(c_d|_{task}, c_r|_{task}) < \gamma_2 \wedge sim(c_d|_{data}, c_r|_{data}) \geq \gamma_3$$

A deviation in execution style occurs whenever the similarity between two tasks is below a threshold but the responsibility and data parts are above a threshold. Consider, e.g., for $\gamma_1 = \gamma_2 = 1$ and $\gamma_2 = $ the constraints $c_d = $ "A worker must glue all product parts." and $c_r = $ "A worker must weld all product *parts"*. Then $sim(\text{``worker''}, \text{``worker''}) = 1 = sim(\text{``all product parts''}, \text{``all product parts''})$ but $sim(\text{``glue''}, \text{``weld''}) < \gamma_2 = 0.17$.

Definition 2 (negation deviation – RCASR6). *A negation deviation for a constraint pair* $(c_d, c_r) \in G$ *occurs if for thresholds* $\gamma_i \in [-1, 1], i = 1, 2, 3$ *holds*
$sim(c_d|_{res}, c_r|_{res}) \geq \gamma_1 \wedge sim(c_d|_{task}, c_r|_{task}) \geq \gamma_2 \wedge sim(c_d|_{data}, c_r|_{data}) \geq \gamma_3$
and there exists a negation for either $c_d|_{task}$ *or* $c_r|_{task}$

A negation deviation occurs whenever a task within a constraint is negated, but all other parts have similarities above thresholds $\gamma_i, i = 1, 2, 3$, e.g., $c_d =$ *"A data subject shall be informed about a data breach."* and $c_r =$ *"A data subject shall <u>not</u> be informed about a data breach."* Then responsibility, task and data similarities are both equal to 1 but the task is negated.

Definition 3 (responsibility deviation – RCASR7). *A responsibility deviation for a constraint pair* $(c_d, c_r) \in G$ *occurs if for thresholds* $\gamma_i \in [-1, 1], i = 1, 2, 3$ *holds:*

$$sim(c_d|_{res}, c_r|_{res}) < \gamma_1 \wedge sim(c_d|_{task}, c_r|_{task}) \geq \gamma_2 \wedge sim(c_d|_{data}, c_r|_{data}) \geq \gamma_3$$

To illustrate the responsibility deviation consider $c_d =$ *"The chief data officer must take care of a data breach."* and $c_r =$*"The data officer must take care of a data breach.".* As $sim(\text{``chief data officer''}, \text{``data officer''}) = 0.9$ is very high, this deviation will only be detected with a $\gamma_1 > 0.9$.

Definition 4 (data deviation – RCASR8). *A data deviation for a constraint pair* $(c_d, c_r) \in G$ *occurs if for thresholds* $\gamma_i \in [-1, 1], i = 1, 2, 3$ *holds:*

$$sim(c_d|_{res}, c_r|_{res}) \geq \gamma_1 \wedge sim(c_d|_{task}, c_r|_{task}) \geq \gamma_2 \wedge sim(c_d|_{data}, c_r|_{data}) < \gamma_3$$

A data deviation can occur if the responsibility and task similarity are above thresholds γ_1 and γ_2, but the data similarity is below γ_3. An example for that case is $c_d =$ *"A data officer should process public data."* and $c_r =$ *"A data officer should process private data.".* Again, task as well as responsibility similarities are equal to 1 but $sim(\text{``public data''}, \text{``private data''}) < \gamma_3 = 0.81$.

Note that, just because none of the deviation definitions holds for a constraint pair, there can still be deviations. Consider, e.g., a constraint pair (c_d, c_r) with $sim(c_d|_{res}, c_r|_{res}) < \gamma_1 \wedge sim(c_d|_{task}, c_r|_{task}) \geq \gamma_2 \wedge sim(c_d|_{data}, c_r|_{data}) < \gamma_3$. In this case neither Def. 3 nor Def. 4 holds but still, the responsibility as well as data aspects do not seem to be correct. Therefore, only a manual inspection of constraint pairs having no deviations can reveal the final overall deviation result. We can only provide deviation statements for unambiguous cases.

Analogously to constraint coverage, notions for the **degree of constraint deviations** can be defined based on the definitions for the deviation types as follows:

1) Full constraint deviation of a regulatory document and a realization holds if for all $(c_d, c_r) \in G$ at most one deviation definition holds. 2) Partial constraint deviation of a regulatory document and a realization holds if for at least one

$(c_d, c_r) \in G$ at least one deviation definition holds. 3) No constraint deviation of a regulatory document and a realization holds if for all $(c_d, c_r) \in G$ no constraint deviation definition holds.

3.3 Post-processing

Based on the findings in Sect. 3.2 we can now assess the overall compliance degree of a regulatory document and a realization. In particular, as depicted in Fig. 1 a detailed analysis on how many and which constraints from a realization, resp. regulatory document were (not) mapped can be provided. Not mapped constraints are considered as not covered by a realization (RCASR3) or not required by a regulatory document (RCASR4). For the group G of mapped constraints, we can provide insights on the number and concrete constraints for which one of the defined constraint deviations (RCASR5–8) occurred. This provides users with appropriate means to identify potential compliance violations or over-compliance. Within the extracted cases 1–3, constraint duplicates can be easily identified (RCASR11). Through the ratio of constraints in case 1 compared to case 2&3 and the count of deviations found, the overall regulatory compliance can be assessed (RCASR12) and the detailed information about the deviation cause aids the mitigation actions (RCASR13). This detailed analysis of a constraint's components not only recognizes a potential constraint deviation, but also indicates the cause of the deviation, which leads to better stakeholder acceptance of the results and aids the improvement of the deviating constraints.

4 Evaluation

The approach is prototypically implemented[2] in Python 3 using (i.a.) the NLP framework spaCy [16]. The approach was implemented for two case studies. Case study 1 was evaluated in a qualitative and quantitative manner and will be discussed in detail in Sect. 4.1–4.3. For Case study 2 we did not create a gold standard due to missing expertise in the field of this regulatory document. Thus, only a qualitative evaluation with regards to cross-regulation application was performed and will be introduced in Sect. 4.4.

4.1 Pre-processing

In Case study 1, the compliance degree of the General Data Protection Regulation (GDPR)[3] and a company's "Data Protection Policy EU" is assessed. For the GDPR articles 1 to 4 and articles 92 to 99 are excluded since they only contain information on when to apply the regulation and a glossary of terms. For the company's policy all text passages are taken into account. Overall, the automatic approach retrieved 423 regulatory constraints, 120 realization constraints with signal words and 264 when taking all sentences from the realization.

---

[2] https://github.com/CatherineSai/compliance_textual_constraints.
[3] https://gdpr.eu/tag/gdpr/.

4.2   Processing

To evaluate Step 1, we manually derived gold standards for case 1 with both options of *Relevance Identification*, i.e., i) using signal words within the realization and ii) using no signal words respectively. Team members independently created a mapping of regulatory-realization-constraint-pairs which were discussed resulting in two gold standards. The gold standard for i) consists of 56 matches while ii) consists of 88 matches. This indicates that selecting ii) is the preferable option as it delivers more constraint pairs than option i). This initial gold standard was later enhanced as further reviews showed, that often multiple realization constraint can individually be a sufficient match for a given regulatory constraint. The enhanced gold standard for step one therefore includes all sufficient regulatory-realization-constraint-pairs. The gold standard for Step 2 was created in the same manner based on the gold standard of Step 1.

Step 1 Keeping in mind NLP challenges like ambiguity, context dependent meaning or implicit (human common) knowledge, it is challenging to implement an automated approach that reaches the exact same understanding of complex regulatory texts as a human. For the intended application of our approach, we thus focused on the recall, i.e., how many of the in the gold standard defined regulatory-realization-constraint-pairs were identified (cf. Table 2). The relatively low precision in Table 2 means that, e.g., for the enhanced Legal-S-BERT the users still have to review 285 proposed pairs for case 1 from the model. Additionally, 175 potentially missing regulatory constraints were identified as case 2 and 186 as case 3. However, 423 regulatory constraints and 264 realization constraints lead to over 100000 possible combinations, so our approach is a major improvement.

Table 2. Step 1 Results best three methods GDPR Case Study

	key phrases (initial)	S-BERT (initial)	L-S-BERT (enhanced)
γ	0.74	0.7	0.72
% precision	12.5	16.9	20.1
% recall	12.5	30.7	70.6

The initial γ−setting for Algorithm 1, was selected after reviewing all highest similarity scores of constraint pairs. Choosing similarity of $\gamma = 0.7$ results in sufficient content-related pairs. Below $\gamma = 0.7$ there are too few content-related constraint pairs. The γ differ across methods because the embeddings and thus the similarity score between the models differ. The selected γ balances the amount of false positive and false negative matches.

Step 2 For the second step of the deviation assessment, we analyzed the 88 identified gold standard constraint matches in further detail. This way Step 2 can be evaluated without influence of the matching performance in

Table 3. Step 2.a) Results GDPR Case Study, % accuracy

	Responsibility	Execution Style	Data	Negation
reg	95.5	89.7	80.5	83.3
rea	94.7	87.7	75.5	100

Step 1. Initially, for Step 2.a), the constraints are decomposed into the four parts defined in Sect. 3.1. The results can be seen in Table 3. This is followed by Step 2.b), the similarity comparison between the identified constraint parts.

Table 4. Step 2.b) Results GDPR Case Study

	Resp	Exec. Style	Data
γ	$\gamma_1 = 0.39$	$\gamma_2 = 0.34$	$\gamma_3 = 0.3$
% acc	92	87.5	97

For the selection of γ_1–γ_3, the variability of the phrases needs to be considered (e.g. responsibility is usually concise with 1–2 words that occur often like "controller", the data phrase on the other hand is likely to cover a longer span of words with higher variance). This also leads to the high accuracy of the similarity computation for the data component: as the text spans are much longer, the similarity computation is less dependent on each word. With the setting in Table 4, we retrieved 11 execution style, 0 negation, 17 responsibility and 1 data deviation.

4.3   Post-processing and Findings

By reviewing the results of Steps 1 and 2, we observed the following: i) the constraint is truly missing in the realization and thus a violation ($\mapsto$ Case 2), ii) multiple deviation definitions hold leading to ambiguous cases that need manual resolution, iii) the constraints are very dissimilar which cause an erroneous automatic analysis. The 17 identified responsibility deviation are caused by three reasons: false similarity calculation and thus a false positive deviation, an unspecific subject in the realization (e.g., "the responsible department" or "management", which could be a controller, processor, or third party vs. "the controller"), or due to the acting role being missing in the constraint as it is formulated in passive style. The data deviation is due to wrong object phrase parsing and the execution style deviations are caused by false similarity calculation and different writing style (e.g. from "obtain [...] the erasure", only "obtain" is the execution style and thus causes a deviation if compared to "be deleted"), these are considered false positives and thus not true deviations. As the unspecific and missing responsibilities are true deviations, we have an overall precision for the deviation detection of 55%. The results of Table 2-4 show, that the approach and technologies used work. However, some of the constraints and their parts being compared are still different (which is especially visible in the true positive execution style deviations) and thus need to be made more comparable (see Sect. 5 Comparability) in the pre-processing to improve the deviation assessment. Thus, this work is just a first step, which does not assess the compliance of all constraints fully automated, but aids a user in directly recognizing the most similar constraint pairs and the deviations within these.

4.4   Cross-regulation Application Through Case Study 2

As second Case study, the regulatory document ISO27001 on information security management systems is compared to "Implementation Guideline ISO/IEC 27001:2013" realization from a company. In the ISO norm, Sections 0–3, Annex and Bibliography are excluded as they contain no constraints. Analogously, for the companies guideline, the preamble, Glossary, References, Index and Appendix were not considered. The ISO Case study differs in many aspects from the GDPR Case study and was analyzed to evaluate the generalizability of the approach. Based on the pre-processing, 139 regulatory constraints and 278 constraints from the realization were extracted. Running the same configuration as in Case study 1, we achieved similar deviation occurrences, leading to the assumption that the choice of thresholds $(\gamma, \gamma_1 - \gamma_3)$ can be transferred from one Case study to another without individual selection for each application. This suggests that if our approach was to be applied to a different use case in practise, there would be no need for the creation of a gold standard. The identified thresholds $(\gamma, \gamma_1 - \gamma_3)$ can be used as a basis and fine tuned to the specific use case via manual inspection of the results, i.e. the similarity of deviation aspects. Generalizability limitations for Case study 2 are further detailed in Sect. 5.

5 Discussion

This section discusses the generalizability to other regulatory documents and their realizations and the comparability enhancement in order to improve the precision in Step 1 and constraint part deviation assessment in Step 2.

Generalizability The applicability to other regulatory documents may require an enhancement of the *constraint signal words*. Thus, for Case Study 2 the predefined set of signal words was enhanced with "duties", "requirements", "require" and its conjugations. Additionally, the *choice of similarity thresholds* needs to be reviewed for other use cases as they strongly influence the results.

Adjustments to Algorithm 1 become necessary if the realization of the use case is formulated in a way, that multiple realization sentences combined are fulfilling one regulatory constraint. In Case study 1, the regulatory document was more extended, resulting in almost 3 times as many constraints from the regulatory document compared to the realization. Therefore, Algorithm 1 is designed to map only one realization sentence to each regulatory constraint. However, in Case study 2, the realization is the more comprehensive document, suggesting that in this Case study a regulatory constraint is represented as multiple realization sentences. Thus Algorithm 1 has to be adjusted to allow multiple realization constraints to be mapped to one regulatory constraint.

Comparability To improve comparability between the two documents, different *levels of abstraction and length* of texts need to be better incorporated in the similarity computations. Transforming *passive formulated sentences to active* writing also poses a major challenge as current solutions do not deliver satisfactory results for long and complex regulatory sentences and can not handle implicit subjects in passive sentences. This is especially important for the deviation assessment in Step 2. Moreover, there is a necessity to *include meta information* such as document structure and referenced content. Regulatory documents and their realizations contain various references to other parts of the same document or other documents, such as *"where the processing is based on point (f) of Article 6(1)"*. Without the information what is contained in *"point (f) of Article 6(1)"*, the constraint is not self-contained and can only be assessed insufficiently.

Additionally, the *inclusion of the documents structure information*, e.g. the section title can improve the meaningfulness of a constraint. The presented approach includes section titles for the key phrase method in step 1 but further investigations how to integrate them in the entire approach are necessary.

6   Related Work

[25] address the compliance between policies and actual scenarios by utilizing a question answering method. [18] train BERT variations with annotated bill pairs to calculate the semantic similarity between bills and the approach compares whole subsections of text, rather than in-depth constraint deviations. Additionally, bills greatly vary from regulatory documents and to the best of our knowledge there is no annotated set available we could use to train such a model for our application area. [7] classify EU laws into topics but perform no comparison calculations, neither between the law nor to their realizations. Within our application use case, [10,17] use BERT and other NLP methods to measure the compliance of policies with the GDPR. However, these approaches calculate the similarity on segment or document level and state "it would be hard to perform rule-by-rule analysis" [10]. Our approach allows for this in-depth deviation analysis. Another line of research focuses on deriving formalized constraints, e.g., [4] or requirements extraction from natural language text operating in a manual, e.g., [6], or (semi-) automatic way [9,27,31].

From a technological point of view compared to string matching approaches like [11], our approach uses more sophisticated text matching and similarity means such as BERT and S-BERT [22] which constitute the current state-of-the art for semantic text similarity [13].

7   Conclusion and Outlook

This paper provides an approach for assessing the compliance degree between a regulatory document and its realization, e.g., a policy. Newly proposed Regulatory Compliance Assessment Solution Requirements (RCASR) build the foundation for a fine-granular assessment of constraint coverage and deviations. The compliance degree assessment approach includes pre- and post- processing steps as well as a processing part where coverage and deviations are determined in an automatic way, still leaving room for users to adapt and control the system. The evaluation demonstrates the importance of finding corresponding constraints in the compared documents (step 1), most accurately extracting their phrase components (step 2) and selecting of the corresponding thresholds for both steps. As future work, we aim to address the RCASRs referring to time and task execution order deviation and plan to provide recommendations on the choice of parameters and support for changes of either regulatory documents or realizations.

Acknowledgement. This work has been partly funded by SAP SE in the context of the research project "Building Semantic Models for the Process Mining Pipeline".

References

1. van der Aa, H., Ciccio, C.D., Leopold, H., Reijers, H.A.: Extracting declarative process models from natural language. In: Advanced Information Systems Eng, pp. 365–382 (2019). https://doi.org/10.1007/978-3-030-21290-2_23
2. Antic, Z.: Python Natural Language Processing Cookbook. Packt, Birmingham (2021)
3. Awad, A.M.H.A.: A compliance management framework for business process models. Ph.D. thesis, University of Potsdam (2010)
4. Bajwa, I.S., Lee, M.G., Bordbar, B.: SBVR business rules generation from natural language specification. In: AI for Business Agility (2011)
5. Bowman, S.R., Angeli, G., Potts, C., Manning, C.D.: A large annotated corpus for learning natural language inference. In: Empirical Methods in Natural Language Processing, pp. 632–642 (2015). https://doi.org/10.18653/v1/d15-1075
6. Breaux, T.D., Antón, A.I.: Analyzing regulatory rules for privacy and security requirements. IEEE Trans. Softw. Eng. **34**(1), 5–20 (2008). https://doi.org/10.1109/TSE.2007.70746
7. Chalkidis, I., Fergadiotis, M., Androutsopoulos, I.: MultiEURLEX - a multi-lingual and multi-label legal document classification dataset for zero-shot cross-lingual transfer. In: Empirical Methods in Natural Language Processing, pp. 6974–6996 (2021). https://doi.org/10.18653/v1/2021.emnlp-main.559
8. Chalkidis, I., Fergadiotis, M., Malakasiotis, P., Aletras, N., Androutsopoulos, I.: LEGAL-BERT: the muppets straight out of law school. CoRR abs/2010.02559 (2020)
9. Dragoni, M., Villata, S., Rizzi, W., Governatori, G.: Combining natural language processing approaches for rule extraction from legal documents. In: AI Approaches to the Complexity of Legal Systems, pp. 287–300 (2017). https://doi.org/10.1007/978-3-030-00178-0_19
10. Elluri, L., Chukkapalli, S.S.L., Joshi, K.P., Finin, T., Joshi, A.: A BERT based approach to measure web services policies compliance with GDPR. IEEE Access **9**, 148004–148016 (2021). https://doi.org/10.1109/ACCESS.2021.3123950
11. Faro, S., Lecroq, T.: The exact online string matching problem: a review of the most recent results. ACM Comput. Surv. **45**(2), 13:1–13:42 (2013). https://doi.org/10.1145/2431211.2431212
12. Friedrich, F., Mendling, J., Puhlmann, F.: Process model generation from natural language text. In: Advanced Information Systems Engineering, pp. 482–496 (2011). https://doi.org/10.1007/978-3-642-21640-4_36
13. Gillioz, A., Casas, J., Mugellini, E., Khaled, O.A.: Overview of the transformer-based models for NLP tasks. Comp. Sci. Inf. Syst. 179–183 (2020). https://doi.org/10.15439/2020F20
14. Han, J., Kamber, M., Pei, J.: Data Mining: Concepts and Techniques, 3rd edn. Morgan Kaufmann, Burlington (2011)
15. Hashmi, M., Governatori, G., Lam, H.-P., Wynn, M.T.: Are we done with business process compliance: state of the art and challenges ahead. Knowl. Inf. Syst. **57**(1), 79–133 (2018). https://doi.org/10.1007/s10115-017-1142-1
16. Honnibal, M., Montani, I.: spaCy 2. natural language understanding with bloom embeddings, convolutional neural networks and incremental parsing. Unpublished software application. https://spacy.io (2017)
17. Kawintiranon, K., Liu, Y.: Towards automatic comparison of data privacy documents: a preliminary experiment on gdpr-like laws. CoRR abs/2105.10117 (2021)

18. Kim, J., Griggs, E., Kim, I.S., Oh, A.: Learning bill similarity with annotated and augmented corpora of bills. In: Empirical Methods in Natural Language Processing, pp. 10048–10064 (2021). https://doi.org/10.18653/v1/2021.emnlp-main.787

19. Ly, L.T., Maggi, F.M., Montali, M., Rinderle-Ma, S., van der Aalst, W.M.P.: Compliance monitoring in business processes: functionalities, application, and tool-support. Inf. Syst. **54**, 209–234 (2015). https://doi.org/10.1016/j.is.2015.02.007

20. Müller, N.M., Kowatsch, D., Debus, P., Mirdita, D., Böttinger, K.: On GDPR compliance of companies' privacy policies. In: Text, Speech, and Dialogue, vol. 11697, pp. 151–159 (2019). https://doi.org/10.1007/978-3-030-27947-9_13

21. Qamar, A., Javed, T., Beg, M.O.: Detecting compliance of privacy policies with data protection laws. CoRR abs/2102.12362 (2021)

22. Reimers, N., Gurevych, I.: Sentence-bert: sentence embeddings using siamese bert-networks. In: Empirical Methods in Natural Language Processing, pp. 3980–3990 (2019). https://doi.org/10.18653/v1/D19-1410

23. Reimers, N., Gurevych, I.: Making monolingual sentence embeddings multilingual using knowledge distillation. In: Empirical Methods in Natural Language Processing, pp. 4512–4525 (2020). https://doi.org/10.18653/v1/2020.emnlp-main.365

24. Rose, S., Engel, D., Cramer, N., Cowley, W.: Automatic keyword extraction from individual documents. In: Text Mining: Applications and Theory, 1st edn., pp. 1–20, March 2012. https://doi.org/10.1002/9780470689646.ch1

25. Saeidi, M., Yazdani, M., Vlachos, A.: Cross-policy compliance detection via question answering. In: Empirical Methods in Natural Language Processing, pp. 8622–8632 (2021). https://doi.org/10.18653/v1/2021.emnlp-main.678

26. Sanchez, G.: Sentence boundary detection in legal text. In: Natural Legal Lang. Proc. Workshop, pp. 31–38 (2019)

27. Sapkota, K., Aldea, A., Younas, M., Duce, D.A., Bañares-Alcántara, R.: Extracting meaningful entities from regulatory text: towards automating regulatory compliance. In: Workshop on Requirements Engineering and Law, pp. 29–32 (2012). https://doi.org/10.1109/RELAW.2012.6347798

28. Williams, A., Nangia, N., Bowman, S.R.: A broad-coverage challenge corpus for sentence understanding through inference. In: Human Language Technologies, pp. 1112–1122 (2018). https://doi.org/10.18653/v1/n18-1101

29. Winter, K., van der Aa, H., Rinderle-Ma, S., Weidlich, M.: Assessing the compliance of business process models with regulatory documents. In: Conceptual Modeling, pp. 189–203 (2020). https://doi.org/10.1007/978-3-030-62522-1_14

30. Winter, K., Rinderle-Ma, S.: Detecting constraints and their relations from regulatory documents using NLP techniques. In: OTM Conferences, pp. 261–278 (2018). https://doi.org/10.1007/978-3-030-02610-3_15

31. Winter, K., Rinderle-Ma, S.: Deriving and combining mixed graphs from regulatory documents based on constraint relations. In: Advanced Information Systems Engineering, pp. 430–445 (2019). https://doi.org/10.1007/978-3-030-21290-2_27

32. Yin, J., Wang, J.: A dirichlet multinomial mixture model-based approach for short text clustering. In: Knowledge Discovery and Data Mining, pp. 233–242 (2014). https://doi.org/10.1145/2623330.2623715

Verification of Quantitative Temporal Compliance Requirements in Process Descriptions Over Event Logs

Marisol Barrientos[✉][iD], Karolin Winter, Juergen Mangler,
and Stefanie Rinderle-Ma[iD]

TUM School of Computation, Information and Technology, Technical University of
Munich, Garching, Germany
{marisol.barrientos,karolin.winter,juergen.mangler,
stefanie.rinderle-ma}@tum.de

Abstract. Process compliance verification ensures that processes
adhere to a set of given regulatory requirements which are typically
assumed to be available in a formalized way using, e.g., LTL. However, formalized requirements are rarely available in practice, but rather
embedded in regulatory documents such as the GDPR, requiring extraction and formalization by experts. Due to the vast amount and frequent
changes in regulatory documents, it is almost impossible to keep formalized requirements up to date in a manual way. Therefore, this paper
presents an approach towards compliance verification between natural
language text and event logs without the need for requirements formalization. This enables humans to cope with an increasingly complex environment. The approach focuses on quantitative temporal requirements
(QTCR) and consists of multiple steps. First, we identify clauses with
temporal expressions from process descriptions. Second, we generate a
set of QTCR by mapping the retrieved clauses to event log activities.
Finally, in the third step, we verify that the event log is compliant with
the QTCR. The approach is evaluated based on process descriptions and
synthesized event logs. For the latter, we implement time shifting as a
concept for simulating real-life logs with varying temporal challenges.

Keywords: Compliance Verification · Temporal Compliance
Requirements · Natural Language Text · Process Descriptions · Event
Logs

1 Introduction

Business process compliance aims at ensuring that business processes adhere to
the constraints that are imposed on them and is a crucial task for companies
as non-compliance can lead to severe fines. Compliance verification as the task
of verifying process models or event logs against constraints and determining
compliance violations has therefore been addressed extensively in the literature.
However, most compliance verification approaches require already formalized
compliance constraints [4,17,27]. Consequently, compliance verification can be

M. Indulska et al. (Eds.): CAiSE 2023, LNCS 13901, pp. 417–433, 2023.
https://doi.org/10.1007/978-3-031-34560-9_25

time-consuming, requires expert knowledge, and might hence be error-prone. Therefore, it is desirable to directly verify compliance of event logs with the source of compliance constraints which are natural language texts, e.g., process descriptions, internal policies, or regulatory documents. Compliance assessment between process models and natural language text has been addressed [28], but approaches for direct compliance verification of natural language text with event logs are, to the best of our knowledge, missing. Due to the complexity of textual descriptions and their interpretation, in this paper, we focus on one aspect of compliance requirements, i.e., temporal requirements, since *"time is one of the most important dimensions that a compliance rule language must tackle"* [17] and second most mentioned perspective in literature after control flow as stated in [27]. Moreover, we consider process descriptions as representative of natural text documents in order to tame the complexity of arbitrary regulatory documents.

The restrictions described in temporal compliance requirements are delimited by temporal information, which is defined as the information used to sequence events and quantify their duration or gaps between them. Temporal information can contain both quantitative and qualitative temporal expressions or relations between these types of expressions [17,20]. An example of a requirement including a qualitative temporal expression is: *activity A must be executed before activity B*. This emphasizes the importance of arranging activities in the proper sequence within the process control flow. Our paper focuses on quantitative temporal expressions, which gave rise to the concept of Quantitative Temporal Compliance Requirements (QTCR) which augment activity executions with temporal conditions, e.g., *activity A must be completed within 10 days*. A QTCR must contain a quantitative temporal expression, however, might not contain qualitative temporal expressions or relations between both of them. This paper aims to explore how to directly verify quantitative temporal compliance requirements expressed in natural language texts over event logs.

The approach takes a process description in natural language text and an event log as input and outputs a set of QTCR violations. The identification of QTCR is a challenging task that involves i) generating one QTCR, which consists of the temporal expression and its related activities, for each temporal expression extracted from the process description, and ii) utilizing event log information to extract a set of unique labels from the *label* attribute. The QTCR are then paired with the most similar label from this set. Once the QTCR are built, the event log is used to extract the desired set of violations, taking into consideration the *label*, *timestamp*, and *life cycle transition* of each event. The latter is essential for reasoning the duration of activities.

The remainder of the paper is structured as follows. First, the problem statement and challenges are outlined in Sect. 2, followed by the foundations for identifying QTCR from natural language texts in Sect. 3. The verification approach is described in Sect. 4 and evaluated in Sect. 5. Section 6 discusses the evaluation results and limitations of the approach, while Sect. 7 outlines related work. The paper concludes in Sect. 8.

2   Problem Illustration and Challenges

Figure 1 depicts an artificial running example illustrating the problem addressed in this paper, i.e., extracting QTCR from a process description (top left) and verifying whether they were violated or not based on an event log (bottom left). The corresponding process model is depicted on the right and will be picked up in the data generation section in Sect. 5.

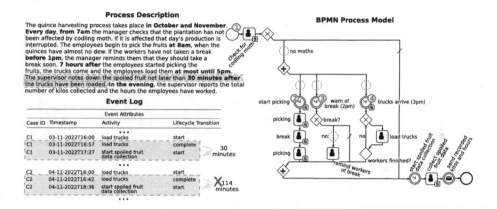

Fig. 1. Running Example: Agriculture Logistics Process

In Fig. 1 all quantitative temporal expressions present in the process description are marked in bold font, e.g., *before 1 pm*. Temporal expressions in our context are parts of text containing temporal information. QTCR are in turn temporal expressions combined with information on activities they refer to. In order to enable compliance verification of QTCR based on an event log, we, firstly, have to identify all sentences containing temporal expressions from the process description. Afterwards, the sentences are processed in order to process activities and their temporal relations resulting in the desired QTCR.

To illustrate this, consider the sentence marked in orange: *The supervisor notes down the spoiled fruit not later than 30 min after the trucks have been loaded.*. The relevant elements for QTCR verification are: i) (not later than) 30 min after, ii) trucks have been loaded, and iii) the supervisor notes down the spoiled fruit. This leads us to *Challenge 1: How to extract and normalize temporal expressions from text*, where first, we need to determine the type of temporal statement which can be either explicit, implicit, relative, or unspecified (for details cf. Sect. 3, Table 2). In the example, the temporal expression is relative because the timestamp is built by counting *30 min after the trucks have been loaded*, indicating the duration of the time lag between two activities (*load trucks* and *start spoiled fruit data collection*). However, if the QTCR would be: *after 4 pm, the supervisor notes down the spoiled fruit*, then it will be an explicit temporal expression, determining the starting of an activity. Together with the temporal extraction, normalization is required, which makes temporal expressions comparable. For instance, the system should automatically deduce that *30 min* and *half an hour* represent the same temporal expression. Once temporal expressions are extracted and normalized, we tackle *Challenge 2: How to extract activities that are related to temporal expressions and their temporal relations.* Some temporal restrictions affect the whole process, a single activity or, as in the example, a set of activities, where in this case, in addition, we need to consider specific signal words like *before* and *after* in order to derive the relations between activities. This challenge also covers identifying the involved life cycle transitions, e.g., *30 min after* refers to the completion of an activity (*load trucks*), but also indicates the starting of another (*start spoiled fruit data collection*).

When having extracted activities and their temporal relations from the textual source, we scan the log for corresponding events. Hereby, we cannot assume to have exactly the same labels in the event log as in the process description. Therefore, we need to cope with text similarity aspects. (→ *Challenge 3: Include a notion of label similarity*). From the event log perspective, at least the event attributes *event label*, *timestamp*, and eventually, *life cycle transition start* and *complete* must be present in order to enable compliance verification. All three attributes are described within the XES standard [2] and constitute rather basic assumptions. Once we have mapped all relevant elements from the process description onto corresponding events of the event log, we can verify the QTCR.

3   QTCR Elicitation from Natural Language Text

One prerequisite of the presented approach is to identify how QTCR are phrased in natural language texts. In order to come up with a holistic view of this aspect we consider multiple sources to derive a set of possible QTCR phrases in natural language texts. In the following, we study literature on patterns for quantitative temporal expressions, also called time patterns, in the business process management and medical context, elicit and compare those time patterns with process descriptions, and propose to use an extension of Heideltime [25] for extracting time patterns from natural language text.

Process Time patterns. [26] presents 15 temporal compliance rules (Petri Net oriented) and [16] 10 time patterns (workflow patterns) where [16] covers all the patterns presented in [26] and includes two additional patterns, i.e., Time-Dependent Variability, and Periodicity, that cannot be fully represented based on Petri Nets. [12] introduce multiple time patterns for BPMN, e.g., *Shifted Duration of an Activity with Reset (Hospitalization must last between 24 and 36 h. If the patient has a fever after 30 h, the duration count is reset and will restart after fever disappears.* [12]), and *Shifted Duration of an Activity (Effective antibiotic therapy for endocarditis should last between 2 and 6 weeks, which are counted starting from the first day of negative cultures.* [12]). These patterns can be constructed as the combination of patterns presented in [16,26], plus an extra constraint that shifts the starting reference to count time, demonstrating the complexity of temporal constraints. The semantic analysis of the predicates with quantitative temporal constraints is not considered in [12,16,26].

Process Descriptions. [14,15] provide a set of well-established process descriptions. First, we select the process descriptions containing QTCR and identify common process time patterns among them. The patterns found in the process descriptions cover 9 out of 10 time patterns presented in [16], and all patterns provided in [26] (cf. Table 1). Note that in [16] the Pattern *Time Lag* is split into two patterns, *Time Lag Between Events* and *Time Lag Between Activities*. However, in our case we have considered them together since in our setting we are abstracting to event labels.

Table 1. Time Patterns Retrieved from the Set of Process Descriptions

Time Pattern	Example taken from Process Description
Time Lag	If no response is received after **five days**, a reminder is sent to the claimant
Duration	If the request is not finished **within 30 days**, then the process is stopped and the employee receives an email cancellation notice and must re-submit the expense report
Fixed Date	Halfway the week, **on**, a staff meeting of the entire medical team takes place
Schedule Restricted	**Every morning**, the files which have yet to be processed need to be checked, to make sure they are in order for the court hearing that day
Time-Based	In a small claims tribunal, callovers occur **once a month**, to set down the matter for the upcoming trials
Validity Period	Every day, **from 7am** the manager checks that the plantation has not been affected by codling moth, if it is affected that day's production is interrupted
Cyclic Elements	**On Day 14**, the Internet service is suspended until payment is received
Periodicity	The process starts periodically **on the first of each month** when Assembler AG places an order with the supplier in order to request more product parts

According to Table 1, *each morning* is classified within pattern *Schedule Restricted* because it refers to a fixed schedule. However, by analyzing the phrase semantically it could also be classified as *Periodicity* because it refers to a periodical recurring process element. Further, we can observe that *five days*, belongs to *Time Lag*, it corresponds to the time between activities, but it could also be seen as a *Validity Period* because after those five days, the reminder is sent.

From the natural language processing point of view, these patterns help to understand the type of data we have, but they do not allow us to reach an automatic classification. Besides, they do not follow a standard temporal pattern nomenclature, which makes it unfeasible to compare with other temporal patterns proposed in the past. [16] emphasize that time constraints often come as a side note, or as text added to the process specification, and might change depending on the process implementation.

Medical Domain. For these reasons, we consider literature outside the business process management community. In the medical domain, the TimeML [21] (ISO-TimeML [22] based on the TIDES standard) has been consolidated, which is used to extract and normalize temporal information, events, and their relations. It follows Allen's interval algebra [13] for reasoning about quantitative temporal information, which defines the 13 possible temporal relationships that exist between two temporal intervals [7]. Temporal information is well defined when, given two points in time or two intervals, the relationship between them can be recognized. [6] survey diverse methods and corpora for the extraction of temporal relations in clinical-free texts. In this survey, those who obtained the best results made use of TimeML, and Time Ontology in OWL [1], among other time-related schemas and ontologies. In [5], they present an ontology of temporal concepts that extend Allen's interval algebra to handle uncertain time intervals, making it possible to solve some of the problems presented in [16].

In order to take advantage of the research done in the medical domain and align the common objectives of both communities, we decided to extract the quantitative temporal expressions from the text following the TimeML patterns, in particular, by following TIMEX3, its sub-standard that describes time. Within the tools used to extract temporal annotations, the following stand out: Heideltime [25] (rule-based), SUTime [11] (rule-based), and spaCy's extension timexy[1]. The last one is not evaluated yet in the existing datasets, such as TempEval-3[2] from SemEval workshop, therefore we excluded it. We used the web interface presented in [8] to test Heideltime and SUTime. The one that was able to identify temporal expressions from [14,15] with a higher scope was Heideltime. To improve the results given by Heideltime, a set of new rules was added, to cover temporal expressions which can be found in the context of business process management, e.g., *first working day of the month* or *day 1*. The new set of rules can be found in the repository. Heideltime introduces the concept of *Realization of point expression* [25], which encompasses all possible temporal expressions that can be found in natural language, allowing its normalization. Table 2 shows an example of each type of realization, together with the four different found types.

Table 2. Realization and TIMEX3 Annotation Example

Realization	Compliance Requirement	TIMEX3	Normalized
Explicit	staff meeting **on Wednesday**	DATE	2022-11-23
Implicit	**in the evening**, the supervisor reports it	TIME	XX-XXTEV
Relative	**30 min** after the trucks have finished	DURATION	PT30M
Unspecified	callovers occur **once a month**	SET	P1M

---

[1] https://pypi.org/project/timexy/, last access: 2023-03-27.

[2] https://paperswithcode.com/dataset/tempeval-3, last access: 2023-03-27.

TIMEX3 of type *DATE* are points of granularity *day, month*, or any greater, while the type *TIME* refers to a granularity smaller than a day (e.g., minutes). The type *SET* represents a periodical aspect of an event, describing a set of times or dates, or frequency within a time interval (e.g.,*once a month*). Explicit realizations of point expressions correspond to *DATE*s or *TIME*s, they do not need further knowledge to be normalized. However, implicit expressions need a point from which to normalize, as for example in the temporal expression *in the evening* it is required to know from and until when is considered to be *evening*, they must be defined by a user. Furthermore, in our particular use case, it is common to see expressions like *working days*, they must be defined by an user. Relative types cannot be normalized unless there is context information, as we can see in Table 2 it is necessary to know when the trucks have finished.

4   QTCR Verification Approach

Figure 2 depicts the proposed QTCR verification approach. The first step involves annotating temporal expressions from the process descriptions. These can be defined as abstract concept that contains the title of the process description, the original sentence, the identified time together with its TIMEX3 type, and its normalized value. Afterwards, we create one QTCR per annotated temporal expression through several intermediate steps (cf. sub-process in Fig. 2). Within this sub-process until the fifth step the knowledge from the event log is not required. In the last step, we determine QTCR violations. The approach is illustrated based on the running example presented in Sect. 2

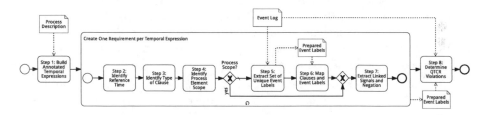

Fig. 2. Overview of QTCR Verification Approach

Step 1 - Build Annotated Temporal Expressions. Within this step, we, first of all, identify all sentences containing at least one temporal expression, i.e., in the case of the running example presented in Sect. 2 all sentences containing terms in bold font. Phrases without temporal expressions are not considered. We annotate each temporal expression using our extended version of Heideltime, as described in Sect. 3, resulting in a set of annotated sentences. Consider, e.g., the sentence from the running example: *The supervisor notes down the spoiled fruit not later than 30 min after the trucks have been loaded.* As we can deduce from Table 2, the identified time *30 min* will be annotated as *DURATION*, with a normalized value equal to *PT30M*. In the next step, we underline that, in order to complete its normalization in this case, context information is needed.

Step 2 - Identify Reference Time. At the end of Sect. 3, it was indicated that the relative realizations of point expressions, those of *DURATION* type, require a reference time in order to be correctly normalized. In our running example, the reference point is the instant (timestamp) corresponding to the activity when the trucks have been loaded (life cycle transition equaling complete). However, if we find expressions, implicit or unspecific, it is not necessary to calculate the reference point because their normalized temporary expressions already contain enough information. In this case, the beginning of each instance of the event log is taken as the reference point, e.g., if the first activity in the event log started on the 21st of November of 2022, then the expression *Wednesday* will be normalized as 23-11-2022. Step one and two address *Challenge 1*.

Step 3 - Identify Type of Clauses. Time constraints that are contained within conditional clauses have to be treated differently than those contained in declarative clauses. Conditions represent decisions that vary the control flow. This prompts us to differentiate between declarative, condition, and consequent clauses. By looking at the running example, in the sentence: *If the workers have not taken a break before 1 pm, the manager reminds them that they should take a break soon*, we can see that the manager reminds the workers, after 1 pm, to take a break only if the workers have not taken a break before 1 pm. This means that if they took the break before 1 pm they should not be reminded. Our approach splits this sentence into two clauses, one containing the condition clause and the other containing the consequence clause. In the following, steps is shown how each of those clauses is mapped with their corresponding activities and restricted time expressions (i.e. a temporal expression plus a signal). From this step until step number seven the *Challenge 2* is addressed. As mentioned in [16], temporal restrictions can be adjusted to different process elements (single activity, activity set, process model, or set of process instances), if the sentence has any conditional clause then the time restriction will affect a set of activities.

Step 4 - Identify Process Element Scope. Temporal expression boundaries can also refer to the general scope of the process by limiting the start and completion time of the first or last activity, e.g., *the quince harvesting process takes place in October and November*. It is clear that the temporal expressions *October* and *November* constitute a boundary for the duration of the process. By looking at Fig. 2, we can see that when the QTCR delimits the full process, then steps five and six of the approach are not needed because for instance, the only involved activities are the first, the last activity, or both. Otherwise, if the sentence refers to a specific activity then steps 5 and 6 cannot be left out.

Step 5 - Extract Set of Unique Event Labels. This step takes the event log as input and identifies all possible unique event labels from all traces. Moreover, the labels are transformed into a lemmatized bag-of-words representation. In the running example, the event label *load trucks* is transformed into {*load, truck*}. As during the next step, i.e., the mapping, we make use of similarity computations between activity and event labels, we ensure via such pre-processing, that noise is reduced and only relevant terms contribute to the comparison. The prepared labels can now be compared with the clauses present in the sentence containing the temporal expression in the next step.

Step 6 - Map Clauses and Event Labels. After extracting the set of unique event labels from the event log, and identifying the different types of clauses present in each temporal expression sentence, each clause is turned into a lemmatized bag-of-words representation. The mapping between the lemmatized clauses and lemmatized event labels is performed by computing the cosine similarities between the embedding of tokens from all the event labels (from the event log), and the clauses (from the sentences containing a temporal expression). This task addresses *Challenge 3* and was carried out by using BERTScore[3] [29], a method used for automatically evaluating the performance of text creation systems. The running example sentence contains these two clauses *the supervisor notes down the spoiled fruit* and *the trucks have been loaded*. If we look at the event log label candidates extracted for the first clause the first top two are *Collect Spoiled Fruit Data* and *Start Spoiled Fruit Data Collection*, while for the second clause, they are: *Trucks Arrive (3 pm)* and *Load Trucks*. After identifying which event log label each clause belongs to, we identify signal words and whether or not negative constraints are present (e.g., *the staff meeting is never on Wednesday*).

Step 7 - Extract Linked Signals and Negation. After knowing which activities are detected for each temporal expression, we proceed to extract their relations. This step is taken after the others in order to know to what activity or temporal expression belongs to each relation, otherwise in cases where in the same sentence there are more than one temporal expressions we could not distinguish between the relations from each of them. For example in the sentence *7h after the employees started picking the fruits, the trucks come and the employees load them at most until 5 pm*, the signal *after* will be linked with the activity *started picking the fruits* and the temporal expression *7h*, while the signal *until* will be linked to *load trucks* and *5 pm*. We summarize the signals in three categories: *AFTER, BEFORE*, and *IN*, which represent all of them. Then we check if the clause is negated to see if the temporal requirement has to be excluded, e.g., *this must not happen in October*. Lastly, we identify based on the extracted data the life cycle transition (start, complete, or both) corresponding to each QTCR.

Step 8 - Determine QTCR Violations. This step takes as input the event log and the extracted requirements and delivers all QTCR violations. For each requirement, it must be verified that the process or activities belonging to the consequence or declarative type have the desired timestamps and states, otherwise, they are considered violations. Consider again the running example Fig. 1. The extracted temporal requirement identified contains the temporal expression of *30 min* (of type *DURATION*, and norm. *PT30M*) Table 2, and the following activities involved Table 3. This allows to automatically check if the event log trace meets the requirement of: by counting 30 min from the timestamp corre-

---

[3] https://github.com/Tiiiger/bert_score, last access: 2023-03-27.

sponding to the complete state of the *load tracks* activity, all the traces from *start spoiled data fruit collection* (both started and finished) should be before.

Table 3. Requirement Extracted from Running Example (short version)

Event Log Label	Type	Status	Signal	Reference
truck load	declarative	complete	in	true
start spoiled data fruit collection	declarative	start & complete	before	false

5   Evaluation

The QTCR verification approach is prototypically implemented[4] in Python 3.10 using the tools and packages mentioned in Sect. 4 and additionally using *NLTK*[5] and the *Python Heideltime Wrapper*[6]. The data set[7] for evaluating the approach is based on 14 process descriptions from [14,15] and the running example. The data generation part is outlined in Sect. 5.1 and the evaluation results are detailed in Sect. 5.2. Each of the 8 steps in the approach has been evaluated independently and in addition, we provide an overall end-to-end evaluation result.

5.1   Data Generation

For the data generation part, we started by modeling the process descriptions using the Cloud Process Execution Engine[8] (CPEE) [18,19,24]. For each of the scenarios, we created executable models with the following properties: i) the labels follow the text as close as possible, ii) the duration of tasks is correct in relation to each other, but is scaled down to seconds, iii) the duration of tasks slightly varies so that both successful executions as well violations are possible (according to the scenario text), and iv) we included some plausible data flow, to aid future work based on the generated logs.

Based on these simple models, which albeit only span the duration of some seconds, we introduced a time-shifting mechanism, to generate logs that span a realistic time frame based on the description in the scenarios. The time-shifting algorithm works based on a set of annotations to the process model:

---

[4] https://www.cs.cit.tum.de/bpm/software/, last access: 2023-03-27.
[5] https://www.nltk.org/, last access: 2023-03-27.
[6] https://github.services.devops.takamol.support/PhilipEHausner/
python_heideltime, last access: 2023-03-27.
[7] https://www.cs.cit.tum.de/bpm/data/, last access: 2023-03-27.
[8] https://cpee.org, last access: 2023-03-27.

– **Start Event:**
  - Multiplication Factor (MF): how much should the duration in seconds be scaled up, e.g., if the value here is"1 h" then every second is scaled up to one hour.
  - Starting Point (SP): a natural language expression for shifting the start of the process, e.g., an arbitrary date and time might be used as a start. Another important requirement is, that this expression can be dynamically set when instantiating this process, to allow for the creation of a series of logs for different days or months.
  - Random +/- Starting Shift (R): a small piece of code that returns the amount of time to add or subtract from the starting point. As this can include logic for random values, instantiation the process multiple times leads to variations in the resulting logs.

– **Activity:**
  - Type (T): an activity might either be shifted to have (a) a specific duration (DUR), or (b) a specific end (END). For both cases all the subsequent task start events have to be shifted, for case (b) the duration of the task has to be adjusted accordingly.
  - Expression (E): a natural language expression. Again code snippets can be provided, to realize randomness.

For the running example presented in Fig. 1, the following values were chosen: ① utilizes a fixed (MF) of 1 h, a fixed starting last (SP) (e.g., 2022-11-01), and a random starting shift (R) of 15 min. In ② (T) is set to (END) and (E) to a random range of 0 to 15 min after 08:00. In ③ (T) is set to (END) and (E) to 13:00. Finally in ④ (T) is set to (END) and (E) is set to 15:00 plus a random range of 0 to 15 min. We then executed this file 50 times, which resulted in a varied set of logs, which contain both violations and successful executions (see footnote 7).

5.2   Evaluation Results

In order to cope with the fact that errors can add up throughout the approach, we provide step-by-step outcomes for each stage of the approach, as detailed in Sect. 4. To do so, we define the following evaluation targets. We measure precision, recall, and F1 score for temporal expression extraction and annotation with evaluation targets a) original Heideltime rules and b) including the updated Heideltime rules covering Step 1. Moreover, we evaluate c) the identification of reference time for Step 2, d) the type of clause for Step 3, e) process element scope for Step 4, f) event log labels mapping for Steps 5 and 6, g) signals and negations for Step 7, and h) identification of QTCR violations for Step 8.

All 14 selected process descriptions from [14, 15] as well as the running example are used for evaluating a) and b). For evaluation target a), i.e., using the original version of Heideltime we received a precision of 0.9091, recall of 0.6452, and F1 score of 0.7547. Updating the Heideltime rules ($\mapsto$ b)) results in a precision of 0.9744, recall of 0.9268, and F1 score of 0.9500. Those scores are an average overall of 15 process descriptions. The included rules provided support for temporal expressions found in business process descriptions, where they talk about workdays, processing times, etc. However, the new rules do not completely allow for the identification of temporal expressions that refer to past or future activities, such as *at the same time as the next activity is being executed.*

Considering the temporal patterns and their possible phrasing as outlined in Sect. 3, we selected 4 process descriptions (including the running example) that are covering all possible QTCR phrases and are therefore representative for further evaluating targets c) to h). For each process description, we generated synthesized event logs with 50 traces each, as stated in Sect. 5.1.

After the evaluation of c) we observed that we were able to distinguish between the requirements that refer to the start or completion of another activity, an activity including shifting, or the starting of the process. In all the scenarios, the different types of clauses (i.e. declarative, condition, and consequence) were identified ($\mapsto$ d)), even for cases where a sentence contained multiple clauses accompanied by conjunctive and disjunctive operators. Moreover, our approach was able to differentiate whether the requirement was referring to the full process or not ($\mapsto$ e)). However, this could bring further challenges e.g., the case of evaluating the events of the log of a sub-process that is embedded in the event log of a general process, where not only the starting and completion of the main process is relevant but also the related sub-process.

The precision scores for evaluation targets f), g), and h) are summarized in Table 4. It can be deduced that the approach delivered in general satisfying results. In particular, for evaluation target f) the precision evaluates on average 0.76. The score for *Billing Process of ISP* is notably lower and that is due to

Table 4. Precision for Targets f), g), and h)

Process Description	f)	g)	h)
Quince Harvesting	0.72	0.81	0.89
Meeting Related Activities	1.00	1.00	1.00
Billing Process of ISP	0.57	1.00	0.10
Expense Report	0.75	0.80	1.00

the appearance of sentences with similar semantics, the differences in meaning are almost negligible even for an expert in the field (e.g., *charge late fee, debit outstanding amount*). For the evaluation of target g) we have at least a precision of 0.80 for the *Expense Report* example and for half of them, we achieved again a precision of 1. The cases that failed were due to the combination of signals, as in the case of *not later than 30 min after.* Of the 200 traces used to evaluate h), 20% of them violated a QTCR. In three of the scenarios, the precision was at least 0.89, however, in *Billing Process of ISP* the performance was affected by the presence of incorrect labels and an unusual QTCR that contained a compound noun referring to data attributes, i.e. *on Day 10, the transaction that failed on Day 8 is re-attempted* demonstrating the accumulation of errors within the pipeline.

The evaluation results demonstrate how our approach is capable of satisfactorily identifying temporal expressions ($\mapsto$ a) and b)) in business process descriptions along with the reference time ($\mapsto$ c)). Each extracted expression gives shape to a QTCR and in all the cases mentioned in Table 4, the clauses and the process element scope, i.e., boundaries of the temporal expression, were correctly identified ($\mapsto$ d) and e)). In the last three steps, the extraction of signals, negations, mapping between extracted clauses with the labels presented in the log, and identification of events that violated the QTCR were evaluated ($\mapsto$ f), g), and h)). Taking the average precision obtained to evaluate these three aspects, *Billing Process of ISP* was the case delivering the lowest precision accounting to 0.55. The case with the highest precision was *Meeting Related Activities* accounting for 1.00. The overall average precision when taking into account all four cases is 0.80.

6   Discussion and Limitations

The applicability and limitations of the approach are discussed below.

Applicability. In the domain of process compliance verification, the applicability of this approach is particularly relevant for organizations that need to ensure their processes adhere to regulatory requirements embedded in natural language text documents, such as the GDPR. For instance, consider the GDPR's requirement for timely notification of data breaches to relevant authorities within 72 h. By focusing on QTCR, the approach can efficiently identify clauses with temporal expressions, map them to event log activities, and verify compliance without relying on the manual formalization of these requirements. Time-shifting can be used in this context to simulate real-life logs by introducing variations in the time taken for organizations to report breaches, assessing the proposed approach's ability to identify compliance issues accurately. This approach is applicable to a wide range of industries and organizations, allowing them to cope with increasingly complex regulatory environments. The evaluation using synthesized event logs and the implementation of time-shifting demonstrate the potential applicability to real-world scenarios, offering a more adaptable way of verifying process compliance and addressing the challenges associated with the manual formalization of regulatory requirements. Additionally, the manual creation of formal rules can be error-prone and time-consuming, making it challenging to maintain up-to-date compliance requirements, further emphasizing the need for an automated solution like the one proposed in this paper.

Generalizability. One crucial part of the approach consists of identifying QTCR from natural language text. In that regard, we need to cope with natural language flexibility and a potential lack of comprehensiveness w.r.t. covering all possible formulations of temporal compliance requirements. In particular, when considering more complex documents like regulatory documents, we might lack generalizability as the possibilities of how QTCR are formulated can be more diverse. During the mapping, one limitation of the approach relates to too similar event labels, e.g., *remind of break* and *take break* as well as *insufficient length of event labels* in the event log. For the latter consider again the running example, i.e., the label in the event log reflecting the activity of the workers needing to take a break is just given as *break*. Such short event labels make it almost impossible to detect the correct mapping between event labels and activities from the process description. This could be overcome by, e.g., including more information from the log file like additional event attributes, in this case, the organizational resource. A similar observation holds for including data attributes which can contribute to extending the semantics of the labels to enhance the mapping.

Ambiguity and Lack of Contextual Information. Moreover, as we realized during modeling the process descriptions for the log generation, missing activity links and references in the texts make it almost impossible to clearly determine which activities are involved in a temporal compliance requirement and what are the reference points to measure compliance violations. Furthermore, according to [9], there is a lack of objectivity in process descriptions, resulting in modelers adopting diverse modeling styles.

7 Related Work

This paper bridges the gap between multiple topics. First, related work on extracting process-related information from natural language text. Imperative model extraction resulting in BPMN models is presented in [15], while [3] extract Declare models from process descriptions and [23] focus on decision model extraction. Most recent approaches exploit deep learning, in particular, GPT-3 models for business process entity and relation extraction from natural language texts [10]. However, those papers do not explicitly address the extraction of quantitative temporal aspects from process descriptions as it is one of the aims of this paper. Moreover, those works solely focus on extracting process models from natural language text and do not touch upon compliance verification at all. Another aspect this paper addresses is ex-post quantitative temporal compliance verification. [4] present an LTL checker. [26] formalize 15 temporal compliance rules allowing for checking temporal compliance rules on a process execution log using alignments. In both cases, the formalization needs to be done manually, i.e., compared to the presented approach it is crucial to have experts formalize the rules based on the given natural language text. As compliance regulations can change frequently, existing approaches such as [4,26] are not as flexible as the approach presented in this paper since both require frequent re-formalization and adding of newly formalized rules. For related work on extracting temporal aspects from natural language text in the medical domain, we refer to Sect. 3.

8 Conclusion and Future Work

Compliance verification constitutes a crucial task within business process compliance management. Typically, compliance requirements are formalized in, e.g., LTL and then checked against an event log. In order to reduce the manual effort, and errors that can arise during the formalization and cope with an increasingly complex regulatory environment subject to frequent changes, we have presented an approach that directly verifies quantitative temporal compliance requirements in natural language text over event logs. For this, we employed a multi-step approach based on natural language processing and evaluated it on a set of well-established process descriptions. The corresponding event logs were generated using the novel concept of time shifting for the cloud process execution engine. For future work, we plan to extend the approach towards more complex documents such as regulatory documents, resource constraint verification, and compliance monitoring at run-time, i.e., on process event streams.

Acknowledgements. This work has been partly funded by SAP SE in the context of the research project "Building Semantic Models for the Process Mining Pipeline" and by the Deutsche Forschungsgemeinschaft (DFG, German Research Foundation) – project number 277991500.

References

1. Time Ontology in OWL (2006). https://www.bibsonomy.org/bibtex/21e7da807dca7f94e75ddcd28567da745/zazi
2. IEEE standard for extensible event stream (XES) for achieving interoperability in event logs and event streams. IEEE Std **1849**, 1–50 (2016). https://doi.org/10.1109/IEEESTD.2016.7740858
3. van der Aa, H., Ciccio, C.D., Leopold, H., Reijers, H.A.: Extracting declarative process models from natural language. In: Advanced Information Systems Engineering, pp. 365–382 (2019). https://doi.org/10.1007/978-3-030-21290-2_23
4. van der Aalst, W.M.P., de Beer, H.T., van Dongen, B.F.: Process mining and verification of properties: an approach based on temporal logic. In: Meersman, R., Tari, Z. (eds.) OTM 2005. LNCS, vol. 3760, pp. 130–147. Springer, Heidelberg (2005). https://doi.org/10.1007/11575771_11
5. Achich, N., Ghorbel, F., Hamdi, F., Métais, E., Gargouri, F.: Approach to reasoning about uncertain temporal data in OWL 2. In: Knowledge-Based and Intelligent Information & Engineering Systems, pp. 1141–1150 (2020). https://doi.org/10.1016/j.procs.2020.09.110
6. Alfattni, G., Peek, N., Nenadic, G.: Extraction of temporal relations from clinical free text: a systematic review of current approaches. J. Biomed. Inf. **108**, 103488 (2020). https://doi.org/10.1016/j.jbi.2020.103488
7. Allen, J.F.: Maintaining knowledge about temporal intervals. Commun. ACM **26**(11), 832–843 (1983). https://doi.org/10.1145/182.358434
8. Aumiller, D., Almasian, S., Pohl, D., Gertz, M.: Online dateing: a web interface for temporal annotations. In: Research and Development in Information Retrieval, pp. 3289–3294 (2022). https://doi.org/10.1145/3477495.3531670
9. Beerepoot, I., Ciccio, C.D., Reijers, H.A., Rinderle-Ma, S.: The biggest business process management problems of our time. In: Proceedings of the International Workshop on BPM Problems to Solve Before We Die (PROBLEMS 2021). CEUR Workshop Proceedings, vol. 2938, pp. 1–5. CEUR-WS.org (2021). http://ceur-ws.org/Vol-2938/paper-PROBLEMS-01.pdf
10. Bellan, P., Dragoni, M., Ghidini, C.: Extracting business process entities and relations from text using pre-trained language models and in-context learning. In: Almeida, J.P.A., Karastoyanova, D., Guizzardi, G., Montali, M., Maggi, F.M., Fonseca, C.M. (eds.) Enterprise Design, Operations, and Computing, vol. 13585, pp. 182–199. Springer, Cham (2022)

11. Chang, A.X., Manning, C.D.: Sutime: A library for recognizing and normalizing time expressions. In: Conference on Language Resources and Evaluation, pp. 3735–3740 (2012)
12. Combi, C., Oliboni, B., Zerbato, F.: A modular approach to the specification and management of time duration constraints in BPMN. Inf. Syst. **84**, 111–144 (2019). https://doi.org/10.1016/j.is.2019.04.010
13. Drakengren, T., Jonsson, P.: Maximal tractable subclasses of Allen's interval algebra: preliminary report. In: Artificial Intelligence, pp. 389–394 (1996)
14. Dumas, M., Rosa, M.L., Mendling, J., Reijers, H.A.: Fundamentals of Business Process Management. Springer, Cham (2013). https://doi.org/10.1007/978-3-642-33143-5
15. Friedrich, F., Mendling, J., Puhlmann, F.: Process model generation from natural language text. In: Mouratidis, H., Rolland, C. (eds.) CAiSE 2011. LNCS, vol. 6741, pp. 482–496. Springer, Heidelberg (2011). https://doi.org/10.1007/978-3-642-21640-4_36
16. Lanz, A., Weber, B., Reichert, M.: Time patterns for process-aware information systems. Requirements Eng. **19**(2), 113–141 (2012). https://doi.org/10.1007/s00766-012-0162-3
17. Ly, L.T., Maggi, F.M., Montali, M., Rinderle-Ma, S., van der Aalst, W.M.P.: Compliance monitoring in business processes: functionalities, application, and tool-support. Inf. Syst. **54**, 209–234 (2015). https://doi.org/10.1016/j.is.2015.02.007
18. Mangler, J., Rinderle-Ma, S.: Cloud process execution engine: Architecture and interfaces (2022). https://doi.org/10.48550/ARXIV.2208.12214
19. Mangler, J., Stuermer, G., Schikuta, E.: Cloud process execution engine-evaluation of the core concepts. arXiv preprint arXiv:1003.3330 (2010)
20. Meiri, I.: Combining qualitative and quantitative constraints in temporal reasoning. Artif. Intell. **87**(1–2), 343–385 (1996). https://doi.org/10.1016/0004-3702(95)00109-3
21. Pustejovsky, J., et al.: The specification language TimeML. In: The Language of Time - A Reader, pp. 545–558 (2005)
22. Pustejovsky, J., Lee, K., Bunt, H., Romary, L.: ISO-TimeML: an international standard for semantic annotation. In: Language Resources and Evaluation (2010)
23. Quishpi, L., Carmona, J., Padró, L.: Extracting decision models from textual descriptions of processes. In: Polyvyanyy, A., Wynn, M.T., Van Looy, A., Reichert, M. (eds.) BPM 2021. LNCS, vol. 12875, pp. 85–102. Springer, Cham (2021). https://doi.org/10.1007/978-3-030-85469-0_8
24. Stertz, F., Rinderle-Ma, S., Hildebrandt, T., Mangler, J.: Testing processes with service invocation: advanced logging in CPEE. In: Drira, K., et al. (eds.) ICSOC 2016. LNCS, vol. 10380, pp. 189–193. Springer, Cham (2017). https://doi.org/10.1007/978-3-319-68136-8_22
25. Strötgen, J., Gertz, M.: Heideltime: high quality rule-based extraction and normalization of temporal expressions. In: Workshop on Semantic Evaluation, pp. 321–324 (2010)
26. Ramezani Taghiabadi, E., Fahland, D., van Dongen, B.F., van der Aalst, W.M.P.: Diagnostic information for compliance checking of temporal compliance requirements. In: Salinesi, C., Norrie, M.C., Pastor, Ó. (eds.) CAiSE 2013. LNCS, vol. 7908, pp. 304–320. Springer, Heidelberg (2013). https://doi.org/10.1007/978-3-642-38709-8_20
27. Voglhofer, T., Rinderle-Ma, S.: Collection and elicitation of business process compliance patterns with focus on data aspects. Bus. Inf. Syst. Eng. **62**(4), 361–377 (2019). https://doi.org/10.1007/s12599-019-00594-3

28. Winter, K., van der Aa, H., Rinderle-Ma, S., Weidlich, M.: Assessing the compliance of business process models with regulatory documents. In: Dobbie, G., Frank, U., Kappel, G., Liddle, S.W., Mayr, H.C. (eds.) ER 2020. LNCS, vol. 12400, pp. 189–203. Springer, Cham (2020). https://doi.org/10.1007/978-3-030-62522-1_14
29. Zhang, T., Kishore, V., Wu, F., Weinberger, K.Q., Artzi, Y.: Bertscore: evaluating text generation with BERT. In: Learning Representations (2020)

Data-Centric Approaches

C-3PA: Streaming Conformance, Confidence and Completeness in Prefix-Alignments

Kristo Raun[1]([✉])[ID], Max Nielsen[2], Andrea Burattin[2][ID], and Ahmed Awad[1,3][ID]

[1] University of Tartu, Tartu, Estonia
{kristo.raun,ahmed.awad}@ut.ee
[2] Technical University of Denmark, Kgs. Lyngby, Denmark
s202785@student.dtu.dk, andbur@dtu.dk
[3] Cairo University, Giza, Egypt

Abstract. The aim of streaming conformance checking is to find discrepancies between process executions on streaming data and the reference process model. The state-of-the-art output from streaming conformance checking is a prefix-alignment. However, current techniques that output a prefix-alignment are unable to handle warm-starting scenarios. Further, no indication is given of how close the trace is to termination—a highly relevant measure in a streaming setting.

This paper introduces a novel approximate streaming conformance checking algorithm that enriches prefix-alignments with confidence and completeness measures. Empirical tests on synthetic and real-life datasets demonstrate that the new method outputs prefix-alignments that have a cost that is highly correlated with the output from the state-of-the-art optimal prefix-alignments. Furthermore, the method is able to handle warm-starting scenarios and indicate the confidence level of the prefix-alignment. A stress test shows that the method is well-suited for fast-paced event streams.

Keywords: Streaming conformance checking · Prefix-alignments · Warm-starting · Confidence · Data streams

1 Introduction

Every organization has processes that need to be executed in order to achieve the organizational goals. Most contemporary processes are built on computer systems—every action leaves a footprint in a database or a log file. This kind of data paves the way for process mining, allowing for the discovery of process models, process monitoring, and measurements of process executions based on organizational data. A key component of process mining is conformance checking, i.e., are processes executed as expected based on a given reference process model?

Traditionally, conformance checking is done in an offline setting: an event log is constructed by filtering events that occurred within a specified time range.

M. Indulska et al. (Eds.): CAiSE 2023, LNCS 13901, pp. 437–453, 2023.
https://doi.org/10.1007/978-3-031-34560-9_26

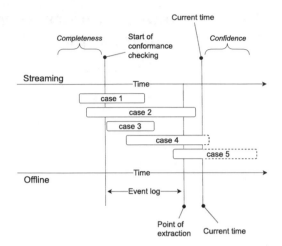

Fig. 1. Differences between streaming and offline conformance checking.

The event log cannot contain any events which occurred after the point of data extraction. These limitations hide several important caveats.

Firstly, process executions commonly exhibit overlap and parallelism. This indicates that some of the process executions from a specified time range are likely to have started before the time range, and some may not yet have concluded. In some cases, this can be remedied by domain knowledge and data preprocessing, e.g., filtering out cases that have not yet concluded. However, such preprocessing induces data loss due to the removal of incomplete process executions and consequently lowers the trustworthiness of the analysis.

Secondly, and more importantly, in an offline setting, the data used for analysis, and the results, are obsolete by design. The longer it takes from data extraction to analysis to decision-making, the less valuable the data becomes. In many real scenarios, such as fraud detection, autonomous driving, malware detection, or health monitoring, making decisions based on stagnant data is impractical, except for high-level trend analysis. Being unaware of discrepancies in individual ongoing process executions can have a broad impact on an organization. This is supported by recent studies, indicating the need for moving towards stream processing and real-time availability of data in process mining [10].

In *streaming conformance checking*, data is observed as an unbounded stream of events rather than a static event log [6]. The organization can receive indications of discrepancies in a continuous manner as soon as these discrepancies occur. This gives the organization the opportunity to remedy the negative impact of observed discrepancies. In order to do that effectively, it is important to know the exact locations of both the wrongly executed and skipped activities.

In long-running processes, an issue that might occur is the *warm-starting* scenario. That is, some process executions are ongoing before the conformance checker is initiated and are thus not completely observable. Examples of such cases can be seen in Fig. 1 with cases 1 and 2. In most conformance checking techniques, this causes a false positive, i.e., a discrepancy is indicated, even if the process followed a conforming behavior. Completeness issues may lower the trustworthiness of the conformance checking method and require a *grace period*, after which a conformance checking method can be expected to output the correct conformance.

Similarly, the ending of a process execution poses a challenge. Streaming conformance checking methods give equal weight to the observed conformance at the beginning of a trace, as they do for conformance that is near the end of a trace's lifecycle. It can be argued that a conforming trace that has seen only a few events has a higher probability of divergence than a conforming trace that has seen most of the expected events. For example, if case 4 and case 5 in Fig. 1 are both conforming, then case 5 has a higher chance of seeing non-conforming behavior. This indicates the need for a confidence measure that would complement the conformance so that organizations can be more alert for traces that are just initializing rather than the traces that are concluding.

The above challenges are especially relevant in the context of complex business processes. When complex processes are deployed, a high level of automation is needed from the computing side, while humans are typically in charge of supervision. In case of deviations, fast decision-making is crucial to keep the systems up and running. To support fast decision-making in such systems, we pose the following two research questions:

- RQ1: can we define a streaming conformance checking algorithm capable of computing prefix alignments with confidence and completeness measurements in warm-starting scenarios?
- RQ2: can the algorithm identified in RQ1 be used in real-world settings?

The paper is structured as follows. Section 2 describes the relevant background. Section 3 discusses the current state of the art. Section 4 introduces the approach and the C-3PA algorithm for computing prefix-alignments enriched with confidence and completeness measures. Section 5 shows the results of the empirical testing, a comparison to existing methods, and a discussion of the algorithm's properties and its matching to the research questions. Section 6 concludes the work and offers ideas for potential further research.

2   Background

In this section, we introduce the main components necessary for understanding the theoretical background of the introduced approach. For further background in process mining and conformance checking, we refer to [1], and [9], respectively.

In process mining terminology, a process model indicates the expected behavior. A process model can be depicted with various semantics. Most conformance checking methods assume the process model to be a Petri net. As is characteristic of real-life processes, a Petri net may exhibit behavior such as sequences, choices, parallelism, and loops [1]. The sequence of fired transitions in a Petri net is an execution sequence $\pi \in M$, where M is the set of behaviors allowed by the Petri net. M is infinite when the model has loops because a loop can unfold an unlimited number of times.

Once the expected behavior is known, the conformance checker also needs to know what is the actual observed behavior. In offline conformance checking, the actual behavior is commonly found in an event log. An event $evt \in \mathcal{U}_{evt}$ is a tuple $evt = (case, act, time) \in \mathcal{U}_{case} \times \mathcal{U}_{act} \times \mathcal{U}_{time}$, referring to a case identifier $case \in \mathcal{U}_{case}$, an associated activity $act \in \mathcal{U}_{act}$, and a timestamp $time \in \mathcal{U}_{time}$. An event log L is a multiset $L \in \mathcal{B}(\mathcal{U}_{case} \times \mathcal{U}_{act} \times \mathcal{U}_{time})$. Informally, L can be considered a container of traces. A trace σ is a finite sequence of events that can be grouped together based on the case id. $\hat{\sigma}$ refers to the prefix of a trace, i.e., the activities seen so far in an ongoing trace.

Streaming conformance checking is done on an event stream $\mathcal{S} : \mathbb{N}_{\geq 0} \longrightarrow \mathcal{U}_{evt}$. Conceptually, a stream is not a collection of events but the natural occurrence of events — at any given time, a new event may be seen, having either a known or a previously unseen case id. An event stream is expected to be unbounded.

A process model and an event log/stream are inputs for a conformance checker. The state-of-the-art output is an alignment between a trace and a model. More formally, an alignment $\gamma = \langle (x_1, y_1), \ldots, (x_n, y_n) \rangle$ is a sequence of pairs, where each pair $(x, y) \in (\mathcal{U}_{act} \cup \{\gg\}) \times (\mathcal{U}_{act} \cup \{\gg\})$ links an activity of the trace σ, or the skip symbol $\gg$, to an activity of the execution sequence π, or the skip symbol, whereas a step $(\gg, \gg)$ is illegal. Alignments allow for an intuitive understanding of the nonconforming activities: they indicate the places where activities match with the expected behavior of the process model (a synchronous move), the places where an activity diverged (a log move), and also the places where the activity expected by the model did not occur (a model move). We denote a conformance cost of an alignment as $\delta(\gamma)$. While different costs can be assigned to log and model moves (non-synchronous moves), in this paper, we assume a cost of 1 for these non-synchronous activities. An alignment can be optimal or suboptimal. An optimal alignment has the minimal cost, i.e., commonly the least amount of non-synchronous moves between a trace and a model. One trace can have multiple optimal alignments. In Petri nets, a silent transition τ indicates a possible skip activity. In accordance with most other research in this area, this paper assigns model moves on τ transitions a cost of 0. Thus, if the model allows for skips and the skip is done, then it is not penalized.

As described in [20], an alignment overestimates the cost of divergence in a streaming setting. Thus, the prefix-alignment $(\hat{\gamma})$ is preferred, as the alignment is not forced to complete the execution sequence on the model. In the rest of the paper, *complete alignment* is used to refer to the alignments from the previous paragraph and to distinguish them from *prefix-alignments*.

While various techniques exist for optimizing the calculation of an optimal alignment, it is still an exponentially hard problem to solve. Thus, approximation methods have been introduced to speed up the calculation. In this paper, the trie data structure is used. A trie $T = (N, E, root, l, \mathcal{F}, min, max)$ where N is a finite set of nodes, $E \subset N \times N$ is a set of edges, $root \in N$ is the root of the trie, $l : N \rightarrow (\mathcal{U}_{act} \cup \{\bot\})$ is a labeling function for nodes, $\mathcal{F} \subset N$ indicates leaf nodes, and $min, max : E \rightarrow \mathbb{N}$ are relations of an edge showing the minimum and maximum distance to reach a leaf node when traversing that edge.

A trie serves as the process model instead of, for example, a Petri net. Importantly, if a Petri net includes a loop, then the Petri net can generate infinite behavior; however, a trie needs to be finite. Thus, the behavior M' allowed by the trie is a subset of the behavior in the Petri net $M' \subseteq M$. Similarly to a Petri net, a trie can be constructed by giving the model constructor an event log - i.e., a *proxy log* (L'). The proxy log serves as a finite representation of behavior allowed in the process. A trie allows for all of the behavior in the proxy log, but no behavior that is outside of it.

A state $s \in S$ is a tuple $(n, \hat{\gamma}, \delta(\hat{\gamma}), \epsilon(\hat{\gamma}), \upsilon(\hat{\gamma}), dt)$, where n is the current node in the trie, $\hat{\gamma}$ is the current prefix-alignment, $\delta(\hat{\gamma})$ is the alignment cost of the current state, $\epsilon(\hat{\gamma}) \in \mathbb{N}$ is the completeness measure, quantifying the behavior not seen at the beginning of the trace, $\upsilon(\hat{\gamma}) \in \mathbb{N}$ is the confidence measure, indicating the amount of behavior not yet seen, and dt is the associated decay time of the state used for releasing states from memory. For a more thorough explanation of *completeness* and *confidence*, we refer to [6], and for a more formal description of *decay time* to [15]. Finally, a state buffer $BS : \mathcal{U}_{case} \mapsto \mathcal{P}(S)$ is a mapping of case ids to the powerset of states. The state buffer is important for keeping track of the latest states of each seen case.

3   State of the Art

One of the first methods for offline conformance checking was token-based replay [16]. The goal is to replay the traces on top of the Petri net. While the method is computationally efficient, it has some important shortcomings: it does not handle well τ transitions nor duplicate labels, and it is not highly informative in terms of the occurred discrepancies.

The alignment-based technique from [2] has been widely accepted as the state of the art for some years. The main benefits of alignments over token-based replay are the deterministic and concise representation of both conforming and non-conforming activities. An unfavorable quality of alignments is the computational complexity. Commonly, a synchronous product net is built between the Petri net model and a model representation of the observed trace to calculate optimal alignments. Then, a search algorithm such as A^* is used for finding the shortest path that minimizes the conformance cost.

Various methods have been introduced to improve memory consumption and computation time. For example, SAT-based approaches have been investigated [5,14], by calculating alignments using SAT formulas. While these methods have generally not outperformed the state-of-the-art implementations yet, they pave the way for easier adoption of such methods in case the SAT solvers are improved in the future. Similarly, planning methods have been investigated [13], utilizing existing knowledge from the domain of planning problems. Planning methods have already shown good results against existing approaches, provided that the process models and event logs are of a large size.

While methods have been introduced to improve the computation time, it is generally still considered impractical to use alignments in large real-life logs, and it remains an active research area to improve the computation complexity of alignments [9].

As mentioned in Sect. 2, complete alignments generally overestimate the cost in a streaming setting, because the methods force the moves on the model to a final state. Prefix-alignments, originally introduced in [3] and adapted to a streaming setting in [20], alleviate the problem by not penalizing traces that have not concluded according to the model. The method introduced in [20] (OCC) calculates prefix alignments on top of event streams. Further, the method includes a window parameter, allowing for a trade-off between computational complexity and approximation error. A window size of 1 has the least computational complexity but the highest possible error, as it only builds on top of the previously calculated prefix-alignment. An infinite window size allows for the computation of optimal alignments at the cost of increased computation time.

Further work in prefix-alignments has mostly attempted to improve the memory footprint of the calculation [17,19]. Recently, [15] introduced an approximate streaming algorithm on top of the trie data structure for the calculation of prefix-alignments that can outperform previous methods for prefix-alignment computation. However, similarly to previous prefix-alignment methods, it cannot handle the warm-starting scenario and does not indicate the confidence of the prefix-alignment.

One of the first computationally efficient streaming conformance checking methods was introduced in [7]. While the method is efficient, it only indicates whether the trace conforms to the model or not. Thus, an extension was introduced in [8] (BP) where the terms *completeness* and *confidence* were introduced for quantifying the warm-starting and trace conclusion, similarly to this paper. More recently, a Hidden Markov Model (HMM) based approach was introduced in [11] that supports warm-starting but not quantifying the confidence.

To generalize, two main paths for streaming conformance checking can be observed. Metrics-based approaches, such as BP and HMM, where additional information is embedded on top of the conformance, have the benefits of a fast computation time and a more holistic view of a trace via completeness and confidence measures. The downside is the vagueness of the conformance metric, which is well-suited for alerting purposes but lacks a clear indication of the discrepant activities. The other path includes prefix-alignment-based approaches, such as OCC. Diametrically, these approaches benefit from a clear representation of both the unexpected and skipped activities. However, they generally exhibit a longer computation time, especially for finding the optimal prefix-alignments. More importantly, they are unable to handle warm-starting nor explain the confidence of the conformance cost.

This paper attempts to bridge this gap by next introducing a method for incorporating the completeness and confidence measures into prefix-alignments.

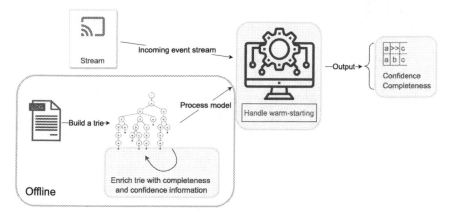

Fig. 2. Approach overview with contributions of this paper highlighted.

4 Conformance, Confidence and Completeness

In this section, we introduce the C-3PA algorithm that is able to consider conformance, confidence, and completeness while outputting prefix-alignments. We first discuss the approach on a high level and introduce how confidence and completeness measures are contrived. Then, we look at the execution steps of the algorithm. Finally, we discuss the space and time complexity of the approach.

4.1 Approach

As discussed in Sect. 2, in order to do conformance checking, it is necessary to know the allowed behavior. In order to be computationally more efficient, the method introduced here uses the trie to represent the allowed behavior. The approach builds upon [4] and [15], with the contribution of this paper highlighted in Fig. 2. To the best of our knowledge, this is the first method that outputs prefix-alignments while handling warm-starting scenarios and computing confidence and completeness.

Confidence shows how much of the trace is expected to still arrive. For this purpose, the building of the trie is modified by supplementing the nodes of the trie with information about their confidence cost. Furthermore, to calculate the confidence measure, the approach looks at all the paths that go from the current node to a leaf node and takes the average of the minimum paths. An example is shown in Fig. 3a. The calculation gives equal weight to all possible paths from the current node and is thus a good indicator of the likelihood of a trace's conclusion. Alternative methods are discussed at the end of Sect. 5 as they are out of scope for this paper.

Completeness quantifies the warm-starting of a seen trace. In other words, how much of the behavior of the trace occurred before the conformance checker was able to observe it. In order to achieve this, the construction of the trie is augmented by creating edges from the root node to every other node in the trie.

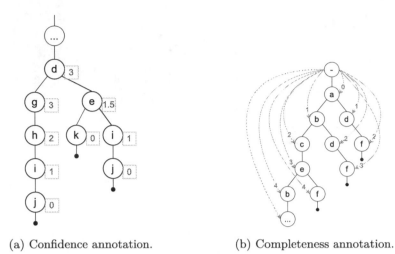

(a) Confidence annotation.   (b) Completeness annotation.

Fig. 3. Trie enrichments.

Essentially, it is a mapping of activities to potential warm-starting nodes. Every known activity has a map of costs associated with warm-starting, which points to the set of nodes with a particular cost and activity label. An example is shown in Fig. 3b.

4.2   C-3PA Algorithm

The pseudocode for the C-3PA algorithm is shown in Algorithm 1. The algorithm takes as input an event, the trie, and a state buffer. Based on the case ID of the arrived event, the algorithm checks in the state buffer whether the case has previously been seen. If a case has not been seen previously, then a new state is instantiated from the root node of the trie.

The algorithm iterates over each state associated with this case and, if possible, then makes a synchronous move on the current activity. If a synchronous move is not possible, then a cost limit is instantiated—a new event cannot increase the cost of the trace by more than 1. Three types of moves are attempted: a log move, model moves, and *warm-starting moves*. The warm-starting moves use the edge augmentation of completeness cost, as shown in Fig. 3b, to try to leap to the currently seen activity from the root node. Importantly, the guiding cost function determines the best states, considering both conformance and completeness. The completeness cost is stored separately from the conformance cost, making it possible to quantify the impact of the warm-starting scenario and paving the way for future work in terms of preferring either warm- or cold-starting.

The guiding cost function does not consider the confidence measure. Confidence is looking into the future, and paths that conclude earlier have a higher confidence value. Thus, using confidence as part of the equation would guide the algorithm to favor the shortest paths through the trie. This may lead to suboptimal paths and is thus not a natural part of what should steer the algorithm.

Algorithm 1. C-3PA

Input: $evt(case, act), T, BS$
1: $S \leftarrow \emptyset$
2: $S_{interim} \leftarrow \emptyset$
3: **if** $case \in BS$ **then**
4:     $S \leftarrow BS(case)$
5: **else**
6:     $S \leftarrow \{s_{root}\}$ ▷ Initialize state with root node
7: **for each** $s \in S$ **do**
8:     **if** $s.syncPossible(act)$ **then**   ▷ Attempt to make a sync move on activity a
9:         $S_{interim} \leftarrow S_{interim} \cup \{s_{new}\}$ ▷ Store a new state with synchronous move
10: **if** $noSyncMovesDone$ **then**
11:     $cost_{lim} \leftarrow minCost(S) + 1$ ▷ Assign a cost limit for non-sync moves
12:     **for each** $s \in S$ **do**
13:         $s_{log} \leftarrow makeLogMove(s, act)$ ▷ New state with log move
14:         $S_{model} \leftarrow makeModelMoves(s, act)$ ▷ A set of new states with model moves
15:         $S_{ws} \leftarrow makeWarmStart(s, act)$ ▷ A set of new warm-starting states
16:         **for each** $s_{temp} \in \{s_{log}\} \cup S_{model} \cup S_{ws}$ **do**
17:             **if** $s_{temp}.\delta(\gamma) + s_{temp}.\epsilon(\gamma) <= cost_{lim}$ **then**
18:                 $S_{Interim} \leftarrow S_{Interim} \cup \{s_{temp}\}$
19: $S \leftarrow manageStates(S)$ ▷ Update decay time, remove old states
20: **for each** $s_{temp} \in S_{interim}$ **do**
21:     $S \leftarrow S \cup s_{temp}$
22: $BS.S \leftarrow S$ ▷ Update the states in the state buffer

---

However, there may be use cases where confidence, with alterations, could be used as part of the cost function. This is discussed at the end of Sect. 5.

The most recent state of a case in the state buffer contains information about the prefix alignment, completeness, and confidence of the trace.

4.3 Complexity

The trie construction happens offline and thus mainly impacts the space complexity. Based on [15], the trie is commonly $O(log(|L'|))$ to the size of the proxy log used to generate the trie. Adding the confidence measure requires a single traversal over all the nodes of the trie, $O(N)$. Warm-starting expects an edge from the root node to every node in the trie. Thus, adding the edges during the construction of the trie is also $O(N)$.

Synchronous moves and log moves can be done in $O(1)$. The biggest impact on the time complexity, thus, comes from handling model moves and warm-starting. Both of these depend on the branching factor of the trie. The branching factor is in the worst case the number of traces in the proxy log $O(|\sigma \in L'|)$. The depth of the search is dependent on the length of the currently seen prefix $O(|\hat{\sigma}|)$. The complexity is thus $O(|\sigma \in L'| \times |\hat{\sigma}|)$. In a process model, this would indicate behavior that allows any activity to occur as the first activity, followed by an infinite loop of a single unique activity. Thus, the amortized complexity is more likely $O(log(|\sigma \in L'|) \times log(|\hat{\sigma}|))$. L' is finite and can thus be considered a constant, leaving the complexity as $O(log(|\hat{\sigma}|))$, i.e., increasing logarithmically with the size of the trace prefix.

In conclusion, this means that the computation should only be hindered if the trace lengths become very large, making it suitable for most streaming use cases. This answers RQ1 from Sect. 1. Next, we will look at the empirical evaluation to answer RQ2.

5   Experiments

In this section, we look at the empirical tests conducted to validate the algorithm's[1] output and to compare it to existing algorithms. First, we look at the experiments related to the warm-starting scenario. Specifically, the goal is to validate whether the algorithm is able to handle warm-starting and what are the possible implications of enabling warm-starting under different settings. Second, we investigate the conformance result of the algorithm, both in terms of the correctness of the prefix-alignment, and correlation with other methods. Then, we look at the computation speeds of various methods and conduct stress testing on the new algorithm to validate its applicability for streaming settings. Finally, we end with a discussion of the results obtained, and the strengths and weaknesses of the introduced algorithm.

For running the experiments, the real-life event logs from BPI challenges in 2012[2] and 2017[3] were used. Additionally, synthetic datasets[4] were included as the datasets include a log and a pre-defined Petri net reference model. In total, 12 original logs were used. Event logs were used to validate the entire behavior of C-3PA and allow for equal comparison against other methods without impact from networking or other outside factors.

For the BPI logs, the Inductive Miner [12] was used with a noise threshold of 0.95 to discover a Petri net model. To build the tries used by the C-3PA algorithm, proxy logs were simulated on top of the Petri net models using the method from [18] with 2000 generated traces, random path simulation, and a looping factor of 3. For warm-starting validation, the event logs were pre-processed by filtering out 20% or 50% of the starting activities of each trace in each log, resulting in an additional 28 logs.

5.1   Warm-Starting

To validate the warm-starting capability of the algorithm, the algorithm was initialized with the following three settings: warm-starting enabled from all states, warm-starting enabled only from the root state, and warm-starting disabled. The three variations were executed on the 28 logs pre-processed for warm-starting. The average conformance costs of these executions are shown in Fig. 4a.

---

[1] https://github.com/MaxTNielsen/ConformanceCheckingUsingTries/tree/current_branch.

[2] https://doi.org/10.4121/uuid:3926db30-f712-4394-aebc-75976070e91f.

[3] https://doi.org/10.4121/uuid:5f3067df-f10b-45da-b98b-86ae4c7a310b.

[4] https://github.com/PADS-UPC/RL-align/tree/master/data/originals/M-models.

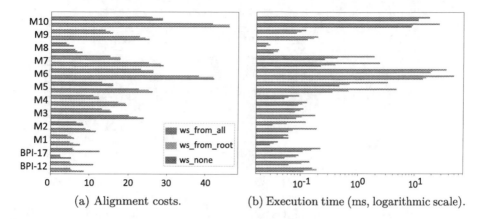

(a) Alignment costs.   (b) Execution time (ms, logarithmic scale).

Fig. 4. Warm-starting experiments.

The conformance cost improvements for warm-starting enabled only from the root state (*ws_from_root*) is moderate compared to the variation with no warm-starting (*ws_none*): across all the datasets, the improvement is 7.3%. An apparent reason for this is that the root state needs to be in memory, and thus once the root state is out of the buffer, warm-starting is no longer an option. An implication of this option is that any chosen warm-starting scenario will be equal to doing model moves on the unseen prefix.

For warm-starting from all states (*ws_from_all*), the change in the conformance cost is much more noticeable. Across all datasets, the improvement is 17.1%. This comes, though, at the cost of execution time. As shown in Fig. 4b the warm-starting across all states is taking noticeably longer. This makes sense because warm-starting is costly, and with warm-starting enabled for all states, the warm-starting will be visited for each non-synchronous move. However, the benefit of warm-starting is one of the algorithm's focal points; thus, in the following experiments, the option with warm-starting enabled from all states will be used.

5.2 Comparison to Existing Methods

The algorithm introduced in this paper is an approximate algorithm. Thus, it is important to validate that the algorithm is actually outputting the correct conformance. In the following, we will investigate how precise the algorithm is for indicating conformance issues by building a confusion matrix with optimal prefix-alignments as the baseline and then analyzing the Spearman correlation of non-conforming results.

Confusion Matrix. To assess the correctness, the first step is to evaluate how often the algorithm reports conformance when actually non-conformance should have been reported and vice-versa. For this comparison, the optimal prefix-alignments from [20] (OCC W-inf) are used as the ground truth. The

Table 1. Spearman correlations against other methods.

Correlations	HMM	BP	OCC W-1	OCC W-inf
Conformance	0.28	0.52	0.95	0.98
Completeness	0.66	0.35	–	–
Confidence	–	0.44	–	–

derived confusion matrix across all 12 original datasets is shown in Fig. 5a. The confusion matrix shows that almost all traces are correctly classified, with most traces being non-conforming to the process models. 243 traces can be considered false positives, where C-3PA indicates a compliant trace, while actually non-conformance is shown by optimal prefix-alignments—this is the result of warm-starting by C-3PA. 8 traces are false negatives, indicating that C-3PA classified the trace as non-conforming while actually, it was conforming.

The interpretation is that generally, the algorithm can classify non-conformant traces well. As the algorithm is dependent on the trie data structure, a potential improvement for the classification could be achieved by increasing the size of the trie. For the purposes of this paper, such an investigation is out of scope. Another thing to note is that there is a high proportion of non-conformant traces present in the datasets. Still, as the ultimate goal for a conformance checker should be to detect non-conformant behavior, this skewness is considered acceptable.

Correlation. Spearman correlation was used to validate that the output from C-3PA behaves similarly to the output from previously existing algorithms. Table 1 shows the correlations, with 1 indicating complete positive correlation, -1 indicating complete negative correlation, and 0 indicating no correlation.

As discussed in Sect. 3, the HMM [11] and BP [8] methods are able to output additional measures in addition to conformance, but they do not compute the prefix-alignments. Thus, the conformance correlation is moderate with these

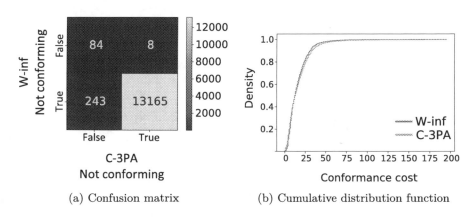

(a) Confusion matrix   (b) Cumulative distribution function

Fig. 5. Comparative experiments.

Table 2. Average processing time per event (ms).

	C-3PA	OCC W-1	OCC W-inf	HMM	BP
BPI2012	2.66	48.95	95.89	2.94	0.04
BPI2017	2.14	40.32	80.66	3.02	0.04
M1	0.51	8.61	13.48	5.35	0.03
M2	1.50	53.94	85.55	17.67	0.03
M3	7.39	-	-	-	-
M4	8.57	164.96	331.38	2.20	-
M5	47.60	-	-	-	-
M6	1871.24	-	-	-	-
M7	29.34	-	-	-	-
M8	1.21	5.67	8.68	1.10	0.02
M9	14.07	443.58	740.48	4.79	-
M10	1028.41	-	-	-	-

methods. Interestingly, the completeness correlation with HMM is relatively strong, while it is much weaker with the BP method. The confidence is also moderately correlated with the output from BP. All in all, it seems that C-3PA is giving output similar to these methods, but due to operational differences, the algorithms are not too strongly correlated.

In comparison with the prefix-alignments with window size 1 (OCC W-1) and optimal prefix-alignments (OCC W-inf) from [20], the conformance correlation is very strong. For further investigation, cumulative distribution functions were constructed as shown in Fig. 5b. The resulting plots indicate a high similarity between the distributions, exhibiting almost identical curves. This indicates that despite the underlying approximations, the C-3PA algorithm is suitable for outputting prefix-alignments describing process deviations.

5.3   Stress Test

Important characteristics of streaming conformance checking are event processing time and memory consumption. The events may arrive in a very fast manner, and it is important to calculate the conformance quickly. At the same time, the stream is unbounded, but the memory of the conformance checker is not. Thus, the method needs to have a good handling of memory.

The event processing time of the C-3PA algorithm and other methods is shown in Table 2. To be noted, the results need to be interpreted with some reservations: HMM implementation is in Python, while all other methods are implemented in Java. Further, such a direct comparison may be influenced by factors deriving from implementation, rather than an algorithm's actual potential. Regardless, it is currently the best indication available for showing the applicability of the various methods in a streaming setting.

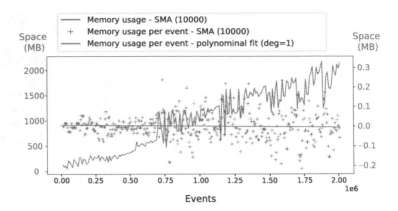

Fig. 6. Memory consumption across 2 million events.

Based on the results, C-3PA outperforms OCC, in some cases by an order of magnitude, while simultaneously being able to handle warm-starting and indicating the confidence of the prefix-alignments. The results are in most cases notably slower than that of BP, but this is expected as BP does not output the prefix-alignments, but rather just gives a trace-level measurement of the conformance. A dash (-) indicates that no response was received within 30 min. This includes the pre-processing time, which is the main factor for HMM and BP (building reachability graphs), and algorithm execution time, which is the main factor for OCC. In the worst case, for dataset M6, the trie generation took 949 ms and algorithm execution total time was 842 s for C-3PA.

The memory consumption of C-3PA is shown in Fig. 6. The memory consumed per event does not increase as the stream progresses, as indicated by the red line. The total memory consumption does increase, as an increasing number of cases are kept in memory. In the current implementation, the user can define how many individual cases can be stored in the memory before the case together with its states is released. In general, the approach is memory efficient while permitting either a smaller or larger memory configuration depending on the organizational needs.

5.4 Discussion and Limitations

The C-3PA is a conformance checking algorithm that outputs prefix-alignments, can handle warm-starting scenarios, and presents a confidence level of the prefix-alignment. Regarding RQ2, the results indicate that C-3PA is well suited for real-life situations by outperforming the state of the art in terms of computation time, handling fast-paced event streams, and correlating well with optimal prefix-alignments.

One of the algorithm's limitations comes from using the trie as the underlying process model. A trie may not be ideally suited for large models with a lot of concurrent behavior and several loop cycles, because such behavior is not as succinctly represented as in a Petri net. It is currently hard to define beforehand what is the optimal size of a trie to sufficiently represent the allowed behavior, and this is something that would require additional research.

From a technical perspective, the handling of warm-starting may still require a grace period. With the current setup, the algorithm would attempt to warm-start infinitely, which is impractical. Similarly, in terms of confidence, further activities within the case could still theoretically occur, i.e., the quantification of confidence may be misleading in some instances. Also, investigating alternative methods for computing confidence may prove interesting. For example, instead of looking at the average lengths of a path to a leaf node, confidence could be calculated as the minimum length to a leaf node. If incorporated into the algorithm's cost function, this could be used to guide the algorithm to prefer the shortest paths in the model.

Finally, it is important to note that all experiments were run on processes that have been designed for static process executions. Such processes may have characteristics that are intrinsically different from processes that are designed for event streams. Unfortunately, to the best of our knowledge, no usable public datasets of process executions on event streams are available. Furthermore, in addition to C-3PA, only the implementation of the BP method is able to calculate conformance on actual event streams rather than static logs. Thus, despite the limitations discussed above, we believe that the results achieved in this paper are as representative as currently possible, with the C-3PA algorithm answering both of the posed research questions.

6   Conclusion

This paper introduced a novel approximate algorithm (C-3PA) for streaming conformance checking. C-3PA is knowingly the first algorithm that fuses together the representability of prefix-alignments, allows for warm-starting scenarios, and is able to quantify the confidence of a prefix-alignment with regard to the conclusion of the trace. Extensive empirical testing was conducted to show the algorithm's ability to handle warm-start scenarios, show its correlation to existing streaming conformance checking methods, and to stress test the algorithm under latency and memory constraints. Future research directions would be to investigate whether confidence could also be integrated into the cost function, for example by utilizing a known stochastic distribution of branches in the trie. Furthermore, a more extensive study could be done in terms of datasets and trie construction, in order to achieve equality with optimal prefix-alignments.

Acknowledgement. This work was supported by the European Social Fund via "ICT programme" measure, the European Regional Development Fund, and the programme Mobilitas Pluss (2014-2020.4.01.16-0024).

References

1. van der Aalst, W.M.: Process mining: a 360 degree overview. In: van der Aalst, W.M.P., Carmona, J. (eds.) Process Mining Handbook. Lecture Notes in Business Information Processing, vol. 448, pp. 3–34. Springer, Cham (2022). https://doi.org/10.1007/978-3-031-08848-3_1
2. Adriansyah, A.: Aligning observed and modeled behavior. Ph.D. thesis, Mathematics and Computer Science (2014). https://doi.org/10.6100/IR770080
3. Adriansyah, A., Van Dongen, B.F., Zannone, N.: Controlling break-the-glass through alignment. In: 2013 International Conference on Social Computing, pp. 606–611. IEEE (2013)
4. Awad, A., Raun, K., Weidlich, M.: Efficient approximate conformance checking using trie data structures. In: 2021 3rd International Conference on Process Mining (ICPM), pp. 1–8. IEEE (2021)
5. Boltenhagen, M., Chatain, T., Carmona, J.: Optimized sat encoding of conformance checking artefacts. Computing **103**(1), 29–50 (2021)
6. Burattin, A.: Streaming process mining. In: van der Aalst, W.M.P., Carmona, J. (eds) Process Mining Handbook. Lecture Notes in Business Information Processing, vol. 448, pp. 349–372. Springer, Cham (2022). https://doi.org/10.1007/978-3-031-08848-3_11
7. Burattin, A., Carmona, J.: A framework for online conformance checking. In: Teniente, E., Weidlich, M. (eds.) BPM 2017. LNBIP, vol. 308, pp. 165–177. Springer, Cham (2018). https://doi.org/10.1007/978-3-319-74030-0_12
8. Burattin, A., Zelst, S.J.V., Armas-Cervantes, A., Dongen, B.F.V., Carmona, J.: Online conformance checking using behavioural patterns. In: Weske, M., Montali, M., Weber, I., Vom Brocke, J. (eds.) BPM 2018. Lecture Notes in Computer Science, vol. 11080, pp. 250–267. Springer, Cham (2018). https://doi.org/10.1007/978-3-319-98648-7_15
9. Carmona, J., van Dongen, B., Weidlich, M.: Conformance checking: foundations, milestones and challenges. In: van der Aalst, W.M.P., Carmona, J. (eds.) Process Mining Handbook. Lecture Notes in Business Information Processing, vol. 448, pp. 155–190. Springer, Cham (2022). https://doi.org/10.1007/978-3-031-08848-3_5
10. Kipping, G., et al.: How to leverage process mining in organizations-towards process mining capabilities. In: Di Ciccio, C., Dijkman, R., del Rio Ortega, A., Rinderle-Ma, S. (eds.) BPM 2022. Lecture Notes in Computer Science, vol. 13420, pp. 40–46. Springer, Cham (2022). https://doi.org/10.1007/978-3-031-16103-2_5
11. Lee, W.L.J., Burattin, A., Munoz-Gama, J., Sepúlveda, M.: Orientation and conformance: A hmm-based approach to online conformance checking. Inf. Syst. **102**, 101674 (2021)
12. Leemans, S.J.J., Fahland, D., van der Aalst, W.M.P.: Discovering block-structured process models from event logs - a constructive approach. In: Colom, J.-M., Desel, J. (eds.) PETRI NETS 2013. LNCS, vol. 7927, pp. 311–329. Springer, Heidelberg (2013). https://doi.org/10.1007/978-3-642-38697-8_17
13. de Leoni, M., Marrella, A.: Aligning real process executions and prescriptive process models through automated planning. Expert Syst. Appl. **82**, 162–183 (2017)
14. Ojeda, J.: Conformance checking artefacts through weighted partial MaxSAT. Inf. Syst. 102168 (2023)
15. Raun, K., Awad, A.: I will survive: An online conformance checking algorithm using decay time (2022). https://doi.org/10.48550/ARXIV.2211.16702. https://arxiv.org/abs/2211.16702

16. Rozinat, A.: Process mining: conformance and extension. Ph.D. thesis, Industrial Engineering and Innovation Sciences (2010). https://doi.org/10.6100/IR690060, proefschrift
17. Schuster, D., van Zelst, S.J.: Online process monitoring using incremental state-space expansion: an exact algorithm. In: Fahland, D., Ghidini, C., Becker, J., Dumas, M. (eds.) BPM 2020. LNCS, vol. 12168, pp. 147–164. Springer, Cham (2020). https://doi.org/10.1007/978-3-030-58666-9_9
18. Vanden Broucke, S., De Weerdt, J., Vanthienen, J., Baesens, B.: An improved process event log artificial negative event generator. Available at SSRN 2165204 (2012)
19. Zaman, R., Hassani, M., Van Dongen, B.F.: Efficient memory utilization in conformance checking of process event streams. In: Proceedings of the 37th ACM/SIGAPP Symposium on Applied Computing, pp. 437–440 (2022)
20. van Zelst, S.J., Bolt, A., Hassani, M., van Dongen, B.F., van der Aalst, W.M.: Online conformance checking: relating event streams to process models using prefix-alignments. Int. J. Data Sci. Anal. 8(3), 269–284 (2019)

Supporting Provenance and Data Awareness in Exploratory Process Mining

Francesca Zerbato[1][(✉)] ⓘ, Andrea Burattin[2] ⓘ, Hagen Völzer[1] ⓘ,
Paul Nelson Becker[2], Elia Boscaini[2], and Barbara Weber[1] ⓘ

[1] University of St. Gallen, St. Gallen, Switzerland
{francesca.zerbato,hagen.voelzer,barbara.weber}@unisg.ch
[2] Technical University of Denmark, Kgs. Lyngby, Denmark
andbur@dtu.dk, {s194702,s194720}@student.dtu.dk

Abstract. Like other analytic fields, process mining is complex and knowledge-intensive and, thus, requires the substantial involvement of human analysts. The analysis process unfolds into many steps, producing multiple results and artifacts that analysts need to validate, reproduce and potentially reuse. We propose a system supporting the validation, reproducibility, and reuse of analysis results via analytic provenance and data awareness. This aims at increasing the transparency and rigor of exploratory process mining analysis as a basis for its stepwise maturation. We outline the purpose of the system, describe the problems it addresses, derive requirements and propose a design satisfying these requirements. We then demonstrate the feasibility of the central aspects of the design.

Keywords: Process Mining · Exploratory Analysis · System Requirements and Design · Analytic Provenance · Data Awareness · User Support

1 Introduction

Process mining comprises methods to analyze event data generated in information systems during the execution of business processes. Process mining is quickly growing in adoption, and so is its business impact [9].

Like other data science disciplines, process mining requires the substantial involvement of humans, e.g., process analysts, to obtain insights from raw event data [7]. Analysts often freely explore the data with the available tools to gain a basic understanding of what it represents, investigate different scenarios, and create hypotheses. Hypotheses can then be tested using best practices, but more exploration is required if the test fails or the results are inconclusive [19]. Each insight that emerges during the analysis informs which subsequent analysis steps are chosen. On the one hand, the choices made during the analysis yield many possible reasonable results that need to be assessed. On the other hand, such choices might give rise to potential inconsistencies in the analysis process [14].

Due to its knowledge-intensive character and emergent course of action, an exploratory analysis includes many manual and error-prone steps that are often

M. Indulska et al. (Eds.): CAiSE 2023, LNCS 13901, pp. 454–470, 2023.
https://doi.org/10.1007/978-3-031-34560-9_27

hard to pre-specify and can be challenging to track and validate over long periods of time without tool support [3]. Existing process mining tools do not explicitly support analysts in tracking, validating, and communicating their analysis process and their insights. As a result, analysts must carry out these activities manually, which can quickly become impractical for extensive analyses [6,19].

Toward establishing a more rigorous and reliable analysis process, we suggest increasing the transparency of the analysis process as a first important step. To this end, in this paper, we propose a system to support process analysts in tracking their analysis steps and the dependencies among them, as well as the results and the goals of their analysis. This aims to support rigor in the analysis process itself as well as communication in reviews, audits, and storytelling activities. The corresponding components of the support system are a *replayable history* of user interactions with a process mining tool and a *provenance view*, which are inspired by reliable system engineering, viz. configuration- and change management [4], and requirements tracing [18]. Moreover, we propose a novel integrated *data view*. The data view aims to support analysts in maintaining awareness of the current data selection, understanding the effect of the data transformations applied to it, comparing the current data selection with previous "states" of the analysis, and increasing the analyst's confidence that each analysis step indeed serves its intended goal or justifies its specified result.

The rest is structured as follows. Section 2 motivates our approach with a realistic process mining scenario. Section 3 presents the requirements of the system, while Sect. 4 describes its core components. Section 5 evaluates the system design. Section 6 discusses related work. Section 7 closes with an outlook on future research.

2   Motivating Scenario

In this section, we present an example process mining analysis derived from behavioral data we collected in two observational studies with more than 50 experienced process analysts overall [21,22]. We will refer to this scenario throughout the paper to illustrate the problems we address and the proposed solution.

An Example Process Mining Analysis. Rob is a process analyst in charge of analyzing an event log recording instances, also known as *cases*, of a road fine management process [5]. Tom, a member of the police acting as a business stakeholder, asks him "What are scenarios in which offenders do not pay their fines?" To answer this question, Rob applies many operations in a process mining tool. Below we describe some steps of his analysis, which we also report in Fig. 1.

(A) Parameter sweeps. First, Rob familiarizes himself with the raw event log (L_0), i.e., the one provided by the police. With the goal in mind to reduce complexity (G1), he removes infrequent behavior with a *variant filter*. He applies the filter three times (cf. o_1-o_3 in Fig. 1) using the relative number of cases as a parameter, i.e., 75%, 85%, and 90%. After applying the filter, he generates descriptives to better understand the effect of the filter on the number of cases (v_1-v_3). While the first two filter configurations remove too much process behavior, o_3 results in a reasonable number of cases. Thus, he settles for o_3 and annotates his choice, also reporting the reasons for discarding the other filters.

(B) Focus on a subset of the log. Then, Rob focuses on the question (G2), starting from cases corresponding to unpaid fines. He applies an *activity filter* to the previously filtered log to select cases with a credit collection (*CC*) activity (o_4), which he hypothesizes correspond to unpaid fines (H1). He then creates and inspects the process map of these cases (v_4). From the map, he notices that some cases still include a payment (*P*) activity; thus, his hypothesis was not precise. He makes a new hypothesis that unpaid fines do not include *P* (H2) and applies the corresponding filter (o_5) to create a new process map (v_5).

(C) Test hypotheses and compare results. Afterward, Rob focuses on partially paid fines. He hypothesizes that these are complete cases that include either *P* and some outstanding amount or both activities *P* and *CC* (H3). To check his hypothesis, he removes incomplete cases (o_6), selects cases that include *P* (o_7), and adds a derived attribute to filter for cases with a positive outstanding amount (o_8-o_9). He also mistakenly re-applies o_7. After inspecting the results, he continues with the second part of H3. He applies an activity filter that works on the conjunction of both conditions (o_{10}). However, he is unsure about the logic implemented by the filter in o_{10} because he finds it difficult to understand the

	U	Id	Operation	I/O		Timestamp	User Annotations	Goals and Hypotheses
(A)	R	o_1	variantFilter(cases, keep, 75%)	L_0	L_1	07/10/22 10:01:18	filtered too much	
	R	v_1	nCases()	L_1	#cases	07/10/22 10:01:50		
	R	o_2	variantFilter(cases, keep, 85%)	L_0	L_2	07/10/22 10:02:03	filtered too much	G1: Reduce
	R	v_2	nCases()	L_2	#cases	07/10/22 10:02:32		complexity
	R	o_3	variantFilter(cases, keep, 90%)	L_0	L_3	07/10/22 10:03:11	good trade-off	
	R	v_3	nCases()	L_3	#cases	07/10/22 10:03:29		
(B)	R	o_4	activityFilter(cases, keep, "CC")	L_3	L_4	07/10/22 10:15:02		G2: Answer Question
		v_4	processMap()	L_4	M_1	07/10/22 10:15:57	there is still P	H1: Unpaid fines include CC
	R	o_5	activityFilter(cases, remove, "P")	L_4	L_5	07/10/22 10:18:32	unpaid fines	H2: Unpaid fines do
	R	v_5	processMap()	L_5	M_2	07/10/22 10:18:56		not include P
(C)	R	o_6	filterIncompleteCases(cases, remove)	L_0	L_6	07/10/22 10:25:10		H3: Partially paid
	R	o_7	activityFilter(cases, keep, "P")	L_6	L_7	07/10/22 10:26:45	paid fines with an	fines are fines that
	R	o_8	addDerivedAttr(amountDue)	L_7	L_8	07/10/22 10:29:02	outstanding	include P and some
	R	o_9	attrFilter(cases, keep, amountDue>0)	L_8	L_9	07/10/22 10:29:49	amount	outstanding amount
	R	o_7	activityFilter(cases, keep, "P")	L_9	L_{10}	07/10/22 10:29:49		or include both P
	R	o_{10}	activityFilter(cases, keep, "P ∧ CC")	L_6	L_{11}	07/10/22 10:31:36	fines with P+CC	and CC
	R	o_7	activityFilter(cases, keep, "P")	L_6	L_{12}	07/10/22 10:33:18		G3: Validate
	R	o_4	activityFilter(cases, keep, "CC")	L_{12}	L_{13}	07/10/22 10:33:44	filter is correct	combined filter
	R	o_{11}	activityFilter(cases, remove, CC)	L_{12}	L_{14}	07/10/22 10:36:51		H4: Some partially paid cases do not include CC
(D)	R	Show results to business stakeholders and auditors						G4: Storytelling
(E)	J	o_5	activityFilter(cases, remove, "P")	L_3	L_{15}	14/10/22 08:33:17	order of filters	G5: Internal auditing
	J	o_4	activityFilter(cases, keep, "CC")	L_{15}	L_{16}	14/10/22 08:33:46	checked	

Fig. 1. The operations applied by Rob and Julie over time. **U** is the user, i.e., (R)ob or (J)ulie. **Id** is an identifier for each operation of the **Operation** column. **I/O** shows the input resp. output of an operation. **Timestamp** is the timestamp of the operation. The last two columns show **User Annotations** and analysis **(G)oals and (H)ypotheses**.

effect of nested operations, and he knows that, in some cases, filters are sensitive to their order. Thus, Rob decides to validate the filter (G3) by applying two separate filters and checking each one of the conditions in o_{10} individually. He documents this check by taking notes. As a result of his analysis, he rejects H3 because the two results don't match as he had expected. Thus, he filters for partially paid cases that do not include CC (o_{11}) as he hypothesizes that the credit collection agency does not handle some partially paid fines (H4).

(D) Storytelling. After the analysis, Rob presents his results to Tom (G4). For each result, Rob points to the supporting evidence from his analysis. In a deeper discussion, he explains to Tom how he obtained the results, including steps that did not directly contribute to the final outcomes but accounted for analysis decisions. For example, when Tom asks why he focused on 90% of the raw event log, Rob shows all the parameter values he had tested in (A) and uses his annotations to share the reasoning behind the decisions he made.

(E) Internal auditing. A week later, Julie looks at Rob's analysis with the goal of auditing it (G5). She inspects Rob's results and runs some validation steps using a different process mining tool. For example, she swaps the filters that Rob applied in (B) to see if their order has any effect on the final result. Indeed, she knows that the semantics of filter operations is often implicit or not communicated unambiguously and that different process mining tools might implement different filter semantics. She also notices that one filter (o_7) does not have any effect on the result and, as such, could be removed in a future step.

Scenario Conclusion. Rob's analysis (A)-(C) reflects typical process mining analysis steps, where multiple operations are combined to analyze different subsets of the event log. Such steps reflect the knowledge-intensive and ad-hoc character of exploratory process mining analysis, which develops based on emerging insights, as shown by the observational study in [21]. While process mining tools allow realizing such steps, they lack support for analysts to track their analysis steps and goals (cf. (A)-(C)), e.g., to maintain a resource of "reflection in action" [20], and to conduct other meta-analysis activities, such as storytelling, validation and auditing (cf. (D)-(E)). However, such activities are crucial to increase the rigor of the analysis and make it more reliable and less prone to errors that can, for example, derive from combining and nesting operations with different or ambiguous semantics. This is the main driver of our paper.

3   Requirements

To support reviews, audits, and other validation activities for process mining analysis, we derived the following non-exhaustive set of requirements for a system supporting the *process of process mining.* Such a support system is thought of as complementing an existing process mining tool, not of replacing it.

(R1) Maintain Provenance Information. The support system should enable analysts to capture and browse provenance information about their analysis process and its results.

Provenance information includes the analysis operations performed, their input and output data, as well as dependency information about which results depend on which operations. With the help of provenance information, analysts can reproduce their analysis for validation, storytelling, and auditing.

(R2) Trace Analysis Goals and Insights. The support system should enable analysts to trace which analysis operations were performed to achieve which analysis goals and which insights were obtained from which operations.

The tracing of goals and insights clarifies to the analyst and the stakeholders why a certain analysis operation or set thereof has been performed, supporting validation, storytelling, and auditing. It also supports the identification of ineffective explorations and helps identify candidates for reuse.

For the next requirement, we note that the user interface of many process mining tools is designed in such a way that multiple UI elements, e.g., the process map or the variant inspector, operate on a specific selection of the event log that is defined through active filters and transformations. Whenever the active selection changes, all UI elements change accordingly. In these rapidly-changing settings, it is often challenging to keep track of which data selection was used to generate any (intermediate) result or artifact produced during the analysis.

(R3) Increase Data Awareness. The support system should help analysts to be aware of the data selection and properties of the data that the process mining tool interfaces are operating on. This should apply not only to the current step of the analysis but also to all previous steps, favoring the comparison among the results produced throughout the analysis from different data selections.

Data awareness, i.e., the awareness of the data selection on which the current analysis step is operating, supports the assurance of the effectiveness of the data selection, as well as the understanding of the effects of the operations performed in each step and the comparison among different data selections over time.

4   A System to Support the Analysis Process

In this section, we describe the design, intended use, and underlying assumptions of the support system. The system consists of three main components: (i) a *replayable history* comprising the sequence of all the performed operations, as well as two complementary kinds of linked views: (ii) a *provenance view*, which captures provenance information about the analysis process, and (iii) multiple *data views*, which capture how the working event log is transformed during the analysis at different levels of abstraction.

4.1   Replayable History of Interactions

The proposed support system integrates with an existing process mining tool through a *replayable history* of interactions. That is an append-only record of all interactions of the process analyst with the tool. Columns 3–6 of Fig. 1 represent such a replayable history, i.e., we use the operations, their input and output and their ordering given by the timestamp. It must be *replayable*, meaning that it contains enough information to reproduce the *state* of the process mining analysis. Based on the design of most process mining tools, we assume that the core part of that state is a *working event log*, i.e., the initially loaded event log, that was transformed through various process mining operations, e.g., filtering, aggregation, and data enrichment. Some operations, which we refer to as *view operations* (cf. Sect. 2), will also produce additional artifacts, e.g., a process map, and consume additional artifacts, e.g., a normative process model, but our main focus within this paper is on the working event log. We discuss the extension of our approach to more complex process mining analysis settings in Sect. 7.

Let L_0 denote the event log initially loaded in the process mining tool in a given session. A *replayable history* is a sequence $op_1, op_2, \ldots$ of *operations* on the working event log, where an *operation* $op_j = (i, o, L_j)$ consists of

(i) an *input log index* $i \geq 0$ such that $i < j$; We say that L_i is the *input log* to operation op_j,

(ii) a parameterized *operation signature* $o = (f, p_1, \ldots, p_k)$ where f is a process mining tool function that accepts an event log L and actual parameters $p_1, \ldots, p_k$, and

(iii) an event log L_j, which we call the *output log of* op_j such that $L_j = o(L_i) =_{\text{def}} f(L_i, p_1, \ldots, p_k)$, i.e., o describes a deterministic[1] process mining tool function f such that the output only depends on parameters $p_1, \ldots, p_k$.

For example, o_4 in Fig. 1 refers to the operation

$$L_4 = \text{activityFilter}(L_3, \text{`cases'}, \text{`keep'}, \text{`CC'})$$

that keeps only cases with the 'CC' activity. We henceforth do not strictly distinguish between an operation and its signature when the difference is clear from the context. Also, we note that the input log to the first operation op_1 of the replayable history must be L_0, which we assume is implicitly part of the history.

In general, the input event log can be any event log produced previously and not just the direct predecessor in history. This means that analysts can navigate back to a previous working event log and continue the analysis from there. This type of navigation might not be a native capability in the process mining tool but can be provided by the provenance view presented in Sect. 4.2.

We consider operations that are "relevant" for process analysts [2], such as data exploration interactions [14], i.e., we choose a level of abstraction comparable to the one in process mining tools. In this way, we can also include view operations, such as v_4 in Fig. 1, which refers to the operation $M_1 = \text{processMap}(L_4)$.

The determinacy in (iii) above guarantees that any intermediate version of the working log can be reproduced recursively. When a replayable history is properly integrated with a process mining tool, then all the analysis artifacts and UI elements that are based on earlier versions of the working log can be

---

[1] Note that determinacy of an operation that calls a pseudo-random function requires the inclusion of the random seed in the operation parameters.

reproduced to support auditing, storytelling, and other communication use cases. Moreover, the replayable history is the basis for constructing the provenance and data views introduced in the following paragraphs.

4.2   Provenance View

The *provenance view* is a rooted, directed tree that reflects the analysis steps performed on the working event log as a branching history [6].

The tree of the provenance view is a visualization of the replayable history where each index $j = 0, 1, \ldots$ of the history is a node labeled with the log L_j and where each operation $op_j = (i, o, L_j)$ creates an edge from node i to node j labeled with o. Figure 2 shows a provenance view derived from the replayable history of Fig. 1, where each node is labeled with an object representing the state current state of the analysis, i.e., the working event log, and each edge is labeled with an operation. For example, node L_3 is the node representing the event log given as input to operation o_4, an activity filter that retains cases with activity CC; L_4 is the filtered event log resulting from o_4.

A path between two nodes represents a sequence of operations that transforms the first node, i.e., the working event log, into the second one. New paths are created via *branching*. We consider tree branches to reflect distinct analysis (sub-)goals, such as testing a specific hypothesis or validating a particular operation, that develop on the same working log. For example, G1 in Fig. 2 recalls the goal of the motivating scenario to reduce event log complexity via variant filters. Analysts can interact with the provenance tree to deliberately create new branches and decompose the analysis into different goals or reuse the results of previously performed steps for further analysis. For example, new branches can be created to test hypotheses or to validate the effects of different operations on the same working log. Also, branching helps visualize the "analysis coverage", i.e., all the steps done in the course of an analysis, highlighting missing steps and discarded results. Discarded results can provide precious information about the

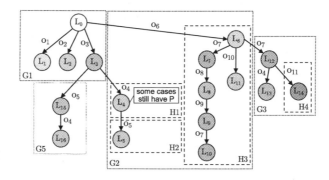

Fig. 2. Provenance view derived from the motivating example of Fig. 1. User annotations, hypotheses (H), and goals (G) are sketched on the tree to exemplify their use.

process of obtaining the final result. For example, the branching realized by o_1-o_3 in Fig. 2 shows that different parameter configurations were tested, indicating that the choice of applying o_3 was informed by the (unsatisfactory) results of o_1 and o_2. Instead, missing steps can indicate unexplored areas needing attention.

One last important feature of the provenance view is annotations. Annotations can be attached to nodes or sub-trees to capture user observations about specific analysis outcomes as well as analysis goals. Annotations are versioned to allow tracking changes in the flow of thoughts as the analysis evolves. Analysts can use annotations to "give meaning" to intermediate results, to document analysis steps and decisions, or to report hypotheses and goals. For example, node L_4 in Fig. 1 is annotated with "some cases still have P", documenting the fact that the filter o_4 did not result in unpaid fines, i.e., cases without a payment (P) activity, as expected (cf. Sect. 2). Similar to literate programming [10], the information included in annotations can support analysts in storytelling tasks.

Overall, the provenance view provides access to analytic provenance information organized into analysis goals via branching and annotation. The provenance view also allows the analyst to reuse previously obtained results, e.g., to extend them or use them as input for further analysis steps, as done with L_6 in Fig. 2. Finally, it provides a transparent view of the analysis process that can help identify unnecessary and missing steps, inform future analyses, and serve as a basis to automate steps that might emerge as repetitive.

4.3   Data Views

Complementing the provenance view, the analysis is also reflected in one or more data views. Figure 3(a) shows a *data view*, which is a rooted, directed multi-graph. Each node is labeled with an object that represents some aspect of the state, i.e., the working event log, and hence some aspect of the effect of the previous analysis step. Figure 3(a) shows a data view, which we call the *complete data view*, where each node is labeled with the complete working event log, not just one aspect of it. However, in contrast to the provenance view, the different sequences of operations represented in the edges can lead to the same node whenever they produce the same working event log. For example, starting from node L_3, both sequences o_4, o_5 and o_5, o_4 commute, i.e., they lead to the same node $(L_{5/16})$.

Different sequences of operations resulting in the same log can be expected or unexpected for the analyst. The previous example of commuting filters (o_4, o_5) might be expected, whereas the observation that starting from L_8 the sequences o_8 and o_8, o_9 result in the same log might be unexpected. Indeed, the fact that o_9 had no effect might depend on specific characteristics of the working event log. This is one way in which the data view can help analysts validate the effect of their actions or spot inconsistencies stemming from unclear operation semantics.

Conversely, analysis steps with different working event logs are represented by different nodes. Again, working logs being different can be expected or unexpected by the analyst, the latter, e.g., for non-commuting permutations of the same filters. Different nodes can then be compared with a dedicated *diff* capability within the

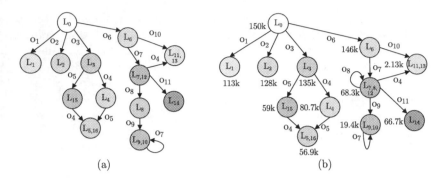

(a)   (b)

Fig. 3. Examples of data views based on the motivating example. (a) *Complete* data view; (b) data view using the *number of cases* as abstraction.

data view, which allows the analyst to investigate an unexpected difference. A full design of such a diff capability is out of the scope of this paper.

We assume that the complete data view is always automatically provided to the user. The complete data view can be computed from the provenance view by unifying nodes that are labeled with equal event logs, as shown in Fig. 2 with the same color, or directly from the replayable history as described below.

Figure 3(b) shows another data view for our example. In general, each data view is created from a pre-defined or user-defined *abstraction*. An *abstraction* α defines, for each working event log L, an object $\alpha(L)$. The set of cases, the number of cases, or the number of case variants are frequently used abstractions in process mining, but abstractions based on data attributes or other event log characteristics may also be defined. *Case abstractions* are of special interest, which are defined through a mapping β that defines an object $\beta(c)$ for each case c and $\alpha(L)$ is then the set or bag of all $\beta(c)$ where c is a case of L. For example, we can disregard the ordering of events in a case c and define $\beta(c)$ as the set of activities that occur in c. A user-defined abstraction may also disregard event data features that are deemed irrelevant for a specific analysis. Figure 3(b) uses the number of cases as data view abstraction. Whenever an abstraction is just a short object, e.g., a number, we can show it directly in the data view.

A data view for an abstraction α is defined as follows for the general case. An abstraction α induces an *equivalence* over working event logs L_1, L_2 by $L_1 \equiv L_2$ whenever $\alpha(L_1) = \alpha(L_2)$. The *data view* generated by α is a directed graph where the nodes are the equivalence classes of this equivalence: Let $[L] = \{L' \mid L' \equiv L\}$ denote the *equivalence class* of working event logs w.r.t. to L. Then, the nodes of the data view are the classes $[L]$ where L is some working event log of the replayable history and there is an edge from $[L]$ to $[L']$ labeled with operation o whenever there exists an $L_1 \in [L]$ and an $L_2 \in [L']$ such that L_2 was obtained from L_1 in the replayable history by applying the operation o. Again, a diff capability on the abstraction can support the analyst in investigating differences. Consider, for example, two nodes connected by an edge that represents a case filter. In that case, the diff consists of two sets: the set of cases removed by the filter and the set of cases kept by the filter. If the diff view allows the analyst to search for specific test cases from the log, then the analyst can determine in which of the two sets of the diff the test case ended up. In this sense, the diff view allows the analyst to test whether the case filter had the desired effect.

Different data views allow analysts to explore the effect of their operations at different abstraction levels. Also, they provide orthogonal and overlapping perspectives into the current data selection. Hence the data views can raise the awareness of the analyst for potential mistakes and ease the comparison among different intermediate results. While the provenance view traces the analysis steps to their goals, the data views can help validate that the results were obtained on the proper data selection. Many useful abstractions and their semantic equivalences, such as the examples above, are generic, i.e., they can be provided off-the-shelf to the user and can be reused across projects. Project-specific abstractions that are deemed useful, such as abstractions that use specific definitions of process outcomes or performance metrics, could be reused in similar projects, e.g., when different projects deal with the same process type.

Requirements Review. The requirements presented in Sect. 3 are addressed by the design of the support system as follows.

(R1), i.e., the maintenance of the provenance information is addressed mostly through the replayable history, which guarantees that analysis steps are recorded and intermediate results can be reproduced. A specific part of the recording is the ability of analysts to navigate back in history and create a new branch of the provenance tree. This feature is supported by the provenance view.

(R2), i.e., the tracing of analysis goals and insights, is realized by the provenance view and its annotation capability. The annotated provenance tree shows which analysis branches serve which goals and which insights are derived from them. These links can be inspected for consistency or for assessing the analysis coverage, thus supporting the reasoning over analysis steps and results.

(R3), i.e., the support for data awareness is implemented predominantly by the data views, which provide multiple cues for the analysts on what data selection they are currently operating on. The equivalence between working event logs and the capability to compare them at different abstraction levels allow analysts to understand and validate various aspects of their analysis.

5 Evaluation

In this section, we evaluate our approach by demonstrating the feasibility of central aspects of the design. Section 5.1 presents tests that evaluate the efficiency of updating the data view based on different equivalences. Section 5.2 presents a proof-of-concept and describes how it informed the next evaluation stages.

5.1 On the Efficiency of Computing the Equivalence in Data Views

To demonstrate the feasibility of our design, we focused on the efficiency of computing event log equivalences in the data views. Indeed, establishing whether two logs are equivalent in a data view is computationally not trivial. Whenever a new analysis operation is performed, it is necessary to decide whether the graph of the data view needs to be updated with a new node, i.e., the working log is different from all the previously computed ones, or with a self-loop, i.e., the working log is *equivalent* to a previously computed one (cf. Sect. 4.3). Since different equivalences could incur different computational costs, which might result in delays if many large logs are compared, we devised some tests to investigate the performance of updating different data views.

We implemented two equivalences for XES-formatted event logs. The first, *size-only*, considers two logs as equivalent if they have the same number of events. The second, named *complete*, considers two logs as equivalent if they have the same set of cases and each case has the same set of events. Two events are the same if they have the same key/value attributes. We implemented this equivalence considering realistic improvements, i.e., we check increasingly restrictive conditions, and as soon as one condition fails, two logs are deemed not equivalent.

For running the tests, we constructed logs of exponentially increasing size, i.e., different *configurations*. Specifically, we generated logs with $100/1\,000/10\,000$ cases and $10/50/250$ events per case, thus ending up with 9 configurations (the smallest event log contains 100 cases with 10 events each $= 1\,000$ total events; and the largest event log contains $10\,000$ cases with 250 events each $= 2\,500\,000$ total events). Each event has 10 attributes. Details are provided in Table 1.

For our tests, we identified five *scenarios* (s1-s5) that represent edge cases from a computational point of view. These scenarios capture differences between event logs that become increasingly subtle and, as such, increasingly harder to compute. In each scenario, we compare a "given" event log with an amended copy, which incorporates the following changes:

s1. One case of the given log is filtered out (for our test, we filtered out the very last case that appears in the given log);
s2. One event of the given log is filtered out (we filtered out the very last event of the last case that appears in the given log);
s3. One attribute of the very last case of the given log is changed;
s4. One attribute of the last event of the last case of the given log is changed;
s5. No changes; the copy is identical to the given event log.

As a result, we obtained 45 event logs (9 configurations × 5 scenarios), where the perturbations represent the worst-case possibility, i.e., finding the difference requires inspecting the entire logs.

Table 1. Cases and events for each configuration used for testing the equivalences.

	c1	c2	c3	c4	c5	c6	c7	c8	c9
Number of cases	100	1 000	10 000	100	1 000	10 000	100	1 000	10 000
Events per case	10	10	10	50	50	50	250	250	250
Events in the log	1 000	10 000	100 000	5 000	50 000	500 000	25 000	250 000	2 500 000

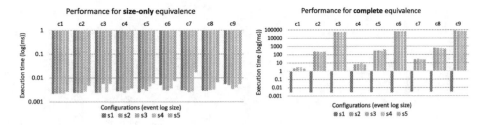

Fig. 4. Performance of the *size-only* and *complete* equivalences against the 9 configurations and 5 scenarios. The y-axes are in a logarithmic scale of milliseconds, i.e., bars below 1 mean that it took less than 1 ms to compute the equivalence.

We computed the *size-only* and *complete* equivalences while monitoring the required time. For the tests, we used a laptop running Windows 10 64bit and equipped with an Intel Core i7-7500U 2.70GHz CPU and 16GB of RAM. From the performance results in Fig. 4, we can see that the time required for processing the *size-only* equivalence is negligible (less than milliseconds in all cases) as it requires verifying only the size of the log. Instead, the time needed to compute the *complete* equivalence grows linearly with the number of events in the log (the worst time reported is 77 s for configuration c9). This holds for all scenarios but S1, where differences are instantly detected. The linear complexity for the *complete* equivalence suggests that the computation of the equivalence between two event logs is scalable. Also, the worst-case scenario is observed only when two logs have no differences, meaning that in other cases the equivalence computation can be more efficient. For example, for the data views of Fig. 3, which both have multiple different nodes, we could imagine a strategy that first computes the *size-only* equivalence and, only if two logs are equivalent, it computes the *complete* equivalence. Besides, since any new node will be equivalent to at most one other node, the worst-case scenario will be observed at most once.

From these tests, we conclude that the equivalences implemented are already promising from a performance viewpoint, despite the fact that no particular optimization was considered. The implementation of the equivalences, the scripts used to generate the logs, the logs, and the detailed results are publicly available.[2]

5.2   Proof-of-Concept Implementation

To better understand how the support system proposed in this paper could be used, we have implemented a conceptual prototype. The implementation, which is available as open source(See footnote 2), consists of a web application with a backend realized in Python and a frontend written in Javascript.

The prototype implements the core functionality of the three components described in Sect. 4. The replayable history is created directly in the prototype from recorded user interactions: the user can upload an event log and apply different filter operations, e.g., activity, directly-follows, or throughput-based filters. In

---

[2] See https://doi.org/10.5281/zenodo.7329844.

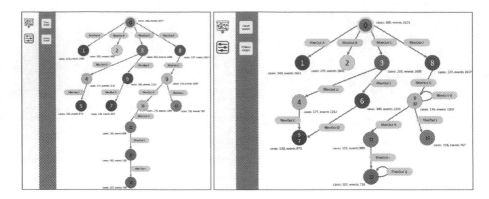

Fig. 5. Screenshots of the developed prototype showing the provenance view (left) and the corresponding data view (right). The yellow ring around a node indicates the "current selection", i.e., the working event log to which operations are being applied. (Color figure online)

this way, the prototype can "simulate" the analysis done in a process mining tool and reproduce a basic yet realistic history of interactions. Based on the replayable history, the prototype can create a provenance view and a corresponding data view and update them whenever the replayable history is extended. The user can navigate the provenance tree, create new branches from any selected node, i.e., to pursue different analysis goals, and annotate the nodes. In turn, in the data view, the user can visualize the working event logs, which are deemed equivalent if they have the same set of case ids. Figure 5 shows screenshots of the prototype with a scenario in which two pairs of equivalent nodes occur.

As part of our evaluation, we used the prototype to replay scenarios from [22]. Our ultimate goal was to identify critical aspects for the implementation of the system that should be addressed before conducting a user evaluation. In particular, we identified the following critical points for the next evaluation stage.

- Tighter integration of the support system with a process mining tool should be considered to enable the automated export of replayable histories. Re-creating a replayable history from a realistic analysis in a fully-fledged process mining tool is error-prone and expensive.
- Although our tests have shown that equivalences in the data view can be efficiently computed, we have learned that the complexity of both the provenance tree and the data view graph can become large with long repayable histories. The support system should provide means to manage such complexity, e.g., by easing frequent branching and the navigation of large trees.
- The branching in the provenance view is done by users based on different reasons, e.g., wanting to reuse an intermediate result or validate a sequence of steps. Further investigation on the reasons for branching should be conducted to enable the system to differentiate them and instruct users accordingly.

6   Related Work

In this section, we discuss related work comparing our system with relevant literature and existing software in the fields of data analytics and process mining.

The idea to increase analytical rigor is inspired by techniques from systems engineering, such as configuration- and change management [4] and requirements tracing [18]. Although such systems are not conceived to support exploratory data analysis, they inspired the design of the provenance view by manifesting the evolution process and the user goals and enabling deliberate branching.

More closely related to our work are systems that capture and visualize *analytic provenance* to assist data analysis and sense-making processes [20]. Among them, *provenance management systems* [13] have emerged in the areas of scientific workflows and visual analytics. Such systems leverage different kinds of provenance information [14] to assist analysts in the creation and management of data analysis workflows. Notable examples are VisTrails [3] for visualization workflows, Chimera [8] for data derivations, and ZOOM [2] for bioinformatics. Provenance management systems capture provenance information in the form of a history or action log, similar to our replayable history, and often allow users to visualize it, similar to our provenance tree. For example, VisTrails [3] allows users to manage visualization workflows and to maintain and navigate the history of their design. However, these systems focus on repeatable analyses, requiring analysts to pre-specify workflows. As such, they do not directly support exploration processes learned from "free" interactions between the analyst and the tool. Moreover, only a small part of such systems use provenance information to support sense-making in terms of improving the analysis rigor [20], which is what we aim to support with the tracing of user goals in the provenance view and the user-defined equivalences in the data view. An example of tools supporting sense-making is InfoVis [15], a framework for maintaining the provenance of visualization states that allows analysts to externalize their reasoning process. Compared to InfoVis, we propose multi-perspective data views as a novel feature to increase data awareness in contexts like process mining, where the data selection changes frequently and, thus, might make it hard to keep track of how the results were generated from the data.

In process mining, the capture and management of provenance information have received little attention so far. Inspired by scientific workflows, some works have focused on supporting the management of changes in *process mining pipelines*. Examples of tools that offer this kind of support are Rapid-ProM [1], buparFlow [16], and PM4KNIME [11] for process mining pipelines or FilterTree [12] for chaining filters into preprocessing pipelines. Although these tools might resemble our work, they support repeated analyses through reusable pipelines but are not designed to assist exploratory analysis. Also, these tools do not manage provenance information, nor do they explicitly support sense-making or meta-analysis tasks, e.g., through the tracing of analysis goals, or data awareness, e.g., with user-defined abstractions on the working event log. Similar remarks can be made for commercial process mining tools [17], which, to our knowledge, do not yet support the recording and management of analytic provenance information. Existing features like the Process Diff of IBM Process Mining could inform the design of the diff capability in data views defined over (discovered) process models as analysis artifacts (cf. view operations in Sect. 4.1). However, the comparison among process mining analysis states, such as working logs, is not supported by existing software.

7   Conclusion and Outlook

In this paper, we have proposed a support system aimed at providing process analysts with a transparent overview of their analysis and making them aware of the data selection they work with at each analysis step. The proposed system can support the provenance and reproducibility of the analysis, ease result validation and auditing, and provide a basis to improve the rigor of the analysis process.

Limitations and Outlook. The first limitation of this paper concerns the notion of state of a process mining analysis, which we have assumed being a single event log. As mentioned in Sect. 4.1, a reasonable extension of the system could manage additional analysis inputs, e.g., a normative process model. This extension is straightforward as long as the interaction between different input artifacts is limited. Each artifact can be managed separately with dedicated provenance and data views. However, with the emergence of multi-process mining[3], multiple event logs may have stronger interactions, i.e., they might change simultaneously in interdependent ways. Such cases might require a generalization of the current definition of provenance view, which we will explore in the future. Another limitation concerns the current evaluation of the support system. On the one hand, the experimental evaluation in Sect. 5.1 is limited to simple equivalences. Future work should investigate the feasibility of other equivalences that might be relevant for process mining practice. On the other hand, the effectiveness and usefulness of the proposed system have not been evaluated by users. Towards a user evaluation, we have used a proof-of-concept implementation of our system to replay realistic scenarios and identify critical aspects for future work that should be addressed before designing such a study. For example, we have learned that a new implementation of the system should consider methods to deal with the complexity of large provenance and data views, such as techniques for tagging and storing milestones or optimizing navigation via scrolling and panning.

Acknowledgment. This work is part of the ProMiSE project, funded by the Swiss National Science Foundation under Grant No.: 200021_197032.

References

1. Van der Aalst, W., Iriondo, A.B., Van Zelst, S.: RapidProM: mine your processes and not just your data. In: RapidMiner: Data Mining Use Cases and Business Analytics Applications. Chapman & Hall/CRC Press (2018)

---

[3] https://multiprocessmining.org.

2. Biton, O., Cohen-Boulakia, S., Davidson, S.B., Hara, C.S.: Querying and managing provenance through user views in scientific workflows. In: 2008 IEEE International Conference on Data Engineering (ICDE), pp. 1072–1081 (2008)
3. Callahan, S.P., Freire, J., Santos, E., Scheidegger, C.E., Silva, C.T., Vo, H.T.: Vistrails: visualization meets data management. In: Proceedings of the 2006 ACM SIGMOD International Conference on Management of Data, pp. 745–747 (2006)
4. Conradi, R., Westfechtel, B.: Version models for software configuration management. ACM Comput. Surv. **30**(2), 232–282 (1998)
5. De Leoni, M., Mannhardt, F.: Road traffic fine management process. Eindhoven University of Technology, Dataset (2015)
6. Derthick, M., Roth, S.: Enhancing data exploration with a branching history of user operations. Knowl. Based Syst. **14**(1), 65–74 (2001)
7. Doan, A.: Human-in-the-loop data analysis: a personal perspective. In: Proceedings of the Workshop on Human-In-the-Loop Data Analytics. HILDA 2018, ACM, New York, NY, USA (2018). https://doi.org/10.1145/3209900.3209913
8. Foster, I., Vockler, J., Wilde, M., Zhao, Y.: Chimera: a virtual data system for representing, querying, and automating data derivation. In: Proceedings of the 14th International Conference on Scientific and Statistical Database Management, pp. 37–46 (2002)
9. Grisold, T., Mendling, J., Otto, M., vom Brocke, J.: Adoption, use and management of process mining in practice. Bus. Process. Manag. J. **27**(2), 369–387 (2020)
10. Knuth, D.E.: Literate programming. Comput. J. **27**(2), 97–111 (1984). https://doi.org/10.1093/comjnl/27.2.97
11. Kourani, H., van Zelst, S.J., Lehmann, B.D., Einsdorf, G., Helfrich, S., Liße, F.: PM4KNIME: process mining meets the KNIME analytics platform. In: Proceedings of CEUR Workshop on ICPM Demo Track, pp. 65–69 (2022)
12. Leemans, S.: Filtertree: a repeatable branching XES editor. In: Proceedings of CEUR Workshop on ICPM Doctoral Consortium and Demo Track, pp. 70–74 (2022)
13. Pérez, B., Rubio, J., Sáenz-Adán, C.: A systematic review of provenance systems. Knowl. Inf. Syst. **57**(3), 495–543 (2018). https://doi.org/10.1007/s10115-018-1164-3
14. Ragan, E.D., Endert, A., Sanyal, J., Chen, J.: Characterizing provenance in visualization and data analysis: an organizational framework of provenance types and purposes. IEEE Trans. Vis. Comput. Graph. **22**(1), 31–40 (2015)
15. Shrinivasan, Y.B., van Wijk, J.J.: Supporting the analytical reasoning process in information visualization. In: Proceedings of the SIGCHI Conference on Human Factors in Computing Systems, CHI 2008, ACM, New York, pp. 1237–1246 (2008)
16. Steukers, B., Janssenswillen, G., van Hulzen, G.A.W.M., Vanhoenshoven, F., Depaire, B.: bupaRflow: a Workflow Interface for bupaR. In: Proceedings of CEUR Workshop on BPM Demo and Resources track, vol. 3216, pp. 102–106 (2022)
17. Viner, D., Stierle, M., Matzner, M.: A process mining software comparison. arXiv preprint arXiv:2007.14038 (2020)
18. Watkins, R., Neal, M.: Why and how of requirements tracing. IEEE Softw. **11**(4), 104–106 (1994). https://doi.org/10.1109/52.300100
19. Wongsuphasawat, K., Liu, Y., Heer, J.: Goals, process, and challenges of exploratory data analysis: an interview study. arXiv:1911.00568 (2019)
20. Xu, K., Attfield, S., Jankun-Kelly, T., Wheat, A., Nguyen, P.H., Selvaraj, N.: Analytic provenance for sensemaking: a research agenda. IEEE Comput. Graph. Appl. **35**(3), 56–64 (2015). https://doi.org/10.1109/MCG.2015.50

21. Zerbato, F., Soffer, P., Weber, B.: Initial insights into exploratory process mining practices. In: Polyvyanyy, A., Wynn, M.T., Van Looy, A., Reichert, M. (eds.) BPM 2021. LNBIP, vol. 427, pp. 145–161. Springer, Cham (2021). https://doi.org/10. 1007/978-3-030-85440-9_9
22. Zerbato, F., Soffer, P., Weber, B.: Process mining practices: evidence from interviews. In: Di Ciccio, C., Dijkman, R., del Rio Ortega, A., Rinderle-Ma, S. (eds.) BPM 2022. Lecture Notes in Computer Science, vol. 13420, pp. 268–285. Springer, Cham (2022). https://doi.org/10.1007/978-3-031-16103-2_19

Bridging Research Fields: An Empirical Study on Joint, Neural Relation Extraction Techniques

Lars Ackermann[✉][ID], Julian Neuberger, Martin Käppel, and Stefan Jablonski

Institute for Computer Science, University of Bayreuth, Bayreuth, Germany
{lars.ackermann,julian.neuberger,martin.kaeppel,
stefan.jablonski}@uni-bayreuth.de

Abstract. Information systems that have to deal with natural language text are often equipped with application-specific techniques for solving various Natural Language Processing (NLP) tasks. One of those tasks, extracting entities and their relations from human-readable text, is relevant for downstream tasks like automated model extraction (e.g. UML diagrams, business process models) and question answering (e.g. in chatbots). In NLP the rapidly evolving research field of *Relation Extraction* denotes a family of techniques for solving this task application-independently. Thus, the question arises why scientific publications about information systems often neglect those existing solutions. One supposed reason is that for reliably selecting an appropriate technique, a comprehensive study of the available alternatives is required. However, existing studies *(i)* cannot be considered complete due to irreproducible literature search methods and *(ii)* lack validity, since they compare relevant approaches based on different datasets and different experimental setups. This paper presents an empirical comparative study on domain-independent, open-source deep learning techniques for extracting entities and their relations jointly from texts. Limitations of former studies are overcome *(i)* by a rigorous and well-documented literature search and *(ii)* by evaluating relevant techniques on equal datasets in a unified experimental setup. The results[1] show that a group of approaches form a reliable baseline for developing new techniques or for utilizing them directly in the above mentioned application scenarios([1]Our code and data: https://github.com/JulianNeuberger/re-study-caise.).

Keywords: Named Entity Recognition · Relation Extraction · Natural Language Processing · Artificial Intelligence

1 Introduction

Due to a dramatic increase in the amount and volume of textual information sources, techniques for automatically extracting and formalizing information from texts play a crucial role in information systems engineering [1,5,15,20,21].

Our work is supported by the Bavarian Research Foundation (grant no. AZ-1390-19).

M. Indulska et al. (Eds.): CAiSE 2023, LNCS 13901, pp. 471–486, 2023.
https://doi.org/10.1007/978-3-031-34560-9_28

Relation extraction (RE) techniques contribute to solving this task, since they aim at extracting entities and relations among them. Our research group has come into contact with RE from the application perspective of process model extraction from human-readable text sources (e.g. [2,8,21]) written in English (e.g. for identifying resources, activities, data objects, and connections among them) [2]. Further exemplary applications are the extraction of UML diagrams (e.g. [7,25]) or entity-relationship diagrams (e.g. [4]). Each of those applications contains a *specific* solution for extracting relations. This raises the question of whether there is a promising *baseline technique* that could be used "out of the box"[1] to solve this task *without* the effort of developing application-specific solutions, which is the standard approach these days?

Most existing techniques are published in isolation and with an evaluation on few, mostly different datasets and with different experimental setups like different evaluation metrics and different usage of training and validation splits. Hence, it is not possible to compare approaches based on their documented evaluation results [27]. To overcome this issue, *Papers with Code*[2] allows for sharing papers along with code and all

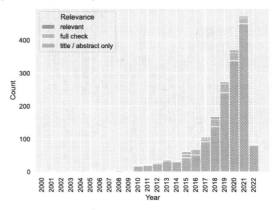

Fig. 1. Publications relevant to RE since 2000.

resources for reproducing experiment results. However, results can be published by the authors themselves, which neither guarantees a uniform experimental design nor obviates the need for reproducing results in order to ensure correctness. Literature surveys [13,14,16,17,29] do not abolish these issues, since they base their discussions on evaluation results from the original publications, a principle which suffers from the same shortcomings. Empirical comparative studies are intended to provide a unified evaluation but former studies [19,27] are incomplete due to irreproducible literature search methods. Consequently, it is not possible to identify the best-performing relation extraction approach directly from existing literature.

Considering the observations above, the contributions of this paper are the following: **(C1)** It comprises a rigorous, reproducible literature search based on well-documented search queries, filter criteria and documented review decisions that is based on PRISMA [18], an established method for literature reviews. **(C2)** It provides a unified evaluation of the RE techniques selected in point **C1**. **(C3)** As a basis for contribution **C2** all raw predictions on the test sets

---

[1] A definition for this term is given in Sect. 3.1.

[2] https://paperswithcode.com/.

are (re-)produced by the authors as an independent party. *(C4)* It identifies a group of relation extraction techniques that show promising results. *(C5)* It uncovers the most likely drivers of performance degradation in neural Joint RE techniques.

The impact of contribution *C1* can be inferred from Fig. 1, which shows an exponential increase in RE publications. Our study thus reveals the applicability of the investigated approaches to a given dataset and allows for a well-founded decision in favor of one of these approaches or, alternatively, the development of a specific solution. Due to the reproducible search method, the study can be extended by adding papers published in recent years through running a documented set of search queries[3] and adding a time restriction. The result of the literature search is a selection of RE techniques that fulfills the specified filter criteria (Sect. 2.2). This paper focuses on the subclass of *Neural Joint RE techniques*. *Joint* means that a single model is trained for extracting both entities and relations instead of training two separate models. The term *Neural* refers to approaches that are based on deep learning. The rationale behind these and other restrictions is discussed in Sect. 2.2.

The remainder of this paper is structured as follows: Section. 2 reifies the RE task and provides an overview of related surveys and comparative studies. Furthermore, it describes the criteria used for selecting RE approaches that are evaluated based on an experimental setup described in Sect. 3. This section also presents the evaluation results along with a thorough analysis. Finally, Sect. 4 summarizes core insights of this study and provides impetus for future research.

2   Research Scope

Consistent with the idea of bridging research fields, the research scope is tailored to two types of readers: *(i)* Contributors to research domains that require an RE technique to solve a specific downstream task and *(ii)* contributors to the research domain of RE who need to reflect on the state of the art. For both types of readers, this study answers the following leading research question for the subset of RE techniques defined in Sects. 2.1 and 2.2:

> *Are there Joint RE approaches that stably achieve better results on diverse datasets, and what data characteristics cause performance degradation?*

RE is a broad term, therefore Sect. 2.1 defines how we use it in this paper. Section 2.2 defines criteria for including a RE approach in experiments.

2.1   Task Description: Relation Extraction

RE in general means to identify entities and relations among them [14,17]. The following describes the understanding of the RE task used in this paper.

---

[3] See https://github.com/JulianNeuberger/re-study-caise#search-queries.

Extraction Scope. RE distinguishes between *mention-level* and *global* [9,11] techniques. *Mention-level* means relation classification for a given sentence and given entities [11]. *Global* means the prediction of relational facts from plain text [9]. This study focuses on global RE (abbreviated with RE in the remainder).

Input Scope. The input scope is either *sentence-*, *document-*, or *corpus-level*, depending on whether the input is a single sentence, multiple sentences, or multiple documents containing multiple sentences [14]. In the latter two cases, relations usually cross sentence boundaries. Our experiment scope is sentence-level (Sect. 3) for mainly two reasons: *(i)* It facilitates the relation extraction task and thus better describes the overall potential for extracting relations in a generalist setting and *(ii)* document- and corpus-level Joint RE are emerging fields. The few documented approaches still produce rather poor results, making it hard to apply them in the information-systems domain.

Output Scope. Some approaches can only extract exactly one relation per *sample* (corresponds to a sentence according to our input scope), but this study also considers approaches that allow for multiple relations per sample. The *arity* of each relation is two, which means that only binary relations are considered, therefore all experiments described in Sect. 3 expect output relations to be triples of the form $\langle E_1, R, E_2 \rangle$, with E_1, E_2 being two entities, and R being the relation among them. Furthermore, all experiments use datasets with *directed* relations [11], meaning the triple $\langle E_1, R, E_2 \rangle$ denotes a relation R with E_1 as source (aka *head*) and E_2 as target (aka *tail*), and $\langle E_2, R, E_1 \rangle$ denotes the same relation with opposite direction. Finally, in contrast to *Open Relation Extraction* [10], all relation types are represented in both training and test data in experiments conducted in this paper.

2.2 Literature Review

To ensure the reproducibility of this study, it is based on a rigorous literature review procedure following the principles of *PRISMA* [18]. In the first stage a set of search queries[4] serves as a coarse-grained filter for selecting neural relation extraction approaches. In the second stage, the title and abstract of all results found by running these queries are manually reviewed for relevance. Finally, the remaining papers are reviewed for relevance using the full text.

Stage 1: Retrieval Stage. To search for relevant RE approaches, Google Scholar and the Scopus database are used. Google Scholar offers the advantage of accessing additional scientific databases (e.g. ScienceDirect, DBLP, ACM Digital Library, ACL Anthology, Springer, IEEE, and arXiv). With duplicates removed, the set of queries mentioned above retrieved *1845* publications potentially relevant to the field of Joint RE. For validation, we check whether the results include all articles previously found by the authors in a manual search (*41* articles). Two additional articles are identified in this way, leading to *1847* results overall.

---

[4] See https://github.com/JulianNeuberger/re-study-caise#search-queries.

Stage 2: Filtering by title and abstract. In this stage, the articles found are matched against several exclusion criteria[5] by analyzing the *title and abstract*. To be considered relevant, an article must not meet any of the following exclusion criteria. The first criterion (EXCL 1) excludes all articles not written in English, while the second criterion (EXCL 2) excludes surveys, comparative studies, or domain-specific applications of existing approaches. EXCL 3 filters out articles proposing an approach that cannot handle English text, since they are not compatible with the application scenarios that led to this study (cf. Section 1). Criterion EXCL 4 excludes all articles that do not propose a deep learning approach. We restrict ourselves to RE approaches that use deep learning for entity and relation extraction, since artificial neural networks usually outperform conventional approaches and are known to have better generalization capabilities [14,31]. EXCL 5 requires that the source code of the techniques is publicly available to enable a fair comparison, as re-implementations based on the descriptions in the article would potentially be error-prone. Another requirement is that entity and relation extraction is jointly trained, i.e. a single model is trained to solve both subtasks [22,27,34] (EXCL 6). One reason is that learning to predict entities and relations simultaneously has been shown to bring synergies to both tasks and increases the extraction capabilities of a model [22]. In addition, it avoids the problem of *error propagation* that occurs when misclassified entities are used as input to a separate relation extraction component, potentially lowering the prediction quality of that component even though it is not primarily responsible for these consequential errors. EXCL 7 excludes approaches that rely on domain-specific knowledge bases such as Freebase or Google Knowledge Graph, since this external knowledge needs to be maintained (Freebase, for instance, is offline) and implies a strong dependency on completeness, correctness and availability (e.g. [28]). Furthermore, it may limit transferability to other domains due to application biases (e.g. Google's Knowledge Graph is used to fill info boxes to summarize search results regarding people, places, etc.). After this stage, 189 articles remain for detailed review by reading their full texts.

Stage 3: Filtering by reading the full text. In the final phase, irrelevant articles are excluded by reviewing the full text, reusing the criteria used in stage 2. This step is necessary because in many cases the abstract is too vague to seriously evaluate the exclusion criteria. Finally, we obtain 31 relevant approaches.

2.3   Related Work

Currently no existing study fully meets our research scope (Sects. 2.1 and 2.2) but there are still several distantly related surveys and comparative studies.

Empirical Studies. [27] analyzes 20 approaches regarding flaws frequently occurring in articles related to RE, including a comparison of different RE approaches. The study described in Sect. 3 avoids aforementioned flaws by using a unified

---

[5] Criteria list: https://github.com/JulianNeuberger/re-study-caise#filtering.

Table 1. Detailed characteristics of the approaches considered. Column *Params* lists the approximate total number of weights, trainable or not. Training durations are given for the smallest dataset (ConLL 04) and largest one (NYT 10). Column *Termination* lists the criterion used to stop training. Column *Input features* lists the inputs a model takes. Here *TOK* means a sequence of tokens, *POS* their part-of-speech tags, *CL* char-level input, and *LM*, *WV* pretrained language models and word vectors respectively.

Approach	Params	Training dur	Machine	Termination	Input features
RSAN [34]	≈8M	1.5 h–6.0 h	Titan RTX	Epochs	TOK,POS,CL
Two [30]	≈7M	1.5h–3.5 h	Titan RTX	Ep., Steps	TOK,CL,LM/WV
CasRel [31]	≈100M	2.0 h–5.0 h	RTX 2080 TI	Epochs	TOK,LM
JointER [33]	≈14M	<1 h–4.5 h	Titan RTX	Epochs	TOK
PFN [32]	≈111M	4.0 h–6.5 h	Titan RTX	Epochs	TOK,LM
SpERT [6]	≈100M	<1 h–10 h	RTX 2080 TI	Epochs	TOK,LM
MARE [12]	≈350M	1.0 h–16 h	RTX 2080 TI	Patience	TOK,LM

experimental setup. In [19], the influence of two main information sources is discussed, namely textual context and entity mentions. Both [19,27] tailor their experiments to answer research questions different from those in our study (Sect. 2). Another study, [26], is exclusively focusing on the biomedical application domain and does not perform a rigorous literature search. Furthermore, the evaluation is limited to three basic neural network architectures and omits, for instance, the established transformer models.

Literature Surveys. In contrast to the few empirical studies, there are various literature surveys that compare RE techniques mainly on a conceptual level [3, 13,14,16,17,29,36]. All of those articles include a quantitative comparison based on evaluation scores. However, due to the nature of a survey, the evaluation scores are an excerpt from different external sources, such as the original publication of an approach. Therefore, the experimental setups differ significantly – in line with the flaws identified in [27] – lowering the validity of the quantitative analysis. Moreover, none of the aforementioned surveys conducts a reproducible literature search, which challenges the completeness of the literature considered.

3   Comparative Study

Addressing the research question posed in Sect. 2, this study evaluates approaches that are able to solve the Joint RE task (Sect. 2.1) and that are selected in the literature review phase (Sect. 2.2). To be able to inspect the performance of approaches from different angles, three different variants of the measures *F1 score*, *precision*, and *recall* are computed. To also vary the application scenario, the approaches are applied to four datasets with diverse characteristics.

3.1   Considered Approaches

As mentioned in Sect. 1, this study focuses on approaches that can be used "out of the box". An approach is considered usable "out of the box", iff *(i)* its executable source code is publicly available, *(ii)* the default hyperparameters are known, *(iii)* hyperparameter optimization is not mandatory, and *(iv)* neither language model re-training nor vocabulary adaptation is required.

To enable consistent evaluation and practical application, all approaches must export their predictions in a structured format. All of these limiting criteria are necessary for an approach to be widely applied without expert knowledge in RE, which is consistent with the intuition of "out of the box".

According to this definition, 31 approaches were classified as relevant. If possible, authors of those approaches as well as authors of this study adapted the code of approaches to the needs of our experiments (Sect. 3.2). However, even with the help of the respective authors, the code of several approaches could not be adapted for various reasons (e.g. incomplete code, lack of reproducibility, missing hyperparameters). Hence, they are discarded. This results in the group of approaches listed in Table 1. Although the above restrictions keep the focus very narrow, approaches that satisfy them have a high practical applicability in terms of availability and documentation for this very reason.

3.2   Experimental Setup

This section provides details on the datasets, their splits, and all the evaluation steps performed.

Datasets. All approaches are evaluated on four prelabled datasets: SemEval 2010 (task 8) [11], NYT10 [23], FewRel [10], and Conll04 [24]. We have chosen these datasets due to their diversity with respect to several characteristics, such as, for instance, number of samples, distance of entities that have a relation or size of the tagset (see Table 2). Datasets that require an external knowledge graph are ruled out (see *EXCL 7* Sect. 2.1). The train/dev/test splits are created as follows: For SemEval 2010 (task 8) and NYT10 the original training data is split into 80% training and 20% dev data by uniform sampling. For Conll04, the corpus is divided into 70% training data, 20% dev data, and 10% test data by uniform sampling. In the case of the FewRel dataset, the provided training and test data (train_wiki.json and valid_wiki.json respectively) are first merged and a stratified split based on the relation type is made into 70% training data, 20% dev data, and 10% test data. Merging training and test data is necessary because the selected RE approaches are not able to handle relations that are not existent in the training data. However, in FewRel, training and test data are disjoint with respect to the relation types they contain. Global dataset statistics are listed in Table 2. The distribution of relation types is visualized in Fig. 2.

Experiment details. For a unified evaluation, the implementations of the approaches are modified in two places[6] First, each approach is modified so that any dataset matching the required input format can be passed in. Second, parts

---

[6] the modified implementations can be found at https://github.com/JulianNeuberger/re-study-caise/#considered-approaches.

478   L. Ackermann et al.

Table 2. Detailed dataset statistics. # *samples* refers to the number of sentences, while # *instances* refers to the number of relation examples. *max dist* and *avg dist* denote the maximum and average number of tokens between relation arguments, measured from the start token of an argument. Average distance is rounded to two decimal places. The minimal distance is 1 for each dataset.

dataset	# samples	# instances	# rel	max dist	avg dist	vocab	# tokens	# entities	# tags
NYT10 (train)	56271	70247	29	128	10.98	75721	2142436	116297	16
NYT10 (valid)	14068	17492	28	102	11.13	37338	536268	29008	15
NYT10 (test)	4006	5859	29	86	11.35	18001	154274	8331	13
Total	74345	93598	29	128	11.03	87014	2832978	153636	17
Semeval (train)	6400	5252	9	26	4.73	18735	123443	12800	15
Semeval (valid)	1600	1338	9	35	4.84	8052	30532	3200	9
Semeval (test)	2717	2263	9	20	4.86	11342	52500	5434	9
Total	10717	8853	9	35	4.78	25194	206475	21434	16
ConLL 04 (train)	3861	1383	5	68	7.77	15218	98390	9928	4
ConLL 04 (valid)	551	216	5	35	7.99	4602	14300	1403	4
ConLL 04 (test)	1104	449	5	82	8.29	7048	27490	2846	4
Total	5516	2048	5	82	7.91	18401	140180	14177	4
FewRel (train)	39120	39120	80	34	8.90	86020	975468	78240	19
FewRel (valid)	5600	5600	80	33	8.84	24427	139423	11200	18
FewRel (test)	11280	11280	80	33	8.88	38681	281523	22560	18
Total	56000	56000	80	34	8.89	107253	1396414	112000	19

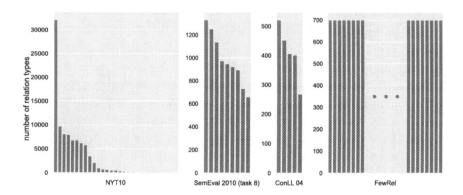

Fig. 2. Distribution of relation types per dataset. Visualization of FewRel is abbreviated, as it contains the same number of examples for all relation types.

of the evaluation functionality are modified to output a unified results file that contains all the information needed for scoring with a variety of metrics. Then, this results file is analyzed using an evaluation component implemented by the authors of this study. Moreover, we also corrected serious errors that prevent a fair comparison (e.g. the use of test data for training).

All data is converted into the required format and approach-specific preprocessing is performed if necessary. The model is then trained on the training set and progress is monitored using the dev data. Training is terminated depending on the criteria defined by the approach (Table 1). The study does not perform hyperparameter optimization, but uses the default parameters specified in the respective approach. Finally, the model is evaluated on the test set. The prediction of the model is stored and later analyzed by the evaluation component. Some approaches limit the input sequence to a maximum size, which is met by filtering out longer sentences. This is treated as an incorrect prediction.

3.3   Evaluation Metrics

Before calculating metrics, the predicted relations must be matched with the ground truth relations. In this study, the *exact match* strategy [35] is used, i.e. a predicted triple (h, r, t) is considered to be correct, iff its relation (r) and the boundaries of its head (h) and tail (t) entities are correct. Furthermore, since a sentence might contain an arbitrary number of relations and a model can predict any number of relations, the number of correct predictions (n_{ok}) for a sample is determined as the cardinality of the intersection of predictions (n_{pred}) and ground truth labels (n_{gold}).

Following this, precision P and recall R are defined as $P = n_{ok}/n_{gold}$ and $R = n_{pred}/n_{gold}$. To capture different perspectives on the results of approaches, we use three distinct ways of calculating n_{ok}, n_{pred}, n_{gold}, as well as P and R:

1. *micro* metrics are calculated over the entire dataset. It shows how well an approach predicts relations in general, without weighting results by the number of supporting instances of a given relation type. Therefore, its is unsuited for imbalanced datasets, e.g. *NYT10*.
2. *macro_{rel}* metrics are calculated for each *relation type* separately and averaged. This allows insight into an approach's ability to predict rare relation types correctly, complementing the *micro* scores and their shortcomings.
3. *macro_{doc}* metrics are calculated for each *document* separately and averaged. Both *micro*, as well as *macro_{rel}* fail to score the ability of approaches to correctly identify documents with no relation, as they score the entire dataset at once, which *macro_{doc}* counter-acts.

3.4   Results

Table 3 shows the scores for each approach and dataset, which are additionally visualized in Fig. 3. In general, approaches struggle with the large number of unique relation types present in *FewRel* which is evident by low F1 scores. *MARE* and *SpERT* score noticeably higher, reaching 47.21% and 40.36% $F1_{macro_{rel}}$ respectively. Some approaches, like *RSAN* score best in regards to recall (53.14%), identifying the presence of a relation, but fail to properly predict the relation type, resulting in a low precision (9.19%) and overall F1 score (15.67%). Similarly, the long-tail phenomenon, i.e. a large number of relation types with very few examples challenges all approaches, apparent by comparing their high *micro* and low *macro_{rel}* scores. *CasRel* performs best ($F1 = 40.20\%$) using *macro_{rel}* and 71.71% using *micro_{rel}*. Two ($F1_{macro_{rel}} = 14.72\%$) and *RSAN* ($F1_{macro_{rel}} = 23.29\%$) perform worst, most likely resulting from imbalanced data.

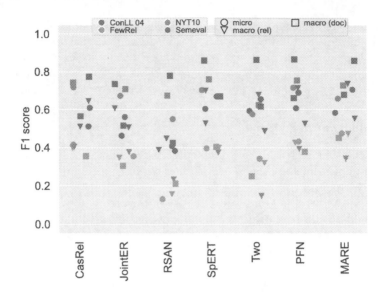

Fig. 3. Overview of the test scores for each considered approach. F1 scores are grouped by the averaging strategy used, cf. Section 3.3.

The $macro_{doc}$ scores of approaches on the *ConLL 04* dataset show that all of them are able to model samples, where no relation is present. *PFN* ($F1 = 86.56\%$) is closely followed by *MARE* (85.83%) and *SpERT* (85.82%). Comparing the $macro_{doc}$ scores to *micro* scores reveals its usefulness, as samples containing no relation would otherwise not be scored, resulting in worse perceived performance, e.g. for *PFN* scoring $F1_{micro} = 60.71\%$.

Semeval contains a large number of NER tags compared to its size, resulting in high linguistic variability of relation instances. We discuss this characteristic in more detail in Sect. 3.5. High variability presents a challenge to *RSAN*, which only scores a $F1_{micro}$ score of 42.37%. All other approaches are able to cope, with *MARE* performing best (70.47%).

3.5   Detailed Analysis

This section analyzes effects of data characteristics on model performance. We selected those by fitting a decision tree to rows of data, consisting of several characteristics present in the dataset and the correctness of the model's prediction results. This allows to only select characteristics with the highest impact.

Distance between relation arguments. The number of tokens between a relation's arguments is a hurdle to most approaches, as they have to reason across longer distances. This effect is visualized in Fig. 4. We binned samples of each dataset separately into 15 bins according to the maximum distance of any relation it contains. For each bin we calculated the F1 metrics discussed in Sect. 3.4 for the results of each approach. With the exception of *Two*, which maintains a fairly

Table 3. Detailed results of all experiments on the test sets of each dataset. Each variant of F1 score, precision (P) and recall (R) is reported as defined in Sect. 3.3

	dataset	$macro_{doc}$			$macro_{rel}$			$micro$		
		F1	P	R	F1	P	R	F1	P	R
CasRel	ConLL 04	77.29%	76.81%	77.78%	51.00%	43.09%	62.47%	51.07%	44.71%	59.55%
	FewRel	35.46%	33.99%	37.06%	39.96%	43.35%	37.06%	41.59%	47.38%	37.06%
	NYT10	74.23%	76.82%	71.80%	**40.20%**	34.60%	47.95%	**71.71%**	76.59%	67.42%
	Semeval	56.48%	56.15%	56.83%	64.49%	71.15%	58.96%	60.90%	62.98%	58.95%
JointER	ConLL 04	73.46%	73.36%	73.55%	50.60%	44.98%	57.84%	46.27%	40.30%	54.32%
	FewRel	30.48%	30.18%	30.78%	34.69%	39.75%	30.78%	35.48%	41.87%	30.78%
	NYT10	70.81%	74.03%	67.86%	37.66%	33.22%	43.45%	67.22%	75.19%	60.78%
	Semeval	51.57%	50.99%	52.15%	60.67%	64.46%	57.31%	56.08%	54.73%	57.49%
MARE	ConLL 04	85.83%	**87.00%**	84.69%	**55.19%**	**58.25%**	52.43%	58.23%	**71.29%**	49.22%
	FewRel	**45.05%**	**45.03%**	**45.07%**	47.21%	**49.33%**	45.27%	**47.43%**	50.04%	45.07%
	NYT10	72.67%	**78.97%**	67.31%	34.22%	**35.67%**	32.88%	65.74%	**83.59%**	54.17%
	Semeval	**67.78%**	**67.65%**	67.91%	73.51%	**78.60%**	69.03%	**70.47%**	71.88%	**69.11%**
PFN	ConLL 04	**86.56%**	86.22%	**86.91%**	52.51%	46.35%	60.55%	**60.71%**	64.34%	57.46%
	FewRel	37.83%	36.94%	38.76%	42.58%	46.87%	39.00%	43.16%	48.69%	38.76%
	NYT10	75.36%	77.13%	73.67%	39.31%	33.04%	48.53%	71.50%	74.44%	68.78%
	Semeval	66.07%	65.75%	66.40%	71.37%	77.65%	66.03%	68.91%	71.66%	66.37%
RSAN	ConLL 04	77.80%	77.70%	77.91%	38.78%	36.43%	41.46%	38.27%	38.86%	37.69%
	FewRel	21.15%	13.20%	53.14%	15.67%	9.19%	**53.14%**	13.16%	7.51%	**53.14%**
	NYT10	67.34%	58.40%	**79.51%**	23.29%	15.15%	**50.39%**	54.95%	43.27%	**75.27%**
	Semeval	42.37%	39.63%	45.53%	44.71%	40.85%	49.38%	40.82%	34.58%	49.80%
SpERT	ConLL 04	85.82%	85.59%	86.06%	52.71%	46.54%	60.75%	60.28%	63.39%	57.46%
	FewRel	40.36%	38.36%	42.58%	39.88%	37.51%	42.58%	39.53%	36.90%	42.58%
	NYT10	**75.88%**	76.90%	74.89%	37.41%	30.17%	49.22%	70.19%	70.21%	70.18%
	Semeval	66.87%	65.94%	67.83%	69.86%	71.19%	68.57%	66.84%	64.94%	68.85%
Two	ConLL 04	86.26%	85.73%	86.81%	48.58%	38.48%	**65.87%**	59.20%	56.34%	**62.36%**
	FewRel	25.03%	24.54%	25.53%	31.87%	42.39%	25.53%	34.12%	**51.42%**	25.53%
	NYT10	62.33%	65.61%	59.37%	14.72%	15.44%	14.07%	57.44%	74.12%	46.89%
	Semeval	61.53%	61.24%	61.83%	67.68%	76.94%	60.41%	65.41%	70.84%	60.76%

consistent performance, all approaches yield significantly lower performance on relations exhibiting longer distance between arguments.

Sample length. Samples with more tokens usually are usually harder to model for mainly two reasons: Firstly more tokens mean more (possible) entities that have to be marked and can participate in relations, secondly longer samples usually exhibit relations where arguments are further apart. For each dataset samples are binned into 15 bins according to the number of tokens they contain. We then calculate the metrics for each bin in the same way as for the *distance between relation arguments*. For the *NYT10* dataset a visualization of the effects of this characteristic can be seen in Fig. 4. In general approaches struggle with longer samples, with the exception of *Two*, which maintains a fairly consistent performance. Results in general are very similar to the *distance between relation arguments* for the aforementioned dependency between a sample's length and the distance between relation arguments it contains.

Relations per sample. If a dataset contains samples with multiple relations it can be harder to model. This effect is founded in the fact that additionally to classifying relations correctly, the number of relations has to be predicted as well. We binned samples of each dataset according to the number of relations it contains. Datasets *SemEval* and *FewRel* contain only samples with exactly one relation, so we exempt them from this analysis. We then calculate the metrics for each bin in the same way as for the *distance between relation arguments.* In our experiments the number of relations per sample is detrimental to performance, though much less pronounced compared to effects discussed previously.

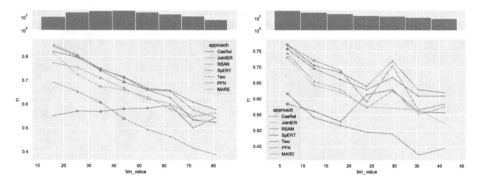

Fig. 4. Micro F1 scores of approaches on NYT10 data in relation to distance between relation participants (*left*) and sample length (*right*) in tokens. Samples were sorted into 15 bins, bins containing less than 25 samples are not drawn, as they suffer from the law of small numbers. Marginal log bar plot shows the number of samples in that bin.

Variability of relation arguments. It is easy to see that classifying relations containing arguments with little to no variation in constituent tokens is less of a challenge than the other way around. To investigate the effect of this observation on the performance of approaches, we calculated the linguistic variability of relation arguments (i.e. head and tail) by dividing the number of unique tokens by the number of total tokens used in all relation arguments for a specific relation type. This will result in 1.0 at best and $1/\#tokens$ at worst, which we then scale to the range $[0.0, 1.0]$. Using linear regression we calculate the correlation between this linguistic variability factor and $F1_{micro}$. Our null hypothesis is that there is no correlation between linguistic variability and performance, which we reject if p is less than our significance threshold of 5%. All approaches exhibit a statistically significant negative correlation between linguistic variability and performance, with the exception of *Two*, which shows a statistically non-significant weak negative correlation, meaning it is not sure there is a correlation at all. *MARE* has the weakest statistically significant correlation, which leads us to believe it can handle linguistic variability in relation arguments best. *JointER* has the strongest negative, statistically significant correlation, implying it is worst suited for this specific data characteristic. A visual comparision between the two can be found in Fig. 5. Analysis results for all approaches can be found in Table 4.

Table 4. Pearson correlation coefficient (r) and statistic significance (p). While *Two* exhibits the weakest negative correlation between linguistic variability and performance, we have to reject the null hypothesis, meaning we have to assume there is no correlation. All other approaches feature a clear correlation between linguistic variability and performance. *MARE* is able to cope best, while *JointER* struggles the most. The correlation for those extremes is visualized in Fig. 5.

Approach	CasRel	JointER	MARE	PFN	RSAN	SpERT	Two
r	-0.5496	-0.6044	**-0.3117**	-0.4822	-0.5779	-0.5242	-0.1127
strength	strong	strong	**medium**	strong	strong	strong	weak
p	$\sim 0.00\%$	$\sim 0.00\%$	0.05%	$\sim 0.00\%$	$\sim 0.00\%$	$\sim 0.00\%$	22.03%
significant	yes	yes	yes	yes	yes	yes	no

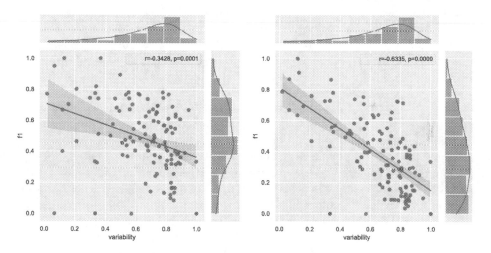

Fig. 5. Micro F1 scores of approaches on all datasets in relation to the linguistic variability present in a sample for *MARE* (*left*) and *JointER* (*right*). 1.0 variability corresponds to a sample consisting of unique tokens only, while 0.0 is a sample with only a single unique token. *MARE* is the approach best suited for coping with strongly varying phrasing of relation arguments, while the performance of *JointER* suffered the most. Detailed results are listed in Table 4.

4   Conclusion and Future Work

Irreproducible literature search and differing experimental setups invalidate the quantitative comparison of RE approaches directly from literature. From an application perspective, however, there is a strong need to identify approaches that work for a wide range of different domains without making major adjustments. In this paper a rigorous, reproducible literature search is conducted to identify all relevant RE approaches and an empirical comparative study with an unified experimental setup is performed to identify a group of jointly trained neural RE approaches that outperform their competitors.

MARE is suitable for most studied datasets, performing best in 21 out of 36 categories and competitively in nearly all other. As such it seems to be applicable to most situations, except datasets with a large number of under-represented relations. Here *CasRel*, *PFN*, and *SpERT* are better choices. *Two* and *RSAN* can be feasible, if the dataset is known to be well balanced. Finally, regarding the research question given in Sect. 2, there are considerations to be made depending on the dataset on hand. Nonetheless, *MARE*, *CasRel*, *PFN*, and *SpERT* form a promising baseline for being fine-tuned to concrete applications.

Currently this study has a few limitations. First, it focuses on neural Joint RE approaches only. Thus, the authors plan a similar unified evaluation of both jointly and separately trained RE approaches. Which approaches are considered in this study largely depends on the selectivity of the search queries used. This potentially causes the systematic literature review to rule out papers that are actually relevant. However, the advantage is that the literature review can be easily extended and thus, missed articles can be added manually. A limitation to the experiments is that datasets without NER tags are artificially enriched using the Stanza Parser, which leads to coarsely labeled entities in some datasets, e.g. SemEval with examples like *"Flowers are carried into the chapel."* and corresponding relation *Entity-Destination*. Thus, automated NER tagging of datasets is potentially error-prone. Another open question is, whether RE approaches could benefit from data augmentation that is used to cope with data quality and quantity issues. Finally, hyperparameters of models have been selected as they were recommended by their authors. This allows us to consider more approaches on multiple datasets, instead of optimizing only a few. Still, this neglects the possibility of achieving a performance boost through a general hyperparameter optimization framework. Due to the long runtime, the authors preceded the hyperparameter optimization with the present study to achieve a smaller preselection of promising approaches.

References

1. van der Aa, H., Carmona, J., Leopold, H., Mendling, J., Padró, L.: Challenges and opportunities of applying natural language processing in business process management. In: Proceedings of COLING. ACL (2018)
2. Ackermann, L., Neuberger, J., Jablonski, S.: Data-driven annotation of textual process descriptions based on formal meaning representations. In: CAiSE. Springer International Publishing (2021)

3. Alshuwaier, F., Areshey, A., Poon, J.: A comparative study of the current technologies and approaches of relation extraction in biomedical literature using text mining. In: ICETAS (2017)
4. Btoush, E.S., Hammad, M.M.: Generating er diagrams from requirement specifications based on natural language processing. In: IJDTA (2015)
5. Dawood, O.S., et al.: From requirements engineering to uml using natural language processing-survey study. In: EJERS (2017)
6. Eberts, M., Ulges, A.: An end-to-end model for entity-level relation extraction using multi-instance learning. In: EACL ACL (2021)
7. Elallaoui, M., Nafil, K., Touahni, R.: Automatic transformation of user stories into uml use case diagrams using nlp techniques. Procedia Computer Science (2018)
8. Friedrich, F., Mendling, J., Puhlmann, F.: Process model generation from natural language text. In: CAiSE. Springer, Berlin Heidelberg (2011)
9. Han, X., Yu, P., Liu, Z., Sun, M., Li, P.: Hierarchical relation extraction with coarse-to-fine grained attention. In: EMNLP. ACL (2018)
10. Han, X., et al.: FewRel: A large-scale supervised few-shot relation classification dataset with state-of-the-art evaluation. In: EMNLP. ACL (2018)
11. Hendrickx, I., et al.: SemEval-2010 task 8: Multi-way classification of semantic relations between pairs of nominals. In: SemEval. ACL (2010)
12. Klöser, L., Kohl, P., Kraft, B., Zündorf, A.: Multi-attribute relation extraction (MARE): simplifying the application of relation extraction. In: DeLTA. SCITEPRESS (2021)
13. Kumar, S.: A survey of deep learning methods for relation extraction. CoRR (2017)
14. Liu, K.: A survey on neural relation extraction. Sci. China Technol, Sciences (2020)
15. López, H.A., Debois, S., Hildebrandt, T.T., Marquard, M.: The process highlighter: From texts to declarative processes and back. In: CEUR Workshop Proc. (2018)
16. Nasar, Z., Jaffry, S.W., Malik, M.K.: Named entity recognition and relation extraction: State-of-the-art. ACM Comput, Surv (2021)
17. Nayak, T., Majumder, N., Goyal, P., Poria, S.: Deep neural approaches to relation triplets extraction: a comprehensive survey. Cogn, Comput (2021)
18. Page, M.J., et al.: The prisma 2020 statement: an updated guideline for reporting systematic reviews. In: Systematic reviews (2021)
19. Peng, H., et al.: Learning from Context or Names? An Empirical Study on Neural Relation Extraction. In: EMNLP. ACL (2020)
20. Qian, K., et al.: Annotation inconsistency and entity bias in MultiWOZ. In: Proceedings of SIGdial. ACL (2021)
21. Quishpi, L., Carmona, J., Padró, L.: Extracting annotations from textual descriptions of processes. In: Fahland, D., Ghidini, C., Becker, J., Dumas, M. (eds.) BPM 2020. LNCS, vol. 12168, pp. 184–201. Springer, Cham (2020). https://doi.org/10.1007/978-3-030-58666-9_11
22. Ren, F., et al.: A novel global feature-oriented relational triple extraction model based on table filling. In: EMNLP. ACL (2021)
23. Riedel, S., Yao, L., McCallum, A.: Modeling relations and their mentions without labeled text. In: Proceedings of ECML PKDD. Springer, Berlin Heidelberg (2010)
24. Roth, D., Yih, W.t.: A linear programming formulation for global inference in natural language tasks. In: CoNLL. ACL (2004)
25. Salih Dawood, O., Sahraoui, A.E.K.: From requirements engineering to uml using natural language processing - survey study. EJIE (2017)
26. Saranya, M., Geetha, T.V., Annie, R.A.X.: Comparative analysis of different deep learning techniques for relation extraction from biomedical literature. In: Proceedings of ICSADL. Springer Singapore (2022)

27. Taillé, B., Guigue, V., Scoutheeten, G., Gallinari, P.: Let's Stop Incorrect Comparisons in End-to-end Relation Extraction! In: EMNLP. ACL (2020)
28. Vashishth, S., Joshi, R., Prayaga, S.S., Bhattacharyya, C., Talukdar, P.: RESIDE: Improving distantly-supervised neural relation extraction using side information. In: EMNLP. ACL (2018)
29. Wang, H., Qin, K., Zakari, R.Y., Lu, G., Yin, J.: Deep neural network-based relation extraction: an overview. Neural Comput, Appl (2022)
30. Wang, J., Lu, W.: Two are better than one: Joint entity and relation extraction with table-sequence encoders. In: EMNLP. ACL (2020)
31. Wei, Z., Su, J., Wang, Y., Tian, Y., Chang, Y.: A novel cascade binary tagging framework for relational triple extraction. In: ACL (2020)
32. Yan, Z., Zhang, C., Fu, J., Zhang, Q., Wei, Z.: A partition filter network for joint entity and relation extraction. In: EMNLP. ACL (2021)
33. Yu, B., et al.: Joint extraction of entities and relations based on a novel decomposition strategy. In: Proceedings of ECAI (2020)
34. Yuan, Y., Zhou, X., Pan, S., Zhu, Q., Song, Z., Guo, L.: A relation-specific attention network for joint entity and relation extraction. In: IJCAI (2020)
35. Zeng, D., Zhang, H., Liu, Q.: Copymtl: Copy mechanism for joint extraction of entities and relations with multi-task learning. ArXiv (2020)
36. Zhang, X., Dai, Y., Jiang, T.: A survey deep learning based relation extraction. J. Phys.: Conf. Series **1601**, 032029 (2020)

Privacy and Security

Designing Secure and Privacy-Preserving Information Systems for Industry Benchmarking

Jan Pennekamp[1](✉) , Johannes Lohmöller[1] , Eduard Vlad[1] ,
Joscha Loos[1] , Niklas Rodemann[2] , Patrick Sapel[3] , Ina Berenice Fink[1] ,
Seth Schmitz[2] , Christian Hopmann[3] , Matthias Jarke[4,5] ,
Günther Schuh[2] , Klaus Wehrle[1] , and Martin Henze[6,7]

[1] Communication and Distributed Systems, RWTH Aachen University,
Aachen, Germany
{jan.pennekamp,johannes.lohmoeller,vlad,loos,
ina.fink,klaus.wehrle}@comsys.rwth-aachen.de
[2] Laboratory for Machine Tools and Production Engineering,
RWTH Aachen University, Aachen, Germany
{n.rodemann,s.schmitz,g.schuh}@wzl.rwth-aachen.de
[3] Institute for Plastics Processing, RWTH Aachen University, Aachen, Germany
{patrick.sapel,christian.hopmann}@ikv.rwth-aachen.de
[4] Information Systems, RWTH Aachen University, Aachen, Germany
jarke@dbis.rwth-aachen.de
[5] Fraunhofer FIT, Sankt Augustin, Germany
[6] Security and Privacy in Industrial Cooperation,
RWTH Aachen University, Aachen, Germany
henze@cs.rwth-aachen.de
[7] Fraunhofer FKIE, Wachtberg, Germany

Abstract. Benchmarking is an essential tool for industrial organizations
to identify potentials that allows them to improve their competitive position through operational and strategic means. However, the handling of
sensitive information, in terms of (i) internal company data and (ii) the
underlying algorithm to compute the benchmark, demands strict (technical) confidentiality guarantees—an aspect that existing approaches fail
to address adequately. Still, advances in private computing provide us
with building blocks to reliably secure even complex computations and
their inputs, as present in industry benchmarks. In this paper, we thus
compare two promising and fundamentally different concepts (hardware-
and software-based) to realize privacy-preserving benchmarks. Thereby,
we provide detailed insights into the concept-specific benefits. Our evaluation of two real-world use cases from different industries underlines that
realizing and deploying secure information systems for industry benchmarking is possible with today's building blocks from private computing.

Keywords: real-world computing · trusted execution environments ·
homomorphic encryption · key performance indicators · benchmarking

M. Indulska et al. (Eds.): CAiSE 2023, LNCS 13901, pp. 489–505, 2023.
https://doi.org/10.1007/978-3-031-34560-9_29

1   Introduction

Benchmarking is either a one-time or continuous process of identifying best practices to improve the performance using indicators [17]. More precisely, *industry benchmarking* is an essential tool for businesses to identify potentials by comparing themselves internally, with partners, or competitors through specific key performance indicators (KPIs). It provides companies with insights into the effectiveness of their processes (qualitatively and quantitatively). Further, it allows them to identify processes that are worthwhile to improve to close the gap between the market leader (best in class) and their own position, e.g., by avoiding a waste of resources [17,30]. To this end, we can distinguish between two common types of industry benchmarks, i.e., internal (involving departments of a single company) and external benchmarking (comparing multiple companies) [17].

From an information systems' perspective, benchmarks build on distributed information systems (ISs) with the goal of improving the overall performance (expressed through use case-tailored KPIs), within certain peer groups [14].

Overall, we identify three crucial dimensions when designing such systems: (1) *benchmarking frequency* (one-time vs. continuous benchmarking), (2) *openness of data* (i.e., open vs. closed data), and (3) *openness of the algorithm* (i.e., open vs. closed benchmarking algorithms). Traditionally, benchmarks utilized labor-intensive, manual interviews [17,23] to collect the required data to compute the defined KPIs by following a fixed algorithm, i.e., we can classify them as one-time benchmarks that source closed data and a closed algorithm. Data-driven approaches increasingly evolve toward continuous benchmarking systems, which might additionally rely on public (open) data and algorithms (e.g., governmental applications). As such benchmarks (open data and open algorithms) do not require elaborate security mechanisms, they are comparably easy to realize.

However, benchmarks in industry require strong security as they operate on sensitive (closed) company data using valuable, use case-tailored, and complex (closed) algorithms. Without sufficient security guarantees, companies fear a loss of control over their sensitive data, and in turn, of their competitive advantages. Thus, privacy-preserving benchmarks increase the number of companies willing to participate, which significantly affects the utility of benchmarks and the revenue of the analyst (the developer of the underlying algorithm). Moreover, such systems also help to ensure the confidentiality of the algorithm. Thereby, they protect the analyst's intellectual property, counteracting potential losses of subsequent compensations through unauthorized and unpaid reuse of algorithms.

Given these confidentiality needs, realizing privacy-preserving industry benchmarks is challenging. Fortunately, developments in the area of private computing provide us with two diametric concepts for designing such privacy-preserving systems. On the one hand, *Trusted Execution Environments* (TEEs) [27] provide hardware-based guarantees through dedicated computing enclaves for the private computation on sensitive data. On the other hand, *Fully Homomorphic Encryption* (FHE) [2] schemes are a software-based approach that enables privacy-preserving computations on encrypted data without revealing any details of the computation or its inputs. The question is which direction is best-suited.

In this paper, we answer this question by studying the suitability and applicability of two diametrical designs to benchmark organizations in industry, i.e., a hardware-based TEE and a software-based FHE approach, with the latter basing on our prior work [23]. Using real-world use cases in the domains of injection molding and global production networks, we evaluate our designs qualitatively and quantitatively. These use cases originate from the interdisciplinary research cluster "Internet of Production" [7,22], which connects researchers from various domains and more than 30 institutes. Thus, we holistically discuss the foundations for and implications of such privacy-preserving information systems.

Contributions. Our primary contributions in this paper are as follows.

- We study two diametrical designs[1] that secure ISs for industry benchmarking with modern concepts from private computing, i.e., using TEEs and FHE.
- We discuss the performance, limitations, and security guarantees of each design to give an intuition of the real-world implications, i.e., we provide a holistic overview for practical deployments of such information systems.

Organization. In Sect. 2, we first introduce industry benchmarking, two real-world use cases, and relevant related work. Subsequently, in Sect. 3, we present the two diametrical private computing concepts, which we build upon when describing our two benchmarking designs (Sect. 4). In Sect. 5, we evaluate these information systems also in light of our use cases before concluding in Sect. 6

2   Company Benchmarking in Industry

The need for privacy-preserving benchmarks motivates us to study existing concepts that promise to secure corresponding information systems. In Sect. 2.1, we first provide essential aspects of industry benchmarking, its actors, benefits, and privacy requirements. Subsequently, in Sect. 2.2, we detail two real-world use cases, which also serve as a basis for our evaluation (Sect. 5), before discussing past efforts to realize secure and privacy-preserving industry benchmarks in Sect. 2.3.

2.1   Company Benchmarking 101

Industry benchmarking usually focuses on practices such as the company's operations and the management of a company or a department [19]. The main objectives are to evaluate the company's current market position to identify the gap between the company and a recognized leader, as well as to adapt local processes to close this identified gap. For example, Xerox, a manufacturer of photocopiers and document management systems, improved its annual productivity gains from 3%–5% to 10% [31] after comparing its processes with L.L. Bean, a retailer of outdoor sporting goods, and addressing the benchmark's findings.

Benchmarks operate on key performance indicators (KPIs), allowing for quantitative comparisons of products, services, or implemented practices [11,14].

---

[1] We open-sourced them at https://github.com/COMSYS/industry-benchmarking.

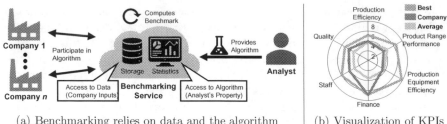

(a) Benchmarking relies on data and the algorithm   (b) Visualization of KPIs

Fig. 1. Using the algorithm and the companies' inputs, the benchmarking service computes all target KPIs, which allows companies to judge their performance.

Thus, we can also understand KPIs as digital shadows [5,12,18], i.e., an abstraction that represents the companies' performance. Nowadays, the sets of relevant KPIs frequently change. For instance, they increasingly cover sustainability, which also allows for comparisons of environmental and social aspects [6].

Figure 1(a) illustrates the process of benchmarking, including the main actors: an analyst, the benchmarking service, and participating companies. First, the analyst develops suitable algorithms to compute meaningful KPIs, which are usually kept private due to their value and intellectual property [10]. For example, the business models of credit scoring agencies, such as Experian or Schufa, largely depend on the confidentiality of the algorithm. The benchmarking service collects the corresponding inputs from participants and computes the KPIs to compare them as part of the benchmark. Eventually, the participants receive the general results and their own KPIs. Companies can then investigate their performance in comparison to the average and "best in class", as shown in Fig. 1(b).

Previous work [4,14,29] frequently outlined the need for confidential KPIs. The prevalence of closed benchmarking algorithms stresses the need to also protect the computation of the compared KPIs as it represents the analyst's competitive advantage who invests significant effort to derive meaningful KPIs [23]. We, therefore, identify two crucial privacy requirements that need to be considered: (1) the provided company inputs *and* computed company-specific KPIs, which we define analogous to personal privacy as *company privacy*, and (2) *algorithm confidentiality*. Mitigating data leaks is a significant challenge. Accordingly, company data should not even be accessible to the benchmarking service. However, neither should the algorithm be public nor (partly) accessible to the companies.

As a further complication, the KPI computation can be very complex in real-world benchmarks, i.e., a single KPI can be based on several formulas with dependencies, diverse operations, and hundreds of inputs [23]. Overall, a single benchmark may consist of up to 200 KPIs [14], thus, demanding computational resources for its operation. Next, we take a look at two real-world use cases.

2.2   Real-World Use Cases of Company Benchmarking

In this paper, we consider two real-world use cases, which we introduce next.

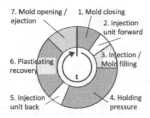

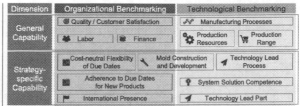

(a) Process steps of an injection molding cycle

(b) The benchmark evaluates organizational and technological dimensions through specifically derived KPIs.

Fig. 2. Our real-world benchmarking use case in the domain of injection molding captures the complexity of the production process through various KPIs.

Benchmarking Companies in Injection Molding (IM). Our first use case is injection molding as primary shaping: It is widely applicable in different industries and domains and allows for the processing of complex part geometries without subsequent rework. The raw plastic material is plasticized by heat and friction and then injected into the mold, which is the negative of the plastic part to be produced. After a pre-defined cooling time, the final part can be ejected from the mold [13]. Given the multitude of steps within a single cycle and their sensitivity, injection molding is a highly complex process, as shown in Fig. 2(a).

This use case bases on a real-world benchmark from 2014 that still utilized a centralized, paper-based approach [23] (cf. Sect. 2.3). Back then, companies in the injection molding industry compared their performance in organizational and technological aspects to advance or consolidate their positions (cf. Fig. 2(b)). The underlying algorithm and hence most of the resulting KPIs are highly specialized for this domain. As we detail in Table 1, the complexity of this example is high, with computations in up to 49 sequential operations, over 600 inputs, and more than 2700 operations, i.e., the analyst's effort is significant. In addition to elementary arithmetic, the KPI computation also sources exponentiation (x^y), roots $(\sqrt[n]{x})$, as well as absolute $(|x|)$ and extrema values (min/max). In return, participants received detailed results due to the large number of KPIs (Fig. 2(b) highlights some of them). As such, this use case is a representative real-world example, and it is along the lines of the number of expected KPIs (cf. Sect. 2.3).

This benchmark must be privacy-preserving as it builds on private inputs and computes sensitive KPIs. Here, prominent examples are data comprising costs of labor or manufacturing processes. For an in-depth presentation of the setup and the benchmark itself within this use case, we refer to previous work [23].

Table 1. Overview of our two real-world use cases and their algorithm complexity.

Dataset	Inputs	KPIs	Depth (Max)	Depth (Avg)	Formulas	Operations
IM	674	48	49	12	627	2704
PN	35 (n-dim)	14	12	6	14	100

Measuring the Efficiency of Global Production Networks (PN). Our second use case [24] benchmarks the performance of production sites in global-ized production networks to exemplarily study another setting and a different type of algorithm. Distributing production sites and supply chains can yield sig-nificant advantages as the geographic, regulatory, and technological conditions of each location can be exploited best [32]. However, a competitive advantage is only given if the beneficial performance is being attested regularly, e.g., through benchmarks where companies compare their inventory, efficiency, and equipment over different days, products, and production sites. The data necessary to gen-erate the KPIs for comparing companies' production networks requires highly sensitive company data. Thus, it must be treated confidentially, as it would allow others to draw conclusions about the corporate strategy and relationships [16].

In this context, benchmarking the performance of individual production sites is particularly interesting to compare the efficiency of companies or even loca-tions within a single company. For example, a KPI can express the unit costs of a product at a specific location for this purpose. By breaking down the unit product costs, companies can then identify the main drivers, such as the degree of automation, the wage level, or even the characteristics of the machine park. In this use case, the product portfolio complexity has been identified as a major driver of unit costs, which can be traced back to the need to interrupt production sequences with setup processes, resulting in reduced machine utilization.

In comparison to IM, the underlying algorithm of PN features three interest-ing differences for the design of an IS: (1) arrays as input values with variable length, which might implicitly reveal sensitive company details, (2) component-wise operations on arrays, and (3) summation (Σ) or extrema over arrays. Hence, despite its small size, with 14 KPIs and 100 operations (cf. Table 1), it is of great relevance for our work due to the complex operations contained within.

With these real-world use cases, we intend to provide a holistic view on the features any suitable design must adhere to while studying their implications. In the following, we look at past efforts in realizing secure benchmarking systems.

2.3   Related Work in Securing Company Benchmarks

Traditional benchmarking services utilize a centralized design that digitizes the paper-based responses of participants before computing the KPIs and compar-ing them [23]. Apart from their labor-intensive realization, such benchmarking services conceptually serve as a trusted third party as they have access to all sen-sitive inputs. Such centralized designs protect the algorithm but fail to account for the sensitive company inputs (*company privacy*). In contrast, local computa-tions by the participants, who only return the computed KPIs, protect sensitive inputs but fail to account for the required *algorithm confidentiality*. In a general direction, advances in privacy-preserving data processing emerge in research [1]. However, they frequently build upon disclosing the algorithms as well. Ongoing developments in the area of private computing promise to privacy-preservingly secure industry benchmarks while reliably mitigating this critical drawback.

Software-Based Approaches with Private Computing. In related work, we discover several software-based designs utilizing secure multi-party computation or homomorphic encryption. The former approaches usually have two major drawbacks: (1) they are commonly round-based, i.e., all participants need to participate simultaneously [4,14], and (2) the scalability is, at best, quadratic [4,15] in the number of participants. Initial homomorphic encryption-based approaches [28,29] come with a limited set of supported operations that challenge the computation of complex operations directly on encrypted data. These approaches have in common that they do not consider *algorithm confidentiality* [23], i.e., they only protect the comparison of KPIs but fail to account for the sensitivity of the KPI computation (the analyst's intellectual property).

In 2020, improved FHE schemes allowed us to propose a Privacy-preserving Company Benchmarking (PCB) [23], which considers *both* privacy requirements. Using FHE-encrypted inputs, PCB locally computes simple operations on encrypted data and locally compares encrypted KPIs, achieving *company privacy*. While PCB offloads complex computations to the participants, it allows for algorithm obfuscation to probabilistically ensure *algorithm confidentiality*. In this work, we refer to an increment of PCB with fewer needs of offloading as SW-PIB.

Hardware-Based Approaches. On the other side of the spectrum of private computing, we have hardware-based concepts, such as TEEs, which only emerged after the *majority* of software-based benchmarking approaches had already been proposed. The range of applications that utilize TEEs to securely execute programs is immense, with them also moving toward mobile devices, such as smartphones, these days. However, we did not discover any approach that utilizes TEEs to secure industry benchmarks. Thus, in this work and based on their secure computing enclaves, we study the opportunities hardware-based designs offer for the secure realization of benchmarking information systems.

3   Preliminaries: Recent Advances in Private Computing

Given the huge potential of private computing for benchmarking information systems, we now introduce the ideas and variants of the corresponding diametrical extremes, i.e., hardware- and software-based concepts, in more detail. Afterward, we study two designs for privacy-preserving industry benchmarking that base on these fundamentally different concepts to evaluate their practical feasibility.

Trusted Execution Environments (TEEs) [27] shield and protect confidential data and code during the processing via *hardware* mechanisms that are implemented in modern CPUs. The core idea is that confidential data and code remain inaccessible for the untrusted part of the system. To this end, TEEs allow attesting the hard- and software for validity such that users then share their data securely with a trusted party. For benchmarking, we can utilize these properties to protect the inputs and the analyst's algorithm. Using remote attestation, participants can verify the configuration of the system they are sending data to, as well as details on the software running in the TEE. Intel SGX is a popular and widely available implementation of this concept, which is also present in commodity hardware and today's cloud environments, such as Microsoft Azure [25].

Fully Homomorphic Encryption (FHE) [2] is a *software-based* approach that relies on the homomorphic property of special cryptosystems that allow for operations on the ciphertext to also be reflected in the plaintext, i.e., FHE enables computations directly on encrypted data even on untrusted hardware. Particularly, the widespread adoption of cloud computing contributes to the increasing application of FHE. FHE schemes can have varying cryptographic foundations that differ in terms of supported operations and encrypted data types (e.g., Booleans, integers, or approximated reals), each with individual overhead and constraints [2]. After a certain number of operations on a single ciphertext, ciphertexts need to be refreshed: either interactively using the owner's key pair or through (local) bootstrapping. In practice, the ideal design choice depends on the specific confidentiality needs and availability of computing resources.

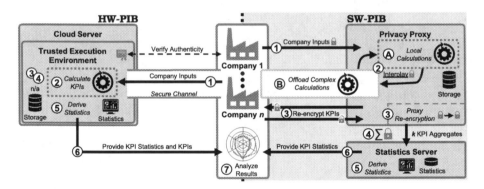

Fig. 3. Our hardware security-based approach **HW-PIB** (left) can be realized with a single server. Contrary, our software security-based approach **SW-PIB** (right) uses two non-colluding servers to ensure the confidentiality of inputs and the valuable algorithm. Eventually, companies analyze the benchmarking results.

4   Privacy-Preserving Company Benchmarking Designs

We propose two reference designs (**H**ardware- or **S**oftware-based) for **P**rivacypreserving **I**ndustry **B**enchmarking (PIB), i.e., HW-PIB and SW-PIB, to study their suitability for real-world information systems through qualitative and quantitative analysis. Apart from the frequently addressed company privacy, our designs also consider algorithm confidentiality (cf. Sect. 2.1). In Sect. 4.1, we provide a high-level overview to express the general processing steps. Subsequently, we discuss crucial details of HW-PIB and SW-PIB in Sect. 4.2 and 4.3, respectively.

4.1   Design Overview

The main difference between our designs lies in the underlying private computing concept (hardware vs. software-based). While TEEs can retain inputs and
computed KPIs of each company within the protected enclave in HW-PIB, SW-
PIB's privacy proxy only operates on encrypted data, and the statistics server
only has access to aggregates. Designing and evolving the actual benchmarking
algorithms is entirely independent of our designs, which focus on securing the
operation of benchmarking algorithms. Thus, the development of benchmarking algorithms remains unchanged. Conceptually, the logical steps to compute a
benchmark are identical in our designs, and the overall steps are largely comparable. However, the individual realizations differ significantly. Thus, we provide
a high-level description at this point. We visualize both designs in Fig. 3.

In ①, the participating companies share their inputs with the benchmarking
service. In HW-PIB, the companies send their sensitive data through a secure
(TLS) channel directly into the TEE. In contrast, SW-PIB requires the participants to homomorphically encrypt their inputs with their own public keys.
Subsequently, in ②, using the analyst's algorithms, the KPIs are computed.
While HW-PIB operates directly on plaintext data within the TEE, SW-PIB
deals with ciphertexts: Thus, in SW-PIB, depending on the operation, the computation is either Ⓐ performed (locally) on the privacy proxy if supported by
the FHE scheme or Ⓑ it is offloaded to the participant. We refer to offloading
as the process where the participant receives the operation and ciphertext(s)
from the privacy proxy to (1) decrypt the input ciphertext(s), (2) compute the
operation on the decrypted plaintexts, (3) homomorphically encrypt the result,
(4) and return it to the privacy proxy. Thereby, we circumvent the restricted set
of FHE-supported computations on ciphertexts and provide analysts with the
flexibility to include arbitrary operations in the benchmarking algorithms.

Steps ③ and ④ are only relevant for SW-PIB as HW-PIB directly operates on plaintext data within the protected enclave, i.e., no additional security
measures are needed. First (③), the ciphertexts must be re-encrypted with the
statistics server's key. Depending on the underlying FHE scheme, we can either
utilize proxy re-encryption directly on the proxy or we have to offload the re-
encryption to the company. Second (④), the privacy proxy aggregates the KPIs
of k participants [23] that are all encrypted with the statistics server's key and
forwards these aggregates to the statistics server, which can decrypt them.

⑤–⑦ are again identical for HW-PIB and SW-PIB. The benchmarking
service derives the KPI statistics (⑤) and shares them with the companies (⑥).
Finally, in ⑦, companies analyze their results to derive management decisions.

Next, we look at the designs' specifics and our prototypical implementations.

4.2   HW-PIB: Shielding the Computations

HW-PIB, our hardware-based design, utilizes TEEs to process the companies'
sensitive inputs while preserving confidentiality. The design builds on the isolation property of TEEs together with memory encryption and storage sealing to
restrict the access to sensitive information to software within the enclave.

Setup. Since the enclave has access to company inputs as plaintext data, the setup first needs to establish trust between the running enclave, the analyst, and participating companies. This trust includes (a) the correct and benign functionality of code running inside the enclave and (b) that the enclave actually runs the intended software on a trustworthy platform. We resolve (a) by open-sourcing the enclave code, such that any interested entity can verify its functionality, and (b) via remote attestation by a trusted certificate authority. Upon successful attestation, it issues and signs an enclave-specific certificate. This certificate serves as an enclave identifier and proves successful attestation to all entities who connect via a secure channel. The analyst and the companies then provision the enclave with their configuration and data (①), respectively.

KPI Computation. Due to the use of a trusted enclave, the TEE may have access to all data in plaintext. Hence, HW-PIB locally supports arbitrary complex operations (②) and does not require any offloading. The TEE's memory encryption ensures that the input and all intermediate computation results remain confidential, i.e., they are only accessible by/within the enclave itself.

Aggregation. Due to HW-PIB's computations on plaintexts, it does not require any preparatory aggregation steps (③–④). Instead, HW-PIB directly calculates the KPI statistics (⑤). Together with their individual KPIs, in ⑥, the general statistics are sent to the companies via TLS. Afterward, the enclave may terminate to ensure that any data and the KPIs are no longer accessible.

Remarks. As a hardware-based design, HW-PIB depends on a TEE-enabled cloud server, which various vendors offer. In this work, we utilize Intel SGX.

4.3   SW-PIB: Realizing Oblivious Computations

Now, we focus on the specifics of SW-PIB and the implications of utilizing FHE.

Setup. During the setup, the analyst (cf. Fig. 1) configures the privacy proxy (by sharing the algorithm and configuring k). Moreover, the statistics server generates an FHE key pair that is used to compute the aggregates in ④. Finally, each participant must generate an FHE key pair as well (used in ①–③).

KPI Computation. To ensure algorithm confidentiality, the privacy proxy tries to compute as many operations on ciphertexts as supported locally (Ⓐ). The support for complex operations (i.e., beyond $+, -$, and $\cdot$) depends on the utilized FHE scheme. Accordingly, unsupported operations need to be offloaded to the client (Ⓑ). Here, the analyst may configure obfuscation strategies (cf. [23]). This continuous interplay (②) concludes once all KPIs have been computed.

Aggregation. The realization of ③ depends on the support of proxy re-encryption in the utilized FHE scheme: Either the KPI re-encryption (to encrypt with the statistics server's key) is offloaded to the participant (who simultaneously learns its own KPIs), or the re-encryption is performed locally at the proxy (while the encrypted KPIs are shared to the participant for decryption). Once the KPIs of k companies have been aggregated (④), these aggregates are then sent to the statistics server, which combines them with existing statistics in ⑤. Eventually, in ⑥, the general statistics are retrievable for all participants.

Remarks. In SW-PIB, we have no requirements on the required hardware, as data is protected through a software-based (FHE) approach. However, this design comes with limitations of the locally supported FHE operations. Furthermore, separating privacy proxy and statistics server is crucial to prevent the decryption of (unaggregated) ciphertexts that contain sensitive company inputs or KPIs.

5 Evaluating Secure Industry Benchmarking Systems

To evaluate the feasibility of our discussed designs, we study their performance (Sect. 5.1) using synthetic measurements and two real-world benchmarking algorithms. We further discuss their respective security guarantees (Sect. 5.2) and compare them (Sect. 5.3). With this overview, we provide insights into concept-specific benefits and their applicability for benchmarking information systems.

5.1 Performance and Overhead Evaluation

We conduct our evaluations using our open-sourced implementations of the designs. In particular, we focus on the performance of the KPI computation as it covers the majority of relevant operations. We do not report any numbers on the aggregation phase (③–⑤) due to its low computational footprint.

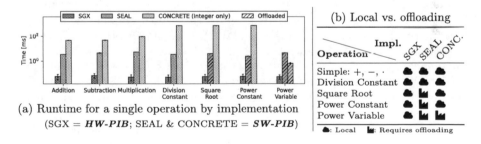

(a) Runtime for a single operation by implementation
(SGX = **HW-PIB**; SEAL & CONCRETE = **SW-PIB**)

Fig. 4. The locally supported (complex) operations differ across implementations.

Implementation. For HW-PIB, we utilize Scone [3], running on Intel SGX. For SW-PIB, we (i) re-implemented and extended PCB [23], which builds on Microsoft SEAL [20], with array computations, as required by our PN use case, and (ii) built a proof of concept that employs CONCRETE [8]. Since Microsoft SEAL does not (yet) implement proxy re-encryption, we resort to offloading in Step ③. However, this limitation of SEAL is not a conceptual issue in SW-PIB.

Experimental Setup. Our implementations run on a commodity computer with moderate resources (Intel i7-7700 with 16 GB RAM and a regular SSD). All entities communicate over the loopback interface. We conduct 50 runs for each measurement, compute the mean, and calculate 99 % confidence intervals. We rely on 128 bit-level security. In SEAL, we configure polynomial moduli of 16 384 (7 levels) and 8192 (4 levels) for IM and PN, respectively (cf. Sect. 2.2). To ensure consistency across the reported numbers and avoid bias in our results, we followed the same evaluation methodology for all conducted experiments.

Performance. To assess the performance, we have to look at the setup and run times. We observe that the setup times are negligible (17.893 ± 0.015 s for HW-PIB and 3.424 ± 1.164 s for SW-PIB). Looking at the run times, we first investigate the performance of single operations. As we illustrate in Fig. 4(a), these synthetic measurements show that HW-PIB is one order of magnitude faster than our SEAL- and CONCRETE-based implementations of SW-PIB, and it does not require offloading (Fig. 4(b)). The performance of the CONCRETE-based version will likely deteriorate once additional datatypes, such as floats or larger integers, are supported. Still, we want to emphasize the potential of programmable bootstraps, i.e., this FHE scheme supports additional complex operations without the need for offloading. While the overhead of computing FHE ciphertexts at the privacy proxy is already significant, the need to offload operations further slows down SW-PIB; especially for constrained network links.

Moving to our real-world examples, we notice that both designs are practical for real-world deployments. For the larger IM example (cf. Table 1), HW-PIB and SW-PIB finish after 0.115 ± 0.019 s and 634.008 ± 0.538 s, respectively. Thus, from a suitability perspective, analysts could even offer significantly larger yet confidential benchmarks. In contrast, our PN example is an order of magnitude faster, with 0.080 ± 0.001 s and 34.409 ± 0.044 s. Overall, the runtimes for single operations, as we have illustrated in Fig. 4(a), amplify in real-world benchmarks. Hence, the performance of SW-PIB remains inferior to HW-PIB.

Accuracy. While HW-PIB is exact by design, our SEAL-based implementation of SW-PIB uses approximate arithmetic, i.e., when processing floats, we encounter precision losses. As we perform computations on approximated numbers, the precision loss amplifies, especially for long chains of operations. When using SW-PIB and suffering from insufficient accuracy, the benchmarking algorithm can be tweaked to better fit the precision of the utilized FHE scheme. For example, numbers can be scaled to account for precision losses of approximate ciphertext representations. Nonetheless, SW-PIB is feasible as we only observe minor deviations. Overall, we measure 4.0 ± 0.3 % for IM and <0.01 % for PN.

Ciphertext Overhead. HW-PIB does not introduce noteworthy storage and network overhead by design. Thus, we now focus on SW-PIB: Relying on FHE introduces storage and network overhead due to comparably large ciphertext sizes. For IM, we measure a size of at most 1.842 MB for a single ciphertext, i.e., even the up- and download of thousands of ciphertexts (when sharing inputs or during offloading) is feasible over bandwidth-constrained network links. Hence, ciphertext overheads do not prohibit real-world applications of SW-PIB.

Moving on, we discuss our designs' security before comparing them in detail.

5.2 Security Discussion

From a security perspective, we expect malicious-but-cautious entities [26], i.e., they want to extract as much information as possible without leaving any traces of the extraction. This assumption is especially reasonable in scenarios with businesses that are bound to specific legislation. Consequently, we exclude collusion attacks that involve multiple entities. Next, we look at our two designs in detail.

HW-PIB. The security builds upon hardware-based security. Consequently, the hardware vendor must be trusted, i.e., it serves as the root of trust. Using remote attestation (a key feature of TEEs), we can establish a trust chain to the enclave and the code running within it. Hence, participants only have to verify this chain and the running code using certificates and cryptographic signatures. If the security has been correctly attested, all information and computations are shielded within the TEE. Thus, in this case, HW-PIB is secure by design. However, the multitude of (past) vulnerabilities in TEEs [9] could negatively impact the trust in this technology. Consequently, we also consider SW-PIB.

SW-PIB. This design protects the company inputs and intermediate results using FHE. Its security builds on the privacy proxy and statistics server not colluding. Then, the privacy proxy never has access to any information in plaintext as it lacks the corresponding decryption keys. Moreover, the statistics server only receives aggregates of k participants, i.e., it cannot deduce any details about specific companies if k is reasonably large (i.e., $k > 3$) [23]. Hence, sensitive company

Table 2. Comparison of hardware- and software-secured benchmarking designs.

Design / Criteria	HW-PIB SGX		SW-PIB SEAL		CONCRETE	
Setting	IM	PN	IM	PN	IM	PN
Performance	★★★		★★☆		★★☆	
▶ Setup	Remote attestation		Exchange of key material			
▶ Run Time [s]	0.11 ± 0.02	0.08 ± 0.00	634.0 ± 0.5	34.4 ± 0.0	Unknown	
Accuracy Loss [%]	Exact		4.0 ± 0.3	0.0 ± 0.0	Unknown	
Ciphertext Overhead	★★★		★☆☆		★★☆	
▶ Offloading [#]	None		↓1487 ↑745	↓53 ↑28	↓84 ↑42	↓0 ↑0
▶ Networking [≤×MB]	No overhead		1.842	1.053	Unknown	
Ease of Use	★★★		★★☆		Unknown	
Security	★★★		★★☆		★★★	
▶ Assumptions	Trusted hardware		Secure FHE scheme			
▶ Trust in Participants	Not required		Non-collusion required			
▶ Privacy Issues	None		Minor (offl.)		Barely any (offl.)	
▶ Own KPIs	After/with agg.		Before agg.		After/with agg.	

data is protected (encrypted) at all times. In both designs, the algorithm is never shared with the participants. However, in SW-PIB, we need to offload specific complex operations (cf. Sect. 4.3). Thus, fractions of the algorithm along with their intermediate results need to be shared with the participants, slightly violating the intended algorithm confidentiality. To mitigate these implications of offloading, the benchmarking service can utilize different obfuscation strategies, such as dummy requests, blinding, and request randomization [23]. Consequently, SW-PIB ensures the privacy needs of real-world benchmarks.

5.3   HW-PIB vs. SW-PIB: Selecting the Fitting Design

We compare both diametrical security concepts when realizing benchmarking information systems in Table 2 to give a concise overview and to allow for well-founded deployment decisions. Now, we briefly summarize the specific properties.

Performance. The benchmarking setup is a one-time task and thus negligible with times below 18 s. Given that benchmarking is not an everyday task, the run time for each company is more than suitable for real-world applications, even with significantly larger benchmarks. The real-world use cases further underline this claim (IM: 634.008 ± 0.538 s and PN: 34.409 ± 0.044 s). The TEE- and FHE-induced overheads are reasonable in light of the confidentiality benefits.

Accuracy. HW-PIB features exact computations by design, and the loss of precision for SW-PIB is tolerable as (i) the deviations affect all companies and (ii) benchmarks primarily concern the relative positioning [19]. Moreover, the evaluated real-world algorithms were not tailored to the use with FHE. Given that the inaccuracies follow from small numbers [23], the analyst could easily scale the inputs and formulas to mitigate such deviations to a large extent.

Ciphertext Overhead. In addition to the noticeable ciphertext overhead in SW-PIB, we further have to rely on offloading to compute a subset of complex computations locally at the companies. Recent advances, such as CON-CRETE [8], even promise to reduce the required offloading. Regardless of such advances, companies receive more ciphertexts than they send, which fits to the imbalance of Internet connections. Even with ciphertext sizes of 1.842 MB, for IM, the upload of 1.391 GB per company is feasible in constrained networks.

Ease of Use. We consider our designs to be practical for real-world use as companies can easily participate through common web browsers. While our implementation of HW-PIB natively features a web-based client, we have shown in previous work [23] that our SEAL-based implementation supports WebAssembly-based web clients as well. Concerning reoccurring operational costs, HW-PIB only requires a server with TEE support, which is commercially available at major (cloud) vendors. In contrast, FHE-based SW-PIB does not introduce specific hardware requirements, but its operations are computationally more expensive.

In real-world deployments, analysts could operate the cloud server and privacy proxy, respectively, and fund them through participation fees. If needed, our designs support scaling out the cloud server and privacy proxy, respectively, e.g., to support a tremendous number of participants. Aside from that, industry associations could fund the statistics server in SW-PIB using their membership fees to prevent collusion attacks [23]. Generally, HW-PIB is cheaper to operate with fewer overheads *if TEEs are trusted*, compared to FHE-based SW-PIB.

Security. HW-PIB requires specific hardware for its operation and is secure and privacy-preserving if the trusted hardware is realized as intended. Given that companies establish a secure tunnel into the enclave, HW-PIB reliably protects the algorithm, all inputs, and the computed KPIs. In contrast, SW-PIB does not depend on specifically trusted hardware but on secure and properly configured FHE schemes. We further require non-collusion between privacy proxy and statistics server to ensure company privacy. Obfuscation strategies can help to prevent offloading-induced information leaks (companies have access to the operator and intermediate data). As indicated before, modern FHE schemes promise to further reduce the required offloading. While our SEAL-based SW-PIB uses offloading for the KPI re-encryption (③), which enables companies to abort the protocol (then, they only have access to their KPIs), implementations that support proxy re-encryption provide the same security properties as HW-PIB.

Takeaways. Nowadays, concepts from private computing are readily available to secure information systems in real-world deployments. Thus, when designing secure information systems for industry benchmarks, the key question is which conceptual technology should serve as the root of trust, i.e., trusted hardware or a secure FHE scheme, mainly because the remaining properties do not prohibit practical realizations, as we briefly summarize in the following.

Looking at the performance, both designs fulfill the needs of real-world benchmarks, with HW-PIB computationally outperforming SW-PIB. While HW-PIB's accurate computations promise quick and precise results, SW-PIB is easier to deploy as it is designed for untrusted hardware (despite requiring two entities, i.e., privacy proxy and statistics server). Thus, industry should indeed be able to offer secure and privacy-preserving benchmarks in practice. The exact realization (design) then likely depends on the availability of a TEE and the willingness to build on its associated security assumptions (e.g., trusting the underlying security concept, the vendors, and remote attestation). Otherwise, FHE-based implementations promise secure and practical real-world deployments. For now, we recommend our revised SEAL-based version, but in the future, CONCRETE-based implementations with fewer offloading needs could outperform it.

6 Conclusion

In industry, companies frequently rely on industry benchmarks to identify potentials that allow them to improve their competitive position through strategic and operational adjustments. Given its benefits, industry benchmarking is a valuable tool. However, benchmarks depend on valuable information: First, the underlying complex formulas to compute meaningful key performance indicators (KPIs) constitute the analyst's intellectual property and must be kept private. Likewise, the KPI computation sources sensitive company inputs. The inputs, as well as the KPIs, must thus remain confidential. Consequently, to increase the number of participants, industry benchmarks must be operated privacy-preservingly.

Confidentiality requirements have hindered the wide use of corresponding information systems (ISs) so far. Given the latest advances in private computing, we compared two fundamentally different concepts (hardware- and software-based security) to realize privacy-preserving ISs that are capable of offering real-world industry benchmarks while ensuring both algorithm confidentiality and company privacy. Our corresponding designs each offer concept-specific benefits: While the performance of HW-PIB and its accurate computations promise quick and precise results, SW-PIB is easier to deploy and does not depend on specific hardware or its associated security guarantees. Our evaluation of two real-world industrial use cases (IM & PN) demonstrates that secure benchmarking deployments are practical with today's concepts from private computing. In the future, we look forward to the rapid evolution of private computing and its implications on information systems beyond our application in industry benchmarking.

Acknowledgments. Funded by the Deutsche Forschungsgemeinschaft (DFG, German Research Foundation) under Germany's Excellence Strategy – EXC-2023 Internet of Production – 390621612. We thank Jan-Gustav Michnia for his initial exploration of the FHE library CONCRETE [8]. We followed an abstract research methodology [21] to structure and organize our research collaborations.

References

1. van der Aalst, W.M.P.: Federated Process Mining: Exploiting Event Data Across Organizational Boundaries. In: IEEE SMDS (2021)
2. Acar, A., Aksu, H., et al.: A Survey on Homomorphic Encryption Schemes: Theory and Implementation. ACM Comput. Surv. **51**(4), (2018)
3. Arnautov, S., Trach, B., et al.: SCONE: Secure Linux Containers with Intel SGX. In: USENIX OSDI (2016)
4. Becher, K., Beck, M., Strufe, T.: An Enhanced Approach to Cloud-based Privacy-preserving Benchmarking. In: NetSys (2019)
5. Bibow, P., Dalibor, M., et al.: Model-Driven Development of a Digital Twin for Injection Molding. In: CAiSE (2020)
6. Boos, W.: Production Turnaround – Turning Data into Sustainability. Tech. rep., RWTH Aachen University (2021), white Paper
7. Brauner, P., Dalibor, M., et al.: A Computer Science Perspective on Digital Transformation in Production. ACM Trans. Internet Things **3**(2), 1–32 (2022)
8. Chillotti, I., Joye, M., et al.: CONCRETE: Concrete Operates oN Ciphertexts Rapidly by Extending TfhE. In: WAHC (2020)
9. Fei, S., Yan, Z., et al.: Security Vulnerabilities of SGX and Countermeasures: A Survey. ACM Comput. Surv. **54**(6), 1–36 (2021)
10. Gunasekaran, A., Putnik, G.D., et al.: An expert diagnosis system for the benchmarking of SMEs' performance. Benchmarking **13**, 1–2 (2006)
11. Herrmann, D., Scheuer, F., et al.: A Privacy-Preserving Platform for User-Centric Quantitative Benchmarking. In: TrustBus (2009)

12. Jarke, M.: Data Sovereignty and the Internet of Production. In: CAiSE (2020)
13. Kamal, M.R., Isayev, A.I., Liu, S.J.: Injection Molding: Technology and Fundamentals. Hanser (2009)
14. Kerschbaum, F.: Practical Privacy-Preserving Benchmarking. In: IFIP SEC (2008)
15. Kerschbaum, F.: Secure and Sustainable Benchmarking in Clouds. Bus. Inf. Syst. Eng. **3**(3), 135–143 (2011)
16. Kerschbaum, F., Oertel, N., Weiss Ferreira Chaves, L.: Privacy-Preserving Computation of Benchmarks on Item-Level Data Using RFID. In: ACM WiSec (2010)
17. Kozak, M.: Destination Benchmarking: Concepts. CABI, Practices and Operations (2004)
18. Liebenberg, M., Jarke, M.: Information Systems Engineering with DigitalShadows: Concept and Case Studies. In: CAiSE (2020)
19. Marti, J.M.V., d. R. Cabrita, M.: Entrepreneurial Excellence in the Knowledge Economy: Intellectual Capital Benchmarking Systems. Palgrave Macmillan (2012)
20. Microsoft Inc: Microsoft SEAL. https://github.com/Microsoft/SEAL (2018)
21. Pennekamp, J., Buchholz, E., et al.: Collaboration is not Evil: A Systematic Look at Security Research for Industrial Use. In: LASER (2021)
22. Pennekamp, J., Glebke, R., et al.: Towards an Infrastructure Enabling the Internet of Production. In: IEEE ICPS (2019)
23. Pennekamp, J., Sapel, P., et al.: Revisiting the Privacy Needs of Real-World Applicable Company Benchmarking. In: WAHC (2020)
24. Rittstieg, M.: Einflussfaktoren der Leistungsfähigkeit von Produktionsstandorten in globalen Produktionsnetzwerken. Ph.D. thesis (2018)
25. Russinovich, M.: Azure confidential computing. https://azure.microsoft.com/en-us/blog/azure-confidential-computing/ (2018 (Accessed March 20 2023))
26. Ryan, M.D.: Enhanced Certificate Transparency and End-to-end Encrypted Mail. In: NDSS (2014)
27. Sabt, M., Achemlal, M., Bouabdallah, A.: Trusted Execution Environment: What It is, and What It is Not. In: IEEE TrustCom (2015)
28. Sahin, C., Kuczenski, B., et al.: Privacy-Preserving Certification of Sustainability Metrics. In: ACM CODASPY (2018)
29. Sohati-Moghadam, S., Fayoumi, A.: Private Collaborative Business Benchmarking in the Cloud. In: SAI (2018)
30. Teicholz, E.: Facility Design and Management Handbook. McGraw-Hill (2001)
31. Tucker, F.G., Zivan, S.M., Camp, R.C.: How to Measure Yourself Against the Best. Harv. Bus. Rev. **65**(1) (1987)
32. Verhaelen, B., Mayer, F., et al.: A comprehensive KPI network for the performance measurement and management in global production networks. Prod. Eng. (2021)

PMDG: Privacy for Multi-perspective Process Mining Through Data Generalization

Ryan Hildebrant[1]([envelope]), Stephan A. Fahrenkrog-Petersen[2,3], Matthias Weidlich[2], and Shangping Ren[4]

[1] University of California, Irvine, USA
rhildebr@uci.edu
[2] Humboldt-Universität zu Berlin, Berlin, Germany
{fahrenks,weidlima}@hu-berlin.de
[3] Weizenbaum Institute for the Networked Society, Berlin, Germany
[4] San Diego State University, San Diego, USA
sren@sdsu.edu

Abstract. Anonymization of event logs facilitates process mining while protecting sensitive information of process stakeholders. Existing techniques, however, focus on the privatization of the control-flow. Other process perspectives, such as roles, resources, and objects are neglected or subject to randomization, which breaks the dependencies between the perspectives. Hence, existing techniques are not suited for advanced process mining tasks, e.g., social network mining or predictive monitoring . To address this gap, we propose PMDG, a framework to ensure privacy for multi-perspective process mining through data generalization. It provides group-based privacy guarantees for an event log, while preserving the characteristic dependencies between the control-flow and further process perspectives. Unlike existing privatization techniques that rely on data suppression or noise insertion, PMDG adopts data generalization: a technique where the activities and attribute values referenced in events are generalized into more abstract ones, to obtain equivalence classes that are sufficiently large from a privacy point of view. We demonstrate empirically that PMDG outperforms state-of-the-art anonymization techniques, when mining handovers and predicting outcomes.

Keywords: Privatization · K-anonymity · Attribute Generalization

1 Introduction

Privacy-preserving process mining [1] enables data-driven analysis of business processes, while protecting sensitive data about the individuals involved in process execution. To this end, existing techniques rely on the anonymization of an event log, which is commonly modeled as a set of traces, with each trace being a sequence of events that denote activity executions. In order to obtain a provable privacy guarantee, the traces of an event log are transformed. Here, existing techniques differ in terms of the adopted privacy guarantee and the properties preserved by these transformations. Anonymization of event logs may guarantee differential privacy [2] or rely on group-based notions, such as k-anonymity and its derivatives [3]. Moreover, the respective transformations

© The Author(s), under exclusive license to Springer Nature Switzerland AG 2023
M. Indulska et al. (Eds.): CAiSE 2023, LNCS 13901, pp. 506–521, 2023.
https://doi.org/10.1007/978-3-031-34560-9_30

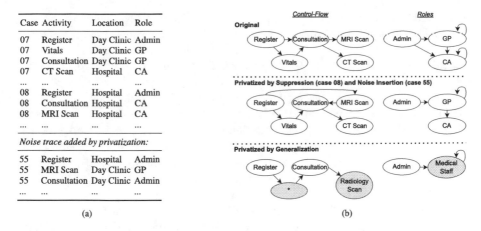

Case	Activity	Location	Role
07	Register	Day Clinic	Admin
07	Vitals	Day Clinic	GP
07	Consultation	Day Clinic	GP
07	CT Scan	Hospital	CA
...	...	...	...
08	Register	Hospital	Admin
08	Consultation	Hospital	CA
08	MRI Scan	Hospital	CA
...	...	...	...

Noise trace added by privatization:

55	Register	Hospital	Admin
55	MRI Scan	Day Clinic	GP
55	Consultation	Day Clinic	Admin
...	...	...	...

(a)

(b)

Fig. 1. (a) Example log of a clinical pathway containing traces for case 07 and 08; (b) the control-flow and the role perspective, when considering the original log, the event log privatized by suppression (case 08 is suppressed) and noise insertion (case 55 is added), and the event log privatized by generalization of activities and roles.

may only suppress behavior in the log or potentially introduce new and noisy behavior in terms of unseen sequences of activity executions.

Most techniques for privacy-preserving process mining [4–6] focus on the construction of a process model from an event log [7]. As such, they target the control-flow perspective of the process, trying to ensure that the anonymized event log includes semantically correct sequences of activity executions from the process. However, event logs also contain information on other process perspectives, such as roles, resources, and case objects. Advanced process mining tasks exploit the relation between the control-flow and these additional perspectives, e.g., to extract hand-overs during process execution [8] or to construct models to predict the outcome of running process instances [9].

As of today, ensuring privacy beyond the control-flow creates a notable research gap. So far, data linked to events is either neglected, or assigned randomly once the control-flow has been anonymized [10]. The latter tends to break any dependencies between the various perspectives, rendering the event logs unsuitable for multi-perspective process mining, as illustrated in Fig. 1. Here, Fig. 1a shows an example event log of a clinical pathway for two patients, cases 07 and 08. Figure 1b (top), in turn, highlights the control-flow dependencies and the hand-overs between the involved roles. Existing techniques for privatization of the control-flow by suppression (of case 08) and noise insertion (of case 55), however, do not only disturb the control-flow, but also break the dependencies between process perspectives, as illustrated for the hand-overs between roles in Fig. 1b (middle). This raises the question of *how to preserve the characteristic dependencies between the process perspectives when anonymizing an event log.*

In this paper, we address this question with PMDG, a framework to ensure privacy for multi-perspective process mining through data generalization. It preserves the dependencies between process perspectives when constructing an event log that meets k-anonymity, a privacy guarantee often adopted in industry [11]. To this end, we adopt data generalization instead of data suppression and noise insertion. Figure 1b (bottom) gives the intuition of this approach: here, sufficiently large equivalence classes of traces are derived by generalizing activities (*CT Scan* and *MRI Scan* become *Radiology Scan*) and role information (*GP* and *CA* become *Medical Staff*). While the generalization incurs some information loss, it arguably preserves general characteristics, such as the conduct of radiologic scans only after the consultation, as well as the handovers between administrative staff and medical personnel.

In sum, our contributions are the definition of PMDG as a first framework to enable privacy for multi-perspective process mining; and its instantiation with specific techniques for (i) the vectorization of traces to facilitate control-flow generalization; (ii) the selection of hierarchies to be used for the abstraction; and (iii) the application of the selected hierarchies to generalize the control-flow and the data assigned to events.

We demonstrate the effectiveness of PMDG for multi-perspective process mining in experiments with three public event logs. When mining handovers and predicting process outcomes, we observe that PMDG significantly outperforms state-of-the-art anonymization techniques in terms of maintaining characteristic hand-overs and classification accuracy, respectively. In the remainder, Sect. 2 reviews related work on privacy-preserving process mining. Section 3 then provides background information. The PMDG framework is outlined and instantiated in Sect. 4, before we present evaluation experiments in Sect. 5. We discuss our approach on a qualitative level in Sect. 6, before concluding in Sect. 7.

2   Related Work

Privacy-preserving process mining has received much attention recently [1]. Several approaches have been proposed to ensure k-anonymity and other group-based privacy guarantees, e.g., by merging similar traces [4, 12] or filtering data [5]. Due to their focus on the control-flow, these methods are not suited for multi-perspective process mining.

Instead of hiding sensitive data within groups of traces, some approaches achieve differential privacy by inserting noise into event logs [6, 13, 14]. Here, the privacy guarantees limits the effect one individual can have on the anonymized data. Yet, the approaches filter behavior from the log or introduce new and formerly unseen behavior.

The importance of the privatization of additional process perspectives has been highlighted in [15], which introduced a technique that is tailored to one particular perspective, i.e. resource assignments. In the general case, the aforementioned approaches for control-flow anonymization may be combined with an enrichment step, which either assigns values randomly [10] or unifies their distribution over an event log [16]. Either way, characteristic dependencies between the process perspectives are compromised and the insertion of new dependencies may lead to wrong conclusions in the analysis.

Another angle is followed in confidential process mining that aims to protect an event log by encryption [17]. This may include several process perspectives, but lacks any formal guarantee on the privacy of individuals in the dataset.

Our approach relies on data generalization to privatize several process perspectives. Generalization is a well-established method to privatize relational, hierarchical, and simple sequence data, see [18–20]. Yet, PMDG is the first use of data generalization for event logs, i.e. multi-variate sequences for which the dependencies between the various dimensions shall be preserved.

3   Background

Event Logs. Process mining is based on events, each representing the recorded execution of an activity, i.e. *Register* or *MRI Scan* in Fig. 1. We denote the universes of activities and events by $\mathcal{A}$ and $\mathcal{E}$, respectively. The activity for which an event $e \in \mathcal{E}$ signals the execution is written as $e.a \in \mathcal{A}$. Events have a schema, defined by a set of attributes, $\mathcal{D} = \{D_1, \ldots, D_n\}$, and we denote the domain of values of attribute D by $\mathcal{V}_D$. For an event e, we write $e.D \in \mathcal{V}_D$ for the respective value of attribute D. In Fig. 1, we have $\mathcal{D} = \{Location, Role\}$. Here, attribute *Role* assumes the values *Admin*, *CA*, and *GP*, whereas the respective domain may also include further values. In particular, it can contain more abstract roles, such as *Medical Staff* or *Staff*.

Events that relate to the same, single execution of a process are grouped into a trace. Each trace σ is a finite sequence of events $\langle e_1, \ldots, e_n \rangle \in \mathcal{E}^*$ of length $|\sigma| = n$. We use $\sigma.A$ to denote the control-flow of a trace σ, meaning the sequence of activities for which the execution is indicated by the events within the trace. For our running example, for instance, we have $\sigma.A = \langle Register, Vitals, Consultation, CT\ Scan \rangle$ for the trace of case 07. All traces with the same control-flow are said to be of the same trace variant, which is identified by one of the respective traces. That is, $[\![\sigma]\!]^A$ is the bag of traces that have the same control-flow as σ. A bag of traces is called an event log, $L = [\sigma_1, \ldots, \sigma_n]$. It represents the input for many process mining algorithms.

k-Anonymity. A well-known way to protect the privacy of individuals is to hide them within a group, which is the aim of k-anonymity [3]. The idea is that, in a dataset (an event log), one individual shall be indistinguishable from at least $k-1$ other individuals. Therefore, the probability of identifying one individual, the so-called problem of *identity disclosure*, can be bound to $1/k$. To achieve that k individuals are indistinguishable, the quasi-identifiers need to be aligned. In general, quasi-identifiers are attributes that enable the identification of an individual, such as a postcode or birth date.

In our setting, we assume that all attributes of all events and the control-flow of a trace can serve as quasi-identifiers. We therefore consider all traces that have the same control-flow and sequence of selected attribute values to be part of an equivalence class. The selected attributes are generated based on a defined perspective required for advanced process mining tasks. In line with the notation introduced for trace variants, we identify an equivalence class by one of its members, i.e. $[\![\sigma \mid \mathcal{D}']\!]$ denotes an equivalence class that comprises all traces that have the same control-flow and attribute values for the specified attributes $\mathcal{D}' \subseteq \mathcal{D}$ as σ. Based thereon, we define k-anonymity as follows: Let $L = [\sigma_1, \ldots, \sigma_n]$ be an event log. Then, the log L satisfies k-*anonymity* with respect to a given perspective, if for every equivalence class $[\![\sigma \mid \mathcal{D}']\!]$ in L induced by a trace $\sigma \in L$, it holds that $|[\![\sigma \mid \mathcal{D}']\!]| \geq k$.

We note that the above definition of equivalence classes, and hence of k-anonymity, induces the strictest possible notion. It assumes the strongest adversary, under which any attribute and the control-flow may serve as quasi-identifiers in an identity disclosure attack. As such, it subsumes attacks in which an adversary possesses only a certain type of background knowledge [5], such as knowing which activities have been executed by an individual, but not their order of execution. To avoid assumptions on the knowledge of an adversary, we adopt the above model that represents the worst case scenario.

4 Generalization of Event Logs

This section first outlines the design principles for our work (Sect. 4.1). Then, we give an overview of our PMDG framework to address the identified research gap (Sect. 4.2). While some steps of it rely on existing techniques, some aspects call for new techniques to ensure high utility of the anonymized event log. Specifically, we introduce strategies for trace vectorization (Sect. 4.3) and hierarchy selection (Sect. 4.4).

4.1 Design Principles of the Framework

We developed the PMDG framework using the design science methodology [21]. The starting point for our problem observation is that existing anonymization techniques for event logs mostly rely on noise insertion and aggregation, but do not incorporate any generalization strategies. To address this research gap, we derived the following design objectives for the artifact: Given an event log with m traces and a privacy parameter $k \leq m$, the artifact (i) shall transform the event log to fulfill k-anonymity through generalization; and (ii) shall minimize the total amount of generalizations that are applied to the log. In this section, we introduce the PMDG framework to realize these design objectives. The evaluation step of the artifact is provided within a later section, while this paper denotes the final communication step of the design science methodology.

4.2 PMDG Framework

As shown in Fig. 2, our framework is applied to an event log that contains information about multiple process perspectives through the attribute values assigned to events (see Sect. 3). In addition, it relies on generalization hierarchies. That is, an *activity hierarchy*, modeled as a function $\rho_A : \mathcal{A} \rightarrow \mathcal{A}' \cup \{\star\}$, which maps an activity to a more abstract activity or a wildcard $\star$. For an attribute D representing an additional perspective, a *value hierarchy* $\rho_D : \mathcal{V}_D \rightarrow \mathcal{V}_D \cup \{\star\}$ maps an attribute value to a more abstract value or a wildcard. Either way, for the control-flow or perspective, the hierarchies are rooted in the wildcard $\star$, meaning that for any activity $a \in \mathcal{A}$ and value $v \in \mathcal{V}_D$, it holds that $\star \in \rho_A^*(a)$ and $\star \in \rho_D^*(v)$, where ρ^* denotes the transitive application of a generalization hierarchy ρ. Moreover, for all process perspectives, multiple hierarchies may be available to generalize the respective information. Using the hierarchies, the PMDG framework transforms the event log given as input, to one such that the resulting log guarantees k-anonymity.

Common strategies for data generalization are based on operations that change individual values of the elements in a dataset [22]. Hence, in order to enable comprehensive generalization, i.e. to achieve that any two elements may end up in the same equivalence class, it is necessary to ensure that all elements assume the same structure. Transferred to our setting, this requires all traces to be of equal lengths and all events to have the same schema. While the latter requirement typically does not impose any challenges in practice and is incorporated in our definition of the model already, differences in the lengths of traces need to be handled. To this end, our framework incorporates *trace vectorization* as a first step, which we explain in more detail in Sect. 4.3.

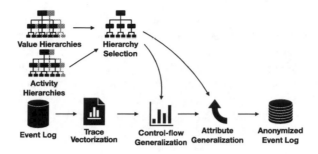

Fig. 2. Overview of the PMDG framework.

Next, the PMDG framework generalizes the control-flow before considering further process perspectives. The reason being that behavioral information serves as the basis for advanced process mining tasks and shall always be protected by k-anonymity. Further perspectives enrich the control-flow and may be subject to more fine-granular control of the privacy guarantee, e.g., adopting t-closeness [23] instead of k-anonymity.

To obtain the privacy guarantee through generalization, however, multiple hierarchies may be available, for the control-flow as well as for other process perspectives. For instance, activities may be generalized according to the artifact that is handled (e.g., all activities related to a *CT Scan* are generalized into a single activity) or by the type of the action that is conducted (e.g., all activities that prescribe different drugs are combined into a single activity). Similarly, roles may be generalized based on some organizational structure (e.g., wards in a hospital) or some ability (e.g., the specialization of a doctor). Each hierarchy will affect the utility of the resulting event log differently. Hence, the PMDG framework includes a step to guide the selection of one hierarchy for the control-flow generalization, and one hierarchy for each attribute representing an additional process perspective, as detailed in Sect. 4.4.

Once the generalization hierarchies have been selected, they are applied to the event log using existing algorithms to achieve k-anonymity [22, 24]. In essence, these algorithms adopt some step-wise generalization until the resulting equivalence classes are sufficiently large. Specifically, in our context, given an activity hierarchy ρ_A and a value hierarchy ρ_D per attribute D, the result of the generalization step can be characterized as follows: For each trace $\sigma = \langle e_1, \ldots, e_n \rangle$ of the original log L, the resulting log L' will contain a trace $\sigma' = \langle e'_1, \ldots, e'_n \rangle$, such that

Traces after trace vectorization:

Case 07	
Activity	Role
Register	Admin
Vitals	GP
Consultation	GP
CT Scan	CA

Case 08	
Activity	Role
Register	Admin
⋆	⋆
Consultation	CA
MRI Scan	CA

Traces after generalization:

Case 07	
Activity	Role
Register	Admin
⋆	⋆
Consultation	Medical Staff
Radiology Scan	CA

Case 08	
Activity	Role
Register	Admin
⋆	⋆
Consultation	Medical Staff
Radiology Scan	CA

Fig. 3. Generalization example.

for each event e_j, $1 \leq j \leq n$, it holds that the activity and each attribute value remains unchanged or has been generalized, i.e. $e'_j.a = e_j.a$ or $e_j.a = \rho_A^*(e_j.a)$ and $e'_j.D = e_j.D$ or $e_j.D = \rho_D^*(e_j.D)$.

For example, consider the traces for cases 07 and 08 from Fig. 1 and focus solely on the control-flow and the role perspective. Trace vectorization will normalize the length of both traces by inserting an event with wildcard values (discussed in Sect. 4.3), see Fig. 3 (top). With an activity hierarchy that generalizes *MRI Scan* and *CT Scan* to *Radiology Scan*, as well as a value hierarchy generalizing *GP* and *CA* to *Medical Staff*, the traces can be generalized to fall into the same equivalence class, see Fig. 3 (bottom). As such, the resulting event log would satisfy 2-anonymity.

4.3 Trace Vectorization

As explained above, comprehensive generalization requires that all elements in a dataset assume the same structure. Furthermore, we want to ensure that an anonymized event log can be generated for every k that is equal or smaller than the number of the traces in the log. However, only traces with the same length can be merged into the same equivalence class. Therefore, we need to unify the length of traces in the event log. To this end, we adopt trace vectorization, which is similar to the idea of sequence encoding in predictive process monitoring [25]. Specifically, given an event log $L = [\sigma_1, \ldots, \sigma_n]$, trace vectorization yields a log $L' = [\sigma'_1, \ldots, \sigma'_n]$, such that:

- All traces have the same length, i.e. for all σ'_i, σ'_j in L', it holds $|\sigma'_i| = |\sigma'_j|$.
- For each trace $\sigma = \langle e_1, \ldots, e_m \rangle$ of the original log L, there is a corresponding trace $\sigma' = \langle e'_1, \ldots, e'_k \rangle$ in L', so that the projection of σ' on the events $\{e_1, \ldots, e_m\}$ yields the trace σ and all events e of σ' that are not part of the projection are wildcard elements, i.e., it holds that $e.A = \star$ and $e.D = \star$ for all $D \in \mathcal{D}$.

One naive approach for trace vectorization would be to extend all traces that are shorter than the maximum length of traces in an event log with wildcard events at the end. However, such an approach cannot be expected to preserve the utility of the traces for process mining, especially considering the control-flow perspective. For instance, for the trace of case 08 in Fig. 3, adding the wildcard event at the end would have severe consequences for the subsequent generalization: Instead of preserving the information on the *Consultation* and *Radiology Scan* activities of both traces, all except the first activity would be generalized to the root element ($\star$).

In PMDG, therefore, we employ a strategy based on multi-sequence alignments (MSA) [26]. In essence, MSA identifies how to insert gaps into sequences of symbols, such that the same symbol is assigned to a certain index in all sequences and the number of gap indices is minimal. In our setting, we adopt MSA for the control-flow perspective, as it serves as the basis for process mining tasks. That is, given an event log $L = [\sigma_1, \ldots, \sigma_n]$, MSA is applied to the set $\{\sigma_1.A, \ldots, \sigma_n.A\}$ to identify where wildcard events shall be inserted.

4.4 Hierarchy Selection

As detailed above, multiple hierarchies may be employed to generalize the control-flow or the data representing additional process perspectives. Below, we first elaborate on types of hierarchies and their origin as well as their implications for the utility of the anonymized event log. We then present a heuristic solution to guide the selection of generalization hierarchies as part of PMDG.

Types of Hierarchies. In general, one can distinguish two types of hierarchies:

(i) *Syntactic hierarchies* are obtained by suppressing a part of an activity label or an attribute value. Common examples for syntactic hierarchies are numeric values (e.g., postcodes *'12489'* and *'12555'* are generalized to *'12—'*) or dates (*'10/2022'* and *'12/2022'* are generalized to *'–/2022'*). However, one may also consider activities and generalize, for instance, *CT Scan* and *MRI Scan* to *Scan* by suppressing the first token of the label.

(ii) *Semantic hierarchies* generalize the meaning of an activity or attribute value. An example would be the generalization of an attribute capturing a city (*'Berlin'*) into a country (*'Germany'*), larger region (*'EU'*), or continent (*'Europe'*). The creation of semantic hierarchies requires domain knowledge and these hierarchies are usually either user-defined or extracted from a knowledge base. For activities in traditional business processes, for instance, the MIT process handbook [27] defines generalization hierarchies of activities.

The selection of a hierarchy will impact the utility of the resulting event log, even when considering only a single type of hierarchy. Taking up the example of syntactic generalizations of dates, *'11.2022'* and *'12.2022'* may be generalized not only to *'–/2022'*, but also to *'11/—'* and *'12/—'*, respectively, depending on which parts to suppress. Either generalization provides a different kind of information, which influences the types of questions that can be answered with process mining for the anonymized log.

Selecting a Hierarchy. Since the selection of certain hierarchies for data generalization has significant implications, ideally, one would test all available hierarchies for the control-flow and all attributes. Measuring the quality of the resulting event logs based on a chosen utility measure, the best combination of hierarchies can be determined. However, such a brute-force approach is typically infeasible, due to the exponential number of hierarchy combinations. Therefore, in PMDG, we incorporate a heuristic strategy to guide the selection of a generalization hierarchy independently for the control-flow and each attribute. The heuristic is based on a notion of utility, for which we consider the following instantiations:

○ The utility is given by the number of equivalence classes within an anonymized event log. Here, the intuition is that a larger number of equivalence classes in the anonymized log yields a better representation of the variance in the original log.
○ The utility is inversely proportional to the differences in size of the equivalence classes, i.e. the number of contained traces. Here, the motivation is to preserve information on common behavior more precisely than on uncommon behavior.

Based on a specific notion of utility, the selection of a hierarchy per process perspective may be guided by an estimated utility, as follows. Let $\{\rho_D^1, \ldots, \rho_D^n\}$ be a set of hierarchies for an attribute D (or, analogously, for the activities). Then, for each hierarchy, we determine the equivalence classes when considering *only* the attribute D and *one* level in the generalization hierarchy (i.e., $\rho_D^1, \ldots \rho_D^n$ are applied only once, not transitively). Let u_1^i be the utility as determined for the equivalence classes obtained with ρ_D^i, which, as mentioned above, may be defined by the number of classes. Afterwards, the equivalence classes obtained with subsequent levels of the hierarchies are assessed iteratively, yielding utility values u_j^i for hierarchy ρ_D^i when incorporating it up to level j. Per hierarchy ρ_D^i, these utility values are summed up in a weighted manner, i.e., $u^i = \sum_{j=1}^{k} w_j \cdot u_j^i$ with k as the maximum depth of the hierarchy. Using the weights w_j enables us to give preference to different levels of generalization, i.e., prioritizing the generalization from a city to a country, over the one from a country to a continent. Finally, we select a hierarchy ρ_D^i for which the estimated utility u^i is maximal over all hierarchies $\{\rho_D^1, \ldots \rho_D^n\}$ for attribute D.

5   Evaluation

Within this section, we investigate how anonymizing event logs with PMDG impacts the utility of advanced process mining tasks. Through an empirical evaluation, we show the feasibility and effectiveness of PMDG. First, we will give an overview of the datasets used in our experiments in Sect. 5.1. Next, we outline our experimental setup, baseline, and evaluation metrics in Sect. 5.2. The results of our experiments in Sect. 5.3.

5.1   Datasets and Implementation

For our experiments, we use three real-world event logs: BPIC 2013 [28], Road Traffic Fines [29], and the CoSeLoG [30]. For each log, we excluded all variants that only appear once. This ensures a reasonable setting for anonymization (where unique traces would be problematic in any case). Certain experiments with advanced process mining tasks required the existence of the same attribute in all events, in that case we performed these experiments only with the BPIC 2013 [28] and CoSeLoG [30] event logs, since road traffic fines is missing such an attribute.

For all of our experiments, we provide an open-source implementation on GitHub.[1] The trace generalization approach is implemented in Python. For the generalizations of attributes, we used Java libraries from the ARX project.[2] For our experiments on mining handovers, we relied on the organizational mining features of PM4Py.[3] For our experiments on outcome prediction, we used scikit-learn.[4]

5.2   Experimental Setup

Parameter Settings. In our experiments, we use different strengths for k-anonymity, with values of k varying from $\{5, 10, 15, 20\}$. Furthermore, we use semantic hierarchies that we created manually. We also tested syntactic hierarchies, but these were always outperformed in terms of the amount of changes applied to the anonymized log. We selected our semantic hierarchies based on retained equivalence classes for the control-flow and minimum generalizations for the attributes. In our experiments regarding predictive process monitoring, we trained decision trees on 1,000 randomly generated 20/80 test-train splits.

---

[1] https://github.com/Ryanhilde/PMDG_Framework/.

[2] https://arx.deidentifier.org.

[3] https://pm4py.fit.fraunhofer.de.

[4] https://scikit-learn.org.

Table 1. Comparison of Control-flow Preservation

Log	Trace Vec	$k = 5$	$k = 10$	$k = 15$	$k = 20$
CoSeLoG	MSA	**17**	**13**	**9**	**8**
	Naive	**17**	**13**	8	**8**
BPIC 2013	MSA	**82**	31	23	**23**
	Naive	65	**34**	**27**	22
Traffic Fines	MSA	**75**	**53**	**43**	**37**
	Naive	12	12	12	12

Baseline. As a baseline for some of our experiments, we used PRIPEL [10], a framework that transforms event logs to achieve ϵ-differential privacy [2]. The provided privacy guarantee is not directly comparable with k-anonymity, i.e. we cannot assume that a specific k-value will ensure the same amount of privacy as a setting in PRIPEL. However, PRIPEL is the best choice for comparison, as it is the only existing technique that is capable of handling all attribute values. In general, a lower value for ϵ corresponds to a stronger privacy guarantee. For our experiments, we consider two settings for PRIPEL in the two event logs, a weak privacy guarantee ($\epsilon = 1.0$) and a strong one ($\epsilon = 0.1$). Furthermore, we set the pruning parameter of PRIPEL to 2 in the weaker setting and to 20 for the stronger one; and always set the maximum prefix-length to the mean of the trace variants. These two parameters are required by PRIPEL, due to the underlying control-flow anonymization technique [6]. Furthermore, we compare our trace vectorization technique based on MSA with a naive approach, that fills up all traces at the end with wildcards.

Evaluation Metrics. We use the number of remaining variants as a metric, to measure the control-flow preservation after the anonymization, which is shown in Table 1. To study the impact of the attribute anonymization on the utility of advanced process mining tasks, we investigated two advanced process mining techniques: the discovery of handovers [8,31] and process outcome prediction [9].

Through handover analysis, an analyst can investigate which attribute values directly follow each other within two events of the same trace. Often this analysis is performed on resource related attributes such as resource role or location. In order to quantify the results of our anonymization, we measure the preserved information of the generalized event logs compared to the original event log. We utilize an information preservation metric to capture the information loss due to generalization. Our metric is based on the intuition that generalizing a handover from its original relation (e.g. in the case of resource locations: Germany to China) to a generalized relation (e.g. Europe to China) still has some utility. Furthermore, this utility is higher than if the handover would have been generalized to an even higher level (Europe to Asia) or the highest level (Europe to World). We therefore define the preservation for generalized handovers p as:

$$p = \frac{[1 - \frac{\alpha(e'_1.D)}{\alpha(*)} + \frac{\alpha(e_1.D)}{|\alpha(*)|}] + [1 - \frac{\alpha(e'_2.D)}{\alpha(*)} + \frac{\alpha(e_2.D)}{\alpha(*)}]}{2} \tag{1}$$

The assumption here is that α is a function that returns the number of potential attribute values that can be represented through a (generalized) attribute value, i.e. the value *'EU'* could represent 27 countries in an attribute D that encodes countries. The special case $\alpha(*)$ returns the number of fine-granular values of an attribute D, i.e. all possible countries. The values e_1 and e_1' represent the original and generalized values for the left-side of the handover, respectively, while e_2 and e_2' represent the right-side, i.e. (China). Our metric only measures the loss of information for existing handovers, since generalization cannot insert new handover relations.

As a second analysis task, we consider process outcome prediction. Here, the utility of an event log is given by the classification results. We assess these results using the well-known classification metrics: *precision*, the fraction of positively labeled instances that are actually correct; *recall*, the ratio of actual positives that are correctly labeled; and *F1-score*, the harmonic mean of precision and recall.

5.3   Results

Control-Flow Preservation. In Table 1, we show that the MSA based trace vectorization usually outperforms the naive approach. We can see, it can provide significant benefits based on the traffic fines event logs. In cases where the naive approach is better, the benefit is comparatively small. Overall, we can observe that higher k lead to a higher loss in control-flow variance.

Handovers. In Fig. 4, we visualize the handovers created from the anonymized BPIC 2013 log based on the attribute *org:role* and $k = 5$. Such an analysis would allow an organization to understand which kind of resource roles usually interact with each other. We can clearly see that the anonymization through PMDG produces a smaller handover graph (middle graph) that contains less information as compared to the original handover graph (left graph). However, more detailed insights can be derived from the results for the information preservation metric as shown in Table 2. Here, we notice that a lot of handover information has actually been preserved. This highlights that the loss illustrated in Fig. 4 is mostly due to the substitution of low-granularity handover relations with handover relations that are on a higher level of generalization.

Fig. 4. (Left) Original Event Log, (Middle) $k = 5$, and (Right) PRIPEL weak setting handover graphs for the org:role attribute.

Table 2. Precision of generalized handovers

Log and Attribute	$k = 5$	$k = 10$	$k = 15$	$k = 20$
BPIC 2013 "org:role"	85.2	80.0	79.3	79.4
BPIC 2013 "organization involved"	100	100	100	100
BPIC 2013 "resource country"	89.7	89.7	89.7	90.2
BPIC 2013 "organization country"	89.2	88.1	88.1	87.6
CoSeLoG "org:resource"	73.1	75.4	75.3	75.3

In contrast, the right graph in Fig. 4 illustrates the results obtained with PRIPEL using the weak configuration. Here, virtually all attribute values are connected. While this, trivially, preserves all existing handovers, it also introduces a large amount of false handovers. Arguably, this is a major loss of information. However, this result is expected for an anonymization technique that is based on noise insertion and that adopts randomization for the attribute values assigned to events.

Let us illustrate the differences between the two anonymization strategies with an exemplary analysis question. That is, Volvo IT, the company from which the BPIC 2013 log was obtained, was interested in understanding ping-pong behavior, i.e., cycles of handovers [28]. Approaching this question based on the attribute *org:role*, the original log reveals handovers between roles E10 and V3_2, while there are no connections for the pairs of roles {E9, V3_2}, {A2_1, C_1}, and {A2_2, C_1}. With PMDG, the roles E9 and E10 are generalized into a single role E*, which is connected to role V3_2. While this hides the fact that E9 was not connected to V3_2, it still suggests to assess the handovers of the set of E roles with V3_2. At the same time, the graph with PMDG does not include the incorrect handovers for A2 and C_1, so that these roles are not considered in the analysis of ping-pong behavior. The noisy result obtained with PRIPEL, in turn, is not suitable for this analysis, as it suggests that all roles are involved in cyclic handovers.

Process Outcome Prediction. Next, we consider the common task of process outcome prediction. Here, we look at the prediction of the ending activities using a decision tree classifier. In Fig. 5, we show the results from the classification experiment. The left heat maps show the results with different values for the privacy guarantee k. We observe that for both the BPIC 2013 log and the CoSeLoG log, higher privacy guarantees lead to better prediction metrics. This behavior is expected, since a more general log contains less control-flow variance, so that prediction becomes easier.

On the other hand, the classifiers trained based on event logs retrieved from PRIPEL provide classification results that have extremely low precision and recall. The results can be seen by observing the right heat maps. The noise inserted into the anonymized logs from PRIPEL clearly has a strong negative impact on the classification results and, hence, renders the anonymized event logs useless for outcome prediction.

6   Discussion

Below, we discuss several aspects of our approach, which will help to understand opportunities and limitations that need to be considered when applying PMDG.

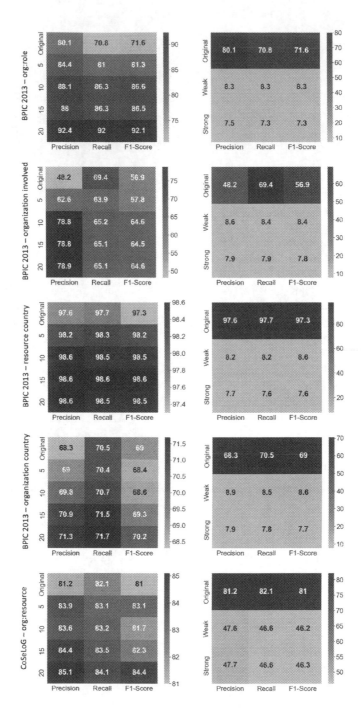

Fig. 5. Decision Tree Results for the **PMDG** (left) and **PRIPEL** (right) approaches.

Limitations of Generalization. The main drawback of generalization is the loss of detail within the anonymized data. As a consequence, the data may no longer be useful for certain analyses. For instance, if individual resources are generalized towards their department, it is no longer possible to check whether the two-man rule was followed. As another example, consider the medical domain, where the dosage of a medication may be generalized. Questions related to the daily dosage limit may become impossible to answer under strong generalization.

The Choice of Generalization Hierarchies. The success of applying PMDG highly depends on the generalization hierarchies that are available. Semantic hierarchies require manual work for their creation, a factor that can limit their availability. Also, for certain attributes, it might not be obvious how to generalize them. A prominent example are activities that often lack an unambiguous generalization hierarchy. Without the knowledge of a domain expert, it is not clear how to assess to which extent a generalization maintains process-specific information. Furthermore, PMDG makes no guarantee that the abstracted results will be useful in all situations. The usefulness of the results is dependent on the quality of the generalization hierarchy provided and the level of abstraction necessary to provide the privacy guarantee.

Different Levels of Abstraction. Based on the generalization technique used, an anonymized log might contain attribute values with differing levels of abstraction, i.e. an attribute encoding a region might contain values that represent a country or a continent. Mixing these different levels of abstraction can be challenging in the analysis, since most techniques do not offer built-in solutions to deal with such heterogeneous abstraction levels. Therefore, event logs that are anonymized with PMDG might require some post-processing before they can be utilized in common process mining solutions.

Risk of Complete Suppression. If an event log only consists of variants with a small number of traces that differ a lot in their attribute values, it is possible that these attribute values are essentially suppressed, i.e., generalizing a region from a value representing a city to the value *'World'*. In such a case, all potential benefits of generalization are lost. This problem can be addressed by providing hierarchies with a large number of generalization levels, so that the attribute values can converge to a level that still offers some utility. However, a large number of generalization levels may lead to an event logs with a lot of variance in its attribute values.

Curse of Dimensionality. A well-known issue for achieving k-anonymity is the curse of dimensionality [32], meaning that an increase in attributes or events makes it harder to achieve the privacy guarantee. As we introduce additional attributes assigned to case and events, the data is partitioned into smaller equivalence classes. Consequently, an anonymized event log can be expected to lose more utility. A potential solution for this problem is the adoption of mixed privacy guarantees [33]. These techniques would allow for the use of noise-based anonymization for some attributes and generalization for others, while this choice is taken based on the requirements imposed in a specific analysis setting.

7   Conclusion

Within this work, we introduced PMDG, an anonymization framework that transforms events logs, so that they are protected by k-anonymity. The novelty our approach comes from (i) its ability to preserve the dependencies between different process perspectives as recorded in an event log, i.e. the control-flow and the attribute values assigned to events; and (ii) the utilization of data generalization techniques as a means to achieve a privacy guarantee. In experiments with real-world event logs, we showed that PMDG outperforms the state of the art in terms of utility preservation for advanced process mining techniques. In future work, we intend to study how to support the construction and application of generalization hierarchies to optimize the utility of anonymized logs.

Acknowledgment. This work was supported by the NSF, grant number 1952225 and the German Federal Ministry of Education and Research (BMBF), grant number 16DII133.

References

1. Elkoumy, G., et al.: Privacy and confidentiality in process mining: Threats Res. Challenges ACM Trans. Mech. Inf. Syst. **13**(1), 1–17 (2021)
2. Dwork, C.: Differential privacy: a survey of results. In: Agrawal, M., Du, D., Duan, Z., Li, A. (eds.) TAMC 2008. LNCS, vol. 4978, pp. 1–19. Springer, Heidelberg (2008). https://doi.org/10.1007/978-3-540-79228-4_1
3. Sweeney, L.: K-anonymity: a model for protecting privacy. Int. J. Uncertain. Fuzziness Knowl.-Based Syst. **10**(5), 557–570 (2002)
4. Fahrenkrog-Petersen, S.A., van der Aa, H., Weidlich, M.: PRETSA: event log sanitization for privacy-aware process discovery. In: ICPM, pp. 1–8 (2019)
5. Rafiei, M., van der Aalst, W.M.P.: Group-based privacy preservation techniques for process mining. Data Knowl. Eng. **134**:101908 (2021)
6. Mannhardt, F., Koschmider, A., Baracaldo, N., Weidlich, M., Michael, J.: Privacy-preserving process mining. Bus. Inf. Syst. Eng. **61**(5), 595–614 (2019)
7. Augusto, A., et al.: Automated discovery of process models from event logs: review and benchmark. IEEE Trans. Knowl. Data Eng. **31**(4), 686–705 (2018)
8. Zhao, W., Zhao, X.: Process mining from the organizational perspective. In: Wen, Z., Li, T. (eds.) Foundations of Intelligent Systems. AISC, vol. 277, pp. 701–708. Springer, Heidelberg (2014). https://doi.org/10.1007/978-3-642-54924-3_66
9. Teinemaa, I., Dumas, M., La Rosa, M., Maggi, F.M.: Outcome-oriented predictive process monitoring: review and benchmark. ACM Trans. Knowl. Discov. Date **13**(2), 17:1–17:57 (2019)
10. Fahrenkrog-Petersen, S.A., van der Aa, H., Weidlich, M.: PRIPEL: privacy-preserving event log publishing including contextual information. In: Fahland, D., Ghidini, C., Becker, J., Dumas, M. (eds.) BPM 2020. LNCS, vol. 12168, pp. 111–128. Springer, Cham (2020). https://doi.org/10.1007/978-3-030-58666-9_7
11. Kessler, S., Hoff, J., Freytag, J.-C.: Sap hana goes private: from privacy research to privacy aware enterprise analytics. VLDB J. **12**(12), 1998–2009 (2019)
12. Batista, E., Martínez-Ballesté, A., Solanas, A.: Privacy-preserving process mining: A microaggregation-based approach. J. Inf. Secur. Appl. **68**, 103235 (2022)
13. Fahrenkog-Petersen, S.A., Kabierski, M., Rösel, Han van der Aa, F., Weidlich, M.: SACOFA: semantics-aware control-flow anonymization for process mining. In: ICPM, pp. 72–79. IEEE (2021)

14. Elkoumy, G., Pankova, A., Dumas. M.: Mine me but don't single me out: differentially private event logs for process mining. In: ICPM, pp. 80–87. IEEE (2021)
15. Rafiei, M., van der Aalst, W.M.P.: Mining roles from event logs while preserving privacy. In: Di Francescomarino, C., Dijkman, R., Zdun, U. (eds.) BPM 2019. LNBIP, vol. 362, pp. 676–689. Springer, Cham (2019). https://doi.org/10.1007/978-3-030-37453-2_54
16. Batista, E., Solanas, A.: A uniformization-based approach to preserve individuals' privacy during process mining analyses. Peer-to-Peer Netw. Appl. **14**(3), 1500–1519 (2021)
17. Rafiei, M., von Waldthausen, L., van der Aalst, W.M.P.: Supporting confidentiality in process mining using abstraction and encryption. In: Ceravolo, P., van Keulen, M., Gómez-López, M.T. (eds.) SIMPDA 2018-2019. LNBIP, vol. 379, pp. 101–123. Springer, Cham (2020). https://doi.org/10.1007/978-3-030-46633-6_6
18. Corpet, F.: Multiple sequence alignment with hierarchical clustering. Nucleic Acids Res. **16**(22), 10881–10890 (1988)
19. Wang, K., Yu, P.S., Chakraborty, S.: Bottom-up generalization: a data mining solution to privacy protection. In: ICDM, pp. 249–256. IEEE (2004)
20. Wong, W.K., Mamoulis, N., Lok Cheung, D.W.: Non-homogeneous generalization in privacy preserving data publishing. In: SIGMOD, pp. 747–758, New York, NY, USA, ACM (2010)
21. Peffers, K, Tuunanen, T., Rothenberger, M.A., Chatterjee. S.: A design science research methodology for information systems research. J. Manag. Inf. Syst. **24**(3), 45–77 (2007)
22. LeFevre, K., DeWitt, D.J., Ramakrishnan, R.: Incognito: efficient full-domain k-anonymity. In: SIGMOD, pp. 49–60 (2005)
23. Li, N., Li, T., Venkatasubramanian, S.: t-closeness: privacy beyond k-anonymity and l-diversity. In: ICDE 2007, The Marmara Hotel, Istanbul, Turkey, 15–20 April 2007, pp. 106–115. IEEE Computer Society (2007)
24. Prasser, F., Kohlmayer, F., Lautenschläger, R., Kuhn, K.A.: ARX-a comprehensive tool for anonymizing biomedical data. In: AMIA Annual Symposium Proceedings, vol. 2014, p. 984. American Medical Informatics Association (2014)
25. Leontjeva, A., Conforti, R., Di Francescomarino, C., Dumas, M., Maggi, F.M.: Complex symbolic sequence encodings for predictive monitoring of business processes. In: Motahari-Nezhad, H.R., Recker, J., Weidlich, M. (eds.) BPM 2015. LNCS, vol. 9253, pp. 297–313. Springer, Cham (2015). https://doi.org/10.1007/978-3-319-23063-4_21
26. Jagadeesh Chandra Bose, R.P., van der Aalst, W.M.P.: Process diagnostics using trace alignment: opportunities, issues, and challenges. Inf. Syst. **37**(2), 117–141 (2012)
27. Malone, T.W., Crowston, K., Herman, G.A.: Organizing Business Knowledge: The MIT Process Handbook. MIT Press (2003)
28. van Dongen, B.F., Weber, B., Ferreira, D.R., De Weerdt, J. (eds.). In: Proceedings of the 3rd Business Process Intelligence Challenge co-located with 9th International Business Process Intelligence Workshop (BPI 2013), Beijing, China, 26 August 2013, volume 1052 of CEUR Workshop Proceedings. CEUR-WS.org (2013)
29. de Leoni, M., Mannhardt, F.: Road traffic fine management process (2015). 270fd440-1057-4fb9-89a9-b699b47990f5. https://doi.org/10.4121/uuid
30. Buijs. J.: Receipt phase of an environmental permit application process ('WABO'), CoSeLoG project (2014). https://doi.org/10.4121/uuid:a07386a5-7be3-4367-9535-70bc9e77dbe6
31. van der Aalst, W.M.P.: Process Mining: Data Science in Action, 2nd edn. Springer, Heidelberg (2016)
32. Aggarwal, C.C.: On k-anonymity and the curse of dimensionality. In: VLDB, vol. 5, pp. 901–909 (2005)
33. Holohan, N., Antonatos, S., Braghin, S., Aonghusa, P.M.: (k, ϵ)-anonymity: k-anonymity with ϵ-differential privacy. CoRR, abs/1710.01615 (2017)

A Case Study on the Impact
of Forensic-Ready Information Systems
on the Security Posture

Lukas Daubner[1]([✉]) [iD], Raimundas Matulevičius[2] [iD], Barbora Buhnova[1] [iD],
Matej Antol[1] [iD], Michal Růžička[1] [iD], and Tomas Pitner[1] [iD]

[1] Masaryk University, Brno, Czechia
{daubner,buhnova,matejantol,mruzicka,tomp}@mail.muni.cz
[2] University of Tartu, Tartu, Estonia
raimundas.matulevicius@ut.ee

Abstract. While approaches aimed at developing forensic-ready systems are starting to emerge, it is still primarily a theoretical concept. This paper presents a case study of integrating forensic readiness capabilities into SensitiveCloud, an information system for storing and processing sensitive data. A risk-based approach to forensic readiness design is followed to achieve it. Consequently, weaknesses in both processes and systems are identified, and forensic readiness requirements are formulated. This case study reports on lessons learned in a practical implementation of a forensic-ready system, its impact on security, and its support towards ISO/IEC 27k.

Keywords: Forensic Readiness · Forensic-Ready Systems · Risk Management · Information Security · Digital Forensics

1 Introduction

Information security is, without a doubt, a key component of information systems, as there is an incentive to keep its data protected against misuse [23]. This incentive stems from regulations, legislation, competitive pressure, contracts, and risks of reputation or financial loss. Security is ever so important for information systems working with highly sensitive data, like biological research or medical records. In these cases, a data leakage could expose the sensitive information of individuals and lead to severe fines, making such systems a very lucrative target.

As such, users might be concerned about security when entering data into the system. Indeed, data breaches have been caused by inadequate security risk mitigation [12]. To dispel such concerns and testify due diligence in security, information systems can work towards security certifications (e.g., ISO/IEC 27k family of standards [21]), demanding continuous improvement of security posture, i.e., security status, resources, and capabilities in the organisation [22].

However, security can never be taken as absolute. Thus, forensic readiness [32] aims to prepare for digital forensic investigations and scenarios requiring digital evidence [7,27], complementing the security practice [17]. Recently, it was

© The Author(s) 2023
M. Indulska et al. (Eds.): CAiSE 2023, LNCS 13901, pp. 522–538, 2023.
https://doi.org/10.1007/978-3-031-34560-9_31

approached from a software engineering perspective, creating the notion of forensic-ready software systems [25] or systems forensic-by-design. They include requirements for conducting sound forensic processes and generating sound evidence.

The methods for designing and developing forensic-ready systems still cannot be considered mature and are mostly theoretical. As many conceptual frameworks feature risk management, we formulated Forensic-Ready Information Systems Security Risk Management (FR-ISSRM) [10], a risk-based design approach, to bridge this gap. Still, a practical demonstration and evaluation are missing.

This paper presents a case study on developing a forensic-ready system following the FR-ISSRM approach. It allowed identifying weaknesses in incident handling and investigation, remediable by implementing forensic readiness requirements and gaining insight into set security processes. Additionally, our contribution serves as material for the information systems engineering community, providing a practical reference for theoretical concepts.

2 State of the Art

Related Work. The importance of implementing forensic readiness was highlighted in a few studies. For example, three security incident investigations in public administration, finance, and manufacturing domain were assessed in [24]. The study exposed inadequacies which led to the failure to investigate the incident or to prevent it. Another study examining devices deployed in smart grid infrastructure showed a severe lack in supporting the investigation of attacks [19].

Traditional forensic readiness controls are organisation-focused, including plans for investigation cost-effectiveness and minimal business interruption [18], escalation policies [27], and personnel training [7]. Then, system-oriented controls address evidence storage [3,30], integrity [33], and proactive preservation [4]. In the cloud domain, forensic-supporting architecture is proposed [34]. Attention is also given to the representation of forensic-ready systems, utilising Sequence Diagrams [26], or Business Process Model and Notation (BPMN) [10].

Implementation of forensic readiness is a topic of numerous guides, standards, and frameworks. Table 1 presents the overview, denoting addressed aspects and focus on a specific domain. It notes their addressing of systems, specifying requirements, including an implementation process, model support, evaluation techniques, and risk assessment, too. Risk management is a part of forensic readiness implementation approaches [1,16,27]. In the area of information systems (IS), there is Information Systems Security Risk Management (ISSRM) [11,23], a model-based approach harmonising the security risk management for IS. It has been practically applied [2], shown to cover ISO/IEC 27k requirements [14], and integrated with enterprise architecture [15]. It supports modelling approaches (e.g., Risk-Oriented BPMN [5]), including extension of ArchiMate [15].

Forensic-Ready Risk Management. From a security standpoint, forensic readiness is considered an add-on [9] to cover residual and low-probable risks,

Table 1. Comparison of related forensic readiness approaches

Paper Reference	Domain	Systems	Requirements	Process	Models	Evaluation	Risk Assessment
Tan [32]	✗	●	●	●	●	●	●
Rowlingson [27]	✗	●	●	●	●	●	●
GPG 18 [7]	✗	●	●	●	●	●	●
Grobler et al. [18]	✗	◐	●	●	●	●	●
Elyas et al. [13]	✗	●	●	●	●	●	◐
Grispos et al. [16]	✓	●	◐	◐	●	○	●
ISO/IEC 27043 [20]	✗	◐	●	●	●	○	○
Bajramovic et al. [6]	✓	●	●	●	●	○	○
AbRahman et al. [1]	✓	●	◐	◐	●	○	●
Simou et al. [29]	✓	●	●	●	●	○	●
FR-ISSRM [8]	✗	●	●	●	●	●	●

○ – *Not addressed;* ◐ – *Limited discussion;* ● – *Addressed; Domain-specific* (✓ – *Yes,* ✗ – *No)*

assuming that an incident eventually occurs. A Forensic-Ready Information Systems Security Risk Management (FR-ISSRM) [8] was formulated to conceptualise risk management in forensic readiness. This allows systematic assessment of forensic readiness and assists in formulating requirements for forensic-ready software.

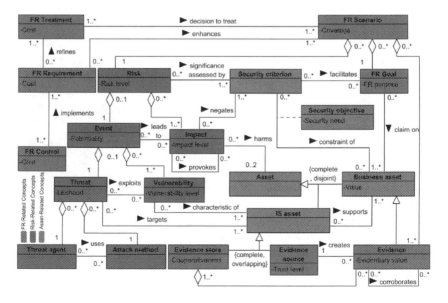

Fig. 1. FR-ISSRM domain model [8] (risk treatment-related concepts omitted)

The FR-ISSRM concepts are organised in a domain model, visualised in Fig. 1, as an extension of the ISSRM domain model [11]. **Asset** is anything valuable that has a part in the organisation's objectives. It is divided into an

Information System (IS) Asset (i.e., a component of an IS) and a **Business Asset** (i.e., information, processes, capabilities, and skills). The **Risk** is a combination of a **Threat** with one or more **Vulnerabilities** leading to a negative **Impact** on Assets. The combination of a Threat and Vulnerabilities represents an **Event** [23]. FR-ISSRM adds **Evidence**, a Business Asset representing a piece of information potentially usable in digital forensic investigation, its point of origin (**Evidence Source**) and retrieval (**Evidence Store**). The purpose of implementation of forensic readiness is captured by **Forensic Readiness Goal (FR Goal)**. Together, they contribute to **Forensic Readiness Scenario (FR Scenario)**, describing how exactly is a FR Goal addressed, using the Evidence, and covering a particular Risk. Then, the **Forensic Readiness Requirement (FR Requirement)** is a condition to be satisfied in the system to meet the FR Goal, and **Forensic Readiness Control (FR Control)** is its implementation.

A model-driven approach of forensic-ready risk management is enabled by BPMN for Forensic-Ready Software Systems (BPMN4FRSS) [10] modelling notation, an extension of BPMN. The models capture the parts of a system, supporting decision-making in the forensic-ready risk management process. Specifically, the analysed part is modelled as a process using BPMN [23]. It describes systems activities (*Task*), happenings (*Event*), exchanged data (*Data Object*), parts of the system and other participants (*Pool*), and communication between them (*Message Flow*). Then, BPMN4FRSS enhances it with forensic readiness aspects, the most important being *Evidence* (stereotyped Data Object) and *Evidence Source* (magnifying glass symbol). Figure 2 shows an example of a BPMN4FRSS diagram. Additionally, model-based metrics are formulated to evaluate evidence quality and their coverage in the process [8].

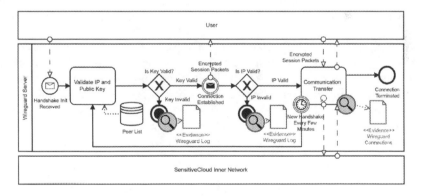

Fig. 2. An asset-level model of the Wireguard VPN Connection scenario

3   Research Method

The case is SensitiveCloud[1], a system run in an academic environment, a platform for the computation and storage of sensitive data. It aims to support medical research implying a security need. Technologically, the system is built on

---

[1] https://www.cerit-sc.cz/infrastructure-services/sensitivecloud.

Kubernetes (K8s), a container orchestration platform managed by Rancher [31], accessible through Wireguard virtual private network (VPN). The Sensitive-Cloud team involved in the study (henceforth Team) consists of three technical specialists (K8s and DevOps), a security manager and an executive manager, where security and executive managers are also co-authors of this paper.

Employed security controls are primarily based on ISO/IEC 27k [21], aspiring for certification. Forensic readiness is considered in conjunction with it to improve the security posture further. It is expected to contribute towards observability (ISO/IEC 27001:2013 Annex A.12.4), incident response (ISO/IEC 27001:2013 Annex A.16.1), and legal compliance involving evidence release.

3.1   Research Questions

The study follows the FR-ISSRM implementation process [8], describing the procedure of specifying forensic readiness concepts. However, the plausible way of implementing forensic readiness in a real system is unknown, as the FR-ISSRM concepts must be instantiated and evaluated from empirical data. Therefore, we derived research questions (RQ) to frame the effort, addressing areas of the FR-ISSRM implementation process vital for the practical development of a forensic-ready system. They divide the problem into the design using FR-ISSRM (RQ1), its assessment (RQ2), and understanding its impact on the system (RQ3).

RQ1: *What data is needed to establish a forensic readiness model of an existing information system?* Forensic readiness relies on information about the system, which can be compiled into a model. However, the feasibility, manner, and implications of its instantiation from available knowledge of a system are crucial in a real environment. The answers shall be built on gathered artefacts and enquiries.

RQ2: *How can the forensic readiness of a system be evaluated based on the established model and empirical knowledge?* While metrics for static analysis of the model exist, they have several limitations in preciseness. Moreover, the model built on empirical knowledge is likely imprecise due to unintentional misspecification or omission. Thus, the evaluation of the system should go beyond the model itself and enrich it with empirical knowledge. The answers shall be based on model-based metrics and simulated incident investigations.

RQ3: *What are the effects of FR-ISSRM process execution and its artefacts on the security posture?* Conduction of the FR-ISSRM process is expected to provide insights into forensic readiness and related subjects regarding the system in question, namely security monitoring and incident handling. Therefore, an inquiry shall be made on those subjects and lessons learned from the stakeholders.

3.2   Research Design

In this study, guidelines for conducting case studies [28] were followed. It is action research, as the main author oversees the forensic readiness implementation.

The foundation of the study is the FR-ISSRM implementation process, supplemented by empirical evaluation. Initially, FR-ISSRM was presented to the Team by the authors of this paper in the level of detail required to perform the study. The study consists of three phases, during which the authors interacted with the Team to collect, create, and analyse materials for the study.

Mapping Phase is concerned with mapping the available knowledge and compiling it into a model of the system. Primarily, security risk management documentation is reviewed for Assets and Risks. Then, concrete incentives for forensic readiness, FR Goals, are established and mapped on the Risks, leading to the definition of FR Scenarios with Evidence Sources. Lastly, a subset of FR Scenarios is selected as units of analysis. Chosen FR Scenarios are captured in BPMN4FRSS [10] notation, supported by our diagramming tool[2]. The authors explained the notation to the Team and consulted the diagrams afterwards.

Evaluation Phase uses the models to evaluate the forensic readiness of the system (both organisational and technical). The aim is to assess that the occurrence of FR Scenarios can be reliably investigated. First, purely model-based metrics are computed by the authors, providing a quick estimation. Then, the models are used to construct a simulated incident by a member of the Team, akin to forensic readiness exercise [7,27], planned based on a protocol[3], prepared by the authors to minimise the impact on a system. It focuses on verifying implemented controls, a sound investigation process, and a discrepancy between expected and actual potential evidence. Lastly, the simulation is executed by the Team.

Feedback Phase processes the results by the authors, based on which treatments, the FR Requirements, are formulated, addressing the shortcomings in the system and adjusting the models. Moreover, a semi-structured interview is conducted with the Team, discussing their perception of the process and results. The aim is to use the results and gained experience to enhance the system.

4   Mapping

The SensitiveCloud's business goal demands security risk awareness by design. This awareness also applies to forensic-ready systems. Identifying what needs to be ready, for what circumstance and why is the first step of the implementation.

Security Risk Management is a prerequisite for conducting FR-ISSRM. Therefore, its documentation must be reviewed for alignment issues with FR-ISSRM. We note two obstacles. The first is a lack of Business Asset (i.e., primary in ISO/IEC 27k [21]) while focusing only on the IS Assets. Remediation is expanding the asset definitions with the Team. The second is a very abstract formulation of risks based on threat catalogue entries. Such risks are instantiated with a concrete Business Asset relation as part of FR Scenario modelling.

---

[2] Tool available at: https://github.com/FREAS-tools/freas-bpmn4frss-library.
[3] Template and guidelines available at: https://doi.org/10.58126/8c9w-eh29.

Table 2. Selected Forensic Readiness Goals

G3	Prove access to user data	Represents the ability to demonstrate that user data was accessed when disputed or assessing impact
G4	Enable investigation of logical perimeter access process breach	SensitiveCloud mandates a strict logical perimeter access policy. A possible breach of this policy should be investigated and explained
G10	Prove misuse of user identity	The user identity represents a claim issued by an identity management. A malicious actor can impersonate the identity to access a protected resource. The aim is to identify malicious impersonation, when it took place, and what was affected
G13	Enable evidence release of perimeter access process	Because owner of SensitiveCloud is public organisation, it might be required to release evidence in accordance with law

Forensic Readiness Goals are formulated to capture the incentive for forensic readiness as a claim towards a Business Asset. In total, 13 FR Goals[4] were conceived from a discussion with SensitiveCloud management. They focus primarily on having trustworthy data in the case of investigating a data breach, addressing the protection of logs and audit requirements of ISO/IEC 27k [21], customer disputes, and legal obligations for evidence release. For this study, FR Goals listed in Table 2 are selected as their investigation is deemed most probable.

Forensic Readiness Scenarios describe a concrete occurrence of a Risk in the system, which generates Evidence addressing an FR Goal. However, the abstract risks made their direct instantiation difficult. Instead, the authors together with the Team created asset-level models, describing a process of regular operation involving the Business Assets, which abstract risks can affect. For example, *Wireguard VPN Connection* can be affected by an Impact *Leaked VPN key* due to a *Physical theft of the admin's laptop* Event. The Asset-level models were captured as a brief textual description (e.g., Establishing access to the SensitiveCloud private network using Wireguard). However, due to criticality, those related to the *Logical perimeter access policy* were modelled as processes using BPMN4FRSS [10] notation (e.g., Fig. 2). Then, their initial Evidence Sources were identified through discussion with the Team.

Proper Risks are created by mapping the abstract ones onto asset-level models, which are then inspected for relevance with FR Goals. The Risk, FR Goal, and Evidence from the asset-level models are sufficient to define an FR Scenario. Notably, multiple FR Goals are found relevant to one Risk with the same Evidence. While it formally leads to multiple FR Scenarios, we merged them to reduce the quantity. In total, 118 FR Scenarios is defined (344 unmerged).

Unit of the Analysis for this study is chosen as a composite from the most high-risk FR Scenarios. Figure 3 shows the BPMN4FRSS diagram, and Table 3 contains descriptions of Risks. The composite combines three FR Scenarios into a complex chain of attack, addressing data leakage and tampering. It is selected by the Team, due to the probability and Impact of the Risk.

---

[4] Full list available at: https://doi.org/10.58126/8c9w-eh29.

5   Evaluation

Initially, the Team did not find an issue regarding forensic readiness, as they followed the standard observability practice. The asset-level models with Evidence, were agreed to reflect the system and set FR Goals are covered. This claim is tested, examining if an investigation can be reliably performed.

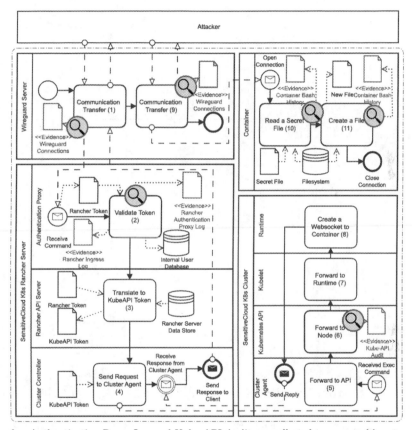

Rancher Authentication Proxy Log and Kube-API Audit are collected to a central log storage.

Fig. 3. Composite Forensic Readiness Scenario of a data manipulation

Model-based Forensic Readiness Metrics [8] derived from the model in Fig. 3 are summarised in Table 4. Relative Evidentiary Value (REV) estimates the Evidence's trustworthiness. It combines tamper resistance of creation TR (the value is proportional to the privilege required), a sum of independent copies $\mathcal{S}_C$, and links from the same $L^=$ and different $L^{\neq}$ contexts (process's participants). Links mean a sum of base values B of other evidence that can be corroborated (e.g., by equality), with the same context being penalised by a sum of managed contexts. Scenario Coverage (SC) is a ratio of components of the

Table 3. Description of risks in the composite Forensic Readiness Scenario

Risk		R1: VPN key leak	R2: Kubeconfig token leak	R3: Container data leak	R4: Container data tamper
	Vulnerability	1. VPN key is unprotected on User Device 2. VPN key is sufficient to access SensitiveCloud network	1. Kubeconfig file is unprotected on User Device	1. Rancher-generated kubeconfig token is sufficient to access computational resource and user data (via kubectl) 2. Rancher-generated kubeconfig token is sufficient to authenticate a user	
Event	Threat	An attacker with the capability to access the VPN key on a User Device steals the VPN key and then uses it to access the SensitiveCloud network	An attacker with the capability to access the kubeconfig file on a User Device steals the kubeconfig token	An attacker uses the kubeconfig token to impersonate a legitimate user and gain access and then reads the contents of a confidential file by executing remote command via kubecl	An attacker uses the kubeconfig token to impersonate a legitimate user and gain access and then creates a new file by executing remote command via kubecl
Impact		1. Loss of User Identity integrity 2. Breach of Perimeter Access Process	1. Loss of User Data integrity	1. Loss of User Data confidentiality	1. Loss of User Data integrity

Table 4. Forensic readiness model-based metrics

(a) Relative Evidentiary Value

$$REV(e) = B(e) + L^=(e) + L^{\neq}(e); \; B(e) = TR(e)\,|S_C(e)|$$

Potential Evidence	B		$L^=$		$L^{\neq}$		REV
	TR	S_C					
Wireguard Connections	2	1	2	3/4	0.75	0	0	2.75
Wireguard Log	2	1	2	3/4	0.75	0	0	2.75
Kube-API Audit	2	2	4	0/4	0	2+2+4	8	12
Rancher Authentication Proxy Log	2	2	4	0/4	0	2+2	4	8

(b) Scenario Coverage

$$SC(s) = \hat{\mathcal{K}}(s)/\mathcal{K}(s)$$

Context	K	$\hat{K}$	SC
Wireguard Server	2	2	1
SensitiveCloud K8s Rancher Server	2	1	0.5
SensitiveCloud K8s Cluster	1	1	1
Container	1	1	1
Global scope	6	5	0.83

process model (divided by message flow) with an Evidence Source $\hat{\mathcal{K}}$ and all its components $\mathcal{K}$, scoped to managed contexts and the whole composite scenario.

While they indicate a good posture, due to corroborability on K8s level, three weak spots are identifiable. Firstly, the value of *Wireguard Connection* and *Wireguard Log* is diminished by non-inclusion in the central log storage, retaining a single copy. Secondly, the links with *Wireguard Connection* are unknown in the prior models, diminishing *REV* and is an issue in the investigation. Lastly, no Evidence of Rancher's response is created, lowering *SC*. Moreover, the metrics do not reflect volatility, which is found to be an issue for *Wireguard Connection*.

Simulated Incident is a more complex validation method. It is based on conducting an artificial attack presented in Fig. 4, from the Risks described in Table 3. The attack deals with disclosed and modified data on the Sensitive-Cloud storage due to leaked access credentials on the user side. The Team's task is to handle the incident and investigate its scale and root cause, which puts the forensic-ready system to the test in a realistic manner.

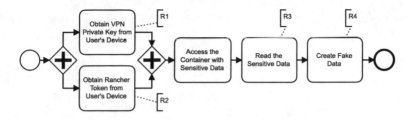

Fig. 4. The attack process of the simulation

Table 5. (Potential) evidence considered during the investigation

Name	P	C	U	Description	Correlation
Wireguard Connections	✓	✓	✗	Result of a "wg" command. Shows the last connection, without history. However, changing the configuration deletes the record	External IP, Internal IP
Wireguard Log	✓	✓	✓	Standard Journald logs. Shows failed handshake attempts. Successful are not logged	External IP, Internal IP
Container Log (MinIO)	✗	✓	✗	Standard logs from MinIO. Did not contain anything usable	-
Rancher Ingress Log	✗	✓	✓	Shows requests to Cluster API (kubectl, Rancher UI). The peer's IP is not visible due to routing	Routed IP, K8s Resource
K8s Cluster Ingress Log	✗	✓	✗	Shows requests to Cluster API, but requests through Rancher bypass it. The peer's IP is visible	Internal IP, K8s Resource
Kube-API Audit	✓	✓	✗	Shows access to a k8s resource by a user. However, it was misconfigured, so pod/exec resources were not recorded	User Name, K8s Resource
Container Bash History	✗	✓	✓	Shows command history. However, it is tamperable	-
Storage Audit	✓	✗	✗	Not confirmed. Deemed unnecessary	-
Rancher Authentication Proxy Log	✓	✗	✗	Not confirmed. Rancher Ingress Log deemed sufficient	-
Rancher Load Balancer Log	✗	✗	✗	Not confirmed. Theoretical way to map Routed IP and Internal IP. Deemed too complicated	Internal IP, Routed IP

P – Considered prior the incident; C – Collected; U – Utilised as evidence

Notably, the simulated incident is performed on the live system, akin to penetration testing. Careful planning is mandatory not to disturb the system's operation. It includes the preparation of Kubernetes deployment and user account, including the full onboarding process and subsequent clean-up.

A successful test means formulating an answer to the investigation query backed by a correlated chain of Evidence. Furthermore, each Evidence should be corroborated by at least one other independent Evidence.

Investigation of the simulated incident sought to answer a compound query: *Which data was accessed, who accessed it and how?* To answer it, the Team used

Evidence compiled in Table 5. It shows which Evidence was recognised before the incident, what was actually collected, and what was used for the answer[5].

The simulation started with an email from a user to the SensitiveCloud contact address, reporting unknown data on the storage and sensitive data published online. First, the Team realised that the user was part of a research group, having a single project utilising a shared service identity with the required permissions. On learning this, Team changed the configuration of Wireguard VPN to deny access with the shared identity in case it was compromised. Likewise, storage permissions were also revoked to restrict further access to sensitive data.

With the access restricted, the Team went through logs to answer the query. First, based on the *Wireguard Log*, they identified an IP address not belonging to the research group. Thus, bolstering the suspicion of credential compromise. Next, aiming to determine accessed resources, the Team found that the *Kube-API Audit* did not record any data due to misconfiguration. They assumed the attacker accessed the container directly, based on *Rancher Ingress Log*, but could not confirm it due to a proxied IP address routed by Rancher. The extent of affected data was determined only from unreliable *Container Bash History*.

Ultimately, the investigation failed to reliably answer the query due to unverified assumptions and dependence on unreliable data. Therefore, a complete chain of Evidence was not established, nor was it corroborated by another source.

6   Feedback

This chapter sums up the results and feedback provided by the Team members. It is used to propose enhancements to the system and its processes.

Table 6. Proposed Forensic Readiness Requirements

FRR1	Integrity of Wireguard Log shall be maintained by an independent copy
FRR2	Successful VPN handshakes shall be recorded
FRR3	Kube-API Audit shall record utilisation of pod/exec resources
FRR4	Kube-API Audit shall be correlable with Internal IP
FRR5	Shell access to Container shall be recorded outside of the Container

Forensic Readiness Requirements, listed in Table 6 are suggested to the Team for implementation to address the shortcomings, thus enhancing the presented composite FR Scenario. The simulation uncovered the following issues to remedy: Used Evidence was not confirmed from another source nor created a complete chain (due to IP hidden behind routing proxy); misconfigured audit logging caused missing, expected, Evidence; Evidence from Wireguard VPN is volatile and thus might be unavailable. Furthermore, combining the results with the model shows reliance on tamperable data from a container, which should be correlated with independent Evidence or coming from a more privileged source.

---

[5] The protocol is available at: https://doi.org/10.58126/8c9w-eh29.

Incident Handling Shortcomings are also to be addressed. The documentation was incomplete for several critical system components (e.g., Wireguard VPN, Rancher internal routing). Thus a single point of failure (parts that only a single person could investigate) was identified. This manifested in the spoilage of *Wireguard Connections* due to changing the configuration before securing the Evidence. An issue was also found in verifying the incident reporter's eligibility.

Interviews with Team members were then conducted to gather opinions on forensic readiness, evaluate the experience with the process, and identify lessons learned. The transcriptions were coded by open coding, followed by axial coding[6].

Primarily, the hands-on experience with the forensic readiness, and namely the simulation, represented a learning opportunity contributing to the general security-related awareness. *"It is basically a form of training for the team, a tool to testify proper workings of the processes."* The simulation, exploiting the benefits of gamification, provided an enlightening and practical perspective on the security of the SensitiveCloud design and operation.

The FR-ISSRM concepts and modelling via BPMN4FRSS diagrams motivated consideration of the system from another angle. *"It somehow pushes a person to think about it from a different angle than before. Or you need to look at it from the security point of view."* It helped to think of hidden relations and interactions, which served as a valuable input to the documentation design and filled gaps in yet undocumented aspects of the system. However, the models are seen as laborious, too formal, and hard to grasp, albeit helpful in the end. *"The formalism is really an overhead, but looking back, when I don't need to do it. It is, in fact, very interesting and valuable."*

Forensic readiness was affirmed as a practical complement to ISO/IEC 27k. *"For me, it is one of the iterations of the Information Security Management System."* It increased the maturity of the Team by shifting towards a security-oriented perspective, and the simulation added structure to the abstract notion of security. *"Suddenly people start to think about the business side of how to make the system somehow transparently, securely, ... "* It was agreed that verifying the forensic readiness of the system should be included in the security plan.

7 Discussion and Conclusion

In this case study, we utilised the FR-ISSRM approach to design and analyse forensic readiness capabilities in SensitiveCloud, an information system for storing and processing sensitive data. Together with the Team, we established the incentives for FR Goals and mapped them onto the system Assets and Risks. Then we evaluated the system to elicit FR Requirements where the FR Goals are unfulfilled. Additionally, we updated the incident handling process.

---

[6] Dataset with codes available at: https://doi.org/10.58126/8c9w-eh29.

7.1   Answers to Research Questions

RQ1: *What data is needed to establish a forensic readiness model of an existing information system?* Assets, FR Goals, Risks, and Evidence, are the basic blocks of a forensic readiness model. Based on them, FR Scenarios can be compiled.

However, we noticed that the Risks need to be described in detail. An abstract, catalogue-like definition is insufficient as it is harder to identify the Evidence. Therefore, we opted for modelling the Assets as scenarios of their regular operation, on which we instantiated the abstract risks into ISSRM Risk.

The FR Goals steer the implementation. However, we note an incentive to focus on IS rather than Business Assets in defining them, which complicates further decisions. A remedy was proposed to first define higher-level business drivers for forensic readiness independent of the system.

BPMN4FRSS notation was used for Asset and, subsequently, FR Scenario modelling. However, the Team found it challenging to describe the system's workings as a process model. Thus, we adjusted the approach to model only high-level interactions (message flows between pools) and resulting Evidence (e.g., a message M to a pool P leads to the generation of evidence E1 and E2). While simpler and still usable for defining the FR Scenarios, the insight is limited. In the end, only the most critical parts of the system were modelled in detail.

RQ2: *How can the forensic readiness of a system be evaluated based on the established model and empirical knowledge?* Static model-based evaluation and empirical simulation both yield insight towards forensic readiness.

The model-based evaluation computes metrics from the BPMN4FRSS model. While a quick indicator, they are not comparable across the FR Scenarios. However, they were able to point out issues (e.g., inadequacy and strong dependence on a single copy of data). But, their explanation is not straightforward as deeper insight is needed to tell which factor influenced the value.

A more complex evaluation combines the model and empirical knowledge by arranging a simulated incident and observing its investigation. Its aim was threefold: (1) to test the actual availability and usefulness of the potential evidence as captured in the model, (2) to identify gaps in the potential evidence, and (3) to observe the cooperation between systems and Team in incident handling. Indeed, flaws were found in all three areas. For evaluation, the gathered potential evidence was compared to the expectations, assumptions, supporting evidence, and impact in answering the investigation query. While costly, the simulation provided the most insight, so future work should aim to improve its effectiveness.

RQ3: *What are the effects of FR-ISSRM process execution and its artefacts on the security posture?* A direct impact on security posture is twofold. First, forensic readiness supports incident handling and investigation process. It is in the form of pre-prepared data pointing to the circumstances of the incident. Forensic readiness is thus concerned with the availability of data when needed. Therefore, the evaluation focused on ensuring that enough data exists. On the other hand, too much data is also undesirable. However, this situation was not encountered in the study, thus remaining unverified. The second impact is essentially an audit of security posture, albeit from a different angle. Both the model but especially the simulated indecent pointed out several weaknesses.

As a side-effect, the Team gained deeper insight into the system as modelling and identifying Evidence requires inspecting the systems' behaviour, causes and effects. This alone was recognised as a valuable, although tedious, result. Naturally, the model was included in the documentation.

7.2   Threats to Validity

Construct Validity is primarily threatened by misunderstandings of forensic readiness concepts and aims within the Team. It was mitigated by supervision during each of the phases and validating sub-results. Indeed, it was found that the theoretical concepts were hard to grasp for the technical team. Thus, the tasks and enquiries were switched to be less abstract and more actionable.

Internal Validity is threatened by the team's low maturity of processes and formalisms in the SensitiveCloud environment and low experience with forensic investigation. Therefore, the gained observations are influenced by this fact. A consistency of BPMN4FRSS models, e.g., the choice of contexts, is critical to metrics. Thus, a session was held with the Team to explain the semantics and establish a common approach. Additionally, some of the Evidence defined in the model was not utilised during the simulation. This issue was explicitly questioned during the feedback interview to capture the reasoning behind the omission.

External Validity is threatened by choice of examined FR Scenario and SensitiveCloud environment. While the FR Scenario was chosen to cover as much of the FR Goals, its main characteristic is that the attacker (except for stealing access credentials) used the system legitimately. Generalisation on scenarios outside this characteristic (e.g., gaining access to a node by container escaping) is not guaranteed. Furthermore, the insights are arguably more relevant for process-wise low-mature environments.

Reliability in this case study depends on the security risk assessment, formulation of FR Scenarios, and interpretation of the evaluation result. The study builds on already performed risk assessments, and each artefact (FR Goals, instantiated Risks, FR Scenarios, models) was validated by the Team to avoid errors. For the topics discussed in the feedback phase, at least two interviewees mentioned them unless explicitly stated. Similarly, at least two technical Team members confirmed the explanation of the potential evidence. The requirements were then proposed to address missing information and validate assumptions.

7.3   Lessons Learned and Future Work

Like all security-related domains, forensic readiness is a continuous effort to improve processes, maturing technologies and training people. Firstly, our evaluation has uncovered several issues in the system (e.g., misconfiguration of *Kube-API Audit*, volatile *Wireguald Log*). Secondly, the execution of the FR-ISSRM process contributed to the overall maturity of the system's secure environment. In particular, the practical experience with the simulated incident investigation led to a sincere recognition of security and incident preparedness. As such, it completed the standard continuous security practices (e.g., those accompanying ISO/IEC 27k). Thirdly, to get forensic readiness and general IT security into the common practice of relevant technological individuals and teams, the framework must be explained to its target audience; the simulation helped to achieve this purpose by being a hands-on exercise. Also, the value of models was understood only after the exercise, albeit limited to simple constructs and semantics.

Future work will continue with the practice and expand on more complex FR Scenarios. Due to the positive experience, forensic readiness is included in security management plans, with periodical exercises planned. But, to do so effectively, research must be made to optimise the FR-ISSRM process, especially the time complexity. Lastly, we aim to expand the tool support to automate and expand the model-based evaluation, bringing more direct value to the models. The work shall focus on how to make the models and process more accessible.

Acknowledgement. This research was supported by ERDF "CyberSecurity, CyberCrime and Critical Information Infrastructures Center of Excellence" (No. CZ.02.1.01/0.0/0.0/16_019/0000822). Computational resources were supplied by the project "e-Infrastruktura CZ" (e-INFRA CZ LM2018140) supported by the Ministry of Education, Youth and Sports of the Czech Republic. A special thanks to the e-INFRA CZ SensitiveCloud team for their participation in the study. This research was also co-founded by the European Union under Grant Agreement No. 101087529. Views and opinions expressed are however those of the author(s) only and do not necessarily reflect those of the European Union or European Research Executive Agency. Neither the European Union nor the granting authority can be held responsible for them.

References

1. Ab Rahman, N.H., Glisson, W.B., Yang, Y., Choo, K.K.R.: Forensic-by-design framework for cyber-physical cloud systems. IEEE Cloud Comput. **3**(1), 50–59 (2016)
2. Affia, A.-A.O., Matulevičius, R., Nolte, A.: Security risk management in cooperative intelligent transportation systems: a systematic literature review. In: Panetto, H., Debruyne, C., Hepp, M., Lewis, D., Ardagna, C.A., Meersman, R. (eds.) OTM 2019. LNCS, vol. 11877, pp. 282–300. Springer, Cham (2019). https://doi.org/10.1007/978-3-030-33246-4_18
3. Afzaal, M., Di Sarno, C., Coppolino, L., D'Antonio, S., Romano, L.: A resilient architecture for forensic storage of events in critical infrastructures. In: IEEE HASE 2012, pp. 48–55 (2012)
4. Alrajeh, D., Pasquale, L., Nuseibeh, B.: On evidence preservation requirements for forensic-ready systems. In: ESEC/FSE 2017, pp. 559–569. ACM (2017)
5. Altuhhova, O., Matulevičius, R., Ahmed, N.: An extension of business process model and notation for security risk management. Int. J. Inform. Syst. Model. Design **4**, 93–113 (10 2013)

6. Bajramovic, E., Waedt, K., Ciriello, A., Gupta, D.: Forensic readiness of smart buildings: Preconditions for subsequent cybersecurity tests. In: IEEE ISC2 2016, pp. 1–6 (2016)
7. CESG: Good Practice Guide No. 18: Forensic Readiness. Guideline, National Technical Authority for Information Assurance, United Kingdom (2015)
8. Daubner, L., Macak, M., Matulevičius, R., Buhnova, B., Maksović, S., Pitner, T.: Addressing insider attacks via forensic-ready risk management. J. Inform. Secur. Appl. **73**, 103433 (2023)
9. Daubner, L., Matulevičius, R.: Risk-oriented design approach for forensic-ready software systems. In: ARES 2021. ACM (2021)
10. Daubner, L., Matulevičius, R., Buhnova, B., Pitner, T.: Business process model and notation for forensic-ready software systems. In: ENASE 2022, pp. 95–106. SCITEPRESS (2022)
11. Dubois, É., Heymans, P., Mayer, N., Matulevičius, R.: A Systematic Approach to Define the Domain of Information System Security Risk Management, pp. 289–306. Springer (2010). https://doi.org/10.1007/978-3-642-12544-7_16
12. EDPB: Data breach: the italian sa fines inail eur 50,000. Decision, European Data Protection Board (2022), https://edpb.europa.eu/news/national-news/2022/data-breach-italian-sa-fines-inail-eur-50000_en
13. Elyas, M., Ahmad, A., Maynard, S.B., Lonie, A.: Digital forensic readiness: expert perspectives on a theoretical framework. Comput. Secur. **52**, 70–89 (2015)
14. Ganji, D., Kalloniatis, C., Mouratidis, H., Malekshahi Gheytassi, S.: Approaches to develop and implement iso/iec 27001 standard - information security management systems: systematic literature review. Int. J. Adv. Softw. **12**, 228–238 (2019)
15. Grandry, E., Feltus, C., Dubois, E.: Conceptual integration of enterprise architecture management and security risk management. In: 17th IEEE International Enterprise Distributed Object Computing Conference Workshops, pp. 114–123 (2013)
16. Grispos, G., Glisson, W.B., Choo, K.K.R.: Medical cyber-physical systems development: A forensics-driven approach. In: IEEE/ACM CHASE 2017, pp. 108–113 (2017)
17. Grobler, C.P., Louwrens, C.P.: Digital forensic readiness as a component of information security best practice. In: New Approaches for Security, Privacy and Trust in Complex Environments, pp. 13–24. Springer (2007)
18. Grobler, C., Louwrens, C., von Solms, S.: A framework to guide the implementation of proactive digital forensics in organisations. In: ARES 2010, pp. 677–682 (2010)
19. Iqbal, A., Ekstedt, M., Alobaidli, H.: Digital forensic readiness in critical infrastructures: A case of substation automation in the power sector. In: Digital Forensics and Cyber Crime, pp. 117–129. Springer (2018). https://doi.org/10.1007/978-3-319-73697-6_9
20. ISO/IEC: Information technology — Security techniques — Incident investigation principles and processes. Standard, International Organization for Standardization, Switzerland (2015)
21. ISO/IEC: Information technology — Security techniques — Information security risk management. Standard, International Organization for Standardization, Switzerland (2018)
22. Joint Task Force Transformation Initiative: Risk management framework for information systems and organizations: A system life cycle approach for security and privacy. Tech. Rep. Special Publication (NIST SP) - 800–37 Rev. 2, NIST (2018)
23. Matulevičius, R.: Fundamentals of secure system modelling. Springer (2017). https://doi.org/10.1007/978-3-319-61717-6

24. Mouhtaropoulos, A., Dimotikalis, P., Li, C.T.: Applying a digital forensic readiness framework: Three case studies. In: IEEE HST 2013,pp. 217–223 (2013)
25. Pasquale, L., Alrajeh, D., Peersman, C., Tun, T., Nuseibeh, B., Rashid, A.: Towards forensic-ready software systems. In: Proceedings of the 40th ICSE: New Ideas and Emerging Results, pp. 9–12. ICSE-NIER 2018, ACM (2018)
26. Rivera-Ortiz, F., Pasquale, L.: Automated modelling of security incidents to represent logging requirements in software systems. In: ARES 2020. ACM (2020)
27. Rowlingson, R.: A ten step process for forensic readiness. Int. J. Digital Evidence **2** (01 2004)
28. Runeson, P., Höst, M., Rainer, A., Regnell, B.: Case Study Research in Software Engineering: Guidelines and Examples. Wiley (2012)
29. Simou, S., Kalloniatis, C., Gritzalis, S., Katos, V.: A framework for designing cloud forensic-enabled services (cfes). Requirements Eng. **24**(3), 403–430 (2019)
30. Singh, A., Ikuesan, R.A., Venter, H.: Secure storage model for digital forensic readiness. IEEE Access **10**, 19469–19480 (2022)
31. SUSE: SUSE Rancher Technical Architecture Guide. White paper, SUSE, Luxembourg (2021)
32. Tan, J.: Forensic readiness. Tech. rep., @stake, Inc. (2001)
33. Wang, J., Peng, F., Tian, H., Chen, W., Lu, J.: Public auditing of log integrity for cloud storage systems via blockchain. In: Security and Privacy in New Computing Environments. pp. 378–387. Springer (2019)
34. Zawoad, S., Hasan, R.: Trustworthy digital forensics in the cloud. Computer **49**(3), 78–81 (2016)

Explainable AI

CREATED: Generating Viable Counterfactual Sequences for Predictive Process Analytics

Olusanmi Hundogan[ID], Xixi Lu[✉][ID], Yupei Du, and Hajo A. Reijers[ID]

Utrecht University, Utrecht, The Netherlands
{o.a.hundogan,x.lu,y.du,h.a.reijers}@uu.nl

Abstract. Predictive process analytics focuses on predicting future states, such as the outcome of running process instances. These techniques often use machine learning models or deep learning models (such as LSTM) to make such predictions. However, these deep models are complex and difficult for users to understand. Counterfactuals answer "what-if" questions, which are used to understand the reasoning behind the predictions. For example, what if instead of emailing customers, customers are being called? Would this alternative lead to a different outcome? Current methods to generate counterfactual sequences either do not take the process behavior into account, leading to generating invalid or infeasible counterfactual process instances, or heavily rely on domain knowledge. In this work, we propose a general framework that uses evolutionary methods to generate counterfactual sequences. Our framework does not require domain knowledge. Instead, we propose to train a Markov model to compute the *feasibility* of generated counterfactual sequences and adapt three other measures (*delta* in outcome prediction, *similarity*, and *sparsity*) to ensure their overall viability. The evaluation shows that we generate viable counterfactual sequences, outperform baseline methods in viability, and yield similar results when compared to the state-of-the-art method that requires domain knowledge.

Keywords: Counterfactual · Explainable AI · Predictive Process Analytics · Evolutionary Algorithm

1 Introduction

Predictive process analytics is an emerging research field in the process mining discipline that focuses on predicting the future states or outcome of running cases of business processes. The proposed techniques often use Machine Learning (ML) models or deep learning models (such as LSTM). These predictive models are trained on historical executions of business processes (i.e., *event logs*) to make predictions of future states or outcomes. Studies have shown that predictive models can forecast the outcome of processes from various domains well [12,20]. For instance, in the medical domain, predictive models are applied to predict the outcome or trajectory of a patient's condition [13].

© The Author(s), under exclusive license to Springer Nature Switzerland AG 2023
M. Indulska et al. (Eds.): CAiSE 2023, LNCS 13901, pp. 541–557, 2023.
https://doi.org/10.1007/978-3-031-34560-9_32

While these predictive models are very powerful, they are usually complex and difficult to comprehend. Therefore, they are also known as *blackbox models*. A lack of comprehension is undesirable for many application domains. For example, not knowing why a mortgage application was denied makes it impossible to rule out possible biases. In critical domains like medicine, the reasoning behind decisions becomes more crucial. For instance, if we know that a treatment process of a patient reduces the chances of survival, we want to know which treatment step is the critical factor we ought to avoid. For the engineering of fair and effective information systems, it is essential to comprehend and explain the reasoning behind predictions.

The Explainable AI (XAI) discipline proposes *counterfactuals* as a human-friendly approach to understanding the underlying reasoning of ML models [14, p. 221]. Counterfactuals can help us answer hypothetical "what-if" questions. In other words, assuming we know *what* would happen *if* we changed the execution of a process instance, we could change it for the better. For example, what if instead of emailing customers, customers are contacted by phone? Would this alternative sequence have led to a different outcome (e.g., instead of rejecting the offer, the customer accepts the offer)?

Existing methods can be divided into two categories: traditional and process-aware. The *traditional* counterfactual methods focus on static, tabular data, such as DICE [15]. These methods aim to minimize the feature changes while maximize the flip in the outcome prediction. These methods do not take the process behavior into account. Applying them directly to event logs may lead to generating *invalid* or *infeasible* counterfactual sequences. The *process-aware* methods adapt the traditional methods for counterfactual generations of event logs [8]. While taking normative process behavior into account, these state-of-the-art methods, however, heavily rely on domain knowledge (e.g., users need to know the flows between milestones of a process) [8].

In this paper, we approach the problem of generating counterfactual sequences for process outcome prediction without domain knowledge. In particular, we propose a general framework that uses evolutionary algorithms to generate sequences. The framework contains three components. The first component is a pre-trained predictive model, which we require to explain using counterfactuals. We assume that the prediction model *accurately* predicts the outcome of a process at any step[1]. The second component implements the evolutionary algorithm, which generates counterfactual sequences that should be of high quality. To quantify the quality of counterfactual sequences and select the best ones, we define a *viability* measure as our third component, which takes four measures into account, namely (1) feasibility of a counterfactual sequence, (2) the delta flipped in the outcome prediction, (3) the similarity between factual and counterfactual, and (4) the sparsity counting the number of changes. As we use evolutionary algorithms to generate our counterfactuals, we refer to

---

[1] The accuracy-condition is favorable, but not necessary. If the component is accurately modelling the real world, we can draw real-world conclusions from the explanations generated. If the component is inaccurate, the counterfactuals only explain the prediction decisions and not the real world.

this framework as CREATED: the CounteRfactual Sequence generation with Evolutionary AlgoriThms on Event Data. The name reflects how our model CREATEs new counterfactual sequences.

To evaluate the CREATED framework, we used ten event logs from three real-life processes and performed two experiments. First, we examined 54 configurations of the CREATED framework to obtain optimal configurations and compared our results with three baseline methods (case-based, sample-based, and random). The results show that we outperform the baseline methods in viability. In the second experiment, we compared our counterfactual sequences to the ones generated by a state-of-the-art method, showing that we yield similar counterfactuals without requiring domain knowledge.

The remainder of the paper is structured as follows. Sections 2 and 3 respectively discuss the related work and preliminary concepts. Section 4 presents our approach. Section 5 explains the evaluation set-up. Section 6 discusses the results, and Sect. 7 concludes the paper.

2   Related Work

As stated before, We divide the existing methods for counterfactual generation into two categories: *traditional* methods and *process-aware* methods. The *traditional* methods concern the classical ML models, and the topic of counterfactual generation as an explanation method was first introduced by [22]. The authors defined a loss function that incorporates the criteria to generate a counterfactual that maximizes the likelihood of a predefined outcome and minimizes the distance to the original instance. A more recent approach by [4] incorporates four main criteria for counterfactuals by applying a genetic algorithm with a multi-objective fitness function [4]. This approach strongly differs from gradient-based methods, as it does not require a differentiable objective function. However, the above traditional methods focus on static data. They do not take process behaviors into account. Applying these methods directly on event logs may result in generating infeasible counterfactual sequences.

Within process mining, the *process-aware* methods for counterfactuals have followed two streams. The first steam uses the Causal Inference techniques to analyse and model business processes, as the causal relationships can be used to understand the effect of decisions in a process on its outcome. However, early work has often attempted to incorporate domain-knowledge about the causality of processes in order to improve the process model itself [2,7,19,23]. Among these, the approach in [16] is one of the first to include counterfactual reasoning for process optimization [16]. Later, the work by [17] uses counterfactuals to generate alternative solutions to treatments, which lead to a desired outcome. However, the authors do not attempt to provide an explanation of the model's outcome and therefore, disregard multiple viability criteria for counterfactuals in XAI. [18] published the most recent paper on the counterfactual generation of explanations. The authors use a known Structural Causal Model (SCM) to guide the generation of their counterfactuals. However, this approach requires a process model which is as close as possible to the *true* process model. Our approach assumes no knowledge of such a normative process model.

The second stream in *process-aware* methods adapts the *traditional* counterfactual methods for process-aware counterfactuals. The DICE4EL approach [8] extends the DICE method [15] to generate counterfactuals for event logs while building on the same notion of incremental generation. The authors recognised that some processes have critical events (mile-stones) which govern the overall outcome. Hence, by simply avoiding the undesired outcome from critical event to critical event, it is possible to limit the search space and compute viable counterfactuals. However, their approach requires concrete domain knowledge about these critical points. We propose a framework that avoids this constraint and does not require domain knowledge. The LORELEY approach [9] extends the LORE method [5] and also uses an evolutionary algorithm. However, this approach focuses on mutating the case/event attributes. More specifically, the approach treats the encoded features representing the control flow as a single attribute in the crossover and mutation steps; thus, no unseen counterfactual sequences are created. In contrast, we generate unseen process sequences. Furthermore, we propose to automatically train a Markov model from the input event log to capture the likelihood of a process sequence. This Markov model is then used to derive the feasibility of counterfactual sequences.

3 Background

We start by formalising the event log and its elements.

Definition 1. Case, Event and Log. Let $\mathcal{E}$ be the universe of the event identifiers and $E \subseteq \mathcal{E}$ a set of events. An event log $L \subseteq \mathcal{E}^*$ is a set of sequences of events. Let C be a set of case identifiers and $\pi_c : E \mapsto C$ a surjective function that links every element in E to a case $c \in C$ in which c signifies a specific case. For a set of events $E \subseteq \mathcal{E}$, the shorthand s^c denotes a particular sequence $s^c = \langle e_1, e_2, \ldots, e_t \rangle$ with c as case identifier and a length of t. Each s is a trace of the process log $s \in L$. Let $\mathcal{T}$ be the time domain and $\pi_t : E \mapsto \mathcal{T}$ a non-surjective linking function which strictly orders a set of events. Each event e_t consists of a set $e_t = \{a_1 \in A_1, a_2 \in A_2, \ldots, a_I \in A_I\}$ with the size $I = |A|$, in which A_i is an attribute and a_i represents a possible value of that attribute.

Definition 2. Attribute Representation. Let $\pi_d : A_i \mapsto \mathbb{N}$ be a surjective function, which determines the dimensionality of a_i, and let F be a set of size I containing a representation function for every attribute. Let $f_i \in F$ be mapping functions to a vector space $f_i : a_i \mapsto \mathbb{R}_i^d$, in which d represents the dimensionality of an attribute value $d = \pi_d(A_i)$. We denote any event $e_t \in s^c$ of a specific case c as a vector, which concatenates every attribute representation f_i as $\mathbf{e}_t^c = [f_1; f_2; \ldots; f_I]$. Therefore, $\mathbf{e}_t^c$ is embedded in a vector space of size D which is the sum of each individual attribute dimension $D = \sum_i \pi_d(A_i)$. In other words, we concatenate all representations, whether they are scalars or vectors to one final vector representing the event. Furthermore, if we refer to a specific attribute A_i, we use the shorthand $\overline{a}_i$.

4 Methods

4.1 Methodological Framework: CREATED

To generate counterfactuals, we need to establish a conceptual framework consisting of three main components. The three components are shown in Fig. 1.

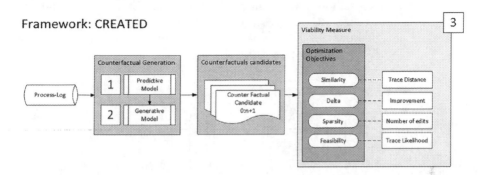

Fig. 1. The CREATED framework: the input is the process log; the log is used to train a predictive model (Component 1) and the generative model (Component 2). This process produces a set of candidates which are subject to evaluation via the validity metric (Component 3).

The first component is a *predictive model*. As we attempt to explain model decisions with counterfactuals, the predictive model needs to be pretrained. We can use any model that can predict the probability of a sequence. The prediction model in this paper is a simple LSTM model using the process log as an input. The architecture is inspired by [8]. The model is trained to predict the outcome given a sequence.

The second component is a *generative model*. The generative model produces counterfactuals given a factual sequence. We implement an evolutionary generator that takes a factual as input and yields counterfactuals candidates as output.

The generated candidates are subject to the third major component. To select the most *viable* counterfactual candidate, we evaluate their viability score using a custom metric. The metric incorporates four criteria for viable counterfactuals. We measure the **similarity** between two sequences using a multivariate sequence distance metric. The **outcome-delta** is the difference between the likelihood of the factual and the counterfactual. For this purpose, we require the predictive model, which computes a prediction score reflecting the likelihood. We measure **sparsity** by counting the number of changes in the features and computing the edit distance. Lastly, we need to determine the **feasibility** of a counterfactual. We measure the feasibility by estimating the probability of a counterfactual. Note that our method was developed for outcome prediction but can be adapted to the next activity prediction task.

4.2   Counterfactual Generators

Generative Model: Evolutionary Algorithm. In this section, we describe
the concrete set of operators and select a subset that we want to explore further.

For our purposes, the *gene* of a sequence consists of the sequence of events
within a process instance. Hence, if an offspring inherits one parent gene, it
inherits the activity associated with the event and its event attributes. Our
goal is to generate candidates by evaluating the sequence based on our viability
measure. Our measure acts as the fitness function. The candidates that are
deemed fit enough are subsequently selected to reproduce offspring. This process
is explained in Fig. 2.

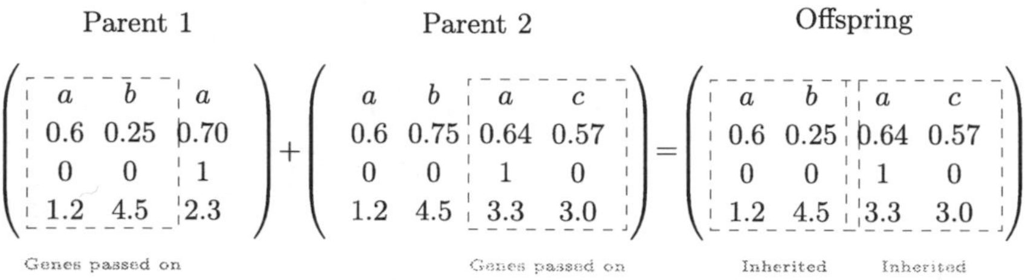

Fig. 2. A newly generated offspring inheriting genes in the form of activities and event
attributes from both parents.

The offspring is subject to mutations. We evaluate the new population and
repeat the procedure until a termination condition is reached. We can optimise
the viability measure established in Sect. 4.3.

Operators. We implemented several different evolutionary operators. Each one
belongs to one of five categories. The categories are initiation, selection, crossing,
mutation, and recombination. Table 1 contains a complete list of the operators.

Naming-Conventions. We use abbreviations to refer to each model configuration. For instance, *CBI-RWS-OPC-RM-RR* refers to an evolutionary operator

---

Algorithm 1. The basic structure of an evolutionary algorithm.

Require: factual,   configuration,   sample-size,   population-size,   mutation-rate,
   termination-point
Ensure: The result is the final counterfactual sequences
   $counterfactuals \leftarrow initialize(\text{factual})$
   while not *termination* **do**
      cf-parents $\leftarrow select(\text{counterfactuals, sample-size})$
      cf-offsprings $\leftarrow crossover(\text{cf-parents})$
      cf-mutants $\leftarrow mutate(\text{cf-offsprings, mutation-rate})$
      cf-survivors $\leftarrow recombine(\text{counterfactuals, cf-mutants, population-size})$
      $termination \leftarrow determine(\text{cf-survivors, termination-point})$
      counterfactuals $\leftarrow$ cf-survivors
   end while

Table 1. An overview of all evolutionary operators used in this paper and a short description.

Label	Name	Description
Initiation		
RI	Random Initialisation	Generates an initial population in which the event sequence was chosen at random based on the log. The event attributes were drawn from a normal distribution
SBI	Sampling-Based Initialisation	Generates an initial population by sampling from a data distribution estimated from the data directly. The event sequence was sampled using the event transition probabilities. The attributes were sampled using distributions conditioned on the emitted events
CBI	Case-Based Initialisation	Samples initial population directly from the Log
Selection		
RWS	Roulette-Wheel-Selection	Selects individuals randomly in proportion to their fitness value
TS	Tournament-Selection	Selects pairs of individuals and compares each pair. The better individual between both pairs has a higher chance of being selected
ES	Elitism-Selection	Selects individual with the highest fitness
Crossover		
UCx	Uniform Crossover	Uniformly choose a fraction of genes of one individual (*Parent 1*) and overwrite the respective genes of another individual (*Parent 2*)
OPC	One-Point Crossover	Chooses a point in the sequence and overwrites the genes of *Parent 2* by the genes *Parent 2* from that point onward
TPC	Two-Point Crossover	Chooses two points in the sequence and overwrites the sequence in between the two points from *Parent 2* with the sequence from *Parent 1*
Mutation		
RM	Random-Mutation	Inserts, changes or deletes activities randomly. Event attributes are drawn from a normal distribution
SBM	Sampling-Based Mutation	Inserts, changes or deletes activities randomly. Event attributes are drawn from an estimated data distribution
Recombination		
FSR	Fittest-Survivor Recombination	Strictly determines the survivors among the mutated offsprings and the current population by sorting them in terms of viability
BBR	Best-of-Breed Recombination	Determines offsprings that are better than the average within their generation and adds them to survivors of past generations
RR	Ranked Recombination	Selects the new population differently than the former recombination operators. Instead of using the viability directly, we sort each individuum by every viability component separately. This approach allows us to select individuals regardless of the scales of every individual viability measure

configuration that samples its initial population from the data (CBI), probabilistically samples parents based on their fitness (RWS), crosses them on one point (OPC), and so on. For the *Uniform-Crossing* (UCx) operator, we additionally indicate its crossing rate using a number. For instance, *CBI-RWS-UC3-RM-RR* uses the *Uniform-Crossing* (UC3) operator. The child receives roughly 30% of the genome of one parent and 70% of another parent.

Hyperparameters. The evolutionary approach comes with a number of hyperparameters. We first discuss the *model configuration*. As shown in this section, there are a 135 ways to combine all operators. Depending on each operator combination, we might see very different behaviours. The decision of the appropriate set of operators is by far the most important in terms of convergence speed and result quality. The next hyperparameter is the *termination point* which determines the duration of the search. Optimally, we find a termination point, which is not too early but not too late, too. The *mutation rate* is another hyperparameter. It signifies how much a child can differ from its parent.

4.3 Viability Measure

Feasibility-Measure. To determine the feasibility of a counterfactual trace, it is important to consider two aspects. First, we have to compute the probability of the sequence of event transitions. This is a difficult task, given the *Open World assumption*[2]. Therefore, we have to assume the data is representative and the underlying process is static. This assumption allows us to estimate first-order transition probabilities by counting event transitions.

Second, we have to compute the feasibility of the individual feature values given the sequence. We can relax the computation of this probability using the *Markov Assumption*. In other words, we assume that each event vector depends on the current activity but on none of the previous events and features. This means that we can model density estimators for every event and use them to determine the likelihood of a set of features.

We define the feasibility measure in Eq. 1, where e_t represents the current event, transited from the previous event e_{t-1}. Likewise, f represents the emission of the feature attributes. Hence, the probability of a particular sequence is the product of the transition probability multiplied by the state emission probability for each step.

$$p\left(e_{0:T}, f_{0:T}\right) = p\left(e_0\right) p\left(f_0 \mid e_0\right) \prod_1^T p\left(e_t \mid e_{t-1}\right) p\left(f_t \mid e_t\right) \tag{1}$$

Delta-Outcome. For the delta measure, we evaluate the likelihood of a counterfactual trace by determining whether a counterfactual leads to the desired outcome or not. For this purpose, we use the predictive model, which returns a prediction for each counterfactual sequence. As we are predicting process outcomes, we typically predict a class. However, forcing a deterministic model to produce a different class prediction is often difficult. Therefore, we can relax the condition by maximising the prediction score of the desired counterfactual outcome [14]. If we compare the difference between the counterfactual prediction score with the factual prediction score, we can determine an increase or decrease. Ideally, we want to increase the likelihood of the desired outcome. We refer to this value as *delta*. For the binary outcome prediction case, we define the function as shown in Eq. 2.

$$delta = \begin{cases} |p(o|s^*) - p(o|s)| & \text{if } p(o|s) > 0.5 \& p(o|s) > p(o|s^*) \\ -|p(o|s^*) - p(o|s)| & \text{if } p(o|s) > 0.5 \& p(o|s) \le p(o|s^*) \\ |p(o|s^*) - p(o|s)| & \text{if } p(o|s) \le 0.5 \& p(o|s) > p(o|s^*) \\ -|p(o|s^*) - p(o|s)| & \text{if } p(o|s) \le 0.5 \& p(o|s) \le p(o|s^*) \end{cases} \tag{2}$$

Similarity Measure. We use a function to compute the **similarity** between the factual sequence and the counterfactual candidates. To incorporate differences in length between both sequences, we use a weighted version of the

---

[2] In theory, we cannot know whether or not any event *can* follow after another event.

Table 2. All datasets used within the evaluation. DiCE4EL is used for the qualitative evaluation, and the remaining are used for quantitative evaluation purposes.

Dataset	#Cases	Min Len	Max Len	% Unique Traces	#Unique Ev	#Data Columns	#Event Attr	#Regular	#Deviant
DiCE4EL	3 051	12	25	0.000328	23	9	7	1 853	1 198
BPIC12-25	3 051	12	25	0.000328	23	23	21	1 853	1 198
BPIC12-50	4 587	12	50	0.000218	23	23	21	2 405	2 182
BPIC12-75	4 677	12	75	0.000214	23	23	21	2 436	2 241
BPIC12-100	4 685	12	96	0.000213	23	23	21	2 442	2 243
Sepsis-25	707	5	25	0.001414	15	75	73	610	97
Sepsis-50	770	5	47	0.001299	15	76	74	662	108
Sepsis-75	777	5	66	0.001287	15	76	74	667	110
Sepsis-100	779	5	88	0.001284	15	76	74	669	110
TrafficFines	129 615	2	20	0.000008	10	40	38	70 602	59 013

Damerau-Levenshtein distance [3]. The Damerau-Levenstein distance applies a cost constant of 1 for each sequential difference. However, as process instances differ not only in event sequences but also in their event attribute values, we use a distance function to weigh the cost. In the case of **similarity**, we apply the euclidian distance. For formal definitions, we refer to [11, p. 42].

Sparsity Measure. For measuring the sparsity, we use the same weighted version of the Damerau-Levenshtein distance. However, to measure the distance, we count the number of differences between event attributes. For formal definitions, we refer to [11, p. 42].

Viability-Measure. We combine the feasibility measure, the outcome delta, the normalised sparsity, and normalised similarity measure by summation. As each measure can have values between 0 and 1, the viability measure ranges between 0 and 4. For more details on the viability measure, we refer to [11, Chap. 3.3].

5   Evaluation

5.1   Datasets

For our evaluation, we use ten event logs of three real-life processes, which were also used in [21]. Each dataset consists of events and contains labels that signify a process instance's outcome. We focus on binary outcome predictions. We include a variation of the BPIC dataset. This dataset was used in [8]. The difference between Hsieh et al.'s dataset and the original dataset is two-fold. First, the authors focus on the generation of two event attributes. Second, the dataset is primarily designed for next-activity prediction, not outcome prediction. We modified the dataset to fit the outcome prediction model. For more information about these datasets we refer to the comparative study by [21]. We list the important descriptive statistics in Table 2.

We list the predictions of our prediction component in Table 3. The F1-Scores on the test sets are generally higher for the BPIC dataset. Furthermore, in the case of the BPIC datasets, the prediction model always predicts the correct outcome if the max-length of the sequence exceeds 25. It is fair to assume that the length of a loan application process determines the chance of getting rejected or not.

Table 3. The evaluation metrics for the prediction component on all datasets. Includes precision, recall and f1 score for test, training and validation data.

Subset Dataset	Precision			Recall			f1-score			Support		
	Test	Training	Validation	Test	Training	Validation	Test	Training	Validation	Test	Training	Validation
BPIC12-100	1.000	0.999	0.999	1.000	0.999	0.999	1.000	0.999	0.999	60.000	1000.000	841.000
BPIC12-25	0.808	0.770	0.765	0.750	0.742	0.733	0.738	0.733	0.723	60.000	1000.000	1000.000
BPIC12-50	1.000	1.000	1.000	1.000	1.000	1.000	1.000	1.000	1.000	60.000	1000.000	819.000
BPIC12-75	1.000	1.000	1.000	1.000	1.000	1.000	1.000	1.000	1.000	60.000	1000.000	841.000
DiCE4EL	0.780	0.806	0.821	0.700	0.755	0.749	0.677	0.744	0.739	60.000	1000.000	1000.000
Sepsis-100	0.259	0.246	0.250	0.509	0.496	0.500	0.343	0.329	0.333	55.000	123.000	42.000
Sepsis-25	0.478	0.511	0.528	0.483	0.508	0.519	0.449	0.482	0.495	60.000	1000.000	873.000
Sepsis-50	0.250	0.240	0.261	0.500	0.490	0.511	0.333	0.322	0.346	60.000	1000.000	1000.000
Sepsis-75	0.207	0.254	0.300	0.455	0.504	0.548	0.284	0.338	0.388	55.000	123.000	42.000
TrafficFines	1.000	0.987	0.984	1.000	0.987	0.983	1.000	0.987	0.983	60.000	1000.000	1000.000

5.2   Preprocessing

To prepare the data for our experiments, we employed basic tactics for preprocessing. First, we split the log into a training and a test set. Then, we filter out every case whose sequence length exceeds 25. We keep this maximum threshold for most experiments focusing on the evolutionary algorithm. The reason is the polynomial computation time of the viability measure. The similarity and sparsity components of the proposed viability measure have a runtime complexity of at least N^2. Hence, limiting the sequence length saves a substantial amount of temporal resources. Next, we extract time variables if they are provided in the log. Then, we normalise the values. Each categorical variable is converted using binary encoding. The activity is label-encoded. As a result, every category is assigned to a unique integer. The label column is binary encoded, as we focus on outcome prediction. Lastly, we pad each sequence towards the longest sequence in the dataset.

5.3   Baseline Models

We use three baseline models and compare them to the evolutionary models. The first baseline generates a random sequence of events and event attributes. Hence, we refer to this approach as **Random baseline** (RGW). We expect most models to perform better than this baseline. Otherwise, it would indicate that a random search would generate better counterfactuals than a guided one. The second baseline resembles the random baseline. However, we use the data likelihood to guide the random search for the generation of counterfactuals. We first generate a random seed of possible starting events $(p(e_0))$. Afterwards, we randomly sample subsequent events by iteratively sampling new activities according to the transition probabilities we gathered from the data $(\prod_1^T p(e_t \mid e_{t-1}))$. Given the sequence, we simply sample the features per event from $p(f_t \mid e_t)$. We call this baseline **Sample-Based** (SBGW). In contrast to both sampling-based baselines, the last baseline leverages actual examples of the data. We refer to this case-based approach as **Case-Based baseline** (CBGW). The idea is to randomly pick traces from the log and evaluate them using the viability measure.

5.4   Experimental Setup

All the experiments were run on a Windows machine with 12 processor cores (Intel Core i7-9750H CPU 2.60 GHz) and 32 GB Ram. The code is written in Python version 3.8. The models were developed with Tensorflow [1] and NumPy [6]. We provide the full code and instructions on Github [10].

In terms of operators, we introduced three initiators, three selectors, five crossers, two mutators, and three recombiners. For the experiments, we exclude the random mutator as preliminary experiments showed that it often leads to results with a feasibility of 0. To reduce the number of model configurations, we initially compare all 135 evolutionary operator combinations. We select the best three models and compare them to the three baseline models. Afterwards, we assess the viability of all the chosen evolutionary and baseline generators. We sample 10 factuals from the BPIC-25 dataset and use our models as well as the baselines to generate 50 counterfactuals for each factual. We determine the mean viability across the counterfactuals. We expect the evolutionary algorithms to outperform the baselines when it comes to viability. In the end, we assess the quality of the generated counterfactuals. In line with [8], we aim to answer the question *what would one have had to change in order to flip the outcome of a process*. The goal is to show that the counterfactuals our models generate are viable without having to rely on domain-specific knowledge. In the current paper, we did not include any results of the individual viability components. Furthermore, we refer to [11, p.64] for more specific and extensive observations.

6   Results

6.1   Experiment 1: Comparing with Baseline Generators

We examined a set of model-configurations containing 135 elements. We choose to run each model configuration for 100 evolution cycles. We randomly sample four factual process instance from the test set. Afterwards, we use the average viability across the instances to evaluate all model configurations. Fig. 3 shows the bottom and top-5 model configurations based on the viability after the final iterative cycle. The figure also shows how the viability evolves for each iteration.

According to Fig. 3, *CBI-ES-UC3-SBM-RR*, *CBI-RWS-OPC-SBM-BBR*, and *CBI-RWS-OPC-SBM-FSR* are the best model configurations. As all best-performing model-configurations use the *Case-Based Inititiation*-operator, we identify it as the most important configuration. The results suggest that the initiation operator governs the starting point of the optimisation. For the following

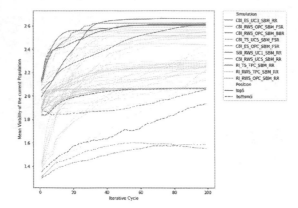

Fig. 3. This figure shows the average viability of the five best and worst model configurations. The x-axis shows how the viability evolves for each evolutionary cycle. The semi-transparent lines are the model configurations that are neither in the best five nor worst five groups. They show the general trend of the viability improvement.

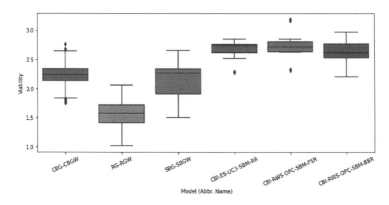

Fig. 4. This figure shows boxplots of the viability of each model's generated counterfactuals.

experiment, we ran each evolutionary algorithm for 200 iterative cycles and set the mutation rate to 0.01.

Next, we employed the baseline models mentioned in Sect. 4.2 and examined their results across all datasets. We randomly sampled 20 factuals from the test set and used the same factuals for every generator. We ensured that the outcomes are evenly divided. The remaining procedure followed the established practice of previous experiments. The results in Fig. 4 show that the evolutionary algorithm *CBI-ES-UC3-SBM-RR* returns better results when it comes to the mean viability. The worst model is the randomly generated model. The Case-Based model appears to be evenly and normally distributed at a viability of *2.25*. The *CBI-RWS-OPC-SBM-FSR* has outliers that far exceed and underperform against other evolutionary algorithms on both ends.

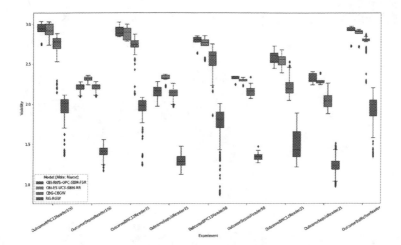

Fig. 5. Boxplots of the viability of each model's generated counterfactuals across a heterogeneous collection of datasets.

Figure 5 displays the results of running each algorithm on a set of different datasets. The figure shows a clear dominance of the evolutionary models across all datasets. Here, *CBI-ES-UC3-SBM-RR* and *CBI-RWS-OPC-SBM-FSR* display a higher median of viability across all datasets. This is unsurprising as the evolutionary algorithm uses initiators based on the baselines. However, it is surprising that the evolutionary models consistently outperform the Casebased-Search Generator (green) across all datasets. In six out of nine datasets, we see an improvement of at least 0.15. The highest median is reached for *CBI-RWS-OPC-SBM-FSR* at 2.94. The Random-Search Generator never manages to come even close to the case-based model. Except for the BPIC12-100 dataset, the Random-Search Generator has a median below 2.

The results for Fig. 5 show that both evolutionary algorithms outperform the competition across *all* datasets and against *all* baselines. This result shows that the algorithm can outperform baselines regardless of the process log and its length. The baseline comparison also shows that we can optimise towards viability successfully. Recall that we defined four criteria for the viability of counterfactuals (similarity, sparsity, feasibility, and delta in likelihood); a model optimising towards those criteria can apparently return superior results.

Table 4. A comparison between the CBI-RWS-OPC-SBM-FSR and D4EL.

Factual Seq.				Our CF Seq.				DiCE4EL CF Seq.		
Amount	Activity	Outcome	Resource	Amount	Activity	Outcome	Resource	Activity	Resource	Amount
5 000	A-SUBMITTED	0	112	7 000	A-SUBMITTED	1	112			
5 000	A-PARTLYSUBMITTED	0	112	7 000	A-PARTLYSUBMITTED	1	112			
5 000	A-PREACCEPTED	0	101	7 000	A-PREACCEPTED	1	112			
5 000	W-Afhandelen leads	0	101					A-SUBMITTED	112	5 000
5 000	A-ACCEPTED	0	111					A-PARTLYSUBMITTED	112	5 000
5 000	O-SELECTED	0	111	7 000	A-ACCEPTED	1	111	A-PREACCEPTED	112	5 000
5 000	A-FINALIZED	0	111	7 000	O-SELECTED	1	111	A-ACCEPTED	1	5 000
5 000	O-CREATED	0	111	7 000	A-FINALIZED	1	111	O-SELECTED	1	5 000
5 000	O-SENT	0	111	7 000	O-CREATED	1	111	A-FINALIZED	1	5 000
5 000	W-Completeren aanvraag	0	111	7 000	O-SENT	1	111	O-CREATED	1	5 000
5 000	W-Nabellen offertes	0	111	7 000	W-Completeren aanvraag	1	111	O-SENT	1	5 000
5 000	O-CANCELLED	0	111					W-Completeren aanvraag	1	5 000
5 000	A-CANCELLED	0	111	7 000	W-Nabellen offertes	1	111	O-SENT-BACK	11259	5 000
5 000	W-Nabellen offertes	0	111	7 000	W-Nabellen offertes	1	111	W-Nabellen offertes	11259	5 000
				7 000	O-ACCEPTED	1	629	O-ACCEPTED	9	5 000

6.2   Experiment 2: Qualitative Assessment

Figure 4 shows the generation of the model-configuration *CBI-RWS-OPC-SBM-FSR* and the model of [8]. Both models also return reasonable counterfactuals. The counterfactual sequence of events of both approaches are almost identical. For instance, our counterfactual and the D4EL counterfactual recognize that after O-SENT, there appears at least one *W-Completeren aanvraag* and one *W-Nabellen offertes* that eventually leads to an acceptance of the counterfactual. We also see that both evolutionary algorithms start the process with the correct sequence of A-SUBMITTED, A-PARTLYSUBMITTED and A-PREACCEPTED. These are strictly the same across all cases. If our generative model had not recognised these, one could question its utility.

In Table 5 we applied the same approach on a different dataset. The generator generates a counterfactual that is close to the original factual and only modifies the number of open cases. Here, we can conclude that a sudden increase in open cases during the *Add penalty* step results in a change of outcome.

The examples show that our generative approach does not rely on domain knowledge, such as milestones. In contrast, the approach by [8] only applies to datasets with clear milestones such as *BPIC-12*.

Table 5. A counterfactual for the Traffic-Fines dataset by the CBI-RWS-OPC-SBM-FSR model.

Factual Seq.				Our CF Seq.			
Open Cases	Activity	Outcome	Resource	Open Cases	Activity	Outcome	Resource
16 318	Create Fine	1	537	15 742	Create Fine	0	537
16 612	Send Fine	1	537	16 504	Send Fine	0	537
16 693	Insert Fine Notification	1	537	16 693	Insert Fine Notification	0	537
16 972	Add penalty	1	537				

6.3   Discussion and Limitations

All models successfully flip the outcome of the prediction model and are close to the factual. In contrast, the model by [8] proposes more changes to the sequence. It is important to recall that the generated counterfactuals focus on explaining the prediction model rather than the true process. More specifically, our generative model shows which events and attributes have to be present or omitted to flip the outcome of the prediction model.

In contrast to [8], we show that we can create these counterfactuals without incorporating domain-specific knowledge, such as an understanding of milestone patterns. Domain knowledge can help to improve or evaluate our solutions. However, they are not strictly required. Furthermore, our models can generate sequences not present within the input event log. Case-based solutions often overlook this aspect, as they are heavily biased toward the input data.

It is worthwhile to discuss that *counterfactual sequences* differ from *counterfactual rules* or *explanations*. To obtain explicit explanations or rules, the generated counterfactuals should be compared to the factual. Our framework enables some alignments between the generated counterfactuals with the factual sequence (see Fig. 4), which may act as an explanation. We consider deriving rules as a post-prior analysis, which is interesting for future work.

Our viability components showed that they can lead to an optimised solution. However, there are most likely other ways to operationalise viability criteria. In addition, what makes an excellent counterfactual and how we can quantify that is still a subject of debate. Currently, there is a lack of standardized evaluation protocols, benchmark techniques, and datasets. As a result, many researchers fall back on defining their custom evaluation methods. In fact, this is still an open research question [8,15]. Therefore, we often have to evaluate the counterfactuals in some subjective and qualitative way. In this paper, we decided to compare the counterfactuals with another approach in the literature and the factual themselves. Because our counterfactuals produced reasonable results, we deemed them viable. As future work, we also see value in incorporating experts to evaluate such an approach.

7   Conclusion

In this paper, we proposed CREATED, a modular framework to generate viable counterfactuals. The framework incorporates an evolutionary algorithm to generate counterfactual sequences while not requiring any domain knowledge other than the log itself. In addition, we proposed a viability measure to quantify and assess the quality of counterfactual sequences when compared to a factual sequence. The viability measure takes four aspects into account: feasibility, the delta in flipping the outcome prediction, similarity, and sparsity. The approach is capable of generating counterfactuals without explicit knowledge about the domain, as we only require the log. We achieve this by incorporating a Markov model trained on the event log. Our evaluation shows that our framework can generate counterfactual sequences which are higher than our naive baselines (i.e., case-based, sample-based, and random baselines). With these results, we demonstrate that optimizing a viability measure does generate higher-quality counterfactuals. We also compared the generated counterfactuals to the state-of-the-art method in the literature and show that our framework can generate similar counterfactuals, without using domain knowledge. The current feasibility measure tends to return lower values than other viability components as it is very sensitive to trace length. In the future, we aim to investigate better feasibility measures.

References

1. Abadi, M., et al.: Tensorflow: a system for large-scale machine learning. In: OSDI. pp. 265–283. USENIX Association (2016)
2. Baker, J., Song, J., Jones, D.R.: Closing the loop: empirical evidence for a positive feedback model of IT business value creation. J. Strateg. Inf. Syst. **26**(2), 142–160 (2017)
3. Damerau, F.: A technique for computer detection and correction of spelling errors. Commun. ACM **7**(3), 171–176 (1964)
4. Dandl, S., Molnar, C., Binder, M., Bischl, B.: Multi-objective counterfactual explanations. In: Bäck, T., Preuss, M., Deutz, A., Wang, H., Doerr, C., Emmerich, M., Trautmann, H. (eds.) PPSN 2020. LNCS, vol. 12269, pp. 448–469. Springer, Cham (2020). https://doi.org/10.1007/978-3-030-58112-1_31
5. Guidotti, R., Monreale, A., Giannotti, F., Pedreschi, D., Ruggieri, S., Turini, F.: Factual and counterfactual explanations for black box decision making. IEEE Intell. Syst. **34**(6), 14–23 (2019)
6. Harris, C.R., et al.: Array programming with numpy. Nat. **585**, 357–362 (2020)
7. Hompes, B.F.A., Maaradji, A., La Rosa, M., Dumas, M., Buijs, J.C.A.M., van der Aalst, W.M.P.: Discovering causal factors explaining business process performance variation. In: Dubois, E., Pohl, K. (eds.) CAiSE 2017. LNCS, vol. 10253, pp. 177–192. Springer, Cham (2017). https://doi.org/10.1007/978-3-319-59536-8_12
8. Hsieh, C., Moreira, C., Ouyang, C.: Dice4el: Interpreting process predictions using a milestone-aware counterfactual approach. In: ICPM. pp. 88–95. IEEE (2021)
9. Huang, T., Metzger, A., Pohl, K.: Counterfactual explanations for predictive business process monitoring. In: EMCIS. Lecture Notes in Business Information Processing, vol. 437, pp. 399–413. Springer (2021)
10. Hundogan, O.: CREATED, https://github.com/Olu93/project_CREATED/blob/a376a41ac51018c43af29a5add7aed6504a37277/README.md
11. Hundogan, O.: CREATED: the generation of viable counterfactual sequences using an evolutionary algorithm for event data of complex processes. Master's thesis, Utrecht University (2022). https://studenttheses.uu.nl/handle/20.500.12932/43117
12. Klímek, J., Klimek, J., Kraskiewicz, W., Topolewski, M.: Long-term series forecasting with query selector - efficient model of sparse attention. CoRR abs/2107.08687 (2021)
13. Mannhardt, F., Blinde, D.: Analyzing the trajectories of patients with sepsis using process mining. In: RADAR+EMISA@CAiSE. CEUR Workshop Proceedings, vol. 1859, pp. 72–80. CEUR-WS.org (2017)
14. Molnar, C.: Interpretable machine learning. Lulu.com (2020), https://christophm.github.io/interpretable-ml-book/

15. Mothilal, R.K., Sharma, A., Tan, C.: Explaining machine learning classifiers through diverse counterfactual explanations. In: FAT*, pp. 607–617. ACM (2020)
16. Narendra, T., Agarwal, P., Gupta, M., Dechu, S.: Counterfactual reasoning for process optimization using structural causal models. In: Hildebrandt, T., van Dongen, B.F., Röglinger, M., Mendling, J. (eds.) BPM 2019. LNBIP, vol. 360, pp. 91–106. Springer, Cham (2019). https://doi.org/10.1007/978-3-030-26643-1_6
17. Oberst, M., Sontag, D.A.: Counterfactual off-policy evaluation with gumbel-max structural causal models. In: ICML. Proceedings of Machine Learning Research, vol. 97, pp. 4881–4890. PMLR (2019)
18. Qafari, M.S., van der Aalst, W.M.P.: Case level counterfactual reasoning in process mining. In: Nurcan, S., Korthaus, A. (eds.) CAiSE 2021. LNBIP, vol. 424, pp. 55–63. Springer, Cham (2021). https://doi.org/10.1007/978-3-030-79108-7_7
19. Shook, C.L., Ketchen, D.J., Jr., Hult, G.T.M., Kacmar, K.M.: An assessment of the use of structural equation modeling in strategic management research. Strateg. Manag. J. **25**(4), 397–404 (2004)
20. Tax, N., Verenich, I., La Rosa, M., Dumas, M.: Predictive business process monitoring with lstm neural networks. In: Dubois, E., Pohl, K. (eds.) CAiSE 2017. LNCS, vol. 10253, pp. 477–492. Springer, Cham (2017). https://doi.org/10.1007/978-3-319-59536-8_30
21. Teinemaa, I., Dumas, M., Rosa, M.L., Maggi, F.M.: Outcome-oriented predictive process monitoring: Review and benchmark. ACM Trans. Knowl. Discov. Data **13**(2), 17:1–17:57 (2019)
22. Wachter, S., Mittelstadt, B., Russell, C.: Counterfactual explanations without opening the black box: Automated decisions and the GDPR. Harv. JL Tech. **31**, 841 (2017)
23. Wang, Z., Zhang, J., Xu, H., Chen, X., Zhang, Y., Zhao, W.X., Wen, J.: Counterfactual data-augmented sequential recommendation. In: SIGIR, pp. 347–356. ACM (2021)

Counterfactuals and Ways to Build Them: Evaluating Approaches in Predictive Process Monitoring

Andrei Buliga[1,2]([✉]) [ID], Chiara Di Francescomarino[3] [ID], Chiara Ghidini[1] [ID], and Fabrizio Maria Maggi[2] [ID]

[1] Fondazione Bruno Kessler, Trento, Italy
{abuliga,ghidini}@fbk.eu
[2] Free University of Bolzano, Bolzano, Italy
{abuliga,maggi}@unibz.it
[3] University of Trento, Trento, Italy
c.difrancescomarino@unitn.it

Abstract. Predictive Process Monitoring (PPM) deals with providing predictions about the continuation of partially executed process executions based on historical process data. PPM techniques have been developed using increasingly complex Machine and Deep Learning architectures, which lack interpretability of the predictions. Recently, explainable PPM techniques have been proposed, thus making them more "trustable" for the users. Amongst these techniques, counterfactuals aim at suggesting, for a given process execution, the minimal changes to be applied to it to achieve a desired outcome. In this paper, we introduce an evaluation framework for evaluating different approaches for the generation of counterfactuals in PPM. The framework is used to evaluate these approaches against several real-life datasets. The results show that, although a clear winner cannot be identified, each approach is suitable for logs with specific characteristics, or for achieving specific objectives.

Keywords: Counterfactual · Predictive Process Monitoring · Explainable AI

1 Introduction

Predictive Process Monitoring (PPM) [8] is a branch of Process Mining [1] that deals with providing predictions about the continuation of partially executed process instances based on a historical log of past process executions. The state-of-the-art efforts for PPM have been focusing on providing accurate predictive models by adopting different strategies such as Deep Learning or Ensemble

This work was partially supported by the Italian (MUR) under PRIN project PINPOINT Prot. 2020FNEB27, CUP H23C22000280006 and H45E21000210001 and PNRR project FAIR-Future AI Research (PE00000013), under the NRRP MUR program funded by NextGenerationEU. The support is gratefully acknowledged.

Learning. Such complex models are known to be black-box models due to the fact that their inner logic is considered uninterpretable by humans. The recent adoption of such black-box models in PPM has synchronously brought upon the adoption of eXplainable Artificial Intelligence (XAI) techniques intending to interpret their predictions. Within PPM, the focus has been mostly on delivering *factual explanations* for understanding *why* a certain prediction was made, such as which features were the most important for providing that prediction [11]. In contrast with such techniques, *counterfactual explanations* (or simply counterfactuals) help users understand rather *what to change* in an input sample (the *query instance*) in order to obtain a desired prediction through what-if scenarios [13].

In PPM, counterfactuals could help users understand how different activities or attributes might affect the outcome of a process execution - hence recommending to them what to change in the process execution in order to achieve a desired outcome. Consider, for instance, the scenario in which Alice wants to obtain a loan of €150 000 to buy her first apartment. Her request gets rejected by the bank. In such a situation, Alice would be interested in knowing how to change her loan request process and data in order to have her request accepted. Counterfactuals could help her in such a scenario. Examples of alternative counterfactuals that could help her obtain the desired outcome could be: (i) *the requested loan should be changed to €135 000*; (ii) *the credit period should be increased by 3 years*; (iii) *an appointment with the bank should be taken before sending the official loan request*; (iv) *the salary of Alice should be increased by €600*. Amongst the alternative counterfactuals she can pick the one that best suits her needs and finally possibly get her loan request accepted.

In this paper, we aim at exploring the task of generating counterfactuals in outcome-based PPM. This exploratory task is far from trivial and presents a number of challenges that must be discussed and addressed. In our opinion three challenges are of uttermost importance. First, the PPM community still lacks a discussion and a consensus on what is a good counterfactual explanation for a trace; second, it lacks agreed-upon evaluation metrics that can be used to establish the quality of a counterfactual; and third, it lacks consolidated methods for generating the desired good counterfactual explanations for PPM tasks. Although few approaches for the generation of counterfactuals in PPM have been proposed in the literature [5,6], a proper evaluation of these approaches is still missing. In order to address the first two challenges and fill this gap, we introduce an evaluation framework that identifies two main dimensions characterizing counterfactual approaches in PPM: the (family of) counterfactual generation methods and the encoding used to represent the process executions. Furthermore, we adapt state-of-the-art evaluation metrics for counterfactual approaches to the PPM domain by introducing a new metrics measuring the compliance of the returned counterfactuals to specific process constraints. We applied the evaluation framework to compare three families of techniques (*case-based*, *generative* and *semi-generative*) and four types of encodings against several real-life datasets. The results suggest that each approach is suitable for logs with specific characteristics, or for a specific purpose.

The main contributions of the work are:

- the definition of an evaluation framework for the evaluation of counterfactuals, extending a principled state-of-the-art XAI evaluation framework for counterfactuals [4] to account for the compliance of the generated counterfactuals with specific process constraints;
- the first extensive comparison and evaluation of different counterfactual generation strategies, related methods and encodings for outcome-based PPM.

The remainder of the paper is structured as follows. Section 2 introduces the main background concepts. Section 3 reports about the evaluation framework that we use in Sect. 4 for a comparison of counterfactual explanation approaches. Finally, Sect. 5 discusses related work, and Sect. 6 concludes the paper and spells out directions for future work.

2   Background

In this section, we introduce the main concepts useful to understand the remainder of the paper.

2.1   Event Logs

An *event log* $\mathcal{L}$ is a set of traces (a.k.a. cases), each representing one execution of a process. A trace $\sigma = \langle e_1, e_2, \ldots e_n \rangle$ consists of a sequence of *events* e_i, each referring to the execution of an activity (a.k.a. an event class). In addition to a timestamp, indicating the time in which the event has occurred, an event in a trace may have a *data payload* consisting of attributes such as the resource(s) involved in the execution of the corresponding activity, or other data specific of the event. Some of these attributes are attributes that do not change for events belonging to the same trace, i.e., they are attributes that refer to the whole trace (*trace attributes*) as, for instance, the personal data of a customer in a purchase process. Other attributes are specific to an event (*event attributes*) as, for instance, the employee who creates an offer, which is specific to the activity Create offer. Traces with payloads can be represented as follows:

$$\sigma = (\{t^1, \ldots t^s\}, \langle e_1\{d_1^1, d_1^2, \ldots, d_1^p\}, e_2\{d_2^1, d_2^2, \ldots, d_2^q\}, \ldots, e_n\{d_n^1, d_n^2, \ldots, d_n^r\} \rangle),$$

where each t^i is a trace attribute and each d_l^k is an event attribute.

2.2   Declare Models

When generating counterfactuals for a process execution, it is critical to determine whether these alternative scenarios preserve specific process constraints (expressed in the form of temporal patterns). The temporal patterns we use in this paper are based on Declare, a language for describing declarative process models first introduced in [10]. A Declare model consists of a set of constraints

Table 1. Main `Declare` templates

Template	Description
EXISTENCE(1,A)	A occurs at least once
RESPONDED_EXISTENCE(A,B)	If A occurs, then B occurs
RESPONSE(A,B)	If A occurs, then B occurs after A
ALT.RESPONSE(A, B)	Each time A occurs, then B occurs after, before A occurs
CHAINRESPONSE(A, B)	Each time A occurs, then B occurs immediately after
PRECEDENCE(A, B)	B occurs only if preceded by A

applied to (atomic) activities. Constraints are, in turn, based on templates. Templates are abstract parameterized patterns and constraints are their concrete instantiations on real activities. Templates have formal semantics expressed in Linear Temporal Logic for finite traces (LTL_f), making them verifiable and executable. Table 1 summarizes the main `Declare` constructs used in this paper. The reader can refer to [10] for a full description of the language.

An aspect of interest for this work is that of trace-based support (or simply *support*), i.e., a normalized measure quantifying how often a constraint is satisfied in the traces of an event log. The support is useful to determine whether the generated counterfactuals satisfy the frequent patterns observed in the whole event log.

2.3 Counterfactual Explanations

Compared to other types of XAI methods, such as feature attribution methods [11], counterfactuals do not attempt to explain the inner logic of a predictive model but instead offer a recourse to the user in order to obtain a desired prediction [13]. When dealing with black-box models, indeed, the internal logic of a model b mapping a sample x to a label y (also called class value) is unknown, or otherwise uninterpretable to humans. A counterfactual c of x is a sample for which the prediction of the black box is different from the one of x (i.e., $b(c) \neq b(x)$). A counterfactual explainer is a function f_k, where k is the number of requested counterfactuals, such that, for a given sample of interest x, a black box model b, and the set X of known samples from the training set, returns a set $C = c_1, \ldots, c_h$ counterfactuals (with $h \leq k$), i.e., $f_k(x, b, X) = C$.

2.4 Diverse Counterfactual Explanations

Diverse Counterfactual Explanations (DICE) [9] is a framework for generating counterfactuals. Given a *query instance* (i.e., a sample) with label y, DICE returns a list of counterfactuals of an alternative class, which are as close as possible to the initial query instance (according to a given distance metrics). As the name of the framework suggests, in the framework, diversity plays a key role, i.e., the framework tries to maximize the pairwise distance between the generated counterfactuals, while minimizing their distance with respect to the query instance (generating multiple similar counterfactuals would result to be redundant). By maximizing the diversity between counterfactuals, the users are provided with multiple scenarios so that they can choose the easiest way to obtain a desired outcome. For instance, in the loan example, Alice may not have the chance to increase her salary but could follow an alternative counterfactual suggesting to *decrease the loan request by* 15 000 *euros*.

To obtain the desired class, DiCE makes use of a pre-trained predictive model in order to predict the class and to determine how to change the query instance to alter the predicted class. Based on the type of predictive model being used, there are different methods available within DiCE. For non-differentiable models, such as Random Forests (used in this paper), three different methods are available: RANDOM, K-D TREE and GENETIC. Amongst the different frameworks for generating counterfactuals (see [12] for a comprehensive review), DiCE was chosen due to its emphasis on generating multiple diverse explanations as compared to other frameworks returning a single counterfactual.

3   Evaluation Framework

In this section, we introduce the *first evaluation framework for evaluating counterfactual approaches in PPM*. As for all frameworks evaluating generic counterfactual approaches [4], approaches, evaluation metrics and other possible dimensions affecting the results have to be taken into consideration. However, differently from the generic counterfactual approaches, in the PPM setting, some more aspects need to be considered. First of all, counterfactual approaches in PPM are characterized not only by the (family of) counterfactual generation methods used, but also by the way in which the log traces are encoded. Moreover, the evaluation metrics have also to consider whether the generated counterfactual is an execution of the considered process, i.e., whether it is compliant with some process constraints characteristic of that specific process. Finally, the length of the prefixes used for making predictions needs to be taken into account, as the generated counterfactuals can vary a lot depending on the point of the process execution in which they are generated.

The proposed evaluation framework relies hence on three dimensions: (i) the **approaches** characterized by the combination of counterfactual generation methods and encodings; (ii) the set of **evaluation metrics** for comparing the approaches (in PPM); (iii) the impact of the specific prefix length on the other two dimensions. In the following subsections, we discuss the first two dimensions. We first identify a set of possible methods for generating counterfactuals in PPM (and possible encodings) and, then, we describe the evaluation metrics used.

3.1   Generating Counterfactual Explanations in PPM

When choosing counterfactual generation methods and encodings, different techniques able to return diverse counterfactuals, and different encodings exist. In the following, we justify and report on the selected families of counterfactual generation methods and considered encodings.

Families of Counterfactual Generation Methods. Within the literature, different techniques able to return a set of diverse counterfactuals exist. Amongst them, techniques such as LORE [3] and LORELEY [6], generate counterfactual rules from which we sample to create diverse counterfactuals. Differently, techniques such as DICE [9] focus on directly generating diverse counterfactual examples. In our evaluation framework, DICE [9] was chosen due to its availability of different strategies for generating a set of diverse counterfactuals.

We identified three different families of counterfactual generation methods: *case-based*, *generative* and *semi-generative*. For each of these families, we selected a method implemented in the DICE framework:

- Methods based on *case-based* reasoning search for counterfactuals of an input query in the sample population. They consider the closest traces in a training event log with respect to a distance function and return the top k traces labelled with the class the user asks for. Within DICE, the only *case-based* method available is K-D TREE. The K-D TREE method finds the closest points in a dataset with predictions in the desired class. To this aim, a K-D TREE, i.e., a binary tree used for space-partitioning k-dimensional data, is built for each of the classes. The K-D TREE divides the parameter space into nested orthogonal regions to minimize the number of queries needed to identify the nearest neighbours with respect to a point.
- Generative methods generate synthetic counterfactuals (i.e., counterfactuals that are not in the sample population) by altering the input query. Within DICE, there is only one generative method available for non-differentiable predictive models, namely RANDOM. The RANDOM method works by iteratively changing one feature at a time, in the input query, until the desired class is predicted. The changed input is provided as a counterfactual. To achieve this, the permitted feature ranges are extracted for each feature and used to avoid generating values outside those ranges.
- The class of *semi-generative* methods lies between *case-based* and *generative* strategies. Within DICE, the GENETIC method is the only *semi-generative* method available. It works by leveraging a genetic algorithm to perform random mating operations to obtain new synthetic counterfactual candidates. The mating operation randomly changes a feature (also taking values inside pre-computed permitted feature ranges) in the initial candidates identified after an initialization phase. Amongst the possible ways for identifying the initial candidates, we selected the one in which a K-D TREE structure is used to generate an initial neighbourhood of traces close to the query instance from a training log.

PPM Encodings. In order to be used by counterfactual methods, traces need to be *encoded* into a format that is understandable for these methods. Three of the encodings are often used when encoding traces for PPM: simple index; simple-trace index; and complex-index encoding. In our study, we include LORELEY as a fourth encoding (rather than a method), as one main contribution of LORELEY [6] is the use of the encoding to generate valid counterfactuals.

More specifically, each trace (prefix) $\sigma_i^m =< e_{i_1}, ..., e_{i_m} >$, $i = 1...k$, has to be represented through a feature vector $g_i =< g_{i_1}, g_{i_2}, ..., g_{i_h} >$.

In the following, we describe the four types of chosen encodings in detail:

- In the `simple-index` encoding [7], the focus is on the events and on the order in which they occur in the trace. Each feature corresponds to a position in the trace and the possible values for each feature are the event classes. The resulting feature vector g_i, for the trace prefix σ_i^m, is $g_i =< a_{i_1}, ..., a_{i_2}, ..., a_{i_m} >$, where a_{i_j} is the event class of the event at position j.

- The `simple-trace index` encoding leverages the same dynamic information related to the sequence of events of the `simple-index` encoding, but it also includes static information related to data (i.e., the trace attributes) in its feature vector. The resulting feature vector g_i, for the trace prefix σ_i^m, is $g_i =< s_i^1, ..., s_i^u, a_{i_1}, a_{i_2}, ..., a_{i_m} >$, where each s_i is a static feature - corresponding to a trace attribute.

- The `loreley` encoding includes the same information as the `simple-trace index`, but encodes the sequence of event classes in a trace as a single feature (each sequence of event classes correspond to a number and the same sequences correspond to the same number). The feature vector, for the trace prefix σ_i, is $g_i =< s_i^1, ..., s_i^u, p_i >$, where each s_i is a static feature - corresponding to a trace attribute - and p_i represents the sequence of event classes of the trace prefix σ_i^m as a single feature. This encoding was introduced in [6] to generate counterfactuals preserving process constraint satisfaction.

- In the `complex-index` [7] encoding, the event classes and both static and dynamic data attributes of a trace are encoded in the vector. This encoding is similar to `simple-index` with the addition of event attributes. The resulting feature vector g_i, for σ_i^m, is $g_i =< s_i^1, ..., s_i^u, a_{i_1}, a_{i_2}, ..., a_{i_m}, h_{i_1}^1, h_{i_2}^1 ...\, _{i_m}^1, ..., h_{i_1}^r, h_{i_2}^r, ..., h_{i_m}^r >$, where each s_i is a static feature - corresponding to a trace attribute, each a_{i_j} is the event class of the event at position j, and each h_{i_j} is a dynamic feature - corresponding to an event attribute.

3.2   Evaluation Metrics

To evaluate the performance of the selected counterfactual approaches in PPM, we adapted the evaluation protocol presented in [4] to the PPM domain. To this aim, we introduced a new metrics assessing to what extent the generated counterfactuals are executions of the process under analysis by evaluating their compliance with some properties, which are assumed to hold in the process and are represented as `Declare` patterns. The reason `Declare` was chosen is that declarative models offer more flexible process representations, making them suitable for checking counterfactual conformance. In particular, `Declare` was used due to the availability of robust tools, such as RuM [2]. We nonetheless need to point out that other choices are possible. Indeed, procedural process model languages, such as BPMN or Petri nets, could be used to evaluate compliance.

The chosen metrics refer to a single query instance x to be explained and consider the returned counterfactual set $C = f_k(x, b, X)$. Four out of the seven metrics evaluate the quality of the returned counterfactuals, *hit rate* focuses on the capability of the methods to return the requested number of counterfactuals (k), *runtime* measures the time required to generate the counterfactuals, while *sat score* focuses on the compliance of the counterfactuals with some given process constraints:

- The *distance* metrics measures the average distance between the query instance x and the counterfactuals in C. This metrics is used to understand the dissimilarity in the feature space between the query instance and the generated counterfactuals. The metrics is a weighted combination of the Jaccard distance J, for categorical features, and the Euclidean Distance d, for continuous features based on the ratio of categorical and continuous features:

$$ J(x,y) = 1 - \frac{|x \cap y|}{|x \cup y|} \qquad d(x,y) = \sqrt{\sum_{i=1}^{n} (y_i - x_i)^2}. \qquad (1) $$

  For good counterfactuals, the *distance* metrics is low.
- The *implausibility* metrics determines how close the generated counterfactuals are to the reference population. This metrics is the average distance between each counterfactual in C and the trace in the training set, which is the closest to it. For good counterfactuals, the *implausibility* metrics is low.
- The *diversity* metrics measures the average pairwise *distance* between the counterfactuals in C. The *diversity* in C should be high.
- The *avg. changes* metrics measures how many features have been changed in each counterfactual with respect to the query instance averaged over the total number of counterfactuals generated. A low number of changed features is preferred.
- The *hit rate* metrics is defined as h/k, where $h = |C|$ is the number of generated counterfactuals, and k the number of requested counterfactuals (see Sect. 2.3). The value of *hit rate* should be high.
- The *runtime* (measured in seconds) is the time to compute the requested number of counterfactuals.
- The *sat score* metrics determines the ratio of counterfactuals that satisfy all the process (`Declare`) constraints underlying the considered process. A high *sat score* indicates a high compliance of the generated counterfactuals with the constraints.

4   Evaluation

In this section, we apply the framework described in Sect. 3 for evaluating the identified counterfactual approaches in PPM. Our goal is to evaluate how they perform, by taking into account: (i) the quality of the returned counterfactuals; (ii) the number of returned counterfactuals with respect to the number of requested ones; (iii) the time required for computing them; and (iv) their compliance with process constraints characterizing the process under examination. In particular, we investigate the following research questions:

Table 2. The constraints used for the labelings

ϕ_1 = EXISTENCE(1.ACCEPT LOAN APPLICATION)
ϕ_2 = EXISTENCE(1.CANCEL LOAN APPLICATION)
ϕ_3 = EXISTENCE(1.REJECT LOAN APPLICATION)
ϕ_4 = RESPONSE(SEND CONFIRMATION RECEIPT.RETRIEVE MISSING DATA)
ϕ_5 = EXISTENCE(1.ACCEPT LOAN APPLICATION)
ϕ_6 = EXISTENCE(1.CANCEL LOAN APPLICATION)
ϕ_7 = EXISTENCE(1.REJECT LOAN APPLICATION)
ϕ_8 = EXISTENCE(1.PATIENT RETURNS TO THE EMERGENCY ROOM WITHIN 28 DAYS FROM DISCHARGE)
ϕ_9 = EXISTENCE(1.PATIENT IS (EVENTUALLY) ADMITTED TO INTENSIVE CARE)
ϕ_{10} = EXISTENCE(1.PATIENT IS DISCHARGED FROM THE HOSPITAL ON THE BASIS OF SOMETHING OTHER THAN RELEASE A)

RQ1. How do different event log characteristics affect the generated counter-factuals (for different prefix lengths) in terms of their quality, number, required time and process model compliance?

RQ2. How does the choice of the trace encoding affect the generated counter-factuals (for different prefix lengths) in terms of their quality, number, required time and process model compliance?

RQ1 aims at identifying how different event log characteristics affect the generated counterfactuals in terms of quality, *hit-rate*, *runtime*, and *sat score*. **RQ2** focuses on how the trace encodings employed affect the same dimensions. In the following subsections, we first describe the event logs used in our evaluation framework, then the experimental setting, and finally discuss the results.

4.1   Datasets

To compare the counterfactual approaches, we selected 4 different real-life event logs, labelled according to the satisfaction of their traces with respect to the 10 `Declare` constraints shown in Table 2. We used, in total, 14 datasets (combinations of event logs and labelings). The event logs were chosen because they contain both static (trace) and dynamic (event) attributes, and present a wide range of different characteristics. Table 3 reports, for each dataset, the number of traces, variants (i.e., unique sequences of event classes), event attributes, and trace attributes of the log,[1] and the constraint used for the labelling.

4.2   Experimental Setting

For each dataset, trace encoding, and prefix length in the range $\{5, 10, 15, 20, 25\}$, we trained a Random Forest (RF) model using the Python library scikit-learn to access all methods available in DICE (which uses scikit-learn in the backend). We split the data into $70\% - 10\% - 20\%$ partitioning for training, validation, and testing, respectively. For the predictive model, hyperparameter optimization was performed using the Hyperopt Python library to identify the best model configuration for each dataset. For DICE, instead, the default setting for each method was used. Then, each of the three methods RANDOM, GENETIC, and K-D

---

[1] The BPIC2015 consists of 5 variants of the same process.

Table 3. Event log statistics and labellings

Dataset	Event Log	trace#	variant#	event class#	trace att.#	event att.#	avg. trace length	labeling formula
BPIC2012_1	BPIC2012	4685	3790	36	1	11	35	ϕ_1
BPIC2012_2								ϕ_2
BPIC2012_3								ϕ_3
BPIC2015_1	BPIC2015 _1	696	677	380	15	14	42	ϕ_4
BPIC2015_2	BPIC2015 _2	753	752	396	15	14	55	ϕ_4
BPIC2015_3	BPIC2015 _3	1328	1285	380	15	14	42	ϕ_4
BPIC2015_4	BPIC2015 _4	577	576	319	15	14	42	ϕ_4
BPIC2015_5	BPIC2015 _5	1051	1049	376	15	14	50	ϕ_4
BPIC2017_1	BPIC2017	31413	2087	36	3	20	35	ϕ_5
BPIC2017_2								ϕ_6
BPIC2017_3								ϕ_7
Sepsis_1	SEPSIS	782	709	15	24	13	14	ϕ_8
Sepsis_2								ϕ_9
Sepsis_3								ϕ_{10}

TREE was run using the same trained RF to obtain the predicted labels of the counterfactuals. The training set used to train the RF model was used as input for the counterfactual generation methods. The query instances were taken from the testing set. DiCE leverages such an input to determine the possible range of values that each feature can take, and, in the case of *case-based*, to build the data structures required and identify the counterfactuals in the training set.

The experiments were performed over traces with variable prefix lengths to determine whether different prefix lengths affect the results of the counterfactual generation process. This was done (similarly to other PPM evaluations) to determine how the technique performs based on the amount of information available up to a certain cut-off point. We also examined different settings for the counterfactual generation process, where we ask for 5, 10, 15 and 20 counterfactual examples to be returned [4]. This was done to determine whether the number of counterfactuals has an impact on the quality of the generated counterfactuals, execution time and satisfiability of the counterfactuals.

Since we did not have knowledge on the process models generating the different logs, the `Declare` process constraints used for computing the *sat score* metrics were discovered from the traces in the event log considering the `Declare` constraints satisfied by all traces in the whole training event log (i.e., with 100% support).[23]

4.3   Results

We now report the aggregated results for each event log and, then, for each encoding (see Fig. 1 and Fig. 2) are available at DiCE_results[4]. In Fig. 1 we report the

---

[2] The discovery was done on complete traces, while the *sat score* was computed for prefixes, where constraints may be temporarily violated but become satisfied as the execution continues.

[3] We used the rule mining tool RuM [2].

[4] The complete results per dataset and discovered `Declare` models are available at DiCE_results.

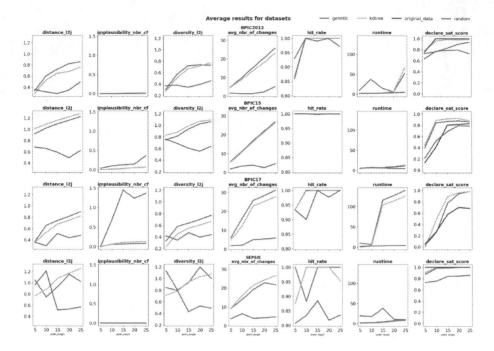

Fig. 1. Results related to counterfactual quality, *hit rate*, *runtime* and *sat score* for each event log, measured over variable prefix lengths.

performance metrics of the investigated approaches for the four event logs aggregated over the encodings and the datasets. For the *sat score* metrics (last column), we also report the *sat score* value related to the query instances.[5] The *sat score* of the query instances is represented by the blue line named *original_data*. This is only shown in the *sat score* column to show how the *sat score* changes with respect to the original traces used for counterfactual generation.

By looking at the figure, we can observe that in terms of *diversity* and *implausibility*, all techniques perform better on small event logs, e.g., SEPSIS, and worse on large and complex logs, e.g., BPIC2012 and BPIC2017. On the other hand, when looking at the *distance* and the *avg. changes* metrics, larger datasets perform best (BPIC2017 has the best performance). Also in terms of *hit rate*, the largest event logs, and in particular BPIC2017, are the best performing ones, especially for GENETIC and RANDOM. As expected, the time required for the computation - especially for K-D TREE and GENETIC- is higher for larger event logs (e.g., BPIC2017). When dealing with *sat score* values, we can notice that BPIC2015 and BPIC2017 have low performance, especially for short prefixes. This is possibly because these event logs have longer traces on average and the discovered patterns are satisfied later in the traces. Amongst the three methods,

---

[5] Since we are considering trace prefixes, it can happen that the prefix does not satisfy a process constraint, which will, instead, be satisfied in the complete trace.

RANDOM performs worst while K-D TREE performs as good if not better than the actual input queries in terms of *sat score*, especially for datasets with a high variant ratio (number of variants over the number of traces).

By focusing on the impact of the prefix length on the results, we notice that the counterfactual quality increases with the length of the prefix, although the quality is lower for RANDOM compared to GENETIC and K-D TREE. As RANDOM only changes a small subset of features to flip the prediction, *diversity* and *implausibility* perform badly, while *distance* performs well (with low values). The opposite happens for GENETIC and K-D TREE, which are bound to the number of variants in the event log, i.e., they achieve good results for *diversity* and *implausibility* and perform worse for *distance*. No clear trend can be devised for the *hit rate* metrics, although, for this metrics, RANDOM performs generally worse than the other methods. Although the *runtime* metrics does not change much across prefix lengths, for large event logs (BPIC2017) there is a sharp increase in the time required for generating the counterfactuals, especially for K-D TREE and GENETIC. The *sat score* metrics significantly increases for BPIC2015 and BPIC2017 around prefix length 15, while it does not vary a lot for the other two event logs. Overall, the trend of *sat score* for the tested methods is close to the one obtained for the *original_data–* and in some cases the value is even higher. The score varies with the prefix length, thus suggesting that this behaviour strongly depends on the point in time in which the process model constraints are checked and confirming the ability of the three methods to generate counterfactuals that maintain the same level of process conformance as the query instances.

To sum up, the different characteristics of the considered event logs have an impact on the considered metrics: large and complex event logs perform better in terms of *distance* and *avg. changes*, while smaller and simpler datasets do better in terms of *implausibility*, *diversity*, *hit rate* and *runtime*. Furthermore, in general, the counterfactual quality increases with the prefix length, i.e., when more information is available in the query instance (**RQ1**).

Figure 2 reports the performance metrics of the investigated approaches for the four encodings aggregated over all the datasets. Also in this case, we report in the last column the *sat score* of the query instances (*original_data*). In terms of encodings, the counterfactuals generated with the `complex-index` encoding present much higher values for *distance*, *diversity*, *implausibility* and *avg. changes* when compared to the other encodings, due to the dimensionality of the data - `complex-index` has a significantly larger feature space due to the inclusion of the event attributes. On the other hand, `loreley` presents the lowest score for *distance*, *implausibility*, and *diversity*, possibly due to the reduced feature space when compared to the other encodings.

In addition, the `complex-index` encoding registers the highest fluctuation, in terms of counterfactual quality, across different prefix lengths. We can also notice that, for this encoding, as the prefix length increases, also the gap between the quality of the counterfactuals generated with K-D TREE and GENETIC, and the quality of the counterfactuals generated with RANDOM increases. For the other

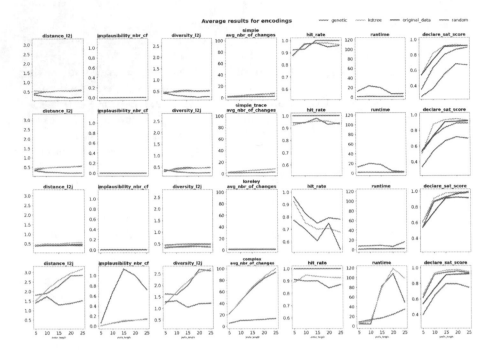

Fig. 2. Results related to counterfactual quality, *hit rate*, *runtime* and *sat score* for each encoding, measured over variable prefix lengths.

three encodings, instead, the quality of the counterfactuals is more stable. From the plots, it is also clear that the *hit rate* remains quite stable for different prefix lengths - except for the `loreley` encoding for which the *hit rate* drastically decreases when the prefix length increases. This behaviour depends on the fact that since `loreley` encodes the sequence of event classes in a trace as a single feature, when the prefix length increases - differently from the other encodings - the number of features remains static. This results in a worse *hit rate* for large prefixes, especially for RANDOM. Finally, the *sat score* increases with the prefix length for all encodings, matching the *original_data*.

To sum up, the encodings impact the quality of the counterfactuals, the *runtime*, and the *sat score* metrics. Enriching the feature space by including data from different perspectives (event classes, trace, and event attributes) increases the overall *diversity* of the counterfactuals, but negatively impacts *distance*, *implausibility* and especially the *runtime* metrics. Moreover, in many cases, the values of the different performance metrics are quite stable for different prefix lengths. The encoding that shows the highest degree of fluctuation, across the different prefix lengths, is the `complex-index` encoding. In addition, for the `loreley` encoding the *hit rate* decreases when the prefix length increases and the *sat score* metrics increases with the prefix length for all the encodings (**RQ2**).

```
Query instance (original outcome : 1)
    AMOUNT_REQ           prefix_1                prefix_2              prefix_3             prefix_4                  prefix_5
3    15000.0  asubmittedcomplete  apartlysubmittedcomplete  apreacceptedcomplete  wcompleterenaanvraagschedule  wcompleterenaanvraagstart

Diverse Counterfactual set (new outcome: 0.0)
      AMOUNT_REQ prefix_1 prefix_2            prefix_3 prefix_4                prefix_5 label
0   75657.5368705       -        -                   -        -  wbeoordelenfraudecomplete     0
1    1838.99697425       -        -  wbeoordelenfraudeschedule        -                       -     0
2   93063.62895225       -        -                   -        -                       -     0
3    45063.9698255       -        -                   -        -                       -     0
4   70369.45523175       -        -                   -        -  wafhandelenleadscomplete     0
```

Fig. 3. Example output of DiCE with `simple-trace index` and RANDOM and k=5 for BPIC2012.

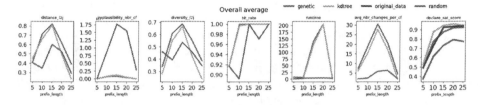

Fig. 4. Average results related to counterfactual quality, hit rate and diversity over all the event logs.

4.4 Discussion

Before moving on to the discussion of the results, we highlight an example output from DiCE, showcasing the modifications made to the original query instance using the RANDOM Fig. 3.

By taking into account the observations above and looking at the aggregated results computed by averaging the results over all datasets and encodings (reported in Fig. 4), we can draw some general findings. The *distance* metrics and the *avg. changes* metrics tend to be higher for the *case-based* and *semi-generative* methods, while *implausibility* is higher for the *generative* ones. This pattern is due to the nature of the *generative* methods that apply changes to a limited subset of features to flip the prediction, thus leading to counterfactuals obtained with a lower number of changes over the query instance and having a lower distance from it. In addition, since these changes are not driven by the historical knowledge of a training set, this results in a higher *implausibility* of the counterfactuals generated with the *generative* methods. For the same reason, the *generative* methods have also a lower compliance with the underlying structure of the process at hand, with respect to the *case-based* and *semi-generative* methods. Therefore, we can state that *case-based* and *semi-generative* based methods represent the best solution if the objective of the analyst is to optimize *diversity*, *implausibility* and *sat score*, while the *generative* ones are to be preferred when the *avg. changes* and the minimality of the *distance* of the counterfactuals from the input instance are more crucial.

We also highlight that, for the *case-based* methods, the results strongly depend on the volume and variety of available training data, which also somehow affect the *semi-generative* methods that use training data in the initialization phase. Therefore, these methods can be effectively applied when historical data of good quality is available. Finally, the *generative* methods return a lower number of counterfactuals in less time. For this reason, the *generative* methods are to be preferred when it is essential to get counterfactuals quickly (e.g., in real-time applications), while the *case-based* and *semi-generative* approaches provide the analysts with more options that can be chosen also at the expense of higher *runtime*.

Reflection on the Challenges and Limitations of the Framework. Given the three challenges presented in the introduction, *insights* and limitations emerged. We believe a trace counterfactual should share the typical properties of a good counterfactual [4], that is, providing an actionable, and plausible alternative to reach a desired outcome by minimising changed attributes. In addition, the counterfactual should maintain process conformance. To account for the multi-dimensionality of process executions, rather than focusing on a single counterfactual, a good technique should provide a set of diverse counterfactuals.

The metrics used in the evaluation assessed the desirable properties of counterfactuals, although limitations emerged during development. The selected distance metrics cannot account for implausible counterfactuals caused by feature value combinations. Sparse counterfactuals are considered more actionable, but sparsity in process mining is challenging as the results may depend on encoding.

Finally, concerning counterfactual generation for PPM, although mature techniques for counterfactual generation are emerging, more process-specific techniques are needed that meet the required properties for trace counterfactuals.

5   Related Work

The existing literature related to XAI applied to PPM can be roughly classified into two groups: the approaches relying on factual explanations and the ones relying on counterfactual explanations. Concerning the first group of works, most of the XAI techniques in PPM focus on providing factual explanations using well-known model-agnostic frameworks, such as LIME or SHAP [11]. This paper focuses on the second group of works, focusing on counterfactual explanations, which can be classified into two categories. The first category poses the counterfactual generation problem as an optimization problem where the input is altered until the desired outcome is reached, while the second one focuses on finding counterfactuals in a dataset, as an example-based explanation [4].

So far, two works have tackled the counterfactual generation problem in PPM. The first paper introduces LORELEY, an adaptation of the Local Rule-Based Explanations (LORE) framework [3], which generates counterfactual explanations leveraging a surrogate decision tree model using a genetically generated neighbourhood of artificial data instances to be trained [3,6]. The prediction task the authors address is the one of multi-class outcome prediction. To ensure the generation of realistic counterfactuals, LORELEY imposes process constraints in the counterfactual generation process.

The second work presents DICE for Event Logs (DICE4EL) [5], which extends the gradient-based method in DICE by adding an optimization function to generate the counterfactuals by maximizing the likelihood that they belong to the training set. The prediction task addressed in the paper is the one of next activity prediction with a milestone-aware focus. Since DICE4EL does not focus on the outcome prediction task, their work was not considered in the evaluation we carried out.

Our work is complementary to the works just described since it provides the first evaluation of approaches for the generation of counterfactuals for the outcome prediction task.

6   Conclusions

This paper tackles the task of comparing approaches for the generation of counterfactuals for outcome-based predictions in PPM. To this aim, we defined a framework for evaluating these approaches and applied it against several real-life datasets. The results show that different approaches can better suit different log characteristics and can face different needs that an analyst could have with respect to the task of generating counterfactual explanations in PPM. In the future, we plan to learn from the analysis carried out in this study to improve the weaknesses of the existing approaches. For instance, besides refining the evaluation so as to ensure the conformance of the query instance prefix, we would like to constrain the *generative* techniques by directly incorporating the temporal process patterns into the counterfactual generation procedure to improve the plausibility and process compliance of the generated counterfactuals.

References

1. van der Aalst, W.M.P.: Process Mining - Data Science in Action, 2nd edn. Springer, Cham (2016)
2. Alman, A., Di Ciccio, C., Maggi, F.M.: Rule mining with rum (extended abstract). CEUR Workshop Proc. **2952**, 38–43 (2021)
3. Guidotti, R., Monreale, A., Ruggieri, S., Pedreschi, D., Turini, F., Giannotti, F.: Local rule-based explanations of black box decision systems. arXiv preprint: arXiv:1805.10820 (2018)
4. Guidotti, R., Ruggieri, S.: Ensemble of counterfactual explainers. In: Soares, C., Torgo, L. (eds.) DS 2021. LNCS (LNAI), vol. 12986, pp. 358–368. Springer, Cham (2021). https://doi.org/10.1007/978-3-030-88942-5_28
5. Hsieh, C., Moreira, C., Ouyang, C.: Dice4el: interpreting process predictions using a milestone-aware counterfactual approach. In: ICPM, pp. 88–95 (2021)
6. Huang, T., Metzger, A., Pohl, K.: Counterfactual explanations for predictive business process monitoring. In: Themistocleous, M., Papadaki, M. (eds.) Information Systems. EMCIS 2021. Lecture Notes in Business Information Processing, vol. 437, pp. 399–413. Springer, Cham (2021). https://doi.org/10.1007/978-3-030-95947-0_28

7. Leontjeva, A., Conforti, R., Di Francescomarino, C., Dumas, M., Maggi, F.M.: Complex symbolic sequence encodings for predictive monitoring of business processes. In: Motahari-Nezhad, H.R., Recker, J., Weidlich, M. (eds.) BPM 2015. LNCS, vol. 9253, pp. 297–313. Springer, Cham (2015). https://doi.org/10.1007/978-3-319-23063-4_21

8. Maggi, F.M., Di Francescomarino, C., Dumas, M., Ghidini, C.: Predictive monitoring of business processes. In: Jarke, M., et al. (eds.) CAiSE 2014. LNCS, vol. 8484, pp. 457–472. Springer, Cham (2014). https://doi.org/10.1007/978-3-319-07881-6_31

9. Mothilal, R.K., Sharma, A., Tan, C.: Explaining machine learning classifiers through diverse counterfactual explanations, pp. 607–617. FAT* 2020 (2020)

10. Pesic, M., Schonenberg, H., van der Aalst, W.M.: Declare: Full support for loosely-structured processes. In: EDOC 2007, pp. 287–287 (2007)

11. Stierle, M., Brunk, J., Weinzierl, S., Zilker, S., Matzner, M., Becker, J.: Bringing light into the darkness-a systematic literature review on explainable predictive business process monitoring techniques. ECIS Research-in-Progress Papers (2021)

12. Verma, S., Dickerson, J.P., Hines, K.: Counterfactual explanations for machine learning: a review. CoRR abs/2010.10596 (2020)

13. Wachter, S., Mittelstadt, B.D., Russell, C.: Counterfactual explanations without opening the black box: automated decisions and the GDPR. CoRR abs/1711.00399 (2017)

Service-Related Approaches

Identifying and Removing the Ghosts of Reproducibility in Service Recommendation Research

Tianyu Jiang[ID], Mingyi Liu[ID], Zhiying Tu[ID], and Zhongjie Wang[✉][ID]

Faculty of Computing, Harbin Institute of Technology, Harbin, China
tianyujiang@stu.hit.edu.cn, {liumy,tzy_hit,rainy}@hit.edu.cn

Abstract. A service recommendation system is an information system that helps build mashups quickly to implement new features in response to environmental changes. With the development of deep learning (DL) in recent years, more researchers have started using DL-based methods to solve service recommendation problem and have achieved remarkable results. However, these works have some common deficiencies on non-unified dataset, pre-trained model, evaluation protocol, and experiment environment. These issues will disrupt evaluating the performance of models accurately and make reproducing them difficult. To solve these problems, we propose a service mashup recommendation benchmark (SMRB) that provides a standard environment to enhance comparability between models and credibility of results. We implement eight models (five from top service computing conferences and journals and three created by ourselves) based on SMRB and compare their performance, which proves the effectiveness of SMRB. After analyzing these results, we found that most DL-based models do not perform as well as they promise; instead, the simplest Multilayer perceptron (MLP) models perform better after tuning the parameters, which inspires us to re-examine whether the particular structure of the model can be helpful for the intended purpose and whether it can really improve the performance of the recommendation.

Keywords: Service recommendation · Reproducibility · Benchmark · Standard environment

1 Introduction

Mashups are ideal for meeting customer requirements because they can quickly create new features by integrating existing web services [20]. The open ecosystem increases the quantity and diversity of available web services, making choosing the right services for a specific mashup difficult [4,9,17]. The Service recommendation system is emerged to address this problem [2]. The core algorithm of this system is receiving the nature language described requirements of mashups as input, and outputting a rating of the APIs relevant to the mashup. Then, developers can choose the relevant APIs from the ranking to reduce their burden.

M. Indulska et al. (Eds.): CAiSE 2023, LNCS 13901, pp. 577–593, 2023.
https://doi.org/10.1007/978-3-031-34560-9_34

Service mashup recommendation has become a research hotspot in the research community, and there are many remarkable methods. Traditional methods for service recommendation can be divided into two classes: *1) collaborative filtering (CF) based methods* [21]. According to the classic CF algorithm, this class regards the mashup as the "user" and the API as the "item". Then, it analyzes the invocation relationship to obtain the similarity between mashups or APIs and finally recommends APIs. *2) content based methods* [7]. This class focuses on the matching degree between Web APIs and the mashup's requirement and recommends Web APIs that are close to the requirement for the mashup. To improve the accuracy of recommendations, such methods often use other additional attributes of Web APIs or mashups, such as tags, topics, popularity, etc.

With the development of deep learning, neural network have been widely used in service recommendation system and an enormous amount of publications have been yielded in recent years. This class of methods extracts the features of mashups and APIs through neural networks, then fuses the two and calculates the score for recommending. The core of this type of approach is learning a valid feature representation. Relying on the high expressive power of neural networks, this class achieves promising results. However, DL methods have more randomness than others, such as random order of training data, random initialization of model parameters, random multi-threaded training of GPU, etc. These bring a ghost of reproducibility existing in the deep learning model. Besides, the service computing community currently does not pay enough attention to the reproducibility of models. As a result, many works have various problems, such as lack of open source code, lack of key parameters, lack of data, unreasonable experimental settings, etc., which further reduces the credibility of these studies.

In this study, we address the research questions:

- **RQ1.** What are the challenges in reproducing service recommendation research? We surveys DL-based studies and summarized them.
- **RQ2.** How do we ensure reproducibility? We provide a standard environment to called SMRB for the service recommendation task.

The main contributions of this paper are summarized as follows:

1. We summarize the problems in service mashup recommendation, including the lack of uniform datasets, pre-trained models, evaluation protocols, and experiment environment, and analyze the consequences they caused. Section 2.
2. We propose a service mashup recommendation benchmark (SMRB) that provides a standard environment to evaluate the performance of service mashup recommendation models and simplify code development for researchers. Section 3.
3. We implement 8 popular state-of-the-art models based on SMRB, compare them in a unified environment, and prove the effectiveness of SMRB. Section 4.

4. We open all code for SMRB and reproduced models[1]. Relevant researchers are free to use it to evaluate their own models in the standard environment.

2   Challenges of Reproducibility

This study surveys some DL-based works in recent years and maps the details into Table 1. By analyzing the results, we found the challenges of reproducibility in these studies, as seen by the following:

1. **Datasets**: *Programmable Web*[2], the largest online Web service registry, provides almost all of the mashups and APIs data utilized in existing service mashup recommendation studies. However, researchers crawled the data independently, resulting in different versions, amounts, etc., and cleaned it through different processes. ProgrammableWeb provides all kinds of metadata for each mashup and API, such as name, description, category, tags, invoked relationship, etc. The usage of metadata varies significantly. Some works rely on description and invoked relationship [9,10], while others include category, tags, and other metadata [3]. In general, more metadata will provide richer information and more feature, but the larger dimension of vectors and more neural cells in the model. Richer information will result in a more excellent performance. Still, it is hard to say does it benefits from more neural cells, especially when they lack well-designed ablation studies.

2. **Pre-trained models**: A mashup or API requirement is usually supplied in textual form and necessitates Natural Language Processing (NLP) technology to convert it into a computable vector. There are various pre-trained models that appear in articles related to service recommendation, such as *LDA* [15], *HDP* [3], *GloVe* [17], *BERT* [9], etc. It's hard to judge whether the differences in experimental results are attributable to the two distinct pre-trained models. For example, BERT is more complicated and effective than GloVe, and it usually has a more significant favorable influence on the experiment's result, which interferes with the evaluation of the model's qualities. Some works attempt to train such pre-trained models from scratch [11], but they do so with the total data, which leads to potential data leaking. At the same time, such training is expensive, and the amount of PW data is too small to obtain an excellent pre-trained language model from scratch.

3. **Evaluation protocol**: Different evaluation protocol will disrupt the measurement of model performance. These differences are mainly manifested in *1) evaluation metrics*: The output of a service mashup recommendation system is a rating of the APIs relevant to the specific mashup requirement. For such form, there are numerous metrics reflecting different aspects. Existing studies usually select some of them to measure the model performance, resulting in a lack of a comprehensive view. Furthermore, the selection of metrics varies between studies and may lead to unfair comparisons between different

---

[1] https://github.com/ssnowyu/SMRB.
[2] https://www.programmableweb.com.

Table 1. Statistics of Community Ground Truth Annotation. - indicates that no relevant information in the work. † indicates that the data is the original crawl data, not necessarily used in the experiment.

Author/Reference	dataset					evaluation protocol			PLM	open source
	source	version	api number	mashup number	metadata	data split	metrics	candidate api		
Wu et al. [17]	PW	Dec-2019	1647	8217	description, invocation matrix	8:1:1	Precision, Recall, NDCG, MAP	all	GloVe	yes
Liu et al. [10]	PW	–	12140†	6976†	description	–	Precision, Recall, F1	200	LDA	no
Yan et al. [18]	PW	Apr-2021	24034†	7974	description, tags	–	HR, NDCG	–	–	no
Ma et al. [11]	PW	25-Jul-2016	728	1979	description, tags, invocation matrix	–	Precision, Recall, NDCG, MAP, F1	all	node2vec	yes
Fletcher et al. [3]	PW	Mar-2018	12879†	–	description, QoS, invocation matrix	7:1:2	Recall, NDCG, MAP	–	HDP	no
Gao et al. [4]	PW	Jun-2014	1559	6339	description, mashup graph, API graph, invocation matrix	–	Precision, Recall, NDCG	all	TF-IDF	no
Liu et al. [9]	PW	10-Oct-2020	720	3379	description	8:0:2	Precision, Recall, F1	all	BERT, Word2vec	no
Shi et al. [15]	PW	Oct-2016	16012	7816	description, mashup-API graph	–	Precision, Recall, F1, Diverstiy	–	LDA	no
Li et al. [7]	PW	–	9192†	6673†	description, category, tags, topic, invocation times	19:1:5	Precision, Recall, F1	–	RTM	no
Qi et al. [13]	PW	–	18478	6146	description, API graph	–	Precision, Recall, Balance, Hit Rate	–	fastText	no
Yao et al. [19]	PW	-	11101†	5658†	name, description, invocation matrix	8:0:2	Precision, Recall	–	TF-IDF	no
Kang et al. [6]	PW	–	100	1993	description, category, popularity	8:0:2	Logloss, AUC	all	Doc2vec	yes
Rahman et al. [14]	PW	–	17564†	6270†	name, description, tags, category, invocation matrix	7:1:2	Precision, Recall, NDCG	–	LDA	no
Jain et al. [5]	PW	–	950	6819	name, description, invocation matrix	–	Precision, Recall, F1	all	LDA	no
Ma et al. [12]	PW	25-Jul-2016	728	1,929	description, tags, invocation matrix	8:0:2	Precision, Recall, F1, MAP	all	LDA	yes
Shi et al. [16]	PW	Oct-2016	12920†	6208†	description, tags	9:0:1	Precision, Recall, F1	–	Word2vec	no

models. Moreover, the reported results usually contain the mean of each metric without mean error or statistical significance, making it difficult to assess the model's robustness and really outperformance. *2) evaluation object*: On the on hand, the model performance should be evaluated using all APIs, i.e., the recommendation is a score ranking of all APIs. If only some APIs are randomly selected to get ranked, it will obtain excellent but inaccurate evaluation results. Furthermore, the uncontrolled random selection process might result in results based on diverse data that are not comparable. On the other hand, the dataset split is also relevant to the model evaluation. Some works configure the validation set, while other works do not. The former can improve the evaluation result by early stopping technique to avoid overfitting. Moreover, the division ratio of the dataset can also affect the evaluation results. The most common division ratio is 7:2:1, but some other ratio divisions exist. Besides, the evaluation results must be obtained on the test set, and there is a high risk of overfitting if they are optimal results on the validation set.

4. **Experiment environment**: Different experimental environments influence the performance of the model. It's hard to standardize the hardware environment for different researchers, but we can control the software environment, such as the same version of the deep learning framework, the same model training process, etc.

The above issues will confuse the evaluation of the actual performance of a model. To be precise, for a good experimental result, we will be unable to explain whether the improvement is due to the model's superiority or other external factors, such as more metadata, better pre-trained models, some specific evaluation protocol, etc. More seriously, these issues increase the work required for reproduction. Even if the reproduction is successful, the results are inconsistent with those reported in the original papers. In response, this study unifieds the datasets, the pre-trained models, the evaluation protocols, and the software environment to build a standard evaluation environment called SMRB for DL-based service mashup recommendation. More details will be described in Sect. 3.

In addition to the problems caused by the substandard environment, coding for a neural network-based service recommendation model for researchers is time-consuming. Some repetitive tasks, such as organizing the dataloader and logging metrics, cost lots of time. In response, we build SMRB based on the open source project *Lightning-Hydra-Template*[3] and encapsulate the provided unified dataset, pre-trained models and metrics into it, which minimizes the code effort for researchers.

3   Introduction to SMRB

Figure 1 shows the architecture of SMRB, with applications, modules, and technologies listed from top to bottom. *1) Applications*: In addition to basic model training, SMRB also supports log, checkpoint, hyperparameter search, and

---

[3] https://github.com/ashleve/lightning-hydra-template.

runtime monitoring. *2) Modules*: SMRB contains seven modules. Datamodule module solves the non-unified datasets, including data source, metadata selection, and dataset split. Pre-trained Model module solves the non-unified preprocessing models. Metric module solves the non-unified evaluation protocol. *3) Technologies*: SMRB relies on PyTorch, PyTorch Lightning, Hydra, and other technologies to minimize development effort and enhance code management.

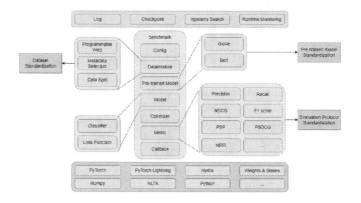

Fig. 1. Architecture of SMRB.

The subsequent parts of this chapter describes in detail how SMRB overcomes the problems described in Sect. 1.

3.1   Dataset Standardization

Programmable Web is favored by researchers according to the literature statistics presented in Table 1. Considering the high recognition, we chose this platform as the data source.

Data Source. We use the *Programmable Web* data crawled by [8], including 6423 mashups and 21633 APIs. Then we deleted mashups that included APIs that were not crawled, yielding 4557 mashups. And delete APIs with no text description, yielding 21495 APIs. Since some APIs have never been used, we provide two types of API data. *1) total data*: 21495 APIs, including some unused APIs. *2) partial data*: 932 APIs, all of which have been used at least once.

Metadata Selection. In the raw data that we obtained, each mashup has name, description, category, tags, url, versions, related APIs, etc., and each Web API has name, description, tags, url, version, etc. Among these metadatas, the description contains the richest information and is most widely used in existing works. So we choose it as the only metadata in our dataset to represent a mashup or a Web API.

Dataset Split. We divide the data into three parts: training set, validation set, and test set, with the ratio of 7 : 2 : 1.

Table 2. Statistical information on different versions of the dataset.

Description	Count(Partial)	Count(Total)
Number of mashups	4557	4557
Number of APIs	932	21495
Number of invocation between mashups and APIs	7139	7139
Average number of APIs invoked by a mashup	1.57	1.57
Average text length of mashup descriptions	27.70	27.70
Average text length of API descriptions	69.34	64.20

After unified processing, we obtained several different versions of the dataset, and Table 2 shows their basic statistical information.

3.2 Pre-trained Model Standardization

Because descriptions are in text form, we must turn them into computable vectors using natural language processing techniques. The typical one is word embedding, which maps natural language words to vectors in space, with each word having only one vector representation. Formally, for a word w, word embedding model converts it into a vector $\mathbf{v}$, where $\mathbf{v} \in \mathbb{R}^d$ and d varies with the models.

Word embedding relies on pre-trained models obtained based on large-scale data training, and we used two popular pre-trained models as alternatives for the benchmark. Notably, we freeze the word embeddings so that they do not change during model training to focus on comparing the model structure while saving computational costs. However, users can also easily use the fine-tune version to accommodate downstream tasks.

1. **GloVe**: A global log-bilinear regression model for unsupervised learning of word representations. GloVe has a pre-trained "word-vector" mapping table, and the representation vector of words can be obtained directly by looking up the table, reducing the computational cost. Since each word gets the representation vector independently, it lacks contextual information and has mediocre semantic expressiveness. SMRB choose Glove.6B.300d[4] pre-trained word vectors which maps a word to a 300-dimensional vector, i.e., $d = 300$.
2. **BERT**: A landmark work in NLP, its full name is Bidirectional Encoder Representations from Transformer. BERT processes the input text by a pre-trained model to obtain a vector representation of each word, which is computationally more expensive than GloVe. It is excellent semantic expressiveness because contextual relationships are taken into account. In this study, we employ the implementation of open source project *transformers*[5], which maps a word to a 768-dimensional vector, i.e. $d = 768$.

---

[4] https://nlp.stanford.edu/projects/glove/.
[5] https://huggingface.co/docs/transformers/model_doc/bert.

We choose 72 words as the norm to deal with varied text lengths of different descriptions and truncate longer text and expand shorter text.

For each text, we obtain a matrix whose size is $(72 \times d)$, where d is the dimension of the word vector. Considering the two most common feature representations in existing works, word-based and text-based, we choose the following two forms: 1) $(72 \times d)$. The original form processed by word embedding model, and each word corresponds to a vector whose size is $(1 \times d)$. This form is suitable for word-based representation. 2) $(1 \times d)$. Pooling the representation whose size is $(72 \times d)$ by averaging to a representation whose size is $(1 \times d)$, with which the whole text is represented. This form is suitable for text-based representation.

3.3   Evaluation Protocol Standardization

We choose metrics widely used in existing work to measure the model performance: precision (P), recall (R), F1 score (F1), Normalized Discounted Cumulative Gain (NDCG), Propensity-score precision (PSP), Propensity-score Discounted Cumulative Gain (PSDCG), and Mean Reciprocal Rank (MRR).

Precision measures the percentage of the Web APIs used by mashup in all the recommended Web APIs. Recall measures what percentage of all APIs used by mashup is included in the recommendation results. Precision and recall are usually mutually constraining, i.e., high precision leads to low recall and vice versa. F1 score is the harmonic mean of Precision and Recall and is more influenced by the extreme low of the two.

Since the recommendation result is an API ranking, it is necessary to consider the API position in the ranking. Discounted Cumulative Gain (DCG) gives high weight to the top-rated APIs. Specifically,

$$DCG@N = \sum_{i \in rank_N(\hat{y})} \frac{y_i}{\log(i+1)} \tag{1}$$

where $rank_N(\hat{y})$ denotes the N lagest indices recommended and $y_i = 1$ if the mashup actually invoked the i-th API, otherwise, $y_i = 0$.

DCG is a cumulative value, and NDCG normalizes it by IDCG. Specifically,

$$NDCG@N = \frac{DCG}{IDCG} \tag{2}$$

$$IDCG@N = \sum_{i \in rank_N(y)} \frac{2^{y_i} - 1}{\log_2(i+1)} \tag{3}$$

where $rank_N(y)$ denotes the N lagest real indices.

Considering the high precision@N and DCG@N can be obtained by directly recommending the APIs with high frequency of use, We introduce Propensity-scored counterparts of precision@N and DCG@N [1]:

$$PSP@N = \frac{1}{N} \sum_{i \in rank_k(\hat{y})} \frac{y_i}{p_i} \tag{4}$$

$$PSDCG@N = \sum_{i \in rank_N(\hat{y})} \frac{y_i}{p_i \log(i+1)} \tag{5}$$

where p_i is the propensity score for the i-th API, which is defined as the ratio of the number of calls to the total number of calls for the i-th API.

In addition, we choose the MRR metric commonly used in recommendation systems, which is expressed as

$$MRR = \frac{1}{|Q|} \sum_{i=1}^{|Q|} \frac{1}{rank_i} \tag{6}$$

where Q is a sample of queries, $|Q|$ is the number of queries, and $rank_i$ is the rank position of the first relevant document for the i-th query.

We apply the early stop technique on the validation set to avoid overfitting and evaluate the model performance on the test set based on all APIs, i.e., the recommendation is a score ranking of all APIs.

4 Experiments

We chose some service mashup recommendation models from the conferences and journals in service computing recent 5 years. Then, we replicated them using SMRB to verify SMRB's effectiveness. Specifically, for works without source code, we write it according to the description in the paper; for work with source code, we migrate them into SMRB. Finally, we compare their results. This chapter describes the selected models, detailed experimental results, and analyses.

4.1 Model Selection

We implemented a total of 8 methods, including 5 replicate models from top service computing conferences and journals in the last five years (e.g., ICSOC, ICWS, SCC, TSC), *MTFM* [17], *coACN* [18], *MISR* [11], *T2L2* [9], *FISR* [12] and 3 self-built models, a variation to T2L2 called *T2L2-W/O-Propagation*, a strong MLP model and a heuristic approach based on API usage frequency. The models are described in detail below:

1. *MTFM* [17]: It uses GloVe for pre-training, extracts semantic features with CNN, processes with feature interaction components to get interaction features, and predicts candidate Web APIs for the mashup.
2. *coACN* [18]: This method classifies Web APIs by service domain using category information and embeds it into the mashup embedding vector. Then, it constructs a service combination graph with the invocation, extracts collaborative relationships using LightGCN, and predicts invocation probability.
3. *MISR* [11]: It uses CNN to extract semantic features. Then, it uses MLP and node2vec to obtain direct and implicit neighbor interaction features separately. The three features are combined and predicted using MLP. The latter two were removed from our study to avoid potential data leakage.

4. *T2L2* [9]: This method consists three linear layers, the first two aligning the representation space of mashups and Web APIs and bridge the semantic gap. The third layer calculates the matching scores. The second layer is part of the propagation component, which incorporates mashup information into the representation vectors of the Web APIs.
5. *FISR* [12]: This model has three layers. Feature Extraction Layer obtains feature representations based on text descriptions. Interaction Layer uses an attention mechanism to learn relevant weights. Output Layer computes the probability of recommending a candidate service to the target mashup.
6. *T2L2-W/O-Propagation*: It doesn't contain the propagation component in *T2L2*. Because T2L2 requires the training data to be ordered chronologically, and our training data is disordered. So we remove the propagation component that may pass error messages.
7. *MLP*: We created it for comparison with other models. It processes the feature of the mashup and the Web API with an MLP with two linear layers to predict the matching scores.
8. *Freq*: It always recommends the top N frequently invoked Web APIs.

4.2   Implementation Details

We trained each model using two copies of the GloVe and BERT datasets, with N in the evaluation metrics set to 5, 10, 15, 20, 25. To rule out chance, we ran each model five times under identical conditions and averaged the results. All experiments ran on a GeForce RTX 3090.

4.3   Results and Analysis

Table 3 and 4 shows the performance comparison of different models on different experiment settings.

The model performs much worse on total API data than on partial API data. Because the former includes more potential APIs, and most lack historical invocation, making recommendations more difficult.

Comparing the results of the two different pre-trained models, it can be seen that for the same recommended model, using BERT as the pre-trained model generally gives better results than using GloVe as the pre-trained model. Since BERT considers the contextual relationship of the text, the representation vector obtained by BERT has more affluent and more accurate semantic information than GloVe, which naturally leads to better results for downstream tasks.

The performance difference between using BERT and GloVe as pre-trained models for T2L2 is minor, indicating that T2L2 is not sensitive to the pre-trained model. On the one hand, this indicates that the model's influence is not vulnerable to changes in the external environment. Still, on the other hand, it makes increasing the model performance by improving the quality of the upstream representation vector difficult.

T2L2's lousy performance is due to the propagation component, which transmits information about past mashups that used an API to the API to enhance

Table 3. Performance comparison of different approaches based on partial data. In each row, the best result is **bolded** and the second best is underline. Due to the limit of pages, the standard error of the mean is not shown in the table.

Metric	N	Freq	MLP		MTFM		coACN		MISR		FISR		T2L2		T2L2-W/O-propagation	
			GloVe	BERT	GloVe	BERT	GloVe	BERT	GloVe	BERT	GloVe	BERT	GloVe	BERT	GloVe	BERT
Precision	5	0.1314	<u>0.1701</u>	**0.1811**	0.1297	0.1407	0.1332	0.1363	0.1363	0.1332	0.1235	0.1200	0.1332	0.1380	0.1538	0.1622
	10	0.0802	<u>0.0991</u>	**0.1062**	0.0778	0.0877	0.0853	0.0824	0.0809	0.0809	0.0776	0.0765	0.0829	0.0844	0.0932	0.0954
	15	0.0576	<u>0.0719</u>	**0.0753**	0.0549	0.0630	0.0614	0.0611	0.0588	0.0568	0.0541	0.0574	0.0607	0.0604	0.0665	0.0684
	20	0.0463	<u>0.0577</u>	**0.0590**	0.0433	0.0511	0.0490	0.0480	0.0467	0.0449	0.0426	0.0452	0.0485	0.0490	0.0529	0.0546
	25	0.0384	<u>0.0478</u>	**0.0489**	0.0360	0.0421	0.0403	0.0405	0.0395	0.0380	0.0351	0.0382	0.0402	0.0409	0.0440	0.0459
Recall	5	0.4456	<u>0.5230</u>	**0.6023**	0.4364	0.4372	0.4062	0.4391	0.4366	0.4385	0.4151	0.4069	0.4220	0.4435	0.4854	0.5097
	10	0.5440	<u>0.6095</u>	**0.7061**	0.5237	0.5451	0.5201	0.5312	0.5183	0.5326	0.5214	0.5186	0.5251	0.5424	0.5881	0.5994
	15	0.5857	<u>0.6635</u>	**0.7515**	0.5547	0.5874	0.5617	0.5907	0.5648	0.5615	0.5451	0.5842	0.5766	0.5819	0.6297	0.6450
	20	0.6274	<u>0.7095</u>	**0.7851**	0.5828	0.6352	0.5979	0.6190	0.5986	0.5919	0.5731	0.6125	0.6142	0.6299	0.6671	0.6865
	25	0.6513	<u>0.7351</u>	**0.8129**	0.6050	0.6544	0.6139	0.6530	0.6324	0.6252	0.5894	0.6483	0.6365	0.6568	0.6949	0.7210
F1	5	0.2030	<u>0.2567</u>	**0.2785**	0.1999	0.2128	0.2006	0.2080	0.2077	0.2043	0.1904	0.1853	0.2025	0.2105	0.2336	0.2461
	10	0.1398	<u>0.1705</u>	**0.1846**	0.1355	0.1511	0.1465	0.1427	0.1399	0.1404	0.1351	0.1333	0.1431	0.1461	0.1609	0.1646
	15	0.1049	<u>0.1298</u>	**0.1369**	0.1000	0.1138	0.1107	0.1107	0.1064	0.1032	0.0984	0.1046	0.1098	0.1094	0.1203	0.1237
	20	0.0862	<u>0.1067</u>	**0.1098**	0.0886	0.0946	0.0906	0.0891	0.0866	0.0835	0.0794	0.0841	0.0898	0.0909	0.0980	0.1012
	25	0.0726	<u>0.0898</u>	**0.0922**	0.0679	0.0791	0.0756	0.0763	0.0743	0.0716	0.0662	0.0722	0.0756	0.0770	0.0828	0.0863
NDCG	5	0.3231	0.5537	**0.6131**	0.3401	0.5467	0.4051	0.3765	0.3372	0.2022	0.2323	0.1952	0.3716	0.4199	0.4856	<u>0.5904</u>
	10	0.3065	<u>0.4760</u>	**0.5071**	0.3153	0.3983	0.3439	0.2970	0.2870	0.2508	0.2765	0.2495	0.3320	0.3677	0.4080	0.4628
	15	0.3212	<u>0.4731</u>	**0.5197**	0.3137	0.3988	0.3428	0.2970	0.2899	0.2616	0.2751	0.2519	0.3335	0.3681	0.4059	0.4632
	20	0.3340	<u>0.4908</u>	**0.5421**	0.3284	0.4087	0.3595	0.3027	0.3087	0.2766	0.2905	0.2710	0.3456	0.3772	0.4223	0.4798
	25	0.3495	<u>0.5040</u>	**0.5584**	0.3526	0.4221	0.3694	0.3162	0.3254	0.2960	0.3106	0.2922	0.3571	0.3904	0.4399	0.4949
PSP	5	1.8055	<u>8.5071</u>	**19.2340**	1.6898	1.9745	1.7803	1.7595	4.4887	1.7690	4.6070	2.6720	1.7437	1.7519	6.5871	7.6427
	10	1.7051	8.6626	**20.1321**	1.7430	2.0164	1.8259	2.1443	3.5737	1.7358	5.2343	2.9416	1.7196	1.8087	7.9635	<u>10.0748</u>
	15	1.6211	8.1835	**18.7009**	1.4855	1.8889	1.7687	2.0865	4.7872	1.5193	3.9588	3.6138	1.7252	1.7561	7.4223	<u>9.1836</u>
	20	1.7373	9.6441	**16.5560**	1.5399	1.9142	1.8408	1.9249	4.5877	1.5697	3.2628	3.0865	1.8033	1.8575	7.7027	9.2319
	25	1.7179	9.5849	**15.7260**	1.4924	1.9573	1.7061	1.9498	4.6032	1.6754	2.7821	2.8238	1.7904	1.8611	8.3733	9.9932
PSDCG	5	5.2281	<u>24.9283</u>	**51.4474**	5.0213	5.5428	5.1878	5.2356	13.0653	5.1426	12.7406	7.4043	5.1307	5.2250	21.5023	21.6099
	10	7.7560	38.9647	**84.7756**	7.8523	8.8182	8.1706	9.1490	17.3868	7.8475	22.8887	12.3341	7.8486	8.1339	36.4466	41.7546
	15	9.6452	48.6466	**105.5939**	9.1392	10.9754	10.3426	11.7665	26.8320	9.2839	24.7177	18.9243	10.1227	10.2977	44.9179	<u>51.6271</u>
	20	12.1049	65.1660	**117.5598**	11.1481	13.3386	12.7619	13.4521	31.5381	11.2952	26.1088	20.6777	12.5279	12.8281	54.9955	62.6343
	25	13.9102	75.3668	**131.1203**	12.5703	15.6652	14.0334	15.6882	36.6556	13.6072	27.0449	22.6120	14.4265	14.8711	66.8632	<u>76.9334</u>
MRR	-	0.5529	0.8218	<u>0.8599</u>	0.5706	**0.8747**	0.7053	0.7067	0.6583	0.3139	0.3731	0.3284	0.5875	0.6977	0.7189	0.8464

Table 4. Performance comparison of different approaches based on total data. In each row, the best result is **bolded** and the second best is underlined. OOM indicates out of memory. Due to the limit of pages, the standard error of the mean is not shown in the table.

Metric	N	Freq	MLP GloVe	MLP BERT	MTFM GloVe	MTFM BERT	coACN GloVe	coACN BERT	MISR GloVe	MISR BERT	FISR GloVe	FISR BERT	T2L2 GloVe	T2L2 BERT	T2L2-W/O-propagation GloVe	T2L2-W/O-propagation BERT
Precision	5	0.1314	<u>0.1451</u>	0.1398	OOM	OOM	0.1358	0.1385	0.1288	0.1332	0.0778	OOM	0.1332	0.1380	0.1398	**0.1578**
	10	0.0802	<u>0.0862</u>	0.0829			0.0851	0.0826	0.0789	0.0789	0.0402		0.0846	0.0835	0.0824	**0.0892**
	15	0.0576	<u>0.0615</u>	0.0596			0.0599	0.0593	0.0583	0.0599	0.0268		0.0607	0.0607	0.0582	**0.0646**
	20	0.0463	0.0489	0.0469			0.0475	0.0478	0.0478	0.0473	0.0201		0.0481	<u>0.0492</u>	0.0460	**0.0511**
	25	0.0384	<u>0.0409</u>	0.0387			0.0395	0.0395	0.0392	0.0386	0.0161		0.0399	0.0408	0.0379	**0.0419**
Recall	5	0.4456	0.4459	<u>0.4649</u>			0.4352	0.4462	0.4075	0.4322	0.2308		0.4220	0.4435	0.4411	**0.4871**
	10	0.5440	0.5297	**0.5512**			0.5451	0.5326	0.4993	0.5121	0.2386		0.5362	0.5367	0.5201	<u>0.5509</u>
	15	0.5857	0.5676	<u>0.5950</u>			0.5761	0.5737	0.5535	0.5835	0.2386		0.5766	0.5847	0.5506	**0.5984**
	20	0.6274	0.6014	0.6243			0.6085	0.6161	0.6050	0.6134	0.2386		0.6100	**0.6328**	0.5811	<u>0.6309</u>
	25	<u>0.6513</u>	0.6284	0.6433			0.6324	0.6360	0.6203	0.6262	0.2386		0.6323	**0.6554**	0.5978	0.6472
F1	5	0.2030	<u>0.2189</u>	0.2149			0.2070	0.2113	0.1957	0.2036	0.1164		0.2025	0.2105	0.2123	**0.2384**
	10	0.1398	<u>0.1482</u>	0.1441			0.1471	0.1431	0.1363	0.1367	0.0688		0.1462	0.1445	0.1423	**0.1536**
	15	0.1049	<u>0.1110</u>	0.1084			0.1086	0.1076	0.1055	0.1087	0.0482		0.1098	0.1099	0.1052	**0.1166**
	20	0.0862	0.0904	0.0873			0.0881	0.0887	0.0886	0.0877	0.0371		0.0892	**0.0914**	0.0853	**0.0945**
	25	0.0726	0.0768	0.0730			0.0743	0.0743	0.0738	0.0727	0.0301		0.0751	<u>0.0768</u>	0.0713	**0.0788**
NDCG	5	0.3231	0.4072	<u>0.5243</u>			0.4513	0.3241	0.2016	0.2051	0.0087		0.3503	0.3762	0.3019	**0.5825**
	10	0.3065	0.3679	<u>0.4161</u>			0.3702	0.2645	0.2452	0.2597	0.0824		0.3172	0.3475	0.2779	**0.4661**
	15	0.3212	0.3654	<u>0.4233</u>			0.3698	0.2738	0.2555	0.2672	0.1023		0.3240	0.3489	0.2908	**0.4580**
	20	0.3340	0.3906	0.4381			0.3864	0.2801	0.2695	0.2815	0.1121		0.3350	0.3605	0.3141	**0.4763**
	25	0.3495	0.4020	0.4487			0.3998	0.2864	0.2807	0.2970	0.1156		0.3476	0.3748	0.3325	**0.4871**
PSP	5	6.4054	8.5486	**17.7200**			6.3094	6.4443	5.9216	6.2704	16.5174		6.1864	6.2154	12.7551	<u>16.6128</u>
	10	6.6491	8.9062	**15.1655**			6.2310	6.5350	6.7328	6.6311	8.8777		6.5479	5.9370	11.7448	<u>14.4231</u>
	15	5.7514	11.6078	<u>13.0102</u>			5.6268	6.2457	7.2615	6.6664	5.9185		6.1205	5.9940	9.2006	**13.0862**
	20	6.1637	11.0371	11.4999			5.8936	6.5463	7.6751	6.2622	4.4389		6.1887	6.6445	8.1707	**14.0720**
	25	6.0947	11.2755	11.3230			5.8814	6.8801	7.0469	6.1464	3.5511		6.0834	6.5427	7.8420	**13.2592**
PSDCG	5	18.5482	27.1171	<u>60.2543</u>			18.5710	19.1293	17.5936	18.2974	**80.2177**		18.3129	18.4980	37.5592	53.2040
	10	27.5165	42.4323	<u>80.3920</u>			28.3722	29.5228	29.4287	29.3888	**82.1704**		29.2486	27.4648	54.3352	54.3352
	15	34.2188	65.3133	**91.9282**			34.2182	36.9599	40.3094	38.3126	82.1704		36.1077	35.5852	59.7940	<u>86.2255</u>
	20	42.9453	76.2281	<u>100.2250</u>			42.0570	45.7928	50.6928	44.2524	82.1704		43.6520	45.7338	65.7709	**106.0466**
	25	49.3502	89.6700	<u>111.8551</u>			48.4661	54.7932	55.6420	50.4235	82.1704		49.8833	52.4367	72.9143	**117.1054**
MRR	–	0.5529	0.6471	<u>0.8423</u>			0.7031	0.6373	0.3694	0.2852	0.1055		0.5451	0.6083	0.5390	**0.8491**

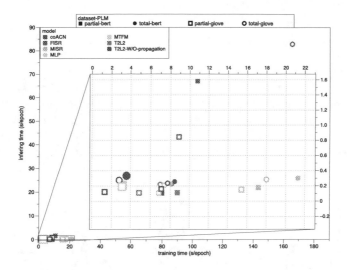

Fig. 2. Comparison of inferring time and training time among DL-based models. The size of point denotes the model size.

their representation. This propagation's efficiency is dependent on temporally ordered training data. However, because of our disordered training data, the propagation component propagates inaccurate information, lowering the T2L2's performance as illustrated by the significantly improved performance vs. T2L2, which may handle this problem by removing the propagation component.

The frequent model directly recommends APIs based on their frequency from highest to lowest. Because of the extreme imbalance in the frequency of API usage, this method does not perform poorly on Precision, Recall, F1, and NDCG. However, its performance on PSP and PSDCG is poor due to the lower weight given to the popular APIs. The performance patterns of MTFM, coACN, and T2L2 on metrics are similar, indicating that these three models also tend to recommend popular APIs.

Surprisingly, despite having only the two essential linear layers, with carefully tuning parameters, the MLP model and the T2L2 model with the propagation component removed obtain strong results in all four metrics, especially when BERT is used as the pre-trained model.

Some models shows obvious biases in different metrics. For example, coACN performs poorly on Precision and F1, but performs well on MRR metrics, which means that the correct results recommended by the model are ranked more highly. MTFM and T2L2 performs well on NDCG, but performs poorly on PSP and PSDCG, which means that these models tend to recommend popular APIs

MISR and FISR are out of memory when trained based on the total dataset, which may be due to the complex structure of the models. These types of models cannot handle large-scale data.

Figure 2 is the comparison of inferring time and training time among DL-based approaches. Among all DL-based approaches, MLP has the fastest inferring speed, the fourth fastest training speed with very little difference between the first spot and the minimum number of trainable parameters.

Taken as a whole, most DL-based models do not perform as well as they promise though they tend to use more complex network structures to extract features; instead, the simplest MLP model performs better after tuning the parameters. This shows that the feature taken from the MLP structure may be more successful than those extracted from the complex network structure for service mashup recommendation. Much of today's work designs special model structures to solve specific problems in service mashup recommendation, but it is difficult to evaluate whether these structures really works. One possible reason is that the text-based descriptions of mashups and APIs generally describe their core functional features in brief terms. These expressions have a small vocabulary, simple grammar, and uniform style. Therefore, simple MLPs have adequately and accurately extracted features from them. Complex models instead harm the original simple features. As a result, we must reconsider which aspect of the problem each model genuinely solves and whether a single-minded pursuit of model complexity can really lead to significant breakthroughs for the service mashup recommendation tasks.

4.4   Discussion

With the increasing popularity of data-driven approaches in various fields, researchers increasingly adopt deep learning. However, blindly migrating existing deep learning models to new domains or stacking complex structures and increasing network depth may not always yield good performance due to differences between domains. For instance, our experiment results indicate that some complex service recommendation models perform worse than the simplest MLPs. Hence, it is crucial for researchers to consider domain-specific characteristics when designing model architectures that fit the domain requirements.

The lack of a benchmark for service recommendations task makes it difficult to find out whether some methods really perform as well as expected. So for academics, creating a benchmark is crucial when introducing deep learning or any other new techniques into a new field. There are several benefits: 1) A benchmark can divide the solution to the task into modules such as datasets, pre-trained models, models, and evaluation metrics. This helps researchers know where to improve. 2) The benchmark provides a fair environment to evaluate the actual performance of models. Based on this objective result, researchers can clarify whether their methods truly address their hypotheses without interference from other parties. 3) A benchmark improves the reproducibility of research, which helps the field grow in a lasting and healthy way.

5   Threats to Validity

Internal Validity. Previous studies used various experiment settings, including different data splits and hardware and software environments. The standard experiment settings in SMRB may conflict with them, leading to differences in reproduced results. We encourage future researchers to adopt the standard experiment settings provided by SMRB to avoid such discrepancies. Additionally, some papers lacked detailed hyperparameter settings, preventing us from reproducing the results with the same hyperparameters as the original study. To address this issue, we used an automated hyperparameter search method in SMRB to tune hyperparameters and report the best results.

External Validity. While we have reproduced five deep learning-based models from recent service recommendation research, it is possible that these models do not fully represent all available approaches. Additionally, SMRB's current dataset only includes text-based descriptions of mashups and APIs since they contain the most information and are commonly used in service recommendation methods. Although some methods use special data, these were not included in our dataset due to the lack of uniform data sources and processing. We have open-sourced SMRB and will provide long-term support. We encourage researchers to contribute their methods to enrich the project.

Construct Validity. To ensure adequate evaluation, we selected commonly used metrics in service recommendations, such as Precision, Recall, F1, NDCG, and MRR. Furthermore, we included PS and PSDCG, two commonly used metrics in recommendation systems, to ensure that methods do not achieve good performance simply by recommending frequently called APIs.

6   Conclusion

In this paper, we propose a service mashup recommendation benchmark called SMRB to deal with the lack of uniform standards in the field of service mashup recommendation. SMRB standardizes the datasets, pre-trained models, evaluation protocol, and experiment environment, which provide a fair environment for comparisons between various methods to enhance comparability between models and credibility of results. Also, the uniform standards accelerate the construction of service recommendation systems. We implement 8 models based on SMRB and compare their performance, which proves the effectiveness of SMRB. By analyzing these results we found that most DL-based models do not perform as well as they promise; instead, the simplest MLP models perform better after tuning the parameters, which will provide some inspiration for service mashup recommendation research in the future.

In our further work, we will create complete documentation for this project based on *Sphinx*, which covers the dataset loader, constructor of DL-based models, detailed tutorial. And we will create a leaderboard to support submission of models/codes for evaluation and ranking.

Acknowledgments. The research in this paper is partially supported by the National Key Research and Development Program of China (No 2021YFB3300700) and the National Natural Science Foundation of China (61832014, 61832004).

References

1. Bhatia, K., et al.: The extreme classification repository: multi-label datasets and code (2016)
2. Bianchini, D., De Antonellis, V., Melchiori, M.: A multi-perspective framework for web API search in enterprise mashup design. In: Salinesi, C., Norrie, M.C., Pastor, Ó. (eds.) Advanced Information Systems Engineering, pp. 353–368. Springer, Berlin Heidelberg, Berlin, Heidelberg (2013). https://doi.org/10.1007/978-3-642-38709-8_23
3. Fletcher, K.K.: A quality-aware web API recommender system for mashup development. In: Ferreira, J.E., Musaev, A., Zhang, L.J. (eds.) Services Computing - SCC 2019, pp. 1–15. Springer International Publishing, Cham (2019). https://doi.org/10.1007/978-3-030-23554-3_1
4. Gao, W., Chen, L., Wu, J., Gao, H.: Manifold-learning based API recommendation for mashup creation. In: ICWS, pp. 432–439 (2015)
5. Jain, A., Liu, X., Yu, Q.: Aggregating functionality, use history, and popularity of APIs to recommend mashup creation. In: Barros, A., Grigori, D., Narendra, N.C., Dam, H.K. (eds.) Service-Oriented Computing, pp. 188–202. Springer, Berlin Heidelberg, Berlin, Heidelberg (2015). https://doi.org/10.1007/978-3-662-48616-0_12
6. Kang, G., Liu, J., Cao, B., Cao, M.: NAFM: neural and attentional factorization machine for web API recommendation. In: ICWS, pp. 330–337 (2020)
7. Li, H., Liu, J., Cao, B., Tang, M., Liu, X., Li, B.: Integrating tag, topic, co-occurrence, and popularity to recommend web APIs for mashup creation. In: SCC, pp. 84–91 (2017). https://doi.org/10.1109/SCC.2017.19
8. Liu, M., Tu, Z., Zhu, Y., Xu, X., Wang, Z., Sheng, Q.Z.: Data correction and evolution analysis of the Programmableweb service ecosystem. J. Syst. Softw. **182**, 111066 (2021)
9. Liu, M., Zhu, Y., Xu, H., Tu, Z., Wang, Z.: T2L2: a tiny three linear layers model for service mashup creation. In: Hacid, H., Kao, O., Mecella, M., Moha, N., Paik, H. (eds.) ICSOC 2021. LNCS, vol. 13121, pp. 317–331. Springer, Cham (2021). https://doi.org/10.1007/978-3-030-91431-8_20
10. Liu, Y., Cao, J.: API-prefer: an API package recommender system based on composition feature learning. In: Kafeza, E., Benatallah, B., Martinelli, F., Hacid, H., Bouguettaya, A., Motahari, H. (eds.) Service-Oriented Computing, pp. 500–507. Springer International Publishing, Cham (2020). https://doi.org/10.1007/978-3-030-65310-1_36
11. Ma, Y., Geng, X., Wang, J.: A deep neural network with multiplex interactions for cold-start service recommendation. IEEE Trans. Eng. Manage. **68**(1), 105–119 (2021). https://doi.org/10.1109/TEM.2019.2961376
12. Ma, Y., Geng, X., Wang, J., He, K., Athanasopoulos, D.: Deep learning framework for online interactive service recommendation in iterative mashup development. CoRR abs/2101.02836 (2021). arXiv:2101.02836
13. Qi, L., Song, H., Zhang, X., Srivastava, G., Xu, X., Yu, S.: Compatibility-aware web API recommendation for mashup creation via textual description mining. ACM Trans. Multimedia Comput. Commun. Appl. **17**(1s), 1–19 (2021)
14. Rahman, M.M., Liu, X.F.: Integrated topic modeling and user interaction enhanced webAPI recommendation using regularized matrix factorization for mashup application development. In: SCC, pp. 124–131 (2020)

15. Shi, M., Tang, Y., Liu, J.: Functional and contextual attention-based LSTM for service recommendation in mashup creation. IEEE Trans. Parallel Distrib. Syst. **30**(5), 1077–1090 (2019)
16. Shi, M., Tang, Y., Liu, J.: TA-BLSTM: tag attention-based bidirectional long short-term memory for service recommendation in mashup creation. In: IJCNN, pp. 1–8 (2019). https://doi.org/10.1109/IJCNN.2019.8852438
17. Wu, H., Duan, Y., Yue, K., Zhang, L.: Mashup-oriented web API recommendation via multi-model fusion and multi-task learning. TSC **15**, 3330–3343 (2021)
18. Yan, R., Fan, Y., Zhang, J., Zhang, J., Lin, H.: Service recommendation for composition creation based on collaborative attention convolutional network. In: ICWS, pp. 397–405 (2021). https://doi.org/10.1109/ICWS53863.2021.00059
19. Yao, L., Wang, X., Sheng, Q.Z., Benatallah, B., Huang, C.: Mashup recommendation by regularizing matrix factorization with API co-invocations. TSC **14**(2), 502–515 (2021). https://doi.org/10.1109/TSC.2018.2803171
20. Yu, J., Benatallah, B., Casati, F., Daniel, F.: Understanding mashup development. IEEE Internet Comput. **12**(5), 44–52 (2008)
21. Zheng, Z., Ma, H., Lyu, M.R., King, I.: QoS-aware web service recommendation by collaborative filtering. TSC **4**(2), 140–152 (2011)

A Resource-Constrained Multi-level SLA Customization Approach Based on QoE Analysis of Large-Scale Customers

Min Li, Hanchuan Xu, Xiaofei Xu, and Zhongjie Wang[(✉)]

Faculty of Computing, Harbin Institute of Technology, Harbin 150001, China
limin19961996@163.com, {xhc,xiaofei,rainy}@hit.edu.cn

Abstract. The user-centered service paradigm has attracted extensive attention from academia and industry. It advocates taking customer requirements as the orientation, maximizing customer satisfaction as the objective, then targeting to carry out market segmentation and multi-level SLA customization. There are two main challenges: personalized preferences of large-scale customers and resource constraints. In this paper, we propose a resource-constrained multi-level SLA customization approach based on QoE analysis of large-scale customers. With a deep generative network, we fit satisfaction mapping functions and infer the customer's personalized preference interval for each QoS. Then, based on the theory of granular computing, a multi-level, multi-perspective and multi-scale granular structure for service customization is constructed. Finally, the best match between users with personalized preferences and resources with differentiated qualities is mined to obtain a reduced and balanced multi-level SLA customization scheme. This paper conducts experiments based on the real data of a hotel booking platform and proves that the method performs well in service customization granularity, preference coverage and matching accuracy. The method is an on-demand optimization and avoids over-optimization. The final customized solutions can not only meet the personalized preferences but also give play to the advantages of different quality resources.

Keywords: Multi-level SLA customization · Personalized preferences · Satisfaction mapping functions · Granular computing

1 Introduction

With the continuous improvement of living standards, customers' requirements tend to be diversified, from basic functions to personalized, experiential and other higher levels of requirements, and the demands for customized services are particularly strong. At the same time, many resources have been opened on online platforms, which have different quality configurations and give support for the satisfaction of large-scale personalized preferences. Service customization is an innovative service paradigm to meet diversified and personalized requirements [1]. The research problem of this paper is, based on differentiated qualities

M. Indulska et al. (Eds.): CAiSE 2023, LNCS 13901, pp. 594–610, 2023.
https://doi.org/10.1007/978-3-031-34560-9_35

of resources and oriented to personalized preferences of large-scale customers, to realize multi-level SLA (Service Level Agreement) customization. It is part of defining and establishing agreements in the SLA management life cycle [6], aiming at subdividing users and integrating resources to provide differentiated service guarantees for large-scale customers. To solve this problem, we face the following challenges:

1. **Identifying and mapping personalized preferences.** The quality of user experience (QoE) and the quality of service performance (QoS) are two different service evaluation standards, and mapping relations between them are unclear that should be reasonably inferred.
2. **Multi-level SLA customization.** On the one hand, the preferences of different customers are generally heterogeneous. On the other hand, different service providers have different quantities and capabilities of resources, which are difficult to meet all the needs of the whole market. Therefore, it is necessary to subdivide users and design multi-level SLA to meet personalized preferences and take advantage of differentiated resources.
3. **Accurate matching between large-scale customers and constrained service resources.** Each category of service has many executable resource instances, which are unevenly distributed at different quality levels. For example, the star rating is one of QoS attributes of hotel service. There are 1,236 hotel resources that can be accessed in the Sanya on Trip.com, 68.93% of the hotels are star-less, and only 9.46% are five-star. It is unrealistic to configure high-quality resources for most customers. So, resource constraints should be considered, and the number of resources should be consistent with the matching customers as much as possible.

This paper proposes a resource-constrained multi-level SLA customization approach based on QoE analysis of large-scale customers, which is summarized in Fig. 1. The main contributions are as follows: 1) Based on the QoE/QoS correlation model, we designed a deep generation network to predict the key parameters of customer satisfaction mapping functions; 2) We proposed a multi-level SLA customization method based on granular computing, which can obtain a multi-level, multi-perspective and multi-scale granular structure; 3) Considering resource constraints, we proposed a method to integrate and reduce the above customization to maintain the balance between the user scale and the number of resources.

The detailed implementation steps are shown in Fig. 2. The method firstly extracts the public information QoE and QoS from online service resource platforms, which can obtain service differentiated qualities (SDQ) but does not know the user personalized preferences (UPP) for each QoS. So, step (1) is to train a deep generation network to infer customer satisfaction mapping functions. Step (2) is to build a multi-level SLA granular structure considering personalized preferences, which takes SDQ and UPP as inputs to segment users and services layer by layer. At each round of segmentation, the method refines the services into high, middle, and low levels of customization by increasing the division scales of QoS intervals, selecting the best QoS configuration and the heuristic factor,

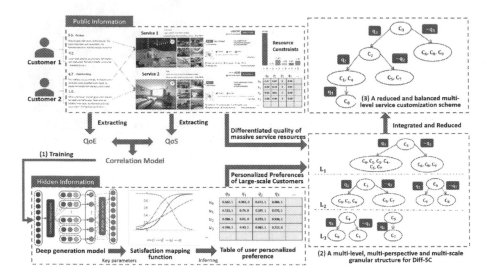

Fig. 1. An overview of the multi-level SLA customization approach

and doing granular calculations. Step (3) is to reduce the granular structure considering resource constraints, which includes two sub-processes: one is to reduce the users for the customized nodes where the number of resources cannot meet the number of users according to the tolerances of users and the redundancies of granules, and get a balanced granular structure; The second is to merge the customized nodes with less partial order QoS to get a reduced granular structure.

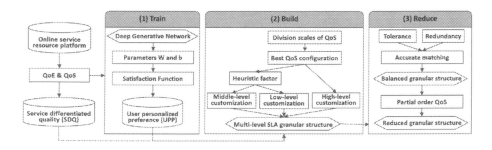

Fig. 2. Implementation steps of the multi-level SLA customization approach

The rest of this paper is organized as follows. The related work is given in Sect. 2. Section 3 explains the model structure, training process and hyperparameters tuning of satisfaction mapping function inference. Section 4 is about the multi-level SLA customization method based on granular computing and the reduction method for accurate matching. Finally, the experimental analysis is in Sect. 5.

2   Related Work

The premise of customization is customer segmentation (also known as market segmentation). Currently, customer segmentation methods are based on two aspects: 1) Customer value. The common practice is to divide users into different levels according to the value generated in the past and future [3,9]. A well-known customer value model is RFM(Recency, Frequency, Monetary) [11]. 2) Customer similarity. Most methods are implemented by clustering. Ernst et al. pointed out a drawback that the choice of initial nodes or the number of categories led to inconsistencies in clustering results, that is, random problems [2]. Hajibaba et al. improved this problem by bootstrap sampling [4]. Saia et al. made representational learning on user preferences and then clustered based on hidden vectors [10], such clustering results are not interpretable.

The second task is to match differentiated service resources for each segmentation to maximize overall customer satisfaction. Some QoS-enhanced service optimization methods were over-optimization and maximized QoS towards the industry peak [5]. However, customers' preferences may not be in the peak area, and the non-peak service quality is already satisfying. The purpose of customization is on-demand optimization and to provide services that are just enough to satisfy customers. In particular, under resource constraints, it can maximize overall users' satisfaction [8,12].

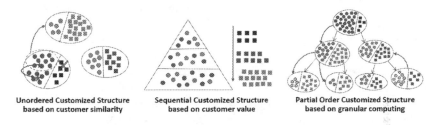

Unordered Customized Structure based on customer similarity **Sequential Customized Structure based on customer value** **Partial Order Customized Structure based on granular computing**

Fig. 3. Comparison of three service customization structures

Service customization can effectively deal with resource constraints while satisfying personalized preferences. However, customized structures of the existing works can not deal with the above two challenges at the same time (Fig. 3). Based on the segmentation results of customer similarity, customizations are unordered, which meet the personalized requirements but cannot flexibly cope with resource constraints. When the resources matching a certain group are insufficient, several users have to be separated from the current cluster to others. Then the cluster center has changed and the solution has to be redesigned. Based on the segmentation results of customer value, customizations are sequential. When the high-quality resources are insufficient, it can be handled by providing low-quality services for low-value customers, but this method only considers customer value and ignores personalized preferences. This paper uses a granular structure to organize multi-level customizations. One user may belong to multiple granules, and a partial path can be determined between these granules. When resources are limited, following this path can find other matching solutions.

3   Satisfaction Mapping Function Inference

The input of the problem is formalized as a five-tuple, $\Gamma = \{U, S, Q, F_u, F_s\}$, where $U = \{u_1, u_2, ..., u_N\}, N \sim 1e5$ is the full set of users, $S = \{s_1, s_2, ..., s_O\}, O \sim 1e3$ is the full set of services, and $Q = \{q_1, q_2, ..., q_M\}, M \sim 1e2$ is the full set of qualities. The large-scale of this paper is reflected in the order of magnitude N, O, M. Personalized preference is quantified as $F_u : U \times Q = \{f(u, q), u \in U, q \in Q\}$, namely, satisfaction mapping function. Differentiated quality of resources is reflected in $F_s : S \times Q = \{f(s, q) = x, x \in \{0, 1\} \ or \ x \in [0, 1]\}$. F_s is known, but F_u is unknown that should be inferred based on the public information.

3.1   Model Structure

Considering that the trend of satisfaction along with quality is usually monotonous and nonlinear, as shown in Eq. 1, this paper quantifies F_u with a sigmoid variant and introduces two parameters W and b, where satisfaction is in $[0, 1]$, W determines the preference direction, b is the offset and $b \in [0, 1]$.

$$Satisfaction = f_{u,q} = \sigma(W_u^q, b_u^q) = \frac{1}{1 + e^{-W(x-b)}} \tag{1}$$

W and b are predicted by a deep generative network. The model structure is shown in Fig. 4, including a generative model R2S and a discriminant model S2E. In our early work [7], we trained a QoE/QoS correlation model from which we can obtain the representation vector of each user's personalized preference, that is, the hidden vector R in this paper. In addition, this model can also predict the QoE of each user for any given service. In this way, the input of R2S and the output of S2E are available. The loss of the model in this paper is calculated by comparing the sentiment polarities of QoE predicted with S2E and the QoE/QoS correlation model. The metric is calculated by the cross-entropy between user satisfaction and dissatisfaction predicted by R2S. If the entropy is too small, it means that the prediction of user satisfaction is too extreme; If the entropy is too large, it means that the training is invalid and the model cannot clearly distinguish whether users are satisfied or not.

3.2   Hyper-parameters Tuning

Since the sigmoid is an S-type saturation function, in order to ensure that the unsaturated interval of F_u falls within the range of quality $[0, 1]$, this paper introduces two hyper-parameters $|W|_{max}$ and δ to reshape F_u. During training, the R2S generates two hidden vectors H1 and H2, H1 is activated with sigmoid to get b in $[0, 1]$, then b is compressed to a reasonable interval by $b' = Max(\frac{\delta}{|W|_{max}}, Min(b, 1 - \frac{\delta}{|W|_{max}}))$; H2 is activated with tanh to get W in $[-1, +1]$, then multiplied by $|W|_{max}$ to expand W to the interval $[-|W|_{max}, |W|_{max}]$. If W is too small, the change of satisfaction is too slow,

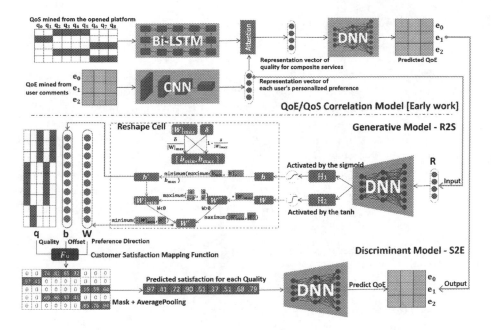

Fig. 4. The deep generative network of satisfaction mapping function inference

and users may be dissatisfied with all services, which is useless for service customization. So, this paper scales W' according to b'. To sum up, it is guaranteed that there is an obvious change from user dissatisfaction to satisfaction within the effective range $[0, 1]$ of q, and the change is not abrupt.

4   Differentiated Service Customization

Introducing a threshold τ to represent the lowest satisfaction that users can tolerate, the critical value $\underline{s}$ and preference direction d of each user u for each q can be inferred, as seen in Eq. 2. If d=1, the user satisfaction interval is $[\underline{s}, 1]$; conversely, it is $[0, \underline{s}]$. Therefore, according to F_u and F_s, we can get the tables of user personalized preference (UPP) and service differentiated quality (SDQ).

$$\underline{s} = \frac{-ln(1/\tau - 1)}{W_u^q} + b_u^q, \ 0.5 < \tau < \sigma(\delta) \qquad d = \begin{cases} 1, \ W_u^q > 0 \\ 0, \ W_u^q < 0 \end{cases} \qquad (2)$$

4.1   Kernel Structure of Granular Computing

Based on the theory of granular computing, this subsection explains the key components of the granular structure for multi-level SLA customization.

- **Basic Granule.** In this paper, the basic granule is extended to a five-tuple $C_i = \left\{ U_i, S_i, \widetilde{Q}_i^u, \widetilde{Q}_i^s, \widehat{Q}_{i \rightarrow j} \right\}$, where U_i is the user subset, S_i is the service subset, $\widetilde{Q}_i^u$ is the equivalent QoS subset of U_i, $\widetilde{Q}_i^s$ is the equivalent QoS subset of S_i, and $\widehat{Q}_{i \to j}$ is the partial QoS of the current granule C_i compared with its parent granule C_j. The relations between them are shown in Eq. 3.

- **Equivalent Relation.** In this paper, equivalent relations are reflected in two aspects: 1) All users in U_i have the same preference for each quality in $\widetilde{Q}_i^u$, which are indistinguishable; 2) All services in S_i have the same value on each quality in $\widetilde{Q}_i^s$, which are indistinguishable.
- **Partial order Relation.** Since different users may have different preference directions for the same quality, the partial order relation is determined according to the public preference direction D (with the principle of the majority following the minority). Partial order means that all services S_i in the current granule C_i are worse than services S_j in its parent granule C_j on qualities $\widehat{Q}_{i \to j}$.

$$
\begin{aligned}
Closure: \ & U_i = \left\{ u \in U \mid \forall \, q \in \widetilde{Q}_i^u, \ I(u,q) = 1 \right\} \\
Closure: \ & S_i = \left\{ s \in S \mid \forall \, q \in \widetilde{Q}_i^s, \ I(s,q) = 1 \right\} \\
Partial \ order: \ & \widehat{Q}_{i \to j} = \left\{ q \in \widetilde{Q}_j^s \mid \forall \, s \in S_i, I(s,q) = 0 \right\} \\
Matching: \ & \forall \, q \in \widetilde{Q}_i^s, \ \forall \, u \in U_i, \ \exists \, q^{(k)} \in \widetilde{Q}_i^s \wedge I(u,q^{(k)}) = 1
\end{aligned}
\tag{3}
$$

4.2   Model Construction of Granular Computing

This paper adopts a top-down approach to construct the granular computing model of multi-level SLA customization, we take UPP and SDQ as inputs and use the breadth-first search to refine the customized services layer by layer. The output is a triple tree, as shown in Fig. 5. Each node is a basic granule, which corresponds to a customized solution, including the quality configuration, matching resources and satisfying users. Each layer represents customized services with different granularity. The higher the layer, the finer the customization granularity, and the higher the customization precision. Each node C_i has three child nodes at most: the midside child $C_{L(i+1)}^M$ represents a high-level customization subdivided from $C_i.S$; the right child $C_{L(i+1)}^R$ represents a low-level customization that its services are inferior to $C_{L(i+1)}^M.S$ in some key qualities; the left child $C_{L(i+1)}^L$ represents middle-level customization that is the same as $C_{L(i+1)}^M$ in some key qualities, but inferior to $C_{L(i+1)}^M$ in other qualities. Finally, we can construct a multi-level SLA customization scheme represented by a multi-level, multi-perspective and multi-scale granular structure, which are specifically reflected in:

- Multi-level. One is the tree hierarchy L_1, L_2, L_3, the other is the partial order of service levels, $M \succ L \succ R$.
- Multi-perspective. During the subdivision of different layers and different granules, the concerned qualities are different, q_0, q_1, q_2, q_3.
- Multi-scale. The range of each quality is divided into multiple subintervals as required, 2-scale, 3-scale and 6-scale.

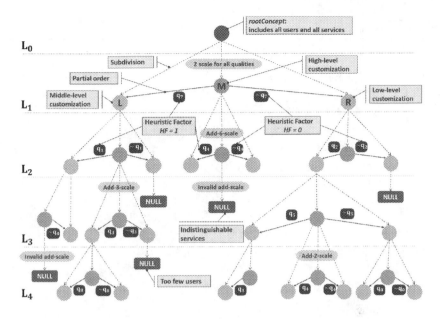

Fig. 5. An example of granular structure for multi-level SLA customization

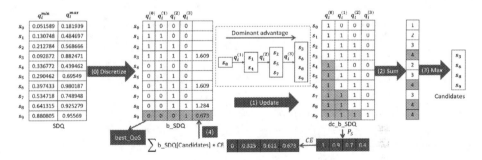

Fig. 6. An example of the selection of the best quality configuration

The granular refinement algorithm is shown in Algorithm 1. First, according to the current multi-scale division of all QoS, the real number matrices UPP and SDQ are converted into boolean matrices b_UPP and b_SDQ. Then, we select the best quality configuration $best\_QoS$ from the current granule $C_{L(i)}$. Considering that multiple subintervals of a QoS are not independent but dominant, this paper updates b_SDQ to dc_b_SDQ, and selects the QoS configuration of a service which is the maximum sum of row vectors in dc_b_SDQ and is the minimum cross entropies of the row vectors in b_SDQ, as the $best\_QoS$, as shown in Fig. 6. $best\_QoS$ is $\widetilde{Q}^s$ of $C_{L(i+1)}^M$. In $C_{L(i)}.S$, services with the same quality configuration as $best\_QoS$ are $C_{L(i+1)}^M.S$. In $C_{L(i)}.U$, users matching $best\_QoS$ are $C_{L(i+1)}^M.U$, and the criterion of matching is the fourth line of Eq. 3. Then we find $\widetilde{Q}^u$ of $C_{L(i+1)}^M.U$ according to the closure operator.

Algorithm 1: Generate finer granules

Input: $C_{L(i)}$, a node to be subdivided at layer i
Output: $[C_{L(i+1)}^M, C_{L(i+1)}^L, C_{L(i+1)}^R]$

1   **if** $C_{L(i)}.concept\_type = 1$ **then**
2   **for** q **in** $C_{L(i)}.\widetilde{Q}^s$ **do**
3       $CE = (CE(q^{(1)}) + CE(q^{(2)}))/2$; add_scale.put(q) **if** CE ¿ 0 ;
4   b_UPP, b_SDQ = Soft_discretize(UPP, SDQ, add_scale, k) ;

5   best_QoS = Select_with_Dominant(b_SDQ) ;
6   $C_{L(i+1)}^M =$ **Function** *generateMidChild()*:
7   S = [s.q = best_QoS for s in $C_{L(i)}.S$] ;
8   U = [best_QoS **match** u.p for u in $C_{L(i)}.U$] ;
9     $\widetilde{Q}^s =$ best_QoS ; $\widetilde{Q}^u =$ **Closure**(U) ; $\widehat{Q} = []$; concept_type = 1 ;
10   condition = CE_add($P_S, P_U, P_{S,U}$) ;
11   **for** q **in** $C_{L(i+1)}^M.\widetilde{Q}^s$ **do**
12   **if** *(q **not in** $C_{L(i)}.\widetilde{Q}^s$) & (q **not in** $C_{L(i)}.\widetilde{Q}^u$)* **then**
13   **if** *condition[q] ¿ condition[HF]* **then**
14   HF = q ;

15   $C_{L(i+1)}^L =$ **Function** *generateLeftChild()*:
16   S = [s.HF = 1 for s in $(C_{L(i)}.S - C_{L(i+1)}^M.S)$] ; $\widetilde{Q}^s =$ **Closure**(S) ;
17   U = [$\widetilde{Q}^s$ **match** u.p for u in $C_{L(i)}.U$] ; $\widetilde{Q}^u =$ **Closure**(U) ;
18     $\widehat{Q} =$ [SUM(S.q) = 0 for q in $C_{L(i+1)}^M.\widetilde{Q}^s$] ; concept_type = 0 ;
19   $C_{L(i+1)}^R =$ **Function** *generateRightChild()*:
20   S = [s.HF = 0 for s in $(C_{L(i)}.S - C_{L(i+1)}^M.S)$] ; $\widetilde{Q}^s =$ **Closure**(S) ;
21   U = [$\widetilde{Q}^s$ **match** u.p for u in $C_{L(i)}.U$] ; $\widetilde{Q}^u =$ **Closure**(U) ;
22     $\widehat{Q} =$ [SUM(S.q) = 0 for q in $C_{L(i+1)}^M.\widetilde{Q}^s$] ; concept_type = -1 ;
23   **return** $[C_{L(i+1)}^M, C_{L(i+1)}^L, C_{L(i+1)}^R]$

$$P_S(q) = \sum_{s \in S} I(dc\_b\_SDQ[s,q],1)/|S|; P_U(q) = \sum_{u \in U} I(b\_UPP[u,q],1)/|U|;$$
$$P_{S,U}(q) = P_S(q)/(P_S(q) + P_U(q)); CE(p) = -[plogp + (1-p)log(1-p)]; \quad (4)$$
$$CE\_add(q) = w_s * CE(P_S(q)) + w_u * CE(P_U(q)) + w_c * CE(P_{S,U}(q))$$

Next, we need to select a heuristic factor HF from $C_{L(i+1)}^M.\widetilde{Q}^s$ to divide the remaining services $C_{L(i)}.S - C_{L(i+1)}^M.S$ into middle-level and low-level customizations. This paper selects HF according to the balance of its subdivided users and resources, corresponding to Eq. 4. Services with $s.HF = 1$ are divided into $C_{L(i+1)}^L$, and services with $s.HF = 0$ are divided into $C_{L(i+1)}^R$. Then the other elements can be calculated with the operators of preference matching, closure and partial order (in Eq. 3).

Since the quality configurations of all services in $C^M_{L(i+1)}$ are *best_QoS*, they are already indistinguishable, so this paper only does data preprocessing of add-scale for high-level customized granules, that is, *concept_type* $= 1$. Add-scale lets originally indistinguishable services to become differentiated. Convergence conditions of the granular construction algorithm are the following two points: 1) If the quality configuration of all services is the same, or 2) the number of users is less than *min_users*, the current granule is no longer subdivided.

The metrics of the algorithm include the coverage of customer preferences, the granularity of customer segmentation, the precision of service customization, and the redundancy of granules, as seen Eq. 5 for their calculation formulas.

$$Granularity = \left| U^M_{L(i+1)} + U^L_{L(i+1)} + U^R_{L(i+1)} \right| / (3 * \left| U_{L(i)} \right|)$$

$$Precision = \left| \widetilde{Q}^M_{s.L(i+1)} + \widetilde{Q}^L_{s.L(i+1)} + \widetilde{Q}^R_{s.L(i+1)} \right| / (3 * \left| \widetilde{Q}_{s.L(i)} \right|)$$

$$Coverage = \left| \widetilde{Q}_s \cap \widetilde{Q}_u \right| / \left| \widetilde{Q}_u \right| \tag{5}$$

$$Redundancy = (\left| U^M_{L(j+1)} \cap U^L_{L(j+1)} \right| + \left| U^M_{L(j+1)} \cap U^R_{L(j+1)} \right|) / (2 * \left| U^M_{L(j+1)} \right|)$$

4.3   Model Reduction of Granular Computing

Section 4.2 only considers the personalized preferences of users, and ignores constrained resources, resulting in some customized solutions where the number of resources is insufficient to meet the matching number of users. In addition, a user may be satisfied with multiple solutions, which leads to high redundancy. So this section gives an accurate matching method and a granular structure optimization method to obtain a balanced and reduced customized scheme.

The accurate matching method reduces the subset of users of each granule to keep the balance of users and resources according to user tolerance and granular redundancy, and it is executed layer by layer from top to bottom in a multi-level SLA granular structure, as shown in Algorithm 2. For the i-th layer, all customized granules of this layer are sorted according to the balance calculated by dividing the number of users by the number of resources. Then, starting with the maximum balance, tolerances of users are calculated. If d=1, *tolerance* $= \bar{q} - \underline{s}$; If d=0, *tolerance* $= \underline{q} - \underline{s}$. In descending order of tolerances, if the user is satisfied with a worse customized service, the user is removed from the current granule; If the current granule is still unbalanced, in ascending order of tolerances, if the user is satisfied with a better customized service, then the user is removed from the current granule.

The optimization of granular structure uses the post-sequential traversal to scan the granular layer from bottom to top, the children of a node consist of four cases: M, ML, MR and MLR. The method calculates the redundancy and quantity of partial order QoS of brother nodes ML and MR. If *redundancy* $>$ *min_R* or *quantity* $\leq$ *min_Q*, they should be merged.

Algorithm 2: Accurate matching algorithm

---

1 children = findChildren(layer_num=i, orderBy='partialOrder') ;
2 balance = calcBalance(children, orderBy='max_balance') ;
3 **for** *i in [0, len(children)]* **do**
4 | concept = balance[i] ;
5 | delete_num = user_number - service_number ;
6 | **if** *delete_num ¿ 0* **then**
7 | tolerance = calcTolerance(concept, orderBy='max_tolerance') ;
8 | **for** *k in [i + 1, len(children)]* **do**
9 | **if** *balance[k] ≺ concept* **then**
10 | In descending order of tolerance, if the user is satisfied with the k solution, then it is removed from the concept ;
11 | delete_num -= 1 ;

12 | **if** *delete_num ¿ 0* **then**
13 | **for** *k in [i + 1, len(children)]* **do**
14 | **if** *balance[k] ≻ concept* **then**
15 | In ascending order of tolerance, if the user is satisfied with the k solution, then it is removed from the concept ;
16 | delete_num -= 1 ;

---

5   Evaluation

This paper conducts experimental analysis based on real user and service data sets, which are crawled from the online travel service platform of Trip.com, including quality configurations of all hotels in Sanya and user comments (Table 1). QoS attributes of hotels include star rating, built time, user scores, surrounding services, infrastructure, additional services, room specifications, etc. And we mine fine-grained QoE on the tour guide, travel arrangement, attraction, gameplay experience, hotel accommodation, group meal, transportation and shopping from user comments. Due to limited length, we publish the detailed list of QoS and QoE (*"/main/QoS.json; /main/QoE.json"*), as well as the intermediate results of the subsequent experimental process, to the GitHub repository[1].

Table 1. The basic information of dataset

Hotels	1236	Room Types	5064	Rooms	79470
QoS	69	Continuous	37	D=1	61
		Discrete	32	D=0	8
QoE	132	Total number of users			65878

---

[1] https://github.com/youcaihua2020/Multi-level-SLA.

5.1 Parameter Analysis of Satisfaction Mapping Function

The input for this step is representation vectors of all users' personalized preferences (64 dimensions, "/main/QoE_Embedding_vectors.csv" in the GitHub repository) and outputs are the parameters W and b of each user satisfaction mapping function (both 69 dimensions, corresponding to 69 QoS attributes, "/main/Weights_W.csv; /main/Weights_b.csv").

We used 8 comparative experiments for hyperparameter tuning and introduced grey relational analysis (GRA) to evaluate. We think that if the change of variances of $W_{u,q}$ and $b_{u,q}$ for all users are synchronized with the change of variance of QoS for all services, then $W_{u,q}$ and $b_{u,q}$ are more accurate. As shown in Table 2, it can be seen that with the increase of $|W|_{max}$, the entropy decreases monotonously, while the loss decreases first and then increases. Because if the $|W|_{max}$ is too large, the change of satisfaction is abrupt, which makes it more difficult for model convergence. When $|W|_{max} = 10$ is fixed and δ is changed, with the increase of δ, the GRA of W and b decreases significantly.

Table 2. The evaluation of satisfaction mapping functions with GRA

Model ID	$|W|_{max}$	δ	Iterations	Loss	Metric	GRA of W	GRA of b
1	4	1	33	1.22937	0.53942	0.9784	0.9448
2	6	1	42	1.24503	0.43775	0.9792	0.9515
3	8	1	96	1.09542	0.42541	0.9831	0.9522
4	10	1	61	1.15391	0.41725	0.9843	0.9561
5	12	1	35	1.23256	0.35955	0.9832	0.9537
6	10	2	35	1.24859	0.37392	0.9785	0.9448
7	10	3	58	1.1574	0.34522	0.9721	0.9317
8	10	4	49	1.31398	0.33038	0.9708	0.8831

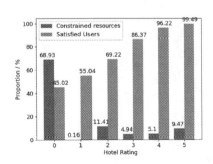

Fig. 7. The proportions of different rating hotels and users satisfied with them

Therefore, in the end, we used model 4 to predict the satisfaction mapping function of each user for each QoS. Taking the QoS of hotel star rating as an example, this paper counted the proportion of resources with different stars and the proportion of users with satisfaction greater than 0.5 for different stars. As shown in Fig. 7, 68.93% of hotels were star-less, and 45.02% of customers were satisfied with them. Although five-star hotels can satisfy 99.49% of customers, their number is small and not enough to meet large-scale customers.

5.2　Algorithm Analysis of Multi-level SLA Granular Construction

There are 4 factors that affect the granular structure, including the minimum number of user segmentation min_users, the satisfaction threshold τ, the maximum extended scales of each QoS k, and the three weights w_u, w_s, w_c in the selection formula of heuristic factors. Based on the τ and all users' satisfaction mapping functions obtained from 5.1, the preference interval and direction of each user can be calculated (i.e., the table of UPP, "/main/UPP_Interval.csv; /main/UPP_Direction.csv"). The QoS of all resources are known, which are normalized into the [0, 1] interval (i.e. the table of SDQ, "/main/SDQ_hotels.csv; /main/SDQ_rooms.csv"). They are inputs for multi-level SLA customization.

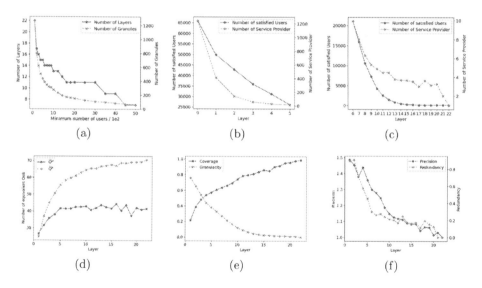

Fig. 8. The trend of the key features of multi-level SLA customization solutions

First, we set $\tau = 0.3, k = 1, w_u = w_s = w_c = 1$ and change min_users. The result is shown in Fig. 8, as min_users increases, both the total number of layers and the total number of granules decrease in (a). The number of users and services contained in each granule are reduced layer by layer, and in the early stage the subdivision of services is more significant (b), and the subdivision of users in the later stage is more significant (c); The number of attributes contained in the equivalent QoS set increase layer by layer, and $\widetilde{Q}^s$ continues to increase until it closes to the full QoS set, while the $\widetilde{Q}^u$ stabilizes at about 41 in the later stage (d); The preference coverage increases and the granularity of user segmentation decreases layer by layer (e); The precision of service customization decreases layer by layer, indicating that the differences among services in the later subdivision are getting smaller and smaller. User redundancy is also decreasing layer by layer (f), because the differences in customer preferences are more pronounced when considering more QoS attributes.

Next, we set $min\_users = 100, k = 1, w_u = w_s = w_c = 1$ and change τ. The increase of τ means that the requirements of users are stricter and the preference intervals are narrower. As shown in Table 3, the coverage and precision are significantly reduced. Moreover, with the increase of τ, the personalization becomes more obvious, so the redundancy at the lowest level is significantly reduced. The number of layers is reduced but the total number of granules is not, because users can be clearly distinguished without too many layers of subdivision.

Table 3. The impact of different satisfaction thresholds on multi-level SLA customization

τ	Layers	Granules	Coverage	Precision	Granularity	Redundancy
0.3	22	1266	0.9767	1.0980	0.002408	0.1250
0.4	19	1220	0.9131	1.0716	0.001914	0.1199
0.5	17	1225	0.8810	1.0290	0.002745	0.0992
0.6	16	1281	0.8519	1.0147	0.002519	0.0641
0.7	14	1259	0.8320	0.9998	0.003649	0.0430

Then, we set $min\_users = 100, \tau = 0.7, w_u = w_s = w_c = 1$ and change k. $k = -1$ means that the scales of all eligible QoS are extended every time. Add-scale makes the granularity finer and the redundancy lower, as shown in Table 4.

Table 4. The impact of different add-scale on multi-level SLA customization

k	1	3	5	7	-1
Granularity/1e-3	3.64917	3.38550	2.84220	1.56591	0.79486
Redundancy	0.04304	0.04213	0.04125	0.02126	0.00339

Finally, with $min\_users = 100, \tau = 0.7, k = -1$, we get a granular structure for multi-level SLA customization, which has 12 layers and 1254 granules. The model instance can be seen "/main/model.pkl" in the GitHub repository.

5.3   Analysis of Granular Reduction Under Constrained Resources

Comparing the balance of each granule, as shown in Fig. 9.(a), most granules are generally greater than 1, especially for high-level customizations, the number of satisfied users far exceeds the matching resources. After accurate matching, the balances of high-level customizations decrease significantly, and the first 5 layers decrease significantly, remaining at about 1. But for the last 10–12 layers, the balance is not down to 1. The reason is that the number of QoS considered in the last layer is large, the differences of users' preferences and services' qualities are obvious, and granular redundancies are very small. After accurate matching, the granular structure is unchanged, and the subset of users matched by each granule can be seen "*/main/model_matching/*"* in the GitHub repository.

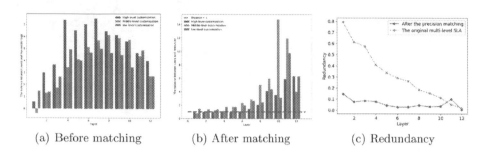

(a) Before matching   (b) After matching   (c) Redundancy

Fig. 9. The performance of the accurate algorithm in this paper on the balance between users and resources

Finally, we compare the two granular reduction strategies: partial order-based reduction and redundancy-based reduction. From the perspective of preference coverages, the redundancy-based reduction is better, as shown in Fig. 10, which delete the rough granules in the first few layers and make the coverage improve from a high starting point. The reduction based on partial order also has a higher starting point but terminates at lower coverage. Because the redundancy-based approach retains the fine-grained customizations with low redundancy in the latter layers, their preference coverages are higher. However, the last few layers have less expansion of QoS, resulting in a smaller number of partial order QoS, so partial order-based reduction will delete these nodes. More detailed results of model reduction can be found on "*/main/model_reduction/*"*.

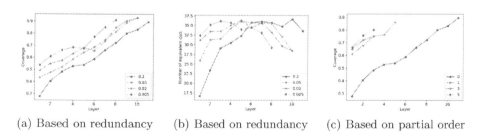

(a) Based on redundancy   (b) Based on redundancy   (c) Based on partial order

Fig. 10. The impact of different granular reduction on the preference coverage

6   Conclusion

In this paper, we trained a deep generation network to extract the hidden QoE information from public user comments and reasonably inferred the satisfaction mapping function. Then, we proposed a granular construction algorithm to obtain a multi-level, multi-perspective and multi-scale SLA customization scheme. Finally, in view of resource constraints, the accurate matching algorithm and the granular reduction algorithm are given, which show the advantage in eliminating the granular redundancy. The multi-level SLA customization in this paper has both equivalence relations and partial order relations, which can provide support for SLA guarantee. In the 12-layer multi-level SLA customization, each user is satisfied with an average of 7.93 customized services, which have different user preference coverage. The number of resources and users matched by each customized service is balanced, averaging 1.24. The user redundancy of customized services in the same layer is very small, only 0.0596. Customized solutions are few but it is enough to cover 92.93% of users' personalized preferences, which can effectively reduce the time of service selection and composition. The limitation of the method is that service customization is based on reasonable inference of customer preferences, but if there is an error between the reasoning results and the real feedback of customers, the quality of customization may reduce. In the future work, we consider fine-tuning the customized structure and solutions according to the real customer satisfaction feedback under the service running environment.

Acknowledgments. Research in this paper is partially supported by the National Key Research and Development Program of China (No 2022YFF0903100) and the National Natural Science Foundation of China (61832014, 61832004).

References

1. Chen, J., Hao, Y.: Mass customization in design of service delivery system: a review and prospects. Afr. J. Bus. Manage. **4**, 842–848 (2010)
2. Ernst, D., Dolnicar, S.: How to avoid random market segmentation solutions. J. Travel Res. Int. Assoc. Travel Res. Mark. Profess. **57**(1), 69–82 (2018)
3. Firdaus, U., Utama, D.: Balance as one of the attributes in the customer segmentation analysis method: systematic literature review. Adv. Sci. Technol. Eng. Syst. J. **5**, 334–339 (2020)
4. Hajibaba, H., Grün, B.: Improving the stability of market segmentation analysis. Int. J. Contemp. Hosp. Manag. (2019)
5. Hayyolalam, V., Pourhaji Kazem, A.A.: A systematic literature review on QoS-aware service composition and selection in cloud environment. J. Netw. Comput. Appl. **110**, 52–74 (2018)
6. Hussain, W., Hussain, F., Hussain, O., Damiani, E., Chang, E.: Formulating and managing viable SLAS in cloud computing from a small to medium service provider's viewpoint: a state-of-the-art review. Inf. Syst. **71**, 240–259 (2017)
7. Li, M., Xu, H., Tu, Z., Su, T., Xu, X., Wang, Z.: A deep learning based personalized QoE/QoS correlation model for composite services. In: IEEE International Conference on Web Services, ICWS 2022, 10–16 July 2022, pp. 312–321 (2022)

8. Liu, Y., et al.: QoE-aware data caching optimization with budget in edge computing. In: 2021 IEEE International Conference on Web Services, ICWS 2021, 5–10 September 2021, pp. 324–334 (2021)
9. Nurma Sari, J., Nugroho, L., Ferdiana, R.: Review on customer segmentation technique on ecommerce. Adv. Sci. Lett. **22**, 3018–3022 (2016)
10. Saia, R., Boratto, L., Carta, S.: Using neural word embeddings to model user behavior and detect user segments. Knowl.-Based Syst. **108**, 5–14 (2016)
11. Wei, J.T., Lin, S.Y., Wu, H.H.: A review of the application of RFM model. Afr. J. Bus. Manag. December Spec. Rev. **4**, 4199–4206 (2010)
12. Xia, J., Cheng, G., Guo, D., Zhou, X.: A QoE-aware service enhancement strategy for edge artificial intelligence applications. IEEE Internet Things J. **7**(10), 9494–9506 (2020)

Request Relaxation Based-on Provider Constraints for a Capability-Based NaaS Services Discovery

Imen Jerbi[1,2,3]([✉]), Hayet Brabra[1], Mohamed Sellami[1], Walid Gaaloul[1],
Sami Bhiri[3,4], Boualem Benatallah[5], Djamal Zeghlache[1], and Olivier Tirat[6]

[1] SAMOVAR, Telecom SudParis, Institut Polytechnique de Paris, Palaiseau, France
imen.jerbi@telecom-sudparis.eu
[2] ISITCom Hammam Sousse, University of Sousse, Sousse, Tunisia
[3] OASIS, National Engineering School of Tunis, University of Tunis, Tunis, Tunisia
[4] University of Monastir, Monastir, Tunisia
[5] School of Computing, Dublin City University, Dublin 9, Ireland
[6] BYO NETWORKS, Orsay, France

Abstract. Network as a Service (NaaS) enables cloud customers to connect their distributed services across multiple clouds without relying exclusively on their infrastructures. The discovery of NaaS services remains challenging not only because of their scale and diversity but also because of the hidden constraints that cloud providers impose on these services at the networking layer. NaaS services are usually offered in the form of service bundles containing underlying services and constraints not requested by the customers. This creates undesirable dependencies and constraints that hamper portability, compatibility and interoperability across providers. The problem of service discovery becomes more challenging when these constraints are the main and first cause that prevents a customer's request from being fulfilled. Without a mechanism that enables customers to identify these constraints and to adjust their requests accordingly, existing service discovery solutions are likely to fall short. We propose to complement existing service discovery solutions by not only identifying unmatched constraints but also recommending relaxing discovery requests to retrieve optimal and compliant services.

Keywords: Network-as-a-Service · Services discovery · Cloud services

1 Introduction

With the emergence of the NaaS [5] paradigm, cloud customers can acquire on a per use basis interconnection and networking services [16]. The increasing demand for network services has pushed cloud services providers (CSPs) to compete for evolving adaptive and programmable interconnection services. This expansion of published NaaS services calls for efficient service discovery solutions [1] to assist users in selecting the most appropriate networking services for their distributed cloud applications. The role of service discovery should be not

© The Author(s), under exclusive license to Springer Nature Switzerland AG 2023
M. Indulska et al. (Eds.): CAiSE 2023, LNCS 13901, pp. 611–627, 2023.
https://doi.org/10.1007/978-3-031-34560-9_36

only to provide such discovery mechanisms to users but also make them aware of constraints and limitations that may come with the providers service offerings.

Over the last decades, service discovery has been actively studied in Web services [8] and cloud computing [9]. A plethora of service description models [13,22,23] have been proposed with the aim of developing efficient service matching and retrieval algorithms. The majority of existing works focus on the description and discovery of services operating at the application layer, i.e., last layer of the OSI model [6]. Some efforts have also been proposed to adapt existing solutions to the network layer [3,12,14,18,21], i.e., third layer of the OSI model. Even if these approaches are valuable, they typically fail to capture, identify and inform users of constraints and limitations that come with the interconnection services offering, especially bundling of multi-layer networking services [11]. *Constraints* refer to rules, conditions or restrictions that prevent a customer from consuming a service in a specific way. *Pure bundling* [25], for instance, is a constraint employed by some CSPs to prevent network services from being purchased separately. In fact, reviewing and analyzing NS offered by popular CSPs, reveals that each networking service is often linked-to/delivered-with other network resources. Another constraint is *location constraint* often used to make a NS highly dependent on its location. A service location refers to the availability zones or regions in which it is located, to the sub-networks to which it is attached, or even to its provider. A service may be available in a region but restricted in another, may be bundled differently according to providers/regions, etc. From a service discovery perspective, such constraints complicate the analysis of NS offers especially when they are *not visible* [25] to the cloud services customers.

The objective of this work is not to propose yet another cloud services matching or retrieval algorithm but to focus on identifying providers constraints, in particular those specific to NaaS and making a customer request partially or unsatisfactorily matched. Our objective is to make the customer aware of these constraints and recommend adapted solutions from the providers offers that comply with the user requirements and remove the network services offering built-in constraints and limitations. Thereafter, we recommend relaxing plans for discovery requests to retrieve compliant networking services.

To illustrate and motivate our approach, we consider the example of a cloud customer requesting a network connection between two *AWS* virtual machines, *VM-1* and *VM-2*, at the data link layer (layer 2 (L2) of the OSI model [6]), i.e. via their MAC addresses. *VM-1* is identified by *mac-0001*, localized in the AWS *Northern Virginia* region-precisely in the *Chicago* availability zone (AZ). *VM-2* is identified by *mac-0002*, localized in the *Oregon* region-precisely in the *Las Vegas* AZ. To realize such L2 connectivity, two cloud network services are required: an L2 endpoint service on each machine to make its corresponding MAC address accessible and an L2 bridging service (i.e. switch) to bridge the data packets between the two given machines.

Network communication rules reveal that neither AWS nor any other cloud services provider can fulfill the customer's request of our example. In fact, a location constraint states that only VMs in the same sub-network, AZ, and region can communicate via their MAC addresses. Hence, the customer request cannot be fulfilled unless she/he takes this constraint into account and places her/his VMs in the same sub-network, AZ, and region. However, such migration may be an expensive solution if the VMs locations are too far apart, sometimes even more costly than purchasing a new VM in the target region. Another solution to this location constraint could be to keep the VMs in their regions and connect them at the L3 communication layer (i.e., through their IP addresses) using an L3 routing service. AWS, for instance, allows to realize such solution using a VPC peering connection[1], which is a networking connection that can be established between two networks in two different regions enabling traffic routing between them using their private IP addresses. This solution does not fully respond to the expressed customer's request. However, it should be considered assuming that some of the non functional requirements (such as speed, rate and latency for instance) can only be fulfilled at the L3 connectivity services layer. As shown in this example, constraints on VMs' location preventing a request from being fulfilled cannot be easily identified by customers especially if they are unfamiliar with networking rules and limitations due to CSPs constraints. Moreover, without assisting customers during service discovery, they might not be able to adjust their request by taking into account the providers' constraints (e.g., location constraint) and discover alternative solutions meeting their needs.

The remainder of this paper is structured as follows. Section 2 looks into related efforts. An overview of our approach is given in Sect. 3. Section 4 introduces preliminary concepts. Section 5 and Sect. 6 detail our contributions. The evaluation details are given in Sect. 7. Section 8 concludes the paper.

2 Related Work

Many approaches tackle the service discovery problem. Depending on the adopted matching method, existing discovery efforts can be organized into semantic-based and content-based (or keyword-based) [1]. Semantic-based matching approaches [3,12,17] rely on the meaning of concepts codified into ontology schema to identify similarities between users requests and offered services. Content-based methods [2,18,20,24] compare keyword composing user request with cloud service textual descriptions. Whether semantic-based or content-based, they have a number of limitations: First, to the best of our knowledge, none of these discovery solutions considers network services in depth; the focus is on computing, platform, and software services. Second, all of these works do not consider the importance of depicting the constraints imposed on networking services in their description models for a more transparent and precise discovery. Considering such constraints adds more complexity to the service description model making the service discovery process more challenging. Other approaches focusing on "recommender systems" have been proposed [15,19] to automatically suggest the most suitable cloud services for customers. While valuable, these systems aim to solve the problem of cloud services selection, rather than the discovery issue. To the best of our knowledge, no work have been proposed not only to identify providers constraints, but also to recommend remedies to lift them.

---

[1] https://docs.aws.amazon.com/vpc/latest/peering/what-is-vpc-peering.html.

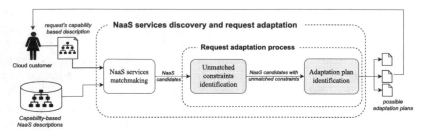

Fig. 1. Approach for NaaS services discovery and adaptation

3   Approach Overview

Our approach for NaaS services discovery and request adaptation relies on three components as illustrated in Fig. 1. It takes two inputs: a cloud customer's request and a repository of NaaS services descriptions. Both inputs are described according to our NaaS capability model [11] introduced in Sect. 4. Based on these inputs, the NaaS services matchmaking component crawls the given repository and returns a set of NaaS services candidates. These laters are those matching the given request with a similarity degree greater than a specific threshold (generally defined by the customer). The so identified NaaS services candidates are then passed to the Unmatched constraints identification component. This later identifies the constraints that are specified in these services to prevent the total matching of the given request. NaaS services candidates with the identified unmatched constraints are then passed to the Adaptation plans identification component. It establishes the possible adjustments, called adaptation plans, that could be applied to the customer's request in order to "relax" his/her requirements vis-a-vis these unsatisfiable constraints. These plans are then recommended to cloud customers as the output of the Request adaptation process based on which they could adapt their requests and re-run the NaaS services discovery and request adaptation process.

   In the following, we introduce our NaaS capability model to describe the inputs of our approach. We detail our contributions: Unmatched constraints identification and Adaptation plans identification in Sects. 5 and 6, respectively. Due to lack of space, the NaaS services matchmaking component is not presented. Nevertheless, this could not impact the understanding of our approach. Indeed, our approach is independent from the used service matchmaking technique. We could rely on existing matching methods [1,8,9,16] to crawl capability-based NaaS descriptions repositories and return NaaS services candidates.

4   Capability Model for Requests and Offers Description

To describe customers requests and NaaS service offers (i.e., our approach's inputs), we rely on our NaaS capability model proposed in [11]. This model is an extension of a previous one presented in [10]. The novelty of our work is not in the model we use but in the techniques we propose. However, their correctness will be heavily dependent on the model. In our work, we rely on the NaaS capability model for two reasons. First, it defines a set of property values types useful to explicitly describe providers constraints and hence offers the means for their identification. Second, to the best of our knowledge, it is the only model that was defined specifically for NaaS discovery. Several standardization initiatives (ETSI NFV [7], TOSCA-NFV [4]) have been proposed for NaaS description. While valuable, these initiatives focus only on describing services from an orchestration perspective. They assume that NaaS are already discovered and made available by the underlying virtual infrastructure managers (AWS, Openstack, etc).

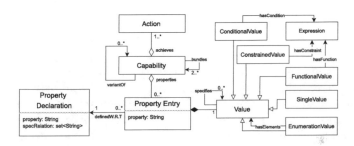

Fig. 2. Capability model for NaaS services description [11]

The key concept of our model is Capability, which corresponds to the description of a service. This description is given in terms of one or many Actions and a set of property entries. A Property Entry (PE) is a (property[2],Value) pair. A property value may be simple as a SingleValue, i.e. literal value (e.g. string, integer), or more complex as a ConstrainedValue (constraint), ConditionalValue (condition), FunctionalValue (function) or Enumeration Value (set of values). Complex values types in our model play two key roles: they allow to capture dependencies between services' properties and they serve as declarative specifications for generating concrete services for a given request.

In Fig. 3, we describe the capability of an L2 connectivity service, whose deployment requires an L2 endpoint and L2 bridging. Its capability, S_{L2C}, is then described as a composition, i.e. bundle, of its required services capabilities: S_{L2EP} and S_{L2B}. The bundles relation allows to explicitly model the packaging of services. As illustrated in Fig. 2, it is defined between a parent capability and at least two children capabilities where the parent capability is a bundle of the children capabilities. A semi-formal definition of this relation and the algorithms to infer it were introduced in [11]. We define the Action of each NaaS service capability as Expose (exp for short) since we consider a NaaS as a mechanism that makes a virtual network resource accessible[3]. For instance, S_{L2EP} describes the capability of a service that gives access to the L2 address[4] of a virtual

---

[2] Property Declaration in the diagram.

[3] Our model enables to define other services' actions.

[4] An L2 address is equivalent to a MAC address if Ethernet is the communication protocol used at the second communication Layer (L2).

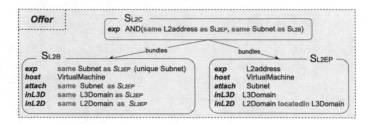

Fig. 3. Capability-based modelling of an L2 connectivity NaaS Service

machine; S_{L2B} describes the capability of a service that makes the machines of a local network accessible; S_{L2C} describes the capability of a service that allows to create a connectivity between machines at the L2 layer. S_{L2C} exposes two types of resources: the machines' L2 addresses and the local network.

In addition to the `Action`, four `Property Declarations` are defined in S_{L2EP} and S_{L2B} to detail each of these services. The property `host` specifies the VM on which a service is hosted. The `attach` property defines the (sub)-network to which the exposed network resources are attached. `inL3D` and `inL2D` specify, respectively, the L3 `Domain` (i.e. regions) and L2 `domain` (i.e. AZs) where these resources are located. Except for the value of the property `inL2D`, which is a `ConstrainedValue`, all values in S_{L2EP} are of type `SingleValue`. All values in S_{L2B} are of type `ConstrainedValue`. The value *"same L2Domain as S_{L2EP}"* captures the dependency between the L2 domain of the L2 bridging service and the L2 domain of the L2 Endpoint service. In addition to the `bundles` relation, our model defines a partial order relation between services capabilities, called *variantOf*, as illustrated in Fig. 2. This relation plays a key role in this paper. In [10], we defined it formally and we proposed rules to infer it[5]. Definition 1 introduces this relation semi-formally.

Definition 1 *(variantOf). Let C_i and C_j two capabilities. C_i variantOf C_j if (1) C_i has the same PEs as C_j with at least one additional PE pe' or (2) C_i and C_j have the same properties and $\forall$ common property p, the value of p in C_i isEqual or specifies its value in C_j.*

The *isEqual* and *specifies* are two relations that may exist between two values. *isEqual* refers to an equivalence relation. *specifies* indicates when a value is more specific than another w.r.t their corresponding types. We formally defined this relation and proposed rules to infer it in [10]. Note that, we implemented our NaaS capability model as an RDF ontology[6]. Services capabilities, their properties as well as their values refer to ontological terms. In our model, we use SPARQL expressions to specify `ConstrainedValues`.

---

[5] https://travailderecherche.wixsite.com/monsite/inference-rules.

[6] https://travailderecherche.wixsite.com/monsite/capability-metamodel.

5 Unmatched Constraints Identification

In this section, we present our approach for identifying constraints preventing a user request from being matched with a set of advertised services (refer to Unmatched constraints identification component in Fig. 1). Recall that, both requests and offers are described according to our NaaS capability model. Through a request, a user may be asking for several services. Thus, depicting the constraints that prevent his/her demand from being matched returns in depicting those preventing each single service requested in this demand from being matched with the advertised services. This identification relies on two key observations: *(i) An advertised service* is abstract and its description represents a declarative specification for generating *service variants* during the discovery. Service variants have the same properties as the advertised service from which they are derived with at least one more specific value, or with equal values and at least one additional property entry [10]. What are invoked and consumed by customers at the end, are service variants with atomic property values. *(ii) A requested service* corresponds to an expected, i.e. desired, service variant. Based on *(i)* and *(ii)*, and considering a requested service s and an advertised one s', we state that no match exists between s and s' if s cannot be generated/derived as a variant from s'. Since services are described according to our NaaS capability model, no match exists between s and s' if $\nexists$ *variantOf* relation between their capabilities C_s and $C_{s'}$. The relation *variantOf* represents one of the cornerstones of our unmatched constraints identification approach (refer to Sect. 4).

We use the *variantOf* relation in Algorithm 1 that we propose for unmatched constraints identification. The proposed algorithm takes two capability-based descriptions as inputs: *Req* for a customer's request and *Off* for a cloud provider's offer. Each description may include several services' capabilities. Algorithm 1 iterates on each requested capability C_i in *Req* and on each advertised capability C_j in *Off* to check if C_i can be generated as a *variantOf* C_j ($\forall i = j$). This verification is accomplished using the *variantOf* relation introduced as a procedure in Algorithm 1. If C_i is not *variantOf* C_j, then C_i and C_j cannot be matched due to a set of constraints that the providers define on the properties of the services they offer and that the customers do not consider when defining the services they request. We refer to these constraints as "unmatched constraints" and we rely on the *variantOf* procedure to identify them and label the properties on which they are imposed. Provider's offer *Off* with the identified unmatched constraints is then returned as output of Algorithm 1.

To illustrate Algorithm 1 execution, we refer to the customer's request introduced in our motivating example and we consider an L2 connectivity service offer whose description is illustrated in the bottom of Fig. 4. The request includes five services' capabilities and the offer only three. We iterate through all capabilities C_i in *Req* (lines 1–8 in Algorithm 1). During the first iteration, Algorithm 1 first checks if each C_{L2EP} in the request is *variantOf* S_{L2EP} in the offer (line 2), which is true as illustrated in Fig. 4. This verification is done using the *variantOf* procedure and is true since each C_{L2EP} has the same properties as S_{L2EP}. Indeed, $properties(C_{L2EP}) \cap properties\,(S_{L2EP}) = \{exp, host,$

Algorithm 1. Identifying unmatched constraints in a NaaS provider's offer

---

Input: $\mathcal{R}eq$, Off : *capability-based descriptions of a request and a provider's offer*
Output: Off: *the offer given as input with identified unmatched constraints*
Parameters: $C_i \in \mathcal{R}eq$; $S_i \in Off$; S_adj set of adjacent capabilities to S_i C_adj set of adjacent capabilities to C_i

1: **for each** *capability* C_i *in* $\mathcal{R}eq$ **do**
2:     $variantOf(C_i, S_i)$
3:     $C\_adj \leftarrow \{C$ such that C_i bundles C in $\mathcal{R}eq\}$
4:     $S\_adj \leftarrow \{S$ such that S_i bundles S in Off $\}$
5:     **if** $C\_adj \setminus S\_adj \neq \{\emptyset\}$ **then**
6:         print(C_i, "can be provided but as a bundle of", S_adj)
7:     **if** $S\_adj \setminus C\_adj \neq \{\emptyset\}$ **then**
8:         print(C_i, "can be provided but with other attached services:", $S\_adj \setminus C\_adj$)

Procedure $variantOf(C_i, S_i)$

1: **if** properties(C_i) $\cap$ properties(S_i) = properties(S_i) **then**
2:     **for each** common property p in C_i **do**
3:         **if** not($v^p_{C_i}$ specifies $v^p_{S_i}$) and not($v^p_{C_i} = v^p_{S_i}$) **then**
4:             label p and its value in S_i as unmatched with an error message
5: **if** properties(S_i) $\setminus$ (properties(C_i) $\cap$ properties(S_i))$\neq \{\emptyset\}$ **then**
6:     **for each** un-common property $p \in$ (properties(C_i) $\cap$ properties(S_i)) **do**
7:         label p and its value in S_i as unmatched with an error message

---

attach, inL3D, inL2D }. Moreover, the value of each common property in C_{L2EP} *specifies* the one in S_{L2EP}. Recall that the *specifies* relation was defined in our previous work [10] with a set of rules[7] to infer it. In line 6 of the *variantOf* procedure, we call these rules. Algorithm 1 then checks that an S_{L2EP} is bundled by an S_{L2C} (lines 3–8). During the second iteration, Algorithm 1 checks if each C_{L2C} in the request is *variantOf* S_{L2C} in the offer, which is false as illustrated in Fig. 4. Using the *variantOf* procedure, each C_{L2C} has the same properties as S_{L2C}. Indeed, *properties*(C_{L2C}) $\cap$ *properties* (S_{L2C}) = \{*exp*\}. However, the value of the common property, i.e. *exp*, in each C_{L2C} is neither equal nor more specific than its value in S_{L2C}. Hence, this property and its value in S_{L2C} is identified and labeled as unmatched (line 4 in the *variantOf* procedure). Algorithm 1 detects then that an S_{L2C} is offered as a bundle of S_{L2EP} and S_{L2B} (lines 3–8); and hence respects the customer's composition need.

During the third and last iteration, Algorithm 1 uses *variantOf* to check if each C_{L2B} in the request is *variantOf* S_{L2B} in the offer, which is false as shown in Fig. 4. In fact, C_{L2B} has only one common property with S_{L2B} (i.e. the *exp* property) and the value of this property in C_{L2B} is neither equal nor more specific than its value in S_{L2B}. Then, the *variantOf* procedure identifies and labels this property and its value in S_{L2B} as unmatched (line 4 in *variantOf* procedure). As for the properties that belong to S_{L2B} but not to C_{L2B} (i.e. *host, attach, inL3D* and *inL2D*), the *variantOf* procedure identifies and labels them as unmatched too (line 7). The execution of Algorithm 1 on the inputs of the given example ends with the identification of the CSP constraints that the customer should consider to adjust his/her request. These constraints are illustrated in text boxes in Fig. 4.

---

[7] https://travailderecherche.wixsite.com/monsite/inference-rules.

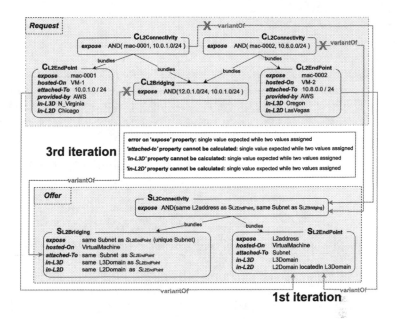

Fig. 4. Iterations of Algorithm 1 on an example of two inputs

6 Adaptation Plans Identification

In this section, we detail how we infer the possible adjustments that could be applied to a customer's request w.r.t the identified unmatched constraints in a provider's offer (refer to Adaptation plans identification component in Fig. 1). In doing so, we rely on two key concepts: graphs and graph rewriting rules. We first represent the offer and the request as NaaS Labeled Directed Acyclic Graphs (NLDAGs). We refer to each NLDAG as dependency graph. A definition of an NLDAG is given in Definition 2.

Definition 2 *(NaaS Labeled Directed Acyclic Graph). A NaaS labeled directed acyclic graph is a triplet NLDAG= (V, E, λ) where:*

- *V is a set of nodes. Each node, v_C^p, corresponds to a value of a property p in a requested/offered capability C_i.*
- *$E \subseteq V \times V$ is a set of directed edges corresponding to dependencies between property values in V. Recall that dependencies between property values are described through their types (i.e., using complex values types in our NaaS capability model as explained in Sect. 4).*
- *λ is a total function that maps each edge to one label from the set of labels L $(\lambda : V \times V \mapsto labels)$. We consider only two labels: "sameAs" and "locatedIn", i.e., L={ "sameAs" , "locatedIn"}.*

By representing the offer as an NLDAG, we can see each identified unmatched constraint in this offer as a couple of nodes and their connecting labelled edges in this NLDAG. Similar to Object Oriented Programming, we see the request's dependency graph as a concrete NLDAG and the offer's dependency graph as a class of concrete NLDAGs. Thus, to identify possible adjustments to a request, we go through the NLDAG representing the offer and we generate the possible concrete NLDAGs considering the atomic values assigned to properties in this request. An adjustment is simply a "rewriting rule" (replacing the value of a property for instance) to be made on the request's NLDAG. An adaptation plan is the set of these "rewriting rules". A definition of an NLDAG rewriting rule is given in Definition 3.

Definition 3 *(NLDAG Rewriting rules: r1, r2 and r3). Let $NLDAG_a = (V_a, E_a, \lambda_a)$ and $NLDAG_r = (V_r, E_r, \lambda)$ dependency graphs representing an offer and a request, respectively. Let $v_{S_i}^p$ and $v_{S_j}^{p'}$ in V_a. $v_{S_i}^p$ refers to an unmatched constraint p in an offered capability S_i. $v_{S_i}^p$ and $v_{S_j}^{p'}$ are linked in $NLDAG_a$ by a sameAs labelled edge, $(\lambda_a : (v_{S_i}^p, v_{S_j}^{p'}) \mapsto sameAs$ **or** $\lambda_a : (v_{S_j}^{p'}, v_{S_i}^p) \mapsto sameAs)$.*

- *An $NLDAG_a$ rewriting rule, $r : \alpha \to \beta$, indicates that $\alpha(\alpha \in (V_a \cup V_r))$ has to be replaced by $\beta(\beta \in (V_a \cup V_r))$. We define three NLDAG rewriting rules: r1 and r2 to rewrite an offer's NLDAG and r3 to rewrite a request's NLDAG.*
  - ***rule r1:*** $v_{S_i}^p \to v$ *is to replace $v_{S_i}^p$ in $NLDAG_a$ by one of the atomic values v assigned to p in the request.*
  - ***rule r2:*** $v_{S_j}^{p'} \to v_{S_i}^p$ *is to replace $v_{S_j}^{p'}$ in $NLDAG_a$ by $v_{S_i}^p$.*
  - ***rule r3:*** $v_{C_i}^p \to v_{S_i}^p$ *is to replace $v_{C_i}^p$ in $NLDAG_r$ by $v_{S_i}^p$ if $v_{S_i}^p$ has been replaced during the rewriting of $NLDAG_a$.*

Note that we do not replace $v_{S_i}^p$ if it is linked to $v_{S_j}^{p'}$ by a *locatedIn* labelled edge, i.e. $\lambda_a : (v_{S_i}^p, v_{S_j}^{p'}) \mapsto locatedIn$ (or $\lambda_a : (v_{S_j}^{p'}, v_{S_i}^p) \mapsto locatedIn$). We rather consider them as ontological terms (see Sect. 4). We then rely on the ontology in which they are described to check if $v_{S_j}^{p'}$ *locatedIn* $v_{S_i}^p$ (or $v_{S_i}^p$ *locatedIn* $v_{S_j}^{p'}$). If not, a backtracking on the previous replacements of $v_{S_i}^p$ (or $v_{S_j}^{p'}$) is required. We illustrate later, how this backtracking avoids the identification of wrong adaptation plans and guarantees that the identified ones are semantically correct. We proposed an algorithm to describe our adjustment identification approach based-on graphs and rewriting rules. Our algorithm takes as input two capability-based descriptions: one of a request and another of a CSP's offer with identified unmatched constraints. It returns possible adjustment plans that could be applied on the request w.r.t these constraints. Due to lack of space, we will not present this algorithm[8]. We only illustrate its steps via the following example.

Example. To illustrate our adjustment identification approach, we refer again to the sample request, the offer, and the unmatched constraints identified in Sect. 5 (Fig. 4). First, we generate the *dependency graphs*, NLDAG$_r$ and NLDAG$_a$, of the request and the offer respectively as illustrated in Fig. 5. NLDAG$_a$ nodes

---

[8] This algorithm and all details related to the source code are available at supplementarymaterials/Algorithms.

Table 1. Properties associated with unmatched constraints and their possible values w.r.t a customer's request

Property in NLDAG$_a$	Possible atomic values in NLDAG$_r$
exp in S_{L2B} and $attach$ in S_{L2B}	10.8.0.0/24 , 10.0.1.0/24
$inL3D$ in S_{L2B}	Oregon, N_Virginia
$inL2D$ in S_{L2B}	Chicago, LasVegas

are values related to the properties of the offered S_{L2C}, S_{L2B} and S_{L2EP}, and edges are dependencies that exist between these values. For instance, $v_{S_{L2B}}^{exp}$ is the value of the property exp in the capability S_{L2B}. The edge $(v_{S_{L2B}}^{exp}, v_{S_{L2EP}}^{attach})$ labelled with sameAs, for instance, indicates that the sub-network exposed by the S_{L2B} is the same sub-network to which the S_{L2EP} is attached. Five unmatched constraints are identified in our example: four in the offered S_{L2B} (i.e., associated with exp, $attach$, $inL3D$, and $inL2D$) and one in the S_{L2C} (i.e. associated with exp). Based on our sample request, we list in Table 1 the possible atomic values of these properties. We iterate on the properties listed in Table 1. Starting by the first property in NLDAG$_a$, i.e. exp in S_{L2B}, we select 10.8.0.0/24 from the set of possible values. We apply the rewriting rule **r1** (given in Definition 3) to replace $v_{S_{L2B}}^{exp}$ in NLDAG$_a$ by this value as shown in Fig. 5 ①. We then apply the rule **r2** (given in Definition 3) to rewrite all values that are linked, either directly or by transition, to $v_{S_{L2B}}^{exp}$ node in NLDAG$_a$: $v_{S_{L2EP}}^{attach}$, $v_{S_{L2B}}^{exp}$ and $v_{S_{L2B}}^{attach}$. Since these values are linked to the $v_{S_{L2B}}^{exp}$ node using "sameAs" edges, they are replaced by the *same* possible value 10.8.0.0/24, as illustrated in Fig. 5 ②.

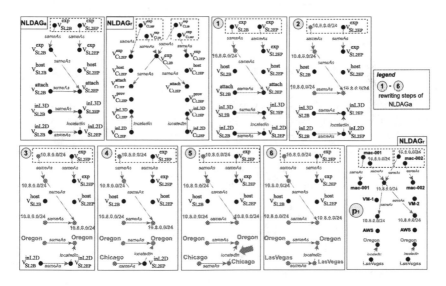

Fig. 5. Rewriting of dependency graphs to generate a possible adaptation plan

Moving to the next property *attach* in S_{L2B}, it does not appear anymore in our NLDAG$_a$ since it was replaced by 10.8.0.0/24 during the previous iteration.

Then, we iterate on the next property, $inL3D$ in S_{L2B}, considering *Oregon* as a possible value. The same process to rewrite $v_{S_{L2B}}^{exp}$ and its linked nodes, is applied to $v_{S_{L2B}}^{inL3D}$. The resulting NLDAG is illustrated in Fig. 5 ③. Coming at the last property, $inL2D$ in S_{L2B}, we select *Chicago* as a possible value. We apply $r1$ to replace $v_{S_{L2B}}^{inL2D}$ in NLDAG$_a$ by this value as shown in Fig. 5 ④. Then, we apply $r2$ to replace $v_{S_{L2EP}}^{exp}$ also by *Chicago* since it is linked to $v_{S_{L2B}}^{exp}$ using a "*sameAs*" labelled edge, as illustrated in Fig. 5 ⑤. Since, this later is linked to *Oregon* in NLDAG$_a$ using a "*locatedIn*" labelled edge, we treat *Oregon* and *Chicago* as two ontological terms. We rely on the ontology in which they are defined to check if *Chicago* is *locatedIn Oregon*, which is *false*. Thus, we backtrack to replace the values of v_{SL2EP}^{inL2D} and v_{SL2B}^{inL2D} by *LasVegas*, i.e. the second possible value of the property $inL2D$, as illustrated in Fig. 5 ⑥. The backtracking step avoids the generation of wrong adaptation plans and hence guarantees that the generated ones are semantically correct. After iterating on the first value of each property in Table 1, we consider the resulting NLDAG$_a$ shown in Fig. 5 ⑥ and we apply the rule **r3** (given in Definition 3) to rewrite NLDAG$_r$ as follows:

- $r3 : v_{C_{L2B}}^{exp} \rightarrow 10.8.0.0/24$ where $10.8.0.0/24$ replaces $v_{S_{L2B}}^{exp}$ in NLDAG$_a$.
- $r3 : v_{C_{L2EP}}^{attach} \rightarrow 10.8.0.0/24$ where $10.8.0.0/24$ replaces $v_{S_{L2EP}}^{attach}$ in NLDAG$_a$.
- $r3 : v_{C_{L2EP}}^{inL3D} \rightarrow Oregon$ where *Oregon* replaces $v_{S_{L2EP}}^{inL3D}$ in NLDAG$_a$.
- $r3 : v_{C_{L2EP}}^{inL2D} \rightarrow LasVegas$ where *LasVegas* replaces $v_{S_{L2EP}}^{exp}$ in NLDAG$_a$.

The rest of nodes in NLDAG$_r$ are not replaced. The set of adjustments lead to the generation of the first adaptation plan illustrated in Fig. 5 ⓟ₁. This plan recommends to place *VM-1* and *VM-2* in the same sub-network $10.8.0.0/24$ located in *LasVegas* (*Oregon*). By re-applying the same process described above on all identified properties (associated with the identified unmatched constraints) and their possible values, we identify three additional plans: P-2, P-3 and P-4. Each of them recommends to place *VM-1* and *VM-2* in the same sub-network: $10.8.0.0/24$, located in *Chicago* (*N. Virgina*) for P-2 and $10.0.1.0/24$, located in *LasVegas* (*Oregon*) for P-3, and in *Chicago* (*N. Virgina*) for P-4. Other plans may be recommended if we rewrite NLDAG$_a$ considering more unmatched constraints. For instance, considering *host* in S_{L2B} as a property associated with an identified unmatched constraint, another plan can recommend to keep *VM-1* and *VM-2* in their locations and to use an L3 service to connect them via their IP addresses.

Note that, considering NLDAG$_a$ and NLDAG$_r$ with respectively n and m nodes, the complexity of rewriting one unmatched property p is less-than or equal-to $2m(n-1)$. In fact, we need to extract all possible values of p (i.e., m values in the worst case) and consider all possible edges (i.e., $n-1$ edges in the worst case) outgoing or ingoing $((n-1) \times 2)$ to the node representing p in NLDAG$_a$.

7   Evaluation

In this section, we evaluate through a user study the effectiveness of our key approach components. Specifically, we aim to evaluate the capability of the

Unmatched constraints identification and Adaptation plans identification components in providing users with understandable and useful outputs that help them to tailor their requests proportionately.

7.1 Method

Experimental Design. We recruited 21 participants (3 PhD students, 3 Master students, 5 engineers and 10 researchers) with different levels of expertise in network services engineering: basic (10), medium (8) and high (3). Of these participants, 40% were members of our research group, and the rest were external. We followed a within-subjects design to evaluate the usefulness and understandability of the proposed two components[9]. Participants were asked to give their feedback on the outputs resulting from testing our approach on three user request examples. Request 1, R1, aims to connect two AWS machines located in different regions via their mac addresses. Request 2, R2, involves three virtual machines VM-1, VM-2 attached to the same subnet in the same AZ and region, and VM-3 attached to a different subnet in a different region. In R2, the customer wants to connect VM-1 and VM-2 via their mac addresses, VM-1 and VM-2, VM-1 and VM-3 via their IP addresses. Request 3, R3, consists of attaching a virtual network interface card (NIC-1) localized in the Virginia region, specifically in the Atlanta AZ to the customer machine VM-1 attached to subnet 10.0.1.0/24, localized in the same region but in the Chicago AZ. To gain feedback on the outputs of our approach, we defined a set of questions (refer to Table 2) for each request, that participants are invited to answer. Specifically, questions Q.1, Q.3, and Q.4, intend to reflect the usefulness of the Unmatched constraints identification component. Questions Q.2, Q.8 and Q.9 aim to examine how understandable the constraints identified by this component for the users. Both Q.5 and Q.6 aim to examine how understandable are the adaptation plans proposed by the Adaptation plans identification component and Q.7 examine its usefulness.

Procedure. The study was conducted using an online form that included an informed consent, all the instructions and links to the components' output for each request. We introduced each request to the participants and asked them to answer the related questions. We performed a qualitative analysis of participant responses to gain insights about the understandability and usefulness of our approach components and to characterize their feedback.

7.2 Results

To evaluate the usefulness of our Unmatched constraints identification component, we relied on the answers to Q.1, Q.3., and Q.4. For question Q.1, some of the participants (7/21 for both R1 and R3) think that these requests can be satisfied

---

[9] Study materials are available at https://userstudy.com/25ad8jv6.

Table 2. User study questions

Questions for Requests R1 and R3	
Q.1	Do you think this request can be satisfied by existing cloud services providers ? If no, why?
Q.2	Looking into the identified constraints, did you understand why this request cannot be fulfilled ?
Q.3	How useful did you find the identified constraints for an eventual adaptation of the request ?
Q.4	Why did you find the identified constraints unuseful/useful for an eventual adaptation of the request?
Q.5	Looking into the proposed plans, did you understand the adjustments to be made on the request to make it satisfiable ?
Q.6	Among the proposed plans, which one(s) did you not understand and why? (multiple plans can be selected)
Q.7	Among the proposed plans, which plan(s) would you select/not select to adjust the request and why?
Questions for Request R2	
Q.8	Do you think this request can be satisfied by existing cloud services providers?
Q.9	If no could you explain why?

by the existing CSPs, when the reality is the request can not be fulfilled (refer to Fig. 6). Our approach, thanks to the Unmatched constraints identification component identifies which constraints from the provider prevent the satisfaction of both requests. Based on the provided answers for Q.3, most of the participants (17/21 for R1 and 16/21 for R3) find the identified constraints useful (Fig. 6). In answering Q.4, many participants expressed their reasons behind this feedback. For instance, P4 explicitly stated "*offer the means necessary for recommending a possible request adaptation*", while, P7 cited that it provides "*Transparent description of services*". Interestingly, P14 said " *it points me directly to the problem in a jargon I understand. I know what to change in my request to be fulfilled.*" The understandability of the Unmatched constraints identification component is evaluated through Q.2, Q.8, Q.9. Based on Q.2's answers, all but one participant were able to understand the constraints making requests R1 and R3 unfulfilled by the existing CSPs (Fig. 6). This observation is also confirmed by answers to Q.8, and Q.9. Indeed, Q.8 tests the participants on a new request with constraints that respect the ones made by the existing CSPs. The expected answer to Q.8 is yes, that is R2 can be satisfied, which was the answer of most of the participants (19/21). This can be justified by the fact that the participants gained knowledge from the identified constraints related to R1, allowing them to properly analyze R2's related constraints. What this and the above tell us is the identified constraints by the Unmatched constraints identification component are sufficiently useful and understandable to users.

As for the Adaptation plans identification component, on the basis of the identified unmatched constraints, it recommends 5 plans for R1 and 2 plans for R3. For request R1, 4 of the 5 plans ($p_{r1.1}$, $p_{r1.2}$, $p_{r1.3}$, $p_{r1.4}$) correspond to the same plans already explained in Sect. 6, while plan $p_{r1.5}$ represents a new recommended plan. Precisely, plan $p_{r1.5}$ recommends the use of a new service instead of L2connectivity service, namely L3connectivity service to link the machines through their IP addresses, thus avoiding the need to change any VM location as the previous four plans suggest. With regard to R3, two plans $(p_{r3.1}, p_{r3.2})$ are proposed by our component, recommending to bring VM-1 and NIC-1 back to the same AZ, that is Chicago for $p_{r3.1}$, and Atlanta for $p_{r3.2}$. Based on Q.5's answers, most of the participants (18/21 for R1, All for R3), find the proposed plans understandable. This observation is also confirmed based on Q.6's answers, in which, a few participants (3/21) expressed that they did not understand plans $p_{r1.1}$, $p_{r1.4}$ and $p_{r1.5}$, (4/21) did not understand $p_{r1.2}$, $p_{r1.3}$ and $p_{r3.1}$, and only (2/21) didn't understand $p_{r3.2}$ (Fig. 6). Unfortunately, we could not figure out the reason behind these participants' answers provided without explanation.

Furthermore, the usefulness of the Adaptation plans identification component, was assessed based on Q.7, where the intent was to prompt participants to select/unselect the plans for an eventual request adaptation. Hence, this implicitly reflects whether or not each proposed plan is useful. For both R1 and R3, the proposed plans were useful to most participants. Specifically, for R1, the five proposed plans were selected by at least 8 participants, with plan $p_{r1.1}$ being the most acceptable (to 12/21) (Fig. 6). Various reasons explaining this diversity in the participants' choices were observed. For instance, participants (P1, P16, P10, P4) who selected plans $p_{r1.1}$, $p_{r1.2}$, $p_{r1.3}$, and $p_{r1.4}$ justified their choice by the fact that these plans are *"viable solutions"* and *"Straightforward"*. One participant P7 who opted for the same plans, cited explicitly *"The communication between the VMs should not go over the internet and less expensive"*. Other participants (11/21) selected the plan $p_{r1.5}$ because their unwillingness to change their VMs localization. The same observations could be seen for R3. Both proposed plans (i.e., $p_{r3.1}$, $p_{r3.2}$) were selected by at least 15 participants, with plan $p_{r3.1}$ gaining greater preference from most of the participants (19/21) due to their willingness to keep their machines in the initially chosen AZ. All the above observations confirm that the adjustment plans proposed by Adaptation plans identification component are sufficiently understandable and useful.

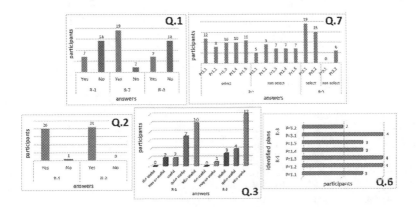

Fig. 6. Statistical measures from Q.1, Q.2, Q.3, Q.6 and Q.7 answers

Discussion. We evaluated so far our approach through a user study but we are pursuing the evaluation to achieve its completeness using a model checker. We also aim to evaluate our proposal's efficiency. To do so, we require a knowledge base of capability-based NaaS descriptions and requests collected from users. These requirements are currently not available and need huge effort to be designed. In fact, the major limitation that may slightly affect the applicability of our approach is that the existing NaaS are not currently described based-on our model. We intend to tackle this issue by proposing a semi-automatic NLP approach to populate a knowledge base of NaaS descriptions, which will not only be useful for evaluating our approach but also for automatically generating the NLDAGs corresponding to the NaaS offers and user requests. Remind that our approach is specific to NaaS, which are low and finite by providers. We have indeed identified in the order of ten NaaS offered by AWS and Azure. Thus, we do not foresee any scalability issue with our proposal for NaaS. This issue might come up when applying it on services operating at higher OSI model layers where combinatorial explosion of services is more likely.

8   Conclusion

This paper focuses on identifying providers constraints that prevent a customer's request from being totally matched, and recommending relaxing discovery requests to retrieve services offers. We plan to extend our approach to select the optimal recommended relaxations w.r.t users preferences. We evaluated so far our contributions based on a user study and we are pursuing the evaluation to achieve its completeness, correctness and efficiency. To do so, we are working on a semi-automatic NLP approach to populate a knowledge base of NaaS descriptions. This knowledge base will be the cornerstone of our quantitative evaluation.

Acknowledgment. This work was partially funded by a French national program via the public private partnership project ISChyO, n° 192906122-RAPID.

References

1. Al-Sayed, M.M., Hassan, H.A., Omara, F.A.: An intelligent cloud service discovery framework. FGCS (2020)
2. Alfazi, A., et al.: Toward unified cloud service discovery for enhanced service identification. In: Service Research and Innovation (2018)
3. Ben Djemaa, R., et al.: Enhanced semantic similarity measure based on two-level retrieval model. Pract. Exper. Concurr. Comput. (2019)
4. Committee Specification: Tosca simple profile for network functions virtualization (NFV) version 1.0. Technical report (2017)
5. Costa, P., Migliavacca, M., Pietzuch, P., Wolf, A.L.: NaaS: network-as-a-service in the cloud. In: 2nd USENIX Workshop (2012)
6. Day, J.D., Zimmermann, H.: The OSI reference model. Proc. IEEE **71**, 1334–1340 (1983)

7. ETSI: ETSI GS NFV-Man 001. Technical report (2014)
8. Hammami, R., et al.: Semantic web services discovery: a survey and research challenges. Int. J. Seman. Web Inf. Syst. **14**, 57–72 (2018)
9. Heidari, A., Navimipour, N.J.: Service discovery mechanisms in cloud computing: a comprehensive and systematic literature review. Kybernetes (2021)
10. Jerbi, I., Bhiri, S.: Definition and induction of a specification order relation between capabilities. In: 2021 IEEE International Conference on Services Computing (SCC). IEEE (2021)
11. Jerbi, I., et al.: Enabling multi-provider cloud network service bundling. In: 2022 IEEE International Conference on Web Services (ICWS) (2022)
12. Kang, J., Sim, K.: Ontology-enhanced agent-based cloud service discovery. Int. J. Cloud Comput. **5**, 144–171 (2016)
13. Kim, I.W., Lee, K.H.: A model-driven approach for describing semantic web services: from UML to owl-s. IEEE Trans. Syst. **39**, 637–646 (2009)
14. Kim, S.I., Kim, H.S.: Ontology-based NSD modeling for NFV service management. In: International Conference on Information Networking (2022)
15. Kunaver, M., Požrl, T.: Diversity in recommender systems-a survey. Knowl.-Based Syst. **123**, 154–162 (2017)
16. Mohammed, F., et al.: Cloud computing services: taxonomy of discovery approaches and extraction solutions. Symmetry (2020)
17. Natarajan, B.E.: New clustering-based semantic service selection and user preferential model. IEEE Syst. J. (2021)
18. el houda Nouar, N., et al.: A semantic virtualized network functions description and discovery model. Comput. Netw. **195**, 108152 (2021)
19. Senyo, P.K., Addae, E., Boateng, R.: Cloud computing research: a review of research themes, frameworks, methods and future research directions. Int. J. Inf. Manag. (2018)
20. Sim, K.M.: Agent-based cloud computing. IEEE TSC (2012)
21. Slawik, M., al.: Establishing user-centric cloud service registries. FGCS (2018)
22. W3C: Semantic annotations for WSDL and XML schema. Technical report (2007)
23. Wang, H., et al.: A formal model of the semantic web service ontology (WSMO). Inf. Syst. **37**, 33–60 (2012)
24. Wheal, J., Yang, Y.: CSRecommender: a cloud service searching and recommendation system. J. Comput. Commun. **3**, 65 (2015)
25. Wu, C., Jin, C., Chen, Y.J.: Managing customer search via bundling. Manuf. Serv. Oper. Manag. **24**, 1906–1925 (2022)

Tutorial Papers

Why Is Coming up with a Research Question Difficult? Mimicking Agile Methodologies for Defining Research Questions in Conversation with the Literature

Oscar Díaz[✉] and Jeremías P. Contell

University of the Basque Country (UPV/EHU), San Sebastián, Spain
{oscar.diaz,jeremias.perez}@ehu.eus

Abstract. Information Systems research commonly addresses ill-structured problems. This means that problems and solutions unfold together, making it difficult for researchers to formulate their research questions from the beginning. This tutorial explores the challenges of coming up with research questions, and proposes an iterative and incremental process for defining their scope. The tutorial provides insights into the operationalization of the process through FRAMEndeley, an extension for research question scoping in Mendeley.

Keywords: Research question scoping · Design questions · Agile literature review · PICO question framework · Double Diamond process model

1 Overview

Information System research rests on the understanding of practical problems and their solution counterparts. Frequently, solutions are not absolute but relative to the context where the problem is observed. This tends to imply that the solution and the problem unveil gradually together, and hence, researchers are not always in the position to state the research question (RQ) at the onset. Like software engineers when facing blurred requirements, researchers might not be familiar enough with the problem in the early phases of a research to properly scope their RQs. Here, the literature may play the role of the stakeholders in Agile methods: keeping the focus on the aspects that are essential (vs. accidental) of the RQ. Informed by Inductive Top-Down Theorizing [4] and the *Double Diamond* design thinking model [1], this tutorial introduces RQ scoping as an iterative and incremental process, moving from systematic literature reviewing to agile literature reviewing. Specifically, this tutorial has three main objectives:

- Raising awareness about the difficulties of coming up with a well-defined RQ.
- Providing insights into the operationalization of the RQ scoping process, which is described in detail in [2].
- Exploring the features of the FRAMEndeley extension for conducting RQ scoping in Mendeley.

© The Author(s), under exclusive license to Springer Nature Switzerland AG 2023
M. Indulska et al. (Eds.): CAiSE 2023, LNCS 13901, pp. 631–632, 2022.
https://doi.org/10.1007/978-3-031-34560-9

2   Relevance

Most of the problems tackled in CAiSE tend to be "ill-defined problems", i.e., they do not have clear goals, solution paths, or expected solutions. This implies that researchers struggle to define the scope of their RQs, a phenomenon termed as the "Goldilocks issue" [3]. Additionally, Information Systems research often targets design questions [5], which bring together aspects from both the problem realm and the solution realm. Therefore, an iterative approach is particularly suitable to this setting, since RQs are gradually refined and elaborated over time as a better understanding of the problem and its potential solutions emerge. This tutorial looks at the literature as a source of guidance for this process, emphasizing its iterative nature. While there is a wide coverage on systematic literature reviewing, agile literature reviewing and the problem of RQ scoping have received less attention, which makes it particularly cumbersome for novice researchers. The fact that the tutorial intermingles theory with its operationalization in Mendeley would allow attendees to apply the new acquired insights right away. At the time of this writing, the FRAMEndeley extension for RQ scoping enjoys over 600 installations.[1]

References

1. Design Council: The double diamond: a universally accepted depiction of the design process. www.designcouncil.org.uk/our-work/skills-learning/the-double-diamond/. Accessed 28 Mar 2023
2. Díaz, O., Contell, J.P.: Developing research questions in conversation with the literature: operationalization & tool support. Empir. Softw. Eng. **27**(7), 174 (2022)
3. Rai, A.: Avoiding type III errors: formulating is research problems that matter. **41** (2017)
4. Shepherd, D.A., Sutcliffe, K.M.: Inductive top-down theorizing: a source of new theories of organization. Acad. Manag. Rev. **36**(2), 361–380 (2011). https://doi.org/10.5465/amr.2009.0157
5. Wieringa, R.J.: Design Science Methodology for Information Systems and Software Engineering. Springer, Heidelberg (2014). https://doi.org/10.1007/978-3-662-43839-8

---

[1] https://chrome.google.com/webstore/detail/framendeley/decpeaebklmmgfhnnhggeikfhhlbcjpf.

The Work System Perspective: An Integrated Approach for Describing, Analyzing, Designing, and Evaluating IT-Enabled Systems

Steven Alter[(⊠)] iD

University of San Francisco, 2130 Fulton Street, San Francisco 94117, USA
alter@usfca.edu

Abstracts. This tutorial explains the most updated version of work system perspective, which extends work system theory (WST) and related ideas that originally emerged from a series of IS textbooks (1992, 1996, 1999, 2002). Those textbooks and subsequent efforts were guided by the aspiration of making analysis and design readily understandable and usable by business professionals. The textbooks articulated the beginnings of the work system method (WSM) whose conceptual basis was clarified in the form of WST in 2013. Subsequent developments articulate a broader work system perspective (WSP), which builds on WST and WSM to provide an integrated approach for describing, analyzing, designing, and evaluating IT-enabled systems that may be sociotechnical (with people performing some of the work), totally automated, or cyber-human (with extensive interaction between people and computerized devices).

Keywords: Work system · Work system method · Work system theory · Work system perspective

1 Goal and Objectives

This tutorial addresses a long-standing issue for information system engineering, business informatics, systems analysis and design, enterprise architecture, and other areas of interest for CAISE attendees. The issue is the lack of readily usable and easily teachable concepts, frameworks, tools, and methods that bridge the gap between two worlds. Those worlds are the people- and business-oriented sociotechnical world of business professionals and the abstract, technology-centric world of IT professionals and IS/IT researchers. That gap contributes to widely recognized difficulties in communicating and collaborating around creating, implementing, and improving IT-reliant systems in organizations regardless of whether the technical approach might be viewed as ERP, CRM, CAD, big data, AI, digital twins, robotic process automation, cyber-human systems, and so on. Some experienced consultants and consulting companies have proprietary methods, but those methods often are not available and readily usable by others.

M. Indulska et al. (Eds.): CAiSE 2023, LNCS 13901, pp. 633–634, 2023.
https://doi.org/10.1007/978-3-031-34560-9

2 Scope

This tutorial will cover the following aspects of the work system perspective (WSP):

- Summary of the main ideas in WST and WSM.
- Important nuances concerning the basic ideas in WST and WSM. Those nuances start with interpretations of basic terms such as customers, product/services, processes and activities, participants, information, technology, environment, infrastructure, and strategies.
- How the WSP extends WST/WSM in directions that touch upon basic understandings of sociotechnical systems, automated systems, human-computer interaction, enterprise architecture, service-oriented thinking, and agile development.
- Analysis and design tools based on WST and its extensions (e.g., performance gaps, key incidents, notable workarounds, resources used by activities, customer and provider responsibilities related to activities, roles of digital agents.
- Theories and frameworks that build on WST/WSM: service value chain framework, theory of workarounds, system interaction theory, facets of work, agent-responsibility framework, smartness of systems and devices, IS usage theory,
- Demonstration of how WST/WSM ideas apply to topics of current interest including shadow IT, AI, BPM, digital transformation, open innovation, agile development, and workarounds and noncompliance.
- Challenges in the continuing evolution of the WSP: alternative metamodels for different purposes, overlaps with BPM, integration with sociotechnical analysis, links to enterprise architecture, creation of a usable IS body of knowledge

References

1. Alter, S.: The Work System Method: Connecting People, Processes, and IT for Business Results. Work System Press, Larkspur, USA. (2006)
2. Alter, S.: Defining information systems as work systems: implications for the IS field. Eur. J. Inf. Syst. **17**(5), 448–469 (2008)
3. Alter, S.: Service system fundamentals: work system, value chain, and life cycle. IBM Syst. J. **47**(1), 71–85 (2008)
4. Alter, S.: Work system theory: overview of core concepts, extensions, and challenges for the future. J. Assoc. Inf. Syst. **14**(2), 72–121 (2013)
5. Alter, S.: Theory of workarounds. Commun. Assoc. Inf. Syst. **34**(55), 1041–1066 (2014)
6. Bork, D., Alter, S.: Satisfying four requirements for more flexible modeling methods: theory and test case. Enterp. Model. Inf. Syst. Archit. (EMISAJ) **15**(3), 1–25 (2020)
7. Alter, S.: Facets of work: enriching the description, analysis, design, and evaluation of systems in organizations. Commun. Assoc. Inf. Syst. **49**(13), 321–354 (2021)
8. Alter, S.: How can you verify that i am using AI? Complementary frameworks for describing and evaluating AI-based digital agents in their usage contexts. In: Proceedings of HICSS 2023 (2023)

Free and Open Source Software: A Brief History

Anthony I. (Tony) Wasserman[(⊠)] [ID]

Software Methods and Tools, San Francisco, CA 94131, USA
tonyw@acm.org

Abstract. This paper provides historical background for a tutorial on open source for information systems, identifying some of the most significant developments that have led to the widespread adoption and use of free and open source software across a broad range of applications in academia, industry, and government.

Keywords: Open source · Free software · Open source project office

The history of distributing program source code dates to the earliest days of computing, when people informally exchanged software at industry group meetings and elsewhere. In the late 1970s, the University of California, Berkeley, released an augmented version of the Unix system [1], known as the Berkeley Software Distribution (BSD), with the included source code known as the 2-clause BSD license [2].

BSD Unix was widely adopted by hardware vendors, especially Digital Equipment Corporation and Sun Microsystems, and by computer science departments around the world. It was very influential, bringing the idea of source code releases to a large audience.

The creation of the Free Software Foundation (FSF) in 1985 was even more influential, and took over the distribution of the GNU software, most notably the GNU Emacs text editor, that was developed by Richard Stallman [3] and released under the GNU General Public License (GPL). The FSF introduced the Free Software Definition, which enumerated the four freedoms of free software:

- The freedom to run the program as you wish, for any purpose (freedom 0).
- The freedom to study how the program works, and change it so it does your computing as you wish (freedom 1). Access to the source code is a precondition for this.
- The freedom to redistribute copies so you can help others (freedom 2).
- The freedom to distribute copies of modified versions to others (freedom 3).

Cygnus Solutions, founded in 1989, was among the first companies to provide commercial support for free software, and was acquired by Red Hat Software in 1999. Red Hat, founded in 1995, offered its own distribution of Linux, developed by Linus Torvalds beginning in 1991 [8]. Another early company in free software was MySQL,

M. Indulska et al. (Eds.): CAiSE 2023, LNCS 13901, pp. 635–637, 2023.
https://doi.org/10.1007/978-3-031-34560-9

founded in 1994, which offered a relational database system under the GPL, as well as under a commercial license [5]. Red Hat Linux and MySQL remain in widespread use today. Netscape Navigator, an early and popular web browser, was released as open source in 1998, which eventually led to the release of the Mozilla browser in 2002.

When the Open Source Initiative (OSI) was founded in 1998, its goals were similar to those of the FSF, but focused more on adoption of open source by industry and government. The OSI created the Open Source Definition [6], and quickly took responsibility for reviewing and approving open source licenses, which it continues to do. The FSF and the OSI share many of the same goals.

In its early days, free and open source software (FOSS) was primarily used by students and hobbyists, but the growing availability of projects such as Linux, MySQL, and Mozilla, along with the dotcom boom of the late 1990s, led to rapid growth in the use of FOSS. Over time, more and more people working for companies began to use open source software, and eventually to contribute code back to open source projects. The rapidly growing community meant that new open source projects were being started and that existing projects were increasingly improving.

FOSS projects were hosted on many different sites, especially SourceForge. However, they were displaced by GitHub [7], founded in 2007, which was not just a software repository, but also a comprehensive platform for software development, offering version control, bug tracking, and more. Today, it is by far the largest hosting site for open source projects, with more than 100 million registered developers. GitHub allows people to choose a license for their work and to rate other projects, making it possible for people to identify popular projects.

Today it is estimated that more than 95% of all software, including proprietary applications, include FOSS code, typically for user interface libraries and database management. The world's fastest supercomputers all run Linux, as do a major share of computers used by cloud computing service providers, and a majority of mobile phones.

Many companies have created Open Source Project Offices (OSPOs) to coordinate their adoption and use of FOSS, establishing and following policies for their business units and their employees [8]. Finally, many governments have established policies for their use of FOSS, often favoring FOSS over proprietary products in their software acquisition procedures. Taken together, these developments assure that FOSS will be central to software development projects for the foreseeable future.

References

1. Ritchie, D., Thompson, K.: The UNIX time-sharing system. Commun. ACM **17**(7), 365–376 (1974)
2. The 2-Clause BSD License. https://opensource.org/license/bsd-2-clause/. Accessed 06 Apr 2023.
3. Stallman, R.M., The GNU Project. https://www.gnu.org/gnu/thegnuproject.html. Accessed 06 Apr 2023.

4. Linus Torvalds. https://www.computinghistory.org.uk/det/1790/Linus-Torvalds/, Accessed 06 Apr 2023.
5. History of MySQL. https://www.datasciencecentral.com/history-of-mysql/. Accessed 06 Apr 2023.
6. The Open Source Definition. https://opensource.org/osd/. Accessed 06 Apr 2023.
7. Let's Build From Here. https://github.com/about. Accessed 06 Apr 2023.
8. Haddad, I.: A Deep Dive into Open Source Project Offices. Linux Foundation (2022)

Author Index

M. Indulska et al. (Eds.): CAiSE 2023, LNCS 13901, pp. 639–641, 2023.
https://doi.org/10.1007/978-3-031-34560-9

Printed in the United States
by Baker & Taylor Publisher Services